I and II ESDRAS

VOLUME 42

THE ANCHOR BIBLE is a fresh approach to the world's greatest classic. Its object is to make the Bible accessible to the modern reader; its method is to arrive at the meaning of biblical literature through exact translation and extended exposition, and to reconstruct the ancient setting of the biblical story, as well as the circumstances of its transcription and the characteristics of its transcribers.

THE ANCHOR BIBLE is a project of international and interfaith scope: Protestant, Catholic, and Jewish scholars from many countries contribute individual volumes. The project is not sponsored by any ecclesiastical organization and is not intended to reflect any particular theological doctrine. Prepared under our joint supervision, THE ANCHOR BIBLE is an effort to make available all the significant historical and linguistic knowledge which bears on the interpretation of the biblical record.

THE ANCHOR BIBLE is aimed at the general reader with no special formal training in biblical studies; yet it is written with the most exacting standards of scholarship, reflecting the highest technical accomplishment.

This project marks the beginning of a new era of co-operation among scholars in biblical research, thus forming a common body of knowledge to be shared by all.

William Foxwell Albright
David Noel Freedman
GENERAL EDITORS

THE ANCHOR BIBLE

I and II ESDRAS

Introduction, Translation
and Commentary by

JACOB M. MYERS

WITHDRAWN

DOUBLEDAY & COMPANY, INC.

GARDEN CITY, NEW YORK

ISBN: 0-385-00426-5
Library of Congress Catalog Card Number 72–84935
Copyright © 1974 by Doubleday & Company, Inc.
All Rights Reserved
Printed in the United States of America
First Edition
Second Printing
1980

To
my wife to whose encouragement and
persistence I am indebted more than
words can express

THE APOCRYPHA

The term Apocrypha (or "Deuterocanonical Books" in Roman Catholic usage) is popularly understood to describe the fifteen books or parts of books from the pre-Christian period that Catholics accept as canonical Scripture but Protestants and Jews do not. This designation and definition are inaccurate on many counts. An apocryphon is literally a hidden writing, kept secret for the initiate and too exalted for the general public; virtually none of these books makes such a pretense. Not only Roman Catholics but also Orthodox and Eastern Christians accept these books, wholly or partially, as canonical Scripture. Roman Catholics do not accept all of them as Scripture, for I and II Esdras and the Prayer of Manasseh are not included in the official Catholic canon drawn up at the Council of Trent. Many Protestant churches have no official decision declaring these books to be non-canonical; and, in fact, up to the last century they were included in most English Protestant Bibles. What is certain is that these books did not find their way into the final Jewish Palestinian canon of Scripture. Thus, despite their Jewish origins (parts of II Esdras are Christian and Latin in origin), they were preserved for the most part in Greek by Christians as a heritage from the Alexandrian Jewish community and their basic text is found in the codices of the Septuagint. However, recent discoveries, especially that of the Dead Sea scrolls, have brought to light the original Hebrew or Aramaic text of some of these books. Leaving aside the question of canonicity, Christians and Jews now unite in recognizing the importance of these books for tracing the history of Judaism and Jewish thought in the centuries between the last of the Hebrew Scriptures and the advent of Christianity.

PREFACE

Any monograph such as this is perforce heavily dependent on earlier studies; its author is like the "householder who produces from his storeroom both old and new things" (Matt 13:52, AB, vol. 26), mostly the former. He is manifestly deeply indebted to all those whose works he has consulted and from whom he has learned as may be seen on every page of his book.

The present translation of I Esdras has been made from Brooke, McLean and Thackeray, *The Old Testament in Greek,* vol. II, *The Later Historical Books,* part IV. I Esdras, Ezra · Nehemiah, or what has been commonly referred to as the Larger Cambridge Septuagint. The A Manuscript has often been followed in preference to that of B, especially where it presents a fuller text, as may be seen from the textual notes. Parallels and/or variations with Chronicles, Ezra · Nehemiah, and Josephus have generally been noted where they appeared to have special significance. The detailed work of Karl-Friedrich Pohlmann came too late for extensive use.

Frequent reference has been made to the writer's earlier work on Chronicles and Ezra · Nehemiah (AB, vols. 12, 13, and 14) where there is generally a fuller discussion of materials involved and various lists and indices of names of persons and places. The unique story of the bodyguards (3:1 – 4:63) has been treated more at length, both for its interest and lack of parallels elsewhere in biblical and apocryphal literature.

The basic text used in the translation of II Esdras was that of Bensly and James with some deviations where other versions or manuscripts were deemed more appropriate. The rather copious textual and other NOTES are by no means exhaustive but may prove helpful to the more serious reader. The commentary attempts to present the thought of II Esdras in running fashion for the reader who may be somewhat puzzled by often enigmatic expressions and allusions.

Limitations of space and time have precluded extensive discussions on the many involvements of II Esdras. But enough has, hopefully, been said to reflect the wide range of sources its author drew upon, either directly or indirectly. Age-old materials were tailored to express his concerns and stimulate his thoughts. If he was a member of the Jamnia school, as was suggested more than a century ago by Franz Rosenthal, we can understand his preoccupation with the problems that beset the Jews between A.D. 66–100. The Jewish scholars of the period were diligent students of the Scriptures in which they found strength and direction that, embellished by their own imagination, they transmitted to their contemporaries in the form of apocalypses. While their compositions were doubtless not wholly satisfactory to themselves or their readers, they did offer hope to buoy the otherwise gloomy prospects for their people. Their works offer vivid testimony to their faith in a God who was alive to the condition of his people but who, at the same time, could not be manipulated or hurried. Judgment and salvation were immanent but the time of neither was susceptible to man's timetable. God would indeed act, but in his time and way. Meanwhile he had taken care of contingencies in a manner that also could not be fully spelled out by scholar or saint. Tracts for the times such as II Esdras have a message for us who in a revolutionary age are obsessed with the impatience reflected by Ezra; it was not that he lacked faith in God but that he, like Job, questioned his ways and the delay, perhaps seeming inactivity, in the face of what appeared to the prophet to be terrible urgencies. The questions posed are still asked in the context of our age.

Apart from some documentary sources, our author manifests acquaintance with and appreciation of apocalyptic materials in the Old Testament prophetic books, certain Wisdom compositions, old poetic pieces heavily freighted with myth and legend, and especially the Book of Job.[1] He follows the creation narrative of Gen 1 (6:38–54), views the Torah as God's revelation to the people for the maintenance of their relationship with him, which reminds the reader of Ezra's conception in the canonical book bearing his name, and at the same time recognizes the powerful impulse of evil that renders men unable to observe the Torah (3:20; 7:72, 119; 8:6). His language and expressions recall similar Canaanite imagery but they were doubtless drawn from the Bible. No attempt has been made here to document the material; that would be the subject for a more extensive investigation and be beyond the scope of the book.

No one is more aware of the inadequacies of this undertaking than the writer. But he has done his best to make intelligible to others what he has learned about I and II Esdras, the latter of which he regards as an exceedingly significant and stimulating piece of work — and indeed quite timely. Hopefully some readers may be inspired, in one way or another, to under-

---

[1] Rosenthal, pp. 42 ff. [BIBLIO II]; and recently F. M. Cross, in *Apocalypticism*, ed. R. W. Funk, pp. 162 ff. [BIBLIO II]; P. D. Hanson, "Jewish Apocalyptic against its Near Eastern Environment," RB 78 (1971), 31–58

[Bibliographical data are provided in the referent Bibliography.]

take a renewed study of II Esdras to their own profit and edification in a rather confused and hopeless world.[2]

The writer wishes herewith to express his gratitude to those who have contributed more or less directly in the execution of this work. First, to Mrs. Mary Miller who typed the original copy from an almost indecipherable manuscript (literally so) and then the final copy; second, to David Noel Freedman for his perceptive suggestions, observations, and corrections; and finally, to the courteous and skillful editors of Doubleday's Anchor Bible who helped measurably in matters of style and clarification of some of the manuscript's obscure and often otherwise unintelligible points. Needless to say, however, the writer bears sole responsibility for the views and judgments expressed.

J. M. MYERS
Gettysburg, Pa.

[2] Cf. D. N. Freedman, in *Apocalypticism*, p. 174.

CONTENTS

II ESDRAS

LIST OF ILLUSTRATIONS

1. Cyrus the Great. Pasargade. Bas-relief with a winged spirit. Palace of Cyrus (sixth century B.C.). From *Persia: From the Origins to Alexander the Great* by R. Ghirshman, figure 174
2. Darius and Xerxes. Courtesy of the Oriental Institute, University of Chicago
3. Artaxerxes I on his throne. Courtesy of the Oriental Institute, University of Chicago
4. Ezra reading the law. Courtesy: Dura-Europos Collection, Yale University
5. Wild boar. Courtesy of the Novosti Press Agency, London
6. Roman eagle. Courtesy of Adler Cameo and Kunsthistorischen Museums, Wien
7. Aurelian. British Museum: Department of Coins and Medals
8. Zenobia. British Museum: Department of Coins and Medals

PRINCIPAL ABBREVIATIONS

1. APOCRYPHAL AND PSEUDEPIGRAPHICAL WORKS

Aboth	Pirqe Aboth (Sayings of the Fathers)
Apoc	Apocryphon of (e.g.) Peter
Asc Isa	Ascension of Isaiah
Ass Mos	Assumption of Moses
I Bar	I Baruch
II Bar	II Baruch (Syriac Apocalypse of Baruch)
III Bar	III Baruch (Greek Apocalypse of Baruch)
Barn	Epistle of Barnabas
Jub	Book of Jubilees
Odes Sol	Odes of Solomon
Pol	Polycarp's Epistle to the Philippians
Pseudo-Philo	*The Biblical Antiquities of Philo,* by Mr. R. James, London: SPCK, 1917
Pss Sol	Psalms of Solomon
Sib Or	Sibylline Oracles
Test	Testament of (e.g.) Levi
Wisd Sol	Wisdom of Solomon

2. MANUSCRIPT MATERIALS

For text of 1 Esdras:

LXX	The Septuagint
LXX^A	Codex Alexandrinus
LXX^B	Codex Vaticanus
LXX^N	Codex Basiliano-Vaticanus (eight–ninth centuries A.D.). Also noted as cursive No. 23 in Rahlfs and as XI in Holmes and Parsons

Note: Greek transcriptions follow system used in H. W. Smyth, *Greek Grammar for Colleges* (New York: American Book Co., 1920), p. 7.

e epsilon	*u* upsilon
z zeta	*ph* phi
ē eta	*ch* chi
th theta	*ps* psi
x xi	*ō* omega
o omicron	

For text of II Esdras:

S   Codex Sangermanensis, in Bibliothèque Nationale, Paris (A.D.
                822)

A   Codex Ambianensis, in Bibliothèque Communale, Amiens (ninth
                century A.D.)

C   Codex Complutensis, in Library of Central University, Madrid
                (ninth–tenth centuries A.D.)

M   Codex Mazarinaeus, in Bibliothèque Mazarine, Paris (eleventh
                century A.D.)

V   Codex Abulensis, in Biblioteca Nacionale, Madrid (early thir-
                teenth century A.D.)

L   Codex Legionensis, in Library of San Isidro de Leon (A.D.
                1162)

Ar.¹   Arabic¹, in Bodleian Library No. 251 (A.D. 1354)

Ar.²   Arabic², in Bodleian Library No. 260 and in Vatican Library
                No. 462 (sixteenth century A.D.)

Armenian   (See Gry, pp. xvi f. [BIBLIO II])

Ethiopic   Ethiopic No. 7 in Bodleian Library (fourteenth or fifteenth
                century A.D.)

Georgian   (See Blake [BIBLIO II])

Syriac   Syro-Hexaplaric Codex, in Ambrosian Library, Milan (sixth
                century A.D.)

3. QUMRAN LITERATURE

From Cave I:

1QGenApoc   Qumran Genesis Apocryphon
1QH   Qumran Hodiyoth (Hymns of Thanksgiving)
1QM   Qumran Milḥamoth (Wars Between the Children of Light and
               the Children of Darkness)
1QpHab   Qumran Pešer (Commentary) on Habakkuk
1QS   Qumran Serek (Manual of Discipline)
1QSa   Qumran Serek a
1QSb   Qumran Serek b

Note: An appended "f" — e.g. 1QHf — signifies "fragments"

From Cave IV:

4QDibHam   Qumran *dbry hm 'rwt,* "The Words of the Lights" (in RB 68
               [1961], 195–250)
4QF1   Qumran Florilegus
4QpNahum   Qumran Pešer on Nahum
4QpPs 37   Qumran Pešer on Psalm 37
4QpIsᵃ   Qumran Pešer on Isaiah a   JBL 75 (1956), 174–87

4QpIs^b	Qumran Pešer on Isaiah b ⎫
4QpIs^c	Qumran Pešer on Isaiah c ⎬ JBL 77 (1958), 215–21
4QpIs^d	Qumran Pešer on Isaiah d ⎭

4. MAJOR WORKS AND JOURNALS

ANET *Ancient Near Eastern Texts Relating to the Old Testament*, ed. James B. Pritchard, Princeton University Press, 2d ed., 1955

APAT *Die Apokryphen und Pseudepigraphen des Alten Testaments*, ed. Emil Kautzsch [BIBLIO II]

APOT *The Apocrypha and Pseudepigrapha of the Old Testament*, ed. R. H. Charles [BIBLIO II]

BZ Biblische Zeitschrift

CAH *Cambridge Ancient History*, XI, *The Imperial Peace*, and XII, *The Imperial Crisis and Recovery, A.D. 193–324*, Cambridge University Press, 1936 and 1965

CD Documents of the Damascus Covenanters cited after Solomon Schechter, *Documents of Jewish Sectaries*, I, *Fragments of a Zadokite Work*, Cambridge University Press, 1910

DJD *Discoveries in the Judaean Desert of Jordan*, 5 vols., Oxford: Clarendon Press, 1955–

EdS *Esra der Schreiber*, by H. H. Schaeder, Tübingen: Mohr, 1930

E-N *Esra und Nehemia samt 3. Esra*, by Wilhelm Rudolph [BIBLIO I]

ES *Ezra Studies*, by C. C. Torrey [BIBLIO I]

HDB James Hastings, ed., *A Dictionary of the Bible*, 5 vols., New York: Scribner's, 1899–1905

HTR Harvard Theological Review

IB *The Interpreter's Bible*, 12 vols., New York and Nashville: Abingdon, 1952–57

JBL Journal of Biblical Literature

JNES Journal of Near Eastern Studies

Jos. *Antiq.* Josephus *Antiquities of the Jews*
  War   *History of the Jewish War*

JQR Jewish Quarterly Review

JTS Journal of Theological Studies

KAT *Die Keilenschriften und das Alte Testament*, by Eberhard Schrader, 3d ed., Berlin: Reuther und Reichard, 1903

LGJV *Louis Ginzberg Jubilee Volume*, English Section, New York: The Jewish Theological Seminary of America, 1945

LS Lex H. G. Liddell and Robert Scott, *A Greek-English Lexicon* (1843), a new edition revised and augumented by H. S. Jones, Oxford: Clarendon Press, 1948

MF *The Missing Fragment of the Fourth Book of Esther*, by R. L. Bensly [BIBLIO II]

MGWJ Monatsschrift für Geschichte und Wissenschaft des Judentums

OLZ Orientalistische Literaturzeitung

PG   Patrologia Graeca, Paris: Migne
PL   Patrologia Latina, Paris: Migne
RB   Revue biblique
RE   *Realencyclopädie der classischen Altentumswissenschaft,* ed. Au-
            gust Pauly (1839 ff.) and rev. by Georg von Wissowa (1894 ff.)
            et alia, Stuttgart: Metzger und Alfred Druckenmüller
RLA   *Reallexikon der Assyriologie,* eds. E. Ebeling and B. Meissner,
            Berlin und Leipzg: Walter de Gruyter, 1932–
SAHG   *Sumerische und Akkadische Hymnen und Gebete,* by Adam Fal-
            kenstein and Wolfram von Soden, Zurich: Artemis-Verlag,
            1953
StB   H. L. Strack and P. Billerbeck, *Kommentar zum Neuen Testa-
            ment aus Talmud und Midrasch,* 6 vols., Munich: Beck, 1922–
            61
TWNT   *Theologische Wörterbuch zum Neuen Testament,* eds. Gerhard
            Kittel and Gerhard Friedrich, Stuttgart: W. Kohlhammer,
            1933–
UT   *Ugaritic Textbook,* 4th ed. (Rome: Biblical Institute Press) of
            C. H. Gordon's *Ugaritic Grammar* (1940)
VT   Vetus Testamentum
VTS   Vetus Testamentum Supplements
ZAW   Zeitschrift für die Alttestamentliche Wissenschaft
ZDPV   Zeitschrift des deutschen Palästina-Vereins
ZNW   Zeitschrift für die Neutestamentliche Wissenschaft

5. Versions

AB   The Anchor Bible, 1964–
CCD   The Confraternity of Christian Doctrine Version, 1944–69
KJ   The King James or Authorized Version of 1611
JB   The Jerusalem Bible, 1966
MT   Masoretic Text
NEB   The New English Bible, 1961, 1970
RSV   The Revised Standard Version, 1946, 1952

6. Other Abbreviations

AB, vol. 14 *Ezra · Nehemiah,* by Jacob M. Myers
NT   New Testament
OT   Old Testament
Akk.   Akkadian
Aram.   Aramaic
Bab.   Babylonian
Heb.   Hebrew
Pers.   Persian

Note: Chapter and/or verse numbers which differ in the Hebrew from the
English are designated by an "H"; e.g. Mal 4:6[3:23H].

INTRODUCTION

I. NAME, CONTENTS, AND RELATIONSHIP TO SOURCES

I Esdras owes its name to the Greek Bible where Esdras A=I Esdras and Esdras B=Ezra and Nehemiah. In some lists Esdras a (alpha), Esdras b (beta), and Esdras g (gamma) stand for I Esdras, Ezra, and Nehemiah. There is no Greek Esdras d (delta) but there is mention of *Esdras o prophetēs* and *Esdras apokalupsis*. The Vulgate (Jerome's Latin Bible) has Esdras 1 (=Ezra), Esdras 2 (=Nehemiah), Esdras 3 (=I Esdras) and Esdras 4 (=II Esdras). In the English Bible we have Ezra and Nehemiah only; in the Apocrypha of the King James (KJ) and Revised Standard Version (RSV) the order is I Esdras, II Esdras (= Fourth Ezra). The Douay-Confraternity Version (CCD) does not contain I and II Esdras, nor does the Jerusalem Bible (JB). My Clementine Vulgate (reprinted in Italy in 1946) has an appendix, at the very end of the volume containing both Testaments, with the Prayer of Manasseh followed by Esdras 3 and Esdras 4. This is the order followed by *Biblia Sacra iuxta vulgatam versionem,* eds. Robertus Weber et al., *tomus* II, Stuttgart: Württembergische Bibelanstalt, 1969:

English	*LXX*	Vulgate
I Esdras	Esdras A (alpha)	Esdras 3
Ezra	Esdras B (beta)	Esdras 1
Nehemiah	Esdras G (gamma)	Esdras 2
II Esdras	--------------	Esdras 4

As it has been transmitted to us, I Esdras tells the story of Judah from Josiah's passover to the reforms of Ezra, with the exception of the work of Nehemiah whose activity is played down (see below). It is essentially the same story as that related in the canonical literature. I Esdras begins in the middle of the reign of Josiah (640–609 B.C.), that is, with his passover (1:1–20) celebrated in the wake of the deuteronomic reformation. The king's piety is noted (1:21–22), followed by the account of his tragic death at the hands of Pharaoh Neco (1:23–31). Continuing the narrative of II Chron 36, there is a short description of the events transpiring in the reigns of Jehoahaz, Jehoiakim, Jehoiachin, and Zedekiah

(1:32–55). As in II Chron 36:22–23 and Ezra 1:1–4, the decree of Cyrus and the response thereto are related (2:1–14). Then the narrative jumps to events that took place in the time of Artaxerxes (2:15–25) — the encounter between the golah and the Samaritan officials, the exchange of correspondence with the Persian court, and the effect of both on the work of restoration of the temple. The story of the bodyguards (3:1 – 4:63) is found only in I Esdras. After that insertion the author returns to the period of Darius which is preceded by an incident revolving around that Persian monarch. Chapter 5 (vss. 1–70) deals with the golah's preparations for and return from captivity. There are the organization of the caravan (1–6), a note on the situation (7–8), the list of those who returned (9–42), the contributions made to the temple building fund (43–45), the erection of the altar (46–49a), the inauguration of worship services (49b–52), arrangements for the temple reconstruction (53), laying the temple foundation (54–62), the offer of assistance by the peoples of the land (63–68) and their obstructive maneuvers (69–70). Chapters 6 and 7 have to do with the state of affairs connected with the rebuilding of the temple. The work began under the inspiration of the preaching of Haggai and Zechariah (6:1–2) but soon came under investigation by the provincial authorities (6:3–6). It was interrupted while the report was sent to the king (6:7–21) and his review of credentials was in progress (6:22–33). Then the work was pursued with vigor, especially after the favorable report from the Persian court (7:1–9). Celebration of the passover marked the successful conclusion of rebuilding the temple (7:10–15). With ch. 8 the scene shifts from the sixth year of Darius to the time of Ezra. Ezra's advent (1–7) was made possible by a royal rescript issued by Artaxerxes (8–24). The work of Ezra began with a service of praise to the Lord (25–27), followed by a list of those who had chosen to return with him (24–40), recruitment of temple personnel (41–48), a farewell service (49–53), and the selection of treasure-bearers (54–59). The journey to and arrival at Jerusalem was uneventful (60–64). But it was soon discovered that not all was well with the Jerusalem community (65–69). The remainder of the book is devoted to the handling of the problem of compromising marriages with the peoples of the land. It begins with a survey of the problem, Ezra's prayer-sermon (70–87), and the community's response (8:88 – 9:2). Agreement on a plan of procedure called for the issuance of a proclamation decreeing an assembly of the people (9:3–17). Following the list of the guilty persons (9:18–36), there was a service of law-reading and rededication of the golah to pursuit of the Torah of Moses (9:37–55).

The above description of the contents of I Esdras may be more easily grasped from the outline with parallels which has been followed in the exposition:

I. The Period of Josiah (1:1–31)
   A. Josiah's passover (1–20 || II Chron 35:1–19; II Kings 23:21–23)
   B. Josiah's piety (21–22)
   C. Josiah's death (23–31 || II Chron 35:20–27; II Kings 23:28–30a)

II. The Last Kings of Judah (1:32–55)
   A. Jehoahaz (32–34 || II Chron 36:1–3; II Kings 23:30b–33)
   B. Jehoiakim (35–40 || II Chron 36:4–8; II Kings 23:34 – 24:7)
   C. Jehoiachin (41–43 || II Chron 36:9–10; II Kings 24:8–17)
   D. Zedekiah (44–55 || II Chron 36:11–21; II Kings 24:18 – 25:12)

III. The Decree of Cyrus and the Response Thereto (2:1–14)
   A. The decree (1–6 || II Chron 36:22–23; Ezra 1:1–4)
   B. The response (7–14 || Ezra 1:5–11)

IV. Correspondence between the Samarian Officials and the Persian Court (2:15–25)
   A. The letter to Artaxerxes (15–20 || Ezra 4:7–16)
   B. The king's reply to Rehum and his associates (21–24 || Ezra 4:17–22)
   C. Effect on the work of reconstruction (25 || Ezra 4:23–24)

V. The Story of the Bodyguards (3:1 – 4:63—cf. Jos. *Antiq.* 11:3:2–6)
   A. The banquet of Darius (3:1–3)
   B. The wager of the bodyguards (3:4–16a)
   C. The address of the first on wine (3:16b–23)
   D. The address of the second on the king (4:1–12)
   E. The address of the third on women and truth (4:13–40)
      1. On women (13–32)
      2. On truth (33–40)
   F. Popular response (4:41)
   G. Dialogue between the king and the third speaker (4:42–46)
   H. The royal decrees (4:47–57)
   I. The song of the youth (4:58–60)
   J. The reaction of the Jews in Babylon (4:61–63)

VI. Preparations for and Return from Captivity (5:1–70)
   A. Organization of the caravan (1–6)
   B. Preliminary statement (7–8 || Ezra 2:1–2)
   C. List of returning captives (9–42 || Ezra 2:3–66)
      1. The laymen (9–23)
      2. The priests (24–25)
      3. The Levites (26)
      4. The temple singers (27)
      5. The gatekeepers (28)
      6. The temple servants (29–32)
      7. Solomon's servants (33–35)
      8. The unrecorded (36–40)
      9. Summary (41–42)
   D. Contributions (43–45 || Ezra 2:68–70)
   E. Erection of an altar (46–49a || Ezra 3:1–3a)
   F. Inauguration of worship services (49b–52 || Ezra 3:3b–6)
   G. Preparations for reconstruction of the temple (53 || Ezra 3:7)
   H. Foundation of the temple laid (54–62 || Ezra 3:8–13)
   I. An offer from neighbors (63–68 || Ezra 4:1–3)
   J. Interference by rejected neighbors (69–70 || Ezra 4:4–5)

VII. Events Associated with the Reconstruction of the Temple (6:1 – 7:15)
   A. Reconstruction of the temple begun (6:1–2 || Ezra 5:1–2)
   B. Intervention by the provincial authorities (6:3–6 || Ezra 5:3–5)
   C. The governor's report to the king (6:7–21 || Ezra 5:6–17)
   D. Investigation by the king and his reply to the report (6:22–23 || Ezra 6:1–12)
   E. Progress of the work (7:1–9 || Ezra 6:13–18)
   F. Celebration of the passover (7:10–15 || Ezra 6:19–22)

VIII. The Ezra Story (8:1 – 9:55)
- A. The arrival of Ezra (8:1–7 || Ezra 7:1–10)
- B. The rescript of Artaxerxes (8:8–24 || Ezra 7:11–26)
- C. Ezra's paean of praise (8:25–27 || Ezra 7:27–28)
- D. List of captives who returned with Ezra (8:28–40 || Ezra 8:1–14)
- E. An appeal for temple servants (8:41–48 || Ezra 8:15–20)
- F. A farewell service (8:49–53 || Ezra 8:21–23)
- G. Selection of treasure-bearers (8:54–59 || Ezra 8:24–30)
- H. Journey to and arrival at Jerusalem (8:60–64 || Ezra 8:31–36)
- I. The scandal of the golah (8:65–69 || Ezra 9:1–5)
- J. Ezra's prayer-sermon (8:70–87 || Ezra 9:6–15)
- K. The people's response to Ezra's prayer-sermon (8:88 – 9:2 || Ezra 10:1–6)
- L. Proclamation and assembly (9:3–17 || Ezra 10:7–17)
- M. List of those cohabiting with alien wives (9:18–36 || Ezra 10:18–44)
- N. The law-reading assembly (9:37–55 || Neh 7:72b – 8:12)

From the above outline it may be seen that I Esdras parallels substantially chs. 35 and 36 of II Chronicles, all of Ezra, and about thirteen verses of Nehemiah. The Ezra order has been altered a bit as the following Ezra parallels indicate:

I Esd	1:1–11	Ezra	6:1–22
	4:7–24		7:1–28
	2:1–70		8:1–36
	3:1–13		9:1–15
	4:1–5		10:1–44
	5:1–17	Neh	7:72b – 8:12

Note, however, the addition of I Esd 1:21–22; 3:1 – 5:6; 5:55; 6:8bc and the omission of II Chron 36:22–23.

It is clear that the time sequence was not a primary concern of the author. There was, therefore, either another frame of reference that is no longer unquestionably discernible, or disorder was already prevalent in the text from which the translation was made, or the compiler followed an order of history peculiar to his period.

C. C. Torrey refers to the historical sequence as "an astonishing example of history stood on its head,"[1] in as much as I Esdras announces the edict of Cyrus with initiation of movements leading to the first returns. Then comes the story of the correspondence between the Samaritan officials and Artaxerxes (and Ahasuerus=Xerxes in Ezra 4:6) in which the progress of wall-building operations is described, together with other construction work. Only then are we introduced to the Darius period in chs. 3 and 4. Ezra 4 appears to be a summary of the Jews' collisions with local imperial authorities in the reigns of Cyrus, Darius, Xerxes, and Artaxerxes and related here for illustrative purposes.[2] So much is evident from the

[1] Torrey, p. 44 [either BIBLIO].

[2] Ezra · Nehemiah, AB, vol. 14, p. XLI. Compare the correct order, with omission of Xerxes, in Ezra 6:14=I Esd 7:4. On the vexed question as to which Artaxerxes, I or II, is meant see ibid., pp. LXVIII–LXX, and compare observation of Josephus Against Apion 1:40: "From the death of Moses until Artaxerxes who succeeded Xerxes as

Masoretic text (MT) of Ezra 6:14 with the addition of "and Artaxerxes king of Persia" (see textual note $q-q$ at 7:4). Note especially the singular of "king." It seems obvious that the author of Ezra was focusing on the Ezra period and that I Esdras accentuated that point by placing Ezra 4:7–24 immediately after the Cyrus account. This suggests an other than purely historical purpose of the original compiler and the author of I Esdras.

II. TEXT, VERSIONS, LANGUAGE

I Esdras is extant only in Greek manuscripts and in Latin, Syriac, Ethiopic, Armenian, and Arabic versions. R. Holmes and J. Parsons, *Vetus Testamentum Graecum cum variis lectionibus,* vol. V, Oxford: Clarendon Press, 1827, cite twenty-four Greek manuscripts, three of which do not contain all of our book. The Brooke-McLean-Thackeray text, on the basis of which the present translation was made, used the great uncials, the Septuagint (LXX) codices Vaticanus, Alexandrinus, and Basiliano-Vaticanus (BAN), except Sinaiticus which does not contain I Esdras, and eighteen minuscules.[3] The editors also drew on Ethiopic (not too useful), Old Latin (from various MSS), and Syriac (the Lagarde edition) versions. The Ethiopic text follows LXX[B] rather than LXX[A],[4] while the Syriac (not extant in the Peshitto which did not have Chronicles and the Ezra material) of Paul of Tella appears to have been made from the LXX column of Origen's *Hexapla* and agrees closely with LXX[B]. The Old Latin version is said to support the Lucianic text.[5]

The problem of language is exceedingly complex. Three possibilities have been conjectured: (a) that I Esdras represents a compilation from LXX of the relevant portions of Chronicles, Ezra, and Nehemiah; (b) that it is based on an earlier Greek rendition; (c) that it represents an independent translation of an original Hebrew text.[6] Each view has had its champions but Thackeray regards none of them as wholly satisfactory, though he seems to lean toward the second. Otto Eissfeldt[7] has expressed

---

king of Persia, the prophets after Moses composed the history of accomplishments down to their times in thirteen books." Note that the Artaxerxes mentioned is the one who succeeded Xerxes. Artaxerxes II is mentioned only twice by Josephus (*Antiq.* 11:7:1).

[3] For details and comparisons see Moulton, ZAW 19 (1899), 209–58; 20 (1900), 1–35 [BIBLIO I]. For the Hexapla of Origen and the Syriac version of Paul of Tella, see Torrey, ES [BIBLIO I], ch 1.

[In footnotes, when a bracketed "BIBLIO I" or "BIBLIO II" follows the first citation of an article, its title is given in the referent bibliography.]

[4] For value of Ethiopic version see Torrey, ES, pp. 100 f.

[5] See Brooke-McLean-Thackeray, II, Part IV, pref. note, p. vi.

[6] H. St. J. Thackeray, in HDB, I, 759–61.

[7] Eissfeldt, p. 575 [BIBLIO I].

the view that it is difficult to determine whether the author was himself the translator of the relevant materials from Chronicles, Ezra, Nehemiah, or utilized an already existent Greek translation, but opts for the former alternative as more probable. He thinks it probable, however, that 3:1 – 5:3 was composed in Greek.[8] R. H. Pfeiffer[9] assumes that I Esdras was translated from the Hebrew-Aramaic and that the story of the bodyguards was Persian in origin, dates from the Persian period,[10] and was translated from Aramaic. He thus agrees with C. C. Torrey whose basic work remains convincing. This is not the place to detail the history of the study of our book since that would prove repetitious, uninteresting, and perhaps confusing to the general reader.

It has been observed that the vocabulary of I Esdras corresponds to a very great extent with that of the second-century B.C. compositions of Sirach, Judith, Esther, I Maccabees, the LXX of Daniel.[11] Twenty-one Greek words occur only here in the Bible and the twenty-eight rare words counted by Moulton are found almost exclusively in the apocryphal books.[12] His study indicates that I Esdras offers a freer, less mechanical translation than the LXX of Chronicles, Ezra, Nehemiah. Articles and pronouns are omitted or supplied with greater freedom. Hebrew parataxis is rendered by hypotaxis, passive verbs are frequently made active. Sometimes the MT is curtailed and the word order changed. The conjunctions are sometimes supplied where wanting and omitted where present in the MT. Moulton's analysis shows that *kol*, "all," is left untranslated twenty-one times, the Greek *pas*, "all," is supplied nineteen times, and *olos*,

---

[8] Schürer, III, 328 [either BIBLIO] — "It appears to be a Greek original and not a translation from the Hebrew." Here he follows Fritzsche, p. 6 [BIBLIO I]. Guthe, APAT, I, 1 [BIBLIO I] also opts for a Greek original for 3:1 – 4:63.

[9] Pfeiffer, pp. 236–50, esp. p. 237 [either BIBLIO]. Pfeiffer believes I Esdras represents a surviving fragment of a Greek translation of Chronicles-Nehemiah which was produced in Alexandria "not later than 150 B.C." (Cf. also Rudolf Kittel, *Geschichte des Volkes Israel*, III, Part II [Stuttgart: Kohlhammer, 1929], 545 f.) This was the Greek version used by Josephus and which, except for our book, was later lost. If that is so, a legitimate question might be why only this fragment, of all the possibilities, was lost. To deal with the Josephus question adequately it would have to be determined which Greek text of the Chronicler's was used elsewhere in his writings where he draws on sources wanting in Kings. Of course the story of the bodyguards in I Esd 3, 4 may have had something to do with its preservation. For latest discussion of the whole problem see Sidney Jellicoe, *The Septuagint and Modern Study* (Oxford: Clarendon Press, 1968), pp. 290–94, and Metzger, p. 12 [either BIBLIO].

[10] Pfeiffer, p. 251. The view that I Esdras was an independent translation from Hebrew-Aramaic is based pretty largely on Nestle, pp. 23 f. [BIBLIO I].

[11] See Fischer, BZ 2 (1904), 351–64 [BIBLIO I], and Bernhard Walde, in *Biblische Studien*, XVIII, Part IV, 1913 [BIBLIO I]. For lexicographic lists see H. B. Swete, *An Introduction to the Old Testament in Greek* (Cambridge University Press, 1900), pp. 310–13.

[12] Moulton, ZAW 19 (1899), 232–34 [BIBLIO I].

"whole," is added once. Often the translator omits *š'r,* "the rest." On the rendering of the divine name he gives the following statistics:[13]

> *'lhym=theos,* "God," 34 times; *kurios,* "Lord," 59 times; 23 times left untranslated; and *theos* is added 5 times.
>
> *yhwh=kurios* 55 times; *theos* 4 times; 5 times left untranslated; and *kurios* is added 23 times.

All in all, it appears that the translator had before him a fuller and perhaps more orderly original than that represented by our MT of Chronicles and Ezra-Nehemiah (cf. the additions in 1:21–22; 3:1–5:6; 5:55; 6:8bc). But in many instances the material has been compressed though nothing essential has been left out. The Greek of I Esdras reads, on the whole, much more smoothly and the structure is superior to that of the LXX of Ezra.

Many years ago Torrey observed that LXX[A] "makes the impression of being surprisingly 'correct', as contrasted with B."[14] He speaks of "erroneous readings" that have been, in almost all cases, allowed to stand. He thought the "variation in Greek texts" was due to corruption. It now appears that many of those variations stem from the original text from which the translations were made. There are some forty substantive additions in LXX[A], as against B. The former follows closely the MT of Chronicles and Ezra-Nehemiah where parallels exist. Interestingly enough, I Esd 3:1–4:63 (the story of the bodyguards) reflects the same kind of pluses found elsewhere in the book. On the other hand, the fifty omissions are relatively insignificant. For example, the article is omitted thirteen times, *kai* eleven times, *de* two times, *kata* two times; others, such as *oun, en, epi, ek,* are omitted only one time each.

Where the Samuel texts from Qumran parallel Chronicles they reflect a text "much closer to the text of Samuel used by the author of Chronicles than to the traditional text of Samuel,"[15] and hence presuppose an earlier underlying recension. The fuller readings of LXX[A] of I Esdras would appear to point to the use of an earlier *Vorlage* than B. Sidney Jellicoe affirms that A represents, in Chronicles, I Esdras, and Ezra-Nehemiah, an early Alexandrian text.[16]

[13] Ibid., pp. 226 ff.

[14] ES, p. 92

[15] F. M. Cross, Jr., *The Ancient Library of Qumran and Modern Biblical Studies,* rev. ed. (New York: Doubleday, 1961), pp. 41, 188, n. 40a; *Bulletin of the American Schools of Oriental Research* 132 (1953), 15–26; cf. P. W. Skehan, "The Biblical Scrolls from Qumran and the Text of the Old Testament," *Biblical Archaeologist* 28 (1965), 87–100, and W. F. Albright, *Yahweh and the Gods of Canaan* (New York: Doubleday, 1968), pp. 34 f.

[16] *The Septuagint and Modern Study,* p. 187; for a discussion of the LXX problem as it relates to Chronicles, I Esdras, and Ezra-Nehemiah, see pp. 290–94. For a convenient parallel print of the original texts of the Chronicles-I Esdras materials involved, with apparatus, see Primus Vannutelli, *Libri Synoptici Veteris Testamenti* (Rome: Biblical Institute Press, 1931), pp. 641–89, 700–1.

III. PURPOSE AND DATE

The purpose and date of I Esdras are closely related. If either could be determined independently it would not be too difficult to fix upon the other. Of course its terminus ad quem is Josephus (*Antiq.* 11:1:1–5:5) who utilized our book as the main source for his history of the period covered by it.[17] He appears to use it also in *Antiq.* 10:4:5–5:2. Pfeiffer[18] thinks I Esdras is part of a Greek translation of the relevant sections of Chronicles, Ezra, Nehemiah produced in Alexandria "not later than 150 B.C." Such external evidence as is available and favoring this date and provenance has been collected by Torrey[19] and is based chiefly on a quotation of II Chron 2:12 ff. by the Greek historian Eupolemus whose work dates ca. 150 B.C.[20] The latter, dealing with preparation for the construction of the Solomonic temple, quotes from the Solomon-Hiram correspondence according to the Chronicles version. That quotation appears to represent the same type of Greek translation as found in I Esdras.

Bertholdt[21] long ago (1812–1819) observed that the compiler of I Esdras brought together from older works a history of the temple from the last period of the legal cultus until its reconstruction and the reinstitution of the prescribed worship. Guthe[22] believed that the purpose of the book is not immediately evident beyond its general concern with the history of the Jerusalem temple. The author has juxtaposed the return from exile and the rebuilding of the temple with the narrative of the destruction of the temple and the beginnings of the exile. Inasmuch as the passover marked the conclusion of the cultic renewal at Jerusalem (Ezra 6:19–22),

[17] Büchler, however, has made much of the fact that Josippon had at his disposal an apocryphal treatise related to the story of the wager of the bodyguards, though not quite identical with it. While he has great respect for those who attempted to show dependence of Josephus on I Esdras he remains unconvinced. His assessment of the story of the bodyguards is indicative of the direction of his thoughts: "It is not to be denied that the story of the wager of the pages creates the impression that the author was a Greek who had acquainted himself with the Persians from sources related to those used by Xenophon, while the author of the story of the victory of Zerubbabel and that of the release of the Jews transmitted for us in III Esdras used the completed extant account of the wager contest of the three bodyguards as foundation for his presentation of Zerubbabel and the departure of the Jews from Babylon and added from it the deduction concerning the power of truth and the king's arrangements for the temple." MGWJ 41 (1896), 66 [BIBLIO I].

[18] Pfeiffer, p. 249.

[19] ES, pp. 82–87.

[20] For date of Eupolemus see Schürer, III, 352, and for the quotation Swete, *Introduction to the Old Testament in Greek*, p. 370.

[21] Quoted by Schürer, III, 328, and by Kellermann, p. 128, n. 150 [BIBLIO I].

[22] APAT, p. 1b. This is, in substance, the view of Eissfeldt, p. 575; Artur Weiser, *The Old Testament: Its Formation and Development* (New York: Association Press, 1961), p. 390; Rudolph, E-N, p. xiv [BIBLIO I], and others. But see Torrey's ridicule of that view of the temple's purpose (ES, pp. 14 f.).

he began his story with Josiah's passover which became authoritative for the future by virtue of the king's order. He thinks 1:21 ff. exhibits threads of the writer's thoughts: do what God has commanded through the prophets. Chapter 5:1–6 is a parenthesis from his hand. So much for chs. 1–7. The second part of the book is incomplete and its purpose remains unclear. Presumably the portrayal of the work of Ezra in the post-exilic community was intended (cf. Jos. *Antiq.* 11:5:5). Thus far Guthe. There is a significant emphasis on the temple, especially in chs. 1 – 7. It is mentioned some forty-seven times, in one way or another, compared with forty-one in the parallels of Chronicles and Ezra. The Greek *naos* occurs nine times in I Esdras, but does not occur at all in the LXX of Chronicles or Ezra. *Ieron*[23] is used twelve times in I Esdras, twice in Chronicles, and once in Ezra. *Oikos,* "house," is found twenty-five times in I Esdras, six times in Chronicles, and thirty-three times in Ezra. The predominant term in I, II, III Maccabees is *naos.* Aristeas has *ieron* five times and *oikos* once. Thus the cultic stress of I Esdras must not be overlooked. This point is further accentuated by the introduction of the story of the bodyguards the purpose of which, as the gloss in 4:13 shows, was to magnify Zerubbabel who was associated with laying the foundation of the temple (Zech 4:19; I Esd 5:55) and even with preparing (anew?) the altar (I Esd 5:47). Then there is the emphasis on cultic concerns reflected by the close association of Zerubbabel with Darius who, in response to the request of the former, sets in motion the series of events whose intent was the restoration of the Jerusalem religious institutions.

Another factor is the clear accent on Ezra whose name occurs twenty times here — the same number of times as in the Ezra-Nehemiah parallels. There appears to be a deliberate attempt to magnify Ezra as may be seen from the fact that in I Esd 9:40, 49 he is referred to as "high priest," *archiereus,* whereas in the parallel passages in Nehemiah he is called "the scribe" (8:1) and "the scribe, the priest" (8:9). Josephus never refers to Ezra as high priest, though he once (*Antiq.* 11:5:1) calls him "the chief priest," *prōtos iereus.* At the same time Nehemiah seems to be downgraded. In I Esd 5:8 (‖ Ezra 2:2) the name occurs in both documents, while in I Esd 5:40 (‖ Ezra 2:63) the name Nehemiah is inserted perhaps as a compromise between the Syriac (has only Nehemiah) and MT (has only Tirshatha). The name Nehemiah is omitted in 9:49 where the parallel (Neh 8:9) has it. The term *Tirshatha,* "governor," is wanting in LXX[B] in the latter passage, although some minor MSS have it.[24] The Syriac of Neh 8:9[10] adds after Nehemiah, "the head of the priests."

---

[23] *to ieron,* "the sanctuary," is rare in the Greek Bible except the Apocrypha. The words *oikos,* "house," and *naos,* "shrine," are used for the Jewish temple in LXX. See article by Gottlob Schrenk in TWNT, III (1938), 230–34.

[24] Cf. Meyer, p. 200, n. 3 [BIBLIO I].

Josephus never mentions Nehemiah in his Ezra material and vice versa. I Esdras thus reflects the opposite of the situation in I Maccabees (1:18, 20, 21, 31, 36; 2:13) and Sirach (49:13)[25] where Ezra is ignored and Nehemiah praised. In II Maccabees (1:18) Nehemiah is even credited with the rebuilding of temple and altar.

The sequence of events following the accession of Cyrus is fraught with difficulty and confusion. No document or solution of the problem is wholly satisfactory if wholesale emendation or rearrangement or both are to be avoided. All texts agree that the original rescript permitting the return of the Jews was issued by Cyrus. There also seems to be substantial agreement that the first Jewish governor or representative of the Jews was Sheshbazzar and that he was succeeded by Zerubbabel. But that is where agreement ends. Just what was accomplished by Sheshbazzar and his group of expatriates cannot now be determined with any degree of confidence. Ezra 1:8, 11 tells us that he was the prince of Judah to whom Cyrus delivered the sacred vessels of the temple expropriated by Nebuchadnezzar and that he brought them to Jerusalem. I Esd 2:11, 14 adds that he was governor of Judah. Ezra 5:14 reaffirms what was said in Ezra 1 but goes a step further and says he was appointed governor by Cyrus. Ezra 5:16 declares that he "laid the foundation of the house of God at Jerusalem,"[26] and that view is repeated in I Esd 6:19. I Esd 6:17 says the temple vessels were delivered to Zerubbabel and Sheshbazzar, named in that order. Josephus mentions the latter only once (*Antiq.* 11:1:3).

There is a tendency thus to confuse Sheshbazzar and Zerubbabel whose genealogy is not consistent. I Chron 3:19=Jehoiachin — Pedaiah — Zerubbabel whereas all the other references make him the son of Shealtiel (Ezra 3:2, 8; 4:2; 5:2; Neh 12:1; Hag 1:1, 12, 14; 2:2, 23; I Esd 5:5, 47, 54; 6:2; Matt 1:12; Luke 3:27). Josephus (*Antiq.* 11:3:10) follows the majority. If these authorities were intent on magnifying Zerubbabel it may be that he was purposely connected with the oldest son of Jehoiachin rather than with the third son of the king as the Chronicles list has it. He too is credited with leading back to Jerusalem a group of the golah (Ezra 2:2; Neh 7:7; 12:1; I Esd 5:5, 8), building or restoring the altar (Ezra 3:2; I Esd 5:47), providing for religious orders and services (Ezra 2:8, 10; I Esd 5:47, 56; 6:28; Neh 12:47). He was approached by the people of the land for permission to assist in the rebuilding of the temple (Ezra 2:8, 10; I Esd 5:65, 67). More significantly, he too is said to have laid

---

[25] On the omission of the mission of Ezra in Sirach see Schaeder, EdS, pp. 37 f., esp. n. 1 where he quotes Smend's explanation.

[26] Ezra 5:16 (MT) has *yhb 'šy' dy-byt 'lh' dy byrwšlm;* LXX[B], *edōken themelious tou oikou tou theou tou eis Ierousalēm.* I Esd 6:19 has *eiseballeto tous thelemious tou oikou Kuriou tou en Ierousalēm.*

the foundation of the temple (Ezra 3:8, 10, 11, 12; I Esd 5:55), so that both he and Sheshbazzar are credited with having laid the foundation of the temple (Ezra 5:16; I Esd 6:19). Zech 4:9 appears to support Zerubbabel.[27] He is generally regarded as initiating the temple building operations (Ezra 3:8 ff.; I Esd 5:54b; 6:2), though he is not mentioned in connection with its consummation except in the Zechariah reference (Ezra 6:13 ff.; I Esd 7:5–9). For some reason the vision of the prophet may not have been fulfilled. Zerubbabel is referred to twice as governor in I Esdras (6:26, 28). In the Ezra 6:7 parallel there is a reference to "the governor of the Jews" (omitted by LXX) who is not named. I Esd 6:28 is wanting in Ezra. Hag 1:2, 14; 2:2, 21 specifically denominate Zerubbabel as governor. Josephus refers to him three times (*Antiq.* 11:1:3; 11:4:1) as *archōn,* "ruler, chief," and once (*Antiq.* 11:3:1) as *ēgemōn,* "leader," and Sirach (49:11b) says "he was like a signet on the right hand" and ascribes to him and Joshua the rebuilding of "the house," that is, the temple.

Just what conclusion may be drawn from this complex situation is uncertain. What happened to Sheshbazzar? What part did he play in the reestablishment of the Jerusalem institutions? Were the names of Sheshbazzar and Zerubbabel confused in the transmission of the accounts?[28] Was there a deliberate attempt to play down the former to the advantage of the latter? All sorts of conjectures are possible but only one appears reasonably certain, i.e. that there were several returns from Babylon and that both Sheshbazzar and Zerubbabel were independent leaders in two of the movements and therefore governors of Judah. It is possible that Sheshbazzar was thwarted by the same forces operative later in the time of Zerubbabel, Ezra, and Nehemiah.[29] In that event, Zerubbabel, who came along later, would have succeeded where Sheshbazzar had failed and hence got the credit for laying the foundations and consummating the project as Zech 4:19 implies. Whatever may be the truth of the matter,

[27] *ydy zrbbl ysdw hbyt hzh wydyw tbṣ'nh,* "the hands of Zerubbabel founded this house and his hands shall complete it." LXX[B] follows MT.

[28] Josephus seems to identify Sheshbazzar with Zerubbabel (*Antiq.* 11:1:3). The Rabbis identified Zerubbabel with Nehemiah (Louis Ginzberg, *The Legends of the Jews,* IV [Philadelphia: JPS, 1913], 352. Syncellus has a great deal to say about Zerubbabel but fails to mention Sheshbazzar. The name of the latter occurs four times each in Ezra and I Esdras and once in Chronicles while that of Zerubbabel occurs twice in I Chronicles, six times in Ezra, three times in Nehemiah, seven times in Haggai, four times in Zechariah, twice in Matthew, once in Luke, and eleven times in I Esdras, or exactly the same number of times as in Chronicles, Ezra, and Nehemiah combined. See further Torrey, ES, p. 306, n. 25. It is said that a late midrash makes Zerubbabel the subject of a little apocalypse on the certainty of the ultimate appearance of the Messiah son of David, on his precursor the Messiah the son of Joseph, and on their friends and foes (Cook, APOT, I, 2, n. 1 [BIBLIO I]).

[29] Cf. Josephus' reference to opposition in the late years of Cyrus and Cambyses (*Antiq.* 11:2:1 f.).

it is certain that Zerubbabel was magnified later on. The hand that introduced parenthetically the phrase "he was Zerubbabel" in I Esd 4:13 certainly thought he was exalted by the story.

Perhaps the most intriguing fact of all is the use of the geographical term Coelesyria and Phoenicia, and Syria and Phoenicia. Coelesyria= Persian satrapy Across the River, a designation not found in I Esdras or Josephus. In I Esdras (2:16, 20; 6:28; 8:64) Coelesyria replaces *peran tou potamou,* "across the river," for Aram. *'br nhrh* (Ezra 4:10, 16; 6:8; 8:36). In I Esd 4:48, where the phrase also occurs, is the story of the bodyguards not found in Ezra. Once (I Esd 2:23) the parallel passage in Ezra 4:20 has *esperas tou potamou,* "west of the river," though the Aramaic is *'br nhrh.* Where the combination Syria and Phoenicia occurs in I Esdras (2:21; 6:3, 7, 26; 8:19, 23), the parallels in Ezra (4:17; 5:3, 6; 6:6; 7:21, 25) have *pera(n) tou potamou.* Aristeas[30] (par. 22) has this expression once. As noted, Josephus always had Coelesyria when he refers to the region indicated, but in *Antiq.* 12:2:3 he has Syria and Phoenicia, quoting the Aristeas passage just mentioned. Coelesyria also occurs in I Macc 10:69; II Macc 3:5, 8; 4:4; 8:8; 10:11; III Macc 3:15; Aristeas, par. 12. Two designations for the district referred to appear to have been combined in I Esdras: (a) Coelesyria and Phoenicia being the Greek (Seleucid) name and (b) Syria and Phoenicia that of the Egyptians of the Ptolemaic period. The descriptive Coelesyria as used by Polybius, Diodorus Siculus, Arrian, and Curtius[31] embraces generally what is included in I Esdras and Josephus, and when linked to Phoenicia covers the same territory as the Persian satrapal term Across the River.[32] Not too much must be made of this except to note that all sources involved reflect a confusion of terminology coincident with the historical situation.

Another indicator may be the consistent use of the word *ierodoulos,* "temple slave," in I Esdras (1:3; 5:29, 35; 8:5, 22, 49) for *Nethinim*[33] throughout the parallels in Ezra. The exception is 1:3 where *ierodoulos* is used for MT *hmbwnym,* "instructors"(?) — Greek *tois dunatois,* "those enabled" — and is probably right as against MT and Greek of II Chron

[30] *Aristeas to Philocrates* (Letter), ed. and tr. Moses Hadas, New York: Harper, 1951.

[31] In the Loeb Classical Library: Polybius, tr. W. R. Paton, 6 vols.; Diodorus Siculus (of Sicily), tr. C. H. Oldfather, vols. 1–6; Arrian *History of Alexander* and *Indica,* tr. E. Iliff Robson, 2 vols.; Quintus Curtius *History of Alexander,* tr. John C. Rolfe.

[32] On geographical conception and political designation see F. M. Abel, *Géographie de la Palestine,* II (Paris: Gabalda, 1938), 132 f.; idem, *Histoire,* I, Part 1 [BIBLIO I]; G. A. Smith, *The Historical Geography of the Holy Land,* 4th ed. (New York: Doran, 1896), pp. 538 ff.; V. A. Tcherikover, *Hellenistic Civilization and the Jews* (Philadelphia: JPS, 1959), pp. 423, n. 36, and 428, n. 55.

[33] The spelling varies — *Natheinim, Natheinin, Nateineim* — but there is no doubt about the word itself.

35:3. The word is not found elsewhere in the LXX and is used only twice by Josephus in the parallel account (*Antiq.* 11:5:1 and 5:2). It is used a number of times in Egyptian papyri from the third century B.C. on. Then there are certain characteristic words of which the following are examples. *Ieropsaltēs*, "temple singers," in 1:14; 5:27, 46; 8:5, 22; 9:24. II Chron 35:15 renders the MT with *psaltōdoi;* Ezra 7:41, 70; 7:7, 24; 10:24 with *adontes.* The term occurs in Egypt from second century B.C. and in Jos. *Antiq.* 12:3:3. *Katalochismos*, "register," is found in the LXX of I Chron 4:33; 5:7, 17; 9:22; II Chron 31:17; I Esd 5:39. The parallel passage in Ezra 2:62 has simply *graphē.* The word appears in the Egyptian papyri from the third century B.C. to the third century A.D. *Meridarchia*, "office," I Esd 1:5, 10; 5:4; 8:28, is rendered in the LXX of II Chron 35:5, 12 by *diaireseis*, "divisions"; I Esd 5:4 is without parallel in Ezra. I Esd 8:28= Ezra 8:1 which has *oi odēgoi*, "guides," though some MSS add *kai ē genealogia*, "and the genealogy." It also occurs in Josephus (*Antiq.* 15:7:3); but *meridarchēs* is found in Egyptian papyri from second century B.C. *Somatophulax* (I Esd 3:4; Judith 12:7; II Macc.) appears in Egypt from second century B.C. and in the historians Josephus, Polybius, Diodorus, and Arrian. *Phorologia* (I Esd 2:18; 6:29; 8:22; I Macc 1:29) occurs in Egyptian papyri from third and second centuries B.C. The parallel Ezra passages (4:13; 6:8; 7:24) have *phoros*, a less colorful word. The use of these and other words reflects a translation some time in the second century B.C.[34] But unless I Esdras is an accidentally preserved fragment of an originally complete translation of Chronicles-Nehemiah, there is still the question of purpose. If it was excerpted there must have been some special reason for it. We noted at the beginning of this section the opinion of scholars as to a possible purpose or purposes of I Esdras. It must have been more than the deliberate preservation of a record of the past, though it was that too. Perhaps it represents a special plea for support for a Jewish religious institution. It has been said that "the charter of Antiochus the Great repeated in short the edict emanating from Artaxerxes II (I?) and brought to Jerusalem by Ezra in 459. Between these two epochs, Alexander and the Lagides had followed the same line of conduct in conceding to the Jews the freedom to live in conformity with the laws of their fathers."[35] Does I Esdras have something to do with the period of Antiochus III, perhaps as a kind of apologia for the Jews who had assisted him in his successful effort to wrest Coelesyria from the Ptolemaic regime[36] and a claim for his favor in return?

Some have suggested that our book was excerpted to gain the support of Ptolemy VI Philometor for the construction and maintenance of a Jewish

---

[34] Oesterley, *An Introduction to the Books of the Apocrypha*, p. 141 [BIBLIO I].
[35] Abel, *Histoire*, I, 91.
[36] Jos. *Antiq.* 12:3:3.

temple in Egypt by Onias IV (the son of the high priest Onias III who was slain at Daphne near Antioch).[37] But Tcherikover[38] has shown that the temple at Leontopolis was related to the military colony there and never commanded the full support of Jews in Egypt. There may, however, be more to this argument than meets the eye. Onias' project may have elicited the support of the Egyptian authorities because it fitted in with their political objectives. The complicated situation in Egypt and Palestine at the time renders a definitive judgment in the matter problematic. That Onias regarded himself as the legitimate high priest after the death of his father is certain, and his moves could thus have been regarded as bearing some weight though one cannot help observing the stress on Jerusalem in I Esdras whereas in Onias' case the site was not Judea or Jerusalem but Egypt and Leontopolis.

This section cannot be concluded without reference to Torrey's revised estimate of I Esdras.[39] He still held to the main tenets developed in his *Ezra Studies* but even more emphatically rejected the idea that I Esdras is a book of an author or compiler with a definite purpose. He regarded it a fragment, "merely a piece of the oldest Greek version of the Chronicler's work" (p. 395). The order or arrangement of the book goes back to the Hebrew original which was revised around the beginning of the second century of our era mainly by eliminating 3:1–5:6. This revised edition became the basis of the Theodotion version now regarded as "the Septuagint." However, some unknown scholar then sought to preserve the older version because of his interest in its deviations from the now orthodox historical materials. One wonders whether it may not have been due rather to the story of the three bodyguards, as Torrey himself suggested, and which had a strong hold on subsequent authors regardless of its time or place of origin. Torrey's work deserves study and consideration but is hardly as fool-proof as he seemed to think.

In summary, no definitive conclusion as to the date and purpose of I Esdras is possible at this time. It may have come from the same general period that gave birth to the final editions of Esther and Daniel. Note, for example, the delimitation of the Persian empire "from India to Ethiopia" and the "127 provinces" (I Esd 3:2 ∥ Esther 1:1; 8:9). The use of *satrapeia* in the LXX of I Esd 3:2 and that of *chōra(os)* to render *medinah* in Esther 1:1 may say something. Ezra 2:1; Neh 1:3; 7:6 employ *chōra(os)* for *medinah*. Then there are reminiscences of Daniel in I Esdras, as noted in the commentary. Its purpose may have had something to do with the support and promotion or both of a Jewish institu-

---

[37] Ibid. 13:3:1 ff.
[38] *Hellenistic Civilization and the Jews*, pp. 276–81.
[39] Torrey, in LGJV, pp. 395–410 [BIBLIO I].

tion.[40] Or it may have been extracted for some liturgical observance as was doubtless the case with other biblical compositions or excerpts.[41]

IV. TEXTUAL AND HISTORICAL SIGNIFICANCE

It is unnecessary to detail here the textual value of I Esdras. The textual and other notes on the translation must suffice. Furthermore, the matter has been amply dealt with by Bayer, Walde, Moulton, and Torrey (see BIBLIO I) and there is little that can be added at present beyond what will be said in the notes.

Despite the fact that I Esdras has been relegated to the Apocrypha, it does make some important historical contributions. Chapter 1:25 supports the MT of II Chron 35:20 whereas the LXX of the latter passage followed II Kings 23:29. Pharaoh Neco did not go to the Euphrates to fight *against* the Assyrians; he went to support them against the Babylonian onslaught.[42] In 4:45 the Edomites are said to have burned the temple in 587 B.C. This is likely to have some truth in view of the intense hatred reflected in biblical sources.[43] The same may be said of the reference to Darius' order to the Edomites to withdraw from the territory they had overrun in the wake of the disorder in Judah following the Babylonian conquest (4:50).[44] The addition of "and its environs" in 5:45, not in the Ezra 2 and Neh 7 parallels, is certainly accurate. Also, I Esdras (6:17) clearly separates Zerubbabel and Sheshbazzar.[45] The date — the twenty-third [day] of the month Adar — in 7:5 rather than the third day of that month in Ezra 6:15 has been shown by F. X. Kugler[46] to be probably correct. Though the story of the bodyguards may be novelistic, the basic elements may not be altogether without a measure of truth.[47] Certainly the Persians held great banquets, as did other courts. Moreover there were doubtless some contests of various kinds sponsored by the participants on such occasions. That there were rewards for the winner also rings true. The reference to the kinsmen of the king sounds credible too inasmuch as the designation occurs elsewhere in the contemporary world. Whether Zerubbabel was regarded as such is another matter or even whether he was

[40] E.g. the controversy of pietists with the Hellenizing party in the time of Seleucus IV (187–175 B.C.) or the early days of Antiochus IV (175–164 B.C.).

[41] Cf. H. St. J. Thackeray, *The Septuagint and Jewish Worship* (London: Oxford University Press, 1923), pp. 16–28, 114–15.

[42] See *II Chronicles*, AB, vol. 13, COMMENT on § 40, par. 12, for details.

[43] See my article in *Near Eastern Studies in Honor of William Foxwell Albright*, ed. Hans Goedicke (The Johns Hopkins Press, 1971), pp. 377–92.

[44] See ibid. p. 392.

[45] Cf. Meyer, p. 75.

[46] *Von Moses bis Paulus: Forschungen zur Geschichte Israels* (Münster in Westf.: Aschendorffsche Verlagsbuchhandlung, 1922), pp. 214 f.

[47] Cf. Pfeiffer, pp. 251 f. He observes that the closest parallel to the story of the bodyguards is that of Ahiqar.

originally the central character of the story. Perhaps the fact that Nehemiah was said to have been the cupbearer of the king[48] served as kind of a model for the attribution of signal honor to Zerubbabel. Interestingly enough there is no mention of Nehemiah in connection with the reading of the law (I Esd 9:49); only "the governor" is specified. In Neh 8:9, the parallel passage, the MT has "Nehemiah the governor" but the LXX omits the descriptive "governor" and retains only the name, Nehemiah. This passage has been employed by some scholars as an argument against the contemporaneity of Ezra and Nehemiah.[49]

V. THEOLOGICAL AND PRACTICAL INTERESTS

Feasts, offerings and sacrifices are stressed — as in the parallels. Passover, tabernacles, and unleavened bread are mentioned. As noted above, the temple is glorified throughout. The author goes beyond Chronicles, Ezra, Nehemiah in his conception of holiness which is a regnant theme. There are holy singers (1:14; 5:27, 45; 8:5, 22; 9:24) where the sources have only singers; holy vessels (1:39, 43, 51; 6:17, 25; 8:17, 55) where the parallels have simply vessels or goodly vessels. The temple is called the holy temple (1:53). Then there are the holy treasury (5:44), holy works (7:3), and the holy garment (8:68, 70) of Ezra. As if to emphasize the liturgical aspect of it, the first day of the month is regularly referred to as the new moon of the month (5:52, 55; 8:6; 9:16, 17, 37, 40) rather than the first day where parallels occur.[50] There is even more stress on the law here than in parallel passages and at several places there is mention of it where it is wanting in the sources. A few examples will suffice to illustrate the point:

1:6   has *prostagma*, "order, command," for *logos*, "word," in II Chron 35:6.

1:46   *nomima*, "customs, usages, statutes=*ḥoq* in MT," is without parallel.

5:48   has *diēgoreumenois*, "expressly declared,"[51] of the sacrifices and offerings commanded in the book of Moses; the parallel in Ezra 3:2 has simply *gegrammena*, "written."

8:7   reads "For Ezra had vast knowledge so that he overlooked none of [the prescriptions] of the law (*nomos*) of the Lord and the

---

[48] Cf. AB, vol. 14, NOTE and COMMENT on Neh 1:11d. It could be added that eunuchs and cupbearers were important officials in the royal household. The former often had a hand in palace intrigues and lent their support to the enthronement of kings. Cf. Tobit 1:22 and Herodotus 3:34.

[49] Cf. Oesterley, *Introduction to the Books of the Apocrypha*, p. 138. For further comments on historical value of I Esdras cf. Lods, pp. 950–53 [BIBLIO I].

[50] Occurs only once, in Ezra 3:5; in Neh 10:33[34]; 1 Macc 10:34; Jub 8:6.

[51] This word appears in Egyptian papyri of the second century B.C.

Commandments (*entolē*)" where Ezra 7:10 has "For Ezra had set his mind on investigating the law of Yahweh."

8:8 adds "of the Lord" (*kuriou*) to the law; Ezra 7:10 has only "the law."

8:21 has "according to the law (*nomos*) of God"; Ezra 7:23 has *en gnōmē theou*, "in the teachings, maxims of God."

9:34, 41 omit the reference to this book and have simply "the law."

9:40 has Ezra bringing out "the law" for the whole congregation "to hear" whereas Neh 8:2 says he read the law to everyone who could listen to it intelligently.

9:42 refers to Ezra as *anagnōstēs tou nomou*, "the reader of the law," while Neh 8:4 has *o grammateus*, "the scribe," thus omitting the objecting of the phrase.

It is possible that a theological interest is present in 1:25 where the author uses the word *exapostellō*, "send out," in preference to *ēkō*, "come," found in II Chron 35:21. Both I Esdras and Chronicles regard Neco as being under divine orders but the former employs a much stronger term; cf. its use in the New Testament.

I Esdras was widely used and quoted in the early centuries of our era. As indicated by the frequent references throughout this introduction and the commentary Josephus used it in preference to Ezra-Nehemiah (see n. 17 above). Justin Martyr (second century) accuses the Jews of removing a passage concerning the passover from Esdras (*Dialogue with Trypho* 72), though what he quotes is not found in I Esdras or anywhere else in the Ezra literature. Clement of Alexandria (second century) refers to Zerubbabel "having by his wisdom overcome his opponents, and obtained leave from Darius for the rebuilding of Jerusalem, returned with Esdras to his native land" (*Stromata* 1:21). Origen (A.D. 182–251) refers to I Esd 4:35, 39 (*Homily on Joshua* 9 and *Commentary on John* 6:1) though that does not necessarily mean that he regarded the book as canonical. Eusebius (A.D. 260–340) quotes I Esd 4:34 (*Comment. on Ps. 76*). Athanasius (A.D. 293–373) refers to I Esd 4:36 (*Orat. II Contra Arianos*, n. 20, and *ad Imp. Constantium Apol.*, n. 11) and to I Esd 4:41 (*ad Imp. Constantium Apol.*, n. 18). The author of *Synopsis scripturae sacrae* (J. P. Migne, *Patrologiae Graecae* [PG], vol. 28, col. 285) quotes I Esd 1:1 and refers to *Esdras protos kai deuteros* (first and second Esdras). Ephrem Syrus (fourth century) quotes I Esd 4:34 ff. in *de Vertutibus et Vitiis* (Sermon 13) and Basilius (same century) quotes I Esd 4:35 (*de Spiritu Sanctu* 7). Chrysostom (A.D. 354–407) in *Synopsis scripturae sacrae* 5 refers to I Esd 4:36. Olympiodorus of Alexandria (sixth century A.D.) in *Comment. in Ecclesiasten*, ch. 1, comments on I Esd 4:34 and John of Damascus (A.D. 700–754) in *Parallel*, I, ch. 19, has in mind I Esd 4:39. Elias of Crete (eighth century A.D.) in *Comment.*

in S. Gregorii Nazianzus twice quotes I Esd 4:34 (*Oration* 1, nn. 109 and 167). The chronographies of Syncellus (ninth century A.D.) and Nicephorus (eighth century A.D.), and the twelfth-century scholiast Zonaras (*Annal.* 1) lean on I Esdras. The former say the history of Esdras begins with the eighteenth year of Josiah, noting especially the passover (Dindorf ed., vol. 1, p. 475).

The early Latin fathers used Esdras 3 (i.e. I Esdras; see Introduction, opening paragraph) freely and without hesitation. Cyprian (A.D. 200–258) quotes I Esd 4:38–40 in *Epistle* 74:9 — *Pompeium* and I Esd 4:34 f. in *de singularitate clericorum,* c. 21. Ambrosius (fourth century) refers to I Esd 4:29 ff. in *Epistle* 7, Bachiarus (a contemporary of St. Augustine) speaks of the spirit of wisdom of Zerubbabel in *Epist. ad Januas de recipiendis lapsis,* and St. Augustine (A.D. 354–430) quotes I Esd 3:12 in *de civitate dei* 18:36. Prosper Aquitanus (fifth century) agrees fully with I Esdras (*de promissionibus et praedictionibus dei II,* c. 36–38) and Sulpicius Severus quotes I Esd 3:4 in *Hist. sacra* II.

After the opinion voiced by St. Jerome[52] I Esdras was relegated to an appendix of the Vulgate. Luther regarded Third Ezra as a "figmentum Iudaicum"[53] and remarked in his Table Talk, "The third book of Esdras I threw into the Elbe. In the fourth book, containing what Ezra dreamed, are beautiful and otherwise good oddities such as wine is strong, the king is stronger, women are still stronger, but truth is the strongest of all."[54] Note his confusion of I and II Esdras (=III and IV Ezra). In his preface to Baruch, he gives this reason for not translating our book: "The same two books of Ezra we simply did not want to translate [into German] because they contain nothing that one cannot find much better in Aesop or still more inferior books; moreover, there are in the fourth book of it [Ezra] idle dreams, as Jerome himself says and that Lyra did not desire to exposit; and it is not found in Greek." Karlstadt (*de canonicis Scripturis libellus*) observed that "Third and Fourth Esdras are scorned."

There is no reference to I Esdras in the Talmud though there are a number of observations on truth that recall the teaching of 4:33–40. For example: "On three things the world stands: on justice, on truth and on peace" (Aboth 1:18). "The seal of the Holy One, blessed be He, is *emeth* [truth]" (Shabbath 55a). "Truth is rare . . . truth has a brick-like foundation. Truth can stand" (ibid. 104a). In Yoma 69b it is said that a tablet fell down from heaven inscribed with the word "truth" and in

---

[52] "You bring before me an apocryphal book which, under the name of Esdras, is read by you and those of your father. . . . I have never read the book (i.e. Esdras): for what need is there to take up what the Church does not receive" — *The Nicene and Post-Nicene Fathers,* Second Series, eds. P. Schaff and H. Wace (New York: The Christian Literature Co., 1893), vol. 6, p. 419.

[53] *Luthers Werke* (Weimar, 1912), No. 268.

[54] Ibid., No. 475.

Yebamoth 105a there is a discourse on the writing of truth in Dan 10:21. Commenting on Exod 34:8, Sanhedrin 111a notes that Moses saw God's attribute of truth.

Tobit refers to truth twice[55] but without connection to I Esdras. The trilogy of wine, women, and truth appears in Testament of Judah (chs. 14, 15, 20) with no more than vague recollections of things said about them in I Esdras. References in Sirach to wine (31:27–28) and women (25:8; 26:1, 13) represent ordinary Wisdom reflections not connected in any way with our book.

[55] Tobit 4:6, "Wherefore if you do truth your works will succeed"; 12:8 (Codex Sinaiticus), "Prayer with truth is good."

BIBLIOGRAPHY I

Books

Abel, F. M. *Histoire de la Palestine,* I. Paris: J. Gabalda, 1952. *Cited as* Abel, *Histoire.*

Ball, C. J. *The Ecclesiastical or Deutero-Canonical Books of the Old Testament commonly called The Apocrypha.* Variorum Reference Edition. London: Eyre & Spottiswoode, n.d.

Bayer, Edmund. *Das dritte Buch Esdras und sein Verhältnis zu den Büchern Esra-Nehemia.* Biblische Studien, XVI, Part I. Freiburg im B.; Herder, 1911. *Cited as* Bayer.

Bertholdt, Leonhard. *Historisch-kritische Einleitung in die sämtlichen kanonischen und Apokryphischen Schriften des Alten und Neuen Testaments.* 3 vols. Erlangen: Palm, 1812–19. In loco.

Eissfeldt, Otto. *The Old Testament: An Introduction,* tr. P. R. Ackroyd. New York: Harper & Row, 1965. *Cited as* Eissfeldt.

Fritzsche, O. F. *Kurzegefasstes exegetisches Handbuch zu den Apokryphen des Alten Testaments.* Erste Lieferung. Leipzig: Weidmann, 1851. Pages 3–66. *Cited as* Fritzsche.

Kellermann, Ulrich. "Das III Esrabuch und die Nehemiaüberlieferung," in *Nehemia Quellen Überlieferung und Geschichte.* Berlin: Töpelmann, 1967. Pages 128–33. *Cited as* Kellermann.

Lods, Adolphe. *Histoire de la littérature hébraïque et juive.* Paris: Payot, 1950. Pages 948–54. *Cited as* Lods.

Metzger, B. M. *An Introduction to the Apocrypha.* New York: Oxford University Press, 1957. *Cited as* Metzger.

Meyer, Eduard. *Die Entstehung des Judenthums.* Halle: Niemeyer, 1896. *Cited as* Meyer.

Mowinckel, Sigmund. *Studien zu dem Buche Ezra-Nehemia.* 3 vols. Oslo: Universitetsforlaget, 1964–65. I, 1–28; III, 10–11.

Nestle, Eberhard. *Marginalien und Materialien.* Tübingen: Heckenhauer, 1893. *Cited as* Nestle.

Oesterley, W. O. E. *An Introduction to the Books of the Apocrypha.* London: SPCK, 1953. Pages 133–41.

Pfeiffer, R. H. *History of New Testament Times with an Introduction to the Apocrypha.* New York: Harper, 1949. Pages 233–57. *Cited as* Pfeiffer.

Pohlmann, Karl-Friedrich. *Studium zum dritten Esra.* Göttingen: Vandenhoeck & Ruprecht, 1970.

Rudolph, Wilhelm. *Esra und Nehemia samt 3. Esra.* Handbuch zum Alten Testament. Tübingen: Mohr, 1949. *Cited as* E-N.

Schürer, Emil. *Geschichte des jüdischen Volkes im Zeitalter Jesu Christi.* 3 vols. 3d ed. Leipzig: Hinrichs, 1898. *Cited as* Schürer.

van Selms, Adrianus. *Ezra en Nehemia.* Groningen-Batavia: J. B. Wolter, 1935. Pages 140–46 deal with the story of the bodyguards.

Tedesche, S. S. "A Critical Edition of I Esdras," Yale Dissertation, 1928. (Edition of Greek text).

Torrey, C. C. *The Apocryphal Literature*. Yale University Press, 1945. Pages 43–54. *Cited as* Torrey.

——— *Ezra Studies*. University of Chicago Press, 1910. *Cited as* ES.

Articles

Büchler, Adolph, "Das Apokryphe Esdrasbuch," MGWJ 41 (1896), 1–16, 49–66, 97–103.

Cook, S. A. "I Esdras," in *The Apocrypha and Pseudepigrapha of the Old Testament,* ed. R. H. Charles. 2 vols. Oxford: Clarendon Press, 1913. I, 1–58. *Cited as* Cook, APOT.

Fischer, Johann, "Das apokryphe und das kanonische Esrabuch," in BZ 2 (1904), 351–64.

Guthe, Hermann, "Das dritte Buch Esra," in *Die Apokryphen und Pseudepigraphen des Alten Testaments,* ed. Emil Kautzsch. 2 vols. Tübingen: Mohr, 1900. I, 1–23. *Cited as* Guthe, APAT.

Howorth, H. H., "The Real Character and the Importance of the First Book of Esdras," *Academy* 43, Jan. 7, 21, Feb. 4, 25, Apr. 15, June 17, July 25, 1893.

——— "Some Unconventional Views on the Text of the Bible," *Proceedings of the Society of Biblical Archaeology* 23 (1901), 147 ff., 305 ff.; 24 (1902), 147 ff., 332 ff.; 25 (1903), 15 ff., 90 ff.; 26 (1904), 25 ff., 63 ff., 94 ff.; 27 (1905), pp. 267 ff.; 29 (1907), 31 ff.

Humbert, Paul, "Magna est veritas et praevalet," OLZ (1928), cols. 148–49.

Klein, R. W., "Old Readings in I Esdras: The List of Returnees from Babylon (Ezra 2 || Nehemiah 7)," HTR 62 (1969), 99–107.

Moulton, W. J., "Über die Überlieferung und den textkritischen Werth des dritten Esrabuchs," ZAW 19 (1899), 209–58; 20 (1900), 1–35.

Riessler, Paul, "Der textkritische Wert des dritten Esdrasbuches," BZ 5 (1907), 146–58.

Rudolph, Wilhelm, "Der Wettstreit der Leibwächter des Darius 3. Esr. 3, 1–5, 6," ZAW 61 (1945–48), 176–90.

Ryan, J. K., "Magna est veritas, et praevalebit," *American Ecclesiastical Review* 135 (1956), 116–24.

Shalit, A., "The Date and Place of the Story about the Three Bodyguards of the King in the Apocryphal Book of Ezra," BJPES 13 (1947), 119–28.

Thackeray, H. St. J., "The First Book of Esdras," in *A Dictionary of the Bible,* ed. J. Hastings (New York: Scribner's, 1899) I, 758–63. *Cited as* Thackeray, HDB.

Torrey, C. C., "The Nature and Origin of First Esdras," AJSL 23 (1907), 116–41.

——— "A Revised View of First Esdras," in *Louis Ginzberg Jubilee Volume,* English Section (New York: The American Academy for Jewish Research, 1945), pp. 395–410. *Cited as* Torrey, LGJV.

——— "The Story of the Three Youths," AJSL 23 (1907), 177–201.

Walde, Bernhard, "Die Esdrasbücher der Septuaginta, ihr gegenseitige Verhältnis untersucht." Biblische Studien, XVIII, Part IV. Freiburg im B.: Herder, 1913.

York, H. C., "The Latin Versions of First Esdras," AJSL 26 (1910), 253–302.

Zimmermann, Frank, "The Story of the Three Guardsmen," JQR 54 (1963–64), 179–200.

I. THE PERIOD OF JOSIAH
(1:1–31)†

JOSIAH'S PASSOVER

1 ¹And Josiah celebrated in Jerusalem the passover[a] to his[b] Lord—they[c] slaughtered the passover [lamb] on the fourteenth day of the first month, ²stationing the priests according to their courses and girded[d] [for service], in the temple of the Lord. ³He specifically charged the Levites, the temple servants[e] of Israel, to sanctify themselves to the Lord when depositing the sacred ark of the Lord in the house which King Solomon, the son of David, had built. ⁴"It is no longer necessary for you to carry it [around] on your shoulders; so now serve the Lord your God, minister to his people Israel, and prepare [the passover] according to your families and tribes in conformity with the decree of David, king of Israel and the grandeur[f] of Solomon his son. ⁵And standing in proper order in the holy place according to your family division, as [the division of] the Levites [serving] before your brothers, the sons of Israel, ⁶slaughter the passover, prepare the sacrifices for your brothers and observe the passover in harmony with the command of the Lord given to Moses." ⁷Then Josiah provided for the people who were present thirty thousand sheep and young goats [and] three thousand head of cattle. These were contributed from the royal bounty, as pledged, to

Note: Translation is from the text of *The Old Testament in Greek,* vol. II, *The Later Historical Books,* part IV: I Esdras, Ezra-Nehemiah, edited by A. E. Brooke, Norman McLean, and H. St. John Thackeray. Cambridge University Press, 1935. Versification follows Greek text; for differences from English versions generally, see KEY TO THE TEXT.

† I Esd 1:1–20 ‖ II Chron 35:1–19, II Kings 23:21–23; 23–31 ‖ II Chron 35:20–27, II Kings 23:28–30.

[a] *pascha.* II Chron 35:1 = *phasech* in LXX.

[b] MT=*lyhwh,* "to Yahweh," without possessive pronoun. I Esdras follows LXX, "to the Lord his God."

[c] LXX^A the sons of Israel.

[d] Rare meaning of *ḥzq* in piel (II Chron 35:2).

[e] *ntynym* for MT *mbwnym,* "instructors." The *nethinim* were a special class of temple employees (cf. I Esd 5:29, 35; 8:5, 22, 48).

[f] For MT of II Chron 35:4 *bmktb,* "decree."

the people, the priests and the Levites. 8 Hilkiah, Zechariah, and Jehiel, the overseers of the temple, also contributed to the priests for [the] passover twenty-six hundred sheep [and] three hundred head of cattle. 9 Chonaniah, Shemaiah, Nethanel his brother, Shebaiah, Ochiel and Joram, the chiefs[g] contributed to the Levites for [the] passover one thousand[h] sheep [and] seven hundred[i] head of cattle. 10 The following then took place: the priests and the Levites [j]with the unleavened[j] bread took their place with proper dignity, according to tribes and family divisions, before the people[k] to offer [the sacrifice] to the Lord as prescribed in the book of Moses — which [they did] in the morning[l]. 11 Then they roasted the passover over fire as required; they boiled the sacrificial victims in copper kettles and caldrons with [m]delectable smell[m], and distributed [them] all to the people. 12 Afterward they provided for themselves and for the priests, their brothers, the sons of Aaron, 13 because the priests served the fat pieces until very late [in the night]; therefore the Levites provided for themselves and for the priests, their brothers, the sons of Aaron. 14 The temple singers, the sons of Asaph, were [stationed] in their posts in accordance with the regulations of David, and Asaph, Zechariah and Eddinos, the royal officials, 15 while the gatekeepers [were in position] at each gateway; not one had to leave his post of daily service, for their brothers, the Levites provided for them[n]. 16 Thus everything pertaining to the sacrifices of the Lord was carried out that day — the passover was celebrated and the sacrifices offered upon the altar of the Lord according to the injunction of King Josiah. 17 So the sons of Israel who were present at that time celebrated the passover and the feast of unleavened bread for seven days. 18 Such a passover celebration had not taken place in Israel since the time of the prophet Samuel, 19 nor had any of the kings of Israel ever celebrated such a passover as Josiah, the priests, the Levites, the Jews and all Israel present [o]in their homes[o] in

---

g LXX of Chronicles=*archontes;* here=*chiliarchoi.*
h LXX[A] has five thousand, as II Chron 35:9.
i II Chron 35:9 five hundred, as some Latin MSS.
j-j *maṣṣoth* for *miṣwoth*, "commandments."
k II Chron 35:12 for MT *lbny h'm,* "the sons of the people."
l reading *boqer* for *bāqār,* "cattle," as does LXX of II Chron 35:12.
m-m Reads *ṣlḥ* for *ṣlḥḥ,* "pots for cooking," in II Chron 35:13.
n So with LXX[A]; B, "themselves."
o-o Probably read *ywšbm,* or as Fritzsche suggests, *bmwšbyhm,* for MT *wywšby yrwšlm,* "and the citizens of Jerusalem."

Jerusalem had [just] celebrated. 20 This passover was celebrated in the eighteenth year of Josiah's reign.

JOSIAH'S PIETY

21 The works of Josiah succeeded before his Lord because of the piety with which his heart was filled, 22 and his story was chronicled in former times because of those who had sinned and acted impiously against the Lord beyond every nation and kingdom and how painfully they grieved him so that the words of the Lord against Israel were confirmed.

JOSIAH'S DEATH

23 Now after all this activity of Josiah, it happened that Pharaoh, king of Egypt, came up to conduct a military campaign at Carchemish on the Euphrates; and Josiah went out to confront him. 24 Then the king of Egypt sent[p] the following message to him: "What have we to do with each other, O king of Judah? 25 [q]I have not been sent out[q] by the Lord God against you; rather my war is on the Euphrates. Now the Lord is with me, and the Lord who is with me is driving me on; so restrain yourself and do not resist the Lord." 26 Nevertheless Josiah did not return to his chariot but attacked[r] him; paying no attention to [the] words of the prophet Jeremiah [which came] from the mouth of the Lord, 27 he engaged him in battle on the plain of Megiddo [s]where the leaders[s] came against King Josiah. 28 Then the king said to his attendants, "Remove me from the battle for I am very seriously wounded." And his attendants removed him immediately from the battle line[t]. 29 He got up into his second chariot and while he was being returned to Jerusalem he died and was buried in the ancestral tomb. 30 In all Judah they mourned for Josiah. Jeremiah the prophet composed a dirge in honor of Josiah, and the prominent men[u] together with the women lament

[p] MT=′th, "come."
[q-q] LXX of II Chron 35:21 reads Hebrew correctly: ēkō, "come." exapestalmai here is much stronger and involves a theological conception.
[r] Lit. "undertook to fight."
[s-s] MT of II Chron 35:23=wyrw hyrym, "and the bowmen shot."
[t] MT of II Chron 35:24=hmrbkh, "the chariot."
[u] hśrym for hšrym, "male singers." The Greek reads "princes, prominent men" for Hebrew "singers," but the reading confirms the text. The context supports the view that the original reading was "singers" rather than "princes."

him to this very day. This has become an established custom for the entire nation of Israel. 31 These things are recorded in the book of the chronicles of the kings of Judah, as well as every single act of Josiah, his splendor, and his understanding of the law of the Lord; both his earlier and later achievements are narrated in the book of the kings of Israel and Judah.

NOTES

1:1. *Josiah*. The Hebrew forms of the names are given where they exist. Otherwise Greek transcriptions are employed.

2. *their courses*. Clerical arrangements for the temple service.

3. *temple servants*. hierodules used only in LXX of I Esdras.

4. *carry it*. I.e. the ark of the Lord.

5. *division*. meridarchian, lit. "office," only in LXX of I Esdras.

8. *Hilkiah*=Chelkeias; *Zechariah*=Zacharias; *Jehiel*=Esyelos.

9. *Shebaiah*=Hashabiah; *Ochiel*=Jeiel; *Joram*=Jozabad.

chiefs. Lit. "commanders of a thousand"; MT has "chiefs of the Levites."

10. This verse represents a resume of II Chron 35:10–12.

in the book of Moses. Cf. 5:48; 7:6, 9; and M. Baillet, J. T. Milik, and R. de Vaux, *Les 'Petites Grottes' de Qumran*, DJD, III (1962), 90.

morning (see textual note *k*) represents a misreading. The passover sacrifice was prepared in the evening (cf. Exod 12:6; Deut 16:6).

11. *roasted*. So the Chronicler (II Chron 35:13) who conflates Exod 12:8 f., which prescribes roasting, and Deut 16:7, which prescribes boiling.

14. II Chron 35:15 has Heman in place of *Zechariah*. Position here may be due to that of Zechariah in I Chron 16:5.

21–22. On these verses see LXX addition between II Chron 35:19 and 20; cf. II Kings 23:24–27. See comments by Torrey, LGJV, pp. 405–10.

23. *Pharaoh*. Neco (cf. II Chron 35:20; II Kings 23:29). The name is omitted here.

24. *Judah*. LXX has "Judea." Freely, "What business do we have to transact or what do our objectives have in common?"

25. *my war is on the Euphrates*. See Benedict Otzen, *Studien über Deuterosacharja* (Copenhagen: Munksgaard 1964), p. 82, n. 14.

26. *words of the prophet Jeremiah*. II Chron 35:22 attributes them to Neco.

29. *he died*. Lit. "he exchanged or yielded up his life."

30. *dirge*. For a dirge still extant in his time, see Jos. *Antiq.* 10:5:1.

COMMENT

[Josiah's passover, 1:1–20] The story related here agrees in general with that transmitted by the Chronicler. Yet the writer has his own way of stressing certain points and glossing over others. One cannot always determine whether a given word of the original has been misread intentionally or inadvertently.

For example, in II Chron 35:3 it is affirmed that the Levites were the instructors (see textual note ^e) of all Israel; I Esd 1:3 makes them temple servants. Was it simply a misreading of the Hebrew or the influence subsequently related of functions of the Levites? However, in 9:48, 49 the author uses a much stronger term for the function of the Levites than the LXX of Neh 8:7, 9: for *mbynym* (Hiphil participle of *byn*) Esdras has *didaskō*, "teach," Nehemiah *sunetizō*, "to cause to understand, interpret." II Chron 35:11 was omitted probably through a misreading of the Hebrew text. Verse 16 was embellished by the insertion of the phrase "the sacrifices of the Lord."

Josiah, acting for or representing the nation, celebrates the passover, ostensibly in response to the demands of the lawbook found in the temple by Hilkiah. As in Chronicles, the date is specified (cf. Lev 23:5) and the place is Jerusalem. Deut 16:5, 6 prescribed a specific place which Josiah and his friends connected with Jerusalem. The priests were stationed according to their cultic order. The Levites were charged with the performance of their duties. They were to sanctify themselves for the proper handling of the ark, perhaps its replacement in the sanctuary after the cleansing of the temple. In any case, the ark was no longer to be carried around in festival processions.[1] Hence the Levites were free for other duties in connection with cultic celebrations "in conformity with the decree of David" (cf. II Chron 8:14 f.). They were given full status as functionaries with the priests and organized, according to families, into service divisions ready for the carrying out of assignments as the occasion demanded. They were to slaughter the passover and prepare the sacrifices as the Mosaic regulations demanded. I Esdras thus follows the Chronicler in normalizing the emergency functions carried out by the Levites in the time of Hezekiah (II Chron 30:17). In view of the description of the Levites as "temple servants" (vs. 3), their service appears to have been restricted to menial tasks. Yet that very term could place them in a position of almost equal service with priests in handling the sacred tasks of the cult.

Contributions for the passover must be regarded as reflecting the generosity of the contributors and the full participation of the community. The numbers of animals of all kinds provided by the king and the chiefs of the house of God are the same for Chronicles as for I Esdras; the number of small animals given by the Levites has been scaled down from five thousand to one thousand, while that of large animals (oxen or bulls) has been increased from five hundred to seven hundred.

The celebrations began with the priests and Levites taking their respectively assigned places for the rites of unleavened bread (vs. 10) which is not mentioned in the Chronicles parallel (II Chron 35:10) until later (vs. 17). Reference to it here is due to a misinterpretation (see third NOTE on 1:10). While both sacrifices were slain at the same time, the indication is that only the unleavened bread rite was performed in the morning (possibly again a misreading of the Hebrew (see textual note ^k). Then the passover was roasted and boiled (a conflation of Exod 12:8 f. and Deut 16:7). Apparently the Levites were busy with paschal duties while the priests were engaged in the pre-

---

[1] According to I Chron 15:2, the bearing of the ark was an exclusive function of the Levites.

senting of burnt offerings, so that the former took care of the needs of the other officiants — priests, temple singers, and gatekeepers. The ubiquity of the Levites is indicative of their place in the sources which I Esdras accepted without question.

If the text of vs. 19 is accepted as it now stands, the reference to "all Israel present in their homes in Jerusalem" does not conform to the MT of II Chron 35:18. Originally the passover was a family feast kept in the home (Exod 12:3, 4, 46); from the time of Josiah (640–609 B.C.) until the destruction of the temple in A.D. 70 except for the period between 587 and 517/16 B.C., it was a pilgrimage feast held at Jerusalem. The celebrations of Hezekiah (II Chron 30) — perhaps to some extent a precedent for the Deuteronomist — and Josiah followed the regulation laid down in Deut 16:1–6 according to which the passover was not to be celebrated in the local communities but "at the sanctuary where Yahweh your God chooses to put his name." Could it be that I Esdras reverts to the priestly regulation of Exodus? Is the passage a simple misreading of the Hebrew? Or does it imply a limitation of celebrants to the cult personnel and the laity who happened to reside at Jerusalem? It will be recalled, however, that Hezekiah invited "all Israel and Judah" and made a special point of urging Ephraim and Manasseh to participate (II Chron 30:1). Josiah too is said to have included "all Judah and Israel" (II Chron 35:18).

[Josiah's piety, 1:21–22] I Esdras prefaces the downfall of Josiah with these verses. They are intended as an explanation as to the reason for the misfortune of the king despite his reforming activity and piety. The wickedness of the nation was so ingrained and persistent that Josiah's good deeds were insufficient to alter its headlong plunge to disaster. II Kings 23:24–27 is doubtless the precedent for this passage as Torrey (ES, pp. 87 ff.) long ago pointed out. He thinks our passage represents what the Chronicler originally wrote but in somewhat "mutilated form," a considerable sentence having fallen out after "because" in vs. 22.[2] Possibly the whole reference was intentionally dropped by the MT because it appeared to put Josiah in the same category as the most evil kings, which he certainly was not.

[Josiah's death, 1:23–31] The campaign of Pharaoh Neco was directed against the Medes and Babylonians (as Jos. Antiq. 10:5:1 asserts) and not against the king of Assyria (cf. II Kings 23:29). I Esdras followed the MT of Chronicles since the LXX of II Chron 35:20 has borrowed the Kings phrase, epi ton basilea Assuriōn, "against the king of the Assyrians." There is more here than meets the eye. The Egyptians maintained a garrison at Carchemish on the Euphrates, which held out against the Babylonians until 605 B.C. and were apparently allies of the Assyrians. Neco's mission was undertaken to support his garrison and so aid the Assyrians. The Babylonian Chronicle refers to an Egyptian crossing of the Euphrates at Carchemish to engage the Babylonians quartered at Quramati[3] from which the latter withdrew forthwith.[4] Josiah was a

---

[2] LXX of II Chron 35:19 inserts II Kings 23:24–27 here.

[3] Quramati was probably situated some fifty miles south of Carchemish, on the east side of the Euphrates. Neco's forces aimed to prevent the army of Nabopolassar from relieving the allies under siege at Harran by the Assyrians.

[4] Cf. D. J. Wiseman, Chronicles of the Chaldaean Kings (London: The Trustees of the British Museum, 1956), p. 67.

supporter of the Babylonians and, despite his defeat at Megiddo, may have altered Neco's timetable to such an extent that the Assyrians failed in their attempt to retake Harran, the capital of Assyria after the fall of Nineveh. Harran had been overthrown by the Babylonians and Medes in 610.

I Esdras regards Neco as an instrument of the Lord. The Chronicler speaks of him as being under divine orders. Josiah refused to heed the words of Neco probably because he did not believe that Neco was an instrument of Yahweh. I Esdras definitizes the source of "the mouth of God," *mpy 'lhym*, by stating that Josiah paid no attention to "the words of the prophet Jeremiah [which came] from the mouth of the Lord," *ek stomatos kuriou*, the Lord here standing for *yhwh*.[5] The question is not about the Lord's use of Neco to perform his purpose (he is said to have done it elsewhere, Isa 7:17–20; 45:1; Jer. 27:6 f.), but Neco's recognition of being in his service, or whether Yahweh would speak through him in a tangible way.[6] If anything, the language here is stronger than in MT. Josiah attacked Neco — perhaps because Josiah was allied with the Babylonians — and thus disregarded the word of the Lord.

The death of Josiah was a profound shock to the nation as may be seen from the uniform reports on lamentation on his behalf by "all Judah." The dirge composed by Jeremiah is said to have been preserved in the official records of the kings of Judah. Josephus (see NOTE on 1:30) has transmitted such a song. It certainly is not our book of Lamentations, nor is it to be found in any of the poems of that composition, though the Chronicler appears to affirm as much (II Chron 35:25). That Jeremiah composed dirges is beyond doubt, as may be seen from Jer 22, especially vss. 28–30, and it is not impossible that words like those in vss. 3–19 could have been used in a dirge for Josiah.

[5] I Esdras has a penchant for Yahweh which he renders *kurios*, "Lord." But where MT has *'lhym*, "Elohim, God," he prefers the same word ca. 34 times; ca. 19 times for the Aram. *'lh*, "God"; ca. 14 times for Aram. *'lh'*, "God." Once *kurios* renders *'dny*, "Lord." The regular Greek term for God, *theos*, is used only ca. 47 times in I Esdras whereas it occurs in the LXX of Ezra 98 times and 75 times in Nehemiah. On the other hand *kurios* occurs 139 times in I Esdras, 43 times in LXX of Ezra, and 26 times in Nehemiah. For a resume of the designation of the deity see Moulton, ZAW 19 (1899), 226–30.

[6] Cf. Wilhelm Rudolph, *Chronikbücher*, Handbuch zum Alten Testament, erste Reihe, 21 (Tübingen: Mohr, 1955), pp. 331 ff.; B. Couroyer, RB 55 (1948), 388 ff.

II. THE LAST KINGS OF JUDAH
(1:32–55)†

JEHOAHAZ

1 32 Then the people *[of the land]* took Jechoniah, the son of Josiah, and made him king in place of Josiah his father when he was twenty-three years old. 33 He was king in Israel and Jerusalem for three months when the king of Egypt dethroned him in Jerusalem 34 and levied upon the nation an indemnity of a hundred talents of silver and one talent of gold.

JEHOIAKIM

35 The king of Egypt elevated King Jehoiakim his brother as king of Judah and Jerusalem. 36 Moreover Jehoiakim imprisoned the chief men and arrested Zarios his brother whom he took along to*b* Egypt. 37 Jehoiakim was twenty-five years old when he became king of Judah and Jerusalem; he too did evil in the sight of the Lord. 38 Nebuchadnezzar, king of Babylon, then came up against him, bound him with copper chains and took him away to Babylon. 39 Nebuchadnezzar also took some of the sacred vessels of the Lord, transported them to Babylon where he deposited them in his temple in Babylon. 40 The tales related about him, his depravity and his impiety are recorded in the book of the chronicles of the kings.

JEHOIACHIN

41 Jehoiakim, his son, then became king instead of him; he was eight*c* years old when he was proclaimed [king]. 42 He reigned

---

† I Esd 1:32–34 ‖ II Chron 36:1–3, II Kings 23:30b–33; 35–40 ‖ II Chron 36:4–8, II Kings 23:34 – 24:7; 41–43 ‖ II Chron 36:9–10, II Kings 24:8–17; 44–55 ‖ II Chron 36:11–21, II Kings 24:18 – 25:12.

a–a With Hebrew of II Chron 36:1.

b So with LXXB,b for LXXB="out of Egypt" (*ex Aiguptou*); with II Chron 36:4 and Jos. *Antiq.* 10:5:2. Apparently a misunderstanding or another tradition for Hebrew.

c I Esdras follows LXXB of II Chron 36:9; LXXA has eighteen, which follows MT of II Kings 24:8.

three months and ten days in Jerusalem and did evil in the sight of the Lord. 43 At the turn of the year Nebuchadnezzar had him brought to Babylon together with the sacred vessels of the Lord

ZEDEKIAH

44 and made Zedekiah[d] king of Judah and Jerusalem, Zedekiah being twenty-one years of age. He reigned eleven years. 45 He too did evil in the sight of the Lord, and disregarded the words spoken by Jeremiah the prophet from the mouth of the Lord. 46 Although he swore an oath to King Nebuchadnezzar in the name of the Lord, he violated his oath, rebelled and with a stiff neck and hardened heart transgressed[e] the laws of the Lord God of Israel. 47 Also the leaders of the people and the priests acted very impiously and lawlessly beyond all the abominations of all the nations, and defiled the consecrated temple of the Lord in Jerusalem. 48 The God of their fathers sent [word] through his messengers to recall them because he wanted to spare them and his dwelling place. 49 But they held his messengers in contempt, and whenever the Lord spoke[f] they laughed his prophets to scorn until he, becoming angry with his people on account of their depravity, incited the kings of the Chaldeans to go up against them. 50 They slew with the sword their youths around the holy temple, sparing neither young man nor maiden, neither old man nor child; but he delivered all [of them] into their hands. 51 And they carried off to Babylon all the sacred vessels of the Lord, both great and small, the treasure chests of the Lord, and the royal stores which they had taken. 52 They set the house of the Lord on fire, broke down the walls of Jerusalem, set fire to its towers, 53 and [g]completely demolished[g] all its glories. The survivors he led away at sword point to Babylon, 54 and they became his and his sons' slaves until the rise of the Persian regime, to fulfill the word of the Lord at the mouth of Jeremiah: 55 "Until the land enjoy[h] its sabbaths, all the time of its desolation it shall celebrate the sabbath up to the completion of seventy years."

---

[d] I Esdras omits 'hyw, "his brother."
[e] parebē for MT šwb, "turn"; so also LXX epistrepsai, a milder term.
[f] II Chron 36:16 has bwzym dbryw, "despising his words."
[g-g] II Chron 36:19 has kl-kly, "all the vessels of. . . ." I Esdras reads klh klw.
[h] Author read rṣh I for rṣh II, "make restitution."

NOTES

1:32. *Jechoniah.* An error for Jehoahaz, corrected by a number of MSS.

34. *talents.* Some old Latin MSS read "ten talents of gold." The ratio of 10:1 between silver and gold may be regarded as normal in the first millennium B.C. There were doubtless exceptions, but in tribute lists this ratio is generally maintained.

35. *Jehoiakim.* So with Hebrew for Joakim of LXX.

36. *Zarios.* A mistake for Jehoahaz. II Chron 36:4 says nothing of the arrest of the nobles but asserts that Jehoahaz was deported to Egypt. Nor is there a hint of it in II Kings 23:34, 35.

41. *Jehoiakim.* Jehoiachin is meant as in Vulgate and as II Chron 36:8 f. and II Kings 24:8 f. show.

43. *turn of the year.* Lit. "at the anniversary." Jehoiachin was taken captive at the beginning of 597 B.C.

44. *Zedekiah.* The brother of Jehoiakim, uncle of Jehoiachin (cf. II Kings 24:17; Jer 37:1). He may have been chosen because none of Jehoiachin's sons was old enough at the time (cf. II Kings 24:15; Jer 22:30).

46. *the laws.* MT of II Chron 36:13 has *miššub,* "from turning."

48. *God.* LXX[B] has "king"; MT "the Lord God."

messengers. So with LXX[b,B] and MT, "messenger."

50. *he delivered.* I.e. the Lord.

53. *he led away.* I.e. Nebuchadnezzar.

54. *word . . . of Jeremiah.* Cf. Jer 25:11; 29:10; and Lev 26:34–35.

55. II Chron 36:21 reads: "Until the land had compensated for the neglect of its sabbaths, all the days of its desolation, it rested until the seventy years were complete."

COMMENT

[Jehoahaz (Jechoniah), 1:32–34] The significance of "the people [of the land]" (*'am hā-āreṣ*) was lost to the writer since the text says simply "those of the nation" (*oi ek ton ethnous*) elevated the new king after the death of his father. Jechoniah is a mistake for Jehoahaz, corrected by LXX[N]. He was the last king of Judah to be enthroned by the landed aristocracy of the nation. Nothing is said in Kings and Chronicles about the circumstances surrounding his reign or why he was deposed in favor of his brother. The amount of tribute laid upon Judah by Neco is the same in all accounts.

[Jehoiakim, 1:35–40] By the elevation of Jehoiakim to the throne by the king of Egypt vassalage to Egypt is clearly indicated. Naturally that meant the imprisonment of the supporters of Jehoahaz. Verse 36b is perhaps a confused version of II Chron 36:4b since no other sources support it; but all agree that Neco exiled Jehoahaz to Egypt. Whether we are to see in Zarios or Zarakes the name Jehoahaz (with Guthe) is uncertain. In view of the context, it is scarcely possible that the writer had in the back of his mind the extradition of the prophet Uriah referred to in Jer 26:23. Jehoiakim remained a vassal of Egypt until after the battle of Carchemish (605 B.C.) when he changed sides. Whether that event was enough to force him to alter his allegiance or that of the destruction of Ashkelon a year later is doubtful (cf. Wiseman, *Chronicles of Chaldaean Kings,* pp. 28, 69), since our sources speak of an invasion of Judah by Nebuchadnezzar. If that was the case, it must have come somewhere around 603/2 B.C. while the forces of Neco were still off balance (cf. Jos. *Antiq.* 10:6:1) for when the Babylonians were checked in 601 B.C. Jehoiakim seems to have shifted policy again as indicated by the withholding of tribute. The running conflict between Babylonians and Egyptians and the strong Egyptian proclivity of Jehoiakim may well have resulted in two invasions of Judah between 603/2 and 597 as reflected by the Chronicler.[1] The assessment of the character of Jehoiakim is more unfavorable than that given by the Chronicler; he is said to have been morally depraved and ungodly.

[Jehoiachin, 1:41–43] I Esdras follows Chronicles almost verbatim. For new information about the fortunes of Jehoiachin in captivity see *II Chronicles,* AB, vol. 13, COMMENT on § 41, 36:9–10. The importance of Jehoiachin for the subsequent history of Judah may be seen from the genealogy of I Chron 3:17–18 and the role of Zerubbabel, his grandson. Despite his short reign — from early December 598 to mid-March 597 — he was still regarded as the legitimate king while Zedekiah was simply a regent. The seals of "Eliakim steward of Yaukin"[2] may point to the maintenance intact of the property of the king in the hope that he would some day return to power (cf. Jer 28:4). That was not to be; though he was ultimately released from prison, he died in exile (cf. Jer 52:31–34, a passage supported, with some qualifications by the Weidner texts). Jehoiachin may have enjoyed popular favor in part because he was the legitimate successor to the throne whereas his uncle, Zedekiah, was an appointee of Babylon.

[Zedekiah, 1:44–55] That Zedekiah was a weak king is demonstrated by his attitudes and decisions recounted in Jeremiah. In fact he was, for the most part, a prisoner of his court (cf. Jer 38:5). The account here does not vary substantially from that of the Deuteronomist or Chronicler. At a few points there may be deliberate exaggeration. I Esdras says Zedekiah "disregarded" the word of the Lord spoken by Jeremiah (vs. 45); II Chron 36:12 says he refused to humble himself before the prophet. More emphasis is here placed on the swearing of an oath of allegiance to and covenant with Nebuchadnezzar (cf. Ezek 17:11–21) and its violation, and there is no specific reference in II Chronicles to the transgression of "the laws of the Lord God of Israel." Condemnation here falls only on the officials (vs. 47) and is not so inclusive as in II Chron 36:14. Their impious acts and lawlessness surpassed those of the pagan nations; in II Chron 36:14 they were said to be just like the nations.

---

[1] See further F. K. Kienitz, *Die politische Geschichte Ägyptens vom 7. bis zum 4. Jahrhundert vor der Zeitwende* (Berlin: Akademie-Verlag, 1953), pp. 23 ff.

[2] Several of these stamp seals have been found, two at Tell Beit Mirsim, one at Ain Shems, and one at Ramat Rahel. See W. F. Albright, JBL 51 (1932), 77–106, and BA 5 (1942), 50 f.; Yohanan Aharoni, *Excavations at Ramat Rahel: Seasons 1961 and 1962* (Rome: Centro di Studi Semitici, 1964), p. 33.

The sermonic character of the passage has been preserved. The preacher emphasized the reason for the difficulties that beset the people of Jerusalem during the reign of Zedekiah. Blame is placed on the king, though not exclusively so, because he disregarded the prophecy of Jeremiah (cf. Jer 37:2), violated his loyalty oath, and transgressed the laws of God. The officials of church and state acted abominably and defiled "the consecrated temple of the Lord" — a particularly significant accusation for the period of I Esdras (see Introduction). Persistent failure to heed the prophets, even ridicule of their message, had frightful consequences not just for the people personally but for the nation. Yahweh was the Lord of nations as well as the God of Judah. Hence he had appointed Nebuchadnezzar to chastize them and rebellion against him was rebellion against Yahweh (cf. Jer 25:19; 27:6-9; Ezek 17:11-21). Yet exile would not be the end; it was a drastic cathartic, as the law (Lev 26) and the prophets (Jer 25:11 ff.; 29:10) declared, but one that would save the patient.[3] The Chronicler has combined the Jeremiah prophecy with that of the Leviticus passage (ch. 26) and reinterpreted them in harmony with his theology.

[3] On the seventy years figure (vs. 55), see Riekele Borger, JNES 18 (1959), 74; Otto Plöger, "Siebzig Jahre," in *Festschrift Friedrich Baumgärtel*, Erlanger Forschungen, Reihe A (Erlangen: Geisteswissenschaften, 1959), pp. 124-30; and P. R. Ackroyd, JNES 17 (1958), 23-27, with other treatments cited there.

THE DECREE

2 ¹ The first year of Cyrus' reign — to fulfill the word of the Lord by the mouth of Jeremiah — ² the Lord aroused the spirit of Cyrus, king of the Persians who issued the following proclamation to his entire kingdom and which he also put in writing: ³ "Thus says the king of the Persians, Cyrus: The Lord of Israel, the *ᵃLord Most Highᵃ* has proclaimedᵇ me king of the world ⁴ and designated me to build for him a house in Jerusalem in the [land of] Judah. ⁵ If now any of you belongs to his people, may *ᶜhis Lordᶜ* be with him; go up to Jerusalem, in Judah and build the house of the Lord of Israel, for he is the Lord who has established his residence in Jerusalem. ⁶ Let all now, no matter where they live, help him — those in his neighborhood — with gold and with silver and with gifts, with horsesᵈ and cattle, together with other things set aside by vows for the temple of the Lord in Jerusalem."

THE RESPONSE

⁷ Following this, the chiefs of the families of the tribe of Judah and Benjamin, with the priests and Levites, indeed all whose spirit the Lord had inspired arose to go up to build the house of the Lord in Jerusalem. ⁸ Their neighbors helped them *ᵉwith everythingᵉ*, with silver and gold, horsesᶠ, cattle and with a *ᵍgreat manyᵍ* [other

† **I Esd 2:1–6** ‖ II Chron 36:22–23, Ezra 1:1–4; **7–14** ‖ Ezra 1:5–11.
ᵃ⁻ᵃ MT of Ezra 1:2 has *yhwh 'lhy hšmym,* "Yahweh, God of the heavens," LXXᴮ follows it.
ᵇ So for MT of Ezra 1:2 — *ntn ly yhwh,* "Yahweh gave me."
ᶜ⁻ᶜ Ezra 1:3 — *'lhyw,* "his God."
ᵈ LXX reads *rkš,* "horse," for *rkwš,* "equipment," of MT of Ezra 1:4. See further note by Hermann Guthe and L. W. Batten, *The Books of Ezra and Nehemia,* The Sacred Books of the Old Testament, ed. Paul Haupt, Part 19 (Leipzig: J. C. Hinrichs'sche Buchhandlung, 1901), p. 57.
ᵉ⁻ᵉ Reading *bkl* for MT *bkly,* "with vessels of."
ᶠ See textual note ᵈ.
ᵍ⁻ᵍ *brb* for *lbd,* "in addition," in MT of Ezra 1:6.

things] vowed by all whose mind had been inspired [to do so]. ⁹ Then King Cyrus brought out the sacred vessels of the Lord which Nebuchadnezzar had taken along from Jerusalem and deposited them in the [temple] of ʰhis idolsʰ. ¹⁰ Having removed them, Cyrus the king of the Persians handed them over to Mithridates his treasurer ¹¹ by whom they were transferred to Sheshbazzar, the governor of Judah. ¹² The number of them was: gold libation bowls, one thousand; silver libation bowls, one thousand; silver censers, twenty-nine; gold bowls, thirty; silver [bowls], two thousand four hundred and ten; other vessels, one thousand. ¹³ The sum of all the gold and silver vessels returned was five thousand four hundred and sixty-nine. ¹⁴ They, together with those [persons] taken captive, were brought back by Sheshbazzar from Babylon to Jerusalem.

ʰ⁻ʰ Cf. Dan 1:2. (LXX Dublinensis [Dublin MS of sixth century] has *en tō eidōleiō autou;* Theodotion, *eis ton oikon thesaurou theou autou*).

NOTES

2:8. *vowed.* Lit. "with very many vowed (things) of all. . . ."
11. *Sheshbazzar* is the common Hebrew form. LXX^B has Sanamassar; LXX^A Sanabassar.
12. The numbers do not correspond with those in Ezra 1:9–11. There they are thirty, one thousand, twenty-nine, thirty, four hundred and ten, one thousand respectively or a total of two thousand four hundred and ninety-nine, though the sum given in the text is five thousand four hundred. I Esdras may be an attempt to harmonize the individual items listed with the total.

COMMENT

[The decree, 2:1–6] The decree of Cyrus is recorded no fewer than three times in the Canonical scriptures (II Chron 36:22–23; Ezra 1:1–4; 6:3–5). I Esdras and Josephus (*Antiq.* 11:1:1) also have it. The Hebrew version in Ezra 1:1–4 and the Aramaic version in Ezra 6:3–5 are, in all probability, not variants of the same document but independent documents dealing with the same official act.[1]

The benevolent act of Cyrus, here and in II Chronicles and Ezra 1, is said to have been inspired by the Lord in fulfillment of the prophecy of Jeremiah. Josephus goes much further when he links it to the Cyrus poems of II Isaiah.

[1] Cf. C. J. Gadd, L. Legrain, and S. Smith, *Royal Inscriptions,* Ur Excavations: Texts, I (London: British Museum, 1928), nos. 194, 307. See. E. J. Bickerman, JBL 65 (1946), 250–53; Roland de Vaux, RB 46 (1937), 56–57; Leonhard Rost, in *Verbannung und Heimkehr: Festschrift für Wilhelm Rudolph,* ed. A. Kuschke (Tübingen: Mohr, 1961), pp. 301–7; and A. R. Burn, *Persia and the Greeks* (London: Edward Arnold, 1962), p. 56, n. 25.

But in each case the decree specified that the purpose of the king was "to build for him [the Lord] a house in Jerusalem." Nothing is said of a returning golah. The decree was announced by official heralds or messengers (for such proclamations cf. II Chron 30:5; Ezra 10:7, Neh 8:15). It was also officially posted in the assembly place of the Jewish community.[2] A kind of bulletin board from the time of Antiochus III (223–187 B.C.) has been found at Jezreel.[3] Not only were the fortunes of the captives and the matter of the temple under the control of Yahweh; he was also the great God who enthroned Cyrus as "king of the whole world."[4] As such he was Yahweh's agent for the construction of his house in his dwelling place at Jerusalem, and it was he who not only gave permission for the enterprise but, as the Aramaic version in Ezra 6:3 affirms, he issued orders directing its undertaking. Whether Cyrus came into contact with prominent Jews in the course of his conquest of Babylon is uncertain, but not impossible, though it is unlikely that he read the prophets as Josephus says. The divine command here must be considered in the light of Cyrus' Cylinder Inscription (ANET, pp. 315 f.) where he speaks of the return, at the behest of Marduk, of "all the gods of Sumer and Akkad" which Nabonidus had removed to Babylon. It is not beyond comprehension that one or another Jewish religious leader interceded for Jerusalem and the temple as Udjahorresnet did for the Neith sanctuary at Sais in Egypt in the time of Cambyses and Darius I.[5] The edict enjoins any one of Yahweh's people who is so minded to go to Jerusalem and assist in the temple reconstruction. His neighbors were importuned to help the cause with money and other gifts; gifts vowed for the temple were also to be contributed.

[The response, 2:7–14] The family heads of "the tribe[6] of Judah and Benjamin" along with the priests and Levites and others who responded to the offer of Cyrus undertook the task of rebuilding the temple at Jerusalem. They were assisted by those of their brethren who, for some reason or other, could not accept the invitation to participate personally in the expedition. I Esdras affirms that these contributors were inspired to do so — we would say everyone who was moved to do so. Cyrus instructed his treasurer, Mithridates, to deliver to Sheshbazzar the sacred temple vessels removed by Nebuchadnezzar (II Kings 24:13; 25:13–16; II Chron 36:10, 18; Jer 52:17–19). Note the official character of the transaction handled through proper channels. Ezra 1:8 is more explicit; it says Mithridates "enumerated" them to Sheshbazzar which implies that a strict record was kept by the Persian treasury officials, a copy of which was given to the Jewish authorities. According to Ezra 5:14 Sheshbazzar was appointed governor (peḥā) by Cyrus and thus became the leader of the first contingent of exiles to return to Judah. Though the tradition

[2] Cf. Bickerman, JBL 65 (1946), 272 ff.
[3] See *The Israel Digest*, December 9, 1960.
[4] The OT characterization of Cyrus is in many ways like that of Xenophon's *Cyropaedia*.
[5] Eberhard Otto, "Die biographischen Inschriften des ägyptischen Spätzeit. Ihre geistesgeschichtliche und literarische Bedeutung," in *Probleme der Ägyptologie*, II (Leiden: Brill, 1954), 169–73.
[6] MT omits "tribe."

of Sheshbazzar's connection with the laying of the foundations of the temple
have been disputed, it appears too strong and persistent to ignore or argue
away (cf. Ezra 1:8, 11; 5:14–16). According to I Chron 3:18 he was the
fourth son of Jehoiachin and was, in all probability, the leader of the exilic
community at the time of Cyrus' edict.[7] He was later succeeded by Zerubbabel,
his nephew.

The emphasis on the cultic vessels of the house of the Lord seems to point
to continuity with the pre-exilic religious institutions. The list is basically
authentic though the figures are unreliable. Those here given may be schematic,
harmonized with the total given in vs. 13. The numbers recorded in Ezra
1:9–11a do not harmonize with the total given there, though the text is far
from clear.[8] The whole tenor of the restoration account of Ezra-Nehemiah
and I Esdras stresses the intimate relationship between the old and new institutions — the sacred vessels of the old temple returned to the new one
(cf. further 6:17, 18, 25), the new temple rebuilt on the old site (cf. Ezra
6:3), the altar set upon its original foundations (5:49; Ezra 3:3). For further
discussion on the parallel passage see AB, vol. 14, COMMENT on Ezra 1:1–11.

[7] For further discussion of the relation between Sheshbazzar and Zerubbabel see AB,
vol. 14, p. LXXVII, n. 20, and COMMENT on Ezra 5:6–17.
[8] Note the marginal "to be changed" which slipped into the text and occurs twice in
vss. 9, 10. On the authenticity of the list see Kurt Galling, ZDPV 60 (1937), 177–83,
and *Verbannung und Heimkehr,* p. 68, n. 7.

THE LETTER TO ARTAXERXES

2 ¹⁵ In the times of Artaxerxes the Persian king, Bishlam, Mithradates, Tabeel, Rehum, Beeltethmos*ᵃ*, Shimshai the scribe and the rest in league with them living in Samaria and elsewhere, wrote the following letter [complaining] against the inhabitants of Judah and Jerusalem: ¹⁶ "To King Artaxerxes, the lord: your servants Rehum, the reporter*ᵇ*, and Shimshai, the scribe, and the rest of their council, [judges] in Coelesyria and Phoenicia; ¹⁷ now let it be known to [our] lord, the king, that the Jews who came up from you to us, have arrived at Jerusalem and have begun to rebuild the rebellious and evil city, to restore its marketplaces and walls, and to lay the foundations of a temple*ᶜ*. ¹⁸ Now if this city is rebuilt and the walls finished, they will not only refuse to pay tribute but even withstand kings. And since the work on the temple has already begun, *ᵈ*we consider it appropriate not to overlook*ᵈ* such a matter but to call it to the attention of our lord the king so that, if it appears proper to you, a search [may] be made in the records of your fathers. ¹⁹ There you will find in the memoranda matters recorded about them and learn that that city was rebellious and an annoyance to both kings and cities, and that the Jews were rebellious and inciters of sieges in former times, on account of which this city was laid waste. ²⁰ Now therefore we are apprizing you, lord king, that if this city is rebuilt and its walls erected you will no longer have *ᵉ*a way of approach*ᵉ* to Coelesyria and Phoenicia."

---

† I Esd 2:15–20 || Ezra 4:7–16; 21–24 || Ezra 4:17–22; 25 || Ezra 4:23–24.
ᵃ A mistake for Aram. *bʻl - ṭʻm,* "commanding officer."
ᵇ *o ta prospiptonta,* "the [one with] the news." Renders Aram. *bʻl - ṭʻm,* "commanding officer." Note similar combination in vs. 15 where the descriptive is given as a proper name.
ᶜ Not in MT || of Ezra 4:12.
ᵈ⁻ᵈ MT has "We eat the salt of the palace," which means "we are under obligation to the king."
ᵉ⁻ᵉ *exodos,* "way out." LXX*ᴬ·ᴺ kathodos,* "way down."

THE KING'S REPLY TO REHUM AND HIS ASSOCIATES

21 Then the king wrote in reply to Rehum the recorder, Beel-tethmos*f*, Shimshai the scribe and the rest of their confederates*g* who lived in Samaria, Syria and Phoenicia, as follows: 22 "*h*I have read*h* the letter which you sent to me. When I ordered a search to be made, it was indeed discovered that that city has resisted kings from of old; 23 men have perpetrated rebellion and war in it and powerful and stubborn kings resided in Jerusalem lording it over and exacting taxes from Coelesyria and Phoenicia. 24 And now I have issued an order to restrain those men from rebuilding the city and to see to it beforehand that nothing is done *i*contrary to these [orders]*i* and that these evil measures go no further to the irritation of kings."

EFFECT ON THE WORK OF RECONSTRUCTION

25 Then when the document of King Artaxerxes was read, Rehum and Shimshai the scribe and their confederates, with horsemen and a host of soldiers marched off in haste to Jerusalem and began to obstruct the builders. Thus the building of the temple in Jerusalem was discontinued until the second year of King Darius, king of the Persians.

f See textual note *a*.
g Aram. *knh*. Akk. *kinatu*, "servant," is not quite so strong a word.
h-h MT *mprš qry qdmy* (was translated "[read] before me"). Here the active voice is used and the king himself does the reading.
i-i *para tauta*.

NOTES

2:15. *Artaxerxes*. Artaxerxes Longimanus (465–425 B.C.). Josephus (*Antiq.* 11:2:1, 2) changes the order from Cyrus, Artaxerxes, Darius to Cyrus, Cambyses, Darius which is historically correct but misses the purpose of the Chronicler.

Bishlam. It is questionable whether this was a personal name originally. LXX of Ezra 4:7 reads *en eirēnē*, "in peace" a greeting. Some see in it a mutilation of *byrwšlm*, "against Jerusalem." See Rudolph, E-N, p. 34, and H. H. Schaeder, *Iranische Beitrage*, I (Halle: Niemeyer, 1930), 214 f.

Rehum=LXX Rathumos. *Shimshai*=LXX Samellios.

16. *[judges]*. Omitted by LXX*B* but present in N, some cursives of Old Latin, Syriac, and Vulgate. A has "powerful, mighty ones," *krataioi*.

Coelesyria and Phoenicia. The combination Syria and Phoenicia occurs fourteen times in I Esdras, all but one (here) rendering '*br nhrh*, "Across the River," the official name of the Persian province across the Euphrates to the west including Syria and Palestine. Five times Syria is qualified with the adjective *koilē*, "hollow," once (8:23) with *olē*, "all." LXX of Ezra has *peran* (*pera*) *tou potamou*, following MT; once *tēs esperas tou potamou*, "on the west [side] of the river." The term Coelesyria was applied by the Greeks to the valleys and depressions west of the Euphrates extending from the Orontes basin south as far as Jerusalem and Ashkelon. For further remarks see Abel, *Géographie de la Palestine*, I, 115 ff., II, 311; Torrey, Es, p. 83, n. 23, and especially O. Leuze, *Die Satrapieneinteilung in Syrien und im Zweistromlande von 520–320* (Halle: Niemeyer, 1935), pp. 365 ff., 387 ff.; Kurt Galling, *Studien zur Geschichte Israels im persischen Zeitalter* (Tübingen: Mohr, 1964), pp. 185–209. Diodorus Siculus 1:30, 31; the latter reference is to Joppa [Iope] in Coelesyria. In 2:2:3 he quotes Ktesias as using the same terminology.

17. [*our*] *lord*. Omitted by MT. So also in vss. 18, 20.

19. *both kings and cities*. *kai basileis kai poleis*. Ezra 4:15, the biblical parallel, has *basileis kai chōras* for Aram. *mlkyn wmdnn*. *chōra* is used exclusively in LXX of Ezra-Nehemiah for *mdynh; polis* is never used in LXX to render *mdnyh*. But in later Greek *polis* is sometimes used as a synonym for *chōra*. Vulg. has *reges et civitates*, "kings and states." The phrase may imply a mistranslation or misunderstanding. One would expect "kings and magistrates" or "kingdoms and cities," but in view of Ezra 4:15 the matter remains uncertain.

21. *recorder*. See textual note[b]. Here with *tō graphonti;* "the one who chronicles [the news]."

Syria and Phoenicia spells out the area of the Persian province Across the River in Ezra 4:17.

23. A considerable simplification of Ezra 4:20.

COMMENT

[The letter to Artaxerxes, 2:15–20] The correspondence[1] between the enemies of Judah and Jerusalem and the Persian court in the time of Ahasuerus (Ezra 4:6)=Xerxes is omitted here and the writer begins his outline of the troubles experienced by the returned exiles with the complaint lodged against them in the time of Artaxerxes. I Esdras ignores the first caveat raised by the opponents and referred to in Ezra 4:7, and telescopes both communications into a single document as shown by the combination of names recorded in Ezra 4:7–8 (cf. I Esd 2:15–16). The text here cannot be used to correct Ezra, but it does bring into sharper focus the purpose of the Chronicler: to point up the similarity between the objections raised against the rebuilding of the city walls and those raised against the rebuilding of the temple in the time of Cyrus and Darius.[2] I Esdras includes here a reference to the reconstruction of the temple (vss. 17, 18) not found in the Ezra parallel which is concerned only with the

[1] See AB, vol. 14, COMMENT on Ezra 4:6–16.
[2] See Rudolph, E-N, pp. 33–45, esp. pp. 40 f.

rebuilding of the city as shown by both the letter of complaint and the imperial response thereto. That Josephus followed I Esdras is indicated by a similar reference to the temple and the fact that his outline of the details of the episode is almost identical (*Antiq.* 11:2:1–2).[3] The extended description of the opposition in Ezra 4:9–10 is sharply curtailed; only the bare essentials are given — almost as if the interracial character of the Samaritan community were deliberately played down. After naming the officials, the only identification is "the rest in league with them living in Samaria and elsewhere" (vs. 15) and "the rest of their council, judges in Coelesyria and Phoenicia" (vs. 16). The latter definition of Coelesyria and Phoenicia appears to broaden the base of the opposition from Samaria to the entire province of Across the River (the fifth satrapy) of the Persian empire. So also the "and elsewhere" in the preceding verse, though, in this instance, nothing more than a misunderstanding of the list of peoples composing the mixed population of Samaria may be involved. Leaving aside the doubtful names of Bishlam and Beeltethmos, the ringleaders of the opposition are said to have been Mithradates (probably the Persian consul at Samaria), Tabeel (the chief Samaritan representative of the people), Rehum[4] (the commanding officer) and Shimshai (the secretary of the consulate).[5] I Esdras does not tell us how or why opposition against the activity of the returned exiles arose (cf. Ezra 4:1–3). Josephus assumes it was motivated by jealousy (*Antiq.* 11:2:1) on the part of the residents of the Samaria area who incited and bribed the Persian officials to lodge complaints against the Jews.[6]

Of course, the most serious attention was given to the building operations of the Jews at Jerusalem. They were regarded as the first step in calculated rebellion and thus of a political rather than religious nature as the Jews claimed and their firman specified. On the basis of past history, the reconstruction of the city with protective walls could only work against the empire if allowed to continue unchecked. Hence the Samaria authorities requested a thorough investigation of the original purpose of the reconstitution of the Jerusalem institutions. This may have appeared to them to be of the utmost importance in view of the almost continuous threats of rebellion in Egypt. If the "way of approach to Coelesyria and Phoenicia" should be cut off the situation could be complicated for the Persian authorities.

[The king's reply to Rehum and his associates, 2:21–24] The communication of the imperial authorities at Samaria was taken seriously by the court and a peremptory order issued that the archives be searched for evidence of the relations between Jerusalem and other capitals in the past. It was discovered that Jerusalem had indeed been governed by powerful kings who lorded it over Coelesyria and Phoenicia and exacted taxes therefrom. The kings referred to cannot be identified with any degree of certainty. They may have been David

---

[3] Cf. Bayer, pp. 87, 94, 102, and Cook, APOT, I, 28, note on vs. 20.
[4] Rehum was apparently the successor of Mithradates. See Galling, *Studien zur Geschichte Israels im persischen Zeitalter*, p. 210.
[5] Cf. Schaeder, EdS, p. 40.
[6] This shows that Josephus may have drawn upon Ezra as well as upon I Esdras for his narrative.

and Solomon, or Hezekiah,[7] or perhaps Josiah (cf. II Kings 23:15, 19–20; II Chron 34:6–7, 9). Perhaps there is more here than meets the eye — a serious rift between urban and rural centers of power.[8] The king acted on the report of his investigators and complainants by issuing an order for the immediate cessation of building operations.

[Effect on the work of reconstruction, 2:25] The Samaria officials hastened to put into effect the cease and desist order of the king. They appeared on the scene with force — "with horsemen and a host of soldiers," an item not spelled out in the Ezra parallel (cf. also Jos. *Antiq.* 11:2:2). Just how the term "obstruct" (*kōluein*) is to be interpreted is not clear. Rudolph (E-N, p. 44) thinks they actually undid the work accomplished thus far and suggests that the intervention took place just before the time referred to by the report of Hanani to Nehemiah (Neh 1:3). The second half of the verse has been the source of difficulty and misunderstanding on the part of many commentators. In its original position in Ezra it marks the connecting link with the following chapter, which deals with the troubles encountered in connection with the rebuilding of the temple under Darius. Since the Chronicler is interested mainly in that situation he uses an illustration of conditions in his time to show how they paralleled one another. The interference of outsiders succeeded for a time in holding up the work of rebuilding the temple in the days of Darius and that of rebuilding the walls in the days of Nehemiah. Chronological order of kings and events, however significant, are less consequential in sermonic illustration.

[7] L. W. Batten, *A Critical and Exegetical Commentary on the Books of Ezra and Nehemiah*, International Critical Commentary (Edinburgh: T. and T. Clark, 1913), p. 179.
[8] On this point see *City Invincible*, eds. C. H. Kraeling and R. M. Adams (University of Chicago Press, 1960), pp. 79 f., and Lewis Mumford, *The City in History* (New York: Harcourt, 1961), pp. 64–70.

V. THE STORY OF THE BODYGUARDS
(3:1 – 4:63)†

THE BANQUET OF DARIUS

3 ¹ Now King Darius held a great reception*a* for all his subjects —
for all his household*b*, all his magnates of Media and Persia, ² all his
governors and commanders, all his subordinate district magistrates,
of the hundred and twenty-seven satrapies from India to Ethiopia.
³ And they ate and drank, and when they had enough they departed,
and Darius the king went to bed; he fell asleep, *c*but soon awoke*c*.

THE WAGER OF THE BODYGUARDS

⁴ Then *d*the three youthful bodyguards*d* who guarded the person
of the king said to one another: ⁵ "Let each of us say what *e*one
thing*e* [he thinks] is the most powerful, and to him whose dictum
appears wiser than that of the others Darius the king will give magnificent gifts and victory trophies; he ⁶ will be clothed in purple, drink
out of gold-plated [cups], and sleep on a golden [couch]; he will

---

† Cf. Jos. *Antiq.* 11:3:2–6.

a doche, "a receptacle," here has the meaning indicated. See also *Eranos* 55 (1957),
145, n. 2.

b oikogenēs may have a meaning like the Aram. *benē bayta* equivalent to Pers.
vispuhrān; cf. *Eranos* 55 (1957), 145–52.

c–c kai expugnos egeneto. Contradicts vs. 13. Fritzsche (p. 25) thinks it means, with
the preceding clause, that he slept fitfully. This Bayer regards as too arbitrary (p.
111, n. 3). Torrey conjectures that the original text may have read *wmt'ryn hww
b'dyn tlth 'lymy',* "then the three youths bestirred themselves" (ES, p. 24); see now
his improved suggestion in LGJV, p. 404. Rudolph (E-N, pp. ix f.) sees an inner
Greek corruption reading *kai kathupnos egeneto,* "and fell fast asleep." Cf. Josephus'
account in *Antiq.* 11:3:2.

d–d Philip had three bodyguards (Diodorus Siculus, xvi 94). Persian kings also
had bodyguards as may be seen from art representations, but so far as the writer is
aware the number is never given. On bodyguards see *sōmatophulakes* by F. Lammert
in *RE,* zweiter Reihe, 5er Halbband (1927), cols. 991–92, and Herbert Donner, "Der
'Freund des Königs,' " ZAW 73 (1961), 269–77.

e–e Note use of indefinite article, *ḥd* in Aramaic.

have a chariot *with gold bridles*, a turban of byssus and a neckband around *his neck*; 7 he shall sit next to Darius by virtue of his wisdom and shall be called a kinsman[h] of Darius." 8 Then they each wrote his own maxim, sealed it, put it under the pillow of Darius the king, and said, 9 "When the king awakes they will give him the piece of writing, and the one whose maxim the king and the three Persian magnates judge to be the cleverest will be given *the prize of victory[i] for[j]* what has been written." 10 The first one wrote, "Wine is the strongest." 11 The second one wrote, "The king is the strongest." 12 The third one wrote, "Women are the strongest, but truth is victorious over[k] everything." 13 So when the king woke up, they took the piece of writing and gave [it] to him, and he read [it]. 14 After he had all the magnates of Persia and Media summoned, together with governors, commanders, district magistrates and consuls, and seated himself in the judgment hall, the piece of writing was read before them. 15 Thereupon he said, "Call in the youths for they [themselves] shall explain their maxims." So they were called, and when they came in 16 they said to them, "Tell us about what you have written."

THE ADDRESS OF THE FIRST ON WINE

Then the first one who spoke of the strength of wine began and said: 17 "O men, how incomparably strong is wine! It confuses the mind

f–f chrusochalinos — "bit or bridle." Occurs only here and II Macc 10:29. On meaning see Herodotus 9:20; Xenophon *Anabasis* 1:2:22 and *Cyropaedia* 1:3:3. Reference here may be to bridles as part of the accouterments of chariots or to the gold-studded body of the chariot.
g–g With LXX[A]; B has "the neck."
[h] *suggenēs.* Cf. *philos tou basileōs* in I Chron. 27:33. *suggenēs* in LXX[B] in II Sam 3:39. For discussion of the term see Donner in ZAW 73 (1961), 269–77, and W. Michaelis, in TWNT, VII (1964), 736–42; Adriatius van Selms, JNES 16 (1957), 118–23. Term occurs frequently in the Apocrypha and in the present story in Josephus. Its use in the papyri would indicate that it was "the highest honorific title introduced by the Ptolemies" (J. H. Moulton and George Milligan, *The Vocabulary of the Greek Testament* [London: Hodder, 1930], p. 595). Cf. translations of Cook and Guthe, in APOT and APAT, respectively — cousin, also an honorific title in England. Georgius Syncellus refers to Ezra as a friend (*philos*) of Xerxes (*Chronology,* Dindorff ed., I, 476).
i–i Reading *nikēma* with LXX[A,N] instead of *nikos,* "victory." Cf. Jos. *Antiq.* 11:3:2, *nikētērion,* "prize of victory."
[j] So for LXX *kathōs,* "as."
[k] On rendering of Aram. *'l* by *uper* see Fritzsche, p. 25, and Torrey, ES, p. 24.

of all the men who drink it; 18 it reduces to the same level the mind of the king and the orphan, the mind of the slave and the mind of the freeman, the mind of the poor man and the mind of the rich man. 19 It turns every thought into gaiety and joviality, and makes one forget every grief and every debt; 20 it enriches all hearts, and makes one forget both king and governor, and makes him speak of everything in colossal figures. 21 When they drink, they do not remember the friendship of friends and brothers, and they soon draw the sword; 22 and when they recover from the influence of wine they do not remember what they have done. 23 O men, is not wine incomparably strong inasmuch as it prompts [them] to act in this manner?" And he was silent, having spoken thus.

THE ADDRESS OF THE SECOND ON THE KING

4 1 Then the second one who spoke of the strength of the king began to speak: 2 "O men, are not men incomparably strong, since they exercise control over land and sea, and all things in them? 3 Yet the king is incomparably stronger; he rules over them and has dominion over them, and to everything he decrees they submit*l*. 4 If he tells them to make war one upon another, they do [so]; if he sends them out against enemies, they go and scale mountains, walls and towers. 5 They kill and are killed, and never transgress the command of the king; when they gain the victory they carry everything to the king, both what they plunder and everything else. 6 Likewise those who neither serve as soldiers nor go to war but cultivate the soil, whenever they sow contribute something of the regular returns to the king; they even force one another to pay tribute to the king. 7 Moreover he *m*is unique*m* — if he tells [them] to kill, they kill; if he tells [them] to desist, they desist; 8 if he tells [them] to strike, they strike; if he tells [them] to destroy, they destroy; if he tells [them] to build, they build; 9 and if he tells [them] to cut down, they cut down; if he tells [them] to plant, they plant. 10 Hence all his subjects and his hosts submit to him. Then too he reclines [at the table], eats, drinks and falls asleep, 11 while they stand guard around him; none dare leave to take care of his own matters, and

---

l enakouousin — elsewhere in LXX only in I Esd 4:10 and Neh 1:12, and rarely elsewhere. It has the meaning of "listen to."

m-m Reading *eis* for *ei*, with LXX[Bab A,N]. Torrey (ES, p. 52) places the clause with preceding verse.

they never disobey. 12 O men, how cannot the king be incomparably strong when he is thus obeyed?" Then he ceased speaking.

THE ADDRESS OF THE THIRD ON WOMEN AND TRUTH

On women

13 Next the third one who spoke about women and truth — he was Zerubbabel[n] — began to speak: 14 "O men, is not the king great, are not men numerous[o], and is not wine powerful? But who now is their master? Who dominates [them]? Is it not the women? 15 Women have given birth to the king and all the people who rule over sea and land. 16 They[p] were born of them, and they[q] reared those who planted the vineyards from which comes wine. 17 They also make men's garments and they give men reputation, so that without women men cannot exist. 18 Indeed, if men accumulate gold and silver, together with anything else that is elegant, and then catch sight of but one woman charming in form and beauty, 19 they let go of all these things to gape after her and open-mouthed stare at her, all preferring her to the gold or silver or any elegant thing. 20 A man will forsake his own father who reared him, and his native land, to cling to his own wife; 21 he 'resigns himself' to his wife and re-members neither his father, nor his mother, nor his native land. 22 Hence you ought to realize that women dominate you; do you not slave and labor hard only to give and convey everything to women? 23 A man takes his sword and proceeds to wage war, to plunder and to steal and 'to sail the sea' and rivers. 24 He confronts the lion and plods through the darkness. And whenever he steals, raids and plunders he carries [it] back to his beloved. 25 A man loves his own wife far more than his father and his mother. 26 Many have taken leave of their senses over women and have become slaves on their account; 27 many have been doomed, deceived and become

---

[n] Syriac and Old Latin add "the son of Salathiel from the tribe of Judah." Torrey (ES, p. 52, n. d) regards the reference to Zerubbabel as a gloss.
[o] *polloi* is an incorrect rendering of Aram. *rbrbyn*, "mighty."
[p] The king and people.   [q] The women.
[r-r] *tēn psuchēn*, lit. "his soul." But probably stands for *npšw* (Hebrew "himself") or *npšh* (Aramaic). Some render, "with his wife he dies," on the basis of Greek of Gen 35:18.
[s-s] Cf. Aram. *prš lym'*, "to go on a voyage"; see Marcus Jastrow, *A Dictionary of the Targumim, The Talmud Babli and Yerushalmi, and The Midrashic Literature* (London: Shapiro, Vallentine, 1926), p. 1242.

sinners for the sake of women. 28 Now, then, will you not believe me? Is not the king sovereign in his authority? Do not all countries fear to approach him? 29 ‘I once saw him and Apame[t], the king's concubine, the daughter of "the eminent" Bartacus, sitting at the right hand of the king; 30 she removed the crown from the king's head, put it on her own [head], and gave the king a slap in the face with her left hand, 31 while[v] the king open-mouthed just looked at her. When she grinned at him, he grinned; when she was irked at him, he humored her that she might be reconciled to him. 32 O men, how incomparably strong are women inasmuch as they can act like this!"

On truth

33 Then as the king and the magnates looked at one another, he proceeded to speak about truth: 34 "Men, are not women strong? Great is the earth, high is heaven, and swift is the sun in its course when it races around its circuit of the heavens and returns again to its place the same day. 35 Is not he who does these [things] great? But truth is great and incomparably stronger than all these [things]. 36 The whole earth appeals to truth, heaven praises her, and all [created] works totter and tremble . . . ; and not a single injustice is "with her". 37 Wine is deceptive, the king is deceptive, women are deceptive, all the sons of men are deceptive, together with all their works, and all such things, and[x] truth is not in them, and because of their deception they will perish. 38 Truth persists and is[y] forever strong; she continues to live and endures[z] "forevermore". 39 With

t–t Torrey (ES, p. 339) suggests as original etheōroun autos Apamēn, "I myself saw Apama."

u–u Could also be a proper name — Thaumastos. Cf. Torrey (ES, pp. 40 ff.; Cook, APOT, I, 31, n. 29. A name Thamasios occurs in Herodotus 7:194. Jos. Antiq. 11:3:5 has Themasios.

v kai pros toutois, "and besides these things," may, as Torrey, ES, p. 25, suggests, stand for Aram. w'm dnh.

w–w met' autou. Lit. with him, but here read "with her" with some hands of LXX[N]. Apparently God is taken as the subject.

x Torrey (ES, p. 25) reads ei, on the basis of a conjectured Aram. hn: "if the truth is not in them."

y LXX[A] reads ischusei, i.e. future tense.

z Or "holds sway or reigns."

a–a eis ton aiōna tou aiōnos is a Semitism. The whole sentence is frequently mis-quoted as "Great is truth and it will prevail" — partly on the basis of the Latin rendering of vs. 41.

her there is neither partiality nor [possibility of] bribery, but she deals fairly, *contrary to* the perpetrators of injustice and evil — so that all approve of her deeds, 40 because there is nothing unjust in her judgment. To her belongs the power, the kingdom, the authority and the majesty for all eternity. Blessed is the God of truth."

POPULAR RESPONSE

41 When he had finished speaking all the people shouted and said, "Great is truth and incomparably strong."

DIALOGUE BETWEEN THE KING AND THE THIRD SPEAKER

42 Then the king said to him, "Ask what you want, above what was proposed, and we will give [it] to you inasmuch as you have been found to be the wisest; you shall sit next to me and be called my kinsman." 43 Then he said to the king, "Remember the vow you made, on the day you received the kingdom, to rebuild Jerusalem 44 and to restore all the vessels taken from Jerusalem and expropriated* by Cyrus when *he vowed* to make an end of Babylon and vowed to send [them] back there. 45 You also vowed to rebuild the temple which the Edomites* set on fire when Judah was devastated by the Chaldeans. 46 Now this is what I request, O lord king, and what I beg of you, for this is [in accord] with your generosity*; I beg of you now that you perform the vow you made to the King of heaven with your own mouth to perform."

THE ROYAL DECREES

47 Then Darius the king arose and kissed him, and wrote letters on his behalf to all the stewards, subordinate district magistrates,

---

b–b apo, "from, by," is probably to be explained on the basis of a Semitic idiom. Cf. Ezra 7:26 — *lhw' mt'bd mnh* "let judgment be executed upon him." Rudolph (E-N, p. ix) suggests for the *apo* phrase "in distinction from the unjust" and evildoers.

c LXX^B has *echōrisen* "set apart"; A, N *exechorēsen*, "go out, away, apart."

d–d Some (Gaab and Torrey) emend to *ērxato*, "began": "When he first took Babylon."

e So with LXX^A,N. B has *oi Ioudaioi*, "the Jews." Josephus (*Antiq.* 11:3:8) adds "Samaritans and those of Coelesyria."

f megalōsunē. II Sam 7:21; II Chron 17:19 renders *gdwlh*.

commanders, and governors to grant safe conduct to him and all those who were going up with him to rebuild Jerusalem. 48 He also wrote letters to all the subordinate magistrates in Coelesyria and Phoenicia, and especially to those in the Libanus, who were to transport cedar logs from the Libanus to Jerusalem and so help him rebuild the city. 49 He further issued letters of immunity for all the Jews who were going up from his kingdom to Judah to the effect that no official, governor, subordinate district magistrate, or steward should force his way into their doors; 50 that all the land which they were to occupy should be free from tribute for them, that the Edomites*g* give up the villages which they took over from the Jews; 51 that twenty talents be given yearly for the reconstruction of the temple until it is finished; 52 that ten talents [be given] yearly toward the daily burnt offering—inasmuch as they are commanded to offer seventeen—; 53 that freedom be given to all who come up from Babylon to build the city, to them and to their children, as well as to all the priests who come up. 54 He stipulated that expenses [be provided] along with the priestly vestments which they use in the [worship] service. 55 He decreed that the expenses of the Levites be paid until the day when the house [of God] was completed and Jerusalem rebuilt. 56 He also allocated land and wages to all the guards of the city. 57 He sent back all the vessels that Cyrus had expropriated from Babylon—everything that Cyrus had ordered to be done, he commanded to be done and sent back to Jerusalem.

The song of the youth

58 Then when the youth departed, he lifted his face toward heaven in the direction of Jerusalem and praised the King of heaven, saying,
59 "From you [comes] victory,
From you [comes] the wisdom,
And yours is the glory*h* —
And I am your household slave.

g So with LXX*A,N*; B has Chaldeans. Josephus (*Antiq.* 11:3:8) adds Samaritans and Coelesyrians. Syncellus follows A, N (Dindorff ed., I, 460 f.).
h L has *ad te consilium et victoriam et sapientiam et gloriam,* "to you belongs counsel and victory and wisdom and glory."

60 "Blessed be you [Yahweh]
Who has given me wisdom;
And I acknowledge you,
Lordⁱ of ^jour fathers^j"

THE REACTION OF THE JEWS IN BABYLON

61 Then he took the letters and went to Babylon where he informed all his brothers. 62 They too praised the God of their fathers because he had given them freedom and permission 63 to go up and rebuild Jerusalem and the temple over which his name was called. So they celebrated^k with joyful music for seven days.

ⁱ L has *Domine*, "Lord."

^{j–j} C has "our fathers." The underlying Hebrew may have run something like this:

  m'tk hyšw'h (Isa 12:2; Ps 3:9)
    m'tk hḥkmh (Job 12:13)
  wlk hkbwd (Isa 42:12; Jer 13:16; Pss 29:1; 96:7; 115:1; I Chron 16:28)
    w'ny 'bdk (1QH 13:18; 14:25)
  brwk 'th ⟨*yhwh*⟩ (Ps 119:12; I Chron 29:10)
    'šr ntt-ly ḥkmh (I Kings 5:21; 8:56; 1QS 11:15; 1QH 10:14; 11:29, 32; 16:8)
  w'ny 'wdk (often in 1QH)
    'dwn h'bwt

The thought, though not necessarily the exact wording, expressed in the several cola is found at various places in the OT and 1QH. See especially the references noted after each colon.

^k *ekōthōnizonto* — elsewhere only in LXX of Esther 3:15 where it is used to render *yšbw lštwt*, "they sat down to drink."

NOTES

3:2. *the hundred and twenty-seven.* Cf. Esther 1:1; Dan 6:1; Additions to Esther A, 1; E, 1; Jos. *Antiq.* 11:3:2.

from India to Ethiopia. Cf. Esther 1:1; 8:9; Add Esther A, 1; E, 1, where phrase is predicated of Artaxerxes.

3. This has been regarded as inspiration for the statement in *Sibylline Oracle* 3, line 393.

4. *three.* Cf. the LXX of Esther 1:14 which mentions three *oi archontes Persōn*, "Persian chiefs." MT has the names of seven.

5. *thing . . . most powerful.* See Erhard Lommatzsch, "Die Stärksten Dinge," in *Akademie der Wissenschaften und der Literatur in Mainz, Jahrbuch* (Wiesbaden, 1961), pp. 236–38, and the Greek expression *ti megiston esti basileias*, "what is greater than royalty?"

6. *byssus.* A very fine linen.

14. *consuls.* Greek is *upatous* used in LXX and Theodotion of Daniel to render several Persian terms. One cannot be sure which one was meant here. It is not used by Josephus in his account of this episode of I Esdras.

16. *they said*. Apparently those who sat in council. Some MSS read "he [i.e. the king] said."

18. For another suggested reading see Zimmermann, JQR 54 (1963–64), 193 f.

20. *colossal figures*. Lit. "in talents."

4:6. *force one another*. Either by spying on one another or by vying with one another.

20. Cf. Gen 2:24. The root verbs are the same in both books but note the compounds in each.

33. *he*. I.e. Zerubbabel.

34. *the sun . . . course*. Cf. Ps 19:4c–6; Eccles 1:5 f. For another rendering of this section see Zimmermann, JQR 54 (1963–64), 189b.

36. *all [created] works*. Cf. Sir 16:24b.

37. Cf. Prov 13:23; Ps 28:3; Ezek 3:18b.

39. *[possibility of] bribery*. Greek *diaphora* here appears to mean cash, price, money, profit. Cf. LS Lex, p. 419a, and J. F. Schleusner, *Novus thesaurus philologico-criticus . . . VT* (Leipzig, 1820). On first part of verse cf. Deut 10:17; II Chron 19:7. Josephus (*Antiq.* 11:3:6) has "It provides us neither beauty that evaporates with time nor wealth of which fortune may deprive us. . . ."

40. *power . . . majesty*. Cf. the doxology at the end of the Lord's Prayer (Matt 6:13, KJ).

Blessed . . . truth. Torrey (ES, p. 56, n. b) may be right in view of the context, "blessed of God is truth." On verse cf. I Chron 29:10; Dan 2:37.

42. *him*. I.e. Zerubbabel.

kinsman. See textual note *h* at 3:7.

46. *King of heaven*. Cf. Dan 4:37; and Lord of heaven (*mr' šmy'*) in Dan 5:23. The same epithet is found also in Tobit 13:7, 11, 16. The term "Queen of heaven" (*mlkt hšmym*) is used in Jer 7:18; 44:17, 18 where it refers to Ishtar.

48. *the Libanus*. Lebanon.

cedar logs. See Ezra 3:7.

him. I.e. Zerubbabel.

49. *force his way*. To collect tribute.

50. *Edomites*. After the exile, the Edomites began to occupy the southern hills because they themselves became the victims of Arab expansion movements into their homeland. Certainly a genuine historical piece.

51. Josephus (*Antiq.* 11:3:8) has fifty, but says nothing of the ten talents stipulated in the next verse.

52. *inasmuch as . . . seventeen*. This is difficult as it now stands and its meaning obscure. For suggestions see Torrey (ES, p. 127).

54. *which . . . service*. Lit. "in which they serve in it" — a Hebraism.

56. Jos. *Antiq.* 11:3:8 has "a fixed amount of silver annually."

57. *he.* Darius.

58. *the youth.* Zerubbabel.

direction of Jerusalem. Cf. Dan 6:10; Tobit 3:11. With this prayer of praise cf. Ezra 7:27; Dan 2:19 ff.

62. *freedom and permission.* Greek *anesin kai aphesin* is *paranomasia*, "God of their fathers." Cf. Ezra 7:27; 8:28; 10:11.

63. *his name was called.* A Hebraism (cf. II Chron 6:33; 7:14; I Esd 6:33) and typically Deuteronomic and Jeremianic.

joyful music. Lit. "with music and joy."

COMMENT

As has been pointed out by all students of I Esdras, the story of the bodyguards is unique.[1] There is not the slightest hint of it in the biblical sources of our book. It is regarded by nearly all scholars[2] as an insert in the story of I Esdras. It may have been designed to introduce Zerubbabel, as the likely gloss of identification in 4:13 and the subsequent events related in chapter 5 seem to indicate (see Introduction for further details) or, as Fritzsche long ago surmised, to answer the question as to why Darius was so friendly to the Jews.[3]

[The banquet of Darius, 3:1–3] The reference is to Darius Hystaspis (522–485 B.C.) not to Darius the Mede of Dan 6:1; 11:1, since the latter is said to have preceded Cyrus whereas in I Esdras the reverse is the order of the two Persian kings. That the story should begin with a great royal banquet

---

[1] Reminiscent of the royal favor shown to the three youths in Dan 1:37 and to Jehoiachin and his sons (I Kings 25:27b). For a discussion of the story see articles by Rudolph, esp. pp. 176–90, Zimmermann, and Shalit in BIBLIOGRAPHY I. Ackroyd thinks the story is popular in nature and cannot be considered "as good historical evidence"; even the name Zerubbabel is hardly original (JNES 17 [1958], 20). Cf. also Torrey, ES, pp. 37–61, who regards it as originally a separate story, "a bit of popular wisdom-literature," with no Jewish historical connections, coming from a Palestinian milieu ca. 300 B.C. It was composed in Aramaic, a judgment supported and elaborated by Zimmermann. See H. P. Müller, "Magisch-mantische Weisheit und die Gestalt Daniels," in *Ugarit-Forschungen,* I (Neukirchen-Vluyn: Butzon & Bercker Kevelaer, 1969), 84. Thackeray (HDB, I, 761) opined that I Esdras was written around this story, and P. A. de Lagarde thought it stood originally after Dan 6:1 (*Mitteilungen,* IV [Göttingen, 1891], 358). The Upanishads record Wisdom contests, sometimes conducted on festival occasions when the king offered prizes for the best contributions (H. M. and N. K. Chadwick, *The Growth of Literature,* II [Cambridge University Press, 1936], 584). Cf. also Herodotus 6:129.

[2] Howorth (*Transactions of the Ninth International Congress of Orientalists,* II [London, 1893], 79; *Academy* 43 [Feb. 4, 1893], 106 [BIBLIO I]; *Proceedings of the Society of Biblical Archaeology* 24 [1902], 335 [BIBLIO I]) and Josef Marquart (*Fundamente israelitischer und jüdischer Geschichte* [Halle, 1896], p. 65) regard it as a portion of the Chronicler's work. Torrey (ES, pp. 26–30, 58–61) thinks 4:47b–56 and 4:62 – 5:6 belong to the Chronicler's composition, though in slightly edited form.

[3] Fritzsche, I, 6. It is to be remembered that other favors granted the Jews in the post-exilic period were due, in some measure, to the position of Ezra and Nehemiah, respectively. On the other hand Bayer, p. 113, thinks of it as unhistorical and a reflection on the events recorded in Esther and Daniel.

is understandable in the light of similar narratives such as Belshazzar's feast in Dan 5; Xerxes' royal banquet in Esther 1; the impressive feast of Assurnasirpal II (*Iraq* 14 [1952], 24–44); and the banquet and conversation of Cyrus described by Xenophon (*Cyropaedia* 8:4:1–27). Josephus says it took place in the first year of Darius.

[The wager of the bodyguards, 3:4–16a] The amusement of guards by various means to reduce the monotony of a tense situation is well known. The initiative for the contest of wits was taken by the guards. Josephus ascribes the whole idea to the king who, being unable to sleep, and entering into conversation with the bodyguards, offered rewards to the one coming up with "the truest and most perceptive response" to the question posed for him by the king. Here the guards themselves write what each thinks is the most powerful and place the sealed document under (or beside) the pillow of the king. What each wrote is stated simply in vss. 10–12. *Ti malista* (=the most powerful) is said to be common in Greek literature (e.g. Herodotus 1:30; Plutarch *Alexander* 64).[4] When the king awoke the document was given to him (by his servants). After reading it, he assembled the royal court where it was read formally in the presence of the magnates of Persia and Media, the governors, commanders, district magistrates, and consuls. Then he gave orders to summon the youths who were permitted to explain their maxims.

[The address of the first on wine, 3:16b–23] It is not quite certain whether the author praises wine or if he endeavors to show merely that it is *malista* (most powerful). It confuses the mind of all who indulge so that they are reduced to the lowest common denominator; it turns their thoughts to frivolity so that grief and debts (normal recollections) are consigned to oblivion; rulers are forgotten; exaggeration in speech reaches colossal proportions; friends and brothers soon become enemies and when they sober up they cannot remember the course of tragedy. Wine was an indispensable concomitant of oriental social life (cf. Esther 1:7 f.; Dan 5:1–4; Test Judah 16:2–4). What inebriation does is spelled out effectively in Prov 23:29–35. On vss. 17–18, cf. the recommendation for Purim (Megillah 7b). Overindulgence in wine is powerful indeed because it makes a fool of one (Prov 20:1; Sir 31:25 ff.). The young Tobit is advised against wine to the point of intoxication (4:15). The observations of Aristeas (250–54) include only women, truth, and the ruler.

[The address of the second on the king, 4:1–12] The strength of the king is based on his position as the ruler of men. While it is men pooling their power who actually do things, it is the king who exercises dominion over them and directs them to do what he determines. Whether men work out of love or fear, they do it for the king. Those engaged in war or in the peaceful pursuits of

---

[4] Richard Laqueur, *Hermes* 46 (1911), 168 ff., thinks the germ cell of the story is a nameless, floating piece of Greek pagan origin that contained only the question about what is most powerful without the Jewish conclusion of 4:43 – 5:6. Cf. Wilhelm Schmid, *Geschichte d. griech Literature* (1912), p. 467. On the other hand, Geo. Widengren suggests it has come from Parthian sources; see his "Quelques rapports entre Juifs et Iraniens à l'époque des Parthes," in *Volume du Congrès: Strasbourg, 1956*, VTS, IV (Leiden: Brill, 1957), 218.

soil cultivation do so in submission to his will. The position and strength of the king is predicated on the obedience thus rendered him (cf. Dan 2:38; 5:19).

[The address of the third on women and truth, 4:13–40. On women, 13–32] The third speaker is none other than Zerubbabel who took the position that women and finally truth were the most powerful. Here is the real purpose of the narrative from the writer's point of view — to introduce Zerubbabel as the really wise youth,[5] who not only won the contest but thereby became the one to remind Darius of his promise and then the king's agent in the reconstruction of the temple. Zerubbabel began his observation by agreeing that wine and the king were indeed powerful. Nevertheless women were even more powerful since they were the mothers of kings and the bearers of those who plant and cultivate vineyards "from which comes wine." Nor is that all. Women make men's clothes and give them reputation. Consider the fact that though men are enamored of gold and silver or any other desirable thing, they will drop them at once upon sight of a charming woman. Do not men leave their parents and even their native land to cling to a wife? Actually women, however unobtrusively, dominate men who slave and labor to support them. Men endure the deprivations of war, the danger of wild beasts, and will even steal for their wives. Indeed men have been known to take leave of their senses over women. There is a host of examples of prominent women in the Bible — Sarah, Rebekah, Deborah, Naomi and Ruth, Esther, Judith, etc., and Proverbs has something to say about the influence of the evil woman (5; 6:20 – 7:27) as well as the sagacious housewife (Prov 31). Women were no less influential among the Persians as the Apame episode illustrates. They were often impressed by women as reflected in the story of Artemesia (Herodotus 8:87, 88, 101–3; 9:109 ff.). It was a woman, Atossa, who beguiled Darius to invade Greece (Herodotus 3:133 ff.). Even Cyrus was wary of Panthea, "the most beautiful woman in the world" (Xenophon *Cyropaedia* 4:6:11; 5:1:9 ff.). Which Apame is meant is uncertain[6] and it is difficult to draw any positive historical relationships from the story. The narrator may well have drawn upon character names known to him and his audience which he then applied to Darius I, though the king actually involved may have been Darius III. But there is no known concubine of either by the name of Apame. That she could thus playfully yet somewhat unbecomingly treat the king in the presence of attendants proves the point that women are stronger than kings.

[On truth, 33–40] To the astonished king and magnates the speaker presented yet another observation. After affirming the incomparable strength of women he speaks of the greatness of the earth, the height of the heavens, and the

[5] Chisian Codex 87 of Susanna (ninth century) affirms that wisdom was sometimes bestowed on an "Israelite" youth without mentioning Daniel. Zerubbabel is an intrusion in the original story but essential for the author of I Esdras in preparation for what follows.

[6] For persons of that name see Ferdinand Justi, *Iranisches Namenbuch* (Hildesheim: Olms, 1963 — reprint of 1895 ed.), p. 19. For a discussion of the problem see further Torrey, ES, pp. 40 ff.; Shalit, *Bulletin of the Jewish Palestine Exploration Society* 13 (1947), 119–28 [BIBLIO I]. The name is of oriental provenance but not found before the Macedonian period.

recurring cycle of the sun, with the declaration that he who is responsible for these things is great. But truth is incomparably stronger. Pfeiffer looks to Ahiqar for the background of the story.[7] Parallels have been observed in the Wisdom of Solomon[8] and in Egyptian Wisdom literature.[9] However, truth was a cardinal virtue elsewhere in the ancient world. Persian youths, for example, were taught to ride, to handle the bow and to speak the truth (Herodotus 1:136). The Persian royal inscriptions are replete with references to the lie (*drauga*) and stress truth (*hašiya*). The predications of truth here, especially the references to natural phenomena (vss. 34, 36) and the strong emphasis on the deceptiveness (*adikos*) of wine, king, women and men, may reflect the conception of the *asha* of Avestan=*arta* of Persian (law, justice, cosmic order, regularity, etc.).[10] The stories of Haman in Esther, and Susanna revolve around the theme of truth.[11] See further the references to truth in Prov 8:7; 20:28; 22:21; 26:28 (particularly LXX); 29:14; II Chron 18:15; 19:9; Test Reuben 3:9; Test Dan 2:1–2. Truth is finally described as persistent, eternal, impartial, and to it belongs "the power, the kingdom, the authority, and majesty for all eternity" (cf. I Chron 29:11–13 and the doxology of the Lord's Prayer; not quite the same Greek words in the latter). There is a similar phrase in Ps 30:6 (LXX) — *kurie o theos tēs alētheras*. For God's love of truth see also Ps 83:11; Sir 41:20 (both LXX). The story is referred to by Origen[12] and is quoted in the ninth homily on Joshua, *a te, Domine, est victoria, et ego servus tuus, benedictus es, Deus veritatis*.

[Popular response, 4:41] The cry of the people, "Great is truth and incomparably strong," is the source of the aphorism "great is truth and it prevails," based on the Latin version, *magna est veritas et praevalet*. For the origin of the substitution of the future for the present tense see the article by Ryan, fn. 11.

[Dialogue between the king and the third speaker, 4:42–46] As hoped by the bodyguards, Darius immediately offered a reward to the winner of the contest. Along with the position of honor at the royal court, the winner was asked to name what he wanted. Zerubbabel recalled the vow of the king on the day of his assumption of power to rebuild the temple and return the sacred vessels which Cyrus was said to have removed from Babylon after his determination to destroy the city. Actually the city was not destroyed by either Cyrus[13] or Darius I. Josephus (*Antiq.* 11:3:7) relates the traditional story of Nebuchadnezzar's expropriation of the vessels from Jerusalem. The

[7] Pfeiffer, p. 252.
[8] Cf. L. E. T. André, *Les Apocryphes de l'Ancien Testament* (Florence, 1903), p. 192.
[9] See esp. Humbert, OLZ (1928), cols. 148–49 [BIBLIO I], where parallels are cited with Ptahhotep and the Complaints of a Peasant. He sees there a model or prototype (*Vorbild*) of our story. See further Lods, pp. 952 f., and "A Piece of Wisdom in Syriac" by S. P. Brock, in JSS 13 (1968), 212–17.
[10] Cf. L. H. Mills, "Asha as The Law of the Gathas," JAOS 20 (1899), 31–53.
[11] For an excellent study of later developments of the theme see John K. Ryan, *American Ecclesiastical Review* 135 (1956), 116–24 [BIBLIO I]. Cf. Ephraim Syrus *Nisibene Hymns* 9:14 and James Russell Lowell's line, "yet 'tis truth alone is strong."
[12] See *Library of the Greek Fathers and Ecclesiastical Historians* (Athens), XII, 12.
[13] See account in Barrel Inscription of Cyrus, ANET, p. 315.

destruction of the temple by the Edomites may have some substance to it.[14] The bestowal of gifts on such occasions was common among Hebrews (cf. Gen 41:42), Babylonians (Dan 5:7, 16, 29), and Persians (Herodotus 3:130; 5:11; Xenophon *Cyropaedia* 8:4:1–27).

[The royal decrees 4:47–57][15] The response of the king to the request of the contest winner was favorable. He issued directives to his officials — probably those who had charge of Across the River — to grant safe conduct to Zerubbabel and his supporters so that they might rebuild Jerusalem, especially the temple (vss. 51, 54). The substance of the Cyrus decree (Ezra 1:2–4; 6:3–5), its reaffirmation by Darius (Ezra 6:6–12), and the permission of Artaxerxes granted to Nehemiah to rebuild the city (Neh 2:5, 8) are combined here. The king ordered that timber from the Libanus be supplied, that immunity be granted to those Jews assisting Zerubbabel in the rebuilding of city and temple, and that annual financial grants be given until the work was finished. Moreover there were to be regular subsidies for worship, perhaps because the Persians were desirous of gaining the support of their subject peoples and were themselves interested in religion. According to Ezra 6:10, Darius requested that sacrifices be offered and prayer made for the king and his sons.[16] The historicity of vs. 50b is highly probable.[17] Josephus has fifty talents (vs. 51) but omits the ten talents of vs. 52. The generosity attributed to the Persians here is supported by other references in the Bible and elsewhere.

[The song of the youth, 4:58–60] The gratitude of the youth naturally finds expression in a hymn of praise, described by Josephus but not given by him. The song is a composite of words and expressions found in many other places.

[The reaction of the Jews in Babylon, 4:61–63] The narrator was a bit too optimistic in his assessment of the response of the Babylonian Jews as attested elsewhere.[18] That the more zealous of them were overwhelmed with joy is beyond dispute; they evidently looked forward to the reconstruction of Jerusalem and the temple. They celebrated for a week.

---

[14] See my remarks in *Near Eastern Studies in Honor of William Foxwell Albright*, pp. 377–92.

[15] Torrey (ES, p. 28) thinks the Chronicler was responsible for this section which is wanting in Ezra. The story continued "from 2:14 (Ezra 1:11) to 4:47," where the name of Darius was substituted for that of Cyrus, and followed by 4:62 – 5:6 and then by 5:7 ff. The interpolator was responsible for 4:43–47a and 4:57–61, of altering the name of the king in vs. 47 as well as in 5:2, 6, and the location of the Artaxerxes correspondence of Ezra 4:6–24 in its present position in I Esdras.

[16] Cf. R. A. Bowman, *Ezra*, IB, III, 617; N. B. Johnson, *Prayer in the Apocrypha and Pseudepigrapha*, Society of Biblical Literature Monograph Series (Philadelphia, 1948), p. 23.

[17] Cf. fn. 13.   [18] AB, vol. 14, p. xxvi.

VI. PREPARATIONS FOR AND RETURN FROM CAPTIVITY
(5:1-70)†

ORGANIZATION OF THE CARAVAN

5 1 *ᵃAfter these thingsᵃ* the family heads, according to their tribes, were selected for return along with their wives, sons, daughters, male slaves, female slaves, and their cattle. 2 Darius sent a thousand horsemen with them to escort them back safely to Jerusalem and, with music of drums and flutes 3 which all their comrades were playing, he ordered them to return with them. 4 Now these are the names of the men who returned, according to their families and tribes in their divisionsᵇ: 5 the priests, the sons of Phinehas, ᶜthe sonsᶜ of Aaron were Jeshua, the son of Jozadak, the son of Seraiah, and ᵈJoiakim, the son of Zerubbabelᵈ, the son of Salathiel, of the family of David, of the line of Perez, of the tribe of Judah 6 who uttered wise words before Darius, the king of the Persians, in the second year of his reign, in the month of Nisan [which is] the first month.

PRELIMINARY STATEMENT

7 These are the Jews who returned from their quarters in exile, whom Nebuchadnezzar, the king of Babylon had expatriated to Babylon: 8 they came back to Jerusalem and to the rest of Judah, each to his own town, coming with Zerubbabel and Jeshua, Nehemiah, Seraiah, Resaiah, Enēnios, Mordecai, Baalsaros, Mispar, Reeliah, Rehum, Baanah, their leaders.

† I Esd 5:7-8 || Ezra 2:1-2; **9-42** || Ezra 2:3-66; **43-45** || Ezra 2:68-70; **46-49a** || Ezra 3:1-3a; **49b-52** || Ezra 3:3b-6; **53** || Ezra 3:7; **54-62** || Ezra 3:8-13; **63-68** || Ezra 4:1-3; **69-70** || Ezra 4:4-5.

ᵃ⁻ᵃ For Hebrew cf. Ezra 7:1, *'ḥr hdbrym h'lh*, "after these things."

ᵇ *meridarchian*. Could perhaps be "official genealogy" rendering Heb. *lhtyhśm* (cf. Ezra 8:1). Greek word occurs only in I Esd 1:5, 11; 5:4; 8:28. *meridarchēs* occurs in I Macc 10:65.

ᶜ⁻ᶜ Plural with LXXᴮ; A has singular which may be better.

ᵈ⁻ᵈ May have arisen from *wyqm bw zrbbl*, "and Zerubbabel arose with him," as Torrey suggests, LGJV, p. 404.

LIST OF RETURNING CAPTIVES

The laymen

9 The number of laymen and their leaders is as follows: the sons of Parosh, 2,172^e; the sons of Shephatiah, 472^f; 10 the sons of Arah, 756; 11 the sons of Pahath-moab^g, those of Jeshua and Joab^h, 2, 812; 12 the sons of Elam, 1,254; the sons of Zattu, 970^i; the sons of Chorbe^j, 705; the sons of Bani, 648; 13 the sons of Bēbai, 633^k; the sons of Azgad^l, 1,322^m; 14 the sons of Adōnikam, 667^n; the sons of Bigvai, 2,606^o; the sons of Adin, 454^p; 15 the sons of Ater, son of Hezekiah, 92^q; the sons of Keilan and Azetas, 67^r; the sons of Azaru, 432^s; 16 the sons of Anneis, 101^t; the sons of Arom^u; the sons of Besai, 323; the sons of Arseiphoureith, 112^v; 17 the sons of Baitēros, 3,005^w; ^{x}the sons of Bethlehem^x, 123; 18 the men of Netophah, 55; the men of Anathoth^y, 158^z; the men of Beth-Azmaweth, 42^a; 19 the men of Kiriatharim^b, 25^c; the men of Chephirah and Beeroth, 743^d; 20 the Chadiasans and the Ammidians, 422^e; the men of Ramah and Geba, 621; 21 the men of Michmas, 122; the men of Bethel, 52; the men of Magbish, 156; 22 the sons of the other Elam and Ono, 725; the sons of Jericho, 245; 23 the sons of Senaah^f, 3,301.

^{e} So with LXX^{A,N} which reads *duo chiliades kai ekaton ebdomēkonta duo uioi saphat terrakosioi ebdomekonta duo*, "2,172, the descendants of Shaphat 472," correctly as may be seen from Ezra 2:3, 4; Neh 7:8, 9, though the figures for Shephatiah vary.
^{f} Some Ethiopic and Syriac MSS have been corrected after MT to 372.
^{g} LXX has *phthaleimōab*. MSS vary greatly in spelling. ^{h} LXX^B has Roboab.
^{i} LXX^{A,N} have 945. So also MT of Ezra 2:8; Neh 7:13 has 845.
^{j} One hand has Zakchai=Zaccai of MT.
^{k} LXX^{A,N} has 623, with MT of Ezra; Neh 7:16 has 628.
^{l} So with some L MSS; LXX^B has Argai.
^{m} Some MSS have 1,222, with MT of Ezra 2:12; Neh 7:17 has 2,322.
^{n} So with LXX^{A,N}; B has 37. Ezra 2:13 has 666; Neh 7:18, 667.
^{o} LXX^{A,N} has 2,066; Ezra 2:14, 2,056; Neh 7:19, 2,067. ^{p} Some MSS have 654.
^{q} So with LXX^{A,N}; some lesser MSS of B and Ethiopic have 98 with Ezra 2:16 and Neh 7:21.
^{r} Omitted in MT. ^{s} Omitted in MT. ^{t} Omitted in MT. ^{u} Omitted in MT.
^{v} Minuscule b has *orai ekaton kai deka duo* (=Jorah, 112); so also MT of Ezra; Neh 7:24 has Hariph, but with same number of persons. A, N have 112.
^{w} Omitted in MT. $^{x-x}$ LXX^B has Ragethlōmān. ^{y} With LXX^{A,N}; B has Enatos.
^{z} Minuscule b has 128 with MT.
^{a} With LXX^{A,N}. ^{b} With some MSS and Ezra 2:25; Neh 7:29, Kiriath-jearim.
^{c} Omitted in MT where the name is linked with the two following names.
^{d} So with LXX^{A,N}; B has 700.
^{e} Whole section of verse omitted by MT of Ezra and Nehemiah.
^{f} LXX^B has Sama.

The priests

24 [The number of] the priests: the sons of Jedaiah, of the house of Jeshua, *g*from the sons of Sanasib*g*, 872; the sons of Immer, 252; 25 the sons of Pashhur, 1,247; the sons of Harim, 217.

The Levites

26 [The number of] the Levites: the sons of Jeshua, Kadmiel, *h*Bannos and Soudios*h*, 74.

The temple singers

27 [The number of] the sons of the temple singers: the sons of Asaph, 128.

The gatekeepers

28 [The number of] the gatekeepers: the sons of Shallum, the sons of Ater, the sons of Tolman, the sons of Akkub, the sons of Hateta, the sons of Sobai, *i*altogether 139*i*.

The temple servants

29 [The number of] the temple servants: the sons of Esau, the sons of Taseipha, the sons of Tabbaoth, the sons of Keros, the sons of Siaha, the sons of Padon, the sons of Lebanah, *j*————*j*. 30 The sons of Akkub, the sons of Utha, the sons of Ketab, the sons of Hagab, the sons of Shemlai, the sons of Hanan, the sons of Koua, the sons of Giddel, 31 The sons of Jairos, the sons of Daisan, the sons of Noba, the sons of Chaseba, the sons of Gazera*k*, the sons of Uzza, the sons of Phinoe, the sons of Asara, the sons of Besai, the sons of Asnah, the sons of the Meunim, the sons of the Nephisim, the sons of Bakbuk, the sons of Hakupha, the sons of Asur, the sons of Pharakim, the sons of Bazluth, 32 the sons of Mehida, *l*the sons of Koutha, the sons of Charea*l*, the sons of Barkos, the sons of Sisera, the sons of Temah, the sons of Neziah, the sons of Hatipha.

Solomon's servants

33 [The number of] the sons of Solomon's servants: the sons of Hassophereth, the sons of Peruda, the sons of Jaalah, the sons of

g–g Omitted in MT.
h–h A corruption of the Heb. *lbny hwdwyh*, "of the sons of Hodaviah."
i–i LXX*B* has The doorkeepers, 400; the men of Ishmael, the sons of Lakoubatos, 1,000; the sons of Tobiah, altogether 139.
j–j Some hands of LXX*A,B* add here "the sons of Aggaba" (=Hagabah of MT of Ezra and Nehemiah).
k With LXX*A,N*; B has Kazēra (=Gazzam).
l–l With LXX*A,N*; B omits.

Darkon, the sons of Giddel, the sons of Shephatiah, 34 the sons of Agia, the sons of Pochereth-hazzebaim, the sons of Sarōthei, the sons of Mesaiah, the sons of Gas, the sons of Addus, the sons of Subas, the sons of Apherra, the sons of Barodis, the sons of Shaphag, the sons of Allōn. 35 All of the temple servants and the sons of Solomon's servants [numbered] 372.

The unrecorded

36 These were the ones who returned from Tel-melah and Tel-harsha; their direction was furnished by Charathalan and Allar, 37 but they were unable to trace their families or descent in Israel: the sons of Delaiah,*m* the son of Tobiah, the sons of Nekoda, 652. 38 Of those who *"laid claim"* to the priestly office and whose official registration could not be found were the sons of Hobaiah, the sons of Hakkoz, the sons of Barzillai*o* who married Augia one of the daughters of Barzillai and was named after him. 39 When the family register was searched without success for a record of these men, they were prohibited from functioning as priests. 40 Nehemiah and the governor*p* ordered them not to partake of the consecrated food until a priest arose clothed with [powers] of *q*direction and the truth*q*.

Summary

41 All the men of Israel, *r*from twelve years of age on*r*, exclusive of male and female slaves, numbered 42,360. They had 7,337 male and female slaves, 245 harpers and singers, 42 435 camels, 7,036 horses, 245 mules, 5,525 asses.

CONTRIBUTIONS

43 Now some of the family heads, when they arrived at the temple of God in Jerusalem, vowed to rebuild the house on its [former] site according to their ability 44 and to contribute one thousand minas of gold, five thousand minas of silver, and a hundred priestly vestments to the temple building fund. 45 The priests and the Levites

---

m LXX[B] has Asan, A, N have Dalan.
n–n *oi empoioumenoi* found in a Sardis inscription of fourth-third centuries B.C.
o LXX[B] has Iaddous, one minuscule, b, has Berzellei.
p LXX[B] has *attharias*, clearly not a proper name but a transcription of *htršt'* of parallel passage in Ezra and Nehemiah. It is the Persian term for "governor," lit. "the one to be feared or respected."
q–q For Heb. *'wrym wtmym*, "Urim and Thummim"; see AB, vol. 14, NOTE on Ezra 2:63.
r–r Wanting in MT of Ezra 2:64 f. and Neh 7:66 f.

and some of the people took up residence in Jerusalem and its environs, while the temple singers, gatekeepers and all Israel [took up residence] in their villages.

ERECTION OF AN ALTAR

46 When the seventh month arrived and the sons of Israel were [located] in their several places, they assembled to a man at the plaza before the first gate facing the east. 47 Then Jeshua, the son of Jozadak, and his brothers the priests, together with Zerubbabel, the son of Salathiel, and his brothers rose and prepared the altar of the God of Israel 48 to offer burnt offerings upon it as prescribed in the book of Moses, the man of God. 49 Some of the other peoples of the land united with them in erecting the altar on its [original] site; even though they were at enmity with them, all the people of the land supported them —

INAUGURATION OF WORSHIP SERVICES

and they offered sacrifices at the proper time and burnt offerings to the Lord, morning and evening. 50 They also celebrated the feast of tabernacles as prescribed in the law, as well as the daily sacrifices, when it was fitting [to do so]; 51 and in addition to these the continual offerings, and sacrifices on the sabbath, new moon, and all other hallowed festivals, 52 *and for all who brought a voluntary offering to God.* From the new moon of the seventh* month on they began to offer sacrifices to God although the temple of God had not yet been rebuilt.

PREPARATIONS FOR RECONSTRUCTION OF THE TEMPLE

53 Moreover they contributed money for the masons and carpenters, and drink, food, and oil* to the Sidonians and Tyrians for bringing cedar lumber from the Libanus, ferrying [it] in rafts to the port at Joppa, in accordance with the permit* issued to them by Cyrus, king of Persia.

s–s So following MT of Ezra 3:5 wlkl mtndb ndbh lyhwh.

t LXXᴮ has tou prōtou mēnos, "the first month."

u LXXᴬ has karra, "carts"; read here with MT of Ezra 3:7 šmn, "oil"; B elaion, "oil." Josephus (Antiq. 11:4:1) reflects LXXᴮ, chara, "joy," rather than chara, "?" He has ēdu kai kouphon, "pleasant and easy."

v to prostagma renders Heb. ršywn, "permit," from ršy, "to give permission" (cf. also J. A. Fitzmyer, The Aramaic Inscriptions of Sefire (Rome: Biblical Institute Press, 1967), p. 112.

FOUNDATION OF THE TEMPLE LAID

54 In the second month of the *w*second year*w* after their*x* arrival at the temple of God in Jerusalem, Zerubbabel, the son of Salathiel, Jeshua, the son of Jozadak, and their brothers, together with the Levitical priests, and all those who had come back from captivity to Jerusalem began 55 to lay the foundation of the temple of God on the new moon of the second month of the second year after [their] arrival in Judah and Jerusalem. 56 They put the Levites twenty years and over in charge of the [building] operations of the Lord. Then Jeshua took his position, together with his sons and brothers, Kadmiel, his brother, the sons of Jeshua Èmadaboun and the sons of Jouda, the son of Eiliadoun with his sons and brothers, all Levites and taskmasters with one accord doing the work on the house of the Lord. So the builders built the house of the Lord. 57 The robed priests stood with musical instruments and trumpets, in conjunction with the Levites, the sons of Asaph, with cymbals, praising the Lord and blessing (him) according to [the prescriptions of] David, the king of Israel. 58 They sang vociferously, blessing the Lord, because his goodness and his glory are eternally over all Israel. 59 And all the people blew trumpets and raised a mighty shout, singing to the Lord, when the house of the Lord was raised. 60 Some of the Levitical priests, and of the family heads, that is the older ones who had seen the former house, came*y* to the building of this one with weeping and great lamentation, 61 while many [others came] with trumpets and a tremendous shout of joy, 62 so that the people were unable to hear the trumpets because of the lamentation of the people, although the multitude blew the trumpets so powerfully that [they] could be heard from afar.

AN OFFER FROM NEIGHBORS

63 When the foes of the tribe of Judah and Benjamin heard [it], they came to investigate the meaning of the sound of the trumpets. 64 And they discovered that the returned exiles had rebuilt the temple of the Lord God of Israel. 65 So coming to Zerubbabel, Jeshua and the family chiefs, they said to them: "Let us join you in building,

---

w-w One MS and L*C* (Versio Altera=Codex Colbertinus) add "of Darius," apparently influenced by Ezra 5:2; Hag 1:1; 2:1; Zech 4:9.
x With LXX*N* and MT of Ezra 3:8; B has "his arrival."
y MT has *wrbym,* "and many," for *wb'ym* here.

66 for we too obey your Lord just as you do and we sacrifice to him
since the days of Asbakaphath, king of the Assyrians, who brought
us here." 67 Then Zerubbabel, Jeshua and the chiefs of the families
of Israel said to them: "You may not share in building the house of
the Lord our God; 68 we alone will build [it] for the Lord of Israel
just as Cyrus, the king of Persia, has ordered us."

INTERFERENCE BY REJECTED NEIGHBORS

69 Then the people of the land impeded the building [operations]
by undermining the morale of those in Judah and restraining [them],
70 and by schemes, demagoguery, and agitation they prevented the
completion of the building during all the lifetime of King Cyrus.
Hence they were prohibited from building for two years until the
reign of Darius.

NOTES

5:1. *family heads.* Lit. "chiefs of the house of the fathers." Heb. *r'šy byt
'bwt.*

2. *a thousand horsemen.* See Neh 2:9.

safely. met' *eirēnēs,* "with peace."

3. *return.* Lit. "go up."

5. *Phinehas.* See NOTE on 1:1.

son of Jozadak. Name occurs in Ezra, Nehemiah and 6Q13.

family. Lit., "house," *oikos.*

8. *Resaiah.* Hebrew of Ezra 2:2 has Reelaiah.

Enēnios=Nahamani of Neh 7:7; wanting in Ezra.

Baalsaros=Bilshan in both Ezra and Nehemiah.

Mispar. Most LXX MSS have Aspharasos, but one has Masphar.

Reeliah with LXX^A,N; B has Boroleios.

Rehum=Roeimos.

9. *laymen.* MT of Ezra and Nehemiah has "the men of the people of
Israel."

11. *2,812.* So with some MSS of LXX^B. Brooke-McLean text has 2,802.

12. *705.* MT for both Ezra and Nehemiah has 760 for Zaccai.

648. Ezra 2:10 has 642; Neh 7:15, 648 sons of Binnui.

14. *Bigvai.* LXX Bosai.

Adin. LXX Adeilos.

454. Neh 7:20 has 655.

15. *Ater.* With LXX^A,N; B has Azēr.

16. *Besai.* LXX Bassai. *Beth-bassi* found at Murabba'at (P. Benoit, J. T.
Milik, and R. de Vaux, *Les Grottes de Murabba'at,* DJD, II [1961], 251).
See Ezra 2:17 and Neh 7:23 — a place name.

17. *123*. So with MT also of Ezra 2:21; Neh 7:26 combines the figures for Bethlehem and Netophah.

18. *55*. Ezra 2:21, 22 (MT) has a total of 179; Neh 7:26 (MT) has 188. LXX[B] for former follows MT. LXX omits latter but Latin MSS follow MT.

19. *743*. Same sum for two here as for three groups in MT of Ezra and Nehemiah.

20. *621*. Same as MT of Ezra and Nehemiah.

21. *122*. Same as MT of Ezra and Nehemiah.

52. Text omits *and Ai* of MT of both Ezra and Nehemiah. The total of the two in MT is 223 and 123 respectively.

Magbish. With some MSS; LXX[B] has Neipheis.

22. *other Elam and Ono*. Former separate in MT Ezra and Nehemiah, but number there is 1,254 for other Elam.

245. Numbers for Jericho vary in different MSS — some of LXX[A], 345, of N, 445; MT of Ezra and Nehemiah have 345.

23. *3,301*. LXX[A,N] have 3,330. MT of Ezra 2:35 has 3,630; of Neh 7:38, 3,930.

24. *872*. LXX[A,N] have 972. Some minuscules have 973 but may be corrections after MT of both Ezra and Nehemiah=973.

252. LXX[N] has 825; A, 1,052 with MT of Ezra and Nehemiah.

25. *217*. LXX[A,N] have 1,017, with MT of Ezra and Nehemiah.

27. *128*. Neh 7:44 has 148, so also LXX[A,N]; but Ezra 2:41 has 128.

28. *139*. Neh 7:45 has 138; Ezra 2:42, 139.

29. *Esau*. MT of Ezra and Nehemiah has Ziha.

Taseipha. MT has Hasupha — some Greek MSS, Asupha.

Keros. Name occurs in Eliashib archives uncovered at Tell Arad (Stratum VI, early sixth century B.C.).

30. *Hagab*. On this as family name see Nigel Avigad, *Israel Exploration Journal*, 16 (1966), 50–53.

31. *Jairos*. Gahar of MT of Ezra and Nehemiah.

32. *Barkos*. An Edomite name=son of Qaus (Edomite deity). LXX[A,N] have Barchoue; B has Bachous.

35. *372*. The figure given in Ezra 2:58 and Neh 7:60 is 392.

36. The place names Cherub, Addan, and Immer of Ezra and Nehemiah parallel omitted here.

37. *652*. So also Ezra. Nehemiah has 642.

40. *Nehemiah*. Not named in MT of Ezra 2:63.

41. *42,360*. Agrees with figures of Ezra and Nehemiah but Josephus (*Antiq.* 11:3:10), emended text, has 48,462.

245. So also Nehemiah. Ezra has 200. Josephus (ibid.) follows I Esdras and Nehemiah here.

42. *7,036*, LXX[N] has 736, as does Ezra. Whole clause wanting in Nehemiah.

5,525. Ezra and Nehemiah have 6,720; Josephus (*Antiq.* 11:3:10) follows I Esdras.

44. *minas*. The light mina=ca. 1.1 lbs.; the heavy mina double that.

One thousand. Ezra 2:69 has sixty-one thousand drachmas (ca. 1,132⁶⁄₇ lbs.); Neh 7:70 has twenty thousand drachmas, or a little less than one-third of the Ezra amount; Josephus (*Antiq.* 11:3:10) has a hundred.

five thousand. So also Ezra and Josephus.

a hundred. So also Ezra. Neh 7:69 has five hundred and thirty, though LXX has thirty; Vulgate follows MT.

45. *Jerusalem and its environs.* Not in parallel chapters of Neh 7 and Ezra 2 but is certainly correct.

46. *east.* Neh 8:1 has Water Gate.

53. *Cyrus.* Josephus (*Antiq.* 11:4:1) adds, "now it was (re)ordered by Darius" to harmonize it with the following verses.

56. *Kadmiel.* So with MT and LXX^N; B has Damadiēl; Josephus has Zodmiēlos.

Ēmadaboun. Josephus reads Aminadabos, apparently *hndd* (Henadad) of MT.

Lord. Some MSS have God.

66. *Asbakaphath.* LXX^B has Asbakaphath; A, N have Asbasareth. Josephus (*Antiq.* 11:4:3) has Salmanassēs (=biblical Shalmaneser), harmonizing it with II Kings 17 (cf. *Antiq.* 9:14:1). The Ezra text reads Esarhaddon.

68. Josephus (*Antiq.* 11:4:3) adds "and now by Darius" to the verse.

69. *undermining the morale.* With MT of Ezra 4:4. LXX *epikoimaomai*, lit. "fall asleep over," may have the same general meaning since it seems to indicate indifference.

70. *two years.* Cf. Ezra 4:24. Ezra 4:6 is omitted in I Esdras.

COMMENT

[Organization of the caravan, 5:1–6] The first step taken by the people after having been granted permission to return to Jerusalem was the careful selection of representatives of the various families and tribes to serve as leaders. After all further arrangements had been completed and the caravan was ready to move, Darius provided an escort for them and sent them on their way rejoicing. Verse 2 is difficult and rendition is quite free, attempting to bring out the meaning as the translator understands it. The meaning appears to be that Darius ordered the cavalry contingent to see the returning exiles safely back to their homeland and sent them off with martial music played by their brethren. The genealogy of vs. 5 is not clear as it stands. According to I Chron 3:19 the sons of Zerubbabel were Meshullam, Hananiah, Hashubah, Ohel, Berechiah, Hasadiah, and Jushab-hesed. Nowhere else does the line of David include Joiakim who is always listed among the priests. The suggestion of Torrey (see textual note $^{c-c}$) may be the explanation, in which case Jeshua and Zerubbabel are representatives of the priestly and Davidic lines. Moreover, Zerubbabel and Jeshua are mentioned together in Ezra 2:2; 3:2, 8; 4:3; 5:2; Neh 7:7; 12:1; Hag 1:1, 12, 14; 2:2. Read perhaps: "of the priests . . . was Jeshua . . . and accompanying him was Zerubbabel . . . who uttered. . . ." Josephus (*Antiq.* 11:3:10) omits names here, though later in the same paragraph he notes that the leaders of the group were

Zerubbabel and Jesus. Josephus (*Antiq.* 11:3:2) says the contest of the body-guards took place in the first year of Darius and he gives no date for the events described here. The month Nisan is mentioned only twice in the Old Testament (Neh 2:1; Esther 3:7), though the expression "the first month" occurs frequently. The Esdras date of the second year of Darius may reflect simply knowledge of Ezra 4:24; Hag 1:1; 2:1, 10; Zech 1:1, 7. In that case it may suggest that some time elapsed between the time of the contest and the decree of Darius and that of the execution of the decree. But it must be used with caution.

[Preliminary statement, 5:7–8 — Ezra 2:1–2] The Ezra list has eleven names, Esdras has twelve and a slightly different order.

Esdras	Ezra
Zerubbabel	Zerubbabel
Jeshua	Jeshua
Nehemiah	Nehemiah
Seraiah	Seraiah
Resaiah	Reeliah
Enēnios	Mordecai
Mordecai	Bilshan
Baalsaros	Mispar
Mispar	Bigvai
Reeliah	Rehum
Rehum	Baanah
Baanah	

[List of returning captives, 5:9–42 — Ezra 2:3–66; Neh 7:7–69.[1] The laymen, 9–23] The list of those who returned from Babylon to Judah and Jerusalem is difficult to evaluate with confidence. It has no doubt been copied from Ezra rather than from Nehemiah since it agrees more frequently with Ezra. But see now Klein, HTR 62 (1969), 99–107. Discrepancies among the three lists may be due to the nature of the records or the method of compilation. It is doubtful if there is a significant lapse of time in the process of compilation. There is some variation in the numbers assigned to some of the families and an apparent attempt at correction in certain instances and MSS, as may be seen from a study of the lists (see fn. 1). It is unnecessary to collate the lists here except to give the totals in each one: the MT has 25,406 for Neh 7 and 24,144 for Ezra 2. The LXX totals are as follows: Neh 7, 22,851; Ezra 2, 26,838; I Esd 5, 25,947.[2] Neh 7 has thirty-one family groups, Ezra has thirty-three in MT. For LXX Neh 7 lists thirty-four; Ezra 2 has thirty-three; I Esd 5 has thirty-five. So no conclusion can be drawn from the relatively small differences which can be accounted for on textual or other grounds.

[The priests, 24–25] There is no variation whatever in the number of family groups of priests, each version listing four. There is a slight difference in totals. MT of Neh 7 and Ezra 2 has 4,289 each. LXX of Neh 7 has 4,289, of Ezra 2, 4,279, of I Esd 5, 2,588 — differences that can be explained on

---

[1] For detailed comparisons of lists see AB, vol. 14, Appendix I, II, ACCORDING TO LXX.
[2] Naturally there is a difference in the figures given by the various MSS of LXX; generally the low ones have been used in arriving at the results here presented.

grounds of bad textual transmission or harmonization (see NOTES). The names are the same.

[The Levites, 26] LXX numbers are same in all three lists and in MT of Ezra-Nehemiah but there is an additional name here due to misreading of underlying Hebrew.

[The temple singers, 27] Only one name occurs here in all lists and versions. MT has 148 for Neh 7 and 128 for Ezra 2. LXX has 148 for Neh 7; B, 148, and A, 128, for Ezra 2; 128 for I Esd 5.

[The gatekeepers, 28] Six names, as in all other versions of the list. Neh 7 has 138 in MT and LXX; Ezra 2 has 139 in both.

[The temple servants, 29–32] LXX[B] has 39; A, 41; of Neh 7, 32; of Ezra 2, 35 — so also MT.

[Solomon's servants, 33–35] LXX has 17; LXX of Neh 7, 11; of Ezra 2, 10. MT has 10 for both. There is thus an expansion of the list in this category though the number has decreased from 392 (MT and LXX of Ezra-Nehemiah) to 372.

[The unrecorded, 36–40] MT of Ezra-Nehemiah has three groups of three names (the same) each and a total of 652 for Ezra 2 and 642 for Neh 7. LXX of Nehemiah has three names with a total of 642, of Ezra 2, four names with a total of 652. On the priests who could not prove their ancestry all lists agree in name and number. Note that in vs. 38 the name of the daughter of Barzillai is given. These priests were barred from functioning and from the consecrated food until such time as they could be authenticated.

[Summary, 41–42] Comparison of figures:

	Jos. Antiq. 11:3:10	Neh 7 MT	Ezra 2 MT	Neh 7 LXX	Ezra 2 LXX	I Esd 5
Laymen	48,462	42,360	42,360	[A]42,360	42,360	42,360
Levites	74			[B]42,308		
Women and children	40,742					
Levite singers	128					
Gatekeepers	110					
Temple servants	392					
Others	652					
Unrecorded Levites and priests	525					
Slaves	7,337	7,337	7,337	7,337 [B]7,334	7,337	7,337
Male and female musicians	245	245	200	245	200	245
Camels	435	435	435	435	435	435
Horses			736	736	736	7,036
Mules			245	245	245	245
Beasts of burden	5,525					5,525
Asses		6,720	6,720	6,720 [B]2,700	6,720	

Josephus gives the figures for each category, possibly because he does not include the names for any class. He is the only one who supplies the figure for women and children. Note also the number of beasts of burden. The number of persons given in the summary does not agree with the sum of the figures arrived at by adding the totals given in each category above.

[Contributions, 43–45] There is some discrepancy in the various versions here, too, as may be seen in the following table[3]:

	MT of Neh 7	MT of Ezra 2	LXX of Neh 7	LXX of Ezra 2	I Esd 5	Jos. *Antiq.* 11:3:10
Governor's gifts	1,000 drachmas of gold		1,000 pieces of gold			
	50 bowls		50 bowls			
	530 priestly vestments		30 priestly vestments			
Gifts of family heads	20,000 drachmas of gold	61,000 drachmas of gold	20,000 pieces of gold	61,000 minas of pure gold	1,000 minas of gold	100 minas of gold
	2,200 minas of silver	5,000 minas of silver	2,200 minas of silver	5,000 minas of silver	5,000 minas of silver	5,000 minas of silver
		100 priestly vestments		100 priestly vestments	100 priestly vestments	
Rest of people	20,000 drachmas of gold		20,000 pieces of gold			
	2,000 minas of silver		2,200 minas of silver			
	67 priestly vestments		67 priestly vestments			

The rationale behind the list is doubtless the precedent of the Exodus tradition (Exod 25:2–7; 35:4–9) when the people offered contributions for the ark, tabernacle, vestments, etc., and the large gifts presented by family heads described in Num 7 for cultic use. The mention of Jerusalem in vs. 45 does not necessarily imply that the city had been rebuilt as Cook suggests.[4] It may refer to the locale of Jerusalem and "its environs," i.e. the villages around the city.

[Erection of an altar, 46–49a — Ezra 3:1–3a] Josephus (*Antiq.* 11:4:1) is more definite than either Esdras or Ezra. He says "the seventh month" refers to the time that had elapsed since the departure from Babylon. There appears to be a telescoping of events here.[5] Ezra 1 gives the impression that they

---

[3] For a discussion of the summary see AB, vol. 14, COMMENT on Neh 7:4–72a.

[4] In APOT, I, 38, note.

[5] It is possible that "seventh month," Tishri (September–October) or Ethanim (II Kings 7:2), may bear some religious import since it was the month of Sukkoth (cf. MS variant of vs. 52, which see).

took place in the reign of Cyrus under Sheshbazzar whereas here and in Ezra 3:1–3a they are attributed to the time of Zerubbabel and hence in the reign of Darius. Those who returned from Babylon might have joined the people of the land at first[6] and, because of the relative inactivity in the years following the arrival of Sheshbazzar, their efforts regarded as unorthodox by the Zerubbabel contingent so that a new beginning had to be made. Ezra 3:3a indicates that "they were afraid of the peoples of the lands," which could mean political or religious fear or both, more likely the latter. Josephus says the erection of the altar incurred their enmity while Esdras asserts that "some of the other peoples of the land united with them (i.e. Jeshua and Zerubbabel and their friends) . . . ; even though they were at enmity with them, all the people of the land supported them" (i.e. Jeshua and Zerubbabel and their friends).

[Inauguration of worship services, 49b–52 — Ezra 3:3b–6] The erection of the altar and the inauguration of cultic services demonstrate the zeal of the golah. The worship services began with the *tamid* (the daily sacrifice), the morning and evening offerings and the celebration of Sukkoth (Lev 23:34; Num 29:12 ff.). Sabbaths, new moons and festivals were stressed by the Chronicler (I Chron 23:31; II Chron 2:4; 8:13; 31:3) and Nehemiah (10:33). Cultic celebrations not requiring the temple, only the altar, could be carried on as soon as the latter was constructed. (On seventh month see fn. 5.) Some MSS have "first month" which is the same month in the autumnal calendar as the "seventh month" in the spring calendar.

[Preparations for reconstruction of the temple, 53 — Ezra 3:7] There is no substantial difference between Esdras and Ezra here. (For comments see AB, vol. 14, COMMENT on Ezra 3:7.) Interestingly enough Josephus (*Antiq.* 11:4:1) says the order was first issued by Cyrus and then carried out by that of Darius which he picked up from I Esd 4:57.

[Foundation of the temple laid, 54–62 — Ezra 3:8–13] Building operations began in the second month of the second year after the first return—not the second return in 520 as may be seen from the fact that many who had seen the first temple were present (vs. 60) which would hardly have been the case sixteen years later. The work progressed so rapidly that, according to Josephus, completion was achieved earlier than might have been expected under normal conditions. The detail of laying the foundation on the new moon is added by I Esdras and is followed by Josephus. There is some confusion of names in vs. 56:

I Esdras	Ezra 3:9	Jos. *Antiq.* 11:4:2
Jeshua	Jeshua	Jesus
Kadmiel	Kadmiel	Zodmiēlos, brother of
Sons of Jeshua	Sons of Judah	Judas
Èmadaboun	Sons of Henadad	Son of Aminadabos
Sons of Jouda		
Sons of Eiliadoun		

[6] Cf. AB, vol. 14, pp. xxv f.

The title of the hymn (vs. 58) is somewhat obscured by the Greek rendering. It ran as follows:

> Praise and give thanks to Yahweh
> For he is good
> Eternal is his devotion toward Israel.

Cf. MT of II Chron 5:13; 7:3; Pss 106:1; 136:1. The reason for the weeping and lamentation here and in Ezra 3:12 appears to be for joy. Josephus, however, says it was due to the memory of the priests and Levites of the magnificence of the old temple and the fact that the new one fell so far short of the splendor of the old.

[An offer from neighbors, 63–68 — Ezra 4:1–3] Follows, in substance, Ezra. According to I Esdras the enemies came themselves to investigate the celebration whereas in Ezra they only heard about it. There is no known resettlement of peoples in Judah under Esarhaddon.[7] The reference is doubtless to the spillover of peoples from Samaria into the vacuum left by the expatriation of Jews by the Babylonians and of whom the golah was afraid (cf. II Kings 17:41). There may be some reflection here of later conditions, in the time of Nehemiah and Ezra, when Yahweh was worshiped by Sanballat as reflected in the names of his two sons who bore Yahweh names. Both Zerubbabel and Jeshua are here connected with the decree of Cyrus rather than with Darius. Josephus set the matter straight (*Antiq.* 11:4:3).

[Interference by rejected neighbors, 69–70 — Ezra 4:4–5] Blame for lack of progress in temple reconstruction rests with the people of the land who were refused a share in building operations with its implications. Haggai and Zechariah accused the golah of lethargy and indifference. The phrase "for two years until the reign of Darius" is certainly a confusion of dates. Cyrus was succeeded in 529 by Cambyses who reigned until 522 B.C. so that the reign of the latter is ignored. The "two years" may reflect "the second year" of Ezra 4:24 which was itself influenced by Hag 1:1.

---

[7] Sidon was reduced by him, and people from the east settled there (Pritchard, ANET, p. 209, and D. J. Wiseman, "An Esarhaddon Cylinder from Nimrud," *Iraq* 14 [1952], 54–60).

VII. EVENTS ASSOCIATED WITH THE
RECONSTRUCTION OF THE TEMPLE
(6:1 – 7:15)†

RECONSTRUCTION OF THE TEMPLE BEGUN

6 ¹ Now in the second year of the kingship of Darius, the prophets Haggai and Zechariah, the son of Iddo, prophesied concerning the Jews of Judah and Jerusalem in the name of the Lord God of Israel [which was] *over them*, ² Then Zerubbabel, the son of Salathiel, and Jeshua, the son of Jozadak, arose and began to rebuild the house of the Lord which was in Jerusalem, with the prophets of the Lord supporting and assisting them.

INTERVENTION BY THE PROVINCIAL AUTHORITIES

³ At that time Sisinnēs, the governor of Syria and Phoenicia, and Sathrabouzanēs, and [their]ᵇ partners came to them and said to them, ⁴ "who gave you an order to reconstruct for yourselves this house and complete this roofed [structure] *and everything else*? And *who are the builders carrying out these things*?" ⁵ Nevertheless the elders of the Jews enjoyed the favor of the watchful eye of the Lord which was upon the captivity; ⁶ they were not interrupted in the building [operations] up to the time that Darius was informed about them and a report could be received [from him].

THE GOVERNOR'S REPORT TO THE KING

⁷ A copy of the letter that Sisinnēs, the governor of Syria and Phoenicia, Sathrabourzanēs, and [their] partners, who were the

† I Esd 6:1–2 || Ezra 5:1–2, cf. Jos. *Antiq.* 11:4:5; 3–6 || Ezra 5:3–5; 7–21 || Ezra 5:6–17; 23–33 || Ezra 6:1–12; 7:1–9 || Ezra 6:13–18; 10–15 || Ezra 6:19–22.
a–a ep'autous=Aram. *'lyhwn.* So also Ezra 5:1.
ᵇ So with K Lᶜ; LXXᴬ, *autou.* (K is a Latin minuscule; Lᶜ, Versio Altera=Codex Colbertinus.)
c–c Omitted in Ezra 5:4.
d–d LXX Ezra has *tina estin ta onomata tōn andrōn tōn oikodomounton tēn polin tauten,* "What are the names of the men who are reconstructing this city?"

officials in Syria and Phoenicia, wrote and sent to Darius: "To King Darius, greetings. 8 Let everything be known to our lord, to the king! Upon coming to the land of Judah and the city of Jerusalem we discovered the elders of the Jews of the captivity in the city of Jerusalem constructing a large new house for the Lord, of expensive dressed stone, [and] rafters are being set on the walls⁰; 9 that work is prosecuted zealously, the project is proceeding successfully at their hands, and will be consummated with all glory and diligence. 10 Then we inquired of these elders, asking, 'By whose permission are you constructing this house and laying the foundation of these works?' 11 We inquired further of them — for the purpose of informing you and registering the instigators — and demanded of them a list of the names of [their] leadersᶠ. 12 They responded to us as follows: 'We are servants of the Lord who created the heaven and the earth. 13 The house was constructed and finished many years ago by a great and powerful king of Israel. 14 When our fathers irritated and sinned against the heavenly Lord of Israel, he surrendered them to Nebuchadnezzar, the king of Babylon, the king of the Chaldeans 15 who demolished and burned the house, and took the people captive to Babylon. 16 But in the first year of Cyrus' kingship over the country of Babylonia, King Cyrus issued a decree [granting permission] ᵍto reconstructᵍ this house, 17 and the sacred vessels of gold and silver which Nebuchadnezzar had removed from the house in Jerusalem and brought into his temple, King Cyrus took out again from the temple in Babylonia and handed over to Zerubbabel and Sheshbazzar the governor, 18 to whom he gave orders to take back all these vessels and put [them] into the temple in Jerusalem, and that the temple of the Lord be rebuilt in its [former] place. 19 So when Sheshbazzar arrived, he laid the foundations of the house of the Lord in Jerusalem and from then until now it has been under construction but has not yet been completed.' 20 Now, therefore, if you prefer, O king, let an examination be made of the royal archives of our lord the king deposited in Babylon, 21 and if it is found that the house of the Lord in Jerusalem was constructed with the consent of Cyrus

---

ᵉ As with LXXᴬ,ᴺ; B has *en tois oikois,* "in the houses." Aramaic of Ezra 5:8, *ktly',* "walls." So also LXX of Ezra 5:8.
ᶠ *ton prokathēgoumenōn,* "leaders" — found in a Cairo papyrus of the second century A.D.; Pierre Benoit, "Fragment d'une prière contre les esprits impurs?" RB 58 (1951), 554.
ᵍ⁻ᵍ LXXᴬ,ᴺ *ton oikon touton aikodomēthēnai,* "that this house be reconstructed."

the king, and if our lord the king prefers, let [his] decision concerning these matters [be relayed] to us."

INVESTIGATION BY THE KING AND HIS REPLY TO THE REPORT

22 Then King Darius ordered a search to be made in the royal[h] archives kept in Babylon. And a roll[i] was found in the fortress[j] in Ecbatana, in the land of Media, on which was the following memorandum: 23 "In the first year of the reign of Cyrus, King Cyrus decreed that the house of the Lord in Jerusalem be rebuilt where they offer sacrifices with continual fire; 24 its height is to be ninety feet, its width ninety feet, with three layers of dressed[k] stones and one layer of ‘new local timber’, and the cost is to be met out of the treasury of Cyrus the king. 25 Also the sacred vessels of gold and silver belonging to the house of the Lord, which Nebuchadnezzar had removed from the house in Jerusalem and brought to Babylon, are to be restored to the house in Jerusalem and placed where they were originally." 26 He gave strict orders to Sisinnēs, the governor of Syria and Phoenicia, Sathrabouzanēs, and their partners, and the provincial appointees in Syria and Phoenicia to keep away from the place and permit Zerubbabel, the servant of the Lord and governor of Judah, and the elders of the Jews to reconstruct that house of the Lord on its [former] site. 27 "I further decree that it be fully rebuilt and that [they] strive diligently to assist the Jews of the captivity until the house of the Lord is completely finished; 28 moreover [I decree that] a regular quota of the taxes levied in Coelesyria and Phoenicia be given to these men for sacrifices to the Lord, to Zerubbabel the governor for bulls, rams, and lambs, 29 as well as a regular yearly [quota] without question, of wheat, salt, wine and oil, as the priests in Jerusalem may declare to be necessary, 30 in order that libations may be offered to the most high God in behalf of the king and his children and that they pray for their life." 31 He decreed also that whoever violates or ignores any one of the written [orders], let a beam be torn out of his own house, let [him] be impaled

h With LXX[A,N].
i LXX[A,N]; B has *topos*, "place." Aramaic has *mglh ḥdh*, "a roll"; Josephus (*Antiq.* 11:4:6) has *biblion*, "book."
j *tē barei* is a simple transcription of the Aram. *byrta*, "the fortress."
k *xustōn*. Ezra 6:4 *gll 'bn*, "hewn stone," LXX[B] *lithinoi*, "of stone," LXX[A] *lithinoi krataioi*, "mighty stones." The Aramaic of Ezra underlies I Esdras.
l-l *xulinou egchoriou kainou*. Ezra 6:4 *dy-' ' ḥdt*, "of wood one layer"; LXX[B] "one layer of timber," though some MSS have "one layer of new timber."

upon it, and *m*his property be [confiscated] for the king*m*. 32 "Therefore, may the Lord whose name is called there annihilate every king and people that extend their hands to impede [the work on] or despoil that house of the Lord in Jerusalem. 33 I, King Darius have issued an *n*[official] decree*n* that it be done precisely so."

PROGRESS OF THE WORK

7 1 Then Sisinnēs, the governor of Coelesyria and Phoenicia, Sathrabouzanēs, and their partners carried out meticulously the orders of King Darius, 2 presiding carefully over the sacred works [and] supporting the elders of the Jews and the *o*temple overseers*o*. 3 And the sacred work flourished because Haggai and Zechariah, the prophets, kept prophesying. 4 They completed the work*p* in accordance with the command of the Lord God of Israel and with the decree of Cyrus, Darius, and Artaxerxes, kings*q* of Persia. 5 The house was finished by the twenty-third [day] of the month Adar in the sixth year of King Darius. 6 The Israelites, the priests, the Levites, and the rest of those of the captivity who had associated themselves with them carried out the prescriptions in the book of Moses. 7 For the dedication of the temple of the Lord they offered a hundred bulls, two hundred rams, four hundred lambs [and] twelve he-goats 8 for the sins of all Israel, corresponding to the number of the 12 *r*tribal chiefs*r* of Israel. 9 The priests and the Levites in their official attire stood in [their proper] positions for the service of the Lord God of Israel as prescribed in the book of Moses, while the gatekeepers [occupied positions] at each of the gates.

CELEBRATION OF THE PASSOVER

10 The Israelites of the captivity celebrated the passover on the fourteenth day of the first month when the priests and the Levites

---

m–m Aramaic of Ezra 6:11 reads *byth nwlw yt'bd*, "let his house be made a dunghill." On *nwlw*, *nwly*, "dunghill, refuse heap," see Dan 2:5; 3:29. But Josephus (*Antiq.* 11:4:6) follows I Esd. LXX of Ezra has *o oikos autou to kat' 'eme poiēthēsetai*, "his house shall become mine."
n–n *dedogmatika* here renders Aram. *śmt t'm*, "issue an official decree." LXX of Ezra has *gnōmēn*, "decree."
o–o Jos. *Antiq.* 11:4:7 *tōn gerontōn archousin*, "chiefs of the senate."
p Text has *tauta*, "these things, this," referring to *ta iera erga*, "the sacred work," in vs. 3.
q With LXX*A,N* *basileōn*, "kings"; so also Ezra 6:14 LXX*B* where some hands have *basileōs*, "king."
r–r *phularchōn*. Ezra 6:17 *phulōn*, "tribes."

were purified together [11] with all the sons of captivity[s]. [12] So they slaughtered the passover [lamb] for all the sons of the captivity, for their brothers the priests, and for themselves. [13] The Israelites of the captivity, that is all who had separated themselves from the impurities of the nations of the land, seeking the Lord, ate [of it]. [14] They also celebrated the feast of unleavened bread for seven days with joy before the Lord [15] because he had changed the attitude of the king of Assyria toward them, thus supporting them in the work of the Lord God of Israel.

[s] The LXX text here has doublets which have been omitted in the translation for the sake of clarity. It has *oti ēgnisthēsan. oti oi Leveitai ama pantes ēgnisthēsan,* "because they were purified; because the Levites had been purified to a man."

NOTES

6:1. *over them.* The name of the Lord "called upon" Israel (cf. Num 6:27; Deut 28:10; II Chron 7:14); the ark (II Sam 6:2); the city (Jer 25:29); the temple (Jer 7:10, 11, 14, 30; 32:34; 34:15); the nations where Israelites are exiled (Amos 9:12). The pronoun in brackets refers to the name of the Lord.

2. *Salathiel.* Ezra 5:2 has Shealtiel.

3. *Sisinnēs.* Tattenai in both Greek and Aramaic of Ezra 5:3.

Syria and Phoenicia. Ezra has Across the River which was the famous fifth satrapy of the Persian empire of which Syria and Phoenicia were local districts.

Sathrabouzanēs is of course the Shethar-bozenai of Ezra.

8. *rafters.* Greek is *xulōn,* "timber, beam"; Aram. *'a'* has the same meaning. But what is meant by the whole clause is uncertain. The emphasis is on completion of the building and so the setting of the rafters is quite probable. See AB, vol. 14, third NOTE on Ezra 5:8.

14. *surrendered them.* Lit. "gave them into the hand of."

17. *Sheshbazzar.* LXX[B] has Sabanassar, A, N have Sanabassar. I Esdras thus separates Zerubbabel and Sheshbazzar, contrary to the views of some scholars who want to regard the names as referring to the same person. Cf. Meyer, p. 75.

20. *royal archives.* Aramaic text has royal treasuries; on their import see Bickerman, JBL 65 (1946), 251, and G. G. Cameron, *The Persepolis Treasury Tablets* (University of Chicago Press, 1948), pp. 9–17, for a detailed description of Persian treasury and its significance.

22. *memorandum.* Aram. *dkrwnh* which was a memorandum of an official decision. Cf. *zkrn* in *Aramaic Papyri of the Fifth Century B.C.,* ed. and tr. A. E. Cowley (Oxford: Clarendon Press, 1923), No. 32, and Jean Hoftijzer, *Dictionnaire des inscriptions sémitiques de l'ouest* (Leiden: Brill, 1965), p. 78. The Greek text here has interpreted the Aramaic correctly. A similar decree was issued by Cambyses for the reconstruction of the Neith temple in Egypt (see Otto, "Die biographischen Inschriften der ägyptischen Spätzeit. Ihre geistesgeschichtliche und literarische Bedeutung," in *Probleme der Ägyptologie,* II, 170 f.).

24. *ninety feet*. Text has sixty cubits.

treasury. Lit. "the house," as also Aramaic of Ezra 6:4.

27. [*they*]. The royal officials in Syria and Phoenicia.

strive diligently. Lit. "to look carefully, to see to it."

28. *regular*. So with Aram. *dy-l' lbṭl*, "without interruption."

30. *the king and his children . . . pray for their life*. Josephus *Antiq*. 11:4:6, "pray for the welfare of the king and the Persians."

32. *Therefore*. The Aramaic of Ezra 6:11 takes *dia tauta* (= '*l-dnh*) with the "whose name is called there" of the preceding verse. Possibly a reference to the figure used in vs. 1.

7:4 *Artaxerxes*. Wanting in Josephus (*Antiq*. 11:4:7) because it was anachronistic.

5. *twenty-third*. Ezra 6:15 "third." Josephus follows I Esdras which according to Kugler's calculations (*Von Moses bis Paulus*, pp. 214 f.) is probably correct since the third day fell on a Sabbath.

Adar. February–March.

sixth year. 515 B.C. But cf. Josephus *Against Apion* 1:21 for other dates.

10. *first month*. Josephus (*Antiq*. 11:4:8) names the month as Nisan — March–April.

13. *the captivity*. I.e. the golah, the exiles.

15. *king of Assyria*. A careless use of the phrase because the reference is certainly to the king of Persia as Josephus recognized (*Antiq*. 11:4:8). Assyria ceased to exist after the sixth century B.C. Herodotus (1:178) refers to Babylon as the capital of Assyria and Xenophon (*Cyropaedia* 2:1:5) speaks of the Assyrians of Babylon.

COMMENT

[Reconstruction of the temple begun, 6:1–2 — Ezra 5:1–2; Jos. *Antiq*. 11:4:5] The author of I Esdras follows his source closely here though he reflects the deuteronomic name theology. The temple was built in the reign of Darius I. The reason for the delay from Cyrus to Darius was owing to interference on the part of local obstructionists, not to the carelessness of the golah as asserted by the prophets. Both Esdras and Ezra agree that Haggai and Zechariah exercised their prophetic function; moreover, Josephus says they encouraged the people in the work and bade them not to be apprehensive of any hostile intervention on the part of the Persians, thus summarizing the message of the prophets. Hence the Jewish authorities overcame their reluctance and began building operations immediately, inspired and assisted by the prophets. In the long run prophetic intervention proved to be the turning point in the enterprise but it also had repercussions. The prophets took advantage of imperial unrest in the wake of the Persian interregnum, even announced the downfall of the empire (Hag 2:22) and whipped up a messianic zeal for Zerubbabel, as indicated by reference to the signet ring (2:23).

[Intervention by the provincial authorities, 6:3–6 — Ezra 5:3–5] The authorities appointed by the new Persian regime[1] lost no time in looking into what looked to them like incipient Jewish revolt. Naturally a bit nervous by virtue of the Babylon revolt after the death of Cambyses, they undertook an immediate investigation of the suspicious activities at Jerusalem. Josephus (*Antiq.* 11:4:6) reports a letter of Cambyses forbidding the rebuilding of the temple which, if true, would have lent weight to their concern.[2] There is a slight hint in vs. 4 — "and everything else" — that there may have been more to Jewish construction than the temple, which might have given the impression of fortification of the city. This deduction is supported by Josephus who tells us that the Samaritans accused the Jews of fortifying the city and that the temple resembled "a fortress rather than a sanctuary." The Persian officials seem to have gotten what information was available by an on-the-spot inquiry and relayed it to their superiors. Nevertheless building operations were not interrupted during the time required for the reaction of the court. This the builders attributed to divine favor.

[The governor's report to the king, 6:7–21 — Ezra 5:6–17] The same general outline of events here as in Ezra. Either on their own initiative or in the course of carrying out an official order, the authorities of the province Across the River (here of Syria and Phoenicia) went to Judah and Jerusalem where they observed the status of the building operations. They interrogated the elders about their authority and demanded, in writing, the names of their leaders. In the course of their response to the questions posed by the provincial officials, the Jews related the history of their situation. Finally they added an appeal that the royal archives be searched to substantiate their story and that the results of the inquiry and the decision of the king be relayed to them as soon as possible. The points made in Ezra are accentuated and expanded on occasion, for instance the addition of "the city of Jerusalem" in vs. 8 and the demand (not "request" as in Ezra) for the list of leaders. I Esdras adds the name of Zerubbabel to the Ezra account in vs. 17. Moreover here (vs. 19) it is Sheshbazzar who lays the foundation of the temple (as in Ezra 5:16) whereas in 5:54–55 Zerubbabel and his associates are said to have performed that act. If anything, this chapter accentuates the position of the Jews vis-à-vis the Persians, but it was for the glorification of the temple—a characteristic of this book.

[Investigation by the king and his reply to the report, 6:22–33 — Ezra 6:1–12] The account of I Esdras sounds a bit less official than that of Ezra. Verse 26 here is a simple declarative statement whereas the parallel in Ezra 6:6, 7 is part of the order issued by Darius and in the imperative mood. Verse 28 decrees a "quota of taxes," where Ezra says the expenses for sacrifices are to be paid fully from taxes levied in Coelesyria and Phoenicia. In the Ezra parallel there is no mention of Zerubbabel; here he is twice mentioned by name (vss. 26, 28). In this context Josephus (*Antiq.* 11:4:6) refers to a communication from Cambyses to the Samaritans to the effect that temple

---

[1] See AB, vol. 14, COMMENT on Ezra 5:3–5.
[2] No such letter is mentioned in I Esdras or in Ezra. The Jewish historian may have had in mind the correspondence referred to in Ezra 4:6 ff. in the reign of Artaxerxes.

reconstruction had been forbidden by him. Perhaps he refers to the correspondence of Ezra 4:7 ff. No such letter is mentioned elsewhere. Furthermore, Josephus states that the Samaritans had themselves informed Darius that the rehabilitation of Jerusalem would be dangerous to his rule. The threat of a curse is found in all three books, and is frequent in ancient documents.[3] Disobedience to a royal decree was a capital offense among the Persians (vs. 31) and involved the confiscation of the offender's property.[4]

Chapter 7 follows closely the general outline of the Ezra parallel, though there are several significant variations. It relates the consummation of the work, the rededication services, the celebration of the passover, and the feast of unleavened bread.

[Progress of the work, 7:1–9 — Ezra 6:13–18] The response of the imperial authorities is more emphatic here. They carried out the orders with great care, even presiding over the work and assisting the elders and overseers of the temple. Ezra does not refer to these matters. Whether Haggai and Zechariah prophesied beyond the dates recorded in their works is unknown (Haggai's prophecy is confined to the second year of Darius; Zechariah's oracles continued until the fourth year of Darius — 7:1) though the implication is that they did so persistently until the temple was completed. Josephus (*Antiq.* 11:4:7) says the rebuilding of the temple was carried out according to "the command of God and the approval of kings Cyrus and Darius," thus omitting the name of Artaxerxes.[5] He noted the anachronism and eliminated the name. The assumption is that the work on the temple began in earnest in the second year, the second month of Darius' reign and was finished in the sixth (ninth according to Josephus) year, twelfth (Adar) month, the twenty-third day (Ezra=third day) of the reign of Darius, i.e. February–March, 515 B.C.

	Josephus	I Esdras	Ezra
Temple work begun	Second month of second year of Darius	Same	Same
Temple completed	Twenty-third of Adar, twelfth month, of ninth year of Darius[6]	Twenty-third of Adar, of sixth year of Darius	Third of Adar, of sixth year of Darius

[3] Cf. E. F. Weidner, AfO 6 (1930), 14 f., and ANET, pp. 500, 502, 504. See especially the invocation by Darius of Ahuramazda against anyone who destroys or fails to protect his inscription and sculptures, in Behistun, col. 4:76–80 (Roland G. Kent, *Old Persian Grammar, Texts, Lexicon,* American Oriental Series, vol. 33 [New Haven: American Oriental Society, 1953], 130, 132).

[4] See A. T. Olmstead, *History of the Persian Empire* (University of Chicago Press, 1948), ch. IX.

[5] Artaxerxes may be a later addition, either because he was king when the Chronicler wrote or because tradition held him to be king when the city wall was erected and the reconstruction regarded as completed.

[6] A variant reads eleventh year of Darius. On what basis the discrepancy between Josephus and I Esdras and Ezra came about has never been satisfactorily explained. It was scarcely possible for Josephus (*Antiq.* 11:4:7) to misread the *ektou etous* (Aram. *šnt št*) of I Esd 7:5; Ezra 6:15. He has *tou d'enatou . . . etous,* "then in the

F. X. Kugler[7] has calculated the third of Adar, 515 B.C., was a Sabbath but that the twenty-third fell on a Friday, and hence I Esdras must be right. Josephus followed the latter but says the temple was finished in seven years. It is rather strange that, apart from Haggai and Zechariah, no names of Jews occur in this chapter. One expects Zerubbabel to be mentioned among the overseers. But that is not the case. Note also the reference to the gate-keepers (vs. 9) — not in Ezra. The priestly and Levitical orders are based on the prescriptions of "the book of Moses" (cf. Exod 29; Lev 8; Num 3:5 ff.; 8:5 ff.), a fairly certain indication that this is not a typically Chronicler composition; he would have quoted the order of David as authority (I Chron 23–26). The number of bulls, rams and he-goats is the same in all versions; Josephus has two hundred lambs whereas I Esdras and Ezra have four hundred.

[Celebration of the passover, 7:10–15 — Ezra 6:19–22] This is a Chronicler addition. Offerings of various types were offered in connection with the dedication of Solomon's temple (I Kings 8:62 ff.; II Chron 7:8–10) and that was the pattern followed in the case of the second temple. However, there was no passover celebration in the earlier dedication because it was not the time for it. At rededications in the time of Hezekiah (II Chron 30:13 ff.) and Josiah (II Chron 35:1 ff.) the passover was observed. The feast of unleavened bread also followed that of the passover in the Hezekiah celebrations. The Levites slew the paschal lambs (cf. II Chron 30:17; 35:11) and the participants were the members of the golah, priests, Levites, and others who had purified themselves, that is, those who remained in the land but had separated themselves from the uncleanness associated with the people of the land and, perhaps, proselytes (Num 9:14).

---

ninth year," which presupposes Aram. *šnt tš'*. Ralph Marcus (Josephus, *Jewish Antiquities, Books* IX–XI, Loeb Classical Library: VI, 365) notes a variant which he does not quote but which probably reads *tou d'endekatou . . . etous,* "then in the eleventh . . . year," the Aramaic of which would be *šnt ḥd 'šr.* Syncellus follows the biblical texts closely (Dindorff ed., I, 449). Josephus himself says elsewhere (*Against Apion* 1:154) that the foundations of the temple were laid in the second year of Cyrus and it was completed in the second year of Darius.

[7] *Von Moses bis Paulus,* pp. 214 f. Perhaps *'šyrn,* "twenty=," somehow dropped out of the Ezra text.

THE ARRIVAL OF EZRA

8 1 Sometime after these events, during the reign of Artaxerxes the king of Persia, Ezra*ᵃ*, the son of Azariah*ᵇ*, the son of Zechrios*ᶜ*, the son of Hilkiah, the son of Shallum 2 the son of Zadok*ᵈ*, the son of Ahitub, the son of Amariah*ᵉ*, the son of Azariah*ᶠ*, the son of Bukki, the son of Abishua, the son of Phinehas, the son of Eleazar, the son of Aaron the chief priest, arrived. 3 This Ezra came up from Babylon as a scribe who was expert in the law of Moses which was given by the God of Israel. 4 The king accorded him honor, inasmuch as he found favor before him in all his requests. 5 Now some of the Israelites, priests, Levites, temple singers, gatekeepers and temple servants came up [with him] to Jerusalem 6 in the seventh year of Artaxerxes' kingship, in the fifth month*ᵍ*; departing from Babylon on the new moon of the first month, they arrived at Jerusalem because a good journey was given them by the Lord for his sake. 7 For Ezra*ʰ* had vast knowledge so that he overlooked none of [the prescriptions] of the law of the Lord and the commandments, teaching*ⁱ* all Israel [its] statutes and judgments.

† I Esd 8:1–7 || Ezra 7:1–10; **8–24** || Ezra 7:11–26; **25–27** || Ezra 7:27–28; **28–40** || Ezra 8:1–14; **41–48** || Ezra 8:15–20; **49–53** || Ezra 8:21–23; **54–59** || Ezra 8:24–30; **60–64** || Ezra 8:31–36; **65–69** || Ezra 9:1–5; **70–87** || Ezra 9:6–15; **88 – 9:2** || Ezra 10:1–6; **3–17** || Ezra 10:7–17; **18–36** || Ezra 10:18–44; **37–55** || Neh 7:72b – 8:12.
ᵃ Some MSS have Esdras, as does Josephus.
ᵇ MT of Ezra 7:1 A has Ezerios. *śryh bn 'zryh*, "Seraiah, son of Azariah."
ᶜ So with LXX*ᴮ*.
ᵈ So with some MSS and MT. LXX*ᴮ* *Saddouloukos.*
ᵉ So with MT and LXX*ᴬ*; B Amartheios.   ᶠ With MT. LXX *Ozeios.*
ᵍ LXX*ᴮ* adds the following clause *outos eniautos o deuteros basilei,* "this was the second year he was king"; A, N, *eniautos ebdomos,* "seventh year," in which case it is a doublet of the earlier reference in the verse.
ʰ LXX*ᴮ* Apsaras; here with A, N.
ⁱ Inserting *didaxai,* "teaching," with LXX*ᴬ,ᴺ*.

THE RESCRIPT OF ARTAXERXES

8 The following is a copy of the order[j] that came from Artaxerxes the king to Ezra the priest and student of the law of the Lord: 9 "King Artaxerxes to Ezra the priest and student of the law of the Lord, greeting[k]. 10 Having decided to act friendly, I have issued orders that those of the nation of the Jews who are so minded, and of the priests, Levites, and of [others] in our realm may, if they choose, go with you to Jerusalem. 11 As many as plan to do so, let them set out together with you, as I and my seven friends, the counselors, have agreed, 12 that they may investigate [affairs] in Judah and Jerusalem in harmony with the law of the Lord, 13 and take back to Jerusalem gifts for the Lord of [Israel][l] which I and my friends have vowed; also all the gold and silver that can be obtained in the land of Babylonia for the Lord in Jerusalem, along with what is being contributed by the nation for the temple of their Lord in Jerusalem, 14 is to be collected — gold and silver, bulls and rams and lambs, with their accessories — 15 so that sacrifices may be offered on the altar of their Lord in Jerusalem. 16 Whatever you with your brothers may desire to do with the gold and silver is subject to the will of your God; 17 so also with respect to the sacred vessels [m]of the Lord[m] contributed for the use of the temple of your God in Jerusalem. And whatever else you may need for the use of the temple of your God that is lacking 18 you must provide from the royal treasury. 19 And, indeed, I, Artaxerxes the king, have ordered the treasurers of Syria and Phoenicia to give him without hesitation whatever Ezra, the priest and student of the law of the most high God, may send for up to a hundred talents of silver, 20 and likewise up to a hundred measures of wheat and a hundred measures of wine, [n]and salt without limit[n]. 21 Let [everything] be accomplished for the most high God according to the law of God so that wrath may not fall upon the realm of the king and his sons. 22 Moreover, you are [hereby] advised that no tribute of any kind or other imposition

---

[j] Reading *prostagmatos*, with LXX[A,N].

[k] LXX of Ezra 7:17 *tetelesto logos kai ē apokrisis*, "the thing/word is finished and the reply," a literal rendering of the Aram. *gmyr wk'nt*.

[l-l] So with some MSS and supported by Josephus.

[m-m] So with LXX[A,N].

[n-n] LXX[A,N] add *alas ek plethous panta*, "salt without limit," following Aram. *wmlḥ dy-l' ktb*, "and salt without prescribed limit."

is to be laid on any priests, Levites, sacred singers, gatekeepers, temple servants, or functionaries of this temple, nor is anyone to have authority to levy [such] on them. 23 And you, Ezra, according to the wisdom of God shall appoint judges and magistrates to render decisions in all Syria and Phoenicia for all those who know the law of your God and to instruct those who do not know [it]. 24 All who violate either the law of your God or that of the king must be punished forthwith[o], whether the [sentence] is death or [some other] punishment, be it monetary fine or ostracism."

EZRA'S PAEAN OF PRAISE

25 [p]Praised be the only Lord who has put these things into the mind[q] of the king to glorify his house in Jerusalem. 26 He has honored me before the king[r] and all his friends[s] and nobles. 27 So I was encouraged by the support of the Lord my God and assembled men of Israel to go up with me.

LIST OF CAPTIVES WHO RETURNED WITH EZRA

28 These are the heads of their families and divisions who went up with me from Babylon during the reign of Artaxerxes the king: 29 of the sons of Phinehas, Gershom[t]; of the sons of Ithamar, Gamelos[u]; of the sons of David, 30 [of the sons of] Parosh, Zechariah and with him 150 officially registered men; 31 of the sons of Pahath-moab, Eliehoenai the son of Zerahiah, and with him 200 men; 32 of the sons of Zattu, Shecaniah the son of Jehaziel, and with him 200[v] men; of the sons of Adin, Obed the son of Jonathan, and with him 250 men; 33 of the sons of Elam, Jeshaiah the son of Gotholios, and with him 70 men; 34 of the sons of Shephatiah, Zaraiah the son of Michael, and with him 70 men; 35 of the sons of Joab, Obadiah the son of Jehiel, and with him 212 men; 36 of the sons of Bani, Shelomith the son of Josiphiah, and with him 160 men; 37 of the

[o] LXX *epimelōs,* rendering *'sprn'* of Ezra 7:26. The idea of the Aramaic-Persian term suggests both speed and precision in the act it qualifies.
[p] LXX^{A,N} preface the statement with *kai eipen esdras o grammateus,* "and Esdras the scribe said."
[q] Omit *mou,* "my," with LXX^{A,N} and MT of Ezra 7:27.
[r] So in part with LXX^{A,N}; B has *tōn basileuontōn,* "of those who rule."
[s] Some MSS have *sumbouleuontōn,* "advisers," as a plus before "friends."
[t] LXX^{B} has Tarosotomos.
[u] Some MSS have Daniel or Gamaliel.
[v] LXX^{B}; A, N has 300, as does Ezra.

sons of Bebai, Zechariah the son of Bebai, and with him 28 men; 38 the sons of Azgad, Johanan the son of Hakkatan, and with him 110 men; 39 of the sons of Adonikam, the last ones, whose names are Eliphelet, Jeiel and Shemaiah, and with them 70 men; 40 of the sons of Bigvai, Uthai son of Istakalkou and with him 70 men.

AN APPEAL FOR TEMPLE SERVANTS

41 Then assembling them at [a place] called the river*w*, where we encamped three days, I scrutinized them, 42 and finding none of the priestly or Levitical families there, 43 I sent to Eleazar, Idouēlos, Maasmas, Elnathan*x*, Shemaiah, Jarib, Nathan, Elnathan*y*, Zechariah and Meshullam*z*, the leading and learned men, 44 and told them to go to Iddo*a*, the official at the location of the treasury, 45 directing them to urge Iddo and his brothers and those employed at the treasury to send us men capable of serving in the priestly office in the house of our Lord. 46 *b*According to the mighty hand of our Lord he brought us*b* learned men of the sons of Mahli, the son of Levi, the son of Israel, Sherebiah with his sons and brothers, 10*c*. 47 *d*Of the sons of Hananiah and their sons, 20 men; 48 and of the temple servants whom David and the leaders had appointed for the service of the Levites, temple servants 220; a name list of all was on record.

A FAREWELL SERVICE

49 Then I proclaimed a fast there for the young men before our Lord, 50 to implore him for a safe journey for us, for our children and cattle. 51 I felt ashamed *e*to request of the king*e* horses and foot soldiers as an escort for security against our enemies; 52 for we had already declared to the king, "The might of our Lord is with those who seek him and will support [them] in all things." 53 So

w LXX*A,N* adds *thera.* Ezra 8:15 has *'l-hnhr hb' 'l- hw'*, "at the canal that runs to Ahava." See also LXX of the latter. Josephus (*Antiq.* 11:5:2) has *eis to peran tou Eupratou*, "other side of the Euphrates."
x LXX Enaatan.   *y* LXX Ennatan.   *z* With LXX*A,N*; B has Mesolabōm.
a With MT of Ezra 8:17; LXX Laadaios, Lodaios.
b–b With LXX*A,N* and MT, partly, of Ezra 8:18.
c Some MSS add *oktō*, "8," thus harmonizing with MT of Ezra.
d Some MSS have at the beginning of the verse "and Hashabiah and Announos and Osiah brother." Cf. also Ezra 8:19.
e–e So with Ezra 8:22 and LXX*A,N*.

we prayed to our Lord again for all these things and ʲfound him to be graciousʲ.

SELECTION OF TREASURE-BEARERS

⁵⁴ Then I selected twelve men of the leading priests, namely Sherebiahᵍ and Hashabiahʰ and ten of their brothers with them ⁵⁵ to whom I weighed out the silver, the gold and the sacred vessels of the house of our Lord, which the king, his advisers and magistrates and all Israel had contributed. ⁵⁶ I weighed out and handed over to them six hundred and fifty talents of silver, silver vessels weighing a hundred talents, and a hundred talents of gold, together with twenty golden bowls and tenⁱ copper vessels of solid, shining copper. ⁵⁷ I told them, "You are holy to the Lord and the vessels are holy, and the silver and the gold is a votive offering to the Lord, the Lord of our fathers. ⁵⁸ Take care of them and guard them until you hand them over to the leading priests, Levites, and family chiefs of Israel in Jerusalem in the rooms of the house of our Lord." ⁵⁹ So the priests and the Levites, taking charge of the silver and the gold and the vessels, brought them to Jerusalem into the temple of the Lord.

JOURNEY TO AND ARRIVAL AT JERUSALEM

⁶⁰ Leaving the location of the placeʲ Thera on the twelfth day of the first month, weᵏ arrived at Jerusalem because the mighty hand of our Lord was with us; he protected us en route from every enemy, and so ˡwe reachedˡ Jerusalem [safely]. ⁶¹ After three days there, the silver and the gold was weighed out and turned over in the house of theᵐ Lord to Meremoth the son of Uriah, the priest, ⁶² with whom was Eleazar the son of Phinehas; with them were also Jozabadⁿ the son of Jeshua and Mōeth the son of Binnuiᵒ, the Levites; all [of it was checked] by number and weight and the total weight recorded on the spot. ⁶³ Those who arrived from the captivity

---

ʲ⁻ʲ Exact wording found also in a third-century B.C. papyrus.
ᵍ With Ezra 8:24; LXXᴮ Eserebia.   ʰ With Ezra; LXXᴮ Assamia.
ⁱ LXXᴬ,ᴺ have 12. LXX of Ezra 8:27 has *diaphora*, "excellent."
ʲ LXXᴬ,ᴺ *potamou*, "river." See textual note ʷ to vs. 41.
ᵏ First person plural with LXXᴬ,ᴺ and to harmonize with the pronoun *ēmin*, "us."
ˡ⁻ˡ First person plural with LXXᴬ,ᴺ.   ᵐ LXXᴬ,ᴺ "our."
ⁿ With LXXᴬ,ᴺ and Ezra 8:33; B has Iosabees.
ᵒ With Ezra 8:33; LXX Sabannos.

offered sacrifices to the Lord God of Israel: *p*twelve bulls for all Israel*p*, ninety-six rams*q*, seventy-two*r* lambs, twelve *s*he-goats for a peace offering*s* — all of them as a sacrifice to the Lord. 64 They also conveyed the orders of the king to the royal stewards and governors of Syria*t* and Phoenicia; so they *u*paid homage to the people and the temple of the Lord*u*.

THE SCANDAL OF THE GOLAH

65 After the conclusion of these events, the officials approached me saying, 66 "*v*The people of Israel*v*, the chiefs, the priests and the Levites have not kept themselves apart from the aliens of the land with their uncleanness — from the Canaanites, the Hittites, the Perizzites, the Jebusites, the Moabites, the Egyptians, and the Edomites — 67 inasmuch as they and their sons have married some of their daughters so that the holy race has been contaminated by the alien peoples of the land; even the leaders and chiefs have shared in this illicit practice from the beginning of the affair." 68 As soon as I learned about these things, I tore my clothes and sacred vestments, pulled some of the hair off my head and out of my beard, and sat down dejected and exceedingly sorrowful. 69 Then all those who were moved by the word of the Lord of Israel congregated to me while I wept on account of the violation and sat crestfallen until [the time of] the evening sacrifice.

EZRA'S PRAYER-SERMON

70 After being aroused from my fast, still in my torn clothes and sacred vestments, [I] fell upon my knees, raised my hands to the Lord and said, 71 "O Lord, I am mortified [and] chagrined before you. 72 Our sins have risen over our heads, our apathies have been more conspicuous than the heavens, 73 from the time of our fathers, and we remain in great sin to this very day. 74 And because of our sins and those of our fathers, we, together with our brothers, our

---

p–p So with LXX*A,N*.
q With Ezra 8:35; omitted by LXX*B*. Perhaps *krios* is to be seen in *kuriō*, "Lord."
r So with a number of MSS and Josephus; LXX*B* has seventy-six.
s–s Ezra 8:35 *ṣpry ḥṭ't*, "he-goats for a sin-offering"; LXX *chimarous peri amartias* (same as MT). I Esdras here has *tragous uper sōtēriou.*
t LXX*A,N* *koilēs Surias*, Coele-Syria.
u–u Cf. Jos. *Antiq.* 11:5:2 for a different syntactic interpretation.
v–v So with LXX*A*; omitted by B.

kings, and our priests, have been consigned in shame to the kings of the earth, to the sword, to captivity, to plunder until this very day. 75 And now how great has been *w*the mercy of the Lord toward us*w*! [because] there is left to us a root and a name in this hallowed place 76 and our light is uncovered in the house of our Lord, to provide for us sustenance in the time of our servitude; for in our servitude we were not abandoned by our Lord 77 but he continued to exercise his favor toward us [even] before the Persian kings so that they provided for us sustenance, 78 glorified our temple, raised the ruins of Zion, and presented us with a *x*solid footing*x* in Judah and Jerusalem. 79 Now, O Lord, having these things, what [more] can we ask? *y*We have transgressed*y* your orders which you issued through your servants the prophets saying, 80 'The land which you are going to possess is a polluted land, polluted by its aliens who have filled it with their uncleanness. 81 Therefore, you must not give your daughters in marriage to their sons, nor take their daughters for your sons; 82 you must never seek peaceful relations with them, so that you may grow strong, eat the good things of the land, and bequeath [it] to your sons forever.' 83 After all that has befallen us, brought about because of our evil deeds and our great guilt — because you, O Lord, have eased the burden of our sins 84 and given us such a root — shall we again violate your law by becoming entangled with the impurity of the peoples of the land? 85 Do not now be so angry with us as to destroy us, leaving neither root, nor seed, nor our name. 86 O Lord of Israel, you are faithful, for we are left a root to the present time. 87 Behold, we are in your presence in our guilt, yet no one can continue in your presence under [circumstances like] these."

THE PEOPLE'S RESPONSE TO EZRA'S PRAYER-SERMON

88 While Ezra was praying and confessing, lying weeping before the temple, there collected around him from Jerusalem a very great crowd of men, women, and youths, for the weeping of the throng was profuse. 89 *z*Jechoniah*z* the son of Jehiel, of the sons of Israel*a*, shouted and said to Ezra, "We have sinned against the Lord; we

---

w-w Omits the second *kuriou*, "Lord"; Rahlfs has "your mercy, O Lord," with LXX*A*.
x-x MT of Ezra 9:9 has *gdr*, "wall"; cf. A. S. Kapelrud, JBL 85 (1966), 254. LXX of Ezra has *phragmon*, "wall," "fence," "hedge."
y-y First person plural with LXX*A,N* and MT of Ezra 9:10; B has third person plural.
z Some MSS have Shecanaiah. So MT and LXX of Ezra 10:2.
a MT and LXX of Ezra have Elam (*'ylm*).

have cohabited with alien wives from the peoples of the land; *but now in spite of everything Israel continues*. 90 Let us swear an oath to the Lord to eject all our wives of foreign origin together with their children, as you and those who are obedient to the law of our Lord have advocated. 91 Rise and act, for the obligation is yours; we are with you to give [you] support." 92 When Ezra got up, he made the family heads of the priests and Levites of all Israel swear to act accordingly, and they swore [to do so].

9   1 Upon leaving*c* the court of the temple Ezra went to the priest-room of *d*Jehohanan the son of Eliashib*d* 2 where he lodged without eating food or drinking water, grieving over the monstrous iniquities of the people.

PROCLAMATION AND ASSEMBLY

3 So a proclamation was issued throughout Judah and Jerusalem for all those of the captivity to assemble at Jerusalem: 4 Anyone who fails to appear within two or three days, in compliance with the summons of the presiding elders, will forfeit his property and he [himself] will be excluded from the people of the captivity. 5 Those of the tribe of Judah and Benjamin assembled themselves at Jerusalem within three days — it was the twentieth day of the ninth month — 6 and all the people sat down in the plaza before the temple, shivering because of the wintry weather. 7 Then Ezra arose and addressed them: "You have acted illegally by cohabiting with alien wives, compounding the sin of Israel. 8 Now, therefore, [make] confession, give glory to the Lord God of our fathers, 9 do his will, and dissociate yourselves from the peoples of the land and the alien wives*e*." 10 All the people shouted and cried with a loud voice, "We will do just as you have said. 11 But the people are numerous, it is winter and we are unable to stand in the open and find it impossible [to do so]; our task cannot be done in a day or two, for we have sinned too greatly in these matters. 12 Therefore let the representatives of the people remain and let all those of our colony who have alien wives appear at a designated time, 13 along with the local elders

---

b–b Some MSS read *nun estin epanō pas elpis tō Israēl,* "now there is, in spite of all, hope for Israel"; see also Rahlfs's text. The parallel Ezra text in LXX^B reads *kai nun estin upomenē tō Israēl epi toutō,* "and now there is a remnant to Israel on this condition."

c Lit. "get up."

d–d So with Ezra 10:6 and LXX^A,N; B has "Jōna the son of Naseibos." The name Eliashib occurs on ostraca from Tell Arad.

e LXX^A and MT of Ezra 10:11.

and judges until the wrath of the Lord turns away from us on account of this infraction." 14 Jonathan the son of Asahel[f] and Jahzeiah[g] the son of Tikvah[h] approved of this [procedure], and Meshullam and the Levite[i] Shabbethai supported them. 15 Thereupon those of the captivity acquiesced in all these things. 16 Then Ezra the priest selected the chief men of their families, all by name, who met together in closed session on the new moon of the tenth month to look into the matter. 17 The consideration of the men who had cohabited with alien wives lasted until the new moon of the first month.

LIST OF THOSE COHABITING WITH ALIEN WIVES

18 Of the assembled priests having alien wives were discovered [the following]: 19 of the sons of Jeshua the son of Jozadak and his brothers: Maaseiah, Eleazar, Jarib[j], and Jodanos[k]. 20 They agreed to put away their wives and [give an offering] of rams in atonement for their mistaken conduct. 21 Of the sons of Immer: Hananiah, Zebadiah, [l]Maaseiah, Shemaiah, Jehiel, and Azariah[l]; 22 of the sons of Pashhur: Elioenai, Maaseiah, Ishmael, Nathaniel, Jozabad[m], Elasah[n]. 23 Of the Levites: Jozabad, [o]Shimei, Kelaiah — that is Kelita — [o], Pethahiah, Judah, and Eliezer[p]; 24 of the temple singers: Eliashib [and] Bakchouros[q]; 25 of the gatekeepers: Shallum and Telem[r]. 26 Of the Israelites: of the sons of Parosh: Ramiah, Izziah, Malchijah, Milelos[s], Eleazar, Asebiah, and Benaiah; 27 of the sons of Elam: Mattaniah, Zechariah, Jehiel, Abdi, Jeremoth, and Elijah; 28 of the sons of Zattu: Elioenai[t], Eliashib, Othoniah[u], Jeremoth, Zabad, and Zerediah[v]; 29 of the sons of Bebai: Jehohanan, Han-

[f] Cf. *Les Grottes de Murabba'at*, DJD, II, 94:12. Name occurs below in vs. 34.
[g] With MT of Ezra 10:15; LXX Ezeias and Ezekias.
[h] With some MSS and MT; LXX[B,A] Thokanos.
[i] Text reads a proper name here — Leueis, but in view of MT it appears better to regard it as a mistake for Levite (Greek Leueites).
[j] With Ezra 10:18; most LXX MSS have Jorib.
[k] Ezra 10:18 has Gedaliah in both MT and LXX.
[l-l] LXX[Bb] *apo tōn uiōn ēiram maasias kai eleias kai samaias kai ieiēl kai ozias*, "of the sons of Hiram: Maaseiah and Elijah and Shemaiah and Jehiel and Uzziah."
[m] So with LXX[Bb]; B has Okailēdos.　　[n] LXX[B] Salthas.
[o-o] LXX[B] Senseis, Kōnos, Kaleitais.
[p] So with LXX[Bb]; B has Jōanes.
[q] Omitted in Ezra 10:24; some MSS of LXX have Sakchour (Zaccur).
[r] LXX[B] Tolbanēs; Bb Telem and Uriah, perhaps a correction from MT of Ezra 10:24.
[s] Ezra 10:25 has *mymn* as do some MSS of LXX for Ezra, but not here.
[t] So for text, Eliada (Heb. *'lyd'*).　　[u] MT of Ezra 10:27, Mattaniah.
[v] MT has *'zyz'*; text of LXX reads Zeraliah.

aniah, Zabdi[w], and Emaththis[x]; 30 of the sons of Bani[y], Meshullam, Malluch, Adaiah, Jashub, Yisal[z], and Jeremoth; 31 of the sons of Addi: Lathos[a], Mōsiah, Lakkunos, Naidos, Beskaspasmus, Sesthēl, Binnui, and Manasseh; 32 of the sons of Annan: Eliōdah, Isshiah, Malchijah, Shemaiah, and Simōn Chosamaos; 33 of the sons of Hashum: Mattenai, Mattattah, Zabad, Eliphelet,[b] Manasseh, and Shimei; 34 of the sons of Bani: Jeremiah, Maadai, Amram[c], Iuel[d], [e]Mamdai, Pediah, Anōs, Karabassiōn, Enaseibos, Mantanaimos, Eliashib, Bannus, Edialeis, Shimei, Shelemiah, and Nethaniah[e]; of the sons of Ezōra: Shashai, Ezriel, Asahel, Shemaiah, Shemariah, and Joseph; 35 of the sons of [f]Nebo: Jeiel[f], Zabad, Jeddai, Joel, and Benaiah. 36 All these had cohabited with alien wives but they now dismissed[g] them together with their children.

THE LAW-READING ASSEMBLY

37 Now the priests, the Levites, and some of the Israelites lived in Jerusalem and in the country. On the new moon of the seventh month, when the sons of Israel [were settled] in their communities, 38 all the people assembled to a man [h]in the plaza in front of the east gate of the temple[h] 39 and requested Ezra, the priest[i] and reader, to bring out the law of Moses which had been given by the[j] God of Israel. 40 So, on the new moon of the seventh month, Ezra, the high

[w] Ezra 10:28 zby (Zabbi).   [x] Ezra 'tly (Athlai).
[y] With a number of MSS and Ezra. LXX[B] has Mani.
[z] Ezra 10:29 wš'l, "and Sheal," probably for yš'l, whence LXX Asaelos, Isaelos, Assael. Hebrew and LXX minuscules are correct as seen now in an Ophel seal (= lḥgy yš'l). Cf. J. Prignaud, "Un sceau hébreu de Jérusalem et un ketib du livre d'Esdras," RB 71 (1964), 372–83, with plate XVI.
[a] With LXX[B]; A has Naathos.
[b] Ezra 10:33 adds here Jeremai. LXX[Bb] also has it, but perhaps misplaced in the next verse.
[c] With LXX[Bb] and Ezra 10:34.
[d] With LXX[A]; B has Iouna.
[e-e] Shimei, LXX[Bb]; has Benaiah, Badaiah, Cheliasoub, Matthaniah, Bennei, and the sons of Bonnei: Selemei, Shemeei, Nathan, Addaiah, Nadabou, Sessei, and Sarouah.
[f-f] With LXX[Bb]; B has Ooma, Zeitias.
[g] apelusan. For meaning "to repudiate" see Les Grottes de Murabba'at, DJD, II, 115:4, in a marriage contract A.D. 124.
[h-h] Neh 8:1 eis to platos to emprosthen pulēs tou udatos, "at the plaza in front of the Water Gate"; Heb. 'l-hrḥwb 'šr lpny š'r - hmym, "to the plaza which is in front of the Water Gate." Cf. I Esd 9:6 en tē euruchōro tou ierou, "in the plaza of the temple," and par. Ezra 10:9 en plateia oikou tou theou, "in the plaza before the house of God" = Heb. brḥwb byt h'lhym. Note the use of tou . . . ierou pulōnos, "the gate of the temple," for to . . . pules tou udatos, "the Water Gate."
[i] LXX[A] archierei, "high priest."
[j] LXX[A] adds kuriou, "Lord."

priest, brought out the law for the whole congregation consisting of men, women, and *all the priests* to hear¹. 41 And he read in the plaza in front of the temple gate from dawn until midday in the presence of the men and women; all listened intently to the law. 42 Ezra, the priest and reader of the law, stood upon the wooden podium that had been constructed 43 and beside him on the right stood Mattathiah, Shema, Ananiah, Azariah, Uriah, Hezekiah*ᵐ*, and Baalsamos*ⁿ*; 44 on the left [stood] Pedaiah, Mishael, Malchijah, Lothasoubos*º*, Nabariah*ᵖ*, and Zechariah. 45 Then Ezra took the book *qof the law*q in his hands in the presence of the people — for he was seated in the most pre-eminent place before all of them — 46 and when he opened the law all [of them] stood up. When Ezra*ʳ* praised *ᵉthe Lord God Most High, God of Hosts,*ˢ 47 all the people shouted Amen, Amen, lifted up their hands, fell to the ground, and worshiped God. 48 Jeshua, Anniouth*ᵗ*, Sherebiah, Jamin*ᵘ*, Akkub*ᵛ*, Shabbetai*ʷ*, Hodiah*ˣ*, Maiannas, Kelita, Azariah, Jozabad*ʸ*, Hanan, and Pelaiah, the Levites, taught the law of the Lord and read the law of the Lord [in translation] to the people, putting meaning into the reading. 49 Then the governor*ᶻ* said to Ezra, the high priest and the reader, and to the Levites who taught the people, with regard to all, 50 "This day is sacred to the Lord — everybody wept when they heard the law — 51 therefore go, eat the fat, *ᵃdrink the sweet*ᵃ, and send portions to those who have nothing. 52 Since the day is sacred to the Lord you must not be sad; the Lord will grant you favor." 53 The Levites too commanded all the people saying, "This day is sacred; do not be sad." 54 Then they all went away to eat, to drink, to rejoice, and to give portions to those with nothing, and to celebrate with exceeding [joy], 55 because they were inspired by the matters in which they had been instructed. Then they assembled. . . .

---

k-k Neh 8:2 *wkl mbyn,* "and all who could understand"; so also LXX there.
ˡ Omit *ton nomon,* "the law," as redundant.
ᵐ Neh 8:4 *ḥlkyh* (Hilkiah). *ⁿ* Neh 8:4 *mʿśyh* (Maaseiah). *º* Neh 8:4 *ḥšm* (Hashum).
ᵖ Neh 8:4 *ḥšbdnh* (Hashabaddanah).   *q-q* So with LXX^A.
ʳ With Neh 8:6 and LXX^A; B Azariah.
ˢ-ˢ So partly with LXX^Bb,A; LXX^B has "the most high God, the Almighty."
ᵗ Some late MSS and Neh 8:7, both MT and LXX, have Bani.
ᵘ So with MT and LXX^Bb.   *ᵛ* With LXX^A.   *ʷ* With LXX^A and MT.
ˣ With MT of Nehemiah; LXX^B has Autais. *ʸ* With LXX^Bb,A; B has Katethzabdos.
ᶻ LXX *attaratē, attharitēs* represents a transliteration of the Persian title *htršt'* and regards it as a proper name; omitted in LXX^B of Neh 8:9, where the name Neemias occurs (as in present MT *nḥmyh hw' htršt',* "Nehemiah who is the governor,") but the title is absent. Syncellus *Chronography* (Dindorf ed., vol. 1, p. 480) follows I Esdras wording, "governor," without the MT qualification.
a-a Insert with LXX^A and with MT and LXX of Neh 8:10.

NOTES

8:6. *his sake.* Ezra's, as next verse indicates.

8. *student.* Lit. "reader"; but *spr* of MT implies more than that. Cf. vs. 7. (Also A. L. Oppenheim, "A Note on the Scribes of Mesopotamia," in *Studies in Honor of Benno Landsberger on His Seventy-fifth Birthday, April 21, 1965* [University of Chicago Press, 1965], pp. 253–56.)

10. *the Jews.* Ezra par.=Israel, the designation before Hellenistic times.

11. *seven friends, the counselors.* Cf. Esther 1:14; Herodotus 5:24; 7:46 ff.; Xenophon *Anabasis* 1:6:4 f.

18. *royal treasury.* See NOTE on 6:20.

19. *treasurers.* Greek *tois gazophylaxi;* Aram. *gzbry'* is a Persian word. For comment on the meaning of the term see Cameron, *The Persepolis Treasury Tablets,* pp. 10 f.

without hesitation. Also a Persian word, meaning exactly, precisely.

a hundred talents. More than 3¾ tons.

20. *a hundred measures of wheat.* For Aram. *kryn m'h*=100 kors or ca. 650 bushels.

a hundred measures of wine. For Aram. *btyn m'h*=100 baths; a bath= 6.073 gallons.

24. A somewhat interpretative verse. Ezra 7:26 lists the possible penalties as death, exclusion, fine and imprisonment. Josephus (*Antiq.* 11:5:1) mentions only death and the payment of a fine.

punishment. Aram. *lšršw;* see Frithiof Rundgren, "Zur Bedeutung von ŠRŠW —Ezra VII 26," VT 7 (1957), 400–4, and Z. W. Falk, "Ezra VII 26," VT 9 (1959), 88 f., where the suggestion is made that it is an Iranian loanword meaning punishment with a stick (*Prügelstrafe*). Pers. *sraušya,* Avestan *sraošya* mean corporal punishment.

26. *friends.* See textual note *h* at 3:7.

27. *go up.* To Jerusalem.

29. *Phinehas.* With Ezra 8:2 and LXX^{A,N}; B has Phoros.

Gershom. With Ezra and LXX^N; B has Tarostomos.

Gamelos. Ezra has Daniel.

David. Some Greek MSS and Ezra add Hattush of the sons of Shecaniah. LXX^{A,N} have *attous o secheniou,* "Attous the [son of] Shecaniah."

31. *Pahath-moab.* LXX has Maathmōab.

32. *Shecaniah.* With LXX^{A,N} and Ezra. B has Eiechoniah.

Jehaziel. With LXX^{A,N} and Ezra. B has Iethēlos.

250. Ezra 8:6 has 50.

33. *Gotholios.* Ezra 8:7 Athaliah.

34. *Zaraiah.* Ezra 8:8 Zebadiah.

70. Ezra 80, both MT and LXX.

35. *Jehiel.* With Ezra 8:9. LXX Iezēlos.

212. Ezra has 218.

36. *Josiphiah.* A seal found at Tell el-Fuḫḫar near Acco bears the name

b'lysp (=Baalyasiph), of similar formation with the divine name Baal (IEJ 14 [1964]), 194.

37. *Bebai.* With LXX^A,N and MT of Ezra 8:11. B=Baiēr and Bēmai.

38. *Azgad.* With Ezra 8:12.

39. *Jeiel.* With Ezra 8:13 and some Greek and Latin MSS.

70. Some MSS have 60.

40. *Bigvai.* With Ezra 8:14 and in view of vs. 36. LXX has Banai.

Istakalkou. Ezra=Zabud.

43. *Idouēlos.* Ezra 8:16 Ariel.

44. *location of the treasury.* Ezra 8:17 *kspy'*, "Casiphia," a place name.

45. *treasury.* Lit. "the place of the treasurers."

46. *Mahli.* LXX Moolei.

Sherebiah. LXX Asebēbiah.

10. Ezra 8:18 has 18; so also LXX^A,N.

56. *six hundred and fifty talents.* A bit over 24½ tons.

a hundred talents. Ca. 3¾ tons. For the value of these gifts see V. Pavlovský, *Biblica* 38 (1957), 297–301.

59. *taking charge.* . . . Could also be read "took charge of the silver and the gold and the vessels that were in Jerusalem and brought . . ."

61. *Meremoth.* Ostraca found at Tell Arad bear names of Meremoth and Pashhur.

62. *Mōeth.* Ezra 8:33 Noadiah.

63. *seventy-two lambs.* MT of Ezra 8:35 has 77. I Esdras is probably right in view of the multiples of 12.

64. *they.* The context indicates "they" refers to stewards and governors. So also Ezra and Josephus (*Antiq.* 11:5:2).

66. *Edomites.* Ezra 9:1 Amorites.

68. *beard.* For reference to a similar incident see Aeschylus *Persians* in J. S. Blackie, *The Lyrical Dramas of Aeschylus* (New York: Dutton, 1906), p. 331, and Neh 13:25.

74. *sins . . . of our fathers.* Corporate liability of nation extends beyond the present back to the fathers. Cf. also Tobit 3:3; Judith 7:28; Bar 3:8.

79. *prophets.* Apparently a general summation of the message of the prophets since the exact passage does not appear in any of the known prophetic oracles. But cf. Deut 7:1 ff. and 23:7.

80. *aliens.* Lit. "aliens of the land."

88. *around.* Lit. "to" (*pros*).

90. *oath.* Ezra 10:3 has covenant.

9:3. *captivity.* The Hebrew of Ezra 10:6 and elsewhere is golah (the people who had returned from exile).

5. *ninth month.* Josephus (*Antiq.* 11:5:4) notes it was the month of Kislev; which would be November–December according to the Julian calendar.

6. *shivering.* Lit. "trembling." Perhaps the emotional state of the people also had something to do with their posture, i.e. being seated.

8. *give glory.* . . . An oath formula (cf. Josh 7:19; John 9:24).

11. *winter.* The rainy season, as Hebrew of Ezra 10:13 makes explicit.

14. *Asahel.* Cf. also vs. 34. Name (*Aazaēlos, Azaēlos*) at Murabba'at. DJD, II, 227.

Shabbethai. Name occurs in Aramaic letters of Hermopolis 4:10.

16. *tenth month.* The month of Tebeth (Esther 2:16), December–January.

17. *first month.* The month of Nisan, March–April.

20. *agreed.* Lit. "put their hands to."

22. *Pashhur.* Name found also at Tell Arad.

31. *Addi.* Ezra 10:30 has Pahath-moab followed by eight names. The same number here but the names are different.

32. *Annan.* Ezra 10:31 has Harim.

Eliōdah, Elionah=Eliezer. Ezra has eight names; here only five.

33. *Hashum.* Text reads Assom.

34. *Ezōra.* Considerable confusion here, as in Ezra 10:35 f.

35. *Nebo.* Ezra 10:43 has seven names; here only five.

36. *dismissed.* On this clause see Schaeder, EdS, p. 10, n. 1. Cf. Ezra 10:44 which is meaningless as it stands in MT.

37. Ezra 2:70; Neh 7:72 add singers, gatekeepers, temple servants (*nethī-nīm*).

seventh month. Tishri, September–October. On position see Rudolf Kittel, *Zur Frage der Entstehung des Judentums* (Univ. Programm Leipzig, 1918), p. 31, n. 34.

41. *listened intently.* Lit. "put the mind to."

43–44. *on the right . . . on the left.* Seven stood on Ezra's right, six on the left side. In view of the emphasis on the number twelve, it is likely that one name should be dropped.

48. *Maiannas.* Maaseiah of Neh 8:7.

putting meaning. Lit. "infusing life into." Cf. also Schaeder, *Iranische Beiträge*, I, 11 [in translation]. See Neh 8:8 and for the meaning Franz Altheim and Ruth Stiehl, *Die aramäische Sprache unter den Achaimeniden* (Frankfurt am Main: Klostermann, 1963), pp. 7 ff.

49. *the governor.* Nehemiah in Neh 8:9 in both MT and LXX.

51. *portions.* For Heb. *mnwt,* "portions of sacrificial offering"; Greek has the meaning of "tribute, gift."

those who have nothing. An interpretation of the Heb. *l'yn nkwn lw,* "to him who has nothing prepared."

55. *Then they assembled.* Some translators read this with the preceding, but it is probably a gloss based on Neh 8:13 inasmuch as some MSS complete that verse here. For comment on the phrase see Bayer, pp. 90 ff.; Rudolph, E-N, pp. xiv ff.; and Cook, APOT, I, 57 f. For Josephus' handling of the story see *Antiq.* 11:5:5. Eissfeldt, p. 575, thinks it represents "a secondary addition" pointing to a sequel to be found elsewhere.

COMMENT

With chapter 8 the Ezra story begins. Up till now I Esdras dealt with events transpiring in the time of Cyrus-Darius. "After these events" (vs. 1) suggests a lapse of time between what has just been related and what follows. Although there may be obscure references elsewhere to the period between Darius and

Artaxerxes they are no longer recoverable. If the seventh year of Artaxerxes I (458 B.C.) is correct there would be an interval of only twenty-seven years. If Artaxerxes II is the king meant (398 B.C.) the interval would be eighty-seven years. The position taken here is that while no certainty exists in the matter of date, the thirty-seventh year of Artaxerxes I (428 B.C.) fits the sequence of events best.[1] Then the work of Ezra would follow closely the conclusion of the final mission of Nehemiah sometime after 430 B.C.

[The arrival of Ezra, 8:1–7 — Ezra 7:1–10] The pedigree of Ezra has been considerably curtailed. Only fourteen names occur, for seventeen in Ezra and twenty-three in Chronicles; see following table.

PRIEST LISTS

I Esd 8:1–2	Ezra 7:1–5 MT	LXX	I Chron 6:3–14 MT*	LXX*
Esras	Ezra	Esdras	Jehozadak	Iōsadak
Adzaraiou	Seraiah	Saraiou	Seraiah	Saraia
Zechriou	Azariah	Zareiou	Azariah	Adzaria
Chelkeiou	Hilkiah	Elkeia	Hilkiah	Chelkeian
Salēmou	Shallum	Saloum	Shallum	Salōm
Saddouloukou	Zadok	Saddouk	Zadok	Sadōk
Acheitōb	Ahitub	Achertōb	Ahitub	Acheitōb
Amartheiou	Amariah	Samareia	Amariah	Amaria
Odzeiou	Azariah	Esreia	Azariah	Adzaria
Bokka	Merioth	Marerōth	Johanan	Iōanas
Abeisai	Zerahiah	Zaraia	Azariah	Adzaria
Pheinees	Uzzi	Saouia	Ahimaaz	Acheimaas
Eleadzar	Bukki	Bokkei	Zadok	Sadōk
Aarōn	Abishua	Abeisoue	Ahitub	Acheitōb
	Phinehas	Phinees	Amariah	Amareia
	Eleazar	Eleadzar	Meraioth	Mareiēl
	Aaron	Aarōn	Zerahiah	Zaraia
			Uzzi	Odzei
			Bukki	Bōe
			Abishua	Abeisou
			Phinehas	Pheinees
			Eleazar	Eleadzar
			Aaron	Aarōn

* Names in reverse order.

The list in Chronicles may have been filled in later from data accumulating in the course of post-exilic investigations. The list does not seem to be purely

---

[1] Following Albright, *The Biblical Period,* p. 64, n. 133. For observations on the date of Ezra see AB, vol. 14, Introduction, The Period of Ezra. For pertinent remarks see J. A. Emerton, "Did Ezra go to Jerusalem in 428 B.C.?" JTS 17 (1966), 1–19; Yohanan Aharoni, *The Land of the Bible* (Philadelphia: Westminster Press, 1967), p. 35; Ulrich Kellermann, "Erwägungen zum Problem der Esradatierung," ZAW 80 (1968), 55–87; Sara Japhet, "The Supposed Common Authorship of Chronicles and Ezra-Nehemiah," VT 18 (1968), 330–71; and for a summary of possibilities and suggestions by various authors to date of his publication see Kugler, *Von Moses bis Paulus,* pp. 215 ff. The canonical position of I Esdras, Ezra-Nehemiah, however, suggests the priority of Ezra though present historical evidence is insufficient to prove it.

artificial; it is rather partial or incomplete, only enough names to illustrate the writer's purpose being given. Its purpose is to authenticate the position of the priest-scribe, as may be seen from the place it occupies in the story and the names given — the first six names are the same in all parallel lists and have always been associated with the high priestly line. Having authenticated the priestly prerogative of Ezra, the author proceeds to describe the other role of the man. That he occupied a dual position can hardly be disputed; he had to do so to deal effectively with problems facing the golah community. It is a matter of proper authority in the two phases of its life — ecclesiastical and civil. So far as the latter was concerned, Ezra achieved recognition by the imperial authorities by virtue of his scribal activity. Ezra may have been sent on a mission similar to that undertaken by Udjeharresnet for an Egyptian House of Life while Darius was in Elam.[2] His standing in royal circles was probably due to some official position.[3] That was the reason for his being entrusted with the responsibility of leading a contingent of laymen, priests, Levites, temple singers, gatekeepers, and temple servants back to Jerusalem.

[The rescript of Artaxerxes, 8:8–24 — Ezra 7:11–26] No substantial difference here between I Esdras and Ezra. There is, however, some variation in tone and emphasis. The king's decision to act in a friendly manner is omitted by the latter. The law of God is found seven times in I Esdras to only five in Ezra, and the provision for a hundred baths of anointing oil is missing from I Esdras.[4] Note that in both recensions the law of God and the law of the king are placed virtually on a par.

[Ezra's paean of praise, 8:25–27 — Ezra 7:27–28] Praise is given to the Lord who inspired the king to act favorably toward Ezra and his project.

[List of captives who returned with Ezra, 8:28–40 — Ezra 8:1–14.] I Esdras follows Ezra 8 closely here.

| | I Esdras | | Ezra 8 | |
			LXX[B]	MT
Parosh	Zechariah	150	150	150
Pahath-moab	Eliehoenai son of Zerahiah	200	200	200
Zattu	Shecaniah son of Jehaziel	200	(300[A])	300
Adin	Obed son of Jonathan	250	50	50
Elam	Jeshaiah son of Gotholios	70	70	70
Shephatiah	Zeraiah son of Michael	70	80	80
Joab	Obadiah son of Jehiel	212	218	218
Bani	Shelomith son of Josiphiah	160	160	160
Bebai	Zechariah son of Bebai	28	78	28
Azgad	Johanan son of Hakkatan	110	110	110
Adonikam	Eliphelet, Jeiel, Shemaiah	70	60	60
Bigvai	Uthai son of Istakalkou	70	80	70
		1,590	1,556	1,496

[2] Cf. A. H. Gardiner, *Egypt of the Pharaohs* (London: Oxford University Press, 1961), p. 367; F. K. Kienitz, *Die politische Geschichte Ägyptens vom 7. bis zum 4. Jahrhundert vor der Zeitwende* (Berlin: Akademie Verlag, 1953), pp. 56 f.; G. Posener, *La première domination Perse en Égypte* (Cairo: L'institut Orientale, 1936), pp. 1–26.
[3] Schaeder, EdS, pp. 39–59, recently disputed by Mowinckel.
[4] See further AB, vol. 14, COMMENT on Ezra 7:11–26.

In both instances the list is not copied from Ezra 2 (I Esd 5) as may be seen from the fact that the priestly line is that of Aaron rather than that of Zadok[5] and that Pahath-moab is represented only by the Jeshua line, that of Joab having attained separate status. It is rather interesting that both recensions of the list (Ezra 8 and I Esd 8) contain twelve family names while those of Ezra 2 (=Neh 7) have only eleven (Neh 10 has nine names; Ezra 10, seven names). The Chronicler's penchant for the number twelve as representing all Israel is clearly in evidence, though only descendants of Judah and Benjamin returned. That this is regarded as a later list appears in the comment, "the last ones" of the Adonikam family (vs. 39) — another indication that there were several returns of golah families between Cyrus and Artaxerxes. Compare the observation of Josephus (*Antiq.* 11:5:2) that the people as a whole continued in Babylon, only two of the tribes being represented "in Asia and Europe." The number of priests is not given; only the names of the family heads.

[An appeal for temple servants, 8:41–48 — Ezra 8:15–20] There are numerous differences in names between I Esdras and the other accounts, for example:

I Esdras	Ezra MT	Ezra LXX
Eleazar	Eliezer	Eleazar
Idouēlos	Ariel	Ariel
Maasmas	Shemaiah	Samaia
Enaatan	Elnathan	Alonam
Shemaiah	Jarib	Areb
Jarib	Elnathan	Elnatham
Nathan	Nathan	Nathan
Ennatan		
Zechariah	Zechariah	Zecharia
Meshullam	Meshullam	Messouam
	Joiarib	Areb
	Elnathan	Eanathan

For explanation of Idouēlos-Ariel and suggestions for other variants, see Bayer, p. 56.

The name of Maasmas is missing in Ezra, and Esdras does not have the last two names of Ezra.

Ezra says only Levites were absent among those gathered at the river in preparation for the return; I Esdras says neither priests nor Levites were there. Casiphia of Ezra is interpreted here as *gadzophulakion,* "treasury," and *gadzophulax,* "treasurer," after the Heb. *ksp.* The number of those who responded according to LXX[B] is ten for the family of Sherebiah, otherwise the numbers are the same — a total of 250 or 258. The whole contingent, with Ezra, Gershom and Gamelos, numbered 1,843 persons. Reference to a record of names indicates that this is an excerpt of that record.

[A farewell service, 8:49–53 — Ezra 8:21–23] There is no mention here of Ahava — perhaps *n'rym,* "young men," was read for MT *nhr,* "river" — or of the fast as an expression of humiliation, or of wrath with the power of God.

[Selection of treasure-bearers, 8:54–59 — Ezra 8:24–30] Verse 55 adds

[5] On the shift between Zerubbabel and Ezra see AB, vol. 14, COMMENT on Ezra 8:1–14.

"magistrates" as a second type of officials. Ezra 8:26 has one hundred vessels of silver with talent value omitted whereas I Esdras has silver vessels weighing one hundred talents. I Esdras has ten copper vessels while Ezra has two. Josephus (*Antiq.* 11:5:2) has 650 talents of silver, silver vessels weighing one hundred talents, gold vessels weighing twenty talents and bronze vessels more precious than gold weighing twelve talents. The presentation of gifts by king, officials, and people parallels the precedent set in connection with the construction of the Solomonic temple (I Chron 26:26) and represents a tacit recognition of the legitimacy of the new temple by the Persian authorities.[6]

[Journey to and arrival at Jerusalem, 8:60–64 — Ezra 8:31–36][7] LXX[B] omits the offering of twelve bulls as a burnt offering for all Israel but other MSS have it.

[The scandal of the golah, 8:65–69 — Ezra 9:1–5] Tendency to compromise is characteristic in difficult times and situations. Ritual and other matters — perhaps preoccupation with the law of God (vss. 7, 23) — took up some time, perhaps as much as four months (cf. Ezra 10:9; I Esd 9:5). There may not have been a full awareness of the problem until after a serious study of the law of God or there may have been efforts to solve it more or less unobtrusively. In any case, Ezra understood quite well that more than a social problem was involved; intermarriage with the peoples of the land would water down the true religion of the golah and spell failure for its objective. The precarious position of the little community (cf. Malachi) demanded resolute action. The method of dealing with the situation adopted by Ezra was by way of self-abasement which dramatized the concern of *the* man of God. He viewed the golah as God's community and the embodiment of his will and way. Hence it was imperative to root out such scandal and forever avoid it.

[Ezra's prayer-sermon, 8:70–87 — Ezra 9:6–15; cf. Jos. *Antiq.* 11:5:3] Ezra's prayer of confession is one of the most remarkable expressions of self-identification in the historical literature of the Bible. The sweep of the prayer too is significant; it embraces the past and the present but looks to the future. There are certain differences in the two recensions. The addition of "our brothers" may not be fortuitous; it appears to refer to those not belonging to Ezra's golah. The divine inspiration of the Persian kings which impelled them to grant the request of *this* golah to undertake the restoration of the ruins at Jerusalem in Ezra is magnified here so that they did more than provide sustenance; they "glorified our temple, raised the ruins of Zion" and provided them with "a solid footing in Judah and Jerusalem." Actually this is a prayer-sermon, the product of a devoted leader who knew the Lord but who also understood people.[8]

[The people's response to Ezra's prayer-sermon, 8:88 – 9:2 — Ezra 10:1 – 6] The popular reaction to his prayer-address was precisely what Ezra hoped for. He attracted a huge crowd of people who immediately fell into the spirit of his

---

[6] See Kurt Galling, "Beiträge zur biblischen Landes- und Altertumskunde," ZDPV 68 (1950), 139.

[7] For interpretation of this passage, see AB, vol. 14, COMMENT on Ezra 8:31–36.

[8] Josephus (*Antiq.* 11:5:3) says Ezra's prostration was a clever way of attracting the attention of the people.

confession and wept profusely. Whereupon Jechoniah (Ezra has Shecaniah; Josephus, Achonias), one of their number,[9] shouted to Ezra an admission of guilt capped with an expression of hope, in spite of everything, for the continuance of Israel. His faith was based on the people's penitence and the conviction that because of it they would commit themselves to obedience to the law of God. After his direct exhortation to the people, Ezra put the whole assembly under solemn oath to do as Jechoniah had demanded (vs. 90). Then he retired for private meditation and to plan for the execution of the people's pledge.

[Proclamation and assembly, 9:3–17 — Ezra 10:7–17] Not all of Ezra's time in seclusion was devoted to prayer and confession. From the sacristy of Jehohanan came the decision to issue a proclamation requesting the golah to assemble forthwith at Jerusalem. The proclamation was relayed by heralds throughout Jerusalem and Judah under the authority of Ezra, the representative of Persia and the interpreter of the law of God. Severe penalties would be invoked upon any who failed to comply in the specified time. Those of the tribes of Judah and Benjamin — a favorite combination of the Chronicler — responded with dispatch, congregating in the temple plaza where they awaited public announcement of the decision of Ezra and the plan for its implementation. He made the following points in his address: (a) the people had sinned, (b) let them confess it and (c) purge themselves of guilt by dissociation from the people of the land. The assembly shouted their consent to do what Ezra demanded but, owing to weather conditions at that time of the year, implored him to put the whole matter into the hands of a committee composed of the people's representatives, local elders and judges who could work it out with deliberate care. Verse 14 reflects the support of the elders and Levites for the proposition. Ezra 10:15 suggests some opposition to the plan of procedure, but the golah itself approved of it. Family heads were carefully selected and the business was conducted in closed session. The committee met from the new moon of the tenth month until the new moon of the first month, or over a period of three months. The procedure followed by the authorities in the resolution of individual cases is set forth in vss. 12–13. To judge from the following list of those declared guilty, they must have had a formidable and distasteful task.

[List of those cohabiting with alien wives, 9:18–36 — Ezra 10:18–44] The names vary somewhat in the recensions of the list. The total number of persons involved (26 clergy and 75 or 76 laymen, a total of 101 or 102) is surprisingly small in view of the extraordinary steps taken by Ezra to purge the community. Even on the basis of the unemended text of Ezra there were only 111 persons out of a population of some 30,000 found guilty. Perhaps the religious leaders overacted, or we do not have a complete list, or the move at exclusion was not so successful as the Chronicler reports. (See Appendix.)

[The law-reading assembly, 9:37–55 — Neh 7:72b – 8:12] Perhaps the inclusion of this passage from Nehemiah was due, in some measure, to the author's feeling for the law and for the temple which occupies such a prominent

9 Ezra also makes him the son of Jehiel but adds "of the sons of Elam." Josephus (*Antiq.* 11:5:4) makes the interlocutor "the chief of the people of Jerusalem."

place in his work. On the other hand it could have stood in the text of Ezra that he used. But one wonders, if the latter was the case, why he did not include Neh 8:13-18 — the account of the celebration of the Feast of Tabernacles. Josephus (*Antiq.* 11:5:5) connects this reading of the laws of Moses with Tabernacles, though he does not specify the day, probably because he was aware of the fact that it was scheduled to begin on the fifteenth day of the seventh month (Lev 23:34; Num 29:12 ff.) whereas this assembly took place on the first day of that month. According to Neh 8 the first reading took place on the first day of the seventh month (vss. 2, 3); on the second day they discovered the law concerning the Feast of Tabernacles, that it was to be celebrated in the seventh month but the day remains unspecified. Only after that was the festival actually celebrated. However, the context seems to indicate that some time must have elapsed before the event could take place. Announcement was made, a proclamation issued in "all their cities and in Jerusalem," materials gathered and booths constructed (vs. 15), all of which took time. It may be that somehow Num 29:1 ff. is involved despite the fact that no reading of the law is mentioned there. The compiler meant to connect the chronology of this passage with that of vss. 16, 17. After the resolution of the marriage problem with its confusion, a period of time was required for the restoration of calm and the settlement of the various families and groups in and around Jerusalem. Yet the seventh month was by tradition one in which significant celebrations took place,[10] and so the date sequence may be schematic. In that case the law-reading ceremony may serve merely as an introduction to the Feast of Tabernacles which was a very important celebration in the religious calendar of Israel and in the theology of the Chronicler (II Chron 8:13; Ezra 3:4; Neh 8:14-17) whose interest in the law of Moses is evident everywhere.[11] The same order of assembly and celebration of Tabernacles is followed here as in I Esd 5:50, 52 (=Ezra 3:1, 4) which may reveal the interest of the leaders of the period. Tabernacles seems to have had some relationship to the convenant renewal celebration[12] and, if so, would signify that the religious officials, perhaps at the behest of Ezra, sought to achieve precisely that effect at this particular time.[13] For description and further implications of the passage see AB, vol. 14, COMMENT on Neh 7:72b – 8:1-12.

[10] See AB, vol. 14, COMMENT on Neh 7:72b – 8:1-12.
[11] Ibid., p. LIX; I Chronicles, AB, vol. 12, pp. LXXVIII f.
[12] Cf. H. J. Kraus, *Worship in Israel* (Oxford: Blackwell, 1966), *passim.*
[13] See also Kellermann, pp. 27, 34, 90 f. Some scholars, however, see here (first day of the seventh month) a New Year's celebration. Cf. Sigmund Mowinckel, *Studien zu dem Buche Ezra-Nehemia,* III, 44–59 [BIBLIO I]; Paul Volz, *Das Neujahrsfest Jahwes,* Tübingen: Mohr, 1912. The problem is exceedingly complex and this is not the place to deal with it in detail. K.-F. Pohlmann, *Studien zum dritten Esra,* pp. 108 ff. [BIBLIO I], thinks Josephus knew nothing of Neh 8:13-18 or of the continuation of Neh 8 in Neh 9 as represented in the canonical book of Nehemiah.

APPENDIX

LIST OF MEN WITH ALIEN WIVES

1. Priests

   a. Line of Jeshua

	Ezra	
I Esdras	MT	LXXB
Maaseiah	Maaseiah	Meessēl
Eleazar	Eliezer	Eliezer
Jarib	Jarib	Iareim
Jodanos	Gedaliah	Gedaliah

   b. Line of Immer

Hananiah	Hanani	Ananei
Zebadiah	Zebadiah	Zabedeia
Maaseiah	Maaseiah	Masaēl*
Shemaiah	Elijah	Eleia
Jehiel	Shemaiah	Samaia
Azariah	Jehiel	Ieēl
	Uzziah	Odzeia

   c. Line of Pashhur

Elioenai	Elioenai	Eliōna
Maaseiah	Maaseiah	Maaseia
Ishmael	Ishmael	Samaēl
Nethaniel	Nethanel	Nathanaēl
Jozabad	Jozabad	Iodzabad
Elasah	Eleasah	Elasa

2. Levites

Jozabad	Jozabad	Iōzabad
Shimei	Shimei	Samon
Kelaiah	Kelaiah	Kōleia
Kelita	Kelita	Kolieu
Pethahiah	Pethahiah	Phadaia
Judah	Judah	Iodom
Eliezer	Eliezer	Eliezer

3. Temple singers

Eliashib	Eliashib	Eleisaph
Bakchouros		

4. Gatekeepers

Shallum	Shallum	Gellēm (SollemA)
Telem	Telem	Telēm
	Uri	Ōdouth

* In Ezra 10, both MT and LXXB, the last five names are attributed to the line of Harim. In I Esdras they are included in the Immer line, though some MSS insert "of the sons of Ieram."

	Ezra	
I Esdras	MT	LXX^B

5. Israelites (laymen)

a. Line of Parosh

Ramiah	Ramiah	Ramia
Izziah		
Malchijah	Malchijah	Adzeia
Milelos	Mijamin	Melcheia
Eleazar	Eleazar	Amamein
Asebiah	Malchijah	Eleazar
		Asabia (LXX^{A,N,S})
Benaiah	Benaiah	Benaia

b. Line of Elam

Mattaniah	Mattaniah	Mathania
Zechariah	Zechariah	Zecharia
Jehiel	Jehiel	Iaēl
Abdi	Abdi	Abdeia
Jeremoth	Jeremoth	Iareimoth
Elijah	Elijah	Eleia

c. Line of Zattu

Elioenai	Elioenai	Eliōna
Eliashib	Eliashib	Eleisoub
Othaniah	Mattaniah	Alathania
Jeremoth	Jeremoth	Amōn
Zabad	Zabad	Zabadab
Zerediah	Aziza	Odzeia

d. Line of Bebai

Jehohanan	Jehohanan	Iōanan
Hananiah	Hananiah	Niana
Zabdi	Zabbai	Zabou
Emathis	Athlai	Thalei

e. Line of Bani

Meshullam	Meshullam	Melousam
Malluch	Malluch	Aloum
Adaiah	Adaiah	Ada
Jashub	Jashub	Iasoud
Yishal	Sheal	Salouia
Jeremoth	Jeramoth	Mēmōn

f. Line of Addi   (Pahath-moab)   (Phaadmōab)

Lathos	Adna	Aidaine
Mōsiah	Chelal	Chaēl
Lakkounos	Benaiah	Banaia
Naidos	Maaseiah	Masēa
Beskaspasmus	Mattaniah	Mathania
Sesthēl	Bezalel	Beselēl
Binnui	Binnui	Thanouei
Manasseh	Manasseh	Manassē

Ezra

I Esdras	MT	LXXB
g. Line of Annan	(Harim)	(Eram)
Eliodah	Eliezer	Eleiezer
Isshiah	Isshiah	Iesseia
Malchijah	Malchijah	Melcheia
Shemaiah	Shemaiah	Samaia
Shimōn	Shimeon	Semeōn
Chosamaos	Benjamin	Beniamein
	Malluch	Malouch
	Shemariah	Samareia
h. Line of Hashum		
Mattenai	Mattenai	Mathania
Mattattah	Mattattah	Atha
Zabad	Zabad	Zabel
Eliphelet	Eliphelet	Eleiphaneth
	Jeremai	Ierameim
Manasseh	Manasseh	Manassē
Shimei	Shimei	Semeei
i. Line of Bani		(Anei)
Jeremiah	Maadai	Modedeia
Maadai	Amram	Marei
Amram	Uel	Ouēl
Iuel	Benaiah	Banaia
Mamdai	Bedeiah	Baraia
Pediah	Cheluhi	Chelkeia
Anōs	Vaniah	Ouiechōa
Karabaseiōn	Meremoth	Ieramōth
Enaseibos	Eliashib	Eleiaseiph
Mantanaimos	Mattaniah	Mathania
Eliashib	Mattenai	Mathanan
Bannus	Jaasu	
Edialeis		
Shimei		
Shelemiah		
Nethaniah		
j. Line of Ezōra	(Binnui)	(Banoui)
Shashai	Shimei	Semeei
Ezriel	Shelemiah	Selemia
Asahel		
Shemaiah	Nathan	Nathan
Shemariah	Adaiah	Adaia
Joseph	Machnadbai	Machadnabou
	Shashai	Sesei
	Sharai	Sariou
	Azarel	Edzerēl
	Shelemiah	Selemia
	Shemariah	Samareia
	Shellum	Saloum
	Amariah	Maria
	Joseph	Iōsēph

| I Esdras | Ezra | |
	MT	LXX[B]
k. Line of Nebo		
Jeiel	Jeiel	Iaēl
Zabad	Mattithiah	Thamathia
Jeddai	Zabad	Sedem
Joel	Zebina	Zanbina
Beniah	Jaddai	Dia
	Joel	Iōēl
	Benaiah	Banaia

II ESDRAS

INTRODUCTION

I. THE NAME OF THE BOOK

Despite the fact that it came considerably later than the other books of the Bible and Apocrypha bearing its name, this composition shows the tenacity of the Ezra-Esdras tradition. (For a description of the nomenclature of the Ezra materials see the Introduction to I Esdras.) There is no really reliable record of the full name of our book in its Hebrew or Greek form. The one adopted by Hilgenfeld[1] is based on a reference by Clement of Alexandria to *Esdras o prophētēs* (*Stromata* 3:16, *Esdras o prophētēs legei* after a quotation of II Esd 5:35), the first verse of ch. 1 (*liber Ezrae prophetae secundus,* "the second book of Ezra the prophet"), and the postscript following 14:50 of the second Arabic version, in addition to some Ethiopic MSS. An Apocalypse of Esdras is mentioned in two Greeks lists but, in all probability, it is not in reference to II Esdras. The list of John of Haghbat (twelfth century) includes, among others, the name *Esdras, Salathiel* which James[2] thinks is probably II Esdras since "I Salathiel, who am also called Esdras" marks the beginning of the Armenian version.

It is probable that II Esdras originally bore a numerical designation. Some Latin MSS, followed by the Geneva Bible and Authorized Version (KJ), designate it as II Esdras. The Armenian version has Third Ezra. Most of the Latin MSS have Fourth Ezra. One Arabic version and the Ethiopic versions designate it First Ezra. The other Arabic version and the Syriac give no number, the latter having only "the writing of Ezra the scribe who is called Salathiel," based on 3:1 of the text. The Clementine edition of the Vulgate has *Liber tertius Esdrae* and *Liber quartus Esdrae,* both of which are in the appendix and, with the Prayer of Manasseh, located after Revelation. In the Revised Version and RSV, I and II Esdras stand first in the apocryphal section.

The Latin MSS vary somewhat in the order of Ezra materials. (For

---

[1] Hilgenfeld, pp. xviii and 36 [BIBLIO II].

[2] Bensly, p. xxv [BIBLIO II]. The Georgian version follows the Armenian but has Syt'iel for Salathiel (see R. P. Blake, HTR 19 [1926], 323 — Latin translation [BIBLIO II]).

the over-all situation see the first table in the Introduction to I Esdras. The most common order is:

> I Esdras=Ezra-Nehemiah
> II Esdras=IV Ezra 1 – 2 (II Esdras 1 – 2 in this volume)
> III Esdras=III Esdras (I Esdras in this volume)
> IV Esdras=IV Ezra 3 – 14 (II Esdras 3 – 14 in this volume)
> V Esdras=IV Ezra 15 – 16 (II Esdras 15 – 16 in this volume)

The order followed here is:

> II Esdras 1 – 2=V Ezra
> II Esdras 3 – 14=IV Ezra
> II Esdras 15 – 16=VI Ezra

II. OUTLINE OF CONTENT

II Esdras, as it stands, is composed of three major parts which are of unequal length and different date. The first section (chs. 1 – 2), also referred to as Fifth Ezra, has to do with Ezra's commission from the Lord. The introductory verses (1:1–3) label the book and give the pedigree of Ezra. Then the author plunges into the mainstream of his purpose: the reception and delivery of the Lord's message for his people. The first word of the Lord is a reminder to his forgetful people of his deliverance of them from Egyptian bondage (4–12) and the provision of leaders for them in the persons of Moses and Aaron (13–14). During the desert period they were divinely fed and provisioned (15–23). Despite the Lord's constant importunity they repudiated him so that he finally resolved to reject them (24–32). They will be replaced by a new people responsive to his direction (33–37). Those coming from the east will be led by the patriarchs and the twelve prophets (38–40). The Lord's judgment upon the people's recalcitrance comes in the form of pillage and dispersion (2:1–7) and woe pronounced over Assur (8–9). In his address to Ezra (10–32) the Lord announces the gift of Jerusalem to his people (10–14) and appeals to mother Jerusalem to embrace her sons; Isaiah and Jeremiah will aid with their counsel (15–32). Then Ezra is directed to go to Israel but when he is rebuffed and the Lord's command rejected, he turns to the heathen with his offer (33–41). The section concludes with Ezra's vision on Mount Zion with its interpretation by the angel (42–48).

The second section (chs. 3 – 14) contains the original material of the book, a series of seven visions of Ezra. The first vision (3:1 – 5:19) is introduced by referring to the mind of Ezra disturbed by the specter of desolate Zion contrasted with the wealth of the Babylonians (3:1–3) which furnished the impetus for his prayer (4–36) wherein he rehearsed the salient elements in Israel's history. All this leads him to ask the crucial questions (32–36) which, in turn are dealt with in the dialogue with Uriel (4:1 – 5:19). Question one: Can the human mind comprehend the way of the Most High? Uriel responds that man cannot hope to comprehend fully the ways of God, even those he himself experiences (4:1–11). Question two: What is the use of exile if people fail to grasp the lesson? Answer: Those of earth can understand earthly points of view only (12–21). Question three: Why can't man then comprehend things below? Answer: In the end-time he will see; there was a grain of evil seed in Adam's heart which is responsible for ungodliness (22–32). Question four: Because our days are few and evil, when will these things come? Answer: When the time is fulfilled; illustration of woman with child (33–43). Question five: Is the time past greater than that to come? Answer: The past is by far the greater (44–50). Question six: Will I (Ezra) live to see it? Answer: Time of his life unknown to the angel but he can interpret certain signs (4:51 – 5:13). The episode ends with the observation of the effect of the vision on Ezra (5:14–19).

The second vision (5:20 – 6:34) presses Ezra's complaint about those who died before the division of the times. Increasingly painful thoughts (5:20–22) give rise to another prayer question (23–30) followed by the angel's reply (31–40). In response to Ezra's observation that those who are alive at the end will be secure but the fate of those who come before and after has not been divulged, the dialogue continues (41–55), explaining why the successive generations were created. Such was the divine plan as may be seen from the successive birth of children (41–47). The earth too is like a womb engendering one generation after another — each smaller and weaker (48–55). By whom will the end come? By the one responsible for the beginning (5:56 – 6:6). As to the interval between first and second times, there will be none (6:7–10). Still probing, Ezra asks for a further revelation and description of the signs of the end-time (11–12). The signs are then given (13–24) and the state of those who survive—the saved—disclosed (25–28). Then the angel assures Ezra that his prayer has been heard and that answer is forthcoming; in the meantime he is warned against undue speculation about former times (29–34).

The third vision (6:35 – 9:25) deals with a whole series of questions by Ezra with answers by the angel, all centering about the enigma of the creation of the world for Israel when worse nations are in control of the world. After another seven days' fast (6:35–37), question one: Why has Israel become the prey of other nations when the world was created for her (38–59)? Answer: This is something for the future, when what was destined from the beginning will come to pass; the end-time is not to be judged by the present (7:1–16). Interestingly enough the second point of the vision (17–61) is introduced by a statement, rather than a question, that has to do with the righteous and the wicked (17–18). The angel asserts the superiority of the law of God over the many who disregard it (19–25). With the revelation of the Messiah, the remnant will enjoy life for four hundred years, after which he and all who are alive will die (26–30). Then will come the judgment of those who are resurrected; without pity, judgment and truth will ensue. The day of judgment will be dark, with only the splendor of the Most High whereby all will see their destiny (31–44). Question three: But all have sinned, so why are only the few saved (45–48)? Answer: Because the few are precious and the many base (49–61). Question four: What use is torment to those who remain alive since all have sinned though they are not to come to judgment after death (62–69)? Answer: Because they have intelligence but did not avoid iniquity (70–74). Question five: What is the state of the soul between death and the new creation (75)? Answer: The souls of the evil are destined to wander about in torment, "unhappy and sad, in seven ways" (76–87), while the souls of the righteous will enjoy rest in seven orders (88–99). Souls separated from the body will be given seven days to see what the angel has just revealed to Ezra (100–1). Question six: May intercession be made by the righteous for the ungodly (102–3)? Answer: Everyone must bear his own iniquity or uprightness (104–5). The Bensly fragment[3] contains questions and answers bearing on certain aspects of the above question. Why was it possible for Abraham to intercede for Sodom, Moses for those who sinned in the desert, Joshua for Israel, Samuel in the time of Saul, David in connection with the plague, Solomon for those in the sanctuary, Elijah for those caught in the drought, Hezekiah for his people (106–11)? In those times the strong prayed for the weak but in the judgment at the end of the world things are different (112–15). Since we are all involved in Adam's sin what good is the promise of the eternal world to us (116–26)? The end result is a matter of choice: those who are victorious in the battle will survive; those who do not believe and fail to heed Moses, the prophets and the angel will suffer unlamented destruction (127–31). Overarching all the dealings of the Most High with mankind is his mercy and compassion for those who live by his law (132–39). The present world was created for the many, the world to come for the few (8:1–3). Question seven: Why was man made with such pains destined to live for so short a time (4–19)? Before the angel's response comes Ezra's prayer for his people, pleading for the exercise of divine mercy (20–36). Answer: Just as not all the farmer's seeds will sprout or all his plants yield fruit, so it is with the people sown

---

[3] Bensly, MF [BIBLIO II]. It is inserted between 7:35 and 7:36 and the present translation and commentary then follow a continuous versification of ch. 7.

in the world (37–41). Question eight: Can man really be compared with seed? Prayer for the deliverance of the Lord's people (42–45). Answer: The Most High does not want man to perish but he has rejected the proffer of his Creator and hence judgment is near (46–62). Question nine: Despite signs already given, what will be the time of judgment (63)? Answer: When a certain number of signs have occurred then the time for the visitation of the Most High will be near. There must be less concern about the punishment of the godless and more about how the righteous are saved (9:1–13). Observation: the number of those that perish is greater than that of those saved (14–16). The angel's explanation of the justification for that fact (17–25) concludes the third vision.

Vision four (9:26 – 10:59) consists of the specter of a mourning woman and the angel's explanation. Chapter 9, vss. 26–28, disclose the recipient's preparation for and meditation before the Most High on the significance of the law (29–37). Lifting up his eyes, Ezra sees a vision of a weeping woman (9:38 – 10:24), and enters into conversation with her, inquiring about the cause of her misfortune which she duly explains to him (9:38 – 10:4). Ezra admonishes her to bear her sorrow bravely; if she accepts the judgment of God in that manner, she will receive back her son and win the praise of women (10:5–17). Her response is negative (18) which brings forth further remonstrance along the same line (19–24). Suddenly the woman is transformed and appears as a city (25–27). Uriel appears in response to Ezra's cry and interprets the figure for the bewildered Ezra. The woman he saw was Zion; the woman transformed was the new building of the Most High (28–59).

Vision five (10:60 – 12:51) is the famous Eagle vision. The eagle has twelve wings and three heads (10:60 – 12:3a), for which the startled Ezra (12:3b–9) requests an immediate interpretation (10–35). The interpreter then orders Ezra to write down the vision and hide it (36–39). Popular lamentation follows the seven days' absence of Ezra (40–45), to which he responds by calling for courage, indicating that he has not left the people in their state of desolation; he has only retreated in prayer for them (46–49). Verses 50–51 are an interlude between this and the following vision.

Vision six (13:1–58) concerns an apparition of the man from the sea. It is in the form of a dream, wherein Ezra sees the figure of a man emerging from the sea; confronted by an innumerable concourse of men, he constructs a mountain for himself. He is attacked by a host of destroyers who fail in their attempt and are themselves vanquished (1–13a). Again there is a request for the meaning of the vision (13b–20). Interpretation: the man from the sea is "my Son"; the innumerable host is the nations gathered to subdue him. But in due time they will suffer defeat at his hands (21–50). In answer to the query why the man came up from the midst of the sea (51), the response is because as no one knows what is in the depths of the sea, so no one on earth can see the Son (52–56). The three days' contemplation in the fields (57–58) serves as preparation for the final vision.

Vision seven (14:1–48) deals with the legend of Ezra. As Moses once heard the voice from a bush at Sinai, so Ezra hears a voice from a bush in front of him (1–17) and enters into conversation with the speaker. He is told what to proclaim openly and what to keep secret. In response to the demand laid down by the bush-speaker, Ezra requests the impartation of the Holy Spirit so as to carry out his orders (18–22). He is then commanded to take forty days leave of absence from the people and take with him five skilled scribes to take down what is dictated (23–26). The people are informed of the plan (27–36), after which Ezra embarks on the work. Given a powerful potion, he pours forth words day and night for forty days during which ninety-four books were written (37–44). After the work was completed, he was commanded to publish the first twenty-four books but to keep the remaining seventy for the select men of wisdom (45–47). The last verse (48) has to do with the time and fate of Ezra.

Chapters 15 – 16, like chs. 1 – 2, are wanting in the eastern versions, and are later additions, sometimes known as Sixth Ezra. They appear to be a curious mixture of oracular and prophetic materials probably intended as Ezra prophecies.[4] There is no manifest order of presentation nor do the various sections move toward a climax. Ezra is directed, just as the prophets were, to speak and write down the words which the Lord was about to put in his mouth (15:1–4). One: The evils to be brought upon the whole world are announced but God's people are to be brought out of Egypt again and Egypt will be smitten with a plague of punishment and so set right (5–19). Two: The oppressors of God's chosen ones and sinners will be subjected to disaster by virtue of their sins (20–27). Three: A vision from the east depicts the letting loose of nations of Arabian serpents and the Carmonians with frenzied anger will lay waste the land of Assyria (28–33). Four: A hurricane with dreadfully threatening storm clouds from east, north, and south will destroy Babylon (34–45). Five: Asia has become like Babylon (46–48). Six: Therefore, evils such as widowhood, poverty, famine, sword and pestilence will be sent against her. She has been guilty of protracted killing of "my chosen" with glee and will suffer worse afflictions than others (49–63). Seven: 16:1–17 is a lamentation over Babylon, Asia, Egypt and Syria, all of which will be visited by unavoidable destruction. Eight: The beginning of sorrows is

---

4 Bensly, p. lxxviii.

already at hand: famine, wars, disasters, pestilence, distress and anguish, but nothing can turn the people away from their wickedness. Just when they think they have peace within their grasp, then sword, famine and great disaster will overtake them (18–35). Nine: An appeal is made to the *servi domini* to listen to and comprehend these things because it is the word of the Lord (36–40). Ten: The word of the prophet is: prepare for the worst (41–51). Eleven: In a short time wickedness will be banished from the earth; sinners will be unable to escape the knowledge of God. He is aware of their tricks and their ways and so they can't hide their sins. God is their judge but, like the prophets of old, this prophet calls upon sinners to mend their ways, for then God will deliver them from distress (52–68). Twelve: God's people will be subject to all sorts of indignities after which will come the testing of the chosen — like gold in fire (69–74). Thirteen: But the Lord promises to deliver them from persecution. They must neither doubt nor fear, for God is their *dux*. Hence they are exhorted to keep his commandments and precepts (75–78).

III. MANUSCRIPTS AND VERSIONS

Unfortunately II Esdras is extant only in translations, the most significant of which are the Latin recensions. For the book in general, nine MS sources are cited by textual scholars; they date from the seventh to the thirteenth centuries A.D. Only a list with dates can be given here. For complete data see Bensly and James, Violet, and Gry noted in BIBLIOGRAPHY II. The oldest and best known are Codex Sangermanensis (S) dated A.D. 822, and Codex Ambianensis (A) in a ninth-century minuscule hand. Codex Complutensis (C) dates from the ninth–tenth centuries. Codex Abulensis (V) comes from the early thirteenth century and appears to be a copy of C; it contains all of our book. Codex Legionensis (L): II Esdras is found here in a Leon copy of the codex dated A.D. 1182 (perhaps A.D. 1300 as Gry suggests); the codex itself dates about A.D. 960. Codex Mazarinaeus (M) dates from the eleventh century; Codex Bruxellensis (N) from the twelfth century. Codex Epternacensis (E) is extant in a Bible of the eleventh century and is closely related to M and N, perhaps a daughter. Finally there is a Palimpsest (P) codex — 15 in the cathedral library at Leon — which contains some sixteen verses of chapter seven; it dates from about the seventh century.

In addition to these repositories there are a number of Latin versions of the confession of Ezra (II Esd 8:20–36), dating from the eighth to the fifteenth centuries. These are Vaticanus (eighth century), Colbertinus (ninth or tenth century), Lyons (ninth century), Mozarabica, Toletana (ninth century), Parisiensis 6 (tenth century), Parisiensis 167, Grenoble,

Phillippsianus (twelfth century), Jenensis (fourteenth century), Dublini-
ensis (fourteenth century), and Oxoniensis (fifteenth century).

The following diagram of Violet (II, xxii) illustrates the textual family
relationship and types of texts. According to textual critics the French
group represents a superior text.

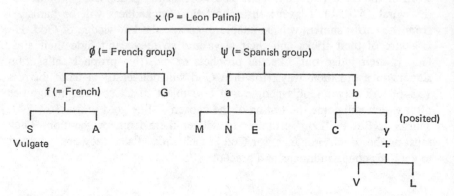

At least six other versions of II Esdras are known. The most important
of these is the Syriac which contains only chs. 3 – 14 — as do the others.
It is represented by only one MS found in the Ambrosian Bible Codex
(sixth century) now in Milan. It was first edited by A. M. Ceriani.[5] A
few verses of II Esdras also appear to be given in lectionaries. This
version is very close to the Latin (Violet, II, xxiv). The Ethiopic version
is represented by eleven exemplars, ten of which were employed by
August Dillmann in *Veteris Testamenti Aethiopici*, V (Berlin, 1894),
152–93. One more text was used by Violet. It too follows the Latin closely
but its renderings are more free and it sometimes reflects readings not
attested elsewhere. There are two independent Arabic versions. Ar.[1] is
represented by two MSS, the one copied from the other but both belonging
to the fourteenth century and probably made from the Greek (Violet, I,
xxxv).[6] Ar.[2] exists in three MSS, also of the fourteenth century, and
produced directly from the Greek according to both Gildemeister and
Violet (I, xxxvii).[7] An Arabic fragment containing 14:38–50 comes from
the ninth century. In addition there is an interesting Arabic note, on folio

[5] *Monumenta sacra et profana*, V, fasc. 1, Milan, 1868. A sample edition of the
Syriac text with emendations has recently been published by the Peshiṭta Institute of
the University of Leiden under the title *The Old Testament in Syriac according to the
Peshiṭta Version*, edited by R. J. Bidawid, Leiden: Brill, 1966.

[6] This text was printed with German translation by H. Ewald, *Das vierte Ezrabuch*
[BIBLIO II].

[7] Edited from the Vatican codex by I. Gildemeister, *Esdrae liber quartus Arabice*
[BIBLIO II]. Text is translated into Latin. Both Arabic texts are translated into German by Violet, I, 2–429 [BIBLIO II]. Both Ar.[1,2] generally expand at some points
the content of the Latin and Syriac.

232b of Latin C, on 5:59–6:6 of II Esdras. There is an array of some eighteen Armenian MSS collated by Michael E. Stone;[8] he gives some details of fourteen of them which date from the thirteenth to the seventeenth centuries. The Armenian version deviates rather widely from the others but, once a critical text is established, will help to determine whether it transmits another Greek tradition and how the Armenian translators operated. The Georgian version appears in two MSS, one the so-called Jerusalem MS,[9] the other that of Mount Athos.[10] According to Blake both MSS go back to the same archetype; they are dependent on the Armenian versions and not directly on a Greek or Semitic original. They belong to the tenth (O=Athos) and eleventh centuries (I= Jerusalem). A small, badly preserved, Coptic (Sahidic) parchment of II Esd 13:29–46[11] said to come from the sixth to eighth centuries strongly reflects a Greek recension. New documents for an assessment of the text of II Esdras were brought together by Donatien de Bruyne in 1920.[12] The report of Peter Galatinus (1561) about a copy of II Esdras in Hebrew circulating among the Jews at Constantinople is hardly to be taken seriously in the light of Violet's investigation (I, xliii f). A retranslation from the Latin into neo-Hebrew in 1487 was found in the de Rossi library at Parma. This may be the source of the Galatinus observation.

IV. ORIGINAL LANGUAGE

It is almost universally acknowledged that II Esdras was composed in a Semitic language, that is, Hebrew or Aramaic. Wellhausen, however, was the first to present a convincing argument for a Hebrew original.[13] He pointed out that parataxis is far more prevalent than syntaxis and the frequent sentences beginning with "and." Here is a list of words, phrases or expressions pointing strongly in the direction of the essential accuracy of

---

[8] Stone, *Textus* 6 (1968), 48–61 [BIBLIO II]. See also Kenneth W. Clark, *Checklist of Manuscripts in the Libraries of the Greek and Armenian Patriarchates in Jerusalem Microfilmed for the Library of Congress, 1949–1950,* Washington, D.C.: The Library of Congress, 1953. For an evaluation of the Armenian texts for II Esdras see further M. E. Stone, "Some Remarks on the Textual Criticism of IV Ezra," in HTR 60 (1967), 107–15, and "Some Features of the Armenian Version of IV Ezra" in *Muséon* 79 (1966), 387–400.

[9] Blake, HTR 19 (1926), 299–375 [BIBLIO II].

[10] Blake, HTR 22 (1929), 57–105 [BIBLIO II].

[11] Johannes Leipoldt and Bruno Violet have published the text with comments in *Zeitschrift für ägyptische Sprache und Altertumskunde* 41 (1904), Heft 2, 138–140. For further comments see Violet, I, xl f.

[12] Donatien de Bruyne, "Quelques nouveaux documents pour la critique textuelle de l'apocalypse d'Esdras," *Revue Bénédictine* 31 (1920), 43–47.

[13] Wellhausen, 234–40 [BIBLIO II]. H. G. A. Ewald (1859) and, still earlier, John Morinus (1633), who was the first to do so, opted for a Hebrew original. See also Box, pp. xiv–xviii [BIBLIO II].

his judgment. *Et factum est,* "and it came to pass" — more than thirty times; *et erit,* "and it shall come to pass" — about fifteen times; *respondere et dicere,* "answer and say" —some fifty times, with slight variations; *et vidi et ecce,* "and I saw and behold" — twenty times, mostly in chs. 11 and 13 reflect Hebrew prototypes. Interestingly enough *et factum est* occurs only once in chs. 1 and 2 and 15 and 16, while *et erit* appears only twice (15:35, 36) in the same chapters. The other expressions just noted do not occur there at all. Sentences or clauses beginning with *quoniam* or *et quoniam,* "for, because," are profuse (about sixty times). Sentences beginning with *ecce* or *et ecce,* "behold," occur about sixty-seven times. *Et non,* "and not," introducing sentences or clauses occurs twenty-four times; those introduced by *nam* (=for) number about sixteen. *Dicens,* "saying" (so frequent in the Hebrew Bible) is found fourteen times. The absolute infinitive with the finite verb is another common occurrence. For example, *pertransiens enim pertransivi,* "I have gone all about" (3:33); *excedens excessit,* "it has completely failed" (4:2); *festinans festinat,* "it is hastening rapidly" (4:26); *odiens odisti,* "you hate exceedingly," (5:30); *vivificans vivificabis,* "you will indeed animate" (5:45); *viventes vivent,* "they shall truly be alive" (5:45); *commotione commovebitur,* "it will be greatly moved" (6:14); *auditu audita est,* "it has surely been heard" (6:32); *loquens locutus es,* "you have indeed spoken" (6:38); *volens voluerit,* "he really wants" (7:5); *ingredientes ingressi fuerint,* "they shall really have entered" (7:14); *mandans enim mandavit,* "for he surely commanded" (7:21); *faciens faciebat,* "he indeed made" (7:70); *vivificans vivificas,* "you really animated" (8:8); *metiens metire,* "measure carefully" (9:1); *ostendens ostensus es,* "truly you revealed yourself" (9:29); *dicens dixisti,* "you indeed said" (9:29); *derelinquens dereliquisti,* "you surely abandoned" (10:32; 12:41); *apparens non appareas,* "you will indeed disappear" (11:45); *revelans revelatus sum,* "I have surely revealed" (14:3); *vindicans vindicabo,* "I will surely vindicate" (15:9). A few others of doubtful construction appear to be based on the same Hebrew phenomenon. The use of *ad* with *dicere* (thirty-one times) and *respondere* (twenty-six times) strongly implies the Heb. *'l,* though it could reflect late Latin. However, there are many instances of those words being followed by the dative (contra Wellhausen) which may indicate the Hebrew preposition *l. Loquere* or *dicere in corde meo* or *suo* (3:28; 8:58; 9:38) is common Hebrew idiom. So are *super cor meam,* "upon my heart" (3:1); *accepisti in corde tuo,* "you took into your heart, considered" (7:16), and *accendam in corde tuo,* "I will kindle in your heart" (14:25). The Hebrew expression *corde maris,* "heart of the sea," occurs in 4:7 and 13:25, 51. Significant too are *nomini suo quod invocatum est super nos,* "his name which is called over us" (4:25), and *nomen quod nominatum est super nos,* "the name which is named over us" (10:22). So also are *dabit vocem,* "he will give his voice" (5:5, 7), and *voce magna,* "great, loud voice" (9:38; 10:26, 27; 12:45). A common Hebrew expression shines through the Latin of *si (enim) inveni gratiam ante oculos tuos,* "if I have found favor before your eyes" (4:44; 5:56; 6:11; 7:102; 12:7) and *si inveni gratiam coram te,* "if I have found favor before you" (7:75, 104; 14:22). Another characteristic expression is *in conspectu* (=*lpny,* "before the face of") in 3:35; 8:28 as may be seen from the Vulgate, but mostly it is rendered simply by *coram. Ante oculos,* "before the eyes" (4:44; 7:102; 12:7) may stand for *lngd 'ynym* as in Pss 5:6; 26:3; 36:2; 101:3 in the Vulgate. *Servus tuus* (5:45, 56; 6:12; 7:75, 102; 8:6, 24; 10:37; 12:8; 13:14) and *familia tua* (9:43), *ancillae tuae* (9:45) may reflect Heb. *'bd. Puer* (1:32; 2:1, 18) expresses the same idea but in a section not belonging to the original book. Other examples could be cited but these are sufficient to show that there was either an underlying original or else the author was very much at home in the Hebrew Scriptures whose idioms he employed freely.

Perhaps this is the place to call attention, briefly, to the rather elaborate argument of A. Kaminka on the origin and composition of II Esdras.[14] He concluded that the original composition of Shealtiel dates from around 556 B.C. and embraces mainly chs. 3 – 10, but also a portion of chs. 12 and 14. The framework of the eagle vision — the motif of the roaring lion for the voice of God is taken from Amos 3:4 and Hos 11:10 — comes from the Persian period. The three heads, the second one of which rules for the longest period, may be Darius II (424–405 B.C.), Artaxerxes II (405–359 B.C.) and Artaxerxes III (359–339 B.C.); the military disorders about which the book is concerned fall in the reign of the last named king. The numerous wings and small, petty wings represent minor Asiatic princes and satraps. The vision of the man from the sea comes from the time of Alexander the Great. The later interpolations, which he notes in connection with translations back into Hebrew, extend down as far as the fourth century A.D.

So far as the writer is aware, no scholar had come out for a wholly Aramaic original until Monsignor L. Gry investigated the matter with great thoroughness in 1938.[15] B. Violet observed the possibility of Aramaisms in 6:18a; 9:17; 10:40, 52; *similitudinem* (=*dmwt,* "form," "pattern",

[14] Kaminka, MGWJ 76 (1932), 121–38, 206–12, 494–511, 604–7; 77 (1933), 339–55 [BIBLIO II]. Some valuable scriptural parallels are given by the author though they may not prove what he intends them to prove.
[15] Gry, pp. xxiii–lxxvi [BIBLIO II]. C. C. Torrey (JBL 61 [1942], 72–74) also favored an Aramaic original.

"likeness") in 10:49; and those suggested in 11:1 – 12:3. But most, if not all, can also be explained on the basis of a Hebrew original or that the Hebrew of the period may have had Aramaic oddities without actually being so or that the fifth vision, drawing heavily on Dan 7, might have been composed in Aramaic from which it was translated by the author of the apocalypse who retained some Aramaisms or that, on the analogy of Daniel, the Hebrew text may have contained one or more Aramaic pieces.[16] The detailed evidence marshalled by Msgr. Gry is too extensive and complex to outline here. The conclusion to which he comes is that "with the exception of the fragment 13:40–48, IV Esdras was written in a mixed Aramaic dialect."[17] He based his proof on examples drawn from vocabulary and morphology, syntax, the text in general (especially scriptural citations of which he claims the received readings, in the majority of cases, correspond to the Targums), and the fact that the original text involved multiple abbreviations that can best be explained on the basis of an Aramaic prototype.

Despite the fact that the Semitic original is no longer extant, most scholars believe that such a composition once existed. There have, however, been those who denied it and held out for an original Greek document. For example, G. C. F. Lücke[18] observed that the argument for a Hebrew original was based on an "extremely superficial judgment." He was followed by G. Volkmar[19] who pronounced it a "reiner Schwindel" (pure fraud). Hilgenfeld,[20] as is well known, translated the Latin text into the Greek to demonstrate the Grecisms. As late as 1871, O. F. Fritzsche[21] wrote: *"Auctor libri nostri procul dubio graece scripsit.* [The author of our book without doubt wrote in Greek]." But no modern scholar champions such a view. Nevertheless, the consensus is that between the Semitic original and the Latin and other versions there is a Greek translation now lost and upon the basis of which they were made. The best evidence for an intermediate Greek version comes from patristic literature with two clear citations and a more doubtful one. Clement of Alexandria (*Stromata* 3:16) cites 5:35, and 8:23 is quoted in the *Apostolic Constitutions* (8:7); 2:4 of the latter may reflect 7:103 of our book. Grenfell and Hunt discovered a papyrus at Oxyrhynchus[22] containing II Esd 15:57–59 which belongs to the additional chapters. Consideration of the suggested Grecisms would take us too far afield here; it

[16] Violet, II, xxxix [Biblio II].   [17] Gry, p. lxxvi.
[18] *Versuch einer Einleitung in die Offenbarung Johannes,* 2d ed. (Bonn, 1852), p. 154.
[19] G. Volkmar, *Handbuch,* Part II, pp. 327–28 [BIBLIO II].
[20] Hilgenfeld, pp. 36–113. Cf. also his discussion of the problem, pp. xlii–xlvi.
[21] Fritzsche, *Libri Veteris Testamenti,* p. vi [BIBLIO II].
[22] A. S. Hunt, *Oxyrhynchus Papyri,* Part VII, no. 1010 (London: Egypt Exploration Society, 1910), pp. 11–15.

is sufficient to refer the reader to Bensly,[23] Box[24] and Gunkel[25] for examples and discussion.

V. The Unity of the Book

With the exception of chs. 1 and 2, and 15 and 16, II Esdras forms a substantial unity. There are, of course, some interpolations or insertions here and there as is pointed out in the commentary with its notes. The documentary hypothesis of the Pentateuch in the Wellhausen period, however, also had repercussions in apocryphal and pseudepigraphic studies. In 1889 Richard Kabisch[26] offered a detailed study on the composition of II Esdras which he subjected to a minute analysis. He concluded that there were two basic documents — a Salathiel apocalypse (S) consisting of Vision I: 3:1–32, 35b; 4:1–51; 5:13b–6:10; Vision III: 6:30–7:25; 8:45–62; Vision IV: 9:13–10:15; 12:40–48; 14:22–35. The other basic section was an Esdras apocalypse (E) which included in part Vision II: 5:1–13a; 6:13–20a, 20c–28, and a fragment of Vision III: 8:63–9:8. There were three minor documents: one, the eagle vision (A): 10:6–57, 60; 11:1–12:8; 12:10–33, 35–38; 13:57–58; two, messianic fragments (M) with almost all of Vision VI: 13:1–15, 25–26a, 27–28, 33–53a; three, another Esdras apocalypse (E²) which embodied 14:1–7, 9–17ab, 18–27, 36–47. These materials were brought together by a redactor (R) who was responsible for 3:1, 35a, 36; 4:52; 6:11, 12, 20b, 29; 7:26, 27, 32b; 9:9–12; 10:58–59; 12:9, 34, 39, 49–51; 13:14, 16–24, 26bc, 29–32; 14:8, 17c, 48–50. Kabisch assigned the following dates: S, A.D. 100; E, 30 B.C.; A, time of Domitian; M, time of Pompey; E², first years after A.D. 100; R, ca. A.D. 120.

G. H. Box[27] also thought our book was a compilation. His scheme follows generally that of Kabisch though it is not so detailed. For him S is the only source preserved substantially and forms the foundation of the whole apocalypse. The Salathiel apocalypse embraces 3:1–31; 4:1–51; 5:13b–6:10; 6:30–7:25; 7:45–8:62; 9:15–10:57. Misplaced fragments in 12:40–48 and 14:28–35 also probably belong to S. E, A, and M were extracted from larger works. 4:52–5:13a and 6:13–29 were taken from E whose present location is due to R who utilized this source also in 7:26–44 and 8:63–9:12. A, with revision by R, is in chs. 11 and 12. M drastically revised and annotated by R reposes in ch. 13. E² is an

---

[23] MF, pp. 17 f.   [24] Box, pp. xi, xviii, and Index v.

[25] APAT, *passim* in notes, where suggestions of Wilamowitz-Moellendorff are frequently given. Pseudo-Philo's *Liber Antiquitatem Biblicarum*, was composed in Hebrew, then translated into Greek and Latin; only the latter translation is extant. See G. Kisch, *Pseudo-Philo's Liber Antiquitatem Biblicarum*, pp. 18 f. [BIBLIO II]. Rosenthal, p. 71 [BIBLIO II], opts for a Greek original because he thinks II Esdras was composed for diaspora Jews.

[26] Kabisch [BIBLIO II].   [27] APOT, II, and *The Ezra Apocalypse*.

Ezra piece contained in 14:1–17a, 18–27, 36–47. R was, of course, the compiler of the book as a whole.

W. O. E. Oesterley,[28] following a somewhat less involved pattern, also holds to the compilation view. He rejects the Salathiel apocalypse idea in favor of an Ezra Apocalypse for chs. 3 – 10. He thinks the author of this section has built around four eschatological passages. They are one, 4:52 – 5:13a which describe the signs heralding the end of the age; two, 6:11–29 which recount the signs preceding the end of this world; three, 7:26–44 which refer to the signs and then proceeds to announce the messiah; four, 8:63 – 9:12 which include a brief sketch of the signs followed by a prediction of the advent of the Most High upon earth. Oesterley notes a certain degree of progress in the author's thought from pessimism to the coming of the messianic age to the resurrection of the dead to the visitation of the Most High. A (the eagle vision) in 11 and 12 is referred to as "a self-contained piece" differing in authorship from the section just described. The vision of the man from the sea (ch. 13) is also regarded as having an independent origin. The same is true of the vision dealing with Ezra and the Scriptures (ch. 14). Chapters 15 and 16 come from the second half of the third century A.D. and chs. 1 and 2 from the middle of the second century A.D.

None of these studies and dissections appears to the writer to carry conviction. Should one accept any of them he would virtually have to regard the compiler or redactor (R) as the author. After a reasonable disposal of the basic argument for a Salathiel apocalypse, M. R. James writes: "The Apocalypse of Salathiel, the centre of all the theories of dissection, is a ghost-book: conjured up by Kabisch in 1899, it has hovered about us long enough. I never liked the look of it, and I earnestly hope that it may now be permitted to vanish."[29] The artistry of the book is superb and the form is preserved throughout. The seven visions reflect an apocalyptic characteristic centering about the number seven. Compare the format of Revelation: the seven letters (1–3), the seven seals (5–8), the seven trumpets (8–9), and the seven plagues (15–16).[30] Naturally the author may have drawn upon memories and observations — such as in the vision of the mourning women (Vision IV), that of the man from the sea (Vision VI) and that of the eagle (Vision V). But such reminiscences do not prove that II Esdras is a compilation from major sources. Perhaps the best assessment of the situation is that of Artur Weiser who observes that "The inconsistencies and the impression at times of a certain mosaic, especially when apocalyptic conceptions are described, are due to

[28] Oesterley, pp. xi–xix [BIBLIO II].
[29] James, "Salathiel qui est Esdras," JTS 19 (1918), 347 ff. Violet (II, xliii) agrees.
[30] For a detailed list of the sevens in II Esdras see Gry, xcvii.

the fact that the author has used current and in part written traditions."[31] Yet the whole book (chs. 3 – 14) represents the author's own conceptions and handiwork.

VI. THE THEOLOGY OF II ESDRAS (chs. 3 – 14)

The theology of II Esdras conforms to that of the Old Testament. God is designated the Most High (*altissimus*) sixty-eight times.[32] The expression *dominator domine*, "Lord, Lord," occurs ten times; *dominus*, "Lord," twenty-eight times, and *deus*, "God," seven times.[33] No particular significance can be attached to these terms except to note the overwhelming preference for *altissimus* and the fact that some nominal form of the divine name occurs on an average of nine and a half times in each of the twelve chapters.

One would expect emphasis on the creatorship of God (3:4; 6:1–6, 38–54; 7:70; 8:1; 9:2, 18b) but special stress is placed on his aloneness in creation as if the author were combating the association of some other agent. For example, "I said, O Lord, Lord, have you not spoken at the beginning, when you, and you alone (*et hoc solus*), formed the earth, and commanded the dust so that it gave you Adam an inert body?" (3:4–5). After a beautiful recital of the works of creation (6:1–5) it is said, "these things were made by me and not by another (*et non per alium*); just so the end (will come) through me and not through another (*et non per alium*)" (6:6). Certainly both passages accentuate the unity of God in both creation and the consummation of the world; perhaps at a time when there was a tendency to associate wisdom or the logos with God in the former and the messiah in the latter. Two other verses reinforce the idea of the aloneness of God. In connection with the affirmation of his creative acts, Ezra says *solus enim es*, "For you are by yourself" (8:7). When the Lord informs him about preparation for creation in primordial time, he notes that *nemo contradixit mihi tunc, nec enim erat quisquam*, "no one opposed me then because none existed to do so" (9:19).

Just as there was one creator God, so there was *populum unum*, "one people," chosen by him (5:27) and "called your firstborn, your only begotten, your confidant, your dearly beloved" (6:58) for whose sake the world was created (6:59; 7:11). He was in covenant relation with

[31] *The Old Testament: Its Formation and Development* (New York: Association Press, 1961), p. 436.

[32] This designation does not appear in chs. 1 – 2, 15 – 16. Cf. Mark 5:7; Luke 8:28; Acts 16:17; Heb 7:1 (a quotation from Gen 14:18–20=*'l 'lyion*); 1QH 4:31; 6:33.

[33] *Dominus* occurs twenty-four times in chs. 1 – 2 and twenty times in chs. 15 – 16; *dominus deus*, five times in chs. 1, 2, 15, 16; *deus* nine times in the same chapters, and once of alien gods; *dominus omnipotens*, six times in chs. 1 – 2, 15 – 16.

them (3:15) through Noah, Abraham, Isaac, Jacob (3:11, 13, 15), and David (3:23). Those who believed in his covenants were the object of persecution (5:29) but would eventually receive their reward (7:83). Ezra prayed for those who kept the Lord's covenants despite tribulations (8:27). Because of God's choice (5:23 ff.) they are "your people" (3:30; 5:30; 6:58; 8:26, 45), the people you chose (*dilexisti*) (4:23), "my people" (5:40; 12:34; 14:4). For their sakes the world was created (6:55, 59; 7:11).

The Lord is a God who is actively concerned about his creation and frequently the old prophetic concept of wider interest crops out as in 4:34 where Ezra is chided for a too narrow conception: "the one above (proceeds) for the many." Or "You will find exceptional individuals who have kept your commandments, but nations (who have done so) you will not find" (3:36), which, despite the context, is as sweeping a statement of universal guilt as any in the prophets (cf. 5:11). The pronouncement in 6:25 appears to include others outside Israel: "Then all who have escaped all these things which I have made known to you beforehand will be saved and they will see my salvation and the end of my world." While the seer is ruthless in his assertion that the heathen will suffer punishment, he is equally hard on those within the nation who have rejected his commandments (ch. 7). God knows best about all mankind (8:15), but "None of those born is without sin, nor are those who exist without fault" (8:35). Yet "the Most High did not want man to perish" (8:59). The world is his world (6:25; 9:2, 20; 11:39).

Hence he is also the Lord of history as may be seen from the prayer discourse of Ezra in 3:7 ff. and the predetermination of the course of the world set forth in 4:28–32. That is also the implication of the famous eagle vision in chs. 11 – 12 which is politically oriented (cf. 12:23). The Lord had appointed the four beasts to hold sway over his world (11:39) but now, since the time has run out, the whole eagle will vanish (vs. 45). He led Israel out of Egypt (3:17; 9:29; 14:4, 29) and was active in the affairs of the ten tribes (13:40–50). Ezra's disillusionment was due to his inability to understand the movements of the Most High (4:34; 5:44); he did not question God's concern for or control over history. He has his own plan and pace, and creation cannot proceed more rapidly than the Creator. No human being can comprehend the ways of God (5:38); he must wait until they are revealed to him or until they become apparent in the outworkings of history.[34] The Most High is at the helm.

In view of man's refusal to take advantage of the ways of God revealed in His commandments, he has laid himself open to the judgment of God

[34] For a discussion on the apocalyptic view of history see Harnisch, pp. 89–177, 249–67 [BIBLIO II].

which is, in the final analysis, an expression of the latter's disappointment with the affairs of men whom he did not want to perish (8:59). The day of judgment (7:102, 104, 113; 12:34) is decisive, "making clear to all the seal of truth." It marks the end of this period of time and the inception of immortal time to come, that is, the necessary separation of the evil from the good so that the latter may live. Then it is that "evil will be destroyed, trickery blotted out, faith flourish, corruption be subdued, and truth, which has been fruitless so long, will be exposed" (6:27, 28). That is the theme pursued in 7:33 ff. Despite the fact that only a few will be saved, the Lord's glory and honor will be vindicated (7:60). Preparation for judgment was arranged at the time of creation (7:70) to take place in the last times (7:87) which were now at hand (8:62). What was about to take place in connection with the eagle vision and the man from the sea indicates as much. Sometimes judgment takes on cosmic dimensions (7:39–44), but it also has individual consequences (7:104–105) in a posthumous context (14:35; 7:76–99). It is, therefore, of dual significance: an ongoing process at work in the world and history, and an event that takes place at the consummation of both. The purpose of judgment was not simply punishment of the wicked; it was rather the salvation of the faithful as may be seen from such passages as 6:27–28; 7:34–35; 13:49 f. From the author's point of view that required radical surgery. Evil will be destroyed (6:27 f.; 7:31, 113 f.; 11:46; 12:33 f.; 13:11, 49 f.) or sealed off (7:95 f.; 8:53).

Concern for his people on the part of the Most High was due to his mercy and love. His love was first manifested through Abraham (3:14). When Ezra expressed vexation about the lot of Israel, the interpreting angel reminded him that he could not love Israel more than his Creator (5:33, 40; 8:47). Israel was his dearly beloved (6:58). But Israel sinned as did other nations, though not quite so much; nevertheless its sins were more irritating because it had the Torah. "When did the inhabitants of the earth not sin before you? . . . You will find exceptional individuals who have kept your commandments, but nations (who have done so) you will not find" (3:35–36). "Who of those now present is there who has not sinned or who of those born is there who has not violated your covenant?" (7:46). "All who are born are entangled in iniquities, full of sins and laden with transgressions" (7:68). "None of those born is without sin, nor are those who exist without fault" (8:35). Because of the universality of sin the only hope for deliverance resided in the Lord's *misericordia,* "mercy," "pity," "compassion." In fact "because of us sinners you are referred to as the merciful one (*misericors*)" (7:132; 8:31). His goodness (*bonitas*) will be evident in his "compassion for those without a treasury of good deeds" (8:36) and when he liberates with mercy "my people who are left in my land . . . and grant them joy until the end" (12:34).

The whole book of II Esdras is shot through with the concept of sin. The problem arises from Ezra's question: "Do those who live in Babylon really do any better?" (3:28), which is essentially what troubled Habakkuk (1:13). Having observed Zion in ruins and God's chosen people in exile he could not understand why they, the more righteous, should have been victimized by the less righteous who were enjoying affluence with the seemingly unhindered role of conqueror and oppressor. He complains that the Lord "bore with them (as) sinners, treated with forbearance wrongdoers, ruined your people, and preserved your enemies" (3:30; cf. 3:8). The nations reveled in prosperity "although they disregarded your commandments" (3:33 f.). Then he reflects on the belief that sin began when Adam transgressed (3:7); sin was what brought on the flood but even the new beginning was of no avail for the descendants of Noah were more wicked than those who preceded them (3:12). After the efforts of David, the city slipped back into the old groove so that it was delivered into the hands of its enemies (3:25, 27; cf. 4:23).

Why, then, could Israel not extricate itself from evil which was responsible for its calamities? It was because Adam was "laden with an evil inclination" (3:21) which was permitted to remain (3:20).[35] No one was informed "as to how this way should be abandoned" (3:31). The evil heart continued to grow (7:48) so that the wicked became ever more numerous (7:51; 4:30–32; 7:116–18). This meant that sin was of universal significance, encompassing all the nations of the world as well as individuals. The whole world was lost (9:20). The spread of sin among the nations and its impact on Israel is clearly portrayed in the eagle vision (ch. 11); the oppressor nations are the agents of sin (11:40 f.; 12:25; 13:37). "All who are born are entangled in iniquities, full of sins, and laden with transgressions" (7:68, 72). Nearly all those sprung from Zion "go straight to perdition and a great number of them will come to doom" (10:10). The whole mortal race has incurred the wrath of God for "None of those born is without sin, nor are those who exist without fault" (8:35). Moreover, "one impaired by the corrupt world [cannot] comprehend incorruption" (4:11). Yet, when all is said and done the inclination to evil remains a mystery. "It would have been better for us not to have been present than to come here and live in sin and to suffer without knowing why" (4:12), complains Ezra. Again he cries, "Why are our years few and evil" (4:33); why cannot a swift end be made of the whole sorry business so that sin's suffering and torment may relax its grip on the Lord's people? He was informed by the interlocutor that judgment had to wait until the times of the Most High, that is, until his

[35] On the origin and perpetuation of sin in rabbinic thought, see Moore, I, 474–96 [BIBLIO II]; Bousset, pp. 399–409 [BIBLIO II].

harvest.[36] The Lord has in mind the many (4:34) which suggests that sin is cosmic in dimension[37] and universal in scope. II Esdras, with other literature of the period, thus exhibits a kind of synoptic view of sin — the sins of Israel and the sins of the nations. The sinfulness of man is revealed by the gap that exists between his thoughts and deeds and the commandments of the Lord which was the standard against which they were measured. "Adam transgressed my orders" (7:11); they scorned, failed to adhere to the ways of the Most High, held his law in contempt, and hated those who reverenced the Lord (7:79); they sinned before the Most High (7:87); they lived scandalously (7:121); they failed to comprehend the ultimate consequences of their defection (7:126); they ignored his ways and contemptuously rejected them (9:9); though they received the law they did not observe it but disregarded its directives (9:32); they as well as their fathers committed iniquity and repudiated the ways the Most High commanded them to observe (14:31). What made matters even worse and their acts more heinous was that as reason or intelligence grew they were increasingly tormented by awareness of perishing and yet appeared unable to extricate themselves from the entanglements of sin (7:64 f.). It is only when the delivered see the glory of the Most High that they will know what should have been done (7:88 ff.) and how "exceedingly sinful" sin is.

II Esdras is, in a sense, a book of lamentation[38] in which the author complains about the oppressions, sufferings and torments of his people. These tragic experiences are manifestations of the Lord's judgments upon evil about which Israel was warned beforehand in the law which was given for its guidance and direction. The law appears to have been regarded as a countermove against the judgment upon disobedience. Yet Adam was warned (3:7) — "you imposed upon him just one commandment (*diligentia*) — which points up another conception, i.e. that it was an act of grace to assist him in avoiding the consequences of error. The trouble was that one violation led to another and that while the law had directive potential man was left without a controlling impulse to follow it. "You did not remove from them their inclination to wickedness so that your law might bear fruit in them" (3:20); "thus the weakness became unremitting and though the law was in the heart of the people, the root of evil remained too. What was good disappeared, while evil stayed on" (3:22). Nevertheless, the fact that a few individuals kept the commandments (3:36) shows

[36] Cf. the parable of the tares in Matt 13, esp. vs. 29.

[37] Observe the cosmic convulsions attendant upon the judgment in 5:1 ff.; 6:19 ff.; chs. 11 – 13. While the language is typically apocalyptic, its world-wide import is abundantly evident.

[38] See also Joseph Klausner, *History of the Second Temple*, V (Jerusalem, 1954), 293–95.

that it could be done by extraordinary efforts. Every man born on earth must wage a struggle during his lifetime; if he is defeated he must endure judgment (7:127–28). There was, therefore, the minimum possibility that the law might be kept but the overwhelming experience of the people demonstrated that, to all intents and purposes, it remained just that — a theoretical possibility. The emphasis on the law (*lex*) is accentuated by the number of times (twenty-six) the term occurs in chs. 3 – 14; it occurs only twice in chs. 1 – 2, and not at all in chs. 15 – 16. The terms "counsels," "precepts," "commandments," "agreements" do occur there, as indeed in chs. 3 – 14. Evidently the law was the standard by which the actions of men and nations were to be judged.[39]

Yet, despite lamentation characteristics, there is *the* dominant theme of judgment and hope. The apocalyptists' sweeping pronouncements of doom upon the historical world must not obscure their more profound belief in the ultimate triumph of God over evil. He was always occupied with his plan of salvation, knowing all along how matters stood and how they would be resolved, but did not reveal it to men. II Esdras is sure of the Most High's condemnation and judgment of evil men and nations, but he is equally certain that paradise awaits the faithful. For him the question is not whether God will move to deliver them but when.

As Gunkel[40] has pointed out, II Esdras centers about two broad aspects of Jewish theological concerns: one, genuine apocalyptic and particular eschatological mysteries similar to those of Dan 7 ff. and Rev 4 ff.; two, religious problems and speculations growing out of eschatology in which they find their resolution or their inception, somewhat analogous to those of Paul. The first three visions deal with religious questions of the time, while the last four are occupied with apocalyptic mysteries. The above treatment on theology is drawn from both sections of the book (chs. 3 – 14). For specifics dealt with, see the outline of contents.

VII. Messianic Implications

Messianic features in II Esdras revolve about the messiah and the messianic age. As expected little can be deduced about the person of the messiah except that he is the anointed one as the name indicates. As the text now stands, he is called "my son Jesus" in 7:28 where "Jesus" is a Christian interpolation. The Syriac and Ar.[1] versions have "my son the messiah"; Ar.[2] has simply "the messiah," to which the Armenian adds "of God." The expression "my son" occurs only here and in I Enoch 105:2

---

[39] Cf. Bousset, pp. 119–41.
[40] APAT, II, 335. Keulers, pp. 22–35 [BIBLIO II], follows Gunkel.

(where it is a late insertion) in late Jewish literature.[41] In 13:3 "something or someone like a man," perhaps after Dan 7:13; elsewhere simply "man" (13:12, 25, 32). In 11:37 and 12:31 he is referred to as a lion, probably after Gen 49:9. According to 7:28 he will reveal himself or be revealed which can hardly be interpreted as preexistent in the usually understood meaning of the word. All it indicates is that he existed before creation and that he was hidden somewhere to appear at a specific point in time (cf. John 7:27; Justin *Dialogue with Trypho* 8). However, 12:32; 13:52; 14:9 may actually hint at pre-existence, in which case 7:28 would have to be interpreted in the same sense.[42] He is also said to be the anointed one (7:28, 29; 12:32).

The function of the messiah is at best somewhat equivocal. 7:28 ascribes to him the activity and leadership of those who are left after the purging, his sole purpose to create joy for them during the messianic interval of four hundred years (cf. 12:34). He thus has no judgmental function as in the New Testament (John 5:22), that task having already been accomplished by the evils preceding his arrival (7:27). He has nothing to do with the appearance of the city and the land of the messianic kingdom (7:26). In ch. 13 the situation is quite different. There the messiah (the man rising from the sea) is the agent of the Most High "through whom he delivers his creation" (13:26)[43] and organizes the new order of the survivors. The signal for the opponents of the Lord to join forces against him will be the voice of the messiah. He it is who will indict the heathen (13:37 f.) and destroy them by the law (fire) (cf. 13:10b). He too assembles the peaceful multitude (13:12). The messiah is thus a more active agent in the latter chapters of our book than in the former.

The messianic age is of four hundred years duration (7:28) and forms a transition period between this present age and that of the world to come. Originally there was no set limit of salvation-time, but II Esdras was not the first to delimit it. The ten-week apocalypse of Enoch (I Enoch 91:12–17; 93:1–14) with its eight weeks of messianic time and two weeks of judgment and the Sibylline Oracle (3:652–660) with its messianic interregnum preceded it. On the basis of Ps 90:15 the rabbis taught that salvation-time was compensation for that of the misfortune of the Jews. It was calculated to be equivalent to that of the sufferings-time.[44] The

---

[41] For an explanation of the probable origin of the expression see James Drummond, *The Jewish Messiah* . . . (London: 1877), pp. 285 ff., and Klausner, p. 358 [BIBLIO II].

[42] See Keulers, pp. 80 f.; Bousset, pp. 228–32, for a description of the person and character of the messiah.

[43] Cf. Klausner, p. 361. On the whole idea of the messiah in II Esdras see M. de Jonge in TWNT, IX (1972), 506–8.

[44] See Volz, p. 236 [BIBLIO II].

four-hundred-year conception coincides with the period spent in Egypt (Gen 15:13).[45] For Esdras the messianic kingdom is included in the new age. The death of the messiah is perhaps related to Dan 9:26, but there he is slain whereas here he dies. Albert Lagrange[46] thought the whole passage to be a Christian interpolation because it is wanting in both Arabic versions and in the Armenian. But Keulers points[47] out that that is unlikely since a Christian could hardly let the messiah die like other humans. Volz thinks the observation is an attempt to counter the Christian doctrine of the divine nature of the messiah.[48] Perhaps the death of the messiah is meant to accentuate as forcefully as possible the radical difference between this age and the age to come. This age thus has to disappear completely together with the messiah (4:29; 7:30).[49]

The messianic age and the world to come were for the few (8:1–3, 41; 9:7–17, 22). They are those who remain or survive the judgmental plagues (6:25; 7:27; 9:7; 12:34; 13:48), the old idea of the remnant or holy seed (Isa 10:20 ff.; 28:5; 37:32; Jer 31:7; Amos 5:15; Micah 4:7; 5:7; Zeph 2:7, 9; 3:13; Zech 8:11; *et alia*). The remnant or survivors are Jews. Included in the group of the saved are the ten tribes and those who are within the limits of his sanctuary (13:39, 48). The heathen and godless Jews are annihilated (9:7 ff.).[50] The criterion for judgment is faith and obedience to the law so that sanctity becomes the sole characteristic of the saved, the members of the messianic company (6:26 ff.). Little is said about material blessings; the main stress falls on spiritual blessings. The wonders attendant upon the messianic age (7:27) are not spelled out here with the exception of the provision of Behemoth and Leviathan. What is meant by them may be seen from II Bar 29:5–8; 73:2–7; 74:1. Behemoth and Leviathan (6:49–52) will become food for the saved.[51]

[45] Bousset, pp. 286–89; Rosenthal, p. 64, n. 2. The Syriac text with its thirty years is a Christian interpolation corresponding to the lifetime of Jesus.

[46] *Le messianisme chez les Juifs* (Paris: Gabalda, 1909), p. 106, n. 3; RB 14 (1905), 615. See L. Gry, in *Mémorial Lagrange*, pp. 133–39 [BIBLIO II].

[47] Keulers, p. 84.   [48] Volz, p. 34.

[49] Incidentally this is the earliest instance in late Jewish literature where the death of the messiah is mentioned. It had nothing to do with the idea of atonement or expiation for human sins. That idea is first broached in second-century Judaism (cf. Schürer, II, 553 f. [either BIBLIO]. When the Christians associated Isa 53 and Zech 12:10 with Christ, the Jews were compelled to confront the atoning death of the messiah in their disputations with Christians. So disagreeable was the idea to them that suffering and death of the messiah was later transferred to the messiah ben Joseph. Note that the Ethiopic version substitutes "my servant the messiah" for "my son the messiah" in 7:29. According to II Bar 30:1 the messiah returns to glory.

[50] II Bar 72:4 f. is far less harsh in his judgment.

[51] May be reminiscent of Ezek 32:1 ff. See Weber, p. 202 [BIBLIO II]. There may be a hint of the same idea in the haoma cult of the Gathas (32:12, 14; 44:20; 48:10) in the practice of which the haoma was drunk and a sacrificed bull was consumed during the orgiastic nocturnal feast (see H. S. Nyberg, *Die Religion des alten Iran* [Osnabrück: Zeller, 1938, reprint 1966], p. 51).

Just when that is to happen remains undisclosed but II Bar 29:4 says it will be in the time of the messiah. Food for the saved is a common conception in apocalyptic literature. II Bar 29:8 refers to a repetition of the manna miracle. Fragment 3 of the Sibylline Oracles speaks of "sweet bread from the starry heavens" as the food of Paradise, and Book 3:746 says honey will fall from heaven and trickle from the rocks (cf. 5:283). Such fare is given for the enjoyment of the saved and often confers immortality upon them (I Enoch 25:5b; Test Levi 18:11 ff.).

VIII. DATE AND PURPOSE

The date and purpose of our book are closely related, as in other books of the Apocrypha and Pseudepigrapha. II Esdras 3 – 14 almost certainly comes from the last decade of the first century A.D. or soon thereafter, as may be deduced from the eagle vision (chs. 11 – 12) and the date mentioned in 3:1. Though that vision may have undergone revision, it appears fairly clear that it received its main thrust from events in the Vespasian-Domitianic period (A.D. 69–96). From 10:20 ff. we learn that Jerusalem had been destroyed (Jos. *War* 6:8:5; 6:10:1; 7:5:2) and its sacred worship paraphernalia plundered (ibid. 6:8:3). The description given here coincides with that of the Jewish historian. To be sure the devastation wrought under Hadrian (A.D. 132–135) was equally violent and fearful, and if we had a description of it such as that provided by Josephus for the one in 68–70 it would appear just as picturesque. Dio Cassius (69:14) says, "All Judea was well-nigh a desert. Fifty fortresses and eighty-five villages were destroyed; 580,000 men fell in battle, while the number of those who perished from their wounds was never calculated." Despite the exaggeration of numbers, the devastation must have been frightful, the suffering and losses enormous. The immediate occasion for the Jewish revolt in the Hadrianic period was the establishment of Aelia Capitolina on the site of Jerusalem and the erection of a shrine to Jupiter Capitolinus on that of the Yahweh temple.[52] It has been suggested that the removal of the seal of Zion (10:23) may have referred to that event.[53] Barry thinks that imbedded in "the Apocalypse of Ezra are yet to be found traces of a lost Hadrian apocalypse, composed after the Bar-Cochba rebellion."[54] Although no conclusive evidence can be cited pro or con, the present writer's impression agrees with that of most scholars as noted above (end of section V).

[52] CAH, XI, 313.
[53] By Phillips Barry in JBL 32 (1913), 270, n. 44. But the substitution of the capital poll tax might have produced an equally reprehensible observation (Jos. *War* 7:6:6).
[54] JBL 32 (1913), 270.

If that impression is substantially correct, II Esdras provides a kind of rationale for the contemporary situation *sub specie aeternitatis*. Other, earlier writers had done the same for their time and situation, especially the apocalyptists from the time of Daniel. He explains why Jerusalem had fallen and Zion was levelled (3:1 ff.), why the Jews were suffering beyond others, and then offers his philosophy of history. The problems he dealt with were almost perennial, but they were rendered more acute now not only by their political involvements but especially by religious events. The advent of Christianity which claimed to be a new Israel was offering eschatological interpretations of the times that shook the infant Church to its foundations but at the same time forced it to look elsewhere for safety and service. One of the significant views of the early Christians was that of the imminent and sudden return of Christ as both savior and judge (Acts 1:11; I Thess 4:13 – 5:10; II Thess 2:7–12; Mark 13; Matt 24; Luke 21) and the end of the world. II Esdras offers a Jewish interpretation of the times. The outward thrust of the Christian movement capitalized on the catastrophe while Jewish communities engaged in self-examination and an inventory of their religious resources. For II Esdras the end of the age was not far off; the world was already old and senile. "My son, the anointed" was about to be revealed and the interregnum to begin. Thus the messianic age of four hundred years was at hand, at whose end a period of primeval silence would ensue to be followed by a new creation. The hoped-for features of the new creation might have obtained for the first one had it not been for the sin of Adam in whose heart an evil seed had been planted that proved to be far more vigorous than the good seed. True, the evil impulse was countered by the law which was given to emancipate the sons of Adam but they failed to respond and hence the destruction that had befallen Israel once more. As Violet[55] has noted, "the author wrestles with the weightiest problems, the reality of sin and the fact of corruption, and endeavors to comprehend God's will for the world and his people." Esdras realizes that the misfortunes suffered by his people were due to the evil heart in man. That is why he wants to know at the very outset (3:20) why the evil heart was allowed to remain in man so that the law had no apparent effect on his transformation. That was the besetting problem of the rabbis in the first century A.D.[56] and that around which the whole book of II Esdras is written. Violet observes succinctly, "Everything contained in the book — parables, questions, visions — is subordinated to it, though they appear at times to predominate and

[55] Violet, II, xxxix f.

[56] For a convenient summary of the handling of the problems in the time of Rabbi Akiba see Rosenthal, p. 51. He thinks that "the murder of the wicked Domitian, the weak rule of his successor, the senile Nerva, and the ensuing revolts" were some of the events uppermost in the mind of the author as he contemplated the problems of the age.

relegate the problem into the background" (II, xl). As posed, it was clearly insoluble for both. Only the individual could be sure of the special pardon of God. Thus it is that the book concludes with the gift of the Holy Spirit and translation into Paradise. II Esdras represents a serious contemporary occupation with the age-old problem of evil that is still with us, though clothed in a different garb but fraught with consequences far beyond the dimensions contemplated by the author. The tragedy of his time and ours is that people choose to remain impervious to the frightful lessons of history.

IX. LITERARY RELATIONSHIPS

On nearly every page of his book, the author of II Esdras demonstrates his familiarity with the thought and verbiage of the Bible. Quotations and allusions thereto are quite extensive. Many of them have been noted in the COMMENTS and observations dealing with specific passages.

He was also keenly aware of contemporary thought and/or literature. A. Hilgenfeld[57] has drawn up a list of what he refers to as citations from the New Testament though it is impossible to determine whether there was direct contact or whether both II Esdras and New Testament writers drew upon floating sources.[58] The same may be said with respect to parallel passages or allusions in other apocryphal literature where the date of final composition remains uncertain. Apart from New Testament references, the following list of correspondences may serve to exhibit the situation.

1. Sibylline Oracles (Sib Or) 3:46–52 (middle of first century B.C.) — II Esd 12:33 ff.
2. Assumption of Moses (Ass Mos) 10:8 (before A.D. 70) — II Esd 11, 12.
3. II Baruch (contemporary with II Esdras) — II Esdras (a great many verbal and ideological similarities as well as differences).
4. Ascension of Isaiah (Asc Isa) 4:5 (end of first or beginning of second century A.D.) — II Esd 5:4.
5. Epistle of Barnabas (early in the reign of Hadrian) — II Esdras.

Barnabas	II Esdras
4:4	12:10 f.
4:7	14:45
4:14	8:3
12:1	4:33; 5:4, 5

The last reference is found also in Gregory of Nyssa (A.D. 332–398) in *Prescriptions against Jews* 7.[59]

[57] Hilgenfeld, pp. lxiv–lxviii, listed by Bensly, p. xxvii.
[58] On the problem in general see Bensly, pp. xxvii; Oesterley, pp. xlii–xliv; Volkmar, *Esdra Propheta*, pp. 395–406 [BIBLIO II].
[59] PG, vol. 46, cols. 213 f., where the Greek translation reads: "and these things will come about, says the Lord, when a piece of wood will be laid on wood and set up and when blood will drop from the wood." Cf. also Pseudo-Jerome *Commentary on Mark* 15:33 (PL, vol. 30, col. 585 — nothing more than a reminiscence at best).

6. *Visions* 1–4 of the Shepherd of Hermas (middle of second century A.D.) bear some resemblance to II Esdras.

7. *Rest of the Words of Baruch* 9:14 ff. with its signs of the approaching messianic age reflect II Esd 4:33; 5:4 ff.[60]

8. The following verbal and material coincidences and expressions in II Esdras and *The Biblical Antiquities of Philo* have been observed by M. R. James:[61]

Pseudo-Philo	II Esdras
23:5; 7:4	3:13
15:6; 23:10; 32:7	3:17–18
32:13	4:35
3:10; 33:3	4:42
53:7; 19:14	4:44
19:14	4:50
34:1, 4	5:4
50:3	5:16
28:9	6:16
19:13	6:18
48:1	6:26
60:2	6:39
15:6	6:42
7:3; 12:4	6:56
3:10; 19:12	7:32
16:3; 32:17	7:75
33:3	7:92
33:5	7:102
18:4; 21:2	8:15
33:3	8:53
19:12; 26:13	9:2
28:4; 19:5	9:22
19:13	12:20
51:5	13:26
21:2; cf. 29:4	13:52
53:8; cf. 15:6; 23:10; 32:7	14:3–4
48:1	14:9

9. Bensly calls attention to common ideas of Hippolytus (first half of third century A.D.) in *Against Plato on the Cause of the Universe* and II Esdras.

II Esdras	Hippolytus
7:84–85	I[62]
7:85–86	I[63]
7:103	III[64]

[60] See further on this matter J. R. Harris, *The Rest of the Words of Baruch,* Haverford College Studies, 2, London, 1889.

[61] *The Biblical Antiquities of Philo,* pp. 54–58. Similarities are based on the Latin texts of both works. But see Violet, II, xlviii.

[62] For original text see *Library of the Greek Fathers,* vol. 6 (Athens, 1956), p. 228, lines 2–7; for translation see *The Ante-Nicene Fathers,* eds. Alexander Roberts and James Donaldson (Buffalo: The Christian Literature Co., 1886 — reprint of Edinburgh edition), V, 222.

[63] *Library of the Greek Fathers,* vol. 6, p. 227, line 9 to p. 228, line 2; *The Ante-Nicene Fathers,* V, 221–22.

[64] *Library of the Greek Fathers,* vol. 6, p. 229, lines 9–11; *The Ante-Nicene Fathers,* V, 223.

10. The first definite quotation from II Esdras is by Clement of Alexandria (A.D. 150–215) in *Stromata* 3:166[65]=II Esd 5:35.

11. Two passages in the Apostolic Constitutions (third century A.D.) deserve notice. The intercessory discourse in 2:14 is quite like II Esd 7:103. In 8:7 we have a quotation from II Esd 8:23 — "whose look dries up the abyss, whose threat melts the mountains, and whose truth abides forever."

12. Tertullian in *On Prescriptions against Heretics*, ch. 3 — "the eyes of the Lord are high" — is said to reflect II Esd 8:20 — "whose eyes are lifted up" — but hardly more than coincidental.

13. Commodianus (third century A.D.)[66] *Instructions* 2:1:28, 29 appear to reflect II Esd 13:42, 47. 2:1:28="fulfilling all laws." 2:1:29="they will be entreated to cross over from these parts to the Lord. He dries up the river for them as before their crossing."

In his *Apologetic Song* he writes: (936 ff.) "But they are Jews who, concealed across the Persian river, are within those borders where God wanted [them] to remain. He will bring back those captives in the same place they may have been out of twelves tribes, nine and a half remain there." (952 f.) "Therefore this people which is now quite remote will return to the land of Judah over a dried-up river." Cf. with these observations II Esd 13:39–47.

14. St. Ambrose (A.D. 340–397) quotes copiously from our book.[67]

de bono Mortis 10	— II Esd 7:32, 33; 5:42, 50–55; 7:80–87
de bono Mortis 11	— II Esd 7:91–101
de bono Mortis 12	— II Esd 7:36–42
de Spiritu Sancto 2:6	— II Esd 6:41
de excessu Satyri 1:2	— II Esd 10:6–24
ad Horontianum, Letter 34	— II Esd 3:5; 7:78
Commentarius in Lucam 1:60	— II Esd 7:28 f.

Two passages are quoted in Pseudo-Ambrosian fragments: "And Esdras declares similarly" followed by II Esd 7:78; "likewise Esdras" followed by II Esd 8:7–11.[68]

15. Cyprian (A.D. 200–258) in a *Treatise to Demetrianus* writes: "You ought to know that in the first place, the world being already old will not endure with those energies with which it endured at first, nor have the same vigor and strength wherewith it prevailed earlier" — a clear reference to II Esd 5:54, 55.[69]

16. Jerome, who was never very sympathetic toward apocryphal books, rebukes Vigiliantius for using it to argue against prayers after death: "As for you, when wide awake you are asleep, and asleep when you write, and you bring before me an apocryphal book which, under the name of Esdras, is read by you and those of your ilk, and in this book it is written that after death no one dares pray for others. I have never read the book."[70]

17. Athanasius (A.D. 293–373) in *Discourse IV*[71] refers to "my son Christ" which has been said to reflect II Esd 7:28–29.

---

[65] *Library of the Greek Fathers*, vol. 8, p. 46, lines 30–32; *The Ante-Nicene Fathers*, II, 400.

[66] For *Instructions* see *The Ante-Nicene Fathers*, IV, 203 ff. For text and interpretation of the *Apologetic Song* see Hermann Rönsch, "Das Carmen apologeticum des Commodian," in *Zeitschrift für historische Theologie* 43 (Gotha: Perthes, 1872), 163–302.

[67] Full excerpts are given, in Bensly, pp. xxxii–xxxiv. Texts may be located in PL, vols. 14–17.

[68] See Bensly, p. xxxv.

[69] PL, vol. 4, cols. 564–65.

[70] PL, vol. 23, cols. 359–60.

[71] Schaff and Wace, *Nicene and Post-Nicene Fathers*, vol. 4 (1892), p. 446.

18. The most extensive use of II Esdras was that of the confession of Ezra (8:20–36) in the Mozarabic Breviary which is of course quite late (see COMMENT on the passage).

19. The story of the reproduction of the scriptures (II Esd 14:20 ff.) was widely known and referred to:

    a. Irenaeus (ca. A.D. 135–200) *Against Heresies* 3:21:2

    b. Clement of Alexandria (A.D. 150–215) *Stromata* 1:21, 22

    c. Tertullian (A.D. 152–222) *Apparel of Women* 1:3

    d. Jerome (A.D. 340–420) *Against Helvidius* 7

    e. Basil (A.D. 330–379) *Letter to Chilo*

    f. Chrysostom (A.D. 344–407) *Homily on Epistle to the Hebrews* 8:9

    g. Leontius of Byzantium (fifth–sixth centuries) *de sectis*[72]

    h. Isidore of Seville (ca. A.D. 560–636) *de libris et officiis ecclesiasticis* 2:12,[73]
and in two other tracts

    i. Jacob of Edessa (A.D. 633–708),[74] who refers to II Esd 14:44.

20. Aphraates (fourth-century Syrian writer), the Persian Sage, in *Demonstratio* XXIII 1 (de Acino) echoes II Esd 9:21, 22.[75]

21. The Ethiopic "Book of the Mysteries of Heaven and Earth" has the eagle refer to the kingdom of the descendants of Esau[76] (cf. II Esd 11:1–8). It speaks of the four books that Esdras wrote.[77] On the day of judgment it says, "On the subject of the day of punishment, Esdras says, 'On the one side it will bring joy, on the other judgment and punishment' " (II Esd 7:38).[78]

The selection above of allusions to and/or quotations from II Esdras indicate the widespread knowledge and appreciation of the book in Christian circles.[79] It is still printed in the Vulgate editions of the Bible, though it has been relegated to the end, after the New Testament. The selection of allusions comes from Schürer, Violet, and Bensley and James, though a few others not mentioned by them have been culled from the vast repertoire of Greek, Latin, Syriac and Ethiopic literature. No doubt the relatively sober imagery of our book commended it to the Church fathers and was responsible for its rather wide use — apart from its breath of hope amid the most trying times that Christianity was to encounter until the present.

Christopher Columbus is said to have been inspired by and got direction from II Esdras.[80]

[72] PG, vol. 86, Part 1, cols. 1211–12.

[73] PL, vol. 82, cols. 233, 235.

[74] See Latin translation of passage in Hilgenfeld, p. 260. For Syriac of *Epistle XIII of Jacob* see W. Wright, "Two Epistles of Mar Jacob, Bishop of Edessa," *Journal of Sacred Literature and Biblical Record* N.S. 10 (London: Williams & Norgate, 1867), 439.

[75] René Graffin, *Patrologiae Syriaca,* II (Paris: Didot et Socii, 1907), cols. 1, 2.

[76] René Graffin, *Patrologia Orientalis,* I (Paris: Didot et Socii, 1947), 83.

[77] Ibid., p. 68.

[78] Ibid., pp. 47 f.

[79] For further uses made of our book in the *Apocalypse of Esdras* see K. von Tischendorf, *Apocalypses Apocryphae* pp. xii–xiv, 24–33 [BIBLIO II], and in the *Apocalypse of Sedrach* see M. R. James, "On the Apocalypse of Sedrach," in *Texts and Studies* [BIBLIO II]. For an idea of the dimensions of influence of II Esdras see Schürer, III, 244 ff.; Violet, II, l–lii; Volkmar, *Esdra Propheta,* pp. 284–96. For Talmudic contacts see Klausner, pp. 349–65, and Rosenthal, pp. 39–71, especially footnotes.

[80] Maria Luisa Ambrosini with Mary Willis, *The Secret Archives of the Vatican* (Boston: Little Brown, 1969), p. 155.

BIBLIOGRAPHY II

Books

Bensly, R. L. *The Missing Fragment of the Latin Translation of the Fourth Book of Ezra.* Cambridge University Press, 1875. *Cited as* MF.
——— and M. R. James. *The Fourth Book of Ezra.* Cambridge University Press, 1895. Reprint, in *Texts and Studies,* ed. J. A. Robinson, III, no. 2. Nendeln/Leichtenstein: Kraus Reprint Ltd., 1967. *Cited as* Bensly.
Bogaert, P. *L'Apocalypse syriaque de Baruch.* 2 vols. Paris: Les Editions du Cerf, 1969.
Böklin, P. *Die Verwandtschaft der jüdisch-Christlichen mit der parsischen Eschatologie.* Göttingen: Vandenhoeck & Ruprecht, 1902.
Bonsirven, J. *La Bible apocryphe en marge de l'Ancien Testament. Textes chosis et traduits.* Paris: A. Fagard, 1953.
Bousset, Wilhelm, and Hugo Gressmann. *Die Religion des Judentums im späthellenistischen Zeitalter.* 3d ed. by Gressmann, 1926. 4th ed., Tübingen: Mohr, 1966. *Cited as* Bousset.
Box, G. H. *The Ezra Apocalypse.* London: Pitman, 1912. *Cited as* Box.
Brockington, L. H. *A Critical Introduction to the Apocrypha.* London: Duckworth, 1961.
Burkitt, F. C. *Jewish and Christian Apocalypses.* Schweich Lectures for 1913. London: Oxford University Press, 1913.
Charles, R. H., ed. *The Apocrypha and Pseudepigrapha of the Old Testament.* 2 vols. Oxford: Clarendon Press, 1913. *Cited as* APOT.
Denis, A. M. *Introduction aux Pseudépigraphes Grecs d'Ancien Testament.* Leiden: Brill, 1970.
Ewald, H. G. A. *Das vierte Ezrabuch: nach seinem Zeitalter, seinen aräbischen Übersetzung und einer neuen Wiederherstellung.* Abhandlungen der königlichen Gesellschaft der Wissenschaften zu Göttingen, XI. Göttingen: Dietrich, 1863.
Fritzsche, O. F. *Libri Veteris Testamenti: Pseudepigraphi Selecti.* Lipsiae: Brockhaus, 1871.
Funk, R. W., ed. *Apocalypticism.* Journal for Theology and the Church, vol. 6. New York: Herder & Herder, 1969.
Gildemeister, Ioannes. *Esdrae liber quartus Arabice e codice Vaticano.* Bonn: Adolphum Marcum, 1877.
Gry, Léon. *Les dires prophétiques d'Esdras (IV Esdras).* 2 vols. (consecutive pages). Paris: Geuthner, 1938. *Cited as* Gry.
Harnisch, W. *Verhängnis und Verheissung: Untersuchungen zum Zeit- und Geschichtesverständnis im 4. Buch Esra u. in der Baruch-Apokalypse.* Göttingen: Vandenhoeck & Ruprecht, 1969. *Cited as* Harnisch.
Hennecke, Edgar., ed. *Neutestamentliche Apokryphen.* Tübingen and Leipzig: Mohr, 1904. (See Schneemelcher, below.)
Herford, R. T. *Talmud and Apocrypha.* London: Soncino, 1933. Reprint, New York: Ktav, 1971.

Hilgenfeld, Adolf. *Messias Judaeorum*. Lipsiae: Sumpto Fuesiano, 1869. *Cited as* Hilgenfeld.

———— *Die judische Apokalyptik in ihrer geschichtliche Entwickelung*. Jena, 1857. Reprint, Amsterdam: Rodophi, 1966.

James, M. R., ed. *Apocrypha Anecdota*. Cambridge University Press, 1893. Reprint, in *Texts and Studies*, ed. J. A. Robinson, II, no. 3. Nendeln/Leichtenstein: Kraus Reprint Ltd., 1967.

———— *Apocrypha Anecdota*, Second Series. Cambridge University Press, 1897. Reprint, in *Texts and Studies*, ed. J. A. Robinson, V, no. 1. Nendeln/Leichtenstein: Kraus Reprint Ltd., 1967.

———— *The Biblical Antiquities of Philo, Now First Translated from the Old Latin Version*. London: SPCK, 1917.

Kabisch, Richard. *Das vierte Buch Esra auf seine Quellen untersucht*. Göttingen: Vandenhoeck & Ruprecht, 1889. *Cited as* Kabisch.

Kahana, Abraham. *ha-Sepharim ha-Ḥitsonim*. Tel-Aviv: The author, 1970.

Kautzsch, Emil, ed. *Die Apokryphen und Pseudepigraphen des Alten Testaments*. 2 vols. Tübingen: Mohr, 1900; reprinted 1921, 1962. *Cited as* APAT.

Keulers, Joseph. *Die eschatologische Lehre des vierten Esrabuches*. Biblische Studien, XX, nos. 2–3. Freiburg im B.: Herder, 1922. *Cited as* Keulers.

Kisch, Guido. *Pseudo-Philo's Liber Antiquitatum Biblicarum*. Publications in Mediaeval Studies. University of Notre Dame Press, 1949.

Klausner, Joseph. *The Messianic Idea in Israel*, tr. W. F. Stinespring. New York: Macmillan, 1955. *Cited as* Klausner.

Metzger, B. M. *An Introduction to the Apocrypha*. New York: Oxford University Press, 1957. *Cited as* Metzger.

Mills, L. H. *Avesta Eschatology Compared with the Books of Daniel and Revelation*. London: Kegan Paul, Trench, Trübner & Co., 1908.

Montefiore, C. G. *IV Ezra. A Study in the Development of Universalism*. London: Allen & Unwin, 1929.

Moore, G. F. *Judaism in the First Centuries of the Christian Era*. 3 vols. Harvard University Press, 1927, 1930. *Cited as* Moore.

Oesterley, W. O. E. *II Esdras*. London: Methuen, 1933. *Cited as* Oesterley.

von der Osten-Sacken, P. *Die Apokalyptik in ihrem Verhältnis zu Prophetie und Weisheit*. Munich: Kaiser Verlag, 1969.

The Peshitta Institute of the University of Leiden. *The Old Testament in Syriac according to the Peshitta Version*. Sample edition. Leiden: Brill, 1966.

Pfeiffer, R. H. *History of New Testament Times with an Introduction to the Apocrypha*. New York: Harper, 1949. *Cited as* Pfeiffer.

Philonenko, Marc, J. C. Picard, J. M. Rosenstiehl, and F. Schmidt. *Pseudépigraphes de l'Ancien Testament et Manscrits la Mer Morte*, I. Paris: Cahiers de la Revue d'Histoire et de Philosophie religieuses, 1967.

Porter, F. C. *The Messages of the Apocalyptical Writers*. New York: Scribner's, 1905.

Riessler, Paul. *Altjüdischen Schriftum ausserhalb der Bibel*. 2d ed. Heidelberg: Kerle Verlag, 1966. *Cited as* Riessler.

Rosenthal, Franz. *Vier apokryphische Bücher aus der Zeit und Schule R. Akiba's.* Leipzig: Otto Schulze, 1885. *Cited as* Rosenthal.

Rössler, Dietrich. *Gesetz und Geschichte in der spätjudischen Apokalyptik.* Wissenschaftliche Monographien zum Alten und Neuen Testament, vol. 3, 2d ed. Neukirchen: Neukirchener Verlag, 1960.

Rowley, H. H. *The Relevance of Apocalyptic.* London and Redhill: Lutterworth Press, 1944. 3d ed., 1963.

Russell, D. S. *The Method and Message of Jewish Apocalyptic* (200 B.C.–A.D. 100). London: SCM, 1964.

Scheftelowitz, J. *Die Altpersischen Religion und das Judentum.* Giessen: Töpelmann, 1920.

Schmidt, J. M. *Die jüdische Apokalyptic.* Neukirchen: Neukirchener Verlag des Erziehungsvereins, 1969.

Schneemelcher, W. E. *Hennecke New Testament Apocrypha,* tr. R. McL. Wilson. Vol. II. Philadelphia: Westminster Press, 1965.

Schreiner, Josef. *Alttestamentlich-jüdische Apokalyptic. Eine Einfuhrung.* München: Kösel-Verlag, 1969.

Schürer, Emil. *Geschichte des jüdischen Volkes im Zeitalter Jesu Christi.* 3 vols. 3d ed. Leipzig: Hinrichs, 1898. *Cited as* Schürer.

Stave, E. *Über den Enfluss des Parsismus auf das Judentum.* Haarlem, 1898.

von Tischendorf, Konstantin. *Apocalypses Apocryphae.* Leipzig, 1866. Reprint, Hildesheim: Olms, 1966.

Torrey, C. C. *The Apocryphal Literature.* Yale University Press, 1945. *Cited as* Torrey.

Violet, Bruno. *Die Apokalypsen des Esra und des Baruch in deutscher Gestalt.* Die griechischen-christlichen Schriftsteller der ersten drei Jahrhunderte, vol. 32. Leipzig: Hinrichs, 1924. *Cited as* Violet, II.

—— *Die Esra-Apokalypse I. Die Überlieferung.* Die griechischen-christlichen Schriftsteller der ersten drei Jahrhunderte, vol. 18. Leipzig: Hinrichs, 1910. *Cited as* Violet, I.

Volkmar, G. *Esdra Propheta.* Tübingen: Sumtibus Ludovici Friderici Fues., 1863.

—— *Handbuch der Einleitung in die Apokryphen,* Part II. Tübingen: Sumtibus Ludovici Friderici Fues., 1863.

Volz, Paul. *Jüdische Eschatologie von Daniel bis Akiba.* Tübingen and Leipzig: Mohr, 1903. Second edition, entitled *Die Eschatologie der jüdischen Gemeinde in neutestamentlichen Zeitalter nach der Quellen der rabbinischen, apokalyptischen und apokryphen Literatur dargestellt,* 1934. *Cited as* Volz.

Weber, F. *Jüdische Theologie.* 2d ed. Leipzig: Dörrfling & Franke, 1897. *Cited as* Weber.

Wicks, H. J. *The Doctrine of God in Jewish Apocryphal and Apocalyptic Literature.* 1915. Reprint, New York: Ktav, 1971.

Willoughby, H. R., ed. *The Study of the Bible Today and Tomorrow.* University of Chicago Press, 1947. Chapters II, XI, XVI.

von Zahn, Theodor. *Geschichte des neutestamentlichen Kanons.* Erlangen: Deichert, 1888–92.

Articles

Bailey, J. W., "The Temporary Messianic Reign in the Literature of Early Judaism," JBL 53 (1934), 170–87.

Blake, R. P., "The Georgian Text of Fourth Esdras from the Athos MS," HTR 22 (1929), 57–105.

———— "The Georgian Version of Fourth Esdras from the Jerusalem Manuscript," HTR 19 (1926), 299–375.

Bloch, Joshua, "The Ezra Apocalypse: Was It Written in Hebrew, Greek or Aramaic?" JQR 48 (1957–58), 279–94.

———— "Was There a Greek Version of the Apocalypse of Ezra?" JQR 46–47 (1954–56), 309–20.

Breech, Earl, "The Fragments I Have Shored against My Ruins: The Form and Function of 4 Ezra," JBL 92 (1973), 267–74.

Brun, L., "Die römische Kaiser in der Apocalypse," ZNW 26 (1927), 133 ff.

de Bruyne, Donatien, "Fragments d'une Apocalypse perdue," *Revue Bénédictine* 32 (1921), 97 ff.

Efros, I., "Prophecy, Widsom and Apocalypse," in *Mordecai M. Kaplan Jubilee Volume*, ed. M. Davis, English Section (New York: The Jewish Theological Seminary of America, 1953), pp. 215–23. *Cited as* Efros, MKJV.

Fohrer, Georg, "Die Struktur des alttestamentlichen Eschatologie," TLZ 85 (1960), cols. 401–20.

Freedman, D. N., "History and Eschatology," *Interpretation* 14 (1960), 143–54.

Frey, J. B., "Le IVe livre d'esdras ou l'Apocalypse d'Esdras," in *Supplement au Dictionnaire de la Bible,* Tome I, Paris: Libraire Letouzey et Ane, 1928.

Ginzberg, Louis, "Some Observations on the Attitude of the Synagogue towards the Apocalyptic-Eschatological Writings," JBL 41 (1922), 115–36.

Gry, Léon, "La 'Mort du Messias' en IV Esdras vii, 29 [iii, v, 4]," in *Memorial Lagrange* (Paris: Gabalda, 1940), pp. 133–39.

Hadot, J., "La datation de l'Apocalypse syriaque de Baruch," *Semitica* 15 (1965), 79–95.

———— "Le problème de l'apocalypse de Baruch d'après un ouvrage récent," *Semitica* 20 (1970), 59–76.

Hanson, P. D., "Old Testament Apocalyptic Reexamined," *Interpretation* 25 (1971), 454–79.

Hauck, A., ed., *Realencyklopädie für protestantische Theologie und Kirche,* 3d ed., vol. 16 (Leipzig: Hinrichs, 1905), 244–49.

Hooke, S. H., "The Myth and Ritual Pattern in Jewish and Christian Apocalyptic," in *The Labyrinth,* ed. S. H. Hooke (London: SPCK, 1935), pp. 211–33.

James, M. R., "On the Apocalypse of Sedrach," in *Apocrypha Anecdota,* Cambridge University Press, 1893. Reprint, in *Texts and Studies,* ed. J. A. Robinson, II, no. 3, Nendeln/Leichtenstein: Kraus Reprint Ltd., 1967.

Kaminka, Armand, "Beiträge zur Erkärung der Esra-Apocalypse und zur Rekonstruktion ihres hebräischen Urtextes," MGWJ 76 (1932), 121–38, 206–12, 494–511, 604–7; MGWJ 77 (1933), 339–55.

König, Eduard, "Die Reste der Worte Baruchs," *Theologische Studien und Kritiken* 50 (1877), 318 ff.

Lambourt, M., "Le cinquième livre d'Esdras," RB 17 (1909), 412 ff.

Metzger, Bruce, "The 'Lost' Section of II Esdras (IV Ezra)," JBL 76 (1957), 153–56.

Mundle, Wilhelm, "Das religiöse Problem des IV Esrabuches," ZAW 47 (1929), 222–49.

Nikiprowetzky, V., "Pseudépigraphes de l'Ancien Testament et manuscrits de la Mer Morte," *Revue des Études Juives* 128 (1969), 5–40.

Oepke, A., "Ein bisher unbeachtetes Zitat aus dem fünften Buche Esra," in *Coniectanea Neotestamentica*, IX (Lund: Gleerup, 1947), 179–95.

Osswald, Eva, "Zum Problem der vaticinia ex eventu," ZAW 75 (1963), 27–44.

Picard, Jean-Claude, "Observations sur l'apocalypse grecque de Baruch," *Semitica* 20 (1970), 77–103.

Plöger, Otto, "Das 4. Esrabuch," in *Religion in Geschichte und Gegenwart*, 3d ed., II (Tübingen: Mohr, 1958), cols. 697–99.

Sigwalt, C., "Die Chronologies des 4. Buches Esdras," BZ 9 (1911), 146–48.

Smith, J. Z., "The Prayer of Joseph," in *Religions in Antiquity: Essays in Memory of Erwin Ramsdell Goodenough*, ed. Jacob Neusner (Leiden: Brill, 1968), pp. 253–94.

Stone, M. E., "The Concept of the Messiah in IV Ezra," in *Religions in Antiquity*, pp. 295–312.

———— "Manuscripts and Readings of Armenian IV Ezra," in *Textus* 6, ed. Shemaryahu Talmon (Jerusalem: The Hebrew University, Magnes Press, 1968), 48–61.

Toma, C., "Jüdische Apokalyptik am Ende des ersten nachchristlichen Jahrhunderts," *Kairos* 11 (1969), 134–44.

Torrey, C. C., "A Twice-Buried Apocalypse," in *Munera Studiosa*, eds. M. H. Shepherd, Jr., and S. E. Johnson (Cambridge, Mass.: The Episcopal Theological School, 1946), pp. 23–39.

Völter, Daniel, "Die Geschichte vom Adler und vom Menschen im 4. Esra nebst Bemerkungen über die Menschensohn-Stellen in den Bilderreden Henochs," *Nieuw Theologisch Tijdschrift* 7 (1919), 241–73.

Wellhausen, Julius, "Zur apokalyptischer Literatur," in *Skizzen und Vorarbeiten*, VI. Berlin: 1899. Pages 215–49.

Westermann, Claus, "Struktur und Geschichte der Klage im Alten Testament," ZAW 66 (1954), 44–80.

Zeitlin, Solomon, "Jewish Apocryphal Literature," JQR 40 (1949–50), 223–50.

Zimmermann, Frank, "Underlying Documents of IV Ezra," JQR 51 (1960–61), 107–34.

I. EZRA'S DIVINE COMMISSION
(1:1 – 2:48)†

The pedigree of Ezra

1 ¹ The second*ᵃ* book of Ezra the prophet*ᵇ*: he was the son of Seriah, the son of Azariah, the son of Hilkiah, the son of Shallum, the son of Zadok, the son of Ahitub, ² the son of Ahijah, the son of Phineas, the son of Heli, the son of Amariah, the son of Azariah, the son of Meraioth, the son of Arna, the son of Uzzi, the son of Borith, the son of Abišua, the son of Phineas, the son of Eleazar, ³ the son of Aaron of the tribe of Levi*ᶜ*. He was a captive in the land of the Medes in the reign of Artaxerxes, the king of the Persians.

The Lord's complaint to Ezra

⁴ Now the word of the Lord came *ᵈto meᵈ* saying: ⁵ Go, inform my people of their misdeeds and their sons of the iniquities which they have committed against me, so that they may inform their grandchildren, ⁶ because the sins of their parents have multiplied in them to such an extent that they have forgotten me [and] offered sacrifices to alien gods. ⁷ Did I not lead them out of the land of Egypt, out of the house of bondage? But they angered me and spurned my counsels. ⁸ As for you, shake out the hair of your head and fling all [their] outrages upon them because they disobeyed my laws. Recalcitrant people! ⁹ How long shall I tolerate them? I have bestowed so many benefits on them! ¹⁰ I have overthrown many kings for their sake; I crushed Pharaoh with his servants, and his

---

† Also referred to as V Ezra. For an evaluation of the French and Spanish texts of these chapters, see Bensly, pp. lxi–lxiii.

ᵃ A has *tertius,* "third."
ᵇ L has *prophete sacerdos,* "prophet priest." C omits the genealogy and has simply *Esdrā filium Cusi,* "Esdras the son of Cush."
ᶜ Hebrew forms of the names are used in all cases except Borith.
ᵈ⁻ᵈ So with S. C has here *ad Esdra filium Cusi, in diebus regis Nabuqodonosor,* "to Esdras the son Cush in the days of King Nebuchadnezzar."

whole army. 11 *e*I destroyed all nations before them; I exterminated the people of two provinces in the east*e*, Tyre and Sidon*f*, and wiped out all their adversaries. 12 You must by all means speak to them, saying: This is what the Lord says:

Rehearsal of the Lord's benefits in the exodus and wilderness

13 As everybody knows, I led you across the sea *g*and laid open for you broad highways through places where there were no roads*g*. I gave you Moses as a leader and Aaron as a priest. 14 I provided you with light by a pillar *h*of fire*h* and performed great wonders among you, but you have forgotten me, says the Lord. 15 This is what the Lord Almighty says: The quail was a sign to you; I gave you camps for protection, yet there is where you complained*i*; 16 and you did not exult in my name by virtue of the destruction of your enemies but have kept right on complaining until now. 17 Where are the benefits I bestowed on you? When you were hungry and thirsty in the wilderness, did you not cry out to me, saying, 18 Why did you lead us into this wilderness *j*to kill us*j*? It had been better for us to serve the Egyptians than to die in this wilderness*k*. 19 I was grieved by your groans and gave you manna *l*for food; you ate the bread of angels*l*. 20 When you were thirsty did I not split asunder the rock, so that waters poured forth in abundance? Because of the heat *m*I clothed you with tree-leaves*m*. 21 I apportioned to you fertile lands; the Canaanites*n*, the Perizzites, and the Philistines*o* I expelled *p*before you*p*. What more can I do for you? says the Lord.

---

e–e C has *nonne propter vos Bethsaydam civitatem everti et ad meridianum duas civitates,* "Have I not destroyed for you the city of Bethsaida and the two cities to the south?" This may be due to Matt 11:21.
f C has *igni cremabi,* "I consumed with fire." The phrase *a facie eorum,* "from before them," looks like a Hebraism=*mlpnyhm.*
g–g C has *et dextera adq. sinixtra muros feci,* "and on the right and to the left I made walls."
h–h C has *nubis,* "cloud."
i C adds *persecutorem vestrum cum exercitu eius dimersi in mare,* "your persecutor with his host I buried in the sea." Perhaps reminiscences of such passages as Exod 15:4; Deut 11:4; Ps 136[135H]:15.
j–j C has *ut moriamur,* "that we die."   *k* C has *solitudine,* "lonely place," "desert."
l–l C has *manducare et manducastis,* "to eat and you ate."
m–m C has *arbores vobis foliis tectis creavi,* "I made trees with covering leaves for you."
n C inserts here *Cettheos,* "Hittites."
o C has *filios eorum,* "their sons," probably a corruption of *Philistinos=Filistinos.*
p–p *a facie vestra=mlpnyk.*

22 This is what the Lord Almighty says: When you were in the desert, thirsty at the brackish*q* river and blaspheming my name, 23 *r*I did not send fire*r* upon you for [your] blasphemies, but made the river sweet by casting wood into the water. 24 What can I do about you, Jacob? You would not listen to me, Judah. I will turn to *s*other nations*s* and give them*t* my name in order that they may keep my decrees. 25 Because you have forsaken me, I will forsake you. When you entreat me for mercy, I will not have compassion for you. 26 When you appeal to me, I will not listen to you; *u*you have stained*u* your hands with blood, and *v*your feet were swift to perpetrate murder*v*. 27 It is not as though you had forsaken me, but you yourselves, says the Lord.

The Lord's appeal to his people

28 This is what the Lord Almighty says: Have I not pleaded with you as a father pleads with his sons, as a mother with her daughters, or [as] a nurse with her babes, 29 that you would be my people and I your God, and that you would be my sons and I your father? 30 Accordingly, I gathered you together as a hen [gathers] *w*her chicks*w* under her wings; but now what shall I do to you? I will thrust you away from me! 31 When you offer sacrifices to me, I will turn *x*my face*x* away from you; for *y*I have repudiated*y* your feast days, new moons and circumcisions*z* *a*of the flesh*a*. 32 I sent to you my servants, the prophets, whom you took and slew, and mangled their*b* bodies; I will demand satisfaction for their blood, says the Lord.

A new people

33 This is what the Lord Almighty says: Your house is deserted; I will blow you away as the wind [blows away] chaff. 34 [Your] sons

---

q With C. S, A have *amorreo*, "Amorites"(?).
r–r C has *non indigne tuli*, "I did not take it ill."
s–s *alias gentes*; Spanish text has *gentem alteram*, "another nation."
t *eis*. Spanish text has *illi*, "to it."
u–u C has *maculaberunt enim animas suas*, "they have stained their lives or souls or themselves." Note change of person and addition of *animas suas*.
v–v C has *pedes vestri non pigri ad effundendum sanguinem*, "your feet not reluctant to shed blood."
w–w So with C, M. S, A have *filios*, "sons," with old Latin tradition transmitted by Cyprian and St. Augustine.
x–x C has *oculos meos*, "my eyes."
y–y C has *non mandavi vobis*, "I did not command you."
z C adds *sabbata*, "sabbaths."   *a–a* Omitted by C.
b C has *apostolorum*, "of the apostles." Cf. Luke 11:49.

will not produce children because they, like you, have disregarded my command and did what is evil in my sight. 35 I am going to deliver your houses to a coming people[c] who, [d]though they have not heard me[d], believe; [those] to whom I showed no signs will do what I decreed. 36 They did not see the prophets, yet [e]they will keep in mind[e] their time-honored [admonitions]. 37 [f]I call to witness[f] the esteem of the coming people, whose little children burst out with delight though they do not see with physical eyes, but in spirit they will believe [g]what I have said[g].

The patriarchs and prophets as leaders of the new people

38 And now, father[h], look with glory and take note of the people coming [i]from the east[i], 39 to whom I will give as leader[s] Abraham, Isaac, and Jacob,[j] and Hosea and Amos and Micah and Joel and Obadiah and Jonah[k] 40 and Nahum and Habakkuk, Zephaniah, Haggai, Zechariah and [l]Malachi, who is also called the messenger of the Lord[l].

Judgment of dispersion

2 1 This is what the Lord says: I led that people out of slavery [and] gave them commandments through my servants the prophets to whom they refused to listen, but rendered my counsels ineffective. 2 [m]The mother who gave birth to them said to them[m]: Go, children, for I have been widowed and forsaken; 3 I reared you with joy but lost you in [n]pain and sorrow[n] because you sinned before the Lord God and did evil[o] in [p]my sight[p]. 4 What more can I do for you, for I have been widowed and forsaken[q]? Go, children, and pray the Lord for mercy. 5 [r]But I[r] summon you, father, as a witness, in addition

[c] C adds *a longe*, "from afar."
[d-d] C has *et qui te non noberunt credent tibi*, "and who did not know you will believe you."
[e-e] *memorabuntur*, "they will be kept in mind." C has *memores sunt*, "they are mindful."
[f-f] C has *testantur apostoli*, "the apostles bear witness."
[g-g] C has *et que dixi audierunt*, "and so they will listen to [what] I said."
[h] Vulgate has *frater*, "brother."
[i-i] *ab oriente*. See "A Prophetic Apocalypse," line 9, in DJD, III, 83.
[j] C adds Elijah and Enoch.   [k] C adds *Mattia* or *Mathothia*.
[l-l] C has *et angelos duodecim cum floribus*, "and twelve angels with flowers." Cf. III Bar 12:1.
[m-m] C has *matrem sibi progeneraberunt que dicit eis*, "they gave birth for themselves to the mother and she said to them."
[n-n] C has *fletu et luctu*, "with weeping and pain."   [o] *malum*. C has *iniquitatem*.
[p-p] *coram me*. C has *in conspectu eius*, "before him."
[q] C adds *a filiis meis*, "by my sons."
[r-r] C has *ego enim desolata sum*, "for I have been made desolate."

to the mother of the children, inasmuch as they have refused to keep my[s] covenant, 6 to confound them and to despoil their mother so that they may have no[t] issue. 7 Let them be scattered among the nations and their names obliterated from the earth because they held my covenant in contempt.

The curse of Assyria

8 Woe to you, Assyria, who conceal the unrighteous ones within you! O evil nation[u], recall what I did to Sodom and Gomorrah 9 whose land [v]lies prostrate as lumps of pitch and piles of ashes[v]. Just so will I do to those who [w]have not listened[w] to me, says the Lord Almighty.

The Lord's address to Ezra

a. The kingdom of Jerusalem is to be given to "my people" instead of to Israel

10 This is what the Lord says to Ezra: Inform my people that[x] I will give them the kingdom of Jerusalem which I would have given to Israel. 11 And I will reclaim for myself their glory and give them the eternal tabernacles which I had prepared for them. 12 The tree of life will become an aromatic perfume for them; they will neither toil nor be fatigued. 13 Ask[y] and you will receive; pray for but a few days for yourselves [and] that they may be shortened; the[z] kingdom is already prepared [a]for you[a]. Watch [for it][b]! 14 Call to witness, call heaven and earth to witness, for I have [c]set aside[c] evil and created good, because I live, says the Lord.

b. Appeal to the mother to embrace her sons

15 Mother[d], embrace[e] your sons, [f]rear them cheerfully[f] as a dove[g] [does her young], strengthen their feet, for I have chosen you, says

[s] C has tuum, "your."   [t] C has ne quando, "none whatsoever."
[u] C has civitas, "city," presupposes Assur.
[v-v] C has descendit usque ad infernum "it has sunk right down to hell."
[w-w] C has obaudierunt, "gave obedience to."
[x] C adds parabi eis manducare, "I have prepared for them to eat."
[y] Vulgate has ite, "go."
[z] C has meum, "my."
[a-a] C has advenire, "to come."
[b] C adds animo, "mind," "self."
[c-c] Vulgate has contrivi "smash," "destroy."
[d] C, M add bona, "good."
[e] C has complexa for complectere (a more literary form with same meaning).
[f-f] C has da illis letitia, "give them joy."
[g] C adds que ducit filios suos, "but he takes care of his sons."

the Lord. 16 Moreover, *I will revive* the dead from their abode and 'lead them forth out' of [their] sepulchers because I acknowledge my name 'in them'. 17 Do not be afraid*, mother of sons, for' I have chosen you, says the Lord. 18 *I will send* you helpers in the person of my servants *Isaiah and Jeremiah* at whose behest I have sanctified and prepared for you twelve trees loaded with different° fruits, 19 and the same° number of fountains flowing with milk and honey, and seven gigantic mountains covered with roses and lilies *with which* I will make your sons replete with joy. 20 Vindicate the widow, judge the fatherless, give' to the destitute, care for the orphan, clothe the naked, 21 heal the crippled and the sick, do not joke about the lame, shield *the maimed*, and permit the blind [to see] the vision of my glory. 22 'Keep safe' within your walls the old man and the youth". 23 Wherever you find the dead°, bury [them there] and "mark the grave", and I will give you* a front seat at my resurrection. 24 Relax° °and rest, my people, for* your repose will come. 25 Good nurse, suckle your sons°, and strengthen their feet. 26 °As for the servants whom° I have given you; none of them shall be lost, for I will seek them from among your number. 27 Don't despair°,°, for when the day of affliction and distress comes, others will weep and be brokenhearted, but you will

---

– C has *suscitabo*, "raise up," for *resuscitabo*.

i–i *eorum*, "their," for *educam illos*.   *j–j* Vulgate has "in Israel" for *in illis*.

k C has *pabere* (*pavere*, "fear") for *timere*.

l C omits.

m–m C has *mitto*, "I send."

n–n C has Jeremiah, Isaiah, Daniel.

o C has *aliis et aliis*, "many different."

p C omits and has *septem*, "seven," bringing it up from after *montes inmensos*.

q–q C has *quos parabi tibi et filiis tuis*, "which I have prepared for you and your sons."

r C has *subministra*, "furnish," "supply" for *da*, "give."

s–s C has *luscu*, "the blind."   *t–t* C has *collige*, "gather."

u C adds, *infantes tuos custodi, servi et liberi tui letentur, et caterua tua omnis cum incunditate erit*, "keep your children, your servants and freedmen shall be gladdened, and all your company shall be with pleasantness."

v C adds *tuos*, "your," after *mortuos*, and *suscitabo*, "I will raise," after *inveneris*.

w–w C has *signa prospiciam*, "I will see the sign, or marker(?)."

x C has *eis*, "them."

y C has *pausate pusillum*, "relax a little."

z–z C omits.

a C adds *confirma quos genuisti*, "strengthen those you have borne."

b–b C has *quia quos*, "because them," omits *servos*.

c Vulgate has *fatigari*, "be weary."

d C adds after *satisagere: conservabo eos*, "I will keep them safe."

be cheerful and prosperous. 28 *The nations will be jealous* but unable to do anything against you, says the Lord. 29 *My hands will protect you, so that your sons will not see Gehenna*. 30 Rejoice, mother, with your sons, *because I* will save you, says the Lord. 31 *Call to mind* your sleeping sons, for 'I will bring them forth' out of the *hidden graves* of the earth and show them mercy, because I am merciful, says the Lord Almighty. 32 Embrace* your sons until I come and proclaim* to them mercy, for my fountains *are overflowing* and my grace will never cease.

The Lord's commands to Ezra

33 I, Ezra, received a directive from the Lord on Mount Horeb* to go to Israel*. *Yet when I came to them they repudiated me* and spurned *the Lord's* command. 34 So I say to you, heathen, who hear and understand: Look forward to your shepherd; he will give you eternal rest, for he is near who will appear at the end of the age*. 35 Be prepared for the rewards of the kingdom, because incessant light will shine upon you forever*. 36 Flee from the darkness of this [present] world, *take possession of the delight of your glory*. *I bear witness openly for my savior*. 37 *Accept the gift of the Lord and rejoice*, be grateful to him who has called you to the celestial kingdoms. 38 Arise, stand erect and observe the number of those marked with a seal *at the Lord's* banquet. 39 Those who have withdrawn* themselves from the darkness of the world* have

---

e–e C has *zelo te habebunt omnes gentes,* "all nations shall have jealousy with reference to you."

f–f C has *me tremunt omnia; oculi mei geennam vident,* "all tremble because of me; my eyes shall see Gehenna."

g–g C omits *quia ego,* "because I."   *h–h* C has *memorabor,* "I will be reminded."

i–i C has *illos exquiram,* "I will search them out."

j–j C has *latitudine,* "breadth"; Vulgate *lateribus,* "concealed places."

k C has *confirma,* "strengthen."

l Vulgate has *praestem,* "I may show"; C, *et aliis praesta,* "show to others."

m–m C has *exuberabunt,* "will overflow."

n C has *cobar, chobar,* "Chebar," the name of a river or canal in Babylon mentioned eight times in Ezekiel. LXX in Ezekiel has *Chobar.*

o C has *Israhel.*   *p–p* Omitted by C, M.   *q–q* C, M have *hoc,* "this."

r C adds *et diminutio hominum,* "and the decimation of men."

s C has *et aeternitas temporum vobis parata est,* "and eternity of times has been prepared for you."

t–t C has *captivitatem gloria vestrae,* "captive of your glory."

u–u C has *testor salvatorem meum mandatum esse a domino,* "I testify that my savior has been commanded by the Lord."

v–v C, M have *vos accipite* to which M adds *iocunditate(m) gloriae vestrae,* "as for you, accept . . . the joy of your glory."

w–w C omits.   *x* C has *tulerunt,* "driven."   *y* C adds *et,* "and."

received dazzling garments from the Lord. 40 [z]Take, Zion, your number and enfold your white-garbed ones who have fulfilled the law of
the Lord[z]. 41 [a]The number of your sons for whom you long is full[a];
implore the council of the Lord that your people who were called
[b]from the beginning[b] may be sanctified.

Ezra's vision and dialogue with the angel

42 I, Ezra, saw a huge throng on Mount Zion which [c]I was unable[c] to count and all praised the Lord vociferously with songs. 43 In
their midst was a young man of towering[d] stature, taller[e] than all
the others; he set crowns [f]upon the heads of each one of them[f],
and was even more exalted[g]. But I [h]was struck with awe[h]. 44 Then
I inquired of the angel as follows: Who are these, sir[i]? 45 His answer
to me was, These are the ones who have laid aside mortal clothes
and put on immortal ones,[j] and have confessed the name[k] of God;
now they are crowned and receive palms. 46 Then I said to the angel:
Who is that young man who has crowned them and put palms [l]in
[their] hands[l]? 47 His answer to me was: He is the son of God
whom they confessed in the world[m]. So[n] [o]I began to praise those
who had so firmly stood for the name of the Lord[o]. 48 Then[p] the
angel said to me: Go quickly, tell my[q] people [r]what sort of[r] and
how many wonders of the Lord God you have seen.

[z–z] C has *accipe, Syon. mons numerum tuum. conclude candidatos tuos servientes tibi in obtemperantia, qonium legem dei suppleberunt.* "Take, Mount Zion, your number, enfold your white-garbed ones serving you willingly, inasmuch as they have fulfilled the law of God."

[a–a] C has *quia olim optabas filios tuos venire inple numerum eorum,* "because you were longing for your sons to come, fill their number."

[b–b] *ab initio.* Occurs about a dozen times.

[c–c] C has *nemo poterat,* "no one was able."

[d] *celsus.* C has *excelsus,* "high," "noble."

[e] C has *eminens,* "eminent," "distinguished," "high," for *eminentior.*

[f–f] C has *in capite illorum coronas singulas ponebat,* "on their heads he put individual crowns."

[g] C has *exaltabantur,* "they were exalted."

[h–h] C has *mirari cepi,* "I began to be amazed."

[i] *domini,* "lord." Omitted by C. [j] C adds *vitam,* "life."

[k] C has *fili,* "of the son." [l–l] Omitted by C.

[m] C adds *mortali,* "mortal." [n] C has *vero,* "indeed."

[o–o] C has *laudare et magnificare coepi dominum,* "I began to praise and magnify the Lord."

[p] C has *et,* "and." [q] C has *ipsius,* "of yourself," "your own." [r–r] *qualia.* C omits.

NOTES

1:1. *The second book*. The only occurrence in OT or Apocrypha of the term "second." The expression forms the title in S.

"Ezra" is the form used in the French texts. The Spanish and Vulgate texts have "Esdras."

the prophet. Ezra is also referred to as a prophet in 12:42 but nowhere in the canonical literature is he so called. There he is referred to as the scribe or the priest or even the high priest. Clement of Alexandria (*Stromata* III 16) refers to *Esdras o prophētēs*, "Esdras the prophet."

3. *land of the Medes*. A rather general term referring to the extension of Medo-Persian rule in the east after the conquests of Cyrus the Great.

Artaxerxes. Which one is meant is still a matter of dispute — Artaxerxes I (Longimanus), 465–425 B.C., or Artaxerxes II (Mnemon), 405–359 B.C. Ezra is mentioned only in connection with Babylon which the author includes in the land of the Medes.

4. *the word of the Lord came to me*. This expression occurs frequently in prophetic literature but never in the canonical Ezra. But note that Ezra is referred to above as a prophet; hence prophetic forms are used.

6. *alien gods*. Cf. Gen 35:2, 4; Deut 31:16; Josh 24:20, 23; Jer 5:19.

8. *shake out the hair . . . and fling*. It is not certain whether the translation ought to be as indicated or "remove," i.e. "cut." The plucking out of the hair was a symbol of mourning (Ezra 9:3), but also of humiliation (Neh 13:25; Isa 50:6).

11. *in the east*. James (Bensly, pp. xlvii f.) suggests that the phrase may have come from Zeph 2:4 (LXX). The author rendered *mesēmbrias*, "at noonday," with *in oriente*, "in the east," thus interpreting it as the quarter of a compass. It does not necessarily reflect the place of writing. The historical situation in the mind of the writer is unknown; it could reflect the conquest of Alexander the Great.

15. *Lord Almighty* (*Dominus omnipotens*). This expression does not occur in OT; "God Almighty" does. It occurs six times in chs. 1, 2. It is found in NT (II Cor 6:18; with God in Rev 4:8; 11:17; 15:3; 16:7; 21:22) and the Greek equivalent *kurios pantokratōr* occurs in LXX. See also Sirach.

16. *exult in my name*. Usually rendered "triumph in my name" but *triumpho* can mean exult, in a figurative sense, which brings out the meaning better here.

17. *benefits*. I. e. recognition of the blessings received on the occasion referred to.

19. *bread of angels*. Cf. Wisd Sol 16:20; Ps 78:25.

20. *heat . . . tree-leaves*. Not in biblical story but may be an application of Exod 15:27. Cf. I Bar 5:8.

24. *turn to other nations . . . them*. There are references in OT, especially in the prophetic literature, castigating Israel for her apostasy but not rejecting her outright. That appears first in NT (Matt 21:43; Acts 13:46) and hence this section reflects Christian influence. Individuals were threatened with rejection (cf. II Chron 15:2; 24:20). This verse is quoted in the works of Augustine (Dialogus a in *De altercatione Ecclesiae et Synogogae* — see Migne, PL, 42, 1133), which may have some bearing on the *terminus ad quem* date of the work. See A. Oepke in *Coniectana Neotestamentica*, XI (Lund: Gleerup, 1947), 179 ff.

25. *entreat me for mercy.* Cf. Prov 1:28.

26. *stained your hands with blood.* Perhaps influenced by Isa 1:15. Cf. Isa 59:7; Rom 3:15; Prov 1:16.

30. *as a hen.* Cf. Matt 23:37; Luke 13:34; Lev Rabba 25 (123b).

31. *feast days, new moons.* Based on Isa 1:13, 15.

32. *my servants.* Pueros for usual *servos* in Vulgate; but same word used also in 2:1, 18. For expression (with *servus*) see Jer 25:4; 29:19; 35:15; 44:4; Rev 10:7; 11:18.

prophets . . . slew. Cf. II Chron 36:15, 16; Matt 23:35–37; Luke 11:50–51; 13:34; Acts 7:52.

33. *deserted.* Cf. Matt 23:38; Luke 13:35.

chaff. Literally the pieces of chopped straw and stubble after threshing (cf. Ps 1:4).

35. *a coming people.* The new community, i.e. Christians. Cf. Isa 52:15; 55:5; Rom 10:14 f.; 15:21.

36. *time-honored* [*admonitions*]. Lit. "their antiquities." Some render "uprightness," "former estate," "their history."

37. *see with physical eyes.* Cf. John 20:29; I Peter 1:8.

38. *father.* Cf. Apoc Paul 20.

from the east. Occurs only here and 15:20, 28, 34, 39.

39, 40. The order of C, M is Abraham, Isaac, Jacob, Elijah, Enoch, Zechariah, Hosea, Amos, Joel, Micah, Obadiah, Zephaniah, Nahum, Jonah, Mattia, Habakkuk, the twelve angels. Note Haggai is missing. Sir 49:10 simply mentions the twelve prophets. Jeremiah and Isaiah are mentioned in 2:18 and Daniel in 12:11. Ezekiel does not appear in II Esdras.

2:1. *commandments . . . prophets.* The commandments are here said to have been given through the prophets rather than through Moses. This is not necessarily a Christian conception as may be seen from II Chron 29:25; Ezra 9:10, 11; Dan 9:10. In the latter passage *toroth* ("laws") are ascribed to the prophets.

my servants the prophets. See second NOTE on 1:32.

2. *mother.* Cf. 10:7 and below vss. 15, 30. The reference is to Jerusalem or Zion. Cf. Isa 50:1; 54:1; Jer 50:12; Gal 4:26, 27 (cf. Pol 3:3); I Bar 4 and 5; II Bar 3:1 ff.; 10:16. Targum to Canticles 8:5 — "At that time [the resurrection of the dead] Zion, who is Israel's mother, will bear her children and Jerusalem receive her children. Pesiqta Rabbathi 26 (132b) — "I answered and said to her [the weeping mother], 'You are no better than my mother Zion, and she has become a pasture place for the beasts of the field.' Then she answered and said to me, 'I am your mother Zion.'"

Go, children . . . forsaken. Cf. I Bar 4:19; lamentation over Jerusalem in *Qumrân Cave 4* by J. M. Allegro, DJD, V (1968), p. 77.

3. *I reared you with joy.* Cf. I Bar 4:11.

Lord God. Occurs five times in chs. 2, 15, 16, but not in chs. 3 – 14.

4. *What more . . . forsaken?* Cf. I Bar 4:17.

pray . . . mercy. Cf. I Bar 4:22.

8. *Sodom and Gomorrah.* Often in Talmud and Midrashim.

9. *lies . . . ashes.* C, M may reflect Matt 11:23 where the same judgment is pronounced against Capernaum.

10. *my people.* Here, the Christians whom the writer regards as displacing Israel. Cf. Hos 2:23.

kingdom of Jerusalem. Not found in Bible.

11. *them . . . them.* The first refers to "my people," the second to Israel.

eternal tabernacles. Cf. Luke 16:9; Eccles 12:5; and "celestial kingdoms," vs. 37 below.

12. *The tree of life . . . perfume.* Cf. 8:52; Rev 2:7; 22:2, 14; Isa 65:22 (LXX); I Enoch 24:4, 5; 25:1 ff.; II Enoch 8:3. In the Apoc Peter (Akhmim Fragment, 15–16) we read of "a great garden . . . full of fair trees and blessed fruits, and of the odor of perfumes. The fragrance thereof was pleasant. . . ." The tree of life is referred to only once in Qumran literature (1QH 8:5), but the theme was common in oriental literature. IV Macc 18:16, "the tree of life is for all those who do his will."

13. *Ask.* Cf. John 16:24.

few days. Cf. Matt 24:22.

kingdom . . . prepared. Perhaps based on such passages as those voicing the eternal nature of the kingdom (cf. Ps 145:13; Dan 2:44; 4:3, 34; 7:14) and on Matt 25:34; Luke 12:32. Reflected also in Pss Sol 5:21; 17:3, 5.

Watch. Mark 13:37.

14. *witness, call . . . earth.* Cf. Deut 4:26; Isa 1:2; II Bar 19:1.

15. *dove.* Used frequently to illustrate certain qualities of Israel; Pseudo-Philo *Biblical Antiquities* 21:6.

strengthen their feet. A figure of speech pertaining to ability to carry the message.

chosen. Cf. Deut 7:6 and often in OT; here transferred to the people in the thought of the writer.

16. *I will revive the dead.* Cf. 2:31; Isa 26:19; Ezek 37:12, 13; Matt 27:53. See *The Excavations at Dura-Europos: The Synagogue,* by Carl H. Kraeling (Yale University Press, 1956), plates LXIX–LXXI, illustrating Ezek 37 which is national in concept rather than personal. Cf. II Bar 50–51; I Enoch 51:1; II Esd 7:32.

my name. Cf. I Enoch 48:7; Rev 14:1.

17. *mother of sons.* See painting of Mater Ecclesia at Montecassiano, Italy, dating from late eleventh century but probably dependent on an earlier model — *Encyclopedia of World Art,* XIII (New York: McGraw-Hill, 1967), plate 343 (top).

18. *twelve trees.* Rev 22:2 speaks of the tree of life with twelve different kinds of fruit (cf. I Enoch 24:4; 25:4. Jubilees 21:12 names twelve types of wood to be used for sacrifices. Cf. twelve leaf-bearing trees of Test Levi 9:12;

the fourteen evergreens of I Enoch 3. The reference here is probably to the twelve apostles viewed as successors of the prophets. Cf. *Geoponica* XI 1.

19. *fountains flowing with milk and honey.* The common OT figure of flowing with milk and honey (cf. Deut 31:20) grafted on the writer's imagery such as reflected in I Enoch 22:9, "bright spring of water," and Rev 21:6.

seven gigantic mountains. Cf. I Enoch 18:6; 24:2.

roses and lilies. Flowers represented the deeds of the righteous (III Bar 12:1–6).

20. *Vindicate . . . judge.* Cf. Isa 1:17.

destitute . . . orphan. Cf. Ps 82:3, 4.

naked. Cf. Isa 58:6, 7; Tobit 1:17.

21. *heal . . . sick.* Cf. Luke 7:22.

23. *bury.* Cf. Tobit 1:17–19; 12:12 f.

mark the grave. May refer to a cross sign placed on grave as a sign of victory; cf. signs of cross in catacombs and on Christian sarcophagi.

front seat. Writer may have had in mind Matt 20:23 or Ps 110:1.

24. *Relax and rest.* Cf. Isa 30:15.

25. *Good nurse.* Perhaps reminiscent of such passages as Num 11:12; Deut 32:18b; Isa 60:4; Hosea 11:3, 4, and the negative reaction of III Macc 1:20. Cf. I Bar 4:8, "the Jerusalem that nursed you."

26. *none . . . lost.* Cf. Isa 40:26; John 17:12. The author probably has in mind the church whose responsibility it was to preserve her own.

27. *the day of affliction.* Cf. John 16:20, 22; I Enoch 96:8.

29. *My hands . . . you.* Cf. Isa 49:2; 51:16; Wisd Sol 5:16; Ps Sol 13:1, 2; Sib Or 3:705.

Gehenna. Valley of Hinnom; literally *gy-bn-hnm*, "valley of the son of Hinnom." Earlier regarded as place of punishment for wicked Jews in full view of the righteous (Ass Mos 10:10; I Enoch 27:2, 3; 54:1, 2; 90:26, 27), later as the abode of all the wicked (cf. II Esd 7:36).

31. *sleeping sons . . . hidden graves.* The resurrection idea is widely prevalent in apocryphal literature (cf. Rev 20:13; II Esd 7:32; I Enoch 51:1; 61:5) but here the context seems to point to the revival of the pious scattered by persecution.

32. *fountains.* Cf. Jer 17:13 where the Lord is said to be "the fountain of living water," and Rev 7:17.

33. *Mount Horeb.* Ezra was regarded as a second Moses, concerned with the Torah; so Mount Horeb would naturally be regarded as the place of his divine instruction.

spurned . . . command. Cf. Jer 6:19; 8:19 — a fairly common complaint of the prophets.

34. *heathen.* Cf. Deut 4:6; Isa 2:2, 3; Micah 4:2; Zech 2:11. Appeal to nations is frequent in the OT.

shepherd. Cf. Heb 13:20; John 10:11; I Peter 2:25; 5:4.

eternal rest. Matt 11:29; Heb 4:9; II Esd 7:91, 95; Rev 14:13 — while the adjective does not appear elsewhere, the idea is present. For use of the idea in gnostic literature see Philipp Vielhauer, "ANAPAUSIS," in *Apophoreta,* eds. W. Eltester and F. H. Kettler (Berlin: Töpelmann, 1964), pp. 281–99.

near. Ps 119:151.

end of the age. Cf. Matt 13:39, 40, 49; 24:3; 28:20 where *sunteleia* (Greek) is rendered *consummatio,* "consummation," by Vulgate; here *finem,* "limit, end," not quite the same. In II Esd 9:5, 6 *consummatio* is used. For same expression as here see II Bar 54:21; 59:8; 69:4; II Esd 6:25. For many expressions with the same general idea see Volz, p. 189 [BIBLIO II].

35. *rewards of the kingdom.* Cf. 7:98; Wisd Sol 5:16; Matt 25:34; Luke 12:32.

incessant light. Cf. Isa 60:19, 20; I Enoch 58; 92:4; *'wr 'wlm(ym),* "eternal light," in 1QS 4:8; 1QM 13:5; 17:6; 1QH 12:15; Cf. Rev 21:23; 22:5; Evangelium Veritas, p. 32:29, 30. On concept of light in apocryphal literature see Friedrich Nötscher, *Zur theologischen Terminologie der Qumran-Texte* (Bonn: Hanstein, 1956), pp. 109–18.

36. *darkness . . . world.* Cf. Wisd Sol 2:5; I Chron 29:15; Eph 6:12.

your glory. Glory is often a substitute for salvation (see Volz, p. 359). For expression see Ezek 24:25; II Bar 15:8; 66:7; II Esd 7:95.

witness . . . savior. See comment by James in Bensly, pp. lviii f.

37. *the gift of the Lord.* Salvation. Cf. I Tim 6:20.

celestial kingdoms. Cf. kingdom of heaven in the NT. See Volz, pp. 299 f.

38. *the number.* Cf. Rev 7:4; I Enoch 47:4; a recurrent theme in apocalyptic literature, applied with reference to creation, the stars, angels, days, weeks, of the righteous, the wicked, etc.

marked with a seal. Cf. Rev 7:3 ff. — the sealing of the 144,000; with reference to those not bearing the seal, Rev 9:4. Also Ezek 9:4, 6 — Vulgate has *signa* in vs. 4 and *taw* in vs. 6, but the same idea is involved; it is quoted in Damascus Covenant Document Text B 9:11b.

Lord's banquet. Cf. Matt 22:2; Rev 19:9. Such a feast was heralded in Isa 25:6 and anticipated in the messianic banquet celebrated by the Qumran community (1QSa II 11–22). The idea of eating or banquet of the pious is found in other Jewish literature; e.g. Zeph 3:13; I Enoch 62:14; Aboth 3:20; 5:21. Jesus refers to such an eating (Luke 14:15; 22:16, 18; Acts of Thomas 7).

39. *dazzling garments.* Cf. Isa 61:10; Rev 3:4; 7:13, 14; Acts of Thomas 7. Accouterments of the saved and the heavenly messengers or servants (cf. Mark 9:3; 16:5; Acts 1:10).

40. *Zion.* Cf. Heb 12:22, 23. Refers to the Church here.

white-garbed ones. Cf. preceding NOTE and I Enoch 71:1; Rev 3:5; 7:13, 14.

41. *number . . . full.* Cf. II Esd 4:36; Rev 6:11; II Bar 23:5. What that number was, was a divine secret (II Bar 21:10; 48:46).

council of the Lord (imperium domini). Refers to the controlling authority or realm of the Lord several times referred to in the OT. The Latin word (*imperium*) does not occur elsewhere in II Esdras. The translation given is therefore not absolutely certain in the context of the sentence. The verb (*impero*) is found only in 3:4; 6:41, 42, 45, 46; 8:10; 14:34.

42. *huge throng on Mount Zion.* The whole verse is strongly reminiscent of Rev 4:1; 7:9 and Heb 12:22; Mount Zion here is the heavenly Jerusalem where dwelt the Lamb and the sealed of the Lord (Rev 14:1).

unable to count. Cf. Rev 7:9 which influenced the Spanish texts (C, M). Here Ezra is the subject, in Revelation it is impersonal (*nemo*).

praised . . . vociferously. Cf. Neh 12:43 (*śmḥh gdwlh*), but in a different context.

43. *a young man of towering stature.* Young man may be a substitute for "son of man" (cf. I Enoch 46:1 f.; Shepherd of Hermas *Similitudes* 9:6:1, "I saw a host of many men approach in whose midst was a man of such gigantic stature that he topped the tower."

set crowns. Shepherd of Hermas *Similitudes* 8:2:1, "then the angel of the Lord ordered crowns to be brought. When the crowns, appearing to be made of palm twigs, were brought, he crowned the men. . . ." See 2:46. The crown was the symbol of victory; here, the crown of salvation is the crown of life, as in James 1:12; Rev 2:10, or the crown of righteousness, in II Tim 4:8; I Peter 5:4. Asc Isa 7:22 speaks of "your clothes and your crown which you will see (in the seventh heaven)"; cf. also ibid., 9:13.

45. *mortal clothes and . . . immortal.* Cf. I Cor 15:53, 54; and "the higher garments" of Asc Isa 9:9. See further Bousset, *Die Religion des Judentums,* pp. 277 f.

palms. Sign of victory. Cf. Pseudo-Melito *Assumption of the Virgin,* Latin Version III.

47. *son of God.* Cf. Christian addition to the Books of Adam and Eve 42:3, 5 (from the Gospel of Nicodemus, ch. XIX).

48. *tell . . . wonders.* Reminds us of Jesus' instruction to the disciples (Matt 11:4 f.; Luke 7:22). Cf. Ps 96:3; Dan 4:2; Acts 2:22; Heb 2:4.

COMMENT

Chapters 1 and 2 are often referred to as V Ezra and sometimes as II Ezra. In the Clementine Vulgate, III and IV Ezra are placed after the New Testament and our chapters stand there at the beginning of IV Ezra. They do not appear in the oriental versions and are extant only in Latin which is markedly different from the Latin in chs. 3 – 14. Scholars generally agree that they were composed in Greek, or at least translated from it. Ezra is here characterized as prophet — a clear indication of the perception of the author, for his work was written in imitation of the prophets. As it stands, it looks like a polemic against Jews on the part of a Christian leader who was himself involved in the conflict between mother and daughter (1:24–37). The strong emphasis on moral precepts as over against ritual (1:31) breathes the same atmosphere as the Barnabas letter (2:4, 10; 9:4). These chapters possess all the marks of apocalyptic but with certain peculiarities such as an exodus from the east, the twelve angels bearing flowers (1:38, 40 — in C, M), the Edenic figures (2:12 ff.), the two servants Isaiah and Jeremiah (2:18) which is an interpretation of Rev 11:3 and a variant of Mark 9:4, the awakening of the scattered

people of the Lord (2:31) and the exalted youth (2:43).[1] Date and authorship
are uncertain and it is difficult to go beyond the general conclusion reached by
Weinel and James[2] to the effect it was written by a Christian some time in the
second century A.D.

[The pedigree of Ezra, 1:1–3] The passage is omitted in C, M. As it stands,
it is somewhat expanded beyond those in I Esd 8:1–2 and Ezra 7:1–5 but is
shorter than the one in I Chron 6:1–14. The following registers illustrate the
point. (Names occurring in all four columns are italicized.)

II Esd 1:1–3	I Esd 8:1–2	Ezra 7:1–5	I Chron 6:1–14
Aaron	*Aaron*	*Aaron*	Levi
Eleazar	*Eleazar*	*Eleazar*	Kehath
Phinehas	*Phinehas*	*Phinehas*	Amram
Abishua	*Abishua*	*Abishua*	Aaron
Borith ?	Bukki	Bukki	Eleazar
Uzzi	*Uzzi*	*Uzzi*	Phinehas
Arna	Amariah	Zerahiah	Abishua
Meraioth	*Ahitub*	Meraioth	Bukki
Azariah	*Zadok*	Azariah	Uzzi
Amariah	*Shallum*	Amariah	Zerahiah
Heli	*Hilkiah*	*Ahitub*	Meraioth
Phinehas	*Azariah*	*Zadok*	Amariah I
Ahijah	*Seraiah*	*Shallum*	Ahitub I
Ahitub	Ezra	*Hilkiah*	Zadok I
Zadok	(14 names)	*Azariah*	Ahimaaz
Shallum		*Seraiah*	Azariah I
Hilkiah		Ezra	Johanan
Azariah		(17 names)	Azariah II
Seraiah			Amariah II
Ezra			*Ahitub II*
(20 names)			*Zadok II*
			Shallum
			Hilkiah
			Azariah III
			Seraiah
			Jehozadak
			(26 names)

At the beginning of the list the names from Aaron to Uzzi (six) are the same
in all of them; so are those from Ahitub to Seraiah at the end. Note that all
the Esdras-Ezra lists make Ezra the son of Seraiah, whereas the list in I Chron
has Jehozadak occupying that place. The priestly tradition plus the one of
Ezra-I Esdras may have influenced L to add *sacerdos,* "priest." The II
Esdras register would seem to indicate that most, if not all, of the lists are
only partial ones, though they carefully preserved the early and late names.

[The Lord's complaint to Ezra, 1:4–12] The word of the Lord came to
Ezra just as it did to the prophets. He was commissioned to bring to the
attention of the people their misdeeds which were becoming more flagrant

---

[1] Cf. Heinrich Weinel in Edgar Hennecke, *Neutestamentliche Apokryphen,* p. 307
[BIBLIO II].
[2] Bensly, pp. lxxix f.

with each passing generation. They forgot the Lord's deliverance, and his guiding counsels were spurned. The divine pathos is as marked as in the prophets (vs. 9). Not only did the Lord free them from Egyptian bondage; he destroyed "all nations before them" and "wiped out all their adversaries." Despite the fact that they were a recalcitrant people, he would not reject his people without warning. That was what Ezra was summoned to do.

[Rehearsal of the Lord's benefits in the exodus and wilderness, 1:13–27] The whole passage reviews salient features of the exodus and wilderness experience from which significant observations are drawn. Besides reminiscences from Exodus, Numbers, and Deuteronomy, there are references to Pss 78 and 106. On the appointment of Moses and Aaron as leader and priest, compare Exod 3:14; 4:14. For pillar of cloud and fire see Exod 14:19, 24. Jeremiah accused Judah of having forgotten the Lord "days without number" (2:32). The author recalls the quail (Exod 16:13) and the camps provided for the people (Num 10:31; Deut 1:33) who nevertheless kept on complaining (Num 14:3; Exod 14:11b), yet the Lord gave them manna (Exod 16:14 ff.; Ps 78:24 f.), the food of angels (cf. Wisd Sol 16:20), split the rock (Exod 17:6) from which issued water, and expelled the inhabitants of Canaan whose land he allotted to them. Despite their blasphemies and grumbling the Lord did not destroy them. But now his patience was at an end and so he will turn to another people and call them by his name.

[The Lord's appeal to his people, 1:28–32] As may be seen from the NOTES this passage too is drawn from biblical materials though it accentuates, perhaps exaggerates, the thought involved. Certainly *after* the proffer of the covenant the Lord pleaded with his people, but to say that he *implored* them to be his people is putting it a bit too strongly. The first half of vs. 29 is reminiscent of Jer 7:23; 11:4; 24:7; 30:22, etc.; cf. Exod 6:7. The father-son relationship between God and Israel could be inferred from numerous passages in the Old Testament (e.g. Ps 89:26; Isa 63:16; 64:8; Jer 3:19; 31:9; Mal 1:6; 2:10). It is applied specifically to David in II Sam 7:14 and to Christ in Heb 1:5. But vss. 28, 29 appear to be closely related to II Cor 6:18 where the Vulgate has *dominus omnipotens dicit* as here. Verse 30 is clearly dependent on the saying of Jesus. The Lord has decided to thrust his people away because they had already severed their filial relationship with him (vs. 27). Thus sacrifices will be of no avail; religious rites are a mere formality because they are no more than the maintenance of appearances after their purpose has been abrogated. Note the phrase "circumcisions of the flesh." With the exception of that phrase, perhaps prompted by such biblical passages as Philip 3:2; Col 2:11; Jer 9:25 f., vs. 31 is based on Isa 1:13–15 and Amos 5:22. The reason given for the rejection of ritual is the people's attitude toward the prophets whom the Lord sent to instruct them. Verse 32 is dependent on Luke 11:49 (cf. Matt 23:34 f.) in view of C, M *apostolorum* found only there.[3] On the whole idea of the treatment of the prophets see II Chron 36:15, 16; Acts 7:52.

[A new people, 1:33–37] Israel's rejection of the Lord rendered its house desolate. Like the ungodly of the Psalmist, they will be blown away like chaff

[3] For a thorough discussion of this verse see Bensly, pp. L f.

from the winnowing floor. What is worse, the repudiated people will remain without issue; their children will remain childless because they were as bad as their fathers.[4] Both alike scorned the commandments and did evil in the sight of the Lord. Hence the heritage will be turned over to "a coming people" who believe without direct hearing or signs. Though they did not enjoy the privilege of seeing the prophets, they recalled their proven admonitions. The regard of the coming people for the Lord will be demonstrated by the joyous acclaim of their little ones in time to come; they will be moved to faith by spirit, not by sight.

[The patriarchs and prophets as leaders of the new people, 1:38–40] Verse 38 is difficult by virtue of the term "father" and the expression "from the east." God is still speaking to the "prophet" who is apparently addressed as father, though Ezra is not so called elsewhere.[5] It may be due to the proximity of the names of the patriarchs who are referred to often as fathers. "From the east" may have been influenced by I Bar 4:35–36, or, if ch. 1 originated in the west, it may refer to Jewish Christians coming from Jerusalem. Or again the author could have had in mind the golah who returned in the time of Ezra, though he actually meant Christians as "the coming people" who were to replace the Jews. In any case, the coming people are regarded as displacing the Jews and the latter's great leaders and prophets as being taken over by this new people. The order of the Twelve Prophets is that of the LXX which points to a Jewish Christian author for the passage. The inclusion of Elijah and Enoch in the Spanish text, on the other hand, reflects Jewish apocalyptic.

[Judgment of dispersion, 2:1–7] Many of the themes of chs. 1 and 2 were developed from chs. 3 – 14. This passage follows on the thought of the first chapter. It continues the complaint of the Lord who refers to his deliverance of Israel from slavery and his proffered direction through the prophets. But the people of Israel would not listen; their refusal rendered the Lord's counsels ineffective to save them from the perils to which such an attitude subjected them. The background here may be the tragic events of A.D. 70 when Jerusalem, Zion — their "mother" — was widowed and abandoned. That state is compared with the happiness of earlier days when the city sang with joy and resounded in festival. Her condition prevents her from doing anything more for her children. All they could now do was pray the Lord for mercy. It is uncertain, as noted above, who is meant by "father," but both father and mother of the children are called upon as witnesses to their refusal to keep the covenant. Hence they have been confounded and their mother has been despoiled so that there will be no more children. The curse pronounced in vs. 7 looks like a Christian judgment uttered against Jews.

[The curse of Assyria, 2:8–9] Babylon in Rev 14:8; 16:19; 17:5; 18:2, 10, 21 and elsewhere is used as a surrogate for Rome. Here it is Assyria which is also employed in other books to designate powers hostile to the Jews.

[4] Cf. Amos 2:7 where n'rh, "young woman," may be corruption of n'dh, "agreement," which would make the observation even stronger. But the Amos word may refer to a pagan goddess, "the Maid," perhaps Anat or Astarte.
[5] But see 2:5. On question of identity see Bensly, MF, p. 24, n. 3.

Ezekiel (32:22) speaks about Assyria in Sheol, and Zechariah (10:11) of laying low the pride of Assyria. The Qumran roll of Milḥamoth (1QM) designates the opponents of the sons of light *ktyy 'šwr*, "Kittim of Ashur" (1:2, 6; 2:12; 11:11; 18:2; 19:10)[6] and Sib Or 3:303 predicts a violent destruction to come one day upon "Babylon and the race of Assyrians." The well-known destruction of Sodom and Gomorrah (Gen 19:24 ff.) was used in Zeph 2:9 as a *māšāl* (proverb, parable, similitude, wise saying) which the writer doubtless drew upon here. The mixture of figures points to the application of biblical phraseology to the current situation. What happened to the foes of Israel in the past will happen to Assyria (Rome).

[The Lord's address to Ezra, 2:10–14] The first part of the address deals with the transfer of the kingdom of Jerusalem from Israel to "my people." The covenant people are now "my people" who have assumed the place of Israel. The expression "my people" is used of Israel in the Old Testament but here of Christians. In Isa 42:8 the Lord asserts that he will not give his glory to another god. But in Isa 48:11 the context indicates that he will not give his glory to another people, a solemn assurance to them that though their sins were grave he nevertheless had not and would not forsake them. What had been reserved for Israel has been taken back to be conferred on "my (new) people." This determination of the Lord with all its implications is to be conveyed by Ezra to "my people."

[Appeal to the mother to embrace her sons, 2:15–32] This is a rather heartwarming appeal to the mother to embrace her sons, to bring them up cheerfully so that they may be able to stand. She has been chosen by the Lord. Even the departed were included among her sons for the Lord's name's sake, that is, because of what he was and because of those who called themselves or were called by his name. The prophets were their assurance as realized in the twelve trees (apostles) and what these had to offer in the semiparadisal situation — a saved, restored people basking among the roses and lilies of the seven gigantic mountains, enjoying the fruits and milk and honey provided for them from the trees and fountains. The exhortations to justice, kindness, and concern for those unable to care for themselves breathe the spirit of the prophets. To be sure, hard times and affliction are inevitable in the present world structure, but those in the Lord's care will be cheerful and prosperous. The nations may be jealous but can do nothing against those under the protective hand of the Lord. Note the strong emphasis on the resurrection of the sleeping sons of the mother who are the recipients of his mercy which never ceases.

[The Lord's commands to Ezra, 2:33–41] Like Moses, Ezra is said to have received the Lord's decrees from Horeb but was no more successful than his predecessor had been. He too was rejected and the commands of the Lord delivered through him spurned. So Ezra appeals to the "heathen," that is, outsiders, to anticipate their shepherd, the harbinger of eternal rest, who will

6 See Yigael Yadin, *The Scroll of the War of the Sons of Light against the Sons of Darkness* (Jerusalem: The Bialik Institute, 1955), p. 255, for comment on the expression, and Matthias Delcor, RB 58 (1951), 526 f.

appear at the end of the age. II Esd 7:112b refers to two worlds — the present world and the eternal world to come.[7] The conception here appears to be Christian, the shepherd being the messiah (Christ). Ezra urges his hearers to look for the rewards of the kingdom. They are to flee from the darkness of this present world and take possession of the joys of their glory. They are urged to accept gratefully the Lord's gift, for those who have rejected this world have received dazzling garments and they will experience the same delights, have access to the celestial kingdom, and participate in the Lord's banquet along with the number of those marked with his seal. Zion (the Church) is exhorted to receive those who have fulfilled the Torah of the Lord. The number of her longed-for sons is full, hence she is to implore the council of the Lord to sanctify those who were called from the beginning.

[Ezra's vision and dialogue with the angel, 2:42–48] Ezra's vision of the heavenly scene of the redeemed was reassurance that his proclamation to Israel (the Church) was not an idle dream. He saw the innumerable throng in heaven praising the Lord incessantly. He witnessed the youth of towering stature crowning those around him. Inquiring about the identity of the throng he was informed that they represented those who had put on immortality. Their reward followed upon their confession of the name of God. Hence they bore the crown of salvation and carried the palms of victory. The one who crowned them was the son of God whom they had confessed on earth. Ezra himself was then moved to praise those who stood firm in their faith in the name of the Lord. He was instructed to relay his vision of the kind and number of wonders quickly to his people. The urgency of the commission was probably due to the precarious situation in which the writer found himself.

[7] For further discussion with references see Volz, pp. 56 f.; Klausner, pp. 413 ff.; Schürer, II, 544 f.; Bousset, p. 249. On the situation at Qumran see Millar Burrows, *The Dead Sea Scrolls* (New York: Viking, 1955), pp. 264 ff., and *More Light on the Dead Sea Scrolls* (New York: Viking, 1958), ch. XXIX; F. M. Cross, Jr., *The Ancient Library of Qumran*, pp. 216–30.

II. THE EZRA APOCALYPSE
(3:1 – 14:51)†

THE FIRST VISION (3:1 – 5:19)
Introduction: the troubled meditation of Ezra

3 1 In the thirtieth year after the *ªoverthrow of the city*ª, I was in Babylon — I, Salathiel, who am also Ezra. Now I was perturbed as I reclined upon my bed so that my thoughts swarmed around in my mind, 2 because I visualized the ruin of Zion [on the one hand] and the affluence of those who lived in Babylon [on the other]. 3 Hence I was so profoundly disquieted that I began to address the Most High in terms reflecting [my] apprehension.

The prayer complaint of Ezra

4 I said, *ᵇO Lord, Lordᵇ*, *ᶜhave you notᶜ* spoken at the beginning, when you, and you alone, *ᵈformed the earthᵈ*, and commanded *ᵉthe dustᵉ* 5 so that *ᶠit gaveᶠ* you Adam an inert body? Yet it was the very creation*ᵍ* of your hands; you breathed into him the breath of life and he was made alive before you. 6 And you led him into paradise*ʰ* which your right hand had planted before ever the earth made its appearance, 7 and you imposed upon him *ⁱjust one commandment of yoursⁱ* which *ʲhe disregardedʲ*. Then you forthwith decreed death

---

† Also referred to as IV Ezra. In view of the exceptional length of this section, each of the seven visions which comprise it is presented as a unit with NOTES and COMMENTS appended.

According to Bensly (p. 6), subscribed to S at end of ch. 2 is *explicit liber Ezrae secundus,* "here ends the second book of Ezra," A has *liber tertius,* "third book." S, ch. 3, then is preceded by *incipit liber Ezrae quartus,* "beginning of fourth book of Ezra."

ª–ª Armenian H has "captivity of Judaia." C, Ethiopic, Syriac, Ar.² add *earum,* "our city." L has *iherusalem et iudaea.*
ᵇ–ᵇ dominator domine. May reflect *'dny yhwh;* Syriac *mry' mr.*
ᶜ–ᶜ nonne. Omitted by S, A but in C, M.
ᵈ–ᵈ Armenian has "the heavens and the earth and everything that is in them." C, M has *plantasti,* "set," "fixed" for S, A *plasmasti* (cf. Bensly, MF, p. 23).
ᵉ–ᵉ pulveri. With Syriac, Ethiopic. S, A have *populo,* "people," C, M *orbi,* "world."
ᶠ–ᶠ dedit. So with Syriac and M. (Cf. Bensly, MF, p. 25).
ᵍ Omitted by A.   *ʰ* L has *horto voluptatis,* "garden of delight"; so also Armenian.
ⁱ–ⁱ Armenian "that they may know he is your work."
ʲ–ʲ Armenian "he transgressed" and adds "and he was deceived."

for him and his descendants—and from him issued nations, tribes, people*, and clans without number. 8 But every single nation followed its own inclination' and behaved impiously*** before you and spurned "your commandments"; °however, you did not restrain them°. 9 Yet in the course of time you brought the flood upon the inhabitants of the world and destroyed them; 10 they underwent the same fate. Just as death [came] to Adam, so the flood [came] to them. 11 Nevertheless you did spare one of them: Noah, with his household, from whom [issued] all righteous men. 12 But when the inhabitants of the earth began to multiply and produced children, peoples and many nations, they began again to be more impious* than their forefathers*. 13 So when they did evil before you, you chose for yourself one of them whose name was Abraham, 14 whom you esteemed* and to whom alone you disclosed, secretly* at night, the end of the times. 15 You offered him an eternal covenant and promised him that you would never abandon his descendants. You gave him Isaac and to Isaac you gave Jacob and Esau. 16 Moreover, you set apart Jacob 'for yourself' but rejected Esau. So Jacob became a vast multitude. 17 Now when you led his descendants out of Egypt and brought them to Mount Sinai

18 You bowed down the heavens,
　　Rocked the earth,
　　And shook the world;
　　You made the abyss quake,
　　And confounded [the order of] "the age".
19 Your glory passed through four gates—fire, earthquake, storm, and frost

　　For you to give to Jacob's descendants the law,
　　And to the generations of Israel the commandment[s]*.
20 Yet you did not remove from them their inclination to wickedness

---

* C adds *ubique*, "everywhere."
' With C, M; S, C have *voluptate*, "pleasure."
*** S has *in ira*, "in anger"; some MSS of C have *mira*, "strangely."
n–n With S, A, omitted by C, M.
o–o Omitted by S, A, but present in Syriac and Arabic; cf. Pss Sol 2:1.
* Armenian adds "before you."
* Armenian H and other Armenian texts expand here: "they were persistent in deeds of injustice" or "their transgressions moved forth and they followed injustice."
* *dilexisti.*   * A has *secreta*, "mysteries."
t–t Omitted by M.
u–u A has *caelum*, "sky," "heavens."
* *diligentiam.* See Bensly, MF, pp. 28, 56 n; a characteristic word in II Esdras (cf. 3:7, 19; 7:37).

so that your law might bear fruit in them. 21 For the first Adam, laden with an evil inclination, transgressed and was overcome; so did all those who issued from him. 22 So the weakness became unremitting and though the law was in the heart of the people, the root of evil remained too. What was good disappeared, while evil stayed on. 23 *w*After the passage of times and the termination of the years*w*, you raised up for yourself a servant by the name of David*x*. 24 You instructed him to build a city for your name where your oblations might be offered to you. 25 This was done for many years; but then those who lived in the city became remiss, 26 carrying on in every way just as Adam and all his descendants had done, for they too had an evil inclination. 27 So you delivered your city into *y*the hands*y* of your enemies. 28 Then I said to myself: Do those who live in Babylon really do any better? And has it for that reason subdued*z* Zion? 29 But when I arrived there and observed [their] innumerable vices, and saw for myself over a period of thirty years*a* so many doing wrong*b* there, I was utterly perplexed, 30 because I came to realize

> How you bore with them [as] sinners,
> Treated with forbearance wrongdoers,
> Ruined your people,
> And preserved your enemies.

31 And you informed no one as to how this way should be abandoned*c*! *d*Does Babylon really act*d* any better than Zion? 32 Or has any other nation except Israel known you? Or what tribes have given credence to your*e* covenants as that of Jacob? 33 Yet their reward has not been evident, nor has their labor produced fruit. I have indeed traversed the nations and observed their affluence although they disregarded your commandments. 34 Now, therefore, weigh our iniquities in the balance against those of the inhabitants

---

w–w Omitted by M.

x All MSS of Armenian but not elsewhere have "After him you raised up his son, Solomon whom you commanded, in a night vision, to build the temple. And [you commanded] all the people to give prayers and offer sacrifices in it" (Stone, in *Textus* 6 [1968], 52). See also Violet, II, 6–7.

y–y Singular in A, M, C.

z dominavit. Note use (S) for deponent; *dominavitur* in C, M. Ethiopic, Arabic, Syriac *abominavit*, "abhor."

a So with Ar.*1* for "this thirtieth year."

b Armenian H, Latin L add "behold," *ecce.*

c Syriac has *mtdrk' 'wrḥk,* "your way comprehended."

d–d A has *faciunt babilonii,* "the Babylonians acted."

e So with M, Syriac, Ethiopic, Arabic; omitted by S, A, C.

of the world; the direction[f] toward which the indicator points will be evident. 35 When did the inhabitants of the earth not sin before you? Or what nation has so well executed your commandments? 36 You will find [g]exceptional individuals[g] who [h]have kept[h] your commandments, but nations [who have done so] you will not find.

Dialogue with Uriel

a. Can the human mind comprehend the way of the Most High?

4 1 Then the angel who had been sent to me [his name was Uriel[i]] replied. 2 He said to me: Since your thinking is so completely wrong with reference to this world, how do you expect to comprehend the way of the Most High? 3 I said, [j]Just so[j], my lord. He replied as follows: I have been sent to show you three ways and to put before you three similitudes. 4 If you can unravel for me [k]one of them[k], I will show you the way you wish to see and teach[l] you why[m] the heart is evil. 5 Speak, my lord, said I. So he said to me:

Go ahead, weigh for me the weight of fire,

Measure for me [n]the measure[n] of the wind,

Or recover for me the day that is past.

6 I responded as follows: What natural-born person can do that, that you should ask me about [o]such things[o]? 7 Then he said to me: Had I asked you, saying,

How many dwelling places[p] are in the depths of the sea,

Or how many fountains are at the source of the abyss,

Or how many ways are above[q] the firmament,

[r] Or where are the exits out of hell,

Or where are the ways of paradise[r]?

---

[f] *momentum* with C, M and Syriac.

[g-g] *homines quidem per nomina*. Cf. *onomata anthrōpōn*, "names of men (persons)" in Rev 11:13, *'nšy šm*, "men of renown" in Gen 6:4; see also I Chron 5:24 *'nšy šmwt*, "famous men."

[h-h] *servasse* in A, C, M for *servare*, "to keep," in S.

[i] *Uriel*. S has *Hurihel*, A has *Orihel*, probably correct.   [j-j] *ita*=Heb. *kēn*.

[k-k] *de quibus . . . ex his*=Heb. *'šr . . . mhm*, "which is from them."

[l] *doceam*, second conjugation future (cf. 10:38) for *docebis* (cf. 12:38).

[m] *quare*. S[a,b] *unde sit*, "whence may be." (S[a,b]=Sabatier, *Bibliorum Sacrorum Latinae Versiones Antiquae*, Rheims, 1743–49.)

[n-n] *saton*=Greek, measure for grain. Cf. Hag 2:16 (LXX), where plural is used twice, and Matt 13:33; Luke 13:21. S, C, M *flatum*, "breath," "blast"; A has *flatus*.

[o-o] *his*. M has *hoc*, "this."

[p] *habitationes*. Syriac, Armenian, and Georgian have *promptuaria*, "storehouses."

[q] *super*. M has *sub*, "under."

[r-r] Reading with Syriac *'w 'ylyn 'nwn mpqnyh d-šywl 'w 'ylyn 'nyn 'wrḥth d-prdys'*.

8 You might have retorted:

I have never descended into the abyss,
Nor as yet entered[s] hell,
Or ever ascended into heaven,
[t]Nor have I looked into paradise[t].

9 But now I have asked you only about fire and wind and the day
through which you have passed, and without which you cannot exist.
Yet you have given me no answer about them. 10 He said to me, you
cannot understand the very things that belong to you, that have
been associated with you, 11 [u]so how can your mortal mind grasp[v]
the way of the Most High or one already impaired by the corrupt[w]
world comprehend incorruption? [x]When I heard this, I fell upon my
face[x],

b. *It is ridiculous to try to comprehend what is unnatural*

12 and I said to him: It would have been better for us not to have
been present[y] than to come here and live in sin and [z]to suffer[z]
without knowing why. 13 He replied to me as follows: Once I went
out to [a]a forest of trees of the field[a] who were holding a consultation.
14 They said, Come, let us proceed to make war against the sea that
it may retreat before us and [that] we may make for ourselves more
forests[b]. 15 But the waves of the sea also held a consultation [c]and
said[c]: Come, [d]let us go up[d] and vanquish[e] the forest of the field
that we may gain for ourselves there additional space. 16 However,
the plan of the forest was [f]in vain[f] because fire came and consumed it;
17 the plan of the waves of the sea too [was in vain], because the
sand stood firm and blocked them. 18 If, now, you were their judge,
which one would you attempt[g] to justify or which one to condemn?

[s] Omitted by Latin; with Syriac *nḥtt*, "descend."
[t–t] So with Ar.[2]; cf. also Ethiopic and Armenian.
[u] Ethiopic has here "the way of the Most High was created from eternity."
[v] *capere*. M has *cognoscere*, "know," "comprehend."
[w] S has *exterius*, "outside." [x–x] Latin corrupt. Translation from Syriac.
[y] So with M; Ethiopic "created"; Georgian *quam hic esse*, "than to be here"; cf. Mark 14:21.
[z–z] With S, A, M; C has *peccatis*, "sinned."
[a–a] Good illustration of Heb. *y'r - 'ṣy - hśdh*.
[b] Ethiopic adds "of trees."
[c–c] *et dixerunt;* C, M have *dicentes*, "saying."
[d–d] So with C, M; S, A have *ascendentes*, "going up."
[e] Reading *consumemus* with S, C for *consumemus*, "bring to completion," of A, M.
[f–f] Some MSS read incorrectly *invanae*. Expression *factus est . . . in vano* occurs fourteen times in Pseudo-Philo.
[g] *incipiebas*. Occurs about three times in Pseudo-Philo.

19 I responded as follows: Both of them *h*concocted a foolish plan*h*, for the land was given to the forest and the locale of the sea to carry its waves. 20 He replied to me: You*i* have judged correctly; why have you not done so in your own case? 21 For just as the land was given over to the forest and the sea to*j* its waves, so also those who inhabit the earth can understand only earthly things and those above the heavens [can understand only] the things that are above the heavens.

c. *But why can't man understand things below?*

22 Then I responded as follows: Pray tell me, O Lord, why has the faculty of perception been given to me? 23 For I did not mean to inquire about the ways above, but rather about those things we experience daily:

*k*Why Israel is subjected*k* to abuse by the nations,
The people whom you chose given up to impious tribes*l*,
The law of our fathers rendered ineffective*m*,
And the *n*written stipulations*n* disregarded.
24 For *o*we leave*o* this world like grasshoppers,
Our life is like a vapor*p*,
And we are unworthy of receiving mercy.

25 But what will he do for his name*q* which we bear? About these things I inquired. 26 He replied to me as follows: If you continue, you will see, and if you *r*go on living*r*, you will often marvel — because the age is *s*speedily coming*s* to an end; 27 for it cannot bear the things promised to the righteous in the times, because this age is full of sorrow and frailties. 28 For the evil *t*concerning which*t* you interrogated me has been sown but its harvesttime*u* has not yet come. 29 If, therefore, what has been sown is not reaped *v*and [if] the place where evil has been sown does [not] pass away*v*, the field where

h–h Heb. *ḥšbw mḥšbwt,* "devise plans."
i tu omitted by C, M.
j M has *cum,* "with."
k–k Some MSS of A have *peccata,* "sin."
l S, C and some MSS of A have *tribus,* "tribe."
m S, A have *interitum,* "destruction."   *n–n* Syriac *dytqs,* "testament," "covenant."
o–o S, A have *pertransivimus,* "we have left."
p So with Syriac, Ethiopic, Arabic, and Georgian. S, A, M have *pavor,* "terror."
q Ethiopic adds "holy."   *r–r* With Syriac *tsg' t'ḥ'.*
s–s festinans festinat. "Hastening it is hastening," a Hebraism.
t–t Text has *de quo . . . de eo,* "concerning which . . . concerning it," a Hebraism.
u C has *detectio,* "uncover," "reveal"; M has *deiectio,* "overthrown," "cast down."
v–v Omitted by M.

good has been sown will not appear. 30 Because a grain*w* of evil seed was sown in the heart of Adam from the beginning, how much wickedness it has brought forth until now and will yet bring forth by *threshing time*ˣ! 31 Calculate now for yourself how great a harvest of wicknedness a [single] grain of evil seed has brought forth. 32 When numberless heads*ʸ* of them have been sown, how large a threshing floor they will require!

d. When will that be?

33 Then I answered as follows: *How long*ᶻ then and when shall this come about? Why are our years few and evil? 34 He replied to me thus: You cannot proceed faster than the Most High, for you want to proceed *at your own pace*ᵃ while the one above [proceeds] for the many. 35 Have not the souls of the righteous in their storehouses*ᵇ* inquired about these things, saying, *How long must we stay here*ᶜ? And when will the crop of our reward upon the threshing floor come? 36 Then Jeremiel, the archangel, replied *to them*ᵈ as follows: When the number of *those like*ᵉ you is full;

> For he has weighed the age in the balance,
> 37 And measured the times*ᶠ* with a measure,
> And counted the times*ᵍ* by number,
> And he will not disturb or rouse [them],
> Until the fixed measure is attained.

38 Then I answered as follows: O Lord, Lord, all of us too are full of wickedness. 39 Is not now perhaps on our account, on account of the sins of the inhabitants of the earth, the crop of the righteous held back? 40 He replied to me thus: Go now and inquire of a pregnant woman if, when she has completed her nine months, her womb can hold back the foetus within it. 41 I said, Certainly not, my Lord. He then said: In the *underworld, the storehouses*ʰ of souls are comparable to the womb; 42 for just as the woman about to

---

w Syriac *prdt'*, "small grain."
x–x Syriac *'dr'*, lit. "threshing place, floor"; Latin *area* (cf. vss. 32, 35, 39; 9:17).
y Syriac *šnn' d-ṭbt*, "head[s] of the good"; so also Ethiopic, Ar.², and Georgian.
a–a Reading with Syriac *mṭl npšk*. Latin A, S *cum et ipsum spiritum*(?).
z–z With Syriac *'dm'* (=*usque ad*); Latin *usquequo*.
a–a Reading with Syriac *mṭl npšk*. Latin A, S *cum et ipsum spiritum*(?).
b prumptuariis. Outside of II Esdras, word occurs only once elsewhere in Vulgate (Ps 144:13).
c–c Reading with Syriac *d'dmh l'mt 'ytyn hrk'*. For an explanation of Latin *usquequo spero sic*, "how long shall I hope thus," see Violet, II, 18.
d–d Reading with Syriac *lhyn;* M has *ad eas*.
e–e Reading Syriac *dmnn* for corrupt Latin *seminum*, S, A, C, M; cf. for expression II Bar 2:1.
f Syriac *lzbn'*, "times."　　*g* Syriac *l'dn'*, "hours," "moments."
h–h Syriac *šywl w'wyṣr'*, "Sheol and the chambers."

bear [a child] strives to bring to an end the inevitable [anguish] of
delivery, so also do these places strive to expel those things committed to them from the beginning. 43 Then the things you want to
see will be shown to you.

e. *Further inquiry about the time — more past than yet to come*

44 I replied as follows: If [i]you please[i], if it is possible, and if I am
capable of it, 45 show me this too, whether there is more to come
than is past or whether we have passed through the major portion of
it, 46 inasmuch as I know what is past [j]but I am ignorant of the
future[j]. 47 He said to me, stand at my right side and I will explain to
you the meaning by [k]a similitude[k]. 48 So I took my place and looked,
[l]and I saw[l] a blazing furnace passing before me; when[m] the flame
had passed by, I looked [again] and saw[n] that the smoke remained.
49 And after this a cloud full of water passed before me that discharged a furious downpour of rain and when the furious downpour
was over, [only] drops [o]of it[o] remained. 50 Then he said to me,
Think it over for yourself! Just as the rain is more than drops and the
fire more than smoke, so the measure that has passed exceeds [what
is yet to come]; but the drops and the smoke remain.

f. *Signs in response to the prayer of Ezra*

51 So I prayed thus: Do you think I will live until that time? Or
what[p] will take place then? 52 He replied to me as follows: [q]The
signs about which you ask me[q] I can tell you in part, but I was not
sent to tell you about your life; I don't even know it.

5 1 But as to the signs: Look now, the days will come when those
who inhabit the earth will be seized by great confusion[r],

And the way[s] of truth will be concealed,
[t]And the country of faith will be barren[t].

[i–i] A polite form of address. See H. M. Orlinsky, *Notes on the New Translation of the Torah* (Philadelphia: Jewish Publication Society, 1969), p. 73.

[j–j] Omitted by M. The whole verse is omitted by some Armenian texts.

[k–k] Omitted by A.

[l–l] *et ecce*. Lit. "and behold" — a blazing furnace passed by.

[m] *et factum est*. Lit. "and it came to pass."

[n] As in [l–l], *ecce*, lit. "behold."

[o–o] *in ea*. Lit. "in it"; Syriac *bh*.

[p] Reading *quid* for Latin *quis*, "who," with Ethiopic and Arabic versions. Georgian *quidquam*, "whatever." Armenian "who of us may be alive especially and who of us may exist in particular."

[q–q] Petrus Cholinus' Latin version of the Syriac has the following: *Praesagitiones eorum de quibus me interrogas*, "the predictions of them concerning which you ask me."

[r] Reading *twht'* with Syriac; Heb. *mhwmh*. Cf. M *ingenti tumultu*, "enormous tumult."

[s] Ethiopic *territorium*, "region."

[t–t] With Syriac *w'qrt' thw' 'r'h dhymnwt;* II Bar 59:10 *regio fidea*, "country of faith."

2 Injustice will be multiplied beyond that which you yourself now see and become incomparably greater than anything you have ever heard about. 3 Waste and trackless*u* will be the nation you now see bearing rule and men shall see it empty. 4 If the Most High permits you to live, you will see [it] utterly confounded after *v*the third [period]*v*.

> The sun will suddenly shine at night,
> And the moon in the daytime.
> 5 Blood will drip from trees*w*,
> Stones will cry out,
> Peoples will be in confusion,
> And *x*the courses*x* will be altered.

6 And one whom the inhabitants of the earth do not anticipate will reign, birds will migrate, 7 the *y*sea of Sodom*y* will produce*z* fish, and one whom*a* the many do not know will cry out by night, but all will hear his voice.

> 8 Chasms*b* will appear in many places,
> And fire often be discharged [therefrom];
> Wild beasts will leave their lairs,
> *c*And women in their uncleanness will give birth to monsters*c*.
> 9 Brackish waters will be found in sweet ones,
> And all friends will assault each other*d*.
> Reason will then be obscured,
> And insight confined to its chamber
> 10 And sought in vain by many.

Injustice and incontinence will be multiplied upon the earth. 11 One

---

u With Bensly, who reads [*et sine*] *vestigio*, the bracketed words are not in the Latin text. But the latter text, "a trackless waste," also makes sense. Syriac *wthw' dl' qym' wdl' mtdyš'*, "a waste without stability and without a track-trodden place."

v–v Reading with C and Syriac *post tertiam turbatam*; A, S have *tubam, tuba*, "trumpet." See R. H. Charles, *The Ascension of Isaiah* (London: Adam & Charles Black, 1900), p. 29, for comment on text and idea.

w Bensly has *ligno*, "wood"; Syriac *qys'*, "wood." But doubtless reflects Heb. *'ṣ*, "tree," "wood."

x–x Bensly has *gressus*. Some (e.g. S) suggest *egressus*, "goings out," indicating Heb. *mwṣ'ym* (cf. Ps 65:9). Syriac *' 'r*, "air," "sky") Ethiopic renders "stars."

y–y Bensly has *mase Sodomiticum*. Syriac *sdwm*. Georgian omits it. But cf. Jos. *Antiq.* 5:1:22 *tēs Sodomitidos limnes*, "of the lake of Sodom."

a Reading *quem* for *quam*, "which" with Box. The alternate reading would be ". . . voice which many do not understand but all will hear its (his) voice." Cf. also Georgian.

b Reading with Syriac *pht'*. Latin *chaus*, "chaos."

c–c Ar.² *et mulieres prodigia parient*, "and women will bear prodigies"; so also Ethiopic *et nascetur prodigium ex mulieribus*.

d Syriac and Ethiopic have "suddenly"; perhaps "without cause."

country will ask its neighbor thus: Has justice *that does right*
passed by you? But the reply will be negative. 12 At that time men
will hope but will not realize [it]; they will exert themselves but their
ways will not achieve their purpose. 13 I am permitted to give you
these signs; if you pray again and weep as now, and fast seven days,
you will hear once more things greater *than these*.

g. The end of the vision

14 When I awoke my body shook feverishly, and I was so distressed that I fainted. 15 But the angel who had come to speak with
me took hold of me, supported me *and set me* on my* feet. 16 Now
the next night Phaltiel*, a leader of the people, came and said to me:
Where were you? And *why is your expression* so gloomy? 17 Or
don't you know that Israel, in the land of their exile, has been
entrusted to you? 18 Get up, then, eat *some food*, so that* you
may not let us down as does the shepherd [who leaves] his flock in
the clutches of savage wolves. 19 I said to him: Go away from me and
do not come near me for seven days, *then you may come to me*.
When he heard what I said, he left me.

e–e Cf. *ta dikaia poiei*, "she does right" in I Esd 4:39, predicated of truth.
f–f horum. Genitive of comparison, as frequently in II Esdras. Cf. Bensly, MF,
pp. 87 f.
g–g Omitted by C.   *h* So with C, M and Syriac.
i Syriac *Pslt'yl;* Arabic *Phaldiel;* Armenian *Phanuel;* Georgian *P'alt'iel;* C *Salatiel.*
j–j vultus tuus. Hebraism: *mdw' pnyk r'ym* (cf. Neh 2:2).
k–k Omitted by A.   *l–l* With Syriac *lhm' qlyl.*   *m* With C, M and Syriac *dl'.*
n–n Syriac *wkd 'mrt lh,* "and then I will speak to him."

NOTES

3:1. *thirtieth year*. Cf. Ezek 1:1 for the same formula. The thirtieth year
would be 557 B.C., since Jerusalem fell in 587 B.C. If the king referred to in
Ezra 7:1, 7 is Artaxerxes I (465–425 B.C.) the date here would be a hundred
years earlier.

Salathiel is the Greek form of Heb. *Shealtiel* given in Ezra 3:2; 5:2; Neh
12:1 as the father of Zerubbabel. (I Chron 3:17–19 makes Pedaiah, the
brother of Shealtiel, the father of Zerubbabel.) Just why Salathiel should figure
here is an unsolved mystery since he figures nowhere else in Jewish literature
in a significant capacity. See however James's explanation in *The Lost
Apocrypha of the Old Testament* (New York: Macmillan, 1920), pp. 79 ff.,
and JTS 18 (1917), 167 ff.; JTS 19 (1918), 347 ff.

I reclined upon my bed. Cf. Dan 2:29; 7:1, 15.

swarmed around in my mind. Lit. "came up upon my heart," a common
expression in the Hebrew Bible. Cf. Dan 2:30 (Vulgate).

2. *ruin of Zion . . . the affluence . . . in Babylon.* While that was to some degree true of the Jews in Babylon and the Jews remaining in Judah during the exile, the reference here is to the increasing gap between the Jews and Romans after the destruction of Jerusalem in A.D. 70.

3. *I.* Lit. "my spirit," "soul."

Most High. '*lywn* in Hebrew. *Altissimus* used by Vulgate for same word in Num 24:16; Deut 32:8; Pss 9:3; 17:14; 20:8; 45:5; 82:19; 86:5; 90:1, 9; 106:11; Lam 3:35, 38; 1QS 4:22; 10:12; 11:15; 1QH 4:31; 6:33.

4. *Lord, Lord.* Cf. Vulgate of Isa 3:1 *dominator dominus* for Heb. *h'dwn yhwh,* LXX *Kurios Pantokratōr* (B); cf. Matt 7:21, 22 *kurie, kurie;* Pseudo-Philo 25:6 *domine, domine,* MS A *domine deus.* The expression occurs nine times in II Esdras (3:4; 4:38; 5:38; 6:11; 7:17, 58, 75[?]; 12:7; 13:51).

formed the earth. Reference is Gen 2:4.

commanded the dust. Cf. II Bar 48:46; 1QH 10:3–5.

5. *Adam an inert body.* Lit. "dead [or lifeless] body." Bereshith Rabba (14:8) says the first man was a lump of earth (cf. 1QH 1:21) into which God breathed the breath of life, as here.

creation of your hands. Cf. Apoc Moses 37:2.

6. *paradise.* Term occurs six times (here, 4:7; 6:2; 7:36, 123; 8:52) and in apocryphal literature is used for both the Garden of Eden and the garden of bliss as the dwelling place of the departed righteous.

before ever the earth. Probably an interpretation of *mqdm,* "from primeval times," of Gen 2:8. According to Jub 2:7 the Garden of Eden was created on the third day. This idea is perpetuated in later Jewish literature (cf. Pesaḥim 54a; Nedarim 39b; Bereshith Rabba 20). Its first literary expression is II Esdras (but cf. 6:2). Apocryphal literature is full of references to Adam's paradise. Paradise is found in conjunction with the heavenly Jerusalem in II Bar 4:2 ff. For early views of the cultic garden, see W. Andrae, "Der kultische Garten," *Die Welt des Orients* (1947–52), 485–94. For location in apocalyptic scheme see II Enoch 8.

7. *one commandment.* The prohibition of Gen 2:17.

disregarded. Cf. I Bar 4:12d, 13a; Jer 6:19.

decreed death. As in the Genesis story death followed upon disobedience; had Adam observed the one prohibition there would have been no death. Cf. II Bar 17:3; 19:8; 23:4; untimely death came to Adam 54:15; 56:6. I Enoch 69:11 indicates that Adam was not created to die. Wisd Sol 1:13–14 says God did not create death but intended everything to exist (cf. 2:23–24). However, Sir 14:17; 17:1–2; 40:11 suggests mortality for everything earthly.

8. *nation.* Could also be rendered "generation" (with Gunkel).

inclination and behaved impiously. Cf. II Bar 51:4. This seems to indicate man's ability to exercise his own will — free will — which is countered by the clause added in Syriac and Arabic texts to the effect that he did so only so long as God did not hinder him.

however, you did not restrain them. May be dependent on Pss Sol 2:1. For a discussion of the whole problem of man's freedom of choice in the Bible and Judaism see Moore, I, 453 ff. The good and evil impulse is perhaps another way of saying that God had invested man with the power of choice, i.e. he is not determined but rather free to choose within limits. He cannot be neutral.

10. *Adam . . . them.* As Adam died for his sin, so did his descendants for theirs. Cf. II Bar 54:15; 56:8. In fact Adam's sin is regarded as the precursor to that of his progeny and hence the cause of their death as well as his own (cf. 4:30 f.; 7:118; II Bar 48:42; Bereshith Rabba 19, on Gen 3:7). On the origin and transmission of sin, see Oesterley, pp. xxvii–xxviii, 22 f.

11. *Noah.* Cf. Gen 6:8 ff.

13. *Abraham.* Gen 12:1. Cf. Pseudo-Philo 23:5.

14. *secretly at night.* Refers to his vision, Gen 15:1, 12.

the end of the times. Cf. II Bar 4:4 and Gen 15:13 ff. Times and seasons are frequently mentioned in the Qumran documents. For a discussion of *'ḥryt hymym,* "end of days," see Johann Maier, *Die Texte vom Toten Meer* (Munich and Basel: Ernst Reinhardt Verlag, 1960), II, 142, and J. Carmignac, "La notions d'eschatologie dans la Bible et à Qumrân," *Revue de Qumrân* 7, no. 25 (1969), 17–27. *Finis tempus* occurs in Vulgate of Dan 8:17, 19. For references in apocalyptic literature see Volz, p. 189.

15. *covenant.* Gen 15:18 ff.; 17:7; II Chron 20:7; Isa 41:8 f.; I Bar 2:35; Pseudo-Philo 8:3; Ps Sol 10:5.

16. *Jacob . . . Esau.* Mal 1:2 f.

vast multitude. Gen 32:12.

18. *You bowed down the heavens.* Reference is to the theophany of Exod 19:16 ff., celebrated also in Ps 18:9 ff. Cf. also I Kings 19:11; Pseudo-Philo 23:10; and Rabbi Akiba in Mechilta on Exod 20:2.

19. *Your glory.* A surrogate for God; cf. Exod 33:18, 22; Ps Sol 12:7; 1QS 10:12.

four gates. Cf. I Enoch 34–36, 76; Rev 7:1 "winds of four quarters." The four gates apparently refers to four heavens through whose portals the glory of God was believed to descend.

fire . . . frost. The first three may have been influenced by I Kings 19:11–12; cf. Ps 148:8.

law . . . commandment[s]. Cf. Sir 45:5.

20. *inclination to wickedness.* Lit. "evil heart"; cf. 3:21, 26; 4:4. For idea in Bible cf. Gen 6:5; 8:21; Deut 15:9; Ps 141:4; Jer 3:17; 7:24; 11:8; 16:12; 18:12. Stubbornness of heart often in Qumran texts; 1QS 1:6 has *bšryrwt lb 'šmh,* "in the stubbornness of an evil [guilty] heart," and *yṣr r',* "evil inclination," in 11 Qumran Psalms 19:15 f. Verse 21 traces the evil heart to Adam who transmitted it to his descendants. The rabbis based their teaching on the *yṣr hr'* and *yṣr ḥṭwb* (evil and good impulses) on the two *yods* of *wyyṣr* in Gen 2:7 but they always regarded the former as the more conspicuous (cf. Solomon Schechter, *Some Aspects of Rabbinic Theology* [1909], pp. 243, 262). John 13:2 and Acts 5:3 attribute certain inclinations to do evil to Satan. For further discussion of the Jewish conception of the origin of sin, see Moore, I, 474 ff.

law might bear fruit. For similar idea with different subject cf. Rom 7:4; Gal 5:22; Eph 5:9.

21. *the first Adam.* I Cor 15:45; the rather different view of II Bar 54:15, 19 — the latter verse is significant. On speculation about the Adam saga see Bousset, pp. 352 ff. and Volz, p. 123. The struggle between the commandment and the inclination of man is the subject of Rom 7. Cf. III Bar 4 where the fall of Adam explains the fall of Jerusalem. For the same general idea see below on 4:30; Sir 15:11–14; Test Asher 1:3–9.

22. *weakness.* Lit. "infirmity," "disease [of sin]." Cf. Rom 6:19; 8:26, etc. in Vulgate. Term occurs also in 4:27; 8:53.

law was in the heart. Cf. Jer 31:33; 1QH 4:10 *šnn*, "engrave."

root of evil. Cf. Sir 3:28; 40:15; I Macc 1:10 where Antiochus Epiphanes is called *ridza amartōlos*, "the sinful shoot."

good . . . evil. The conflict between the law and the evil root was a perennial problem. Cf. Rom 7 and 8; Babylonian Sukkah 52b; Sifre Deut 45 on Deut 11:18. See NOTE on 8:53, below.

24. *build a city.* Apparently based on II Sam 5:9; I Chron 11:7 f.

oblations . . . offered. The whole purpose of Jerusalem was to offer sacrifices which continued to be the hope of the writer, though the city had already been destroyed. Cf. the seventeenth benediction of the Amidah prayer of the synagogue.

27. *your enemies.* Oesterley (pp. 27 f.) thinks the reference is to the Roman conquest by Pompey in 63 B.C. He bases his view on the theory that the author was dependent on Ps Sol 2:1 ff. (cf. Ps Sol 2:7 *oti egkatelipen autous eis cheiras katischuontōn*, "for he gave them into the hands of oppressors," since it (Ps Sol 2) reflects the situation depicted by Josephus, *War* 1:7:1–6; *Antiq.* 14:4:4.

28. *Babylon.* Pseudonym for Rome. See Sib Or 5:143, 159; II Bar 11:1; Rev 14:8, etc. For thought expressed in the verse cf. Hab 1:13; Jer 12:1; II Bar 14:4–15; Apoc Shadrach 3:7 – 4:1.

30. This little psalm of complaint echoes such outbursts as found in Ps 106:40 ff. and Lam 1:5, 10; 2:16, 17; 4:16; II Bar 11:3; 82:3–9; II Esd 12:34. Ezra is faced with the same problem that troubled Habakkuk. For explanation see II Bar 78:5. See further Rosenthal, p. 62.

31. *way . . . abandoned.* Cf. Isa 55:7; Rom 11:33; Eccles 3:11; II Bar 14:8, 9, 15b; 20:4b; 44:6b.

32. *known you.* The reverse of Amos 3:2.

covenants. Author insists upon Israel's acceptance of the Lord's proffer but apparently attributes her failure to carry out the covenant obligations to his lack of instruction as to how they may be "comprehended" (with Syriac).

33. *reward.* Expresses the view of late Judaism that the observance of the Torah deserves reward (cf. Rom 11:6b; Gal 2:16, etc.).

labor. To keep the Torah is no longer a delight (Pss 1:2; 40:8; 119:14, 16, 24, 35, 47, etc.) but a chore. Complaint of vs. 30 is reiterated in slightly different form.

34. *weigh our iniquities.* Cf. Job 31:6; Dan 5:27; Prov 16:2; 21:2; 24:12; I Enoch 41:1; 61:8; Pseudo-Philo 40:1 (see Volz, p. 95, for figure of scales and for possible origin, ibid. and Wilhelm Bousset, "Himmelsreise der Seele," ARw 4 [1901], 136–69, 229–73).

35. *When . . . not sin.* Cf. Rom 5:12.

inhabitants of the earth. Cf. Luke 16:8.

36. *exceptional individuals.* Cf. Ezek 14:14, 20 — Noah, Daniel and Job. The emphasis appears to be on extraordinary persons rather than on few as over against the many as in Matt 7:14; II Bar 21:11. Rosenthal thinks the reference is to proselytes (p. 42, n. 1).

4:1. *Uriel.* Name occurs in I Chron 6:24; 15:5, 11; II Chron 13:2, and also in Assyrian (*ilu-urri*), though not in reference to the angel. It means "God is my light [fire]." See Martin Noth, *Die israelitischen Personennamen im Rahmen der gemeinsemitischen Namengebung* (Stuttgart: Kohlhammer, 1928), p. 168. Uriel was the second of the four archangels named in I Enoch 9:1. According to I Enoch 20:2 he was set "over the world and over Tartarus." He figures in the Book of Adam and Eve (48:4, 6, 7), Apoc Moses (40:1), I Enoch (often), and II Esdras. As Gabriel, another archangel, was sent to Mary (Luke 1:26), so Uriel was sent to Ezra here. For a discussion of the seven archangels see Schrader, KAT, p. 625. See further J. Z. Smith, "The Prayer of Joseph," in *Religions in Antiquity* [BIBLIO II], pp. 271 ff.

2. *your thinking.* Lit. "your heart." Cf. John 3:12 where same idea is expressed.

3. *three ways.* Apparently the three propositions set forth in vs. 5. There is nothing here like the frequently mentioned two ways of the Bible (e.g. Deut 30:15, 19; Ps 1; Didache 1:1; 5:1; II Esd 4:23; or those mentioned in the Qumran documents (see Nötscher, *Zur theologischen Terminologie der Qumran-Texte, passim*).

three similitudes. Parables.

4. *unravel for me.* Cf. II Bar 22:8.

why the heart is evil. The MSS generally followed have this reading but the real meaning may be suggested by the S manuscript. As Oesterley (pp. 31 f.) has pointed out the question concerns the origin of evil not the reason for the evil heart.

5. *weigh . . . fire.* See NOTE on 3:34.

measure of the wind. I Enoch 60:12 "weighing of winds"; II Esd 4:36 "measuring the times." But see Job 28:25. Wind and fire are often mentioned together (8:22; Wisd Sol 13:2; Job 1:16, 19; 15:30). The wind was regarded as mysterious, beyond the comprehension of man (Eccles 11:5; John 3:8); the four winds are a common theme (e.g. Ezek 37:9; Dan 7:2; 8:8; 11:4; Zech 2:6; 6:5; Rev 7:1) and were thought to be kept in storehouses (Jer 10:13; 51:16; Ps 135:7).

the day that is past. See Ps 90:4; II Peter 3:8; Barn 15:4 for the divine view of it. On the whole verse cf. II Bar 59:5; I Enoch 41:4; II Enoch 40:11; Pseudo-Philo 19:14.

6. *ask me.* Recall questions of Job 38; II Bar 14:8; 21:8, cf. 48:3–5.

7. *dwelling places . . . in the depths of the sea.* Lit. "heart of the sea." Cf. Job 38:16.

fountains . . . at the source of the abyss. 1QH 3:15 f. speaks of the boiling of the abyss; 1QM 10:13 has *mbq' thwmwt*, "division of the abysses," and 1QH

10:34 *wbḥdry š'wl,* "and in the rooms of Sheol." The idea is found in Canaanite literature from Ugarit: *mbk nhrm ‖ apq thmtm,* "the source of the two rivers ‖ the outlet of the two deeps" (UT, 49:ı:5–6; 51:ıv:21–22; 2 Aqht vı:47–48).

ways are above the firmament. Cf. Pseudo-Philo 19:10; I Enoch 18:2, 12 where firmament is above the abyss. Perhaps the orbits of the heavenly bodies are meant.

exits out of hell. Cf. Job 38:17b *š'ry ṣlmwt,* "gates of deep darkness"; Pss 9:14; 107:18, "gates of death"; Isa 38:10, "gates of Sheol"; Wisd Sol 16:13.

ways of paradise. I.e. the ways to paradise. Cf. Pseudo-Philo 13:9; 19:10; gates of paradise (Book of Adam and Eve 37:1); the heavenly paradise is meant here, rather than the earthly one of II Enoch 8:5.

8. *descended into the abyss.* Cf. Ps 139:8; Rom 10:7.

entered hell. III Bar 4:4 — hell was shown to Baruch.

ascended into heaven. Cf. Deut 30:12; Prov 30:4; Rom 10:6.

paradise. See M. E. Stone, "Paradise in IV Ezra 4:8 and 7:36; 8:52," *Journal of Jewish Studies* 17 (1966), 85–88.

9. *without . . . exist.* The three qualities mentioned were thought to be essential for man's existence. Cf. Wisd Sol 9:16.

10. *things that belong to you . . . associated with you.* There may be reference here to the four primordial elements — earth, air, fire, water — two of which are mentioned above: fire and wind. See Wisd Sol 7:17; 13:1; 19:18. Gunkel (APAT, II, 355, note p.) refers to belief that the microcosm was composed of the four elements (see 8:8). Oesterley (p. 32) quotes the Bunde-hesh 30:6 (Persian writing). Gunkel's translation is suggestive — "wie wirst du dann das Gefäss sein können, dass des Höchsten Walten fasst" ("how then can you be the vessel that contains the ordinances of the Highest"). Cf. Rom 9:22 f.

11. Verse is exceedingly difficult. See various translations, especially of Gunkel (in APAT) and Violet.

the way of the Most High. Cf. I Cor 2:9.

12. *present.* See II Enoch 41:2; II Bar 3:1; Wisd Sol 8:19, 20; Assumption of Moses 1:14. The expression occurs in Pseudo-Philo at least seven times. According to Erubin 13b, Shammai and Hillel argued two and a half years as to whether it would have been better never to have been created. The former took a pessimistic view which the latter disputed. The optimistic view is supported by John 1:9. Jonah 4:3 shares the view of II Esdras here.

13. The fable-parable of the forest and the sea is reminiscent of Judg 9:8–15 and the vision of Baruch (II Bar 36–37). Such contest fables were common in Babylonian wisdom literature (see W. G. Lambert, *Babylonian Wisdom Literature* [Oxford: Clarendon Press, 1960], pp. 150–212), and originated in mythology.

14. *Come, let us proceed.* Cf. ibid., p. 161.

17. *sand . . . blocked them.* Cf. I Enoch 69:18; Ps 104:9; Jer 5:22; Job 26:10; 38:11; Marduk establishes a bar to keep back the waters of the seas after slaying Tiamat (ANET, p. 67, lines 139 f.) Conflict between sea and land is extremely early and persistent in the literature of the ancient world (see

Hermann Gunkel, *Schöpfung und Chaos in Urzeit und Endzeit* [Göttingen: Vandenhoeck & Ruprecht, 1895], pp. 419 ff.). Here that conflict of nature is sublimated under the figure of sea and forest.

18. The conclusion of the story with dialogic question and answer reflects a parabolic style (cf. Luke 7:42 f.; 10:36 f.) as Adolf Jülicher (*Gleichnisrede Jesu,* I [Tübingen: Mohr, 1910], 93) noted.

22. *O Lord.* Reference is to the divine messenger who is always so addressed. (Cf. Dan 10:17, 19).

faculty of perception. Cf. Prayer of Manasseh 10; Isa 55:8. This is really wisdom in the definition of IV Macc 1:16. The Latin *sensus intellegendi,* "power of knowing"; cf. Test Job 38:6.

23. *Why Israel.* The age-old question as to why the chosen people were the object of conquest by the nations (cf. e.g. Joel 2:17; Hab 1:3, 13; Pss 43:2; 44:24; Lam 5:20; Pss Sol 8:36; 9:1, 2; Test Job 38:6).

The law . . . ineffective. Cf. 14:21 ff. One would expect the law of God, of Moses, etc.; law of the fathers is relatively rare — cf. I Macc 2:20, 50 "covenant of our fathers"; II Macc 6:1; 7:37 "law (*nomos*) of the fathers"; Ezek 20:18 *bḥwky 'bwtykm,* "in the statutes of your fathers." On its ineffectiveness or breach of covenant see Gen 17:14 and the many complaints of the Deuteronomist in Samuel and Kings and those of the prophets.

written stipulations. In parallelism here with "the law of our fathers." For Syriac interpretation see Berakoth 48b; cf. also Rom 9:4; Sir 44:12; Wisd Sol 18:22; II Macc 8:15.

24. *like grasshoppers.* Cf. Ps 109:23; Nahum 3:17. Reminiscent of sweeping away of the locusts after the plague (Exod 10:19); or so valueless as to be stepped on and swept away by others.

a vapor. II Bar 14:10; 82:3; James 4:14; Pss 39:11; 144:4 *hbl;* Eccles 6:12.

unworthy of receiving mercy. Opposed to Ps Sol 9:16 and many of the Psalms whose refrain is "his mercy endures forever." But cf. Gen 32:10; Jer 13:14; Hosea 1:6; Zech 1:12; II Bar 13:9.

25. *do for his name.* Quotation from Josh 7:9. Cf. Jer 14:7; Ezek 36:22; II Bar 5:1; I Enoch 55:2.

which we bear. Lit. "which is called over us," a common expression in OT indicating possession. Cf. Isa 43:7; 63:19; II Chron 7:14; etc.

26. Perhaps a little *mašal,* "proverb," as Violet (II, 16) suggests.

age . . . end. Cf. I Cor 7:31; II Esd 6:20; II Bar 20:1; 54:1; 83:1, 6.

27. For whole verse cf. II Bar 21; 85:1–10.

age is full of sorrow, etc. Cf. I John 5:19; I Enoch 48:7. As might be expected, the idea is expressed in the gnostic writings of Nag Hammadi (see A. Böhlig and P. Labib, *Die koptisch-gnostische Schrift ohne Titel aus Codex II von Nag Hammadi* [Berlin: Akademie-Verlag, 1962], par 169:33). Heb 9:9–10 also contrasts the present temporary age with the one to come.

28. *sown . . . harvesttime.* Common idea in the Bible, especially the harvest as the time of judgment. Cf. Jer 51:33 — of Babylon; Hosea 6:11; Joel 3:13; Matt 13:24 f., 39; Rev 14:15 f.; Gal 6:7 f. Cf. W. Zimmerli, *Die Weltlichkeit des Alten Testaments* (Göttingen: Vandenhoeck & Ruprecht, 1971), p. 75.

29. The thought occurs already in Isa 65:17; 66:22 where a new heaven and earth will displace the old. Cf. also I Enoch 45:4–5; 51:5; Ps 37:9, 34.

30. *grain of evil seed.* Or "seed of evil." Cf. Sir 10:19; Philo *Legum Allegoriae* 3:242; Plutarch *Moralia* 10 ("seed of discord").

in the heart of Adam. Cf. 3:21; 7:11.

from the beginning. See textual note *b–b* at 2:41.

31. *Calculate now.* See NOTE on 4:18.

how great . . . a [single] grain. For comparative idea see James 3:5; Heb 11:12.

32. *numberless heads.* The reference is to innumerable heads of grain (wheat, barley, spelt) as over against the single, little grain referred to in vs. 31. "The argument *a minori ad maius* is characteristically Jewish" (APOT, II, 566).

33. *How long . . . when.* The question propounded is fraught with the same impatience as reflected in Mark 13:4; Barn 12:1.

Why . . . evil. Perhaps Syriac reading should be considered here — *mṭwl* (=*propter*). For expression see Gen 47:9; II Bar 16:1.

34. Cf. II Peter 3:9. The exhortation to patience is a common feature of apocalyptic literature and submission to the will of God a great virtue.

the many. Cf. Jeremias in TWNT, VI, 539.

35. *storehouses inquired.* Cf. Pseudo-Philo 32:13; I Enoch 22:4; 100:5; II Bar 21:23. Cf. Klaus Koch, "Der Schatz im Himmel," in *Leben angesichts des Todes. Beiträge zum theologischen Problem des Todes, H. Thielicke zum 60. Gbt.* Tübingen: Mohr, 1969.

36. *Jeremiel.* Heb has *yrḥm'l* (cf. Jer 36:26). Syriac has Ramiel. Cf. II Bar 55:3; 63:6 — the angel who presides over visions. Georgian version has Uriel. The name of Remiel appears as that of the seventh archangel in I Enoch 20.

the number . . . full. Cf. Rev 6:11; according to Rev 7:4 the number was 144,000. Man's destiny fixed before birth (II Enoch 49:2). II Bar 21:10 says God alone knows the number. On the full number see II Bar 23:4–5. The idea of full measure and full number is continued in Mandean Left Ginza 45:7–15, and Pistis Sophia (see W. C. van Unnik, "Die 'Zahl der vollkommenen Seelen,'" in *Abraham Unser Vater: Festschrift für Otto Michel* [Brill: Leiden, 1963], pp. 467–77). For the whole idea of measuring, weighing, numbering cf. Dan 5:25–27; Test Naphtali 2:3; Wisd Sol 11:20. It is repeated by Philo *De Somniis* 2:29. Cf. Rosenthal, pp. 61 f.

41. *underworld, the storehouses.* Sheol in Hebrew. Cf. Prov 7:27; Isa 57:2. II Esdras apparently regards it as the receptacle for the righteous dead (cf. vs. 35). For a discussion of the locale of the living and the righteous dead see Moore, II, 390. For meaning here see Volz, p. 33.

44. *If you please.* A common expression in OT (cf. Gen 47:29; Ruth 2:10, 13 etc.).

if I am capable. I.e. if I can grasp it (cf. Pseudo-Philo 19:14; 53:7).

45. *whether.* Such questions were common coin of apocalyptists. The same question appears in the prayer of Moses in Pseudo-Philo 19:14: *ostende mihi, quanta quantitas temporis transiit, et quanta remansit,* "show me how much time has passed and how much remains." See Léon Gry, "La date de la fin des

temps, selon les révélations ou les calculs du pseudo-Philon et de Baruch," RB 48 (1939), 337–56; cf. 9:1.

46. *I know what is past.* From history.

47. *side. Partem*=position with reference to the speaker. See second NOTE on 9:38.

48. *blazing furnace . . . smoke.* Figure similar to Gen 15:17; Zech 12:6. The moving oven, *aliku tinuru,* occurs in Maqlu II, 190 and IV, 134 (cf. Wolfram von Soden, *Orientalia* 26 [1957], 127 f.).

49. *cloud.* Cf. cloud of black and white water in II Bar 53.

50. *drops.* Cf. 9:16 where drops and flood are compared; Job 36:27–29.

51. *I will live.* Cf. Ps 39:4. Is there a subtle implication here of the question asked by the Psalmist?

what . . . then. Cf. Matt 24:3; Mark 13:4; Luke 21:7.

52. *signs.* Something may have fallen out of the text since there is no mention of a request for signs to which the angel is responding. Signs were, however, regarded as significant and the indicator of things to come (cf. Mark 13:14, 22; Matt 24:15). *Signum* occurs about thirteen times; all but once it is rendered by *'wt* in the Syriac version (Greek *sēmeion*). For meaning in II Esdras see TWNT, VII, p. 230 f.

5:1. *signs.* To be understood in an apocalyptic and not in an historical sense as in vss. 3, 4.

days will come. Cf. Jer 7:32; see further II Esd 6:18.

confusion. Cf. 13:30.

way of truth . . . concealed. Cf. II Bar 39:6.

country of faith. Cf. II Bar 59:10; Volkmar, *Esdra Propheta* (p. 22), reads "the land will be devoid of truth." See Hosea 4:1 with knowledge of God as subject.

2. *Injustice . . . multiplied.* The increase of unrighteousness is frequently regarded as the harbinger of the messianic age (cf. Joel 4:13 [Hebrew]; Sir 47:24; I Macc 1:40; Matt 24:12; Sota 9:15; Jub 23:16–25; Sib Or 3:796 ff.; I Enoch 80:2–8; Ass Mos 10:5–6; Test Levi 4:1).

3. *Waste and trackless.* Cf. Ps 107:40; Jer 4:23; Isa 34:10; for expression Job 12:24b.

nation. The nation "now bearing rule" was the Roman empire.

4. *the third [period].* The texts vary here on interpretation as to what noun goes with the numerical adjective. Ethiopic has third month; Armenian, third vision; Ar.*¹*, three signs; Georgian, the thirtieth day. All of them probably reflect the same original, which each interpreted differently or indefinitely as Ar.*²*. Behind it lies apocalyptic imagery, perhaps going back to the Tiamat myth where the number three or three and a half occupies a significant role. See Gunkel, *Schöpfung und Chaos,* p. 268, n. 1 and p. 269, n. 1. Cf. Rev 12:14 where the figure is applied to Rome, as here. See further Jub 23:12; Sib Or 3:796–807; and below II Esd 6:14–18, 20–24.

sun . . . night. Cf. I Enoch 80:5; Amos 8:9; Pseudo-Philo 34:1.

moon . . . daytime. Cf. I Enoch 80:4; Joel 2:10; the two lines are paralleled exactly as in Asc Isa 4:5. All sorts of signs involving natural phenomena are found in apocalyptic literature, e.g. Amos 8:9; Joel 2:31; Matt 24:29; Luke 21:25; Acts 2:19b.

5. *Blood . . . trees.* Cf. Barn 12:1; Sib Or 3:803 f. An old benediction reflects the same idea when it speaks of "the abundance you have caused to flow from the tree of the Cross." For a discussion of this line see Bensly, pp. xxviii f.

Stones. . . . See Hab 2:11; Luke 19:40.

courses. . . . The reference is apparently to the gates (the place of outgoings) of the planets (cf. 6:1; I Enoch 72–82). These courses were regarded as fixed (Ps Sol 19); though the planets might conspire with God's people (Josh 10:12b; Judg 5:20) against their enemies, nowhere in the Bible is it said that they left their orbits. I Enoch 80:2–8, however, speaks of the disorder of the planets due to the sins of men (cf. Volz, pp. 180 f.). See also 1QH 1:12. Whole passage recalls the complaints voiced in the Petersburg Papyrus translated by Sir Alan Gardiner in *Journal of Egyptian Archaeology 1* (1914), 103, and the Potter's prophecy in Hugo Gressmann, *Altorientalische Texte zum Alten Testament,* 2d ed. (Berlin und Leipzig: Walter de Gruyter, 1926), pp. 49 f. The latter is preserved in a third-century A.D. Greek translation. Cf. prophecy of Theocylmenus in Homer's *Odyssey* 20:423 ff.

6. *one . . . will reign.* Perhaps the antichrist or Armilus (Weber, pp. 365 f.). Cf. Sir 11:5; II Bar 40:1, 2; Sib Or 3:63; Ass Mos 8:1; Asc Isa 4:2.

birds . . . migrate. Birds were thought to have supernatural powers and therefore to move away instinctively from a hostile environment. Cf. Jer 8:7; Job 35:11; Volz, p. 181. See Targum of Jer 4:25 and Hosea 8:1.

7. *sea of Sodom.* Name of Dead Sea in Talmud. The underlying scripture may be Ezek 47:7 ff. Throughout our passage the convulsions of nature produce the opposite of the normal order — sun shines at night, the moon in daytime, mute stones cry out, normal courses (of planets?) are altered, waters previously without marine life teem with it.

one . . . will cry out. Cf. Jos. *War* 6:5:3; the strange man in vision of Daniel (Dan 10:4 ff.); Joel 2:11. Gunkel takes the voice to be that of the sea.

8. *Chasms.* Cf. Zech 14:4; I Enoch 21:7.

fire. I Enoch 18:11; 89:7; 90:26; II Bar 27:10; 70:8; Rev 9:2.

Wild beasts. Whether they leave their places to do harm to people (Ezek 14:15), to replace the areas left vacant by the depopulation (Isa 13:21) or to fraternize as in the messianic age (Isa 11:9; II Bar 73:6) is not clear.

women . . . monsters. Cf. 6:21; Jub 23:25 — not monsters but prodigies — II Esd 6:21 which Box places after 5:8. Perhaps the idea expressed here is somehow drawn out of such passages as Matt 24:19; Mark 13:17. The idea of women bearing monsters occurs also in the Oath of Plataea said to have been sworn by the Greeks before the battle (479 B.C.). See Peter Green, *The Year of Salamis, 480–479 B.C.* (London: Weidenfeld & Nicolson, 1970), p. 240.

9. *Brackish waters . . .* Cf. IV Bar 9:16 *ta glukea udata almura genēsontai,* "the sweet waters will become brackish."

friends wil assault. . . . See Sir 37:2; Mark 13:12; passage is paralleled in 6:24. Armenian adds details such as fathers and children, children and fathers, etc.

Reason . . . insight. Cf. II Bar 48:36; I Cor 1:18; etc. On personification of Wisdom see Prov 8; Wisd Sol 7:22 – 8:1; Ps 154 (Syriac) also found in Psalms scroll from Qumran (11QPsᵃ, col. 18).

10. *sought in vain.* Cf. Prov 14:6; Jer 49:7.

Injustice. Cf. I Enoch 42:3; reason and injustice with their appeal may have been influenced by Prov 9.

multiplied. Cf. 7:111.

11. *justice.* See preceding NOTE. Cf. also Ps 85:10 ff.; Job 28:12–14; Matt 24:23, 26; Amos 6:10.

reply . . . negative. Cf. Ps 14:1, 3 with *ṭb,* "good," but equally sweeping in its assertion. For personalizing of justice (righteousness), see Ps 85:10, 11, 13.

12. *men will hope but will not realize.* Cf. Job 41:9; Ps 116:11; Jer 23:16; Rom 5:5 (hope that does not disappoint); James 4:2, 3; II Bar 70:5. On hope in apocalyptic literature see Bousset, pp. 206–42.

ways . . . purpose. Often in Pseudo-Philo.

13. *signs.* Signs of the approaching end.

fast. Preparation for revelation (cf. Neh 1:4; Dan 9:3).

seven days. Cf. II Bar 20:5. In II Esdras four such periods of fasting are commanded (5:13, 20; 6:35; 9:26 f.; 12:51). The marks of cultic piety in later times were prayer (Tobit 12:12), fasting and weeping (Joel 2:12).

14. *I awoke.* The preceding visionary experience took place during sleep.

I was so distressed. Lit. "my soul or mind"; stands for Heb. *npšy,* "myself or I."

I fainted. Lit. "it fainted," referring back to soul.

15. *with me.* Latin has *in me* (Heb. *by,* as in Hab 2:1).

set me on my feet. Cf. Dan 8:17, 18; 10:8–10, 15–18.

16. *Now.* Lit. "and it came to pass."

Phaltiel. Occurs in Num 34:26; II Sam 3:15; *Plṭyh* in I Chron 3:21; 4:42; Neh 10:23; and several times in Elephantine papyri. Neh 10:15 refers to one of the *r'šy h'm* by the latter name.

why . . . gloomy. Cf. Pseudo-Philo 50:3; I Esd 8:71.

17. *Or.* Cf. Paul's use of *ē* in Rom 3:29; *'w* in Mal 2:17.

land of their exile. Cf. Neh 3:37 (LXX 4:5) and Tobit 3:15 *en tē gē aichalōsias autōn,* "in the land of our captivity." Once again the Babylonian exile forms the prototype of the writer's time and Ezra the symbol of Israel's leadership in the new captivity.

18. *you . . . let us down.* Cf. 12:44; Ass Mos 11:9; Matt 10:14; Acts 20:29.

shepherd. Cf. Pseudo-Philo 19:3.

19. *Go away.* Cf. II Bar 32:7.

COMMENT

[Introduction: the troubled meditation of Ezra, 3:1–3] In accordance with general apocalyptic imagery, the seer adopted the Babylonian prototype in his treatise. He appropriated the name of Ezra and Babylon as pseudonyms. The whole of our book is composed of visions of Ezra which took place during the troubled repose of the seer. What he saw must be interpreted in the light of the period in which the author lived and wrote and not in that of the exile. Revelation by vision is almost a stereotyped form in late Hebrew literature, especially in developing apocalyptic, though it is not unknown earlier.[1] What Ezra saw in his vision disturbed him so profoundly that he was impelled to address the Most High with fear and trembling.

[The prayer complaint of Ezra, 3:4–36[2]] As is the case with apocalyptic writers generally, the author of II Esdras reflects a keen sense of justice. That is why his observation (vs. 2) led him to a survey of the course of his people's history and experience. So he calls the Lord's attention to the fact that he had created Adam from a lump of clay and animated him with the breath of life. He placed him in the protected garden (paradise) prepared before the appearance of the earth. He laid only one command upon Adam which he promptly disregarded, and for the transgression received the sentence of death which engulfed his descendants as well. History shows that the nations, tribes, clans, etc. that issued from Adam followed in his footsteps. They too behaved impiously and spurned the divine commandments. Since no restraint was placed upon them, matters got out of hand so the Lord destroyed them with a flood — with the exception of Noah who was the progenitor of supposedly righteous men. But the more further generations developed and mankind multiplied the more wicked and irresponsive to the commandments of the Lord they became. In fact they were more impious than their forefathers who had suffered destruction.[3]

Then the Lord endeavored to deal with the problem in another way. He chose Abraham to whom he disclosed the end of the times but to whom he also proffered an eternal covenant which included a promise never to abandon his descendants. From Abrahm issued Isaac to whom were born Jacob and Esau. Jacob was set apart to carry forward the covenant while Esau was rejected. Jacob not only expanded and multiplied as time went on, but was the recipient of the special grace of deliverance by personal intervention as well as being the beneficiary of the Torah and the commandments. The seer then noted that the mere gift of deliverance and Torah-commandments did not include automatic response. The inclination to wickedness persisted so that the Torah remained virtually fruitless. Just as Adam fell victim to an evil inclination, so did the generations after him. Though they were reminded constantly

---

[1] Cf. Jacob's dream at Bethel (Gen 28) and his night vision at Beersheba (Gen 46:1). The prophets too received visions which in later times tended to be night visions, especially as eschatological aspects came into prominence. Cf. Zech 1:7 – 6:15 with its eight night visions, with questions put to an interpreting angel and answers received from him. The concept is most common in Daniel; I Enoch (13:7, 8; 85:3; 90:40, 42); and Shepherd of Hermas *Visions* 3:1, 3. See also II Bar 36:1, 2; 53:1; Test Levi 2:5; and for a vision while awake, Test Joseph 10:1.

[2] On the form of the visions see Introduction. They are cast in the form of laments as shown by Westermann, ZAW 66 (1954), 77–79.

[3] The emphasis on Adam's sin (vs. 21) is reminiscent of Paul's struggle (Rom 5:12 ff.). While there is no specific statement here that Adam's sin was transmitted to his posterity, the matter is again taken up in 4:30–31 and 7:118 where he is charged with guilt regarded as hereditary.

of the peril of their ways, they could not steer clear of evil. The Torah was indeed in their hearts but the roots of evil remained and flourished to the point where the commandments were totally overcome. Despite the course of events, the Lord continued his efforts on behalf of his people by eventually choosing another servant, David, through whom he provided a city where amends could be made by sacrifices. But again his efforts were to no avail. The people of that city, in time, became as remiss as Adam and his descendants, because they still had within them the evil inclination. Though the sentence was the same as before — destruction — this time it was carried out by the national enemies of the Lord's people.

This explanation leads Ezra to reflect on a much wider situation. Why were the less wicked destroyed by the obviously more wicked? The Babylonians (Romans) were even worse than their victims so that the seer was utterly perplexed. The nations of his time were far more successful and affluent than the Lord's people. How could that be in the light of orthodox theology? Israel was ruined while its enemies were preserved — and blessed! Moreover, the Lord had revealed to no one how that process could be halted.[4] No other nation occupied the position Israel did vis-à-vis the Lord or even so much as gave credence to his commandments. Jacob was unique in that respect. And yet Israel remained without reward and without the fruit of its peoples' labor — i.e. without the national stability or affluence of other nations contemplated by Ezra. So he requests the balancing of the iniquities of Israel against those of the inhabitants of the world. The result will surely be evident to the unbiased observer. The other nations were always sinners, while Israel had abided by the commandments of the Lord to a far greater degree. Finally the Lord does admit that a few persons may have kept his commandments but that that was not true of other nations.

The author is, in reality, wrestling with the problem of God quite as much as with that of man. God had indeed created man and provided him with every-

---

[4] The interpretation of vs. 31 depends somewhat on the term "abandoned" or "comprehended" (with Syriac). In the latter case the meaning would be how the Lord's way was to be understood; in the former how the course of the existent situation might be reversed. If a broader, over-all view is intended the problem might be how the way of the evil inclination might be overcome. On the problem of Israel's sufferings see G. Bornkamm, "Sohnschaft und Leiden," in *Judentum Urchristentum Kirche: Festschrift für Joachim Jeremias,* ed. W. Eltester (Berlin: Töpelmann, 1960), pp. 188–99, esp. pp. 191 f. The OT more than once speaks of God's giving men hearts of wisdom (Exod 36:2; I Kings 10:24; II Chron 9:23), perception (Deut 29:3), understanding (I Kings 3:9), the Torah (Ps 37:21), righteousness (Ps 40:10). Ezekiel (18:31; 36:26) prophesies the gift of a new heart and a new spirit and Jeremiah (24:7; 31:33) of a "heart to know me." Ezra's observation in vss. 20 ff. may hint at those promises which remained unfulfilled, even though God could change (*hpk*) a man's heart (I Sam 10:9). The thought is pursued further in 4:26 ff. where Uriel responds to Ezra's observation of Israel (the people God loved) suffering at the hands of the heathen, the ineffectuality of the law of the forefathers, and the eclipse of the agreements. The distraught Ezra is told that God still cares for his people and will continue to do so but evil must run its course until the time of judgment when punishment will be visited upon the wicked and the righteous will be rewarded. See P. Volz, *Die Eschatologie der jüdischen Gemeinde* (Hildesheim: Olms, 1966), pp. 392 ff. — an updated edition of the Volz work listed in Bibliography II.

thing needed for the maintenance of a covenant relationship with Himself. But that was not enough because of the presence of an evil inclination which rendered man unable to carry out the commandments (cf. Paul's struggle related in Romans 5 – 8). The Torah was good and Israel was, in the view of Ezra, somewhat better than other nations. Yet one would not recognize it in terms of historical experience. How could the divine action be justified? Later Jewish theology postulated a *yṣr ḥṭwb* and a *yṣr hrʿ* in man which was really no resolution of the problem because the latter always seemed to prevail. The attraction to the way of the commandment was weaker than the evil inclination. Nevertheless, for II Esdras the focal point of complaint, for the moment, is the justice of God.

[Dialogue with Uriel, 4:1 – 5:19. Can the human mind comprehend the way of the Most High? 4:1–11] The angel appears quite abruptly, in response to the prayer of Ezra in the preceding chapter, and immediately addresses the questioner of the Most High. The tenor of Uriel's discourse is reminiscent of Job 38, though not so grand and sweeping as the exalted poetic conceptions and expressions of that chapter. Since Ezra cannot account for things of this world, how can he comprehend the ways of the Most High? (Cf. Isa 55:8–9). His attitude is just what it ought to be: he responds with an emphatic assent to the observation of Uriel. The whole stance is a familiar one in apocalyptic literature in general (e.g. John and the guiding or interpreting angel in the Book of Revelation), with the angel as mediator (interpreter) or preceptor to the troubled inquirer. Nevertheless, the author follows the prophetic tradition and rejects the grossly fantastic imagery of many of the apocalyptists. The lesson begins with a statement of the credentials of the instructor and the posing of questions for the learner which he is to contemplate if he would gain the knowledge he seeks. The three ways and similitudes (vs. 5) put forth are declared to be beyond human comprehension. That admission by Ezra is followed by further postulates embodying cosmological speculations so often engaged in despite man's lack of first hand experience. Generally II Esdras refrains from such excursions but the aim here seems to be to apprize Ezra of the greatness of God on the one hand[5] and the limitations of man on the other. How can he hope to understand the mysteries of God's ways in areas beyond his experience if he cannot even explain the commonplace in his life? Mortal man whose mind has been corrupted by the corrupt world is not in a position to contemplate and comprehend the incorruptible. That declaration cleared the way for further pursuit of the more immediate questions in Ezra's mind.

[It is ridiculous to try to comprehend what is unnatural, 4:12–21] This passage has to do with Ezra's complaint about the irrationality of existence; the reason for some of the most frustrating experiences of life is not known. Surely, he observes, it would have been better not to have been born than to be exiled, to live in an environment worse than the one before exile, and to

---

[5] See Bousset, *Die Religion des Judentums*, p. 359. The angel's question and comment in vss. 7–11 recall that of Jesus with reference to John's baptism in Mark 11:30 ff. and parallels.

suffer all sorts of hardship and deprivation without any reasonable explanation To some extent, what is voiced here is a variation on the theme of the age-old problem of human suffering, especially that of the righteous or at least of the less wicked — a problem which has not yet been solved with any degree of confidence. The little fable-parable offered to put Ezra's problem in perspective does just that, but no more. Just as the trees of the forest cannot encroach upon the sea or the waves of the sea upon the land reserved for the forest — each must remain in its domain — so earth-bound beings are limited to earthly things and heavenly beings to heavenly things.[6] The same sentiment is expressed in Wisd Sol 9:16 and John 3:12. (Cf. the comment of Rabban Gamaliel in Sanhedrin 39a). The solution for Wisd Sol (7:15–20) was in God's gift of wisdom; for John it was the new birth. For the author of II Esdras it was much more limited: it resided in comprehending that which was natural without attempting to understand what was beyond one's grasp.

[But why can't man understand things below? 4:22–32] It is clear from this little pericope that the author was not overly concerned with speculation about supermundane matters; he was concerned with making some sense out of the direction of history as it evolved in his time, more or less contemporary history which appeared as unintelligible as past history. What he wanted to know had been hinted at before but the realities of the situation made the problem more acute.[7] He has the faculty of perception as may be seen from the questions he poses but he doesn't understand why the course of history cannot be altered, indeed why the ethic implied by the covenant was not applied. His viewpoint is a bit more affirmatively expressed than that of Qoheleth but essentially it is the same (vs. 24) with the exception of the last line which reflects the conception of the prophets. Yet he cannot quite refrain from wondering how the reputation of God will fare for it is, to a large degree, identified with the people he chose. The conclusion reached (the response of the angelic interlocutor) is that human wisdom (knowledge) is inadequate to explain the course of events; faith in the ultimate outworking of things at the end of the age is what counts.[8] The prayer of the Psalmist (25:4) is not answered here (cf. also Rom 11:33 and Eccles 3:11). The reason the righteous (if there are such; see 3:36) cannot "bear the things promised" in this time is due to its sorrows and frailties. Time for judgment has not yet come, hence it is impossible for the good to flourish. That is somewhat more pessimistic (vs. 29) than Jesus' parable of wheat and darnel (Matt 13:24–30— darnel, a type of rye grass, resembles wheat). The idea expressed here is that a little darnel overwhelmed the wheat insofar as growth in this present world is concerned. The little seed of evil sown in the heart of Adam[9] has

---

[6] Cf. Volz, pp. 7, 32, and Bousset, p. 245, for a discussion of the this-worldly and other-worldly conceptions.

[7] See S. B. Frost, "Apocalyptic and History," in *The Bible in Modern Scholarship,* ed. J. P. Hyatt (New York: Abingdon Press, 1965), pp. 98–113, esp. pp. 103 f.

[8] Alfred Bertholet, *Biblische Theologie des Alten Testaments* (Tübingen: Mohr, 1911), II, 414, and I. Efros, "Prophecy, Wisdom, and Apocalypse," in MKJB, pp. 215–23, esp. p. 221, and n. 30 [BIBLIO II].

[9] See Moore, I, 477, and Walther Eichrodt, *Theology of the Old Testament* (Philadelphia: The Westminster Press, 1967), II, 411 f.; Bousset, p. 407.

produced prolifically — and continues to do so until harvesttime (judgment). Ezra is invited to contemplate that fact in view of the "numberless heads" of grain sown through the ages. Truly an enormous judgment (threshing floor) will be required to deal with the harvest.

[When will that be? 4:33–43] Here is reflected the impatience characteristic of many of the apocalypses which in turn evokes an exhortation to patience — also a characteristic teaching of this type of literature. The response of the angel to Ezra's query as to the time when the threshing floor scene will take place reminds one somewhat of Isa 55:8–9, though the context is different. The Most High does not move at the same pace as individuals; he takes into account the many. Just exactly what is meant is uncertain — does it point in the direction of an inclusiveness not contemplated by Ezra? In any case, he is informed that the souls of the righteous "in their storehouses" have already inquired about the duration of their stay and when they will receive the reward of their righteous deeds. According to I Enoch 20, Uriel was the archangel in charge of those who rise (will be resurrected) and so would naturally respond to their inquiries. They have been told that the threshing floor event is conditioned by the number of ages and world empires which vary according to the apocalyptist and his time and by the full number of souls to be born. Everything is carefully balanced, measured, counted, and the saints will not be roused until the "fixed measure" (*praedicta mensura*) is reached, i.e. until the predetermined time.[10] The judgment is inevitable but the time is contingent upon the filling of the number which is known only to God. But the question posed by the seer then is, in effect, how can the number of the righteous be fulfilled when the world is peopled mostly by the wicked? That is, the reward of the righteous is seemingly held up by the wicked (among whom Ezra includes himself) and can therefore never be realized. The angel then puts forth another similitude — that of the pregnant womb whose time of emission has been set and cannot hold in the foetus beyond it. The time of judgment-salvation is like that. Yet the figure is altered from that of the passive character of the woman to that of active participation in the birth of the child. The implication is clear: the storehouses of souls too strive to discharge their foetus. The pace of time and its determination are thus set forth. Judgment will come about under the same preset conditions. Sinners cannot inhibit the relentless forces of divine judgment. At the end of the age Ezra will see what he desires.

[Further inquiry about the time — more past than yet to come, 4:44–50] But when will that be? With all the normal apologies offered by a suppliant, Ezra presses for further revelation as to the time when he will see what the angel promised (vs. 43). The broad base of the query (vs. 45) receives an equally broad answer. The visions of the blazing furnace and smoke and the downpour of rain and the drops signify simply that while most of the time is past, a bit still remains before the end. The method employed here is some-what like that found in Matt 24; Mark 13; Luke 21, where the disciples

[10] For determinism of this kind in apocalyptic thought see R. H. Charles, *The Book of Enoch* (Oxford University Press, 1912), pp. 91 ff., and Harnisch, pp. 281 ff.

inquire of Jesus when the destruction of Jerusalem he has just announced will take place. He points to certain signs of the end but confesses ignorance of the exact time (Matt 24:36; Mark 13:32; this observation is wanting in Luke) which is known only to God who has not revealed it to anyone. But the impression is, in this passage, that the focal point of Esdras' concern is the imminent collapse of the Roman hegemony. Hence the whole vision appears to reflect the climax of his book, i.e. the eagle vision.

[Signs in response to the prayer of Ezra, 4:51 – 5:13] The interpreting angel responds to Ezra's request for understanding of daily (historical) experiences (vs. 23) and how God will justify Israel's bearing of his name in view of these circumstances. If Ezra continued and went on living, the angel answers, he would see, often marvel at the outcome (26). But really the chief concern is the speedy coming of the end of the age which would not only bring understanding but the adjustment of things according to divine standards. Now the question is, will Ezra live to see it? Not the resurrection as such was in doubt but the proximity of the end,[11] i.e. of the judgment. The more serious issue here is whether vs. 52 is responsive to the question asked in vs. 51 or whether something has dropped out. Box [12] thinks there is some indication here of the composite character of the text inasmuch as there is no mention of signs in the question and only the last half of vs. 52 is responsive to vs. 51. One cannot be sure whether the Latin *quis,* "who" or the Ethiopic and Arabic *quid* is original in vs. 51. If the latter is the correct reading there would be less doubt. Perhaps something has fallen out of the text. Note that both time and signs are included in the query of the disciples in Mark 13:4; Matt 24:3; Luke 21:7.

The signs of the approaching end are similar to those found elsewhere in this type of literature. Just as the prophets expected the end of historical periods, the apocalyptists looked for the end-time.[13] On the whole the former spoke of historico-ethical signs of it, while the latter spoke in mythological terms, often with a mixture of the ethical. The angelic interlocutor points to the time when the people of the earth will be thrown into confusion and the country of faith (Judah?) will be barren of its distinctive quality. Injustices of the past, though spectacular, will not compare with what is yet in store. The ruling nation will become a desolate waste and depopulated. The end will come after the third period. The evident signs[14] will be the reversal of the natural order. The sun will shine at night, the moon in the daytime, blood will drop from trees,[15] stones cry out, the normal courses (of the planets?)

[11] Cf. Harnisch, pp. 270 ff.
[12] APOT, II, 568.
[13] Cf. S. B. Frost, *Old Testament Apocalyptic* (London: Epworth Press, 1952), pp. 248 ff.
[14] Bertholet, *Biblische Theologie,* II, pp. 438 ff.; Volz, pp. 162–88.
[15] There may be more here than meets the eye. Could it refer to *martyrs,* as Jesus was "hung on a tree" (wood). On the whole passage see Klausner, pp. 350 ff. Josephus (*Life* 420) notes the crucifixion of many prisoners during the siege of Jerusalem in A.D. 70. In *War* 5:11:1 he says, "so great was their number that there was not room for the crosses, nor crosses for the bodies." Perhaps another indication that II Esdras reflects the events that transpired during the Roman conquests in the east between A.D. 66–73.

altered. The little pericope in vs. 6, in all probability, has to do with the anti-Christ. Then the main theme is continued — the Sodom sea will yield fish, a mysterious voice will be heard in the night, chasms spouting fire will appear, wild animals leave their normal habitats, women bear monsters, brackish waters mix with sweet, normal friends attack one another, and reason and insight disappear though men seek it. Injustice will become rampant and justice will nowhere be found. Hope will remain unfulfilled, and endeavors to achieve it will end in failure. The passage ends with a promise of further, greater revelation.

[The end of the vision, 5:14–19] The seer's experience appeared like a sleep from which he awoke, though the effects were like those of one who has had a hair-raising nightmare. The psychological shock produced physical exhaustion,[16] so that he required assistance from the angel. The appearance of Phaltiel on the night after the conclusion of the vision is part of the symbolical context appropriated by the author. As one of the popular leaders, he calls upon Ezra to fulfill his commitment to Israel in exile, but Ezra then urges him to go away for a period of time, possibly so that the seer could meditate on his experience.

[16] One is reminded of the state of terminal exhaustion found in some techniques of religious conversion. See William Sargant, *Battle for the Mind* (New York: Doubleday 1957), ch. 5. Though couched in traditional terms, the passage reflects a real experience. Cf. Oesterley, pp. 42 f.

THE SECOND VISION (5:20 – 6:34)

Introduction

5   20 Then I fasted for seven days, lamenting and weeping, just as the angel Uriel[a] had commanded me [to do]. 21 But after the conclusion of the seven days, the thoughts of my mind began once more to trouble me intensely; 22 however, I recovered the spirit of understanding and resumed my discourses[b] before the Most High.

Prayer complaint to the Most High and the angel's response

a. The prayer

23 I said, O Lord, Lord! From *all the forests* of the earth and from all its[d] trees, you have selected *a single vine; 24 from all the

[a] Syr. *rm'yl*, "Ramiel"; Ar.[1] and Armenian omit name; Ar.[2] "Suriel"; some exemplars of A have "Oriel."
[b] Omitted by Ethiopic, Georgian, and Ar.[2]
c-c Reading with Syriac and C, M; S, A, Ethiopic have *omni silva*, "every forest."
[d] *eius.* Referring to earth, though it could refer to *silva* if S, A, Ethiopic are correct.
[e] C adds *tibi*, "for yourself."

lands of the globe, you have selected for yourself *an insignificant one*, *and from all the flowers of the world, you selected for yourself a single lily*; 25 from all the deeps of the sea, *you have filled up* for yourself a single brook*, and from all the cities that have been built, you have dedicated Zion for yourself; 26 from all *the winged creatures*, you designated for yourself a single dove, and from all created animals, you provided* for yourself a single sheep; 27 from all the multitudinous* peoples, you acquired* for yourself [only] one people, and you gave a law esteemed by all to this people whom you called. 28 And now, Lord, why have you *handed the one over* to the many, and, having prepared one shoot* above others, [why] have you dispersed your only one among the many? 29 Those who resisted your commandments* have trampled on those who believed in your covenants*. 30 If you really dislike your people so much, *it ought to be* chastized by your [own] hands.

b. *The response*

31 Now* when* I had spoken these words, the angel who had come *to me* before, on an earlier night, was sent to me. 32 He said to me:

Listen to me* and I'll teach you,

Give attention to me and *I'll tell you more*.

33 Then I said: Say on, my lord. So he continued: *Are you as terribly disturbed* about Israel [as his Creator] or do you love him more than his Creator? 34 No, lord, I replied, but *I had to speak out of pain*, for my heart torments me every hour I seek to com-

---

f–f Reading *folium,* lit. "leaf," with C, for *foveam,* "small pit" in S, M, A; Syriac *'tr' ḥd,* "one place."

g–g Omitted by Syriac and Ethiopic.

h–h Syriac *'sqyt lk,* "you have increased for yourself."

i Armenian and Georgian add Jordan.   *j–j* Syriac *prḥt',* "birds."

k Syriac *ṣbyt,* "select," "desire."   *l–l* With Syriac *swg' '.*

m Probably for Heb. *qnyt,* "acquired"; Syriac *qrbt,* "brought near," "acquired."

n–n Reading *tradisti* with M, for *dedisti,* "give."

o Latin *radix,* also in Vulgate at Isa 11:10, for *šrš* which, in Ugaritic and Akkadian can mean "sprout," "shoot," as well as "root."

p sponsionibus, "promises," "stipulations"; Syriac *pwqdnyk,* "your commands."

q testamentis, as Syriac *dytq'* (Greek, *diatheke,* "covenant").

r–r C, M=*debes,* "you ought," with active of *castigare.*

s et factum est, "it came to pass." Syriac, Ethiopic, Ar.*1* omit.

t Syriac *mn btd,* "after."   *u–u* Omitted by C, M.

v Syriac adds *'zr',* "Ezra."

w–w adiciam coram te. Probably stands for Heb. *'wsyp ldbr lpnk,* "I will add to speak before you."

x–x Syriac *sgy 'ttzy't,* "you are terribly disturbed," omits question.

y–y Syriac *mḥš hw ḥšt wmllt,* "suffering it is that I suffered and I spoke."

prehend *the way* of the Most High and to examine the direction of his judgment. 35 You cannot do it, he said. I said, Why, lord? *To what end was I born? Why, then, was not [my] mother's womb my grave,

>that I might not see Jacob's suffering,
>and the weariness of Israel's descendants?

36 He said to me:

>Count for me those *not yet come*ᵇᶜ,
>Collect for me the spattered drops,
>Make green again for me the withered flowers,
>37 Open up for me closed chambers
>And release for me the winds shut up in themᵈ,
>Show me the picture of a sound,

then I will disclose to you [the reason for] *the misfortune* you asked to see. 38 Then I said: Lord, Lord, who can know ᶠthese thingsᶠ except he whose habitation is not among men? 39 But I am dull-wittedᵍ; so how can I speak about those things concerning which you asked me? 40 He replied to me: Just as you are unable to do one of these things suggested, so you will be unable to discover my judgment or the purpose of the love I promised my people.

Why successive generations were created

a. *The divine plan is for successive generations*

41 I said: But then, lord, you ʰgive preferenceʰ to those who are [alive] at the end; so what will those who preceded us do, or we, or those who come after us? 42 He said to me: I will compare my judgment to a circleⁱ:

>As there is no disadvantage to the slow,
>So there is no advantage to the fast.

43 I replied, sayingʲ, Could you not have created [all] those who have been created at the same time — both those who now exist and

---

ᵍ⁻ᵍ Syriac *gzr dyn'*, "decree of judgment."
ᵃ Syriac adds here *l' mṣl' 'n'*, "I am not pleading," but text is not clear.
ᵇ⁻ᵇ S has pluperfect tense.   ᶜ Ar.¹ adds "gather for me the scattered grains."
ᵈ A line may have fallen out here; Syriac *whwny dmwt' dprṣwp' 'ylyn d'dkyl l' ḥzyt*, "show me the image of form (or face) which until now you have not seen." So also Ethiopic and Ar.¹.
ᵉ⁻ᵉ Syriac follows Latin *'ml'* (=*laborem*); but Latin can mean "suffering," "pain," "hardship," etc.
ᶠ⁻ᶠ S has *hoc*, "this."   ᵍ Syriac=*skl' wdwy'*, "stupid and wretched."
ʰ⁻ʰ Latin *praees* for probable Heb. *qdmt*. See Jastrow, *Dictionary of the Targumin*, p. 1316. Syriac *'štwdyt*, "you promised."
ⁱ Latin *coronae;* Syriac *klyl'*, "circle, crown"; so also Ar.².
ʲ *et dixi* omitted by M.

those who shall exist in the future — *k*so that you might display your judgment more quickly*k*? 44 He answered me, saying, Creation cannot proceed more rapidly than the Creator, nor could the world contain at the same time [all] who have been created in it. 45 I said: How then can you say to your servant that you will indeed make alive at the same time [every] creature created by you? *l*If indeed they will be alive at the same time*l* and the creation support [them], *m*it might even now be able*m* to support [all] those present at the same time. 46 He said to me: Ask a woman's womb this*n*: If you give birth to ten [children], why [only one] at a time? Ask it, therefore, to produce ten [children] at the same time. 47 I replied: Impossible! But [it can do it at regular] intervals of time.

b. *The earth is like a womb, engendering one generation*
after another — each smaller and weaker

48 He said to me: I have made *o*the earth*o* a womb for those who at their peculiar time have been impregnated in it*p*. 49 For just as a child cannot yet give birth or one who is old [do it] any more, *q*so I have regulated the world I created*q*. 50 Then I inquired *r*as follows*r*: Inasmuch as you have now revealed to me the way, let me speak *s*before you*s*: Is our mother about whom you spoke to me still young or*t* is she now approaching old age? 51 He replied to me as follows: Ask [a woman] *u*who gives birth*u* and she will tell you. 52 If you say to her: Why are those to whom you have given birth recently not like those [to whom you gave birth] before, but smaller of stature*v*? 53 She herself will tell you, that those who were born in the virility of youth are different from those who were born in the period of old age, when the womb is impaired. 54 Consider, too, that you also are

k–k Partly on the basis of Armenian; Violet renders: "so that your judgment might take place more quickly, and your sentence appear."
l–l So Syriac; omitted by S, C, A, M.
m–m Ar.*1*, Armenian have question form.
n Latin *dices ad eam*, "say to it"; doubtless Hebrew idiom, with imperative followed by a finite verb (cf. *lk w'mrt* in II Sam 7:5).
o–o Reading with Syriac *l'r'' mrb''* for Latin *matricem terrae*, "womb of the earth."
p Ar.*2* adds "I provide for and exert myself for the world I created, since I have made things by degrees in their time and according to their measure."
q–q Latin *sic ego disposui a me creatum saeculum*, "so I have arranged the world created by me"; "regulate" based, in part, on Ethiopic *per tempus* and Ar.*2* *in suo . . . tempore*, "in its time."
r–r Syriac, Ethiopic, Ar.*1* have "him," as suffix plus "I said."
s–s Hebraism: *lpnyk*.   *t* *an*, "or" inserted into Latin text.
u–u Perhaps from Heb. *ywldh*, "the woman who bears a child"; cf. Syriac *yld'*.
v Ethiopic "less virile [or manly]." Texts vary greatly here. Reading here *statura* with some S manuscripts and C, M; A has *statu*, "rank," "condition," etc.

smaller of stature than those who were before you, [55] and those who follow you [will be smaller] than you, because the creation is already old and the vigor of her youth already past.

The end will come through God alone

[56] Then I said: I implore you, lord, *w*if you please*w*, show your servant through*x* whom you are going to visit your creation.

6 [1] He said to me:

*y*In the beginning of the terrestrial world,
Before the portals of the world *z*were established*z*,
Before the wind-blasts*a* blew,

[2] Before the *b*crashes of thunder*b* resounded*c*,
Before the *d*flares of lightning*d* flashed,
*e*Before the foundations of paradise*e* were laid,

[3] Before the *f*beauty of the flowers*f* appeared,
Before the *g*forces of motion*g* were determined,
Before the innumerable hosts*h* of angels were mustered,

[4] Before the heights of the air were raised up,
Before the measures*i* of the firmaments were defined*j*,
Before Zion was designated*k* as a footstool,

[5] Before the existing years were designed,
Before *l*the tricks*l* of those now sinning were thwarted,
And those who stored up*m* faith were sealed —

w–w Common in Hebrew (*'m-n' mṣ'ty ḥn b'ynyk* in Gen 18:3).
x Ar.*1* *propter quem*, "on account of whom."
y Syriac inserts *qdmy byd br-'nš' swlm' dyn b'ydy dyly;* "the beginning is in the hand of man but the end is in my own hands." Perhaps misplaced from vs. 9 from which it is omitted. Violet (II, 43) places it here and omits it from vs. 9. Cf. also Ethiopic, Ar.*1,2* and Georgian.
z–z Reading *statuerentur* with M, for *starent*, "stand," as S, A, C.
a Gunkel (in loco) reads *convectiones* (Greek *sumphoras*, "convocation"); Syriac *ywqrhyn*, "the weights."
b–b Ar.*1* "cherubim."
c Omitted by A.
d–d Ar.*1* and Georgian have "stars." "Flares" occurs in various forms about six times in Pseudo-Philo.
e–e Omitted by Ar.*2*; Ar.*1* "pillar of the foundations," and has *terrae* for "paradise."
f–f So with Syriac. Latin "beautiful flowers."
g–g So with Syriac *'wšn' dzw'na*.
h *militiae* occurs about five times in Pseudo-Philo.
i Gunkel reads the Greek of Hilgenfeld: *metra*, "the thing measured," then rooms or chambers.
j S has *nominarentur*, "were named"; A, C, M have *numerarentur*, "were numbered." Syriac *nštmhn*, "named."
k Reading with Syriac *nštrr*, "laid," "appointed," "designated" rather than the less forceful Latin verbs. Ethiopic corrupt.
l–l So with Latin. Syriac "follies."   *m* C, M insert *merita*, "merits."

6 even then I gave thought [to it]; these things were made by me and not by another; [n]just so the end [will come] through me and not through another[n].

The division of the times

7 Then I responded as follows: What will [indicate] the division of the times, or when will be the end of the first or the beginning of the second? 8 He said to me: From Abraham [o]to Isaac[o], [p]since Jacob [q]and Esau were born of him; for [r]the hand of Jacob[q] held fast to the heel of Esau from the beginning[r]. 9 [s]Now Esau [represents] the end of this age while Jacob [represents] the beginning of the following one[s]. 10 [t]The beginning of a man is his hand and the end of a man is his heel[t]. [u]Do not bother, Ezra, to inquire[u] about anything between the heel and the hand.

Request for and revelation of signs of the end-time

a. Introduction

11 Then I spoke as follows: O Lord, Lord, if you please, 12 show your servant the last of your signs, a portion of which you showed me last night.

b. Revelation of the signs

13 He replied to me as follows: Get up on your feet and you will hear an exceedingly loud voice. 14 If[v] [w]the place where you stand[w] is [x]violently convulsed[x] 15 when it speaks [y]with you[y], you must not be terrified, for the message concerns the end, and the foundations of

---

[n]–[n] Omitted by Syriac, Ethiopic, Ar.[1,2] and Georgian.

[o]–[o] With Ethiopic "to Isaac," and C, M; S, A "to Abraham."

[p] Ar.[1] "the generation of Abraham and his family"; Ar.[2] appears to have considerable interpretive expansion.

[q]–[q] Omitted by C. Syriac has after Abraham: *mn 'brhm 'tyld 'yshq wmn 'yshq 'tyld y'qwb w'sh*, "from Abraham was born Isaac and from Isaac was born Jacob and Esau"; so also Ar.[1].

[r]–[r] Omitted by Ethiopic and Ar.[1]

[s]–[s] Syriac *'qb' dqdmy' 'sh w'yd' dtnyn' y'qwb*, "the heel of the first (age) is Esau and the hand of the second (age) is Jacob."

[t]–[t] Latin is corrupt. Here with Syriac *qdmyh gyr dbr ns' 'ydh wswlmh dbr ns' 'qbh*. Cf. Hilgenfeld's emendation (p. 131): *hominis membra inter calcaneum et manum*, "a man's members between heel and hand."

[u]–[u] S, C, A, M have *querere*, "complain"; reading here with Syriac *tb''* "seek" "demand," "request." Ar.[1] "and here the heel and the hand have been united."

[v] Omitted by Syriac *et erit*, "and it shall come to pass."

[w]–[w] Note Hebrew construction, lit. "place in which you stand upon it."

[x]–[x] Hebrew absolute infinitive.

[y]–[y] With Syriac *'mk*; Latin *in eo*, perhaps due to Greek *en tō lalein*, "in its speaking."

the earth *will comprehend* 16 that the speech is about them; they will quake and be agitated, for they know that ªtheir end requires changeª. 17 When I heard that I got up on my feet and listened. Thenᵇ a ᶜvoice whose sound was like the sound of many waters spokeᶜ. 18 It said,

Look, the days are approaching;

Whenᵈ I begin to draw nigh to judge the inhabitants of the earth,

19 When I shall begin ᵉto avengeᵉ those who have unjustly

    injured [others] by their injustice,

When ᶠthe humiliation of Zionᶠ shall have reached [its] fullness,

20 When the age which is about to pass away will be [finally] sealed, I will give these signs: The books will be opened ᵍbefore the firmamentᵍ where all may see [them]ʰ at the same time. 21 Year-old infants will talkⁱ, and pregnant women will give birth to premature infants at three or four months who will live and ʲskip [about]ʲ. 22 Sown fields will suddenly appear unsown, full storehouses will suddenly be found empty, 23 the trumpet will resound; all, when they hear it, will suddenly be terrified. 24 At that time friends will fight with friends as [though they were] enemies, the land with its inhabitants will be terrified, and springs will cease to run for three hoursᵏ.

c. The state of those who survive: the saved

25 Then all who have escaped all these things which I have made known to you beforehand will be saved and they will see my salvation

---

ᵍ⁻ᵍ Plural with Syriac; Latin *intellegetur* (singular passive). Cf. A. So also in vs. 16, with some MSS of A.

ª⁻ª Violet points to a late Hebrew construction: *ky swpm lhlwp* and Greek *oti telos autōn dei allagēnai*, "because it is necessary for their end to be altered." Syriac *rgšn gyr dšwlmhyn mthlp*, "for they know that their end will be changed."

ᵇ Latin *ecce*=Heb. *hnh*.

ᶜ⁻ᶜ Latin *vox loquens* (Heb. *qwl dbr*) "voice speaking." So also Syriac. Armenian has "its sound is like that of a great tumult or like the sound of the flux of many waters."

ᵈ Latin *et erit*=Heb. *whyh*, "it shall come to pass"="when."

ᵉ⁻ᵉ Latin *inquirere . . . ab*=Heb. *drš mn* — cf. Deut 18:19. "To seek from," in this construction, means "to require of," in the sense of avenge (see lexicons).

ᶠ⁻ᶠ Armenian "when the tribulations of my servants shall be complete."

ᵍ⁻ᵍ From Gen 1:20 *'l pny hrqy'*.   ʰ Syriac *dyny*, "my judgment."

ⁱ Latin *loquentur vocibus suis*, "speak with their voices"; Syriac for *vocibus suis* is *wntlwn qlhwn*, "and give their voices"; as in Hebrew.

ʲ⁻ʲ Latin *scirtiabuntur* probably a Grecism from *skirtaō*, "leap," "spring," "bounce." Cf. Syriac *nšwrwn*, "leap." Box thinks vss. 21, 22 are misplaced and belong between vss. 8, 9 of ch. 5.

ᵏ As in vs. 19, Armenian has greatly expanded the text here.

and the end of my[l] world. 26 Then the persons who have been admitted[m], who have not tasted death from their birth, will appear, and the mind of the inhabitants [n]of the earth[n] will be converted to a different spirit[o].

27 For evil[p] will [q]be destroyed[q],
And trickery blotted out;
28 Faith will flourish,
And corruption[r] be subdued

and truth, which has been fruitless for so long, will be exposed.

Advice concerning things to come — warning against speculation

29 While he was talking with me, suddenly[s] the place where I was standing [t]began to move to and fro[t]. 30 He said to me: I have come to show you these things tonight[u]. 31 If, therefore, you will pray again and fast again seven days, I will again declare to you greater [things] than these [v]by day[v], 32 because your prayer has indeed been heard before the Most High; for the Almighty has taken note of your righteousness and recognized the virtue that you have practiced since your youth. 33 On account of this he has sent me to reveal to you all these things and to say to you: Believe, do not fear, 34 and [w]do not be overanxious[w] to speculate uselessly about former times [x]that you may not be taken by surprise in the last times[x].

[l] Syriac '*lm*', "the world."   [m] Syriac '*t'lyw*', "raised up."   [n-n] So with Syriac, '*r'*'.
[o] Syriac *md''*, "notion," "understanding." Perhaps the *sensum alium* reflects the *spiritum novum* of the Ezekiel passages noted below.
[p] Ar.[1] "evil heart," perhaps under influence of rabbinical theology.
[q-q] Syriac variants here are *mt'ty*', "be extinct," and *mtt'y*', "cover over," "obliterate."
[r] Ethiopic *mortale*, "transient," "mortal."
[s] *ecce=hnh* in Hebrew, as in Gen 37:7 (cf. *The Torah* [Philadelphia: The Jewish Publication Society of America, 1962], p. 67).
[t-t] Cf. Syriac *qlyl qlyl z''*, "move little [by] little."
[u] Latin *et ventura*, "and the things that will come." Reading here with Syriac *bhd' lly*', lit. "in this night."
[v-v] Omitted by all versions but present in S, A, C, M of Latin.
[w-w] Latin *noli festinare*. Georgian adds *malum*, "evil."
[x-x] Ar.[1] "in desiring the acceleration of the end." Georgian "that you may not begin to tremble in these last times."

NOTES

5:20. *Uriel.* See textual note [t] at 4:1.
commanded. Cf. 5:13.
21. *But . . . conclusion.* Lit. "but it came to pass after."
mind. Lit. "heart."

CYRUS THE GREAT Winged figure dressed as an Elamite wearing an Egyptian crown. It guards one of the entrances to the ensemble of the Palaces of Cyrus. The upper part of the monument bears a cuneiform inscription of which only the following words remain: "I Cyrus . . ." Perhaps something like "built this palace" followed. See R. D. Barnett, "Anat, Ba'al and Pasargadae," in *Mélanges de l'Universite saint-Joseph*, XLV (1969), fasc. 25, 407–22, and Max Mallowan, "Cyrus the Great (558–529 B.C.)," in *Iran* 10 (1972), 1–17. See I Esdras 2 ff. The name Cyrus occurs nineteen times in I Esdras. Cyrus, Darius, and Artaxerxes were intimately involved in postexilic affairs.

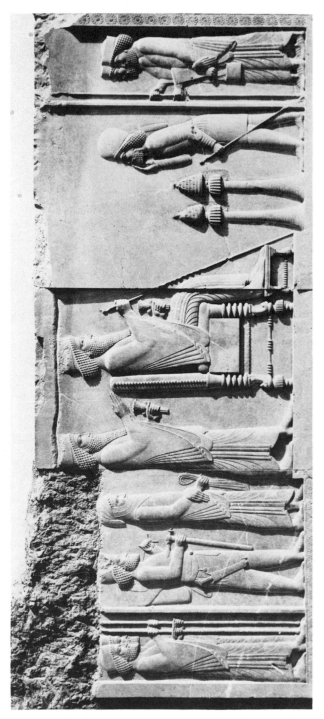

DARIUS AND XERXES   From the Persepolis treasury, without inscription but identified by archaeological context by E. F. Schmidt in *The Treasury of Persepolis*, Oriental Institute Communications 21 (University of Chicago Press, 1939), pp. 21–33. Darius is mentioned some nineteen times in I Esdras. The name of Xerxes is not found there.

ARTAXERXES I ON HIS THRONE The name Artaxerxes occurs nine times in I Esdras. There is, of course, the difference of opinion as to whether it is that of the first or second king bearing the name. See Introduction on date. The. relief is from the Hall of Columns at Persepolis.

EZRA READING THE LAW   See I Esdras 8:25 ff. From the later building of the third-century A.D. Dura-Europos synagogue, second stage, Wing Panel III. See Carl Kraeling, *The Synagogue*, The Excavations at Dura-Europos, Final Report VIII, Part I, Yale University Press, 1956. While there have been other identifications of the figure, Kraeling's appears to be the most reasonable.

WILD BOAR Gold figurine of wild boar from a tomb near Ordzhonikidze in the Dnepropetrovak region in southern Russia, dating between the fourth and third centuries B.C. See II Esdras 15:30.

ROMAN EAGLE The symbol of Rome. See II Esdras 12.

AURELIAN   Coin in the British Museum, third century A.D. See COMMENT on
Section III, specifically on II Esdras 15.

ZENOBIA   Coin in the British Museum, third century A.D. See COMMENT on Section III, specifically on II Esdras 15.

thoughts of my mind. Lit. "thoughts of my heart," the heart being the seat of understanding.

22. *I recovered.* Lit. "my soul recovered." See first NOTE on 5:14.

spirit of understanding. Cf. Heb. *rwḥ tbwnh* (Exod 31:3; 35:31; LXX has *pneuma suneseōs*); *rwh bynh* in Isa 11:2. For significance see Paul Volz, *Der Geist Gottes u. verwandten Erscheinungen im Alten Testament u. im anschliessenden Judentum* (Tübingen: Mohr, 1910), pp. 21 f.; TWNT, VI, 382 ff. (for Qumran and Apocrypha) and Bousset, p. 396.

23. *vine.* The figure of Israel as a vine or vineyard occurs six times in Pseudo-Philo. Cf. Ps 80:9 ff.; Isa 5:1–7 (figure of Israel as vineyard); 27:2 ff.; Jer 2:21a; Hosea 10:1; 14:7. III Bar 1:2 refers to the land as "thy vineyard." Cf. II Bar 36.

24. *an insignificant one.* This is a difficult passage and the rendering is by no means certain. The land is *not* insignificant so far as quality is concerned but rather as to size and tradition as over against the land of Mesopotamia and the Nile valley — the same idea here, in a broader sense, as reflected in Micah 5:2. Box has "planting-ground," Violet, "Garten" (garden), Gunkel "Pflanzgrube" (a trench for planting).

lily. Cf. Hosea 14:5; Song of Songs 2:1, 2; Midrash on Song of Songs 2:1b. Violet thinks a line referring to the olive has fallen out because our verse is based on the Hosea verse. See further Volz, pp. 107 f.

25. *deeps of the sea.* Cf. 1QH 3:32 *mḥšby thwm*. Expression does not occur in OT in sense of *tᵉhōmōth yām;* but cf. *mṣlwt ym*, "depths of the sea," in Micah 7:19; Ps 68:23. Matt 18:6 *en tō pelagei tēs thalassēs*, "in the depths of the sea," as a number of times in classical Greek; cf. Isa 51:10.

filled up. Cf. Addition to Esther 1:10; II Bar 36:3 f.

brook. Cf. Isa 8:6; Song of Songs 4:15. On 25a cf. Ezek 47:1–12; Sir 24: 30 f.; Ode Sol 6:7 ff.

Zion. Cf. Ps 132:13.

26. *dove.* Frequent in Song of Songs which was interpreted allegorically (2:14; 5:2). Cf. Midrash Rabba on Song of Songs 1:15; 4:1. See also II Esd 2:15.

sheep. Cf. Pss 74:1; 79:13; 80:2, 23; I Enoch 85–90.

27. *acquired . . . one people.* Cf. Gen 17:4; Pss 105:6; 106:5; Isa 43:20; I Chron 16:13; Sir 46:1. On the idea of a select people see Exod 19:5; Deut 7:6; I Peter 2:9; etc.; II Bar 48:20.

a law. Cf. Pss 12:6; 18:30; Deut 4:8; Rom 1:32a; 2:15. All nations had law (II Bar 77:3) but Israel's was the best. Late Wisdom writers came to equate wisdom and law and hence it was easier to conceive of the latter's universality while at the same time affirming the superiority of Israel's (cf. Bertholet, *Biblische Theologie*, II, 176 f., 414 f.). This is evident from I Bar 3:36 – 4:1; IV Macc 5:16 ff.; 15:9b; and the *bios nomikos* of 7:15.

28. *shoot.* Cf. 1QH 6:15–16; 8:6, 7, 10, etc.

dispersed. A reference to the dispersion of the Jews (cf. Sib Or 3:271; Jos. *War* 2:16:4[2:398]; 7:3:3).

your only one. For figure cf. *'ḥt hy' l'mh,* "the only one (darling) of her mother"; *yḥyd,* "only," in Gen 22:2, 12, 16; Ps 22:21.

29. Violet, Gunkel, Box, and Oesterley carry over the question of vs. 28 (*utquid*) into this one, but the reading adopted here appears more in harmony with the Latin text elsewhere. Where questions are continued there is usually some interrogative particle. On verse cf. Rom 1:18, 28; Heb 3:10.

30. *chastized . . . hands.* Based on II Sam 24:14; cf. Sir 2:18; Ps Sol 7:3; Jer 10:24; 1QpHab 5:3 ff. As in the Samuel passage, the thought is that the Lord would use pestilence, famine, earthquake or other natural means but avoid the use of the enemy's sword.

31. *on an earlier night.* Not the night immediately preceding but one possibly long past. Cf. Ps 90:4.

32. *Listen . . . teach.* Wisdom appeal underlies the expression (cf. Job 32:10; 33:1, 31; Ps 34:11).

Give attention. Cf. Ps 39:12; Prov 4:1, 20; etc.

I'll tell you more. Cf. the Hebrew construction *ysp 'wd l—,* "add yet to—."

33. *disturbed about Israel.* Cf. Amos 7:2, 5.

love . . . more. Cf. 8:47. A forceful expression of God's incomparable love for his people.

34. *pain.* Cf. Job 16:6; 30:17.

my heart. Lit. "my kidneys" — the seat of emotions and affections (cf. Job 19:27; Pss 16:7; 73:21) which the Lord is said to test (Jer 11:20; 17:10; 20:12). Cf. Jer 15:7 to be rendered "thou didst fill me with concern (or anxiety)." Cf. II Esd 8:16.

comprehend the way. Cf. Rom 11:33; Job 9:10.

direction of his judgment. Cf. Isa 26:8 has "way . . ."; II Bar 44:6; 75:3 ff.

35. *born.* Cf. Jer 20:18.

womb my grave. Job 3:11; 10:18, 19; Jer 20:17. This verse is quoted by Clement of Alexandria *Stromata* 3:16. Cf. II Bar 10:6; Eccles 4:3. Characteristic of psalms of lamentation (Westermann, ZAW 66 [1954], 76, n. 1 [BIBLIO II]).

36. *Count . . . yet come.* Cf. Sir 1:2. Perhaps as some commentators suggest, "days" has fallen out, with Ethiopic. Cf. Georgian "hours." See Job 36:27.

Collect . . . drops. Cf. Sir 1:1, 2; Job 36:27.

withered flowers. Cf. Ezek 17:24.

37. *closed chambers . . . winds shut up in them.* Cf. Job 37:9; I Enoch 41:4; Rev 7:1. Some (Violet and Wellhausen) render spirits for winds with Ethiopic and Ar.[1]. See NOTE on 4:35; cf. 7:95. But references in apocalyptic literature seem to be limited to the repository for the souls of the righteous (cf. however 7:32 below and see discussion by Volz, pp. 134 f.). Storehouses (chambers) of darkness are referred to in 1QS 10:2; of glory in 1QM 10:12; of snow and hail in 1QH 1:12 (cf. Job 38:22).

the picture of a sound. For the ancient world everything was conceived in a corporeal sense; Isa 55:10b the word is conceived as a messenger with a mission to perform. The Virgil passage *saxa sonent vocisque offensa resultat imago* (*Georgics* 4:50) is not quite similar.

38. *habitation is not among men.* Cf. Dan 2:11; III Macc 2:15; I Enoch 14:21; I Tim 6:16.

39. *dull-witted.* Cf. Ps 73:22; Prov 30:2.

40. *my judgment.* I.e. the judgment of the Lord (cf. Dan 7:9, 10; I Enoch 47:3; 100:4; II Esd 7:33); the author has forgotten that the speaker is the angel, not God.

purpose of the love. The vindication of Israel; for the world was created for Israel, according to our author (6:55, 59; 7:11). Cf. Wisd Sol 11:24 ff.

41. *But then.* Heb. *hnh.*

give preference . . . at the end. Cf. Pss Sol 17:50; 18:7; II Esd 6:25; 7:27; 13:16–24; Dan 12:13; Luke 2:29 ff.; Sir 48:11. Those living at the time of the end were always regarded as more fortunate than those who lived before — the latter being the subjects of hope whereas the former were the actual recipients of salvation.

42. *slow . . . fast.* Cf. I Thess 4:15; II Bar 51:13; Barn 6:13. This marks an advance in thought over the old idea noted in preceding verses. Cf. Matt 19:30 and parallels Mark 10:31; Luke 13:30. The doctrine of resurrection put a different construction on things. Note also Eccles 1:11 with a different perspective. 1QpHab 7:2 God told his prophets what would happen to the last generation but not when the end would come (cf. Mark 13:32). The last age may be prolonged (1QpHab 7:12), for all his times come to the end designated for them (cf. 1QS 4:17; CD 1:12). The Qumran documents are vitally concerned about the end of days (the expression occurs about a dozen times).

43. *more quickly.* The day cannot come prematurely. Jesus warned his disciples against possible deception regarding signs of the end (Mark 13, and parallels; II Peter 3:9).

44. *more rapidly than the Creator.* He works according to a time plan.

45. Harks back to vs. 42. Divine judgment is there declared to occur for all at the same time, while in vs. 44 it is said that the world cannot contain all the creations at the same time.

alive at the same time. Presupposes the resurrection. Cf. 7:32; 14:35; II Bar 42:7; 50:2.

50. *mother . . . still young.* Another form of the question posed in 4:33, 45.

52. *smaller of stature.* The biblical view was that the aboriginals were giants (cf. Gen 6:4; Num 13:33; Amos 2:9). Philo (*Creation* 49) was of the same opinion. Cf. T. H. Gaster, *Myth, Legend, and Custom in the Old Testament* (New York: Harper, 1969), pp. 311 and 403, n. 17. The Babylonian Theodicy has the opposite view: "The first child is born a weakling / But the second is called an heroic warrior." Lambert, *Babylonian Wisdom Literature,* pp. 86–87.

55. *creation . . . old.* The apocalyptists believed the world was already old (4:44 f.; 14:10, 16; II Bar 85:10) as did Lucretius *de rerum natura* II. 11.1150 f.

56. going to visit. With Syriac (participle), the reference being to judgment at the approaching end of the present age.

6:1. *In the beginning.* Cf. 3:4; Prov 8:23 ff.; Ps 90:2; I Enoch 48:6b; 60:11–12; II Bar 48:7–10. On entire passage (vss. 1–6) see II Bar 59:5–12; *Enuma Elish* 1:1 ff. For a discussion of the passage in the light of Babylonian mythology, cf. Gunkel, *Schöpfung und Chaos,* pp. 401, 419.

the terrestrial world (*terreni orbis*). Cf. the *terra et orbis* of Ps 89:2 (90:2) in Vulgate and *'prwt tbl* of Prov 8:26. R. B. Y. Scott, *Proverbs · Ecclesiastes,* AB, vol. 18, has "soil of earth" in loco.

portals of the world. Gunkel (APAT) renders "before the portals of heaven stood." He bases his interpretation on 3:18; 8:20; and I Enoch 34, 35. If the Hebrew were available the reference could be traced more certainly. Cf. 1QH 6:31 *š'ry 'wlm,* "eternal gates"; II Sam 22:16; Ps 18:16 *msdwt tbl,* "the foundations of the world."

the wind-blasts. Cf. 13:2, 10 (Ar²); II Bar 59:5; I Enoch 34; Rev 7:1; Enuma Elish 4:42 ff. On the whole of 6:1–6 see I Enoch 17.

2. *crashes of thunder.* Exod 19:16; Rev 4:5; Pss 77:18; 104:7; also in Ugaritic literature (cf. UT, 51:v:70) and figure of Baal hurling his thunderbolt (*Der alte Orient* 33, Heft 1/2 [1933], plate 2).

foundations of paradise. Whether reference is to heavenly or earthly paradise, see Andrae, *Die Welt des Orients* I (1947–52), 485–94, since mythological elements are involved in any case. For conception in later Judaism see Volz, pp. 374 ff. Cf. 4:7; *et alia.*

3. *beauty of the flowers.* No exact parallel but cf. Sir 43:9 and II Esd 6:44. Gunkel thinks the reference is to the flowers of the heavenly paradise which were originally the stars.

forces of motion. Unclear, and probably not so abstract as translation makes it appear. Cf. *mzlwt* of II Kings 23:5; *ai dunameis tōn ouranōn,* "the powers of the heavens," of Matt 24:29 and *ē exousia tou aeros,* "the power of the air" of Eph 2:2; I Enoch 80:7. The Syriac suggests earthquakes but doubtful here.

innumerable hosts of angels. Cf. II Thess 1:7; Heb 12:22; Rev 5:11; 1QM 7:6; 12:1, 8; etc.; Job 25:3; for discussion of intermediaries see Bertholet, *Biblische Theologie,* pp. 374 ff.

4. *heights of the air.* Cf. 4:21; *enuma eliš . . . šamāmu,* "when from above . . . the heavens," the first line of the Babylonian Creation epic.

measures of the firmaments were defined. Lit. "were named"; cf. the immediately preceding reference. Cf. further 6:41; Sir 1:3; Wisd Sol 11:20. The firmaments were the demarcations of the heavens, some of which are referred to in II Enoch 21:6; 22:1.

Zion . . . footstool. Isa 66:1 "the earth is my footstool." Cf. Pss 99:5; 132:7; I Chron 28:2; Lam 2:1; Makkoth 24b.

5. *existing years.* I.e. time.

tricks . . . thwarted. God had set limits to the cunning devices of sinners.

stored up faith were sealed. Rev 7:4 expresses the same idea. The insertion of "merits" in some texts points to this interpretation since it clearly indicates the storing up of merits accruing from obedience to the law (cf. 7:35, 114).

6. *gave thought [to it]*. I.e. the question posed in 5:56. Commentators point out that the thought of Creation was superior to the word that brought it about. Cf. also 1QS 3:15.

end . . . through me and not . . . another. Some think oriental versions omitted this clause for dogmatic reasons. But perhaps nothing more is meant than is expressed in Barn 6:13, "Then I make the last like the first," i.e. the outworkings will conform to the plan. Pseudo-Philo (11:2) speaks of an ever-lasting law given to Moses "whereby I will judge the world." For end-time cf. 1QpHab 7; I Peter 1:20. This is a Jewish view; in Christianity judgment has been committed to the son (John 5:22).

7. *the division of the times*. The Ethiopic has "signs" of the times (cf. Matt 16:3; 24:3). Really what Ezra has in mind is the interval between the beginning and the end, as may be seen from the sequel to the verse.

8. *From Abraham to Isaac*. I.e. as there was no interval or break from Abraham to Jacob and Esau so there will be none between the beginning and end-times. The two are connected, as the Syriac recognized. (Cf. Pseudo-Philo 19:13).

Jacob and Esau. Represent the two ages, the future and that of this world. Both were intimately related from the beginning, for Jacob held fast to the heel of Esau; see Weber, p. 401, for quotation from the Yalḳuṭ on Gen 25, 26. (The Yalḳuṭ is an anthology of Haggadic Midrashim by Machir b. Abba Mari of uncertain date, probably late in the Middle Ages.)

9. *end . . . beginning*. Note again the emphasis on continuity between the two ages. See Hilgenfeld, *Die jüdische Apokalyptik,* p. 195, for possible historical reference.

10. *Do not bother . . . to inquire*. Stresses the author's conception of the inconsequence of the interval, which really doesn't exist as Ar.[1] suggests. See vs. 34 *noli festinare,* "do not hasten," i.e. don't bother about former happenings. But cf. I Enoch 60:10.

12. *your signs*. Cf. 5:56 a. The signs of the end just related were regarded as but a portion of those available if the following passage is more than a parallel to 5:56 – 6:10. Cf. Barn 6:13.

13. *Get up*. Cf. Num 23:18; Judg 3:20; Ezek 2:1; Dan 7:4; 10:11. A common expression.

an exceedingly loud voice. Cf. Exod 19:16; Ezek 3:12; Dan 10:6; Rev 19:6. Associated with apocalyptic events. I Thess 4:16 associates the coming of the Lord with a shout.

14. *convulsed*. One of the phenomena associated with the divine theophany is the convulsing of the earth (II Sam 22:8; Pss 18:7; 68:8; Isa 13:13; Joel 3:16).

15. *terrified*. Cf. Matt 24:6 for warning about things to come so that the faithful may not be alarmed when the time comes for the end. Cf. Daniel for references to end time.

foundations of the earth. Isa 24:18; Ps 82:5.

16. *change.* See Pseudo-Philo 28:9.

17. *a voice.* The heavenly voice was heard on significant occasions — cf. Matt 3:17; 17:5; Rev 6:6.

sound of many waters. Cf. Isa 17:13; Jer 51:16, 55; Ps 65:7, etc. The writer implies that the voice is that of God but does not say so directly because of religious scruples.

18. *the days are approaching.* Cf. Jer 7:32; Luke 17:22; 21:6.

to judge. Lit. "to visit" in the sense of coming to judge. Cf. Pseudo-Philo 19:13.

19. *to avenge.* Lit. "to investigate with idea of taking vengeance upon sinners." Cf. 1QS 10:19; 1QM 7:5; and day of judgment often in Qumran.

the humiliation of Zion. Cf. II Bar 20:2 where it is said that Zion has been taken away so that the day of judgment may come more speedily. See further Matt 24:2, 3; Luke 21:20–28.

20. *to pass away.* Latin *pertransire,* used fifteen times, has the double meaning of passing straight through and of passing away.

books . . . opened. Records were thought to be kept of the deeds of men (Rev 20:12; I Enoch 89:61–64). These were the books opened at the time of judgment (Dan 7:10; Rev 20:12; 5:2; I Enoch 47:3; 90:20; II Bar 24:1; Asc Isa 9:21, 22; Test Abraham 10:11). But perhaps Gunkel is right in regarding the one referred to here as the book of plagues whose very opening signaled the beginning of their operation. Cf. Schrader, *Keilinschriften,* pp. 404 f.

before the firmament. May be a surrogate for the heavenly host. In that case the "all" would refer to them. If, however, the firmament is a giant screen on which the content is flashed (as Gunkel thinks) it would involve all people.

21. *Year-old infants.* Cf. Jub 23:25 f. A continuation of prodigies listed in 5:4 ff. See Gospel of Thomas, 81:5–10.

22. *Sown fields.* Lit. "sown places." Cf. I Enoch 80:2; Sib Or 3:542.

23. *trumpet will resound.* Cf. Isa 27:13; Matt 24:31; I Cor 15:5; I Thess 4:16; Apoc Abraham 31. Sometimes used to summon for celebration (Ps Sol 11:1); here for alarm. Often in 1QM.

24. *springs will cease.* Lit. "arteries, or courses, of springs, or fountains." Cf. Test Levi 4:1; Ass Mos 10:6; Ps Sol 17:21.

25. *escaped.* Lit. "left over," "remain." Cf. I Thess 4:15, 17; Mark 13:13.

be saved. Cf. 7:27; 9:7, 8; 13:23; I Enoch 99:10.

see my salvation. Cf. Ps 98:3; Isa 52:10; Luke 2:30.

end . . . world. See H. Kosmala in *Annual of the Swedish Theological Institute,* II (Leiden: Brill, 1963), 27–37.

26. *persons.* Lit. "men."

admitted. Lit. "taken up."

who have not tasted death. The reference is to Enoch and Elijah in particular (cf. Sir 44:16; Wisd Sol 4:10 f.). Ezra is promised separation from sinners to live with "my Son" (II Esd 14:9). Josephus reports a legend to the effect that Moses was taken without death (*Antiq.* 4:326); it may be inferred also from the Assumption of Moses. For further discussion on the subject see Bousset, p. 233.

appear. Reading passive for active, *yēra'u* for *yir'u.*

converted to a different spirit. Cf. Mal 4:6[3:23H]; Ezek 11:19; 36:26 f.

27. Cf. I Enoch 5:9; Rom 2:7 on this and next verse.

evil . . . destroyed. Cf. I Enoch 69:29.

28. *truth . . . exposed.* Cf. II Enoch 63:4 which has to do with the abolition of falsehood.

29. *place where I was standing.* Construction is Hebrew, lit. "the place upon which I was standing upon it." Cf. III Bar 6:13; Acts 4:31.

31. *seven days.* Seven days' fast occurs before second, third, fourth, and sixth visions.

32. *prayer.* Lit. "voice."

virtue. Lit. "chastity," perhaps referring to asceticism.

34. *taken by surprise.* Lit. "make haste."

COMMENT

[Introduction, 5:20–22] The seven days of flagellation only served to intensify the concern of Ezra. His thoughts became even more perplexed, but he composed himself enough to resume his discourses with the Lord.

[Prayer complaint to the Most High and the angel's response, 5:23–40. The prayer, 23–30] Like the prayer address in ch. 3, this one too is in the form of a national lament and assumes the character of accusation of God. From the whole realm of trees he has selected only the humble vine; from the lands of the earth, only a small, insignificant parcel; from the innumerable flowers of the world, only the lily; from the immeasurable sea, only a small brook of water; from all the cities man has built, Zion alone; from the bird kingdom, only the dove; from the bovine kingdom, only a sheep; from the countless peoples of the world, only one people to whom he entrusted a law when he called them — a law recognized by all others. In view of what appeared to the writer as an unmistakable purpose, why the exile now suffered by this select people? Why has the shoot-root been dispersed among the many?[1] That is, perhaps, the clue to the form of the passage. Verses 23–27 spell out what Israel originally believed its status to be; vss. 28–30 inquire about what has gone wrong. Almost all of the national lament characteristics mentioned by Gunkel[2] appear here: the address begins with a vocative (note double *dominator domine*), has a political aspect, and is an implicit prayer to take note of and resolve the misfortune, etc. Of particular import is the "why" of

---

[1] Could this be a reference to both the Isaianic conception of the shoot-root (11:1) and the servant mission of Isa 49:6 which had somehow miscarried? The only one, the chosen one, had indeed been dispersed among the many but the many rejected him, resisted the commandments, and crushed those who believed in the Lord's covenants. This aspect of messianism had not worked in the author's view. A lot more may be implied here than meets the eye.

[2] Hermann Gunkel and Joachim Begrich, *Einleitung in die Psalmen* (Göttingen: Vandenhoeck & Ruprecht, 1933), pp. 117–39.

vs. 28 which represents the groping of one who is at a loss as to what to make of the situation and expresses the desire to find his way. The author recognizes that misfortune is due to alienation from God.[3]

[The response, 31–40] In response to the observation of the seer, the archangel appears again in an endeavor to lead him to a recognition of his lack of understanding of the profound problem with which the Lord was wrestling. He cannot be more deeply troubled about Israel than the Lord nor can he, a mere human, love Israel more than the Creator does. But as every prophet before him, Ezra confesses to inner pain and anguish whenever he tries to discern the way of the Lord or the direction of his judgment. If he cannot make sense out of it all, why was he born to see nothing but misfortune for God's people? The angelic riddles appear to be patterned after the Wisdom style and represent a series of impossibles for man. Certain things cannot be materialized, much less understood in those terms. The seer acknowledges as much in vs. 38. The whole passage ends on a pessimistic note. Since he is limited to the human level, he cannot comprehend the ways of the Eternal, he cannot fathom the judgment of God nor the design of the love he promised to Israel.[4]

[Why successive generations were created, 5:41–55. The divine plan is for successive generations, 41–47] The dialogue goes on with the main question still being that of judgment at the end of the age. The author, not sure when the end will come and, in view of the preference given to those alive then, wonders what will happen to those who lived before him, to those of his own generation and those of future generations. The reply of the angel is to the effect that one group will not enjoy advantage over another by virtue of the accident of time.[5] The concept of resurrection had actually accorded precedence to earlier generations — those who died before — as may be seen from the Thessalonian passage cited above in NOTE on vs. 42. Hence the old idea voiced in vs. 41 was superseded by the concept set forth in vs. 42. All pious individuals will participate in salvation, which is also the New Testament view. The exigencies of the time may be responsible for pressing the issue in the following verses. Why was not the creation a once-for-all affair so that judgment might come more quickly, that is, without the intervention of time which certainly favors those alive at the moment and discriminates against those who have been put off over a long period of time? The answer: successive generations are a concession to space and time with their limitations. Just as the womb cannot, due to natural limitations, bear ten children at one impregnation, so all the generations of mankind cannot be produced at the same time and for the same reason.

[The earth is like a womb, engendering one generation after another — each smaller and weaker, 5:48–55] Here the conversation shifts from the angel to God himself, who observes that he has made the earth like a womb. Uppermost in the mind of the seer is still the proximity of the end when judgment

---

[3] Cf. Westermann, ZAW 66 (1954), 52 f.
[4] Harnisch, pp. 38 f.
[5] Harnisch, pp. 293 f.; Bousset, pp. 271 f.; Volz, pp. 131–33.

will take place. In the early days, generations were stronger, more virile and larger in stature; future generations will continue the diminution process.[6] As Walther Eichrodt has pointed out, this conception is embodied already in the P genealogy of Gen 5.[7] The question as to whether "our mother" is still young or approaching old age is answered by the observation "the creation is already old and the vigor of her youth already past." Since that is the case, Ezra proceeds to inquire as to the agent of the parousia.

[The end will come through God alone, 5:56 – 6:6] Here God is addressed directly by the seer and he himself responds directly rather than through the intermediary angel. Perhaps the very form of the passage is meant to convey a message as to the directness which characterizes the divine relationship with creation. The question "through whom are you going to visit your creation?" sets the stage for the firm declaration of the divine plan that was conceived and will be actualized by God alone and no other. Some scholars regard this as a polemic against the messianism of the Christians, as pointed out in the NOTE on vs. 6. But it may equally well be directed against the elaborate angelology of Judaism.[8] In any event the thought was father to the deed. In this beautiful poem the author joins the pre-existent with the end-time so that the intervening history doesn't count for much.[9] The important thing is when judgment will come and through whom. The answer is — in the end-time and through God alone. The course that was determined before history will be actualized at history's end. Of particular interest is the fourteen line structure (i.e. 7+7) which is frequently employed in II Esdras.[10] Seven is the characteristic number in apocalyptic literature (see Introduction).

[The division of the times, 6:7–10] This little allegory of the heel and the hand apparently reflects the view current in the author's time and circle with respect to the proximity of the beginning and end-times. It answers the implied conception of an interval of time between them (7b). As Gunkel[11] notes, "the 'wisdom' of the mystery is that this aeon with the hegemony of Esau=Rome is concluded and that of the hegemony of Jacob=Israel is beginning and that Israel's hegemony will follow on the heels of Rome without a break." Accordingly, the time of Israel's rule is regarded as the beginning of the coming age,

---

[6] Multiple births are now relatively frequent. There are numerous instances of the birth of triplets, quadruplets, and quintuplets. Recently a woman in Australia gave birth to nine children, none of whom survived. There must have been multiple births in antiquity, though traditions about them, except for twins, are lacking. Perhaps they did not persist because multiple births beyond twins failed to survive.

[7] Theology of the Old Testament, II (Philadelphia: Westminster, 1967), 401, esp. n. 1. Genesis — see E. A. Speiser, AB, vol. 1, p. XXII.

[8] So also Bousset, p. 331; Volz, p. 237.

[9] Cf. Frost, "Apocalyptic and History," in Bible in Modern Scholarship, ed. Hyatt, pp. 108 f., 111. II Esdras is occupied with the age of the world — it is approaching old age — and hence the concern about time, especially messianic time. A. J. Heschel has pointed to the persistent fear of old age as "the fear of time" (The Christian Ministry 2, no. 2 [Chicago: Christian Century Foundation, 1971], 34). Perhaps the author's fear is due less to personal morbidity than to being swept away somewhat unjustly by it.

[10] Cf. Keulers, pp. 21, n. 1, and 164.

[11] APAT, II, 365. For the equation of Esau-Edom with Rome see Schürer, III, 236.

contrary to 7:29, 31 where the rule of "my son" marks the conclusion of this age. Such vacillation occurs elsewhere, and indicates that this "messianic" age represents a transition period and therefore admits a dual judgment. The remarkable feature about this little pericope is its view of history *sub specie aeternitatis*.[12] Here the two aeons or ages are coupled together, though they may still be different.[13] The result is the virtual disappearance of history — the interval between the ages. Hence Ezra is told not to inquire about it further.

[Request for and revelation of signs of the end-time, 6:11–28. Introduction, 11–12] The introduction begins in much the same way as that in 5:56 ff. Many commentators believe this passage is parallel to 5:56–6:13a, since it also deals with signs of the end. But the two sections are not duplicates because the signs are different and may represent the author's conflation of two traditions.

[Revelation of the signs, 6:13–24] In response to the seer's request for the last of the signs, he is exhorted to give special attention to what is about to be revealed. He will hear a very loud voice accompanied by the convulsion of the place upon which he stands. Nevertheless he must not be afraid, for the voice is announcing the end[14] for which the foundations of the earth have been prepared and will understand. The message is for them; they will shudder and quake because their end means change. Then the interlocutor changes from the interpreting angel to "a voice like the sound of many waters." The voice is that of the Lord himself. In the manner of the prophets, the voice announces the coming days of judgment when the inhabitants of the earth (note universalism) will be subject to his decision. He will bring vengeance upon those who have dealt unjustly with their fellow men. A significant sign is the humiliation of Zion, perhaps somewhat like that mentioned in Matt 24:15 ff. Seven signs will be given to indicate that the time has arrived. (1) The books recording the names and deeds of those to be judged will be opened in the presence of the heavenly host and, possibly, cast on the screen of the firmament for all others to see. (2) Infant prodigies will appear. (3) Produce of the fertile fields will disappear, (4) full storehouses will suddenly be depleted, and (5) the trumpet summons will resound. (6) Friends will attack one another like enemies so that the land will be in terror, and (7) hitherto unfailing springs will cease to run for three hours. This is the only dating attempt but the interpretation is uncertain. I Enoch uses the hour terminology to describe the aeon or age; Gunkel interprets literally.

[The state of those who survive: the saved, 6:25–28] Having been given the signs that will mark the inauguration of the end, the author now directs his attention to the persons involved. Apparently circumstances connected with

---

[12] See Frost's article referred to in fn. 9.
[13] Cf. Harnisch, pp. 93 ff., and n. 2, pp. 301 f. For the conception of the messianic time situation at Qumran see Nötscher, *Zur theologischen Terminologie der Qumran-Texte*, pp. 164–69. For discussion of Esau-Rome see Bousset, p. 218.
[14] For a convenient summary of the characteristic of the end as viewed by apocalyptists see Volz, par. 31, pp. 173–88, and the theology underlying the judgment at the end see Bousset, pp. 242–86. On the conception of the two ages cf. Harnisch, pp. 89 ff.

the appearance of the signs will take their toll so that only those who have survived "all these things" will experience the Lord's salvation and see the end of the world. Among the saved will be those "who have been admitted" or taken up (to heaven) without having passed through the normal gate of death. The concatenation of events will work a mighty change upon the minds of earth's inhabitants so that they will "be converted to a different spirit." As a result, heavenly conditions of life will prevail. Three points developed here are of special interest. First, there is the conversion to a different spirit, a subject that occupied the rabbis. They regarded it as the main proof that in the messianic age God will abolish all evil, that is, the desire for doing evil (the *yṣr hr'*); that is the second point to be observed.[15] The third point is of great importance; it is the flourishing of faith. There is a question as to whether *fides* should here be rendered "faith" or "faithfulness." Volz[16] has distinguished four main types of faith: (1) the common monotheistic faith as over against paganism, (2) eschatological faith, (3) ethical faith, and (4) religious faith (the latter two types are often inseparable). The Hebrew term here may have been *'mwnh,* the Greek *pistis* which includes both faith and faithfulness. It is this double meaning which the translation attempts to convey. Certainly the context indicates that *fides* takes in more than what is involved in the Christian dogmatic understanding of the term (cf. also II Esd 13:23; 9:7).[17] The writer certainly has in mind not only confidence, trust and belief in God but also devotion, loyalty, and faithfulness as the positive side of life in the new age.

[Advice concerning things to come — warning against speculation, 6:29–34] While the Lord was speaking, the earth began to quake. Then the interpreting angel reappeared with further instructions. Ezra is urged to pray and fast seven days more after which he will receive even more astounding revelations. He has been observed by the Most High and found worthy to receive them. In the meantime he is warned not to worry too much about the evil or the happenings of former times lest he be misled and be totally unprepared for the last times and what they may bring.

[15] See Volz, pp. 292 f., and Harnisch, pp. 127 f.
[16] Volz, pp. 317 f.
[17] Bousset, pp. 195 f.

THE THIRD VISION (6:35 – 9:25)

Introduction — after the seven days' fast

6 35 Now after this[a] I wept again[b] and fasted for seven days [c]as [I had done] earlier, so as to complete the three weeks prescribed for me[c]. 36 [d]Then on the eighth night[d] when my heart was again dis-

[a] C, M add *mox,* "soon."
[b] Omitted by M. Armenian omits "I wept again."
[c-c] Omitted by Armenian. Ar.[1] adds at end of verse *finitae erant,* "were completed."
[d-d] Omitted by Armenian.

quieted within me, I began to address the Most High directly. 37 *My spirit was intensely excited and my mind uneasy*.

Question: Why has Israel become the prey of other nations if it was for its sake that the world was created?

38 I said, O Lord, you have indeed spoken from the beginning of creation; on the first day you said: "Let heaven and earth be made" and your word accomplished the work*. 39 At that time, a wind was blowing fiercely, *darkness and silence were everywhere*, and the sound of man's voice was not yet *before you*. 40 Then you directed *a ray of light* to *go forth* from your treasury so that your works could be seen. 41 On the second day* you created the spirit of the firmament and commanded it to separate and make *a division between the waters* that a part might recede above and a part remain below. 42 On the third day you commanded the waters to be collected in *the seventh part* of the earth, but six parts you made dry and preserved that some of them might serve before you for sowing and cultivating. 43 So your word went out and the work was done forthwith. 44 For immediately there was

An immeasurable* quantity of fruit
    appetizing to the most varied tastes,
And inimitably colored flowers*
    with scents of indescribable fragrance.

These things were made on the third day. 45 On the fourth day you commanded the splendor of the sun to be made, the light of the moon, and the order of the stars; 46 and you commanded them to serve man *yet to be formed*. 47 On the fifth day you issued orders

e-e Omitted by Armenian.
f Ar.[1] adds "and governed everything that was made"; Ar.[2] "for you ordered everything."
g-g Syriac *ḥšwk' mḥp' wštq' dql'*, "darkness covered [it] and silence of sound." Armenian omits "a wind was blowing" and the last clause.
h-h Omitted by Syriac, Ethiopic, Ar.[1,2]; Ar.[2] adds "because man was not yet created."
i-i With Syriac *zhr' dnwhr'*, "radiance of light"; Latin *lumen aliquod luminis* "some light of light."
j-j Reading *proferre* with C, M for passive *proferri* of S, A.
k Omits *iterum*, "again" with S, A; Bensly follows C, M.
l-l Syriac *pwršn' byt my' lmy'*, "division between the waters and of the waters."
m-m Syriac *lḥd' mn šb' mnwth*, "one of the seven parts."
n With Syriac *dl' mnyn'*; Latin *immensus*, "immense."
o Syriac adds *w'yln' dbḥzwhwn l' mtpḥmyn*, "and trees of incalculable variety"; Ar.[1], Ethiopic, Armenian, and Georgian all have a reference to trees described differently.
p-p Omitted by Armenian. Syriac (*mnk*) and some other versions add "by you."

to the seventh part where the water was collected that it should produce living creatures, birds and fish; 48 and so it was that the mute
and lifeless water, *as it was commanded*, produced living creatures
for which the nations may extoll your wonderful works. 49 Then you
preserved two living creatures'; you named the one Behemoth and the
other you called Leviathan. 50 You separated* the one from the other
because the' seventh part, where the water was collected, was unable
to contain [both of] them. 51 You gave to Behemoth the one part,
which was dried up on the third day, to live in [and] where there are
a thousand mountains. 52 But to Leviathan you gave "the moist
seventh part". You kept them "to be consumed" by whomever you
wish and when you wish. 53 But on the sixth day you commanded the
earth to bring forth before you cattle, wild animals" and reptiles".
54 Over them you [placed] Adam whom you had put in charge of all
the works which you had created'; and from him all of us whom you
chose as a people are descended. 55 I have spoken about all these
things before you, Lord, because you said that you created *the firstborn world* for us. 56 As for the rest of nations sprung from Adam,
you declared them to be as nothing, like spittle, and you have likened
their profusion to drippings from a bucket. 57 Now, then, O Lord,
these nations that are reckoned as nothing bear rule over us and
devour" us, 58 while we, your people whom you have called [your]
firstborn, [your] only begotten, [your] confidant', [your] dearly
beloved, have been delivered into their hands. 59 So if the world was
created for us, why do we not enjoy possession of the heritage of our
world? How long will this continue?

Response to the question by the interpreting angel

7 1 Now' when I had finished speaking these words, the angel who
had been sent to me "on previous nights" was sent to me [again].

q–q Omitted by all but Latin version.
r Syriac adds *dbryt*, "which you made"; so also Ethiopic.
s Syriac adds *'nyn*, "them."   t Syriac adds *rṭybt*, "moist."
u–u Syriac *ḥd' min*, "one of — the seven moist parts."   v–v Syriac *m'kwlt*, "food."
w Ethiopic adds "of the field."
x Ethiopic "winged creatures of the sky"; Ar.¹ omits.
y Syriac adds *mn qdym*, "from before."
z–z Syriac *l'lm' hn'*, "this world"; so also Georgian; Ar.¹ "first world."
a Syriac *dyšyn*, "trample"; so also Ethiopic, Ar.¹.   b Syriac *qryb'*, "kin."
c Omitted by C, M.
d–d Ethiopic "preceding night"; Armenian "who had spoken before with me." Omitted
by Ar.¹.

2 He said to me: Get up, Ezra, and listen to the words that I have come to speak to you[e]. 3 So I said, Speak my lord. Then he said to me: If[f] a sea is located in a spacious place, broad[g] and limitless, 4 but the entrance[h] to it is[i] confined to a narrow space like a river, 5 how can one[j], seriously desiring to get to the sea to see it or [k]to sail it[k], reach the broad [space] except by passing through the narrow [space]? 6 Again[l], If a city is built, located on an open plain, and is full of all good things, 7 but the road[m] to it is narrow and precariously[n] located because there is a fire on the right (side) and deep water on the left, 8 and there is but a single narrow path between them, that is between the fire and the water, so narrow that it could accommodate the footsteps[o] of only one man [at a time] — 9 if that city has been bequeathed to a man, how can the heir claim his inheritance if he does not traverse the dangerous [path] [p]set before him[p]? 10 I said, Yes[q], Lord. He said to me: That too is Israel's lot[r]. 11 For I did make the world for their sakes and when Adam transgressed my orders what was made was judged. 12 The ways[s] of this world have been made narrow, painful and difficult; [t]they are few and evil[t], full of perils and fraught with great hardships, 13 but the [u]ways of[u] the greater[v] world are spacious and secure and produce the fruit of immortality. 14 If, therefore, those alive do not really enter [through] these narrow and vain things they will be unable to obtain the things stored up [for them].

[e] Armenian adds "and I got up and stood."
[f] Reading with Syriac ('n), Armenian and Georgian.
[g] Reading with Syriac (pty' for pt'); most Latin texts have altum, "deep."
[h] Ethiopic has "way" which may be right.
[i] Latin erit, "will be" but context requires est, "is."
[j] All versions have some form of "if," omitted here for smoothness.
[k-k] dominari, lit. "master"; but, as Gunkel (in loco) points out, probably a mistaken reading of lirdot, "to rule over" for liredet, "to go down." For meaning see Ps 107:23. Ar.[g] omits "to see . . . sail it."
[l] Latin item aliud, "another thing." Syriac šm' twb mdm 'ḥrn, "hear again another thing."
[m] Latin introitus, lit. "entrance"; Ar.[1] adds via (way) introitus.
[n] Syriac brwm', "high." Cf. the bmwrd, "steep place," in Micah 1:4.
[o] Plural with C; all other MSS and versions have singular.
[p p] Ethiopic "rough," "uneven"; Georgian "narrow and terrible," both modifying "path."
[q] Latin sic, "so."   [r] Latin pars, "part," "share"; Syriac mnth, "its lot."
[s] With Ethiopic and Ar.[1]; others have introitus, "entrances," perhaps a misreading of Greek eisodoi for odoi, "ways."
[t-t] Latin text is doubtful; Syriac wmlyn tnḥt' w'ml', "and full of pain and hardship."
[u-u] So with Ethiopic "ways"; text has introitus, "entrances."
[v] Syriac 'tyd, "future."

15 Why then do you agitate yourself, *w*although you are perishable*w*?

Why do you torment yourself, *x*although you are mortal*x*?

16 Why don't you think about what is to come, rather than what now is?

Question and answer on lot of the righteous and the wicked

17 I responded as follows: Lord, Lord, now you have decreed in your law that the just will inherit these things but that the wicked will perish. 18 The just, therefore, can*y* bear with the narrow [contingencies] because they have hope for the spacious [circumstances] but those who have behaved wickedly*z* endure the narrow [contingencies] and yet will not see the spacious [circumstances]. 19 He said to me,

You are not *a*a judge*a* superior *b*to God*b*,

nor more discriminating than the Most High.

20 *c*Let the many who exist perish rather than that the law of God which has been communicated [to them] be slighted*c*. 21 For God has solemnly commanded those coming [into the world] when they came what to do to live and what course to take to avoid being punished. 22 But they remained unconvinced and resisted him;

They invented *d*deceitful ideas*d* for themselves,

23 They contrived devious tricks for themselves,

They even denied the existence of the Most High

And they did not acknowledge*e* his ways;

24 *f*They scorned his law,

They disavowed his covenants*f*,

They had no faith in his commandments,

And they did not accomplish his work.

25 Hence, Ezra,

Emptiness to the empty,

Fullness to the full.

---

w–w Armenian "because you are perishable."

x–x Armenian "because you are mortal."

y Syriac adds *špyr*, "well"; so also Ethiopic.

z Ar.[1,2] and Georgian insert "not," perhaps because of the belief that it was always the just that suffered while the wicked prospered.

a–a Omitted by Syriac.   *b–b* Ethiopic and Georgian have *unicus*, "only one."

c–c Syriac *n'bdwn hkyl sgy' ' 'ylyn d'tw 'l d'tbsy bhwn nmws' d'tsym mny*, "therefore the many who came will perish because the law given by me was disregarded in them."

d–d Syriac *mḥšbt' sryqt'*, "worthless thoughts."

e Syriac *yd'w*, "know," a common expression in Hebrew.

f–f Omitted by M.

The appearance of the messiah with accompanying events

26 For indeed the time *ᵍis comingᵍ* when the signs about which I have told you earlier will occur, *ʰthe invisible city will appearʰ* and the land which is now hidden*ⁱ* will be made manifest, 27 and everyone who has been delivered from the evils mentioned before will see my wonders. 28 For my son Jesus*ʲ*, together with those who are with him, will be revealed and *ᵏhe will bringᵏ* joy for four hundred*ˡ* years to those who have been spared. 29 Then, after those years*ᵐ*, my son Christ will die, as will all *ⁿwho have human breathⁿ*, 30 and the world will return to primordial silence for seven days just as it was at the very beginning; thus nobody will remain.

Judgment of the resurrected

31 Then after the seven days, the world that is not yet awake will be aroused and what is corruptible will pass away.

32 The earth will give up those asleep in it,

The dust will [let go] those who repose in it,

And the storehouses will give up the souls entrusted to them.

33 The Most High will appear on the judgment seat:

ᵒThen the end will comeᵒ,

*ᵖAnd compassion will vanish;

Pity will ceaseᑫ*,

And forbearance will be withdrawn.

34 Only *ʳjudgment will remain;

Truth will stand,

ᵍ–ᵍ Reading *venit*, with C, M; S, A have *veniet*, "will come," with most versions. Georgian follows C, M.

ʰ–ʰ Reading with Armenian, Ar.*¹*, Ethiopic, Latin, lit., "and the bride will appear and the appearing city." The parallelism of the second colon, similar in most versions, requires it.

ⁱ A has *subditur*, "put under"; M has *dicitur*, "spoken about." Syriac omits "land."

ʲ Ar.*¹* *wldy 'lmsyh*, "my child, the messiah." Syriac and other versions have "the messiah," *mšyḥ'*).

ᵏ–ᵏ So with S; A, M, C have "they will be rejoiced."

ˡ Syriac has thirty (Christian interpolation corresponding to the thirty years of Jesus); Ar.*¹* and Georgian have four hundred; Ar.*²* one thousand; Ethiopic and Armenian omit. Latin A has CCC (three hundred) with *trecentis* (three hundred) written above.

ᵐ Omitted by A; Ethiopic and Syriac "after these things."

ⁿ–ⁿ Armenian "who have continued in faith and in patience."

ᵒ–ᵒ With Syriac *wn't' šwlm'*. Cf. Ar.*²*. Omitted by Latin and other versions.

ᵖ Cf. Ar.*¹* for the three following cola.

ᑫ Syriac *wrwḥp' nrḥq*, "and pity will be distant."

ʳ Syriac here *dyny*, "my judgment"; Ar.*¹* "judgment of the Lord."

And faith *regain strength*.
35 Reward[t] will follow,
  And recompense appear;
  "Good deeds" will awake,
*36 *The pit of torment* will appear,
  And evil [ones] will sleep no more.
  And opposite it will be the place of rest;
  The oven of Gehenna will appear,
  And opposite it the paradise of joy.
37 Then the Most High will say to[w] the excited nations:
      Consider[x] and know those whom you denied,
      Or whom you have not served,
      Or whose faithfulness[y] you have spurned.
    38 Look hither and yon:
      Here is joy and repose,
      There is fire and torment.
But these things *he will say* to them on the judgment day: 39 It will
be like this:
      It has neither sun, nor moon, nor stars,
    40 Nor cloud, nor thunder, nor lightning,
      Nor wind, nor water, nor air,
      Nor darkness, nor evening[a], nor morning,
    41 Nor summer, nor spring[b], nor heat,
      Nor winter, nor frost, nor cold,
      Nor hail, nor rain, nor dew,
    42 Nor moon, nor night, nor dawn[c],
      Nor brightness, nor clearness, nor light;

---

s–s Gunkel renders "triumph."
t Latin *opus*, "work," but as Wellhausen plausibly suggests this is likely a Hebraism —
p'lh, "work," "reward"; cf. use in 1QS 4:15, 25; Isa 40:10; Ps 109:20[H].
u–u Plural. Cf. LXX of Tobit 2:14; 12:9; Sir 44:10 has *dikaiosunai*.
* The missing fragment — see Introduction, fn. 3, above — begins here with vs. 36
and continues to vs. 105.
v–v Missing in S; A, C, M, V have *locus*, "place"; here with Syriac *'wb' dtšnyq'*.
w Syriac *lwql*, "against."
x With Syriac *ḥwrw*, a bit stronger than Latin *videre*, "see," "look."
y With C, M, V; Syriac *pwqdnwhy*, "commandments." For Latin *diligentias* see on
3:19.
z–z With Syriac *nmll* (third person); so also Ethiopic and Ar.[1]; Latin *loqueris* (second person).
a *sero* (on adverbial form see Bensly, MF, p. 57). Syriac *rmš*, "evening."
b Syriac *ryš šnt*, "beginning of year."
c *ante lucem*, "before light," for *antelucium*, "dawn"; see Bensly, MF, p. 57, note.
Syriac *'ymm'*, "day."

except for the splendorous brightness of the Most High whereby all will be able to see what was appointed [for them to see]. 43 The time period will be, as it were, a week of years. 44 This is my judgment and its disposition; but to you alone have I revealed these things.

Question: How many are saved, with response

45 I replied: I said then, Lord, and I say now, Fortunate are ᵈthose who are now present and observe the preceptsᵉ ᶠlaid downᶠ by you. 46 But concerning those for whom my prayer was offered, who of those now present is there who has not sinned or who of those bornᵍ is there who has not violated your covenant? 47 Now I see that the world to come will serve to bring joy to the few, but torment to the many. 48 ʰThe evil heart in us has grownʰ,

> That has alienated us from them,
> And has driven us into corruption;
> ⁱIt has brought to our attentionⁱ the ways of death,
> Pointed out to us the paths of perdition,
> And took us far away from life,

and that not merely a few but just about all who were created. 49 He responded to me as follows: Listen to me that I may teach you and ʲset you right againʲ. 50 Because of this the Most High made not one world but two. 51 Inasmuch as you said that the just are not many but few [and that] assuredly the wicked are numerous, ᵏlisten to thisᵏ: 52 ᶫIf you should have just a very few precious stones, ᵐwould you now add to them lead and clayᵐ? 53 Lord, I said, how can that be? 54 He said to me: Moreoverⁿ,

> Inquire of the earth and she will tell you
> Speakᵒ to her and she will enlighten you.

55 You must say to her, you yieldᵖ gold, silver, copper as well as iron,

---

ᵈ Syriac adds *kl*, "all."   ᵉ With Syriac *pwqdn'*.
ᶠ⁻ᶠ Cf. Syriac *mtsymyn*, "fixed," "set," "posited."
ᵍ Ar.¹ adds "of the sons of man," i.e. mortals.
ʰ⁻ʰ Syriac *bn lbk byš'*, "an evil heart is in us." Reading here with Latin, Ethiopic; Ar.¹ "the evil in our hearts"; Ar.² "our heart has fallen into wickedness."
ⁱ⁻ⁱ Reading with Syriac *ḥwyn*.
ʲ⁻ʲ Syriac *wmdryš 'rtyk*, "and I'll set you right again."
ᵏ⁻ᵏ Omitted by Ethiopic and Georgian; Syriac *šm' lwqbl hlyn*, "listen on the other hand to these things."
ᶫ Verse is difficult and rendering here follows Ar.¹ and Armenian in part.
ᵐ⁻ᵐ *'tqn lk 'br' wḥṣp'*, "put for yourself lead and potsherds."
ⁿ For Latin *non hoc solummodo*, "not this only."
ᵒ With Syriac *w'mr lh;* Latin *adulare ei*, "fawn upon her" is used only here in II Esdras. Reminiscent of Hebrew expression of speaking to the heart, *dbr lb*, though the Vulgate does not use *adulare* in translating it.
ᵖ With Syriac *dhb';* Latin *creas*, "produce."

lead and clay*q*; 56 but silver is more abundant than gold, copper than silver, iron than copper, lead than iron and clay than lead. 57 Decide*r*, therefore, for yourself*s* which are more valuable and desirable, *t*what is abundant or what is found [to be] scarce*t*. 58 I said, Lord, Lord, what is plentiful is less valuable, what is rare is more costly. 59 He responded to me as follows: Compare*u* for yourself, now, what you have reflected upon; for he who possesses what is hard to come by rejoices more than he who has what is plentiful. 60 So it is with my promised judgment*v*, because I will rejoice over the few who will be saved inasmuch as they are the ones who confirm*w* my glory now and by whom my name is even now named. 61 I will not lament over the multitude of those who are lost; they are the ones who even now

> Are made like vapor,
> Regarded as smoke;
> *x*Just like flames
they were kindled*x*, blazed up, and have gone out.

Lamentation of Ezra, with response

62 I replied as follows: O earth, what you have given birth to! If reason*y* has been made out of dust just as other creatures, 63 it would have been better if the dust itself had not been born so that reason might not have been produced from it. 64 Nevertheless reason grows up *z*with us*z* and so we are tormented because we are aware of perishing.

> 65 Let the human race lament*a*,
> The beasts of the field rejoice;
> Let all who are born lament*a*,
> Quadrupeds*b* and cattle rejoice.

---

q Syriac *ḥṣpt,* "potter's day."

r Syriac *pḥm,* "compare," "weigh."   *s* Syriac adds *wḥzy,* "and see."

t–t Syriac *sgy't' 'w z'wryt',* "the many or the few."

u Reading *pḥm* with Syriac.

v Reading in part with Syriac *dynh,* "his judgment"; here *dyny,* "my judgment." Latin has *creatura,* "creation," a confusion of Greek *krisis,* "judgment," and *ktisis,* "creation."

w With Syriac *dḥš' tšbwḥty mšrryn,* "who now confirm my glory."

x–x Following Syriac *w'yk šlhbyt' 'tpḥmw.*

y Syriac *md''* according to Ceriani (MS has *mr''* but mistake is easy in Syriac, involving only a misplaced dot). Greek *nous,* Latin *sensus,* "reason," "understanding," "intelligence," etc.

z–z V has *vobiscum,* "with you."

a Syriac has *'bl* for colon 1 and *'l'* for colon 3, both having the same meaning; Latin has same word for both, *lugeo.*

b Syriac *b'yr',* "beasts of burden."

66 They are far better off than we because they do not expect judgment and are unaware of torment*c* or *d*salvation in turn promised
them after death*d*. 67 For what advantage is there to us to *e*be kept
alive*e* only to *f*be severely tormented*f*? 68 All who are born

> are entangled*g* in iniquities,
> full of sins,
> and laden with transgressions.

69 So, if after death we should not come into judgment, *h*it might
have been much better for us*h*. 70 He replied to me as follows: When
the Most High made the world and Adam and all his descendants,
he first ordained judgment *i*and matters pertaining to judgment*i*.
71 Now, therefore, *j*take cognizance of*j* your own words! You declared that reason grows up with us. 72 Hence those who dwell on the
earth will incur torment because, though they possessed reason, they
committed iniquity, and though they received the commandments,
they did not observe them, and though they accepted*k* the law, they
circumvented*l* what they accepted. 73 So what will they have to say
at judgment or how will they reply in the last times? 74 How long the
Most High has exercised patience with those who live in the world,
not on account of them but because of the times *m*he has predetermined*m*!

> *Question: What is the state of the soul between
> death and the new creation (judgment)?*

75 I responded as follows: If you please, *n*Lord, Lord*n*, also make
this clear to your servant; whether after death, or when each one of

---

c Syriac *tšnyq'*, "vexation."
d–d Syriac *ḥy' mn btr mwt'*, "life after death." Ar.² "after death they expect neither
reward nor punishment and know not what the resurrection is."
e–e Syriac *dmḥ' ḥyyn ḥnn*, "living we live."
f–f Omitted by Ethiopic.
g Syriac *mtplplyn*, "bespattered"; verse is omitted by Armenian.
h–h Reading with Syriac. Latin *melius fortassis nobis venisset*, "it might possibly go
better with us." Ethiopic "we would be better off if we did not come to judgment
after death." Ar.² "it might be better for us not to have been created since our way
after death leads to punishment."
i–i Ethiopic "and its damnation"; Ar.² "on account of the wickedness of their works."
j–j Syriac *'štkl*, "take note of," "understand."
k Syriac *'ttsym*, "imposed," with law as subject. Considerable variation among different versions without substantial difference in meaning.
l So with Latin; Syriac *ṭlmwhy*, "they rejected it."
m–m Syriac is impersonal, *zbn' dsymyn*, "the predetermined times."
n–n With Syriac.

us has to surrender his soul, we will really *be kept in repose* until those times come when you are to renew the creation, or [whether] we will be tormented immediately*? 76 He replied to me as follows: I'll show you this too. But you must not get entangled with scorners nor reckon yourself with those who are tormented. 77 For indeed you have a treasure of works stored up with the Most High but it will not be revealed to you until the last times. 78 For the conception of death is this: when the final sentence of death has emerged from the Most High that man is to die,

> when the spirit withdraws from the body,
> *to return* again to him who gave it,

it first of all entreats the glory of the Most High. 79 If it should be one of those who scorned,

> Who did not adhere to the ways* of the Most High,
> Who held his law in contempt,
> Or who hated those who feared God;

80 *such spirits will not enter habitations* but will roam around *henceforth in torment*, ever unhappy and sad, in seven ways. 81 The first way: because they have *spurned the law* of the Most High. 82 The second way: because now they are unable truly to repent that they may live*. 83 The third way: they will see the reward deposited for those who were faithful to *the covenants* of the Most High. 84 The fourth way: they will contemplate the torment deposited for themselves in the last [times]*. 85 The fifth way: they will see the habitations of others* guarded by angels *in complete freedom from disturbance*. 86 The sixth way: they will see how immediately

o–o Ar.² "without bliss [joy]."
p Reading with A, M *amodo;* C, V have *quomodo,* "in what manner."
q–q Latin *demittatur,* "send down [away]"; Syriac *tštdr,* "sent"; Ethiopic, Ar.¹ "return"; Ar.² omits.
r With Syriac *'wrḥth,* "ways"; so also Ethiopic, Ar.¹: Latin *viam,* "way"; wanting in Ar.² and Armenian.
s–s Ar.² "those souls will come to hell and to torment, and for them and their kind a place has been set apart."
t–t Syriac *'l' mn hš' hwyn btšnyq',* "but they are already in torment."
u–u Ar.² "rebelled against the Most High"; cf. Syriac *'ṣy,* "resist."
v Armenian adds "while they were in this world."
w–w So with Latin, Ethiopic, Ar.¹: Syriac and Ar.² omit.
x Syriac adds *hw dbh mtkwnn npšthwn dršy'' mṭl dkd 'yt hw' lhyn zbn' dpwlḥn' l' 'št'bdy lpwqdnwhy dmrym',* "whereby the souls of the wicked are reminded that while they had time for salvation, they did not submit to the commands of the Most High."
y Syriac adds *npšt',* "souls."
z–z Syriac *bnyḥ' sqy' ',* "in great [much] rest."

[some] of them will pass over into torment. 87 The seventh way, which is worse than all the above mentioned ways:

> because they will languish in confusion,
> they will be consumed in shame[a],
> and they will [b]pine away[b] in fears,

when they see the glory of the Most High before whom they sinned while living and before whom they are to be judged in the last times. 88 For those, on the other hand, who have adhered to the ways of the Most High, this order obtains when they are to be separated from [this] crumbling vessel. 89 [c]While they remained in it[c] they served the Most High diligently and encountered danger every hour in order to observe perfectly the law of the lawgiver. 90 This, then, is the direction[d] concerning them: 91 In the first place, they will view with great joy the glory of him who receives[e] them, for they will come to repose in seven orders[f]. 92 The first order: that they have, with great diligence, done their utmost to overcome the evil thought molded with them that it might not mislead them from life to death. 93 The second order: that they see [g]the entanglements[g] in which the souls of the wicked roam about and the punishment that is in store for them. 94 The third order: they see the witness that he who made them bore to them, that while alive they observed the law which was entrusted to them. 95 The fourth order: they comprehend the rest which, gathered in their storehouses, they now enjoy [h]in complete freedom from disturbance[h], guarded by angels, and the glory in store for them in their last [times]. 96 The fifth order: they rejoice because now they have escaped the corruptible and will have the future as an inheritance, but in addition they will see the narrowness and difficulties[i] from which they have been extricated and the expanse they are to receive [j]in joy[j] and immortality. 97 The sixth order: when it is

---

[a] Reading with Syriac *bthmṣt'*; so also Ethiopic. Latin *in honoribus,* "in honors"; A** has *horroribus,* "terrors." (A** refers to second hand of MS, A.)
[b-b] Syriac *ḥmyn,* "burn up."
[c-c] So with Syriac *bhw gyr zbn' d'mr bh; zbn'*=Pers. *zvan,* "time."
[d] Syriac *nmws',* "law," "teaching." Verse is omitted by Ar.[1,2] and Armenian.
[e] Syriac *ddbr,* "who led."
[f] Syriac *'wrḥn,* "ways," and so throughout series. So also Ar.[2] and Armenian; Ethiopic and Ar.[1] follow Latin.
[g-g] With Latin. Syriac *hwpk',* "turning."
[h-h] See textual note [z-z] at 85.
[i] Latin A, C, M, V have *plenum,* "much." Syriac correctly adds *d'ml',* "of toil."
[j-j] Rare Latin word: *fruniscentes,* "enjoyment," "joy."

revealed to them how their face is to shine like the sun and how they are to be like the light of the stars, no longer corruptible. 98 The seventh order, which is superior to all those mentioned above: because they will rejoice with assurance, because they will believe without confusion, and they will *be genuinely happy*, for they make haste to see the face of him whom they served while living and from whom they are to *receive the reward of glory*. 99 This is the order of the just souls pointed out above and of the previously mentioned ways of torment which those who failed to observe will suffer from now on*. 100 I responded as follows: Will, therefore, time *be given to the souls after they are separated from the body to see what you have told me about? 101 He said to me: They will be at liberty for seven days, to see during the seven days the things spoken of above and afterward they shall be gathered into their habitations.

Question: May the righteous intercede for the ungodly?

102 Then I replied as follows: If you please, also make clear to me, your servant, if perchance on the day of judgment the just will be able to intercede for the wicked or to plead with the Most High on their behalf — 103 fathers for sons, or children for parents, or brothers for brothers, relatives for next of kin, and *friends for those dearest [to them]*. 104 *He answered as follows: Yes, I will grant you this favor and make it clear to you. The day of judgment is decisive*, making clear to all the seal of truth. Just as now a father cannot commission a son, or a son a father, or a master a slave*, or a friend one dearest [to him], *to be sick* for him, or to sleep or to eat or to be restored to health, 105 so nobody can pray for another*, for all will

---

k–k Omitted by Syriac.

l–l See note by Bensly, MF, p. 71.

m Syriac adds *hlyn npšt' l'wṣr' l' 'ln ('lyn) 'l' mn hš' hwyn mtṭrpn btšnyq' wmttnḥn wmt'bln bšb' 'wrḥn*, "these souls will not rise into the storehouses but from now on will writhe in torment and groan and lament in seven ways."

n Syriac adds *'tr*, "opportunity," "place."

o–o Syriac *rḥm' ḥlp rḥmyhwn*, "friends for their friends"; so all versions except Georgian which follows Latin.

p–p Omitted by A.

q Reading with Syriac *gzyr'* from *gzr* which means "to cut," "to divide," and not "magistrate" here as Brockelmann and Gunkel say; cf. Ugaritic "to devour." Latin *audax*, "bold," "daring," "violent."

r–r With Syriac *dḥlpwhi ntkrh*, "that he may be sick for him"; Latin *pro eo intellegat*, "he understands for him"; perhaps something like the saying "feel for him."

s Syriac adds *bhw ywm' 'pl' dnwqr 'nš 'l 'nš*, "on that day, nor one lay a burden on another"; so also Ethiopic and Ar.*1*.

bear, each, then, his own injustice or justice. 106 I replied as follows:
How is it then that we find that first Abraham interceded for the
Sodomites, Moses in behalf of the fathers who sinned in the desert,
107 Joshua, ʲafter him, for Israel in the days of Achanᵘ, 108 Samuel
ᵛin the days of Saulᵛ, David on account of ʷthe plagueʷ, Solomon
on behalf of those who were in ˣthe sanctuaryˣ, 109 Elijah for those
who received rain and for the dead that he might live, 110 and
Hezekiah for the people in the days of ʸSennacherib, as well as many
[others] for many [more]? 111 If now, therefore, when corruption
has increased and injustice has multiplied, the just have prayed for
the wicked, why can't it be so then? 112 He responded to me as
follows: ᶻThe present world is not the endᶻ and its glory is transi-
toryᵃ; hence those who were strong have prayed ᵇfor the weakᵇ.
113 But the day of judgment will mark the end of this time ᶜ[and the
beginning]ᶜ of immortal time to come, in which

> corruption has come to an end,
> 114 Intemperanceᵈ has been abolished,
> Faithlessness has been cut off,
> But justice has grown up,
> And truth has arisen.

115 Then no one will be able to have compassion for him who is convicted in the judgment or to cast down him who is victoriousᵉ.

ᵗ Syriac adds *br nwn*, "son of Nun"; so also Ar.².
ᵘ So with MT of Josh 7; Syriac, Latin, and Ar.¹ have Achar; Ethiopic, Ahas; (MT
has Achan for references in Joshua but LXXᴮ and Syriac have Achar in 7:1 and
22:20; I Chron 2:7 MT has Achar, though some MSS have Achan; Syriac has
Achar). Ar.² omits Achar-Achan and Armenian omits the whole reference to
Joshua.
ᵛ⁻ᵛ Inserted into Latin by Bensly; it is found in Syriac, Ethiopic and Ar.¹; Ar.² and
Armenian omit.
ʷ⁻ʷ Syriac *ʼl tbrh dʼmʼ*, "concerning the breach of the people"; so also Ar.²; others
follow Latin.
ˣ⁻ˣ Reading with A *sanctificationem* (Heb. *mqdš*); with Syriac, *mqdš*, and Ethiopic;
Ar.¹,² "dedication of the house [temple]."
ʸ Ar.² adds "the siege [plus] Sennacherib, the king of Babylon."
ᶻ⁻ᶻ Syriac *hnʼ ʻlmʼ ʼyt lh šwlmʼ*, "this world has an end."
ᵃ Latin "the glory in it remains constant," but Bensly, on basis of Syriac and other
versions, inserts *non*, "not," before "constant"; the Syriac has *lʼ hwʼ ʼmynʼyt mqwʼ bh*,
"not does it remain constant in it." That is the basis for our rendering, stated posi-
tively.
ᵇ⁻ᵇ Syriac *dlyt bhwn ḥylʼ*, "in whom there is no strength."
ᶜ⁻ᶜ Omitted by S, A, C, but inserted by Bensly on basis of Syriac, *wryšh*, and Ethiopic.
ᵈ Ethiopic "weakness."
ᵉ Syriac adds *bdynʼ*, "in the judgment."

Question: What is the use of living, if everybody is doomed to sin? Answer:
It is necessary to fight; if victorious there is salvation, if not, then death.

116 I answered as follows: This is my first and last comment, then it would have been better for the earth not to have generated Adam or when it did generate him at least to have constrained[f] him not to sin. 117 What good is it for any [g][of us] [h]to live in grief now and with the expectation of punishment after death? 118 O Adam, what have you done? Although you [alone] sinned, [i]the fall[i] was not yours alone, but ours, too, who descended from you. 119 What benefit[j] is it for us that an immortal time has been promised to us when, in fact, we have done death-dealing works; 120 that perpetual[k] hope has been held out for us when, in fact, we have acted in utter futility; 121 that [l]sound and secure habitations[l] have been prepared [m]for us[m] when, in fact, we have lived so scandalously; 122 that the glory of the Most High is to protect those who have lived virtuously, though we have conducted ourselves most impiously; 123 that paradise, whose [n]incorruptible fruit[n] has been preserved [for us] and in which are abundance and healing, will appear, 124 [but which] we, in fact, cannot enter because we have lived [o]in unacceptable ways[o]; 125 and that the faces of those who have exercised self-restraint shine more brilliantly than the stars, though, in fact, our faces [will be] blacker than the darkness [of night]. 126 For during our lifetime when we committed sin we did not realize what we were to endure after death. 127 He responded as follows: This is the purport of [p]the struggle[p] which man born on earth must wage; 128 if he is defeated, he will

---

[f] Syriac *'rtyth*, "taught"; Latin *coercere;* the former read the Greek *katēchein*, the latter *katechein*. Ethiopic follows Syriac. Verse from "or" missing from Ar.[2].
[g] S, A**, M, C add *hominibus*, "men," on margin.
[h] With Ethiopic.
[i-i] Syriac *byšt'*, "evil"; so also Ethiopic; Armenian *calamitas*, "mischief," "misfortune."
[j] Latin *prodest;* Syriac *ywtrn'* (noun), "utility," "benefit."
[k] Ethiopic "good."
[l-l] Syriac *'wṣr' dl' ṣpt' wdl' kwrhn'*, "storehouses without care and without malady"; so also basically Ethiopic.
[m-m] With C, M; omitted by S, A.
[n-n] Syriac *dl' ḥmyn p'rwhy*, "whose fruits do not dry up." So also Ethiopic and Ar.[1].
[o-o] Latin "in unacceptable places"; rendering here based on possible confusion of Greek *topois*, "places," with *tropois*, "ways," "manners"; cf. Ethiopic "as we were not promised" — perhaps Greek *acharistois tropois*, "unlikely [or unseemly] ways."
[p-p] Ethiopic and Ar.[1] "this world"; Ar.[2] "battlefield."

suffer what you have said; but if he is victorious, he will receive what I say. 129 For this is *the way* about which Moses, when he was yet alive, spoke to the people; he said, Choose for yourself life that you live*. 130 However, *they did not believe* him or the prophets after him, or me who have spoken to them. 131 Hence, there may not be so much sorrow in their destruction as there will be joy over *the salvation of those who have believed*.

> Question: Does the mercy and compassion of God mean that many will be saved? Answer: This world was made for the many, the world to come for the few.

132 I replied as follows: I know, lord, that the Most High is now referred to as the merciful one because he has compassion for *those who have not yet come into the world; 133 *the gracious one* because he is gracious* to those who return* to his law; 134 *the long-suffering one* because he manifests patience for those who have sinned inasmuch as *they are his creatures*; 135 *the generous one* because he certainly prefers to give *rather than to exact*; 136 *the one of many mercies* because he multiplies *ever more* [his] mercies for those of the present, the past, and the future — 137 for if he had not multiplied [them]*, the world, together with those who live in it, could not continue — 138 the giver, for if he would not give out of his goodness so that those who committed iniquities could be relieved of

---

q–q M has *vita,* "life."

r Syriac adds *h' yhbt qdmykwn ywmn' ḥy' wmwt' ṭbt' wbyšt' gbw lkwn hkyl ḥy' dtḥwn 'ntwn wzr'kwn,* "behold I have set before you today life and death, good and evil; choose for yourselves, therefore, life that you and your descendants may live," cf. Deut 30:19.

s–s Syriac *w'ṣw wl' 'ttpysw lh,* "and they resisted and were not convinced [by] him."

t–t So with Latin. Syriac *ḥyyhwn d'ylyn d'ttpysw,* "the lives of those who were convinced."

u–u Omitted by M; cf. Ar.*1,2*.

v–v Syriac *ḥnn',* "the gracious one."

w With Syriac *dmtpnyn;* Latin *qui conversionem faciunt,* "who have made a change in relation to."

x–x Syriac *ngyr rwḥ',* "long of spirit"; cf. Latin *longanimis.*

y–y Syriac *d'bdwhy ḥnn,* "we who are his works."

z–z Latin of Bensly *munificus;* S, A, C, M have *muneribus,* "gifts," "favors." Syriac *yhwb',* "the giver," so also Ethiopic, Armenian and in vs. 138.

a–a Omitted by M.

b–b Apparently Latin is a literal rendering of Heb. *rb rḥmym* as Syriac *sgy rḥm'* indicates (cf. Pss 51:3; 69:17; 119:156; 1QS 4:3; 1QH 4:32; 7:27.)

c–c Latin *magis* omitted by M.

d Syriac *lrḥmwhy,* "his mercies."

their iniquities, *the ten-thousandth part of mankind* would be unable to live; 139 and *the judge*, for if he did not pardon those who were created by his word and annul* [their] multitudinous offenses* there would doubtless be left only a very few of the innumerable multitude.

8 1 He responded to me as follows: the Most High made this world for the many but the world to come for the few. 2 But let me tell you a parable, Ezra. Just as, should you inquire of the earth and it would tell you that it yields a large amount of clay from which earthen vessels are made, but little dust from which gold comes, so too is the way* of the present world: 3 Many have been created but few *will be saved*.

Why was man made to live such a short time?

4 I replied as follows:

       Imbibe*, my soul, perception,
       Feast, *my heart*, on discernment.
    5 For you entered the world involuntarily*,
       And are leaving [it] without [your] consent;

because only a short span* of time has been allotted to you to live. 6 *O Lord above us*, if you will grant permission to your servant, that *we may pray* before you: give us *seed of heart and cultivation of perception* whence fruit may come, so that every mortal who bears

---

e-e Syriac *ḥd mn rbw*, "one out of ten thousand."

f-f Gunkel reads *šmṭ* for *špṭ*, i.e. "the forgiver" for "the judge." But see note in Box, p. 169. The word with meaning of pardon or remission does not occur in biblical Hebrew, though it is found with that meaning in later Hebrew (see Jastrow, *Dictionary of the Targumim*, p. 1594); the root occurs in *šmṭh*, "release," in the year of release.

g Syriac *nṭ'*, "forget."

h With Syriac *'wlhwn;* Latin *contemptionum*, "of contempts," "disdains."

i Syriac *'bdh*, "work"; Ar.[2] "people."

j-j Syriac *hww ḥyyn*, "are alive"; so also Ethiopic.

k With Syriac *srwpy;* Latin S, A, C, M have *absolve*, "acquit" but later MSS have *absorbe*, "drink."

l-l With Syriac *lby;* omitted by Latin.

m With Syriac *l' bṣbynky*, "without your will," for Latin *obaudire*, "to obey."

n-n With Syriac *w'zl' 'nty kd l' ṣbyty;* Latin *et perfecta es nolens*, "and you end it unwillingly."

o Syriac *šwlṭn'*, "power."

p-p Syriac *mry' mry*, "Lord, Lord," Hebrew may have been *'lywn*, "Most High," which Latin read *'lynw*, "over us."

q-q Syriac *'b' '*, "I may pray," which is better here; omitted by Ethiopic, but Ar.[1] follows Syriac.

r-r Ethiopic "understanding and thought."

the likeness[s] of man can go on living! 7 [t]For you are by yourself[t] and we are the one formation[u] of your hands, just as you said. 8 Now when you [v]bring to life[v] the body molded in the womb and provide [it] with members, your creation subsists in fire and water, and for nine months your handiwork bears your creature which [w]was formed in it[w]. 9 So that which shelters and that which is sheltered are both sheltered [x]by your shelter[x]. When the womb discharges what has evolved[y] in it, 10 you have commanded that out of the members themselves, [z]that is out of the breasts[z], milk, the fruit of the[a] breasts, should be provided 11 to nourish [b]for a time[b] what was fashioned.

> Afterward you direct[c] it with your mercy,
> 12 Nurture it with your justice,
> Instruct it in your law,
> And temper[d] it with your wisdom.
> 13 Then you kill it — it's your creation —
> And restore it to life — it's your handiwork!

14 If, therefore, you can [e]so readily do away[e] with [him] who was molded with [f]such [great] pains[f] by your command, [g]why then was he made[g]? 15 Now [h]let me emphasize[h] that you know best about the [i]totality of mankind[i], but about

> Your people I am dejected;
> 16 I lament over your heritage,
> I sorrow because of Israel,
> And I am perturbed on account of the seed of Jacob.

17 So[j] I want to pray before you for myself and for them because I

---

[s] Latin *locum*, "place," possibly a misreading of Greek *tupon*, "form," "image"; Syriac *lbš*, "form," "likeness," as here.

[t–t] Lit. "you are the only one"; Syriac *ḥd gyr 'ytyk*, "for you are one."

[u] Syriac adds *ḥnn 'bd*, "we are the work . . ."

[v–v] *vivificans vivificas*, infinitive absolute construction.

[w–w] Syriac *bryt*, "you created."   [x–x] Omitted by C, M.

[y] Singular, with A; Bensly has *creata fuerint*, "have been created."

[z–z] Omitted by Syriac and Ethiopic. Cf. Ar.[1] "what is necessary for the need."

[a] Syriac adds *dmlywt*, "full."

[b–b] Syriac *lzbn' qlyl*, "for a short time."

[c] Latin *dispono*, "order," "arrange"; Syriac *mdabar*, pael "manage," "govern."

[d] Latin *corripio*, lit. "reprove," "take hold of"; Syriac *mrt'*, "instruct," "train."

[e–e] Latin *perdideris . . . facile ordine*, "easy order"; Syriac *b'gl wqlyl'yt mwbd 'nt*, "you can destroy quickly and easily"; omitted by Ethiopic, Ar.[1,2].

[f–f] Syriac *l'wt' sgy't'*, "many labors."

[g–g] Reading with Syriac, Ethiopic, Ar.[1,2]; Latin *utquid fiebat*, "to what purpose was it [he] made?"

[h–h] Infinitive absolute of Hebrew.

[i–i] Lit. "every man"; Syriac *kwl 'nš*.   [j] *ideo*.

see *the faults* of us who inhabit the earth, 18 and I have heard
about the swift*l* judgment which is to come. 19 So
<blockquote>
Listen to me,

Mark my words,

And let me speak before you*n*!
</blockquote>

Ezra's prayer for his people and the divine response

20 *The beginning of the words of Ezra's prayer before he was
taken ⌈up⌉*. He said:
<blockquote>
Lord, who *lives forever*,

Whose eyes are lifted up,

⌈Whose⌉ dwelling places are in the air,
</blockquote>
21 Whose throne is indescribable*r*,
<blockquote>
⌈Whose⌉ glory is incomprehensible,

Before whom angelic hosts stand with trembling,
</blockquote>
22 And at whose word*s* they are converted to wind and fire;
<blockquote>
Whose word is trustworthy*t*,

⌈Whose⌉ decrees are steadfast,
</blockquote>
23 Whose orders are mighty,
<blockquote>
⌈Whose⌉ commands are fearful,

Whose glance dries up the depths,

⌈Whose⌉ wrath makes mountains melt away,

And ⌈whose⌉ truth *abides forever*.
</blockquote>
24 Listen, Lord*v*, to *the prayer* of your servant,
<blockquote>
Lend an ear to the entreaty of your production,

Give attention to my words!
</blockquote>

k–k Syriac *šwr'tn*, "our sins, faults."

l So Latin; Syriac *gzrh ddyn'*, "decree of judgment."

m–m Syriac *ṣwt lmly ṣlwty*, "pay attention to my words of prayer."

n Syriac adds *mry' 'lhy*, "Lord, my God."

o–o There is no substantial variation in the Latin, Syriac, Georgian, and Ethiopic
texts. Armenian "prayer of the prophet Ezra"; Ar.*1* "I answered saying"; Ar.*2* "I,
el-Uzzir, pray to you and implore you."

p–p With Syriac *d'mr 'nt l'lm;* so substantially Ethiopic and Ar.*1*; Ar.*2* "who lives in
the world of worlds"; Latin "who inhabits the world," *saeculum.*

q–q Syriac *hw dmrwmwhy rmyn*, "whose heights are exalted"; cf. Psi group of Violet.

r Latin, Syriac "immeasurable"; here with Ar.*1* *l'yh'z.*

s With Syriac (*mltk*) and Ethiopic, Armenian and Latin Psi group; S, A have *servatio*,
"observance."

t With S, A *verum;* C, Syriac *mhymn'*=Latin *firmum*, "fast," "firm."

u–u With Ar.*2* *l' yzwl*, "immutable," "without ceasing." Others *testificor*, "certain,"
"attested," probably based on a misreading of Heb. *le'ed* for original *la'ad.*

v Omitted by M, Syriac, Ethiopic, Ar.*1,2*, Armenian.

w–w With Latin and Ar.*2*; Psi group, Syriac (*bqlh*), Ethiopic, Ar.*1*, Armenian,
"voice."

25 So long as I live I must speak,
　　And so long as I have discernment I must be responsive.
26 Do not gaze upon the offenses of your people,
　　But [upon those] who have truly*a* served you.
27 Do not take note of *y*the impious in their pursuits*y*,
　　But [of those] who have kept your covenants *z*despite
　　　　tribulations*z*.
28 *a*Do not think*a* [of those] who have conducted themselves
　　　　wickedly before you,
　　But remember [those] who have voluntarily acknowledged
　　　　*b*respect for you*b*.
29 Do not decree destruction [for those] who have lived like cattle,
　　But be mindful of those who have taught*c* so nobly*d* your law.
30 Do not be indignant with those who have been judged*e* worse
　　　　than beasts,
　　But esteem [those] who have always manifested confidence*f* in
　　　　your glory.
31 For we and our fathers*g* have pursued the ways of death, yet because of us sinners you are referred to as the merciful one. 32 If you
want to have mercy upon us who are without works *h*of justice*h*,
then you will be called the merciful one. 33 For the just whose *i*many
good*i* deeds are on deposit with you will receive their reward by virtue
of their deeds.
34 What is man that you should be angry with him,
　　Or the mortal race that you should be so embittered against it?
35 For in truth
　　　　　　None of those born is without sin,
　　　　　　Nor are those who exist without fault.
36 Thereby, Lord*j*, your justice and your goodness will be revealed,
when you have compassion for those without a *k*treasury of good
deeds*k*. 37 He responded to me as follows: On some matters you
have spoken correctly and it will turn out according to your words;

a Latin *in veritate*, "in truth."
y–y Syriac *bsklwt' dṣn'thwn d'wl'*, "on the follies of their tricks of the impious."
z–z Lit. "in tribulations."　　*a–a* Ethiopic and Ar.*1* "be angry."
b–b *timor*, lit. "fear," but here interpreted in sense of awe.
c Syriac *qblw*, "received."　　*d* Some versions have "clearly."
e Syriac *'bšw*, "acted worse"; cf. also Ar.*1*.　　*f* Psi group *sperantes*, "hope."
g Syriac *mn qdmyn*, "from those before us."
h–h Omitted by Syriac; Ethiopic, Ar.*1,2* "good."
i–i Omitted by Syriac.　　*j* Syriac *mry', mry*, "Lord, my Lord."
k–k Syriac *ḥyl' d'bd'*, "a power," "potential," "treasury of works."

38 for, indeed, I will disregard *the creation* of those who have sinned, or [their] death, or [their] judgment, or [their] destruction, 39 but I will rejoice over *m*the creation of the just, over [their] pilgrimage too, [their] salvation*m*, and the reception of [their] reward. 40 Hence it is just as *n*I have said*n*. 41 Just as the farmer sows an abundance of seed *o*upon soil*o* and plants a multitude of plants, but not all that has been sown will come up at the time or all [the plants] that have been planted take root, so not all who have been sown in this world will be saved.

Question: Is man to be compared with seeds and plants?

42 I responded as follows: If you please, let me speak. 43 As for the seed *p*of the farmer*p*, if it does not come up because it has not received*q* your rain at the right time *r*or has been damaged by too much rain*r*, 44 *s*it perishes*s*; but man who *t*has been molded*t* by your hands and has been referred to as your image because he has been made like [you], for whose sake everything was made—would you compare him to farmer's seed? 45 *u*No, Lord, above us*u*,

> Spare your people,
> Be compassionate with your inheritance,
> For you do have sympathy for your creatures.

46 He replied to me as follows:

> The present is for those present,
> The future is for those to come.

47 *v*You are quite incapable*v* of loving my creature more than I [do], inasmuch as you have frequently reckoned yourself*w* among the

---

l–l plasma, a Greek word.
m–m Syriac *m'tyt' dgbylthwn dzdyq' w'l ḥyyhwn*, "the coming of their forms of the righteous and over their life." The genitives in Latin are probably influenced by *iustorum figmentum*, "creation of the just."
n–n Ethiopic "as you have said."
o–o Omitted by Syriac and Ethiopic, but present in Ar.*1,2*.
p–p Omitted by M.
q Syriac *msb* . . . *nsb*, "receiving . . . received" (infinitive absolute).
r–r Omitted by Ethiopic, Ar.*2* (slight variation), Armenian; Georgian text broken.
s–s S, A, C have *hic pater et filius*, "this is father and son"; M has *sic pat=sic patitur*, "so will perish" which our rendering follows.
t–t plasmatus est, a Greek word meaning "fashioned," "formed," "molded."
u–u Syriac *l' b'' 'n' mnk mry' mry*, "No, I beg from you. Lord, my Lord." For *super nos*, "above us," M has *super nos irascaris*, "concerning us you be angry"="Do not, Lord, be angry over us."
v–v multum enim tibi restat, "for much is left to you," i.e. "lacking to you"; so also Syriac. Vss. 46–49 are missing in Armenian.
w Syriac *npšk*, "your soul [self]."

unjust*. *By no means*! 48 But in this too you will be [regarded] as commendable* before the Most High, 49 because you have humbled yourself, as is proper for you, and did not reckon yourself* among the just so as *to have gloried* over much. 50 For those who live in the world in the last times will be afflicted with many deplorable misfortunes *because they conducted themselves so arrogantly*. 51 But you must consider yourself* and inquire about the glory of those like you. 52 For you

> Paradise has been opened,
> The tree of life has been planted,
> The world to come has been readied,
> An abundance* has been provided,
> The city has been built,
> Repose has been prepared,
> Goodness has been achieved,
> Wisdom has been pre-established*.

53 The root has been *sealed from you*,
> Infirmity has been abolished from you,
> And death* has been removed;
> Hell has fled,
> Corruption [gone] into oblivion,

54 Afflictions have disappeared,

and at the end *the treasure of immortality* is disclosed. 55 Therefore, ask no further questions about the multitude of those who are lost, 56 for when they had the opportunity*,

> They spurned the Most High,
> They held his law in contempt,
> And abandoned* his ways.

ª Ethiopic adds "though you are no sinner"; so also Ar.*¹*.
ʸ⁻ʸ Omitted by C, M; Syriac *l' nhw' hkn'*, "let it not be so."
ᶻ Latin *mirabilis;* Syriac *tštbḥ*, "be praised," "glorified."
ᵃ See textual note *ʷ* at 47.
ᵇ⁻ᵇ With C, M; S, A have *glorificeris*, "that you glory."
ᶜ⁻ᶜ Syriac *šwbhr' sgy'' d'štbhr*, "many arrogances of [their] arrogance." Vss. 50 ff. are missing in Arabic versions.
ᵈ See textual note *ʷ* at 47.
ᵉ Latin *habundantia*, i.e. "a superabundance of bliss."
ᶠ Syriac *šlmt ḥkmt'*, "wisdom has been ended [perfected]"; Ethiopic "the root of wisdom plucked off."
ᵍ⁻ᵍ Syriac *'qr' 'tḥtm mnkwn*, "the root has been sealed from you."
ʰ Not in Latin; supplied from Syriac *mwt'*.
ⁱ⁻ⁱ Syriac *šymt' dḥy'*, "treasures of life."
ʲ *libertatem*, "freedom," "liberty," here rendered a bit more broadly.
ᵏ Syriac *bṭlw*, "destroy," "make to cease"; perhaps reading Greek *kateluon*, "destroy" for *katelipon*, "abandon," "forsake."

57 Moreover, they trampled upon ^l his just ones^l, 58 and thought there was no God although they ^m knew quite well^m that ^n they must die^n. 59 Just as the things said above ^o await you^o, so thirst and affliction already prepared [await them]; yet the Most High did not want man to perish^p, 60 but those who were created themselves polluted the name of him who made them and displayed ingratitude toward him^q who had prepared life^r for them. 61 For that reason my judgment ^s is now approaching^s. 62 I have not disclosed it to everybody, but only to you and a few like you. I responded as follows:

Signs for the seer's time

63 Look, now, Lord, you have told me about a multitude of signs which you are about to perform in the last days but you have said nothing to me about the time.

9 1 He answered me as follows: ^t Note [that] carefully^t for yourself^u. When you observe that a certain part ^v of the predicted signs^v have occurred, 2 then you will know that it is indeed the time when the Most High is about ^w to judge^w the world he has made. 3 So when there will appear in the world

> Tremors^x ^y in places^y,
> Disorder of peoples,
> Intrigues of nations,
> Fickleness of leaders,
> Confusion of rulers,

4 then you will realize that these are the things about which the Most High has spoken ^z from the very beginning^z. 5 For just as everything

---

^l-l Syriac lḥsywhy, "his saints."

^m-m scientes sciunt, "knowing they knew," infinitive absolute as Syriac mdʿ ydʿyn indicates; sciunt is omitted by S, A, C.

^n-n Also infinitive absolute in Syriac mmt mytyn.

^o-o vos suscipient is interpreted here with the help of the Syriac mskyn lkwn.

^p Armenian "I made him to keep my commands and to avoid eternal death."

^q Syriac adds wl' 'wdyw ly, "and they did not acknowledge me."

^r M has hanc vitam, "this life."

^s-s Ethiopic "their judgment will overcome [seize] them."

^t-t Lit. "count," "measure," "reckon," with infinitive absolute construction (cf. Syriac mmšḥ mšwḥ).

^u Syriac bnpšk, "in your soul."

^v-v With S, A pars quaedam, Syriac; cf. Ethiopic "some of the past signs."

^w-w Latin visitare, "visit," which goes back to Heb. pqd, as Syriac npqwd shows; it means "to visit in judgment."

^x So S, C, M and other versions; A has munitio, "defense."

^y-y Lit. "of places."

^z-z Lit. "from the days which have been before from the beginning"; Syriac mn qdym, "from the beginning."

that *has taken place* in the world, *[from] beginning to end as well as the end [itself], has been made known*, 6 so also have the times of the Most High; the beginnings have been attested by portents* and powers, the end by deeds*, and signs. 7 Now, everyone who will be saved*, who is able to escape by virtue of his works or the faith in which he trusted — 8 *he will survive* the above noted perils and enjoy* my salvation in my land and within the territory I have *set apart* for myself from eternity. 9 Then those who now have ignored my ways will marvel* and *those who have contemptuously rejected them will linger* in torment. 10 Those* who did not appreciate me while alive, *though they received my blessings*, 11 and those who despised my law when they were still *free to do so*, 12 and while *the opportunity* for repentance* was yet open to them, nevertheless failed to recognize [it], even spurned [it], they will have to acknowledge [it] *by torment* after death. 13 Therefore you must no longer be so inquisitive as to how the wicked will be afflicted but rather inquire how the just will *be saved*, to whom the age belongs, for whose sake it [was created] *and when*.

Few saved, with justification

14 I responded as follows: 15 *I said before*, say now, and will say hereafter,

More numerous are the lost *than the saved*,
16 As *the tide* is greater than *a drop*.

a–a *factum est*, "was made"; Syriac *dhw' b'lm'*, "that is in the world."
b–b Syriac *ydy' ryšh wswlmh gl'*, "its beginning is known and its end revealed."
c Syriac adds *'twta*, "signs"; Ethiopic "in words, and signs and powers"; Ar.¹ "the obscure beginning will be revealed in powers and miracles."
d Syriac *tb't'*, "penalties." Ethiopic and Ar.¹ follow Latin.
e Syriac *dnḥ'*, "who will survive."
f–f Syriac *nšthr mn*, "he will be spared from."
g Latin *videbit*, "see" in this sense here; so also Ethiopic, Ar.¹.
h–h Latin *sanctificavi;* Syriac *qdšt*, "sanctified."
i Ethiopic "be purified."
j–j Syriac *bsrw wšdw 'nyn*, "held in contempt and rejected them"; Ethiopic "who scorned my law and held me in contempt."
k Latin *quodquod* or *quotquot;* MSS vary.
l–l Syriac *mt'b hwyt lhwn*, "I was good to them."
m–m Latin *libertatem*, "freedom."   *n–n* Latin *locus;* Syriac *'tr'*, "place."
o Syriac *ngyrwt rwh'*, lit. "longness of spirit," i.e. "patience"; so also Ethiopic.
p–p Omitted by Syriac and Ethiopic, but retained by Ar.¹.
q–q Syriac *ḥ'yn*, "live."   *r–r* Latin *et quando;* others omit.
s–s Omitted by Syriac.
t–t Syriac *mn 'ylyn dḥ'yn*, "than those who live."
u–u Syriac *gll'*, "waves"; Ethiopic "flood."
v–v Syriac *twpt' z'wrt'*, "little drop"; Ethiopic "drops"; Ar.¹ "rain drops."

17 He replied to me as follows:

As *w*the field*w*, so the seed,
As the flowers, so the colors,
As the workman*x*, so *y*the product*y*,
As the farmer, so the harvest*z*.

18 *a*For in primordial time*a*, when I was preparing for those who now are, before the world was made for those who inhabit it, no one opposed me then because none existed to do so. 19 But now those created in this world, *b*though provided with an unfailing table and luxuriant pasture*c*, have become disreputable in their conduct*d*.

20 Then I looked at my world and it was decadent*e*,
And at *f*my land*f*, and it was imperiled*g*

because of the plots*h* that had come into it. 21 Although I was aware*i* of it, I spared them *j*with great difficulty*j* and saved for myself [one] grape out of a bunch and a shoot*k* out of a *l*great forest*l*. 22 Therefore let the multitude that was born *m*in vain*m* perish but let my grape and my shoot which I have perfected with much effort be preserved. 23 Now, then, if you will wait for another seven days, without fasting in them 24 but go into a field of flowers where no

---

w–w Syriac *'tr'*, "place"; Ethiopic "land"; so also Ar.*1*.

x Latin *opera*, "work"; Syriac *'bd'*, "toil," "work" but could be pointed as participle. Perhaps a misreading of Heb. *po'al*, "work," for *po'el*, "workman."

y–y Syriac *ryḥn'*, "odor," "fragrance"; Ethiopic and Ar.*1* "judgment," "sentence," presupposing a Syriac *dyn'*, Greek *krisis*, for *ktisis*, "creation," "creature."

z Latin *area*, "threshing floor"; Syriac *'dr'* (in Ruth 3:2 the grain heaped up on the threshing floor, hence harvest); Ar.*2* *kl 'nš'n y'' qb bqdr 'mlh*, "every man will be chastised for his own deed."

a–a So with Syriac *mṭl dbzbnh hw' d'lm'*, lit. "for in the time of eternity"; Latin reads: "for there was a time of the world." M adds, perhaps rightly, *ante*, "before." See also notes by Gunkel and Box in loco.

b Syriac adds *dmtqn*, "which is fixed [ordered]."

c Latin *lege*, "law," and Syriac *nmws'*, "law," misread Greek *nómos*, "law," for *nomós*, "pasture."

d Lit. "manners," "morals"; Syriac *'bdyhwn*, "their works"; Ar.*1* "evil deeds."

e Lit. "lost."

f–f Omitted by S. Latin *orbis*; Syriac *ṭbyl*, Heb. *ṭbl*, "land," "habitable world."

g Syriac *bqyndwnws*, a Greek loanword, *kindunos*.

h Lit. "agreements"; Syriac *hwpkyhwn*, "their conduct"; Box suggests *coagitationes*, "tumults" for *cogitationes*; Ethiopic and Ar.*1* "work," "deed"; perhaps the underlying Hebrew was *mḥšbt*, "plan," "device."

i Lit. "saw."

j–j S omits *vix*, "difficulty." An alternative reading then might be "I spared a few [of] them."

k Syriac *nṣbt'*, "plant," "shoot"; Latin *plantationem*, "cutting."

l–l Latin *tribu multa*, "great tribes"; Syriac *'b' sgy''*, "great forest"; so also Ethiopic and Ar.*1*; behind Latin is misreading of Greek *ulē*, "woods," for *phulē*, "tribe."

m–m Syriac *'l dhw' lsryqwt'*, "because it is useless."

house has been built and eat only of the flowers*n* of the field, and taste no meat and sip no wine, but only flowers*º*, 25 and pray to the Most High *ᵖwithout ceasingᵖ*, then I will come and speak with you.

n Ethiopic "fruit."
º Ethiopic "fruit of trees"; Ar.*1* "fragrant herbs"; Ar.*2* adds "stalks of grass."
ᵖ-ᵖ Syriac *ḥpyṭ'yt*, "zealously"; so also Ar.*1,2*, the latter adding "humbly."

NOTES

6:35. *three weeks.* Dan 10:2. Only two periods of seven days are mentioned thus far (5:20 and here). Perhaps the author was thinking of a seven-day period preceding the first vision. Cf. the seven months' illness and seven years' penance of Reuben (Test Reuben 1:9) and the seven years' fast of Joseph (Test Joseph 3:4).

36. *my heart was again disquieted within me.* Pss 38:9; 39:4.

37. *my spirit was intensely excited.* Luke 24:32; 1QH 7:5.

38. *Let heaven and earth be made.* Cf. Ps 33:6, 9; Heb 11:3; II Peter 3:5; II Bar 14:17.

your word accomplished the work. Cf. Sir 42:15; Wisd Sol 9:1; 18:15. A common idea in the Bible and Jewish theology.

39. *a wind was blowing fiercely.* Cf. Speiser, AB, vol. 1, third NOTE on Gen 1:2.

silence. See Pseudo-Philo 60:2 on the voice of silence.

sound of man's voice. The author plays on Gen 2:19b here.

40. *ray of light.* Cf. Sir 43:1 ff.; II Enoch 25:3. Though the light of the heavenly bodies was not created until the fourth day, the rabbis believed light itself emanated from God on the first day and that by its illumination Adam saw the whole world (cf. Tractate Baba Ḥagiga 12a). For Gnostic speculation see Böhlig and Labib, *Die koptisch-gnostische Schrift,* 146:23 – 147:2. It is said that Pistis Sophia put out her finger and poured over him (deathless man) "light from her light" (152:5). In the Mandean Book of John it is said: ". . . before the sun and moon existed and came into the world, splendor already burned in its receptacle." Mark Lidzbarski, *Das Johannesbuch der Mandäer* (Giessen: Töpelmann, 1915), pp. 222. For theology of verse see Weber, p. 201.

treasury. See textual note *b* at 4:35.

41. *spirit of the firmament.* Gunkel thinks "spirit" here means "angel" as in I Enoch (15:10). Cf. Jub 2:2. The biblical reference is to Gen 1:6. For the Hebrew everything was alive and responsive to God. Hence the firmament here was thought to be capable of receiving and executing a command. Passage is quoted by Ambrose in *de spiritu sancto* 2:7.

to separate . . . division. Cf. Job 9:8; Jer 5:22. Here the firmament is personalized and acts on the divine command. In Genesis it is simply an object of God's creation and the barrier separating the waters above and below it.

42. *seventh part.* Cf. the seven mountains of I Enoch 18:6. According to the *Recognitions* of Clement (9:26) the mathematicians of the day regarded "Genesis" as divided into seven parts called climates over each of which an angel presided. Gunkel points out that this was also the tradition of India and Persia. Cf. also Philo *de opificio mundi* 34:38 f. and Schrader, *Keilinschriften,* p. 618. For the third day of creation see further II Enoch 30:1; Jub 2:5b.

six parts . . . cultivating. Interpretation will depend on textual tradition followed. Box (in loco) thinks the reference is to the divine sanction believed accorded agriculture. Gunkel, however, is of the opinion that, in view of vs. 44, paradise is meant.

43. *word . . . work.* See second NOTE on vs. 38 and Böhlig and Labib, *Die koptisch-gnostische Schrift,* par. 164:3.

44. Based on Gen 1:11 f.; 2:9; 3:6; I Enoch 29–32; Jub 2:7. The Syriac inclusion of trees and the poetic exaggeration of the piece points to Eden as the object of the author's thought. On flowers see first NOTE on 6:3.

fragrance. Cf. I Enoch 24:3 ff.; 32:4; II Bar 29:7.

45. *the fourth day.* Cf. Gen 1:14 ff.; Jub 2:8; I Enoch 72–82; II Enoch 30:2b.

order of the stars. Sir 43:9 ff.; Judg 5:20; UT, 1 Aqht 52, 56, 200, has *hlk kbkbm,* "course of the stars."

46. *to serve man.* A sublimation of the common oriental idea that the stars were gods. Cf. Clementine *Recognitions* 5:29; *Homilies* 10:25.

47. *the fifth day.* Gen 1:20 ff.; Jub 2:11 f.

48. *wonderful works.* Idea not from the Genesis account of this phenomenon but stressed elsewhere with reference to all God's activity (cf. e.g. Ps 105:5; Job 38–39).

49. *two . . . creatures . . . Behemoth . . . Leviathan.* Cf. Job 40:15–41; 34; Ps 148:7; Isa 27:1; II Bar 29:4; I Enoch 60:7–10. Come from Babylonian mythology where they are the semidivine monsters of chaos (cf. Schrader, *Keilinschriften,* pp. 507 ff.; Gunkel, *Schöpfung und Chaos,* pp. 41–69). For their role in apocalyptic literature see Klausner, pp. 298 ff. Note the emphasis on God's creation of these monsters. For a recent discussion of them see M. H. Pope, AB, vol. 15, NOTES on Job 40:15a and 41:1.

50. *You separated the one from the other.* I Enoch 60:7 ff. also speaks of their being separated to occupy the same regions as here. But Leviathan is said to be the female, Behemoth the male. Cf. Baba Bathra 73–75.

seventh part. Cf. Philo on creation, *de opificio mundi* 34:38b, and Clementine *Recognitions* 9:26.

unable to contain [both of] them. Since they were too big. Originally, in mythology, they were oceans. In Ugaritic (UT, 67:I:1) Baal is said to have crushed *Ltn* (Leviathan).

51. *a thousand mountains.* There may be a covert reference to Behemoth in Ps 50:10.

52. *moist seventh part.* Both monsters were sea creatures originally.

to be consumed. . . . . For tradition of a great eschatological feast prepared by the Lord, see Isa 25:6; Ps 74:14; Baba Bathra 74. II Bar 29:4 explains further that the monsters shall be food for the saved. Cf. I Enoch 62:14 and Frost, *Old Testament Apocalyptic*, pp. 152 ff. This is the background for the messianic banquet.

53. *the sixth day*. Gen 1:24 ff.; Jub 2:13b.

54. *Over them*. Cf. Gen 1:26 ff.; 2:15; II Bar 14:18.

55. *created . . . for us*. Cf. 7:11; Ass Mos 1:12; II Bar 15:7; 21:24. For discussion of this view see Charles's note on II Bar 14:18 (APOT, II, 491). Cf. further Hermas *Visions* 1:1:6, for the sake of the Church.

firstborn world. Reflects the two-eon conception of the author (see Volz, pp. 56 f.).

56. *rest of nations . . . nothing*. Isa 40:17.

like spittle. Cf. Isa 40:15 (LXX has *ōs sielos logisthēsontai*, "they shall be reckoned as spittle"); II Bar 82:5; Pseudo-Philo 7:3; 12:4; the Greek misread the Heb. *dq*, "fine dust" as *rq*, "spittle." Ar.[1] *pulvis*, "dust." Cf. Pseudo-Philo 7:3.

drippings from a bucket. Here the author of II Esdras may have depended on LXX of Isa 40:15a.

57. *bear rule over us*. Cf. also question of Hab 1:13 and the observation of 1QpHab, col. 3.

58. *firstborn*. Exod 4:22; Ps 89:28; Jer 31:9 (of Ephraim) — the Hebrew has *bkwr*.

only begotten. Cf. 4QDibHam, col. 3:5 (RB, 68 [1961], p. 202); Ps Sol 18:4 *monogenē;* but application of descriptive to Jesus in John 1:18 indicates that it was already applied to Israel by Jewish interpreters and theologians earlier.

confidant. Refers to the chosen one (cf. Isa 42:1; 43:20).

dearly beloved. Cf. Deut 33:12; Pss 60:5; 108:7; Isa 5:1; II Bar 5:1; Ps Sol 13:8.

59. *why . . . world*. Question often asked by the Psalmists, cf. 4:2; 13:2; 94:3. A characteristic of the psalms of lamentation.

7:1. *previous nights*. The nights before each vision.

2. *Get up*. A Hebrew expression indicating call to attention and respect (cf. e.g. 6:13; Ezek 2:1).

3. *sea*. Cf. Test Levi 2:7. Here it symbolizes the world to come.

4. *entrance*. See textual note *h–h* but observe this is the expression used in Matt 7:13 f. and parallel in Luke 13:24 where Jesus speaks of entering by the narrow gate. Here it is the way or entrance that is narrow. This is the only place the idea occurs in apocalyptic literature. For rabbinic parallels see StB, I, 460 f. The idea of the way made a significant impact on the Mandeans, as may be seen from the many references to it in their literature (cf. e.g. Mark Lidzbarski, *Ginza* [Göttingen: Vandenhoeck & Ruprecht, 1925], pp. 433, 473, 519, and *Mandäische Liturgien* [Berlin: Weidmann, 1920], p. 101). There the way is broad and endless without milestones to mark off the distance. At or beside the way is an impassable sea. The way is full of thistles and briars, surrounded with seven walls impregnable and without breach. Adam too is connected with the way, as here, though with different motive. What the Mandeans did with the sea concept is interesting (see index in Lidzbarski's

works). References to entrance and gate are frequent. On the implications see references in COMMENT on Section II A, The First Vision, fn. 4.

5. *sail.* Lit. "to rule over," "master." See textual note *k–k*.

broad . . . narrow. The former is the world to come, the latter is this world through which one must pass to enter the broad space. Note the opposites here and in the Mandean writings.

6. *city.* Cf. Lidzbarski, *Ginza,* p. 317, and *Mandäische Liturgien,* p. 134 — the city of Uthras, the dwelling place of light.

open plain. Corresponding to the spacious place of vs. 3.

full of all good things. Ar.¹ interprets: "located in a garden and a plain with fruitful, green fields, and its streets are filled with good things." So also Ethiopic.

7. *road.* See textual note *m–m*. But cf. Hermas *Similitudes* 9:12:5.

fire . . . deep water. Cf. Ps 66:12 and the Matthew and Luke references in NOTE on vs. 4. Reminiscent of Scylla and Charybdis in Homer's *Odyssey* Book 12, and, as Gunkel points out, of the passage to Hades, which may also lie in the background of the preceding parable.

8. *only one man.* Perhaps a covert reference to Israel.

9. *bequeathed to a man.* Lit. "is given to a man as an inheritance."

claim his inheritance. Cf. Luke 19:12; Gal 4:1–7; Hermas *Similitudes* 5:2:6. The whole verse has in mind Israel (the heir) whose inheritance lies in the broad place where the sea is located or the city set in an open plain full of good things. To claim it, it is necessary to pass through this world — narrow, dangerous, and beset with all kinds of difficulties. Cf. II Bar 15:8.

10. *Israel's lot.* Ar.¹ "So it has happened (or fallen) to Israel"; Armenian "For this reason the portion of inheritance was given to Israel." The future world, therefore, belongs to Israel.

11. *for their sakes.* Cf. Ass Mos 1:12; II Esd 6:55, 59. Elsewhere for man (8:1, 44; II Bar 14:18) or the righteous in Israel (II Bar 14:19; 15:7; 21:24). Cf. Moore, III, 146, n. 197, for incisive comment on the difference between *saeculum* and *mundum.*

Adam transgressed (I Bar 4:12 ff.). Perhaps Moore is right in pointing to the Christian doctrine of Adam's fall as having left its mark on interpretations here. But what was judged was not the world God made or what Adam was; it was what was made by virtue of the order of things growing out of Adam's *malum.* It was the order of Adam and not the order of God that was judged. For rabbinic views see StB, III, 250. Cf. biblical references — Gen 3; Ps 37:23; Job 24:18.

12. *ways of this world.* I.e. this world as a passageway to the broad place and city set in an open plain — the world to come.

few and evil. See textual note *t–t*. Cf. Gen 47:9 where Vulgate reads *parvi et mali,* "short and evil"; here *pauci . . . et mali,* "few [in number] and evil." See II Bar 16:1.

fraught. Lit. "stiffened."

13. *greater world.* Cf. II Enoch 61:2 f.; Rev 22:2.

fruit of immortality. This may refer to the tree of life. Cf. I Enoch 25:4, 5; Test Lev 18:11; II Esd 7:123; 8:52.

14. *narrow and vain things.* Cf. Matt 7:14; Acts 14:22; Barn 7:11.

things stored up. Cf. I Cor 2:9; Col 1:5; II Tim 4:18. See further TWNT, V, p. 57, n. 43.

15. In view of better things to come, the seer is chided for his brooding over the fact that he is perishable and mortal; this is but the narrow and hard way he has to pass through to life (cf. also I Cor 15:53 f.).

16. *Why don't you think about.* Cf. Isa 43:18; Job 37:14. Gunkel (in loco) rightly observes the significance of this verse for the coherence of the book because it marks the transition of the author's thought from the present to the future. There may be a concealed historical reference here to the fall of Jerusalem in 587 B.C. which was not the end of things; neither would its fall now be the end. There was a return and reconstruction. But the writer now has a different perspective as will become apparent later.

17. *in your law.* Cf. Deut 8:1.

the just . . . the wicked. This was the belief of both Jews and Christians of the first century A.D. The conflict between them arose on how to become just.

18. *bear . . . have hope.* I Enoch 102:4; II Bar 14:12 ff.

19. *God.* Employed three times in vss. 19–21 and elsewhere only in 8:58 (a quotation of Ps 14:1) and 9:45. See Violet's long note in loco. Ethiopic and Georgian substitute "only one" in vs. 19; Syriac omits it in vs. 20. Armenian follows Latin.

discriminating. Lit. "intelligent," "wise," "understanding." On 19b, cf. Apoc Paul 33 — "Are you more merciful than God?" and the rhetorical questions in Job 8:3; 21:22; Acts 4:19.

20. *law of God.* Occurs only once so far in Qumran texts (1QpH 1:11). Cf. n. 3, p. 248, in Lidzbarski, *Ginza* (on use of term in Syriac version).

21. *those coming [into the world] when they came.* Ar.[1] "when they were born." How wide is the reference? To all who are born, i.e. everybody, Jew and Gentile or only to those Jews who were born? Cf. John 1:9; Sir 15:14–20; I Enoch 38:2.

22. *unconvinced and resisted.* Lit. "not persuaded and spoke against."

23. *denied the existence of the Most High.* Cf. 8:58; Pss 14:1; 53:1.

acknowledge his ways. Cf. Prov 3:6; 1QS 5:19 "they do not acknowledge his covenant," where those who follow vanity are characterized. On Qumran conceptions see Nötscher, *Zur theologischen Terminologie der Qumran-Texte*, p. 113, and *Gotteswege und Menschenwege in der Bibel und in Qumram,* Bonn: Hanstein, 1958.

24. *law . . . covenants . . . commandments.* On biblical conceptions cf. Pss 19:7 ff.; 119; James 2:25 f.

accomplish his work. Cf. John 4:34; 17:4 (see Latin); 1QS 4:25; CD 1:1–2; 2:14–15.

25. Cf. Eccles 1:14; Jer 2:5b; Matt 13:12; Mark 4:25; Hermas *Mandates* 11:1:3, 13, 15; 12:5:1 ff.

26. *signs.* See 6:20–24.

invisible city. Cf. 13:36; II Bar 4; Rev 21:2 which may indicate how the Latin translator got his reading of the bride (see Gunkel's suggestion, in loco). The city is Jerusalem.

land which is now hidden. I.e. paradise; the city and land are mentioned together elsewhere.

27. *evils mentioned before.* Lit. "predicted evils" — cf. 6:25.

my wonders. Cf. II Bar 29:6; Sir 18:6; 1QH 1:21; 4:28 ff.

28. *my son Jesus.* A Christian alteration for "my messiah"; cf. I Enoch 105:1; *Christos kyrios* of Ps Sol 17:36.

those who are with him. Cf. I Thess 3:13; II Thess 1:7; Jude 14; but the author has in mind 6:26 above.

revealed. Cf. II Bar 29:3.

joy. Cf. Sir 35:19.

four hundred years. See textual note¹. Gunkel (in loco) thinks this is a combination of Ps 90:15 and Gen 15:13. For rabbinic calculations see Oesterley, pp. 70 f.; StB, III, 826; JBL 53 (1934), 170–87, and the references in Rosenthal, p. 64, n. 2. Rev 20:4 speaks of Christ's interregnum as lasting a thousand years. II Bar 40:3 is indefinite. On whole idea, with variations, see Bousset, pp. 286–89.

29. *Christ will die.* Cf. I Cor 15:28; II Bar 30:1; and on the death of the messiah see Schürer, II, 553 ff.

all who have human breath. Lit. "breathing organs of man." Cf. Gen 7:22; Ps 150:6; Isa 2:22; Eccles 3:19.

30. *primordial silence.* Cf. II Bar 3:7; II Esd 6:39; and silence after the flood in Gilgamesh epic Tablet XI, line 132.

the very beginning. Lit. "the first of the beginning." The implication seems to be that things will revert to the condition preceding creation (apparently against the conception of II Baruch), and "nobody will remain." See Klausner, pp. 355 f.

31. *world . . . not yet awake.* The world still to come.

corruptible . . . pass away. Cf. I Cor 15:26, 53, 54; Rev 20:14; 21:4; the corruptible here comes close to meaning death.

32. *earth will give up those asleep in it.* Cf. Dan 12:2, I Thess 4:13, 15; Pseudo-Philo 3:10; 19:12; I Enoch 51:1.

storehouses. Cf. I Enoch 22:4; 100:5. The origin of the conception of resurrection is obscure but it has been of immense significance in the history of religion. As Gunkel (in loco) points out, it really marks a watershed in the religious history of Israel.

33. *Most High . . . on the judgment seat.* Dan 7:9; Rev 20:11; I Enoch 45:3; Test Levi 5:1.

Then the end. Cf. I Cor 15:24; I Peter 4:7.

compassion will vanish; Pity will cease, And forbearance . . . withdrawn. Cf. Isa 59:9, 11; I Enoch 38:6; 50:5; 101:3; Sib Or 5:353, 510; Jer 13:14; Ezek 5:11 et al.; Zech 11:6 (the prophetic passages refer to the incorrigibly wicked); 1QS 2:7; 10:20; 1QH 9:3 — where these are attributed to the confessor.

34. *Truth . . . faith.* In the sense of loyalty, dependability, and faithfulness — the criteria upon which judgment is based. It will be impartial and strict (cf. Deut 16:19 f.). See I Esd 4:38, 41.

35. *Reward will follow*. Cf. Rev 14:13; reward and recompense in parallelism in Isa 40:10.

Good deeds will awake. Cf. Matt 6:4; 25:31–46; they will be revealed, and so will the evil ones (cf. I Tim 5:4 f.).

36. *pit of torment*. Cf. *topos basanou*, "place of torment," in Luke 16:28; Ezek 31:16; Ps 40:3. Cf. "lake of fire" (Rev 19:20; 21:8); "bottomless pit" (Rev 9:2); "abyss of fire" (I Enoch 10:13; 90:26); "eternal fire" (II Enoch 63:4); "tormented" (II Bar 51:6).

place of rest. Cf. Abraham's bosom in Luke 16:23.

oven of Gehenna. "Mouth of Gehenna," II Bar 59:10; in Pirqe Aboth, Gehenna is referred to as the pit of destruction (5:22).

paradise of joy. Cf. II Bar 51:11; Test Levi 18:10; Pirqe Aboth 5:20 where the lots of the righteous and wicked are contrasted, and NOTE on 4:8.

37. *Consider and know*. For combination of such attention-calling terms see Isa 41:20; Jer 2:19. On thought of verse see I Enoch 60:6.

38. *Look hither and yon*. Cf. Luke 16:23, 24.

joy and repose . . . fire and torment. Frequently found in apocryphal literature in describing the fate of the righteous and wicked. Cf. Test Judah 25:3 ff.; I Enoch 103; II Bar 50, 51.

39–42. The poetic form is clearly evident, originally composed of three stanzas, each with a tricolon. For thought parallels see Gen 8:22; Zech 14:6; Ps 74:16 f.; Sib Or 3:89–92; II Enoch 10:2; Eccles 12:2; and for convenient table of order in the versions see Gry, I, 159. The whole list is doubtless based on the Genesis and Ecclesiasticus passages (cf. Rosenthal, p. 65, where Midrashic materials are cited. Mandean literature is full of the same expressions and allusions.

42. *splendorous brightness of the Most High*. Cf. Isa 60:19 f.; Rev 21:23. The divine light before the creation of light, which will continue when the latter ceases.

43. *a week of years*. Cf. vs. 30 above and Dan 9:24 ff. The world was created in a week from which grew the tradition underlying the passage. Primordial time and that of the end were alike in duration.

45. *I said then*. See vs. 17 above.

Fortunate . . . observe the precepts. Cf. Ps 119:1, 2; Prov 28:19; Luke 11:28; Rev 22:7; Sir 25:7 ff.

46. *my prayer*. See vs. 18.

sinned. Rom 3:23; I John 1:10; note emphasis on the universality of sin here and in 8:35.

who of those born . . . your covenant. The broad assertion that all who are born have violated or transgressed the covenant is sweeping in its inclusiveness (cf. I Kings 8:46; II Chron 6:36; Gal 3:22). See Moore, I, 468 f.; II, 322, n. 1. In a Sumerian Wisdom text it is said: "Never has a sinless child been born to its mother, . . . a sinless *workman* has not existed from of old." (J. B. Pritchard, ANET: *Supplementary Texts and Pictures* [Princeton University Press, 1969], p. 154.)

47. *few . . . many*. This was always a problem, even when the future world

was not contemplated (cf. Jer 42:2; Ezek 12:16). Here the thought is similar to that expressed by Jesus in Matt 7:13 f.; Luke 13:23.

48. *evil heart*. See COMMENT on Section II A, The First Vision, at 3:20. There is some question of translation here. Does the writer mean to say that the impulse to do evil has grown (our rendering) or simply that an evil impulse is present among us? The Syriac indicates the latter, the Latin *increvit* the former — the evil heart in us has been augmented, increased. Cf. 4:30 the grain of evil seed.

from them. Probably refers to the commandments above. Violet (in loco) has suggested that the Hebrew thought may have been *m'lhym*, "from God" which the author, to avoid using the term God, changed to *mhm*. Abraham Kahana, *Has-s^epharim Haḥitsonim*, II, 628 [BIBLIO II], has *y^enakk^erenu le'loah*, "we were strangers to God." Cf. Eph 4:18; Col 1:21.

driven us into corruption. Cf. II Peter 2:19.

ways of death. Cf. Deut 30:19; Prov 14:12; Jer 21:8.

paths of perdition. *'bdn'*, "Abaddon," in Syriac. Cf. Job 28:22; Prov 15:11.

took us far away. May contain a historical reference to exile as appears to be indicated by the final clause of the verse.

50. *not one world but two*. Esdras' two-world conception, this world being the one leading into the world to come, spoken about in vss. 1 ff. Cf. vs. 112.

52. Text is unclear as may be seen from the wide variations of the versions but the meaning seems to be that the value of a few precious gems cannot be increased by the addition of lead and clay vessels. For figure of the precious and less valuable see I Enoch 65:7 f.; in another context, Jer 15:19. Note use of economic terms for purposes of comparison. It was apparently a well-recognized conception, not a novel one as Gunkel and Box think.

54. *Inquire of the earth*. Cf. imaginary conversational form in Hosea 2:21 f.; Job 12:7 f.; 16:18; also II Esd 8:2.

57. *more valuable and desirable*. Supply and demand is the principle expressed here.

59. *Compare for yourself*. The idea is to weigh carefully. The same terms are found in Prov 3:15 in the Syriac Bible (*yqr*, "precious," and *phm*, "compare").

60. *the few*. See NOTE on vs. 47 above.

confirm my glory. Cf. Pss 29:1 f.; 96:3; 1QS 10:9; 1QH 11:6; 12:30, and often elsewhere.

my name is even now named. I.e. in praise. Cf. 1QH 1:30; 3:23; 11:25; 12:3; 11QPs 19:8; for Israel called by the name of the Lord see Deut 28:10; Jer 14:9; a wider import in Amos 9:12.

61. *I will not lament*. Cf. I Enoch 89:58; 94:10; 97:2; Pss 2:4; 37:13; Qoran, Sura 7.

vapor. Ps 144:4; Hosea 13:3; Wisd Sol 2:4; James 4:14; II Bar 82:3.

smoke. Hosea 13:3; Ps 37:20; II Bar 82:6.

flames . . . kindled, blazed up, and have gone out. Like a brush fire, it blazes furiously but burns out quickly. Perhaps the idea of the fleeting character of the multitude with its destruction is meant to be conveyed.

62. *reason.* Both reason and Adam came from the same source: the earth (cf. 7:116 f., a significant parallel). The question is what is meant by the Latin *sensus?* The word in this verse occurs only in Latin and Syriac; in the next verse the Ethiopic substituted "heart," while Ar.² has *fqr,* "reflection," "reason," "understanding," twice in its addition to vs. 63. The different renderings indicate the uncertainty of correct interpretation. Goodspeed has "understanding," "intelligence"; Violet, *"Verstand";* Gunkel, *"Vernunft";* Box, "mind"; Oesterley, "mind"; Gry, *"raison";* Kahana, *"leb"* (heart); RSV and NEB have "mind" in vs. 62 but the latter has "power of thought" in vs. 63. Harnisch (pp. 156 ff.) discusses the possibility that the underlying original might have been *yetser,* "impulse." NEB makes a question out of 7:62. The complaint voiced by Ezra is reflected also in Rom 8:22 f. For an analysis of the terminology involved at Qumran see Nötscher, *Zur theologischen Terminologie der Qumran-Texte,* pp. 52 ff.

63. *reason . . . produced from it.* On thought cf. II Enoch 41:2; I Enoch 38:2; II Bar 10:6; Matt 26:24, where the idea is expressed that it would have been better, under the conditions given, if man had not been born. Here the complaint is directed against reason or the quality that makes man knowledgeable or responsible.

64. *tormented because we are aware of perishing.* Knowledge of what is coming creates increasing agony for an already troubled conscience.

65. The more favorable lot of the animals voiced here is the opposite of the biblical conception where man is said to have dominion over them (cf. Gen 1:26, 28; Ps 8:5–8; 1QS 3:17–18). See, however, also Tischendorff, *Apocalypses apocryphae,* p. 25 (Apoc Esdrae, 13). The author's reasoning is given in vs. 66.

66. Cf. Eccles 4:2–3; II Bar 10:6.

67. *to us.* Note the author's inclusion of himself (see vs. 48), but cf. 6:32 f.; Ezek 33:12.

68. *entangled . . . full . . . laden.* Potent description of the complexity of involvement in sin. Cf. II Bar 21:19. The universality of sin (Eccles 7:20; Prov 20:9) was stressed by the rabbis (cf. Sanhedrin 101a). See also II Esd 8:34 f. and vs. 46 above.

69. Despite assertions elsewhere by apocalyptists that due to their peculiar situation the judgment was for them, i.e. they were the righteous ones, Ezra here expresses his skepticism. Paul had the same view (Rom 7:13–24); he cried out, "O wretched man that I am" and despaired utterly of himself without Christ. For Ezra's solution see 8:48b. Cf. further Luke 17:10.

70. *he first ordained judgment.* I.e. the judgment has been predetermined since in preparation for it paradise and Gehenna were created before the world, according to rabbinic theology (Pesaḥ 54a). The inevitability of judgment is due to the above-noted entanglements of sin.

72. *torment because.* Cf. II Bar 15:5, 6; 19:3; 48:40; Barn 5:4; Luke 12:47 f. Here the concept of reason is, in effect, turned around, and renders man accountable for his acts because he knows right and wrong. He willingly re-

ceived the commandments and accepted the law but circumvented what he had received and accepted. Cf. strong emphasis on guilt incurred deliberately in 1QS 7.

73. *say at judgment.* Cf. I Enoch 62:10; 63:11; Matt 25:37, 44; 1QH 1:25.

74. *patience.* Cf. 1QH 1:6.

on account of them. Occurs about five times in Pseudo-Philo.

times . . . predetermined. Cf. 4:37; 6:6; 1QS 3:15 f.; the *mw'd mšpṭ nhrsh,* "appointed time of judgment," in 1QS 4:20; or *'d qṣ nhrsh,* "until the appointed time," of 1QS 4:25; 1QpHab 7:7, 12; et al.

75. *If you please.* Lit. "if I have found favor before you."

renew the creation. Greek *kainē ktisis.* For the expression see Gal 6:15; II Cor 5:17. For the conception of a recreated world, cf. Matt 19:28; II Peter 3:13; Rev 21:1; II Bar 32:6 (cf. 44:12; 57:2); Isa 65:17; 66:22; 1QH 11:13; Pseudo-Philo 3:10; 16:3; 32:17; 1QS 4:25 *'swt hdš.*

76. *entangled with scorners.* Cf. II Peter 2:20 f. Cf. renunciations of confessor in 1QS 10:20 ff.; for the involvement of the righteous one with sinners in the world, 1QH 3:24 f.

77. *treasure of works.* Cf. 8:33; II Bar 14:12; Matt 6:20; Ps Sol 9:9; Test Levi 13:5; Moore, II, 91; Schrader, *Keilinschriften,* p. 405, n. 4. See NOTE on 4:35.

last times. Cf. Qumran expression *'hryt hymym,* "end of days," e.g. 1QpHab 2:5; 9:6; 1QSa 1:1; 4QpNahum 2:2; 3:3 *b'hryt hqṣ.*

78. *return again to him. . . .* Cf. Eccles 12:7; Apoc Moses 31:4; for God's giving of spirit see 1QH 12:11; 13:19; 16:11; 4QFl 3:14.

79. *scorned.* Cf. 1QH 2:11.

ways . . . Most High. Cf. 1QS 3:10; 8:13; CD 20:18.

held his law in contempt. 1QpHab 1:11; 5:11; 1QS 3:5; CD 8:19; 19:5.

hated those who feared God. Cf. II Chron 19:2. On whole verse see 1QH 15:17–19; 1QpHab 2.

80. *spirits.* For references to the interpretation of this verse, especially "spirits" see Bensly, MF, p. 64, n. 80.

habitations. Latin varies in words used for the dwelling place of the righteous after death. Here it is *habitationes;* vss. 85, 101, 121 *habitacula;* 4:35; 7:32, 95 *promptuaria.* See NOTE on vs. 77, the original Hebrew for treasury-treasure of works and storehouse was doubtless *'wṣr,* "storehouse."

roam around. Cf. Matt 12:43; Luke 11:24.

seven ways. May be origin of seven-hell conception (cf. Gunkel, *Schöpfung und Chaos,* p. 309; Qoran, Sura 15, on seven gates of hell).

81. Cf. Wisd Sol 5:1; 16:16 (on former see Johannes Fichtner, *Weisheit Salomos* [Tübingen: Mohr, 1938], p. 23).

law of the Most High. Cf. 11QPs Col 18:12 (Syriac Apocryphal Psalm 2) *btwrt 'lywn;* Sir 9:15; 19:17; 23:23; 39:1; 41:8; 42:2; 44:20; 49:4.

82. *unable to truly repent.* They apparently want to repent but that is now denied them. Cf. I Enoch 63:5–8; 65:11; Heb 12:17.

83. *see the reward.* See Luke 16:23; Ps Sol 4:8 f.

faithful to the covenants. . . . Cf. 1QpHab 2:4, 6, 14; 1QH 9:31.

84. *torment.* Cf. Job 15:20; for the victim of the wicked seeing their end, Ps 91:8.

deposited. I.e. the torment stored up against them for the future.

85. *guarded by angels.* Cf. I Enoch 100:5, 6; II Bar 30:2.

complete freedom from disturbance. Lit. "with great silence."

86. *immediately.* Latin *amodo* is a Grecism, *apo nun*, "from now." Some of the wicked will thus pass into punishment at once, in contrast to vs. 84.

87. *consumed in shame.* Cf. 1QS 4:23; Pss 35:26; 40:14.

pine away. II Bar 30:4; 51:5; Lev 26:39; Ezek 24:23b; Pseudo-Philo 16:3.

glory of the Most High. Cf. 1QS 10:9; CD 20:26.

judged in the last times. Only one reference to posthumous judgment in OT — Ps 1:5.

88. *ways . . . Most High.* See second NOTE on vs. 79.

crumbling vessel. Lit. "corruptible vase." Cf. 4:10; *kly 'bd* in Ps 31:13; II Cor 4:7; I Cor 15:53; 1QH 4:9. The body is the prison of the soul.

89. *observe perfectly the law of the lawgiver.* Cf. I Macc 2:50; I Enoch 108:7 ff. (Fragment of the Book of Noah). The reference is to the Torah of the Lord given through Moses. See second NOTE on vs. 79 and Pseudo-Philo 33:3.

91. *seven orders.* The seven joys (Gunkel), steps or grades (Violet), of the spirit. See fourth NOTE on vs. 80. Cf. Test Levi 2:6 ff. on the stages or gradations of heaven. Cf. Schrader, *Keilinschriften,* pp. 617 ff., and references there.

92. *the evil thought molded.* Cf. Gen 8:21; Pseudo-Philo 33:3; 1QS 5:5; CD 2:16. This is the *yṣr hr'*, "evil impulse." The Syriac *mḥšbt' byšt'*, "evil thought," "tendency," is almost like the Qumran and Damascus Covenant citations and I Chron 28:9; 29:18 *yṣr mḥšbwt.* This impulse could be for good (*yṣr ḥṭwb*) or evil. But the law was created as a help to counteract the latter (cf. Bereshith Rabba 27 and Kiddushin 30b). For the whole matter of the evil impulse see Moore, I, 479 ff.

93. *they see the entanglements . . . of the wicked.* Cf. Ps 118:7; I Enoch 62:12; Ass Mos 10:10; Apoc Peter 11:13; II Clem 17:7; 4QpPs 37, 4:11.

roam about. Common belief that the evil spirits remained at large because they had no resting place (cf. Matt 12:43 — not parallel but idea of wandering spirit is clear).

94. *witness.* I.e. what they now see.

entrusted to them. Lit. "the law was given to them in [or by] faith."

95. *comprehend the rest.* I.e. understand and appreciate it (cf. 4QpPs 37, 4:11). In their storehouses they are undisturbed by the trials endured in life (vs. 89) because their place of abode is guarded by angels — cf. great gulf fixed of Luke 16:26.

96. *escaped the corruptible.* Gunkel has noted that the author believed corruptibility did not belong to the essence of man but was foreign to it. Cf. also W. O. E. Oesterley, *Immortality and the Unseen World* (London: SPCK. 1921), pp. 190–99.

difficulties. Lit. "full of hardship," "pain," "labor."

97. *face is to shine like the sun and . . . the light of the stars.* Cf. vs. 125; I Enoch 104:2; II Enoch 1:5; II Bar 51:3, 10; Dan 12:3; Matt 13:43. As Gunkel has pointed out the stars of heaven were originally regarded as angels. Our author affirms the resurrected are like them. They are no longer corruptible, subject to corruption (cf. I Cor 15:53, 54, KJ), but are "like angels in heaven" (Matt 22:30; Mark 12:25). See discussion of subject by Efros, MKJV, pp. 222 f.

98. *with assurance.* Lit. *fiducia*, "with self-confidence," "boldness," "trust" (cf. *en parrēsia pollē*, Wisd Sol 5:1).

genuinely happy. Lit. "rejoice without fear."

see the face. Cf. Matt 5:8; Rev 22:4; I John 3:2.

reward. Cf. Rev 22:12 where the Syriac uses the same word as it does here.

100. *souls.* I.e. the souls of the just, in preceding verse. The souls of the wicked are not gathered into the heavenly storehouse but roam about (vs. 93).

101. *seven days.* This conception is probably based on an old tradition. See references in Bousset, pp. 297 ff.; note especially Book of Adam and Eve 51, which warns against mourning for more than six days because on the seventh day the departed is the subject of the rejoicing of God and angels, i.e. he has entered the portals of heaven.

102. *If you please.* Lit. "If I have found favor before your eyes."

the day of judgment. Not necessarily a Christian conception (cf. III Bar 1:7; Test Levi 3:3; I Enoch 10:6; 22:11; Jub 4:19; II Enoch 39:1; Ps Sol 15:13; Judith 16:17. *ywm hdyn* is common in rabbinic literature. See 7:113 and 12:34.

intercede. Cf. Pseudo-Philo 33:5.

103. *fathers for sons.* Cf. Pseudo-Philo 33:5.

104. *yes, I will grant . . . this favor.* Lit. "because you have found favor before my eyes."

seal of truth. I.e. the seal of the judge which guarantees the validity of the sentence. Cf. Sir 45:12.

105. *nobody can pray for another.* Cf. II Enoch 53:1; II Bar 85:12. II Bar 84:10 exhorts persistent and diligent prayer that the sins of those praying may not be reckoned against them but that the Mighty One may "remember the rectitude of your fathers." Cf. also Apostolic Constitutions 2:14. The whole passage appears to be based on Ezek 18:20.

106. *Abraham.* Gen 18:23.

Moses. Exod 32:11.

107. *Joshua . . . Achan.* Cf. Josh 7.

108. *Samuel.* I Sam 7:9; 12:23.

David. II Sam 24:15 ff.

Solomon. I Kings 8:22 f., 30 f.

in the sanctuary. His prayer for Israel at the time of the dedication of the temple.

109. *Elijah . . . rain.* I Kings 18:36 f., 42.

dead . . . live. I Kings 17:20 f.

110. *Hezekiah.* II Kings 19:15 ff.

112. *its glory*. The Syriac has *tšbwhth d'lh'*, "the glory of God," which is probably right. In that case the reference is to the Shekinah (cf. vs. 122). For the significance of the presence of the Shekinah and the conditions of its withdrawal see Solomon Schechter, *Some Aspects of Rabbinic Theology* (New York: Schocken, 1961), p. 223.

116. *it would have been better*. Cf. 7:66; II Bar 10:6; 48:12, 16; Eccles 4:3; Job 10:18; Jer 20:14–18.

generate. I.e. produced Adam (cf. 3:5).

not to sin. Cf. 1QH 14:17; also II Esd 7:63.

117. See NOTES on vss. 65–66.

any [of us]. Lit. "all [of us]"; Heb. *kl* which means "any" as well as "all."

118. *O Adam*. Cf. II Bar 48:42; Apoc Moses 14.

the fall. Cf. Moore, III, 146, n. 198, who holds that *casus* ought not be translated "fall" but "disaster." He thinks the idea of "Adam's fall" cannot be dissociated from the Christian doctrine of the "fall." Note the different renderings of *casus* by the versions — Syriac and Ethiopic have "evil"; Ar.[1] "sentence," "judgment"; Ar.[2] "damage," "loss"; Armenian "suffering." Passage is not in Georgian due to a lacuna. The idea here seems to be that the descendants of Adam experience the same fate he suffered but not necessarily because of it.

but ours, too. Cf. 1QS 11:9. See M. J. Lagrange, *Saint Paul. Épitre aux Romains* (Paris: 1950), p. 116.

119. *immortal time . . . promised to us*. Cf. 7:113; Heb 4:1; Volz, p. 368 f.

death-dealing works. Cf. Heb 6:1; 9:14 *nekra erga*.

120. *perpetual hope*. Cf. I Peter 1:3 *elpis dzōsa*, "living hope"; and Efros, MKJV, p. 222, n. 33.

in utter futility. Cf. 1QS 5:19 where the expression is *m'śy hbl*, "deeds of vanity."

121. *habitations*. See second NOTE on vs. 80.

122. *glory of the Most High*. See NOTE on vs. 112.

conducted . . . impiously. Lit. "we have walked in wicked ways." Cf. Wisd Sol 5:7; 1QS 4:9–11 *lrwḥ 'wlh*, "of the spirit of wrong-doing"; 1QS 5:11 *bdrk hrš'h*, "in the way of wickedness"; and often elsewhere.

123. *paradise . . . fruit*. Cf. Ezek 47:12; Rev 22:2.

124. *unacceptable ways*. Cf. IV Macc 4:1 *panta tropon diaballōn*, "every kind of slander"; Eph 2:3.

125. *exercised self-restraint*. Cf. II Enoch 66:6; Titus 1:8.

shine . . . stars. See NOTE on vs. 97.

blacker than the darkness. A reminiscence of Sheol, the place of darkness without light (Job 10:21b). Cf. Matt 8:12, etc.; I Enoch 10:4 f.; 46:6; 62:10; 63:11; Jude 13; IQH 12:6; and generally the sons of darkness.

127. *struggle*. The struggle is with evil, or rather against the evil inclination.

128. *if he is defeated*. I.e. if the evil inclination gets the upper hand.

if he is victorious. I.e. if the good impulse or inclination prevails. Cf. Sir 15:14–17: "God from the beginning created man, and put him in the hand of his despoiler, and gave him into the hand of his inclination (*yṣrw*). If you desire [to do so] you can keep the commandment, and it is understanding to do his delight; if you have confidence in him, you will live. Poured out before you are fire and water; stretch out your hand for what you desire. Before man are life and death [and] what he desires will be given to him" (literal translation of Hebrew).

129. *the way.* This refers back to the victory gained in the struggle which everyone born must wage, and forward to the means by which it can be achieved. As Gunkel has pointed out, while Ezra looks at life from the vantage point of the sinner, the interpreting angel always views it from that of the saved (APAT, II, p. 378).

Choose . . . life . . . live. Cf. Deut 30:19; Ass Mos 3:11 f.; II Bar 19:1 f.; 1QSb 3:25 (not an exhortation here). Of course the term "life" here refers to life after death. The addition of the Syriac is the translator's inclusion of the fuller text of the OT passage.

130. *or me.* Here the interpreting angel thinks of himself as the bearer of the word of God just as Moses and the prophets were. Cf. name of Malachi which means "my messenger." On the place of Moses, the prophets, and the angelic interpreters in apocalyptic, see Volz, pp. 190 ff.

131. See NOTES on vss. 60, 61.

132. *the merciful one.* This is the first in a series of seven descriptives of the Lord probably based on Exod 34:6, 7; cf. also Ps 145:8–9. Several of the series occur together in Neh 9:17 — (1) *sylḥwt,* "forgivenesses," (2) *ḥnwn wrḥwm,* "gracious and compassionate," (3) *'rk 'pym,* "long suffering," (4) *rb ḥsd,* "great in steadfast love," (5) *rb ḥsd w'mt,* "great in steadfast love and devotion."

Joel 2:13	(2), (3), (4)
Jonah 4:2	(2), (3), (4)
Ps 86:15	(2), (3), (5)
Ps 103:8	(2), (3), (4)

D. Simonsen, "Ein Midrasch im IV Buch Esra," in *Festschrift zu Israel Lewys 70 Geburtstag* (Breslau: M. and H. Marcus, 1911), pp. 270–78 and Moore, I, 390 f. regard vss. 132–39 as a Midrash on Exod 34:6–7. The characterizations are nominal, as in Syriac, rather than adjectival, as Latin. Some of them occur also in Qumran literature — e.g. 1QH 1:31 f.; 4:37; 6:9 f.; 10:14; 11:9, 29 f.; 1QM 14:8; CD 2:4; etc.

not yet come into the world. Cf. Midrash Rabba on Gen 21:17 — despite foreknowledge, God will exercise compassion for those not yet born before they sin.

133. *the gracious one.* Cf. Exod 22:27; II Chron 30:9; Pss 111:4; 116:5; I Peter 2:3; Ass Mos 4:6.

return to his law. Two interpretations are possible: (a) repentance, (b) conversion of *gerim,* "outsiders." Cf. II Bar 41:4.

134. *the long-suffering one.* Lit. "slow of anger." Often in Bible. Cf. 1QS 4:3; CD 2:4.

they are his creatures. Cf. appeal in Isa 64:7, 8, especially as transmitted by LXX; cf. *m'śy 'l,* "works of God," in 1QH 5:36; CD 1:2; 2:15.

135. *the generous one.* Latin *munificus* which Violet (in loco) thinks may be a translation of original *donator,* "giver"; cf. Ps 145:15 *nwtn,* "the one who gives," "giver."

give . . . exact. Cf. Acts 20:35.

136. *the one of many mercies.* See textual note *b–b*.

multiplies . . . [his] mercies. Cf. Pss 86:5, 13, 15; 106:7, 45; Lam 3:32.

present . . . past . . . future. Those now living, the dead, and those yet to be born.

137. *could not continue.* Cf. Ps 119:77; Ps Sol 15:15.

138. *the giver.* There is some question as to the original here. M reads *et donat,* "and he gives." But how is the giver related to forgiveness?

relieved of their iniquities. Cf. Acts 5:31; 11:18; II Tim 2:25; Sir 18:13; Ps Sol 5:5. Some of those references are to the giving of repentance and forgiveness and may have some bearing on the divine descriptive at the beginning of the verse.

139. *the judge.* See textual note *f–f*.

pardon. The function of the judge is to indict or release.

annul. Probably the Hebrew was *nś'* (cf. Ps 32:5; Exod 32:32; 34:7; CD 3:18 of Text A¹ [the text of CD as edited by Leonhard Rost in his *Die Damaskusschrift,* Berlin: Walter de Gruyter & Co., 1933]; 1QH 16:16).

multitudinous offenses. Cf. Hosea 9:7; Jer 30:14, 15; Lam 1:5; 1QH 1:32; 4:19.

8:1. *the Most High.* Cf 1QH 6:33.

the many . . . the few. See NOTES on 7:47–61.

3. Cf. Matt 20:16; 22:14.

4. *Imbibe, my soul.* Cf. Prov 3:5. The seer here expresses his doubts about an intellectual solution for his problem. The passage is strongly reminiscent of Wisdom as the words perception, heart, discernment indicate. The figures of speech are materialistic in tone (cf. also Ps 34:8; Heb 6:4, 5; I Peter 2:3) but the significance runs deep because the writer is probing the ways of the Lord.

5. *involuntarily.* Cf. Pirqe Aboth 4:29: "For not of your own will were you molded and not of your own will will you die, and not of your own will are you to give a just account and reckoning before the King of the kings, the Holy One, blessed be he." Cf. also II Bar 14:11.

leaving . . . without . . . consent. Cf. II Bar 48:15.

only a short span of time. Cf. II Bar 48:12.

6. *seed of heart.* The Syriac rendering (*lb' ḥdt',* "new heart") coupled with the cultivation of perception echoes Paul's conception (Rom 12:2; Eph 4:23, 24) of the renewal of heart and mind. "The *cor malignum* (evil heart) is to be replaced by a *cor novum* (new heart) and the *granum seminis mali* (grain of evil seed) (4:30) by the *semen cordis novi* (seed of a new heart)," Box, in APOT, II, 593.

fruit may come. Cf. Lidzbarski, *Mandäische Liturgien,* p. 141, and *Ginza,* p. 534; W. C. Till, *Die gnostischen Schriften des koptischen Papyrus Berolinensis 8502* (Berlin: Akademie Verlag, 1955), 104:14 ff.; 122:12 ff.

likeness. Cf. Gen 1:27; Rom 5:14.

7. *you are by yourself.* Cf. Deut 4:35; 6:4; Isa 43:11; 44:6, 8; 45:6, 21.

formation of your hands. Man was the direct production of the hand of God (Gen 2:7); the other creation was called into being by the word. (II Bar 48:24; 1QH 3:21; Job 10:8 regard man as the work of God's hands.)

just as you said. Cf. references in opening NOTE on this verse.

8. *molded in the womb.* Cf. Ps 139:15 ff.; Job 10:10 ff.; 31:15; Isa 44:2, 24; 49:5; 1QH 9:30; 15:15, 17; 1QS 11:21; Wisd Sol 7:2.

fire and water. Refers to the constituent elements of man. Cf. 4:10; for latter element see also 1QH 1:21; 3:24. One wonders if the liquidity and color of blood had something to do with origin of this conception. For Philo's idea see his *On Creation of the World* 51 and on rabbinic views Weber, p. 210 f.

nine months. Period of gestation before birth. Nowhere mentioned in Bible; Wisd Sol 7:2 has ten months (see comments and references by Fichtner in *Weisheit Salomos*, p. 29).

9. *shelters.* Note play on words. The womb and foetus are both kept by the Keeper (God). For idea (*ḥasah*) see 1QH 9:29.

evolved. Lit. "what shall have been created in it"; Syriac "what was in it."

10. *fruit of the breasts.* Cf. 1QH 9:30 "from the breasts"; Isa 66:11 "her consoling breasts" — of Jerusalem.

11. *direct it with your mercy.* Cf. 1QH 9:30b "from the breasts of her who conceived me, your mercies were [over] me and in the bosom of my nurse. . . ." On *direct* cf. Ar.[1] *dbr*, "manage," "govern," and use of *yrh* in Hebrew, though not with *rḥm* or *ḥsd*. For Latin meaning see textual note [c].

12. *law . . . wisdom.* Cf. Sir 17:11; I Bar 3:37 – 4:1; II Bar 38:2 — where the law and wisdom are associated but where the former appears as basis for latter.

temper. Cf. Ar.[1] *'lm*, "informed." On whole verse see Pseudo-Philo 33:3.

13. *kill . . . restore.* Cf. Deut 32:39; I Sam 2:6; II Kings 5:7. Yahweh has the power to bring the dead back to life. That is what the writer celebrates. The sequence is the same as in I Sam 2:6, "Yahweh kills and makes alive, he brings down to Sheol and brings up (from Sheol)." The resuscitation narratives of Elijah and Elisha point in the same direction, i.e. Yahweh's power made available to the prophet to revive the dead or the mortally ill. The important point is the sequence and Yahweh's power to revive the dead or the near dead. See comments by Box and Oesterley, in loco.

14. *so readily do away.* Lit. "facile order."

molded with such [great] pains. Cf. Ps 139:14–16; see NOTE on vs. 8.

15. *emphasize.* Lit. "saying let me say."

you know best. tu plus scis, tu prae omnibus scis occur (18:3; 21:2) in Pseudo-Philo (cf. 53:7).

totality of mankind. I.e. mankind outside of Israel, whose fate the seer does not worry about too much. He is content to leave it to the Lord.

your people. Cf. Deut 9:26; Ps 28:9; 1QH 4:6, 11, 16, 26; 6:8; and frequently in Pseudo-Philo.

16. *your heritage.* Cf. 1QM 12:12; 19:4; 1QH 6:8.

seed of Jacob. Ps 22:23; Isa 45:19; 65:9; Jer 33:26.

17. *inhabit the earth.* There is some question whether *terram* here means

earth or land. Oesterley (in loco) argues for the latter since Israel has been "particularized," but note the address to the Lord in vs. 20.

18. *swift judgment.* Cf. 5:43 *celerius iudicium,* here *celeritatem iudicii;* cf. II Peter 2:1.

19. Cf. Ps 5:2 on whole verse.

Mark my words. Lit. "comprehend," "understand," "perceive"; the Psalm verse noted has *intellige clamorem meum* which renders Heb. *bynh hgygy,* "understand my moaning."

20. For a discussion of the so-called confession of Ezra see Bensly, lxxx–lxxxvi; Violet, I, xxvi–xxix — where textual matters especially are treated. The special introductory note is found in the versions too, an indication of its early use for liturgical purposes. One Ethiopic MS has the sentence in red.

before he was taken [up]. There must have been a tradition that Ezra, like Enoch and Elijah, was taken to heaven without going through the normal process of death.

Lord . . . forever. Cf. Pss 9:8a; 102:13; Isa 57:15; Tobit 5:16; 13:1.

eyes are lifted up. Original reference is to the stars. Cf. Pritchard, *Supplementary Text and Pictures,* p. 137 — Hymn to Enlil.

dwelling places are in the air. Based on the idea of a two-storied world, in the upper one of which God dwells (cf. Amos 9:6; Gunkel, *Schöpfung und Chaos,* pp. 401 ff.).

21. *throne.* Cf. I Enoch 14:18; Ass Mos 4:2; Test Levi 5:1 — all probably based on the description of Ezek 1; I Kings 22:19; II Chron 18:18.

glory. Cf. I Esd 4:59. The effulgence of light surrounding God (Rev 21:23; 22:5).

angelic hosts. Cf. II Bar 48:10; I Enoch 61:10; Dan 7:10; 1QM 12:1.

22. *converted to wind and fire.* Cf. Ps 104:4; II Bar 21:6; one of the seven "souls" in the Apoc John (Codex II, 20:35 ff.) is fire.

word is trustworthy . . . steadfast. Cf. Dürr, *Die Wertung des göttlichen Wortes,* p. 59; for descriptives of the divine word see Pss 19:8 ff.; 119. The old Synagogue Liturgy prayer following the Shema‘ begins with: "True (sure) and constant, established and enduring . . . is this your word," referring to the Shema‘. The same prayer contains the words: "And his throne is established, and his kingdom and faithfulness endure forever." Box (in loco) thinks we have in these verses a reminiscence of this Synagogal Liturgy. Cf. also the great Hymn to Shamash — "Whose command is unalterable" (Falkenstein and von Soden, SAHG, p. 247).

23. *commands are fearful.* Cf. Marduk's word *seqarka palḫu,* "your word is fearful."

glance dries up the depths. See Dan 3:54 (Theodotion); passage is quoted in Apostolic Constitutions 8:7; cf. further Isa 50:2; 51:10. Perhaps a mythological reference reflected in the fearful glance of the gods — in Numushda hymn we read, "your glance is fearful" (SAHG, p. 113).

mountains melt away. Cf. Micah 1:4; Ps 97:5; Sir 16:19.

truth abides forever. Cf. I Esd 4:38, 41); Apostolic Constitutions 8:7; 1QS 9:4; 1QSb 2:2 *'mt 'wlm.* The terms "glance," "tremble," "melt" occur together in LXX of Micah 1:4.

24. One or more of the phrases are common in the devotional literature of the Bible.

25. *So long as I live.* Cf. Ps 116:2.

be responsive. Perhaps Hebrew was *šwb dbr,* frequent in OT.

26. *Do not gaze . . . people.* Cf. Pss 25:7; 51:9; II Bar 48:19. See Bousset, p. 198.

27. *kept . . . despite tribulations.* Box refers to the Maccabean martyrs. Cf. Rev 7:14; et al.

28. *conducted themselves wickedly.* Cf. Isa 59:8; Prov 10:9; 28:18.

respect for you. Lit. "your fear," i.e. "those who fear you."

29. *lived like cattle.* Cf. Ps 73:22, though there may be a veiled meaning — the heathen were sometimes referred to as being like cattle.

those who have taught . . . your law. If we agree with the above (that the cattle refers to the heathen), then this colon would refer to the orthodox Jews. There may be some moral implications in view of the mention of the law and vs. 31.

30. *judged worse than beasts.* Cf. I Enoch 89:10 ff. Box suggests an allusion to informers against the righteous.

confidence in your glory. Cf. Rom 4:20; 1QH 3:35 *'mt kbwdw.* This, and preceding verses focus attention on the righteous rather than on the wicked (cf. II Bar 14:7).

31. *we and our fathers.* Cf. Ps 106:6; Ezra 9:7; Jer 3:25; an Akkadian penitential prayer has the following expressions: "Who is it, who has not fallen into sin against his god, who at all times has observed his command?" SAHG, p. 272).

referred to. Lit. "is called."

32. This verse sounds very much like Paul's doctrine in Rom 3:19–26. Cf. Hans Lietzmann, *An die Römer:* Handbuch zum Neuen Testament 8, 3d ed. (Tübingen: Mohr, 1928), pp. 50 f. It is justification by mercy or compassion. Cf. also this from the Akkadian prayer noted in vs. 31:

> Though my sins be ever so numerous, absolve my guilt;
> Though my wickedness be screened, may your heart be peacefully
>   inclined (toward me)!
> Though my wickedness be ever so numerous, grant me the more mercy!

Cf. James 2:12; and the prayer of Habakkuk (3:2).

33. *good deeds are on deposit.* Cf. 7:77; II Bar 14:12 f.

receive their reward. Cf. Ps Sol 17:11; and the Baruch passage just noted. The classical Hebrew teaching. See Weber, par. 61. I Enoch 38:2a; 50:3; Ps Sol 9:7 ff. Cf. Moore, II, 91.

34. Cf. Ps 8:4; Job 7:17 f.; note the author's interpretation.

35. Verse is quoted in the Ezra Apocalypse (Tischendorff, *Apocalypses apocryphae,* p. 30); cf. 7:46, 68; 9:19 f.; Eccles 7:20; Prov 20:9; Job 15:14–16; 25:4 f.; Moore, I, 468. For rabbinic discussion see Rosenthal, p. 60.

36. Cf. Rom 5:8; I Tim 1:15.

treasury of good deeds. Matt 6:19 f.; 19:21 f.; II Bar 24:1; Test Levi 13:5.

37. *some matters . . . correctly.* Reference is to vss. 20 ff.

according to your words. I.e. what was said in vss. 26–36.

38. *God will disregard or ignore the situation of the wicked.* Cf. II Bar 72:4–6. Their death, judgment, and destruction will indeed take place but the chief concern is for Israel.

39. *pilgrimage.* Synonymous with "death" in vs. 38; cf. II Cor 5:6–8.

reward. Cf. Sir 35:19; 1QS 10:17 f.; Apoc Moses 13:3–5; Eccles 12:5.

40. Cf. 8:1 ff.

41. Cf. Mark 4:1–9, 14–20.

at the time. Cf. Ps 1:3; Matt 24:45; Luke 20:10; it refers to the harvesttime as the root-taking refers to the promise of growth and ultimate fruitage. For eschatological figure see 1QM 1:5. The application is clear — not all seed germinates, not every plant grows. So it is with reference to mankind — not all will be saved.

42. *If you please.* Lit. "if I have found favor before you."

43. *seed.* Cf. Isa 61:11.

44. *but man.* Syriac *br nš'*, "son of man," more effectively brings out the caveat of the seer who cringes at the comparison of seed with humankind (but see also 4:28 ff.).

for whose sake . . . made. Cf. NOTE on 6:54.

45. *Spare your people.* Joel 2:17; Amos 7:2, 5; Ps 28:9; 4QF1 1:13 "to save Israel."

sympathy. Lit. "to feel compassion," "pity." The writer is deeply troubled, as the lamentation indicates. Apoc Shedrach (13) and Apoc Esdras (Tischendorff, *Apocalypses apocryphae*, pp. 25, 26) express the same sentiment — have mercy on your work, and have pity on your work — following the idea here.

46. For the form of the verse cf. 7:25. Note the sharp dualism between the present and the future age.

47. *You are quite incapable.* Lit. "much is lacking to you that you are able." Cf. Hermas *Visions* 3:1:9. See NOTE on 5:33. A remarkable confidence in the incomparable love of God which is "broader than the measure of man's mind," since man, a sinner, cannot even contemplate its fullness.

48. *commendable.* Cf. Hermas *Visions* 2:3:1 f. If the Syriac is correct here it would indicate the promise of entrance into heaven (cf. Efros, MKJV, p. 223).

49. *humbled yourself.* Cf. Matt 23:12; Luke 18:13 f.; 4QpPs 37, 2:8 f.

to have gloried. I.e. he did not boast of his peculiar position; rather like the Ezra of the Bible (9:6 ff.) he associated himself with those for whom he prayed.

50. *conducted themselves.* Lit. "walked in."

51. *glory . . . like you.* Cf. 14:9; Luke 24:26; Rom 8:18. Cf. Efros, MKJV, p. 222, n. 35 for further references.

52. *Paradise has been opened.* See last NOTE on 4:8. Cf. 7:36, 123; II Bar 4:6; 51:11; Test Levi 18:10; II Enoch 65:10.

tree of life . . . planted. Cf. II Enoch 8:3; I Enoch 25:4–5; Test Levi 18:11; IV Macc 18:16 "the tree of life is for all those who do his will"; Ezek 47:12; Rev 2:7; 22:2 f.; 1QH 6:15; 8:5 *et passim;* 1QS 8:5; 11:8.

city . . . built. Cf. Sir 24:11; II Bar 4:2 ff.; Heb 11:10; Rev 3:12; 21:2, 10; II Esd 10:42.

Wisdom . . . pre-established. According to Prov 8:23 f. Wisdom was "set up" before the earth was made; cf. I Cor 2:7. Moore, II, 342, thinks the antecedent to this and similar passages in apocalyptic literature was Ezek 40 ff.

53. *root.* I.e. root of evil. See third NOTE on 3:22; cf. I Enoch 91:8.

sealed. For idea see Dan 9:24; II Bar 21:23; Wisd Sol 2:5; Pseudo-Philo 33:3. The colon may refer to the removal of the evil inclination, *yṣr hrʿ.*

death . . . Hell. Cf. Isa 25:8; 28:15; I Cor 15:26, 54 f.; Rev 6:8; 20:14; 21:4; 1QH 3:8, 9, 28; 6:24; 9:4, and frequently in pseudepigraphic literature.

53–54. *Corruption . . . Afflictions.* Cf. Rom 8:20 ff.; II Enoch 65:9.

54. *treasure of immortality.* Cf. Isa 33:6; 1QM 10:12 *'wṣrwt kb[d]*, "treasures of glory." See NOTE on 4:35.

55. *ask no further questions.* Lit. "do not add to ask."

56. *had the opportunity.* I Enoch 98:4; Sir 15:17 speaks about every man's choice which makes it possible for him to have what he desires. Cf. below 9:11.

spurned the Most High. Cf. Num 14:11; 16:30; Deut 31:20; Isa 1:4.

held his law in contempt. Cf. Lev 26:43; Ps 107:11; CD 8:19; 1QS 5:19; Sir 41:8.

abandoned his ways. Cf. Prov 2:13; II Peter 2:15; 4QF1 1:14 *swr;* CD 1:12. On the whole verse cf. 9:10–11; III Macc 7:10.

57. *trampled upon . . . ones.* Cf. 1QH 6:32; 1QpH 3:10; Amos 5:11; Jer 12:10.

58. *and thought.* Lit. "they said in their heart."

there was no God. Pss 14:1; 53:1.

they must die. Cf. Isa 22:13; Wisd Sol 2:5 f.; I Cor 15:22; Rom 8:13; Heb 9:27.

59. *thirst and affliction.* Cf. Luke 16:24; II Bar 59:2. See Volz, p. 284, for further references to what awaits sinners.

not want man to perish. Cf. Ezek 18:21 f.; Matt 18:14; John 3:15; II Peter 3:9; I Tim 2:4.

60. *themselves polluted the name.* Cf. Ezek 43:8; I Enoch 45:2; CD 15:3; it was an act of will, not something beyond their control. See vs. 36. Cf. Harnisch, p. 176, for discussion of the problem involved.

displayed ingratitude. Cf. Rom 1:21. The importance of giving thanks and praise to God by both word and deed may be seen from the frequent passages in the OT and Qumran documents that deal with it.

prepared life. Cf. John 14:2b.

61. *judgment is now approaching.* A characteristic of eschatological literature (cf. Ezek 7:7; 30:3; Joel 3:14; Obad 15; Zeph 1:14; Matt 24:34, and parallels).

62. *disclosed it . . . only to you and a few like you.* I.e. these disclosures have been made only to Ezra and men like him, apocalyptists or prophets (seers). Contrast Mark 13:32 and parallels.

63. *multitude of signs.* Apocalyptists were profuse with signs of the end but none were more specific than that, as may be seen even from the relevant discourses of Jesus (Matt 24 and parallels). Cf. above NOTE on 4:33; Acts 1:7; II Bar 22:1 ff.; Apocryphon of John, 17:4 ff. The expression occurs frequently in Qumran literature but again without specifics.

in the last days. See Kosmala, *Annual of the Swedish Theological Institute* 2, 27–37.

9:1. *Note* [*that*] *carefully.* The idea of measurement or calculation of times and seasons is common in apocalyptic literature.

part. Note emphasis on "part" here and see 5:1–12; II Bar 27.

predicted signs. Cf. 5:1–12; 6:13–28; 9:1–6; 13:16 ff.

2. *then you will know.* Only those who know will be able to understand the time (Dan 12:10), i.e. those who are in possession of the secret books (cf. II Bar 28:1; I Enoch 99:10; 100:6).

to judge the world. Cf. II Bar 25; 1QH 14:24, "the wicked"; CD 5:15, "deeds of the wicked"; 8:3. Observe the universality of judgment, more pronounced in apocalyptic than in the Bible itself.

3. *Tremors in places.* Cf. 5:8; 6:14 f.; Mark 13:8; 1QH 3:35; II Bar 70:8.

Disorder of peoples. Cf. 5:1, 5; Isa 17:12 f.; II Cor 12:20.

Intrigues of nations. Cf. 16:31; Matt 24:7; Ezek 38:10; 1QM 13:4; 1QH 4:12.

Fickleness of leaders. Ethiopic "the leaders will fight among themselves"; cf. Ezek 30:4 ff.

Confusion of rulers. Cf. III Macc 6:18 f.

4. *from the very beginning.* The writer here refers to what he believes to be old traditions, perhaps to ideas expressed in the Apocalypses bearing the names of such worthies as Adam, Seth, Enoch, Noah, and others.

5–6. Gunkel's rendering (in loco) follows the Ethiopic at significant points and is still worthy of consideration: "For as everything that has taken place in the world, had a [hidden] beginning in word, but a visible end, so also are the times of the Most High: their beginning in word and omen, but their end in deeds and miracles." He calls attention to Justin's *Apology* (1:12:10): "Whence we become more assured of all things He taught us, since whatever He beforehand foretold should come to pass, is seen in fact to come to pass; and this is the work of God, to tell of a thing before it happens, and as if it were foretold so to show it happened." On the conception of the word, associated with revelation and activity as here and elsewhere affirmed, see Dürr, *Die Wertung des göttlichen Wortes,* pp. 40 f. (with reference to this and other passages of similar import). The meaning seems to be that from the beginning everything was contained in the word; the end, with the signs of its approach, is discernible by the initiate while others must await the inception of the signs. The seer was one of the choice spirits to whom was communicated the word of the Lord.

7. *will be saved.* Cf. 7:60 and textual note *e–e* here; for conception see Test Levi 18:10–14.

escape by . . . works or the faith. Cf. 13:23; James 2:14 ff. II Esdras thus proclaims the doctrine of faith and works as does James. (But cf. 7:77; 8:33.) II Baruch (51:3; 67:6; 84) promulgates the idea of salvation by the law. Paul goes in the direction of *sola fidei* (Rom 3:27 f.; 4:4, 5; Gal 5:4–6), which was followed by the Mandeans — "everyone who stands genuinely and reliably in the first faith receives endurance for eternity" (Lidzbarski, *Ginza,* p. 42).

8. *enjoy my salvation.* Lit. "see my salvation." Cf. CD 20:34. "My salvation" refers to the messianic age.

in my land and within the territory. I.e. the chosen land where "my salvation" will take place (cf. 12:34; 13:48 f.; II Bar 29:2; 40:2). How old the tradition is is not clear but it is as early as Joel 2:32; "my land" in 1QH 4:8; "his land" in CD 1:8. For further references and discussion see Volz, pp. 308 f. The political eschatology here voiced may be based on vs. 3; apocalyptists, like some writers of the NT, did not always distinguish clearly between this and the one having to do with heaven and hell. Direct expressions are rare in OT; cf. Jer 2:7; 16:18; Ezek 36:5; 38:16; Wisd Sol 12:3, "your holy land"; Sir 45:22, "the land of the people" seems to regard it as a special place. "My territory" (referring to God's land) does not occur in the OT.

9. *marvel.* Cf. Wisd Sol 5:2. Gunkel renders *Ehrfurcht,* i.e. "get respect," based on Hilgenfeld's conjecture of the Greek *thaumasousai,* but in view of Wisd Sol passage this is doubtful.

linger in torment. Cf. Gen 3:19; Ezek 26:20 f.; Sir 40:1 ff.

10. *appreciate me.* Lit. "know me." Cf. 1Q 27, 1, lines 3, 4; 1Q 34, 3, col. 2, lines 3 f.; CD 8:4. [1Q references follow those listed in DJD, I, 1955.]

blessings. Lit. "benefits" (Heb. *ṭwbwt*).

11. *despised my law . . . free.* Cf. 8:56; II Bar 85:7; I Cor 7:37a; Acts 5:4; Ps Sol 9:7 with discussion by H. E. Ryle and M. R. James, *Psalms of the Pharisees commonly called the Psalms of Solomon* (Cambridge University Press, 1891), pp. 95 f., and references to other literature.

12. *opportunity for repentance.* Lit. "while the place of repentance was yet open to them." Cf. II Bar 85:12; this is a general conception in I Enoch and our book (I Enoch 63; 65:11); see also Sanhedrin 97b; Heb 12:17; Apocryphon of John 70:15; Wisd Sol 12:10; I Clement (Rome) ch. 7.

they . . . acknowledge [it] by torment. Cf. Zech 12:10; John 19:37; for the inspiration to courage by torture see IV Maccabees *passim.* On one occasion Antiochus recommended the example of the seven youths and their mother to his soldiers (17:23).

13. *how the wicked . . . afflicted.* Cf. II Bar 48:48.

how the just . . . saved. This becomes the theme of the next three visions.

15. *I said before.* At 7:47.

More numerous are the lost. This is the persistent lament of the seer (cf. 7:49–61; 8:1–13). See Bousset, pp. 386 f.

16. *a drop.* Cf. 4:50.

17. The crisp poetic form is reminiscent of 7:24. The author was fond of expressing his thoughts in striking poetry (cf. 7:114; 8:52 ff.). The productiveness of the seed depends (II Enoch 42:11–13) on the quality of the field; the color of the flowers on that of the flowers (5:36b; 6:44); the quality of the products is determined by the skill and interest of the craftsman, and the harvest is dependent on the industriousness of the farmer. For an interesting reconstruction in Aramaic see Violet, II, 127; and for a biblical example see Isa 24:2.

18. *in primordial time.* With Syriac. Lit. "in its time of eternity" or "world." Cf. *l't 'wlm* in 1QSb 4:26; *qṣy 'wlmym* (1QS 4:16); *qṣy nṣḥ* (1QH 1:24). The idea appears to refer to the period before the creation when it existed in the word (thought) of God. See rendering of Gunkel, Box, Violet, and Harnisch, pp. 104 f.

before the world was made. Cf. Ps 90:2; John 17:5; Pseudo-Philo 28:4.

no one opposed . . . none existed. Note emphasis on the aloneness of God;

hardly the Satan here but sinners (cf. Sir 12:5 f.) as indicated by the preceding clause.

19. *unfailing table and luxuriant pasture.* Cf. Ps 78:19–20, but reference is to paradise which those created in (for) this world would have enjoyed in the world to come had they remained above reproach in their conduct (cf. I Enoch 62:14; Pseudo-Philo 19:5; the hidden manna of Rev 2:7, 17; Matt 8:11; Ps 23:1, 2, 5).

disreputable. Corrupt. Cf. Gen 6:11 f.

20. *Then I looked.* Cf. Gen 6:5, 12. The whole first colon appears to be a reflection of the Genesis verse.

plots. For the plots of the wicked see 1QpHab 3:5; 1QM 13:4; 1QH 4:12; 6:22; Isa 59:7.

21. *with great difficulty.* See textual note *ʲ–ʲ*. Oesterley has "but not greatly"; Violet *ein klein wenig,* "a very few." But Gunkel and Box read as above based on Lupton's Greek conjecture *panu mogis.* See NEB translation. For God's abortive efforts see Isa 65:2; Pseudo-Philo 28:4.

grape . . . shoot. Cf. Isa 17:6; 60:21; 1QH 6:15; Pseudo-Philo 28:4. In fact vss. 18–22 are very close to Pseudo-Philo 28:4. On identification of the shoot see remarks by Maier, *Texte vom Toten Meer,* II, 90.

22. *multitude . . . born in vain.* Cf. Sir 41:5–9; Wisd Sol 2:1 ff.; 5:13. I.e. they were born only to be lost through their own misdeeds and corruption.

23. *without fasting.* Because of what the interpreter has already exhorted the seer to think about (vs. 13) it is no longer fitting to fast. This is essential for the structure of the book as Gunkel has pointed out (APAT, II, 348).

24. *eat only of the flowers of the field.* Interpretation is somewhat uncertain because of Ethiopic rendering. Flowers figured extensively in ancient thought. Sons were compared to flowers (Sir 39:13 f.), as was Simon, the son of Onias in Sir 50:8. According to III Macc 7:16 the saved wore crowns of flowers. Judas was said to have eaten only what grew wild (II Macc 5:27). Whether flowers were consumed directly is not clear, though Herodotus (2:92) speaks of lotus bread made and eaten by the Egyptians, and their consumption of the lotus root. They also ate the seeds of a certain species of lily about the size of an olive stone, and the lower part of the papyrus stems. The reference here may be figurative—the eating only of that which was regarded as most precious and beautiful so as to reflect its character. See the fare of Daniel and his companions (Dan 1:12–16; and *Lives of the Prophets* on Dan 16). Cf. Paul Volz, *Die biblischen Altertümer* (Stuttgart: Calver, 1925), pp. 248 f.

25. *pray . . . without ceasing.* See textual note *ᵖ–ᵖ* and cf. I Sam 7:8; I Thess 5:17; et al.

COMMENT

[Introduction — after the seven days' fast, 6:35–37] The seer had been advised to fast seven days more and hence was eager to continue his quest for further revelations. As may be seen from the last clause of vs. 35, this vision is not only a continuation of the preceding ones but really marks a climax thereto. If anything Ezra is "intensely excited" in anticipation of the answers he will receive in response to further probing. There is a certain parallel between 5:20 ff. and this passage. Prayer and fasting were thought to be of special import for the quickening and intensification of the ecstatic state (cf. Luke 2:37).[1]

[Question: Why has Israel become the prey of other nations if it was for its sake that the world was created? 6:38–59] As in the earlier visions, the author's method is to pursue his point through a series of questions and answers, really a colloquy between the seer and the interpreting angel. After recounting the steps and works in creation, he concludes by inquiring why, if the world was created "for us,"[2] the elect people were not enjoying their rightful heritage. The glowing description of the wonders of creation accentuates its purpose and the position of God's people in it. While a national background pervades the whole passage, it doubtless received a much broader interpretation (8:44; II Bar 14:18). In a sense this vision climaxes the series up till now and carries the argument a step further. The first vision posed the question as to how the divine purpose can be achieved if the only people bearing God's name have been laid low by the nations. The second vision asked why the elect nation or people has to be delivered into the hands of those worse than themselves to be chastised. The third one carries the argument a bit further by emphasizing the contrast between Israel and the nations and at the same time laying stress on the former's place in the incomparable scheme of creation.

The magnificent description of creation, based on biblical conceptions and expressions and elaborated by current Jewish exegesis, prepares the way for the sharp focus of the author's thought — the purpose of it all in view of present historical circumstances. Throughout there is constant and designed emphasis on the divine word. Perhaps the most striking observation is vs. 43 which summarizes the work of God accomplished by his word. In paraphrasing the six works of creation, the prominent feature is "you commanded."[3] Twice (vss. 38 and 43) the author affirms that the word was the divine agent that brought about the creation. How is it that the material aspects of creation have been carried out so minutely and strikingly while the main word — decreeing that creation's ultimate design was for Israel (vs. 59) or for man (vs. 46) — has failed to accomplish its end? For the bolstering of his lengthy query, the writer has drawn upon conceptions from numerous biblical sources as interpreted in contemporary documents.

[Response to the question by the interpreting angel, 7:1–16] The divine response to Ezra's prayer came first through the medium of the interpreting angel bearing the divine word. The form taken by the revelation is common in both Jewish literature and the New Testament: the parable. Both parables used here have the same thrust and purpose. The elements are: (a) a spacious, limitless place (sea, city), (b) the narrow, treacherous way to get to it, and (c) the desire to reach the sea or city. Specifically stressed are (a) and (b). The end is taken generally to be desirable; the way to reach it is the problem — one which gave all theologians a great deal of difficulty. The author's thought here expressed is remarkably similar to that of Robert G. Ingersoll: "Life is

---

[1] See references in Bertholet, *Biblische Theologie,* II, 357, 425 ff.
[2] "For us" refers to Israel or the upright of Israel. Cf. Volz, pp. 70, 107 f.
[3] Lorenz Dürr, *Die Wertung des göttlichen Wortes,* . . . (Leipzig: Hinrichs, 1938), pp. 40 f.

a narrow veil between the cold and barren peaks of two eternities. We strive in vain to look beyond the heights. We cry aloud, and the only answer is the echo of our wailing cry. From the voiceless lips of the unreplying dead there comes no word; but in the night of death hope sees a star and listening love can hear the rustle of a wing." (From oration delivered at the funeral of his brother, quoted in the *New York Times Book Review,* July 5, 1970, p. 23). The way was hard and perilous and, of course, represented this world brought to its present state by Adam's transgression (vs. 11). Since then it has been Israel's lot to traverse that narrow and painful way. Just what it entails for the thinkers of the writer's age may be seen from II Bar 56:1–16. The sum and substance of the passage is conveyed by the direct word of the Lord (he speaks from vs. 10 on; apocalyptic is fond of shifting between an intermediary and the Lord himself). The world was indeed made for Israel but Adam's violation of the divine stipulations brought about another world which was judged. As Rössler has observed, "The transgression of Adam was followed by withdrawal of salvation from this world and transferred to the future coming age."[4] Now "the ways" of this world are constricted while those of "the greater world are spacious and secure" and productive of fruits of immortality. Yet it is absolutely requisite for those who are alive (born into this world) to endure narrow and vain things in order to obtain the things stored up for them in the spacious world. The affairs of this world, which were the absorbing concern of many groups, must be placed in proper perspective. The direction of one's thought is important for the writer. Apocalyptists had lost faith in this world which they believed would soon pass away. They concentrated on the future world where wrongs would be absent and where the righteous would enjoy the blessings intended for them from the beginning.

[Question and answer on lot of the righteous and the wicked, 7:17–25] This is rather more of an observation than a direct question in which the law (*lex*) occupies an important role. The decree of the law to the effect that the just will be saved and the wicked punished marks the point of departure. The former can afford to endure passing through the narrows of this world with all its impediments because of the hope of enjoying the broad places. But the wicked have to suffer the same hardships without hope of reward. That would seem to lean somewhat in the direction of faith as over against just reward for hardships endured in this life (cf. Luke 16:19–31). It is, therefore, not the experiences of life that determine one's destiny but his attitude toward the law (vs. 20). As Bousset remarked, sin is not a predetermined condition; the individual is responsible for his deeds and the difference between the destiny of the just and the wicked is due to their free choice based on their decision for or against the law.[5] The broad universalism of sin[6] is here narrowed down to faith in and faithfulness to the law. Inasmuch as the law is held to be the criterion against which people are judged, it would appear that the subjects of judgment are the individual members of Israel (cf. Rom 2:12–16). Verse 21 is

---

[4] Dietrich Rössler, *Gesetz und Geschichte, Untersuchung zur Theologie der jüdischen Apokalyptik und der pharisäischen Orthodoxie* (Neukirchener Verlag, 1960), p. 74; Bousset, pp. 407 f.
[5] Bousset, p. 405. Cf. also Volz, p. 101, and Harnisch, p. 154.
[6] Cf. Harnisch, pp. 49 ff.

somewhat ambivalent. Is "those coming [into the world] when they came" a reference to Israelites or to all peoples? Most scholars think it is to the former, in which case it would follow the complaint of the prophets who accused Israel of precisely the attitudes and activities denounced in vss. 22–24. The same is true of the Qumran teachers who accused the people again and again of "stubbornness of heart." The issue of the situation for the faithful and faithless is summarized by the aphorism in vs. 25.

[The appearance of the messiah with accompanying events, 7:26–30] Some scholars regard this passage and the following one as belonging to the redactor (R) of the book because they supposedly introduce a subject extraneous to the argument pursued in the vision.[7] However, on closer inspection, these passages appear to accentuate the theme of the preceding: judgment is decreed for those who reject the law. "Emptiness to the empty." One would expect something of the messianic theme to be injected here whatever course its particular direction may take. Here it takes the form of an interregum[8] between the present period and the final judgment and partakes of a conception somewhat analogous to Jewish thought expressed in the II Isaiah — the period of restoration. It is, of course, presented in more colorful apocalyptic terms and therefore more specific in its descriptives — the four hundred years and the death of the messiah. The messianic age is thus a harbinger of the splendor and wonder of the coming world and of the universal judgment of this world. The appearance of the invisible city sounds as if the old city lay in ruins. All those who have succeeded in escaping the convulsions connected with the signs will enjoy the wonders of the limited messianic age. At the end of that age the messiah and all human beings will die. The world will assume its primordial character; nobody will remain. Only then will the resurrection and the final judgment take place. As the passage now stands; Christian tampering can be detected from the insertion of "Jesus" in vs. 28 and "son" in vss. 28, 29 (cf. Gunkel in APAT, II, 350).

[Judgment of the resurrected, 7:31–44] Here the writer explains his idea of what will take place after this world has been put to silence for seven days. First there will be a general resurrection followed by the final judgment. The Most High on his judgment seat will be absolutely impartial, without favoritism. The criteria are truth and faithfulness, or good deeds. Evil deeds cannot be hidden and they will form the basis for the rejection of their perpetrators. The respective ends of both are now visible — the one, joy and repose, the other, fire and torment.[9] Apparently the same state or condition will prevail as before the creation of the world.

[Question: How many are saved, with response, 7:45–61] To return to the question handled before the messianic age interlude (7:26 ff.), concern for the fate of the many as over against the few is expressed — perhaps an attempt on the part of the author to justify the ways of God to man, both to the few and the many. Beatitude for those who keep the divine precepts is voiced. But there

---

[7] See, e.g. Kabisch, Oesterley, and Box.
[8] Cf. Keulers, *Die eschatologische Lehre,* p. 40. See NOTE on vs. 28. For a discussion of the whole passage with its implications see C. C. Torrey, "The Messiah Son of Ephraim," JBL 66 (1947), 253–77, esp. 259–63.
[9] See comments by Moore, II, 385 and Bousset, ch. XIII.

was still the troublesome problem of the end result in view of the admission that all were sinners and violators of the covenant in one form or another. In the world to come the few will be saved, the many lost. There is a slight retraction in vs. 48 where the growth of the evil heart (impulse) has had a deleterious effect on "just about all" who were created — all of which opens the door to the divine response. Because the just were few and the wicked many, not one world but two were created.[10] Vis-à-vis the Eternal, the situation can be compared to the precious and base minerals of the earth. While there is no certainty as to the rendering of vs. 52, the meaning is fairly clear from the verses that follow. The few are the precious who are cherished by the Lord; the world to come is for them. The many are the plentiful, base minerals; no amount of accumulation can change their value and they cannot be compared with the precious ones. When all is said and done, gold, silver, copper, iron, lead and clay are just that. The possessor of the rare metals cherishes them far more than those that are plentiful. In the judgment, the Lord reflects the same attitude. The multitude were content with base substitutes for the precious — a relative righteousness. The few, on the other hand, endured suffering and hardship, because they had the real thing. For the former, judgment brought death and destruction; for the latter, deliverance and reward. The former blazed brightly in their world but had even now burned out; the latter stood the assaying test whose precious metal was indestructible.

[Lamentation of Ezra, with response, 7:62–74] The complaint revolves around the concept of *sensus*, "reason," which makes man aware of his condition and end. *Sensus* is regarded as having the same origin as other creatures and is coterminous with the individual of whom it forms a part. It grows up within and along with him and presumably sharpens as time goes on, so that there is no cessation of torment as man progresses in life. Animals without it can rejoice because they have no *sensus* and hence are better off than man. He is really at a disadvantage, despite the vaunted conception of dominion over God's other creatures inasmuch as his life is a living hell of torment because he knows that he will be brought into judgment and that he can do little about his condition. He is somehow entangled in sins from which he cannot extricate himself. If there were no judgment after death, he might indeed be better off. The angelic response, however, turns the whole matter around. Since the *sensus* grows up with man, he is tormented by the fact that he has failed to heed it and hence suffers remorse because he has used it for circumventing the very gifts that otherwise would have given him comfort and assurance. So what can his reply be "in the last times"? God has been patient, not on man's account, but because of his own predetermined plan and time. The author, in this passage, has not yet arrived at the place reached by the Qumran sectarian.[11]

[Question: What is the state of the soul between death and the new creation (judgment)? 7:75–101] The question posed by Ezra was a live one when the

---

[10] For a discussion and implications of the two-world doctrine of the apocalyptists, see Bousset, pp. 244 f.
[11] Cf. 1QS 11:10–14; 1QH 4:30–32. 1QS 11:17 consigns everything to God's will, as does John 15:5.

doctrine of resurrection was first enunciated[12] and in some circles is still so. Are the dead kept in repose until the time of the new creation, or do they immediately enter upon their destined courses? It is really a discourse following the foregoing discussion about judgment, though it interrupts the theme of the chapter. The response of the interpreter is that first, all those who die, good and bad alike, pay their respects to the glory of the Most High. Then the seven degrees or stages or ways of the lot of the wicked are outlined. (1) They are in torment and grief now because they scoffed at the law of the Most High; (2) the time for repentance is past though they might earnestly desire to repent; (3) they are even more remorseful because they see the rewards of the faithful and (4) the torments stored up for them in the last times; (5) they see, on the other hand, the peace and protection of those now enjoying bliss; (6) they will witness the immediate torment of some of them; (7) the sight of these things causes them confusion and shame, and brings home to them their worst fears under the impact of which they simply pine away.

But what about the righteous, those who adhered to the ways of the Most High by resisting the evil inclination through the law which had been given to them? They too are subject to seven orders, steps or degrees of joy by virtue of their lot. (1) They have the satisfaction of having done their utmost to overcome the evil thought or inclination, that is, have utilized what God provided them; (2) they will see the entanglements of sin in which the wicked were caught but from which they escaped, and catch a glimpse of the unrepentant roaming about and the punishment in store for them; (3) they see the divine attestation to their faithfulness; (4) they appreciate their intermediate state of peace and security and see the glory awaiting them after the judgment; (5) they rejoice in their escape from corruptible things and the difficulties from which they have been extricated, and look forward to the joys of immortality; (6) they see how they are to shine in incomparable splendor; (7) they see the reward of glory with all its blessings, the opposite of those of the wicked (vs. 87). As Box[13] notes, these descriptives surpass in perception, taste, and discernment anything found in other apocalypses. Their psychological character is apparent but the majestic portrait of the pathos of the soul is not beyond the bounds of credibility to those who have been deeply involved in the religious experiences of life.

The passage ends with a reference to the seven days' freedom granted to the souls of the righteous immediately after death. It must be remembered that we have here only a description of the intermediate state of the soul. Nothing is said about the method by which all souls are finally judged. II Bar 30 points to the resurrection of all the dead as a prelude to the final judgment.

[Question: May the righteous intercede for the ungodly? 7:102–15] Having asked the question about the intermediate state of the dead and received the interpreter's reply, the seer is still not satisfied because he seems to have thought of himself as belonging to the unrighteous group. He was shocked by the terrible fate that he was told awaited the wicked in the judgment and now pursues the question as to whether all avenues of intercession for them are

12 Cf. Harnisch, p. 125, n. 2, and references there; TWNT, VI, 377 f.
13 Charles, APOT, II, 587.

blocked. Was it absolutely impossible for relatives or friends of the deceased still living to intervene with the Most High on their behalf? The response is a flat yes. Each one must bear the responsibility for his own actions. But Ezra protests that history plainly records examples of those who interceded success-fully for others — why can't it be so now? The interpreter points out that all the examples quoted took place in the temporary order but on the day of judgment nothing can be changed. "No one will be able to have compassion for him who is convicted in the judgment or to cast down him who is victorious." The day of judgment thus marks the strict division between "the end of this time and the beginning of immortal time to come." Corruption, intemperance, faithfulness have ceased by then, and justice and truth set in. At the judgment everything is decisive here, as in II Bar 85:12–15.[14]

Our author here reaches the acme of individualism. National, racial, in-stitutional distinctions are wiped out. The individual soul stands in all its nakedness before the Judge and no one can change his situation now. Box's comment is to the point: "It would appear from the emphatic way in which it is insisted that intercession by the living for the living is alone possible while the present order lasts, that the Apocalyptist is aiming at some counter-doctrine of intercession for the dead. Certainly no room seems to be left in his theology for prayers for the dead. The eternal destiny of the soul is fixed by the course of the earthly life. Those who died enter immediately upon an existence of bliss or woe which but anticipates the final doom of Judgment; and this doom, according to our present passage, is fixed and unalterable."[15]

[Question: What is the use of living, if everybody is doomed to sin? Answer: It is necessary to fight; if victorious, there is salvation, if not, then death. 7:116–131] As the dialogue between Ezra and the angel continues, Ezra appears to have been convinced of the inevitable destiny of the mass of sinners and bursts out in great lamentation. It would have been better for Adam and his descendants never to have been generated from the earth than to suffer that fate. Could not some restraint have been placed upon him to prevent the catastrophe? Like Job 3 and Jeremiah 20:18, he asks, "What is the use to live one's life in grief under the dismal threat of punishment after death?" Ezra, including himself with the company of sinners, wonders just what benefit it is to have the promise of eternal life when they have been guilty of deadly works. Expressions of hope are tragically deceptive when held out to those whose lives are lived in vanity, and knowledge of eternal storehouses for souls is a travesty to persons who live scandalously. What good is it to be told of the protection of the Most High for those who live victoriously when one has lived impiously; or to be made aware of paradise when he can't get in by virtue of his unacceptable life? The trouble is that the many in their lifetime failed to grasp the meaning of what they would have to suffer after death — not that they were unaware of it but they had no way of appreciating its awfulness.

---

[14] See Harnisch, pp. 218 f. The rabbis believed that the merits of pious sons will be effective in the salvation of the fathers (see Ecclesiastes rabba on Eccles 4:1), a doc-trine repudiated by II Esdras. Cf. remarks by Roger Le Déaut, "Aspects de l'interces-sion dans le Judaisme ancien," *Journal for the Study of Judaism* 1 (Brill: Leiden, March 1970), 45 f.
[15] Box, pp. 153–56.

The interpreting angel admitted that life is a struggle, even a battle, which all men must wage with utmost seriousness. Some of the combatants are victorious, some defeated — the many in Ezra's view. But the odds are not so one-sided as Ezra has made them. All have been shown the way, that is, they have the Torah on their side. Given the presence of the good and evil inclination,[16] there is always the Torah, which is the way. The difficulty is people do not believe those who have promulgated the way. The underlying problem is that of freedom and determinism; Ezra mentions the latter in vs. 116. There is freedom, but not without direction. Our passage here could almost be considered as a commentary on the conception expressed in I Cor 10:13: "No temptation has overtaken you that is not common to man. God is faithful, and he will not let you be tempted beyond your strength, but with the temptation will also provide the way of escape, that you may be able to endure it" (RSV).

[Question: Does the mercy and compassion of God mean that many will be saved? Answer: This world was made for the many, the world to come for the few. 7:132–8:3] It will be noted that here, as often elsewhere, Ezra's question is stated declaratively. It is in the form of an interpretation of certain qualities of God as reflected in the epithets applied to him. Whether the passage *as it stands* is original with the author is not certain, but there is a definite play on the number seven. Throughout, the emphasis falls on the goodness and compassion of God. The implication is that there will be salvation despite the presence of the evil inclination and the many who yield to it. For (a) God is the merciful one because of his compassion for those not yet born; although he knows that a man may succumb to evil, he is nevertheless active in his life until the man has cut himself off.[17] (b) He is the gracious one because of his grace (ḥn) exemplified in dealings with those who return to the Torah, follow God's directions, and with those who turn to it from the outside (strangers) without consideration of merit. (c) He is the patient or long-suffering one as may be seen from his infinite patience displayed for sinners; he knew man because he was his creature. (d) He is the generous one since his gifts outweigh his exactions. (e) He is the one of many mercies, the one plenteous in mercy, the all-merciful because of the extent of his sympathy and pity; they are not just coextensive with time and persons involved in it but are heaped up on them in each situation in every generation. (f) The concept of God as the giver is shown by his goodness; he is responsible for forgiveness, and the deadly consequences of sins without whose relief none could exist; all would be victimized by their transgressions. (g) God, as judge, grants pardon and annuls offenses so that more than "a very few" will be left. As seen from these observations, the author is still troubled by the question of the many who will die and the few who will live, attempting to reconcile that problem with the character of God.

The response of the interpreting angel to these observations follows the same line of reasoning set forth in 7:49–61. As elsewhere in our book,[18] the

---

16 Cf. Ps Sol 9:7.
17 See NOTE on vs. 132.
18 Life is regarded as an eschatological phenomenon in II Esdras (cf. 7:48, 60, 66 f., 82, 92, 129, 131, 137 f.; 8:3, 6, 39, 41, 54; 9:13, 15; 14:22, 30). See further Harnisch, pp. 53 f.

emphasis falls on the present and future *saeculum* (world or age). The parable and lesson drawn from it still maintain the doctrine of the many and the few, the former being the inheritors of this world, the latter of the world to come. This doctrine must not be confused with that of the many in the Qumran materials where the term refers to those of the community who have excluded themselves from the rest of mankind.[19]

[Why was man made to live such a short time? 8:4–19] The piece begins with the seer's colloquy with his soul, reminding himself of the necessity to comprehend his position in life. The state of life is not an enviable one since man's course is totally uncontrollable. He has nothing to say about his coming into the world nor about his leaving it, and the span of his life is short. Yet within the confines of his life there is a possibility of ordering its direction so that man may go on living. There is some indication that Ezra is thinking more about Israel than about those outside. Just as the individual is first sheltered in the womb, tenderly nurtured immediately after birth and then instructed for life by the parents, so Israel was conceived in the choice of the Lord, sheltered and nurtured by him into maturity, and then instructed in his law. Because of what God is, he holds over his creature the power of life and death — which he exercises. That observation leads to the all-important question as to why man (Israel?) was made to exist for such a limited time. Vs. 15 points to the writer's basic concern. He is not questioning the Lord's dealings with the totality of mankind, but he is vitally concerned about Israel. He is aware of the nation's faults and the judgment to come and hence implores the Lord to hear what he is about to say in his prayer, much as the Psalmists did.

Verse 6 may be of more than passing significance by virtue of Ezra's express prayer for "seed of heart and cultivation of perception" which comes close to the idea of a new birth. The Syriac addition of the adjective "new" may point to Christian influence. The new heart expression does not occur so far in the Qumran documents but there is some reference to change of heart or illumination of heart (cf. 1QS 2:3; 1QH 2:18; 10:31; 1QHf 4:12).[20] There is thus some affinity of thought between II Esdras and Qumran on this matter. The direction or purpose of "the seed of heart" was that "every mortal . . . can go on living," that is, attain immortality.[21]

[Ezra's prayer for his people and the divine response, 8:20–41] This remarkable prayer (vss. 20–36) played a significant role in the liturgy of the early church as may be seen from its quotation in the Apostolic Constitutions, its separate status in numerous manuscripts of the Vulgate and the Mozarabic Liturgy, and its transmission in two recensions. It is often entitled the Confession of Ezra, imitating the confessional prayer of Ezra 9 and I Esd 8:74–90. It begins by invoking the eternal, incomprehensible, faithful, all-powerful God to hear the prayer of his servant who is compelled, by virtue of deep inner commitment, to his God and to his people, to voice his concern for their wel-

---

[19] See caveat of Otto Plöger, *Theology and Eschatology* (Richmond: John Knox Press, 1968), p. 18, n. 16.
[20] See Nötscher, *Zur theologischen Terminologie der Qumran-Texte,* p. 95. See further Sir 45:26; 50:23; I Bar 2:31; II Macc 1:3 f.
[21] Cf. Volz, pp. 306, 364; Wisd Sol 8:17.

fare. His plea is somewhat reminiscent of Abraham's prayer for Sodom (Gen 18:23–33). Ezra appeals to the Lord to think of the righteous who have truly served him, kept his covenants despite tribulations, maintained a reverent stance before him, taught his law, and always reflected confidence in him, rather than to base his judgment solely on the vexations brought upon him by the wicked.[22] Just as in the Ezra prayer (Ezra 9), the seer includes himself among the sinners (vs. 31) and stresses the evangelical principle of the mercy of God demonstrated by his forgiveness. But this can hardly be regarded as Christian influence because the idea is present in many verses of the Old Testament (cf. e.g. Pss 25:7; 79:8; Isa 43:18, 25; 63:9; Hab 3:2). God is implored not to be too meticulous with man (interpretation of Ps 8:4 in vs. 34) since all have sinned. The main emphasis in the prayer falls on the merciful and compassionate nature of God.[23]

The interpreter's answer is not really responsive to the concerns of the seer. His chief worry was about the lost but the angel once more shunts that problem aside by turning attention to the saved. He acknowledges that God rejoices over "the creation of the just" but first affirms his disregard of sinners, probably outsiders here. Yet that is precisely the thrust of the Bible as well as the complaint of Ezra. The little parable of the farmer reinforces the interpreter's method of dealing with the paramount problem of the seer — the seeds that grow and the plants that take root accentuate the saved but completely ignore the mass of unsaved.

[Question: Is man to be compared with seeds and plants? 8:42–62] Ezra is horrified that man should be compared to the seed of the farmer. But even the seed is dependent for germination on the moisture provided by God, but too much of it will prove equally damaging. In no sense is man like seed because he bears the image and likeness of the Creator. Moreover, all the seeds and plants have been provided for man's sake. The seer's protestation is well expressed in the entreaty uttered in vs. 45, which is turned aside by the interpreting angel. He reminds Ezra that there are two world levels — this world and the world to come. The conversation centers about the latter. Then the interpreter takes his pupil to task for seemingly loving man more than the Creator does, but in the same breath he is both commended and rebuked — he must not reckon himself with the wicked, though his humility reflected by so doing is commendable. He is further exhorted to pay less attention to the fate of the worldly minded — that is determined, fixed already, and well known to him. Let him consider himself and the glory (life) that awaits him and those like him. What is in store for them is detailed in the remarkable poem in

---

[22] On apocalyptic prayers of intercession see Le Déaut, *Journal for the Study of Judaism* 1 (1970), 35–57 and Lods, *Histoire de la littérature hébraique et juive*, pp. 990–92. Cf. also II Esd 12:48 below. On the appeal to the merits of the just see A. Marmorstein, *The Doctrine of Merits in Old Rabbinical Literature*, New York: Ktav, 1968. For Mozarabic liturgy see PL, vol. 85 (1891), Canticum LXI, cols. 878–79. Perhaps the prayer of Ezra is a reflection of the penitential prayer of Ezra (Ezra 9:6–15) and that of the congregation in Neh 9:6–37.

[23] The roots *rḥm*, "compassion," and *ḥsd*, "devotion," "mercy," together, occur about one hundred times in the Qumran literature.

vss. 52–54.[24] He is told to ask no more questions about the lost. They had their opportunity but used it to evil ends, knowing all the while that a time of judgment would come. Nevertheless they acted as if there were no God. So bliss is in store for the seer, but eternal deprivation with all its horrors awaits them. That is not the will or desire of God and he can in no way be charged with injustice or lack of concern. They *themselves* polluted his name and displayed their ingratitude by their evil deeds, thereby flaunting the very life that was prepared for them. That is why judgment was approaching, though that fact was revealed only to the seer and his comrades.

[Signs for the seer's time, 8:63 – 9:13] The response of Ezra to the preceding observations is one of silence but not satisfaction. He now presses for specifics about the inception of the last days. Like others before him, he is given a lot of generalities but the time itself is never revealed. Apocalyptic literature is full of all sorts of calculations aiming to provide just the information the seer seeks but in the end they are as indefinite and cryptic as the host of signs to which the interpreter invites his attention.[25] Our author never indulges in celestial arithmetic. More exact times are given, for example, in Daniel, especially in the last chapter, vss. 11 and 12. Of course, such exact numbers gave rise to further interpretations when the times indicated had elapsed. The analysis in Daniel of the seventy years of Jeremiah is a good case in point. No doubt the refusal to be precise was in the past a reaction to the other group; in this way the obvious difficulties of precise dating could be avoided, but adherents were left in a state of mild frustration. Apparently both Jesus and II Esdras belonged to the school that preferred to leave the mystery of the date to God himself. There has never been a lack of the other kind, however, as evidenced by the Millerites and others in this country during the past century.

The answer to the question posed by the seer here receives some, though still inconclusive, consideration. He is told to mark carefully the happenings of the time and then compare them with the signs already disclosed. When a certain portion of those signs has taken place, then he will know that the time of God's judgment is at hand.[26] The more prominent of the signs are then listed (vs. 3). The tenor of the passage indicates that in the author's opinion the time for divine intervention has come. The interpreter repeats his belief that the Most High has revealed to his servants the course of history from beginning to end. The times are characterized by portents and powers at the beginning and by deeds and signs at the end. In other words, the end is inherent

---

[24] Box (APOT, II, 598) has called attention to the striking progression of thought in vss. 53–54. First is the reference to the eradication of the root of evil, then to the removal of the consequences of sin (infirmity, death, Hell, corruption, affliction), and finally to the treasures of immortality.

[25] Exact times were not to be known by man but signs were given him to judge for himself. See Volz, pp. 171 f., for details and references.

[26] Rosenthal (p. 54) refers this verse to the reign of Nerva. But as early as the sixth century B.C., Solon too was concerned about judgment and the end. "Zeus is forever watching the end, and strikes of a sudden. . . . He does not, like a mortal, fall in a rage over each particular thing. And yet it never escapes him all the way when a man has a sinful spirit; and always, in the end, his judgment is plain." Quoted by Michael Grant, *The Ancient Historians* (London: Weidenfeld & Nicolson, 1970), p. 49.

in the word spoken at the time of creation when the divine purpose and method of operation were determined. Once more the situation of the saved and the lost is described. The former escape the tragedies of the end by virtue of their works and faith. They will enjoy the salvation of the Lord in *his* land, within *his* borders which have been set apart from eternity. On the other hand, the wicked must endure the added torture of seeing the bliss of the saved while lingering in torment.[27] They had their opportunity[28]; though they received his benefits (cf. Matt 5:45), they neglected God's law, even spurned it. In the torments after death they will have to acknowledge that his laws were valid; their tragic experience is proof of it. Ezra is again admonished to give attention to the way of salvation rather than to the experiences and affliction of the wicked.

[Few saved, with justification, 9:14–25] The seer asserts again, in forceful terms, his contention that few are saved and many lost, insisting upon an explanation. The retort of the interpreter reasserts the responsibility of man for his condition (cf. vs. 7) by the poetic vs. 17. As the fate of the seed depends on the field, the beauty of the flowers on the quality of the stalk, the creation of the craftsman on his skill, and the harvest on the industriousness of the farmer, so is that of man dependent on the quality of faith and works exemplified in his life. In the thought of God there was no opposition because there was no one to do so before the world was made or before the existence of man. Things are different since the thought of God has issued in creation. Though provided with a law and the promise of an unfailing table and luxuriant pasture (paradise), man chose the path of disreputable conduct. And so, when God considered his creation, he could see nothing but decadence and the threatening peril of his land by virtue of the evil machinations rampant in it. He tried with great difficulty to spare his creation but actually succeeded in preserving for himself a very small portion. Note the hint that even the few were spared only by his grace. It is upon these few that he depends to modify the well-nigh complete frustration of his creation despite his great and protracted efforts. The angel's discourse does not, therefore, answer the question of Ezra. It simply states the facts as he sees them and attempts to justify the ways of God with his world.

There follow directions, however, for further dialogue. The seer is put off another seven days during which he is exhorted to withdraw to a place unspoiled by the buildings of man and nurture himself on the flowers (fruits) of the field. He must abstain from the "goods" of man and so prepare himself for the coming conversations. Perhaps this is the writer's way of saying that man can consider the ways of God only when he divests himself of human impediments; another level of divine-human communication is essential for the conservation of life.

---

[27] Cf. the story of the rich man and Lazarus in Luke 16:19–31.
[28] For further discussion of this point see Harnisch, pp. 175 ff.; Volz, p. 303.

THE FOURTH VISION (9:26–10:59)

Preparation for the vision

9 26 I then proceeded into the field as he commanded me — the field is called Ardat[a] — where I sat among the flowers and ate of [b]the wild plants of the land[b]. Their fare satisfied[c] me. 27 After seven days, while I lay on the grass, I experienced the same mental anguish as before. 28 [d]Then my mouth was opened[d] and I commenced to speak before the Most High as follows:

Audible meditation on the permanence of the law

29 [e]O Lord[e], you have [f]indeed revealed[f] yourself to us through our fathers in the desert[g]. When they left Egypt and entered the trackless[h] and unfruitful desert[i] you said,

30 You, O Israel, listen to me;
    O seed of Jacob[j], give attention to my words.

31 Now[k] I am sowing in you my law and it will produce fruit[l] in you and [m]you will be eternally glorified[m] by it. 32 However, our fathers who received the law did not observe[n] it but disregarded [its] directives; nevertheless the fruit of the law was not destroyed — it could not [be destroyed] because it was yours — 33 but those who received it were destroyed because they did not observe [the seed] that was sown in them. 34 [o]Now it is generally true[o] that when the soil receives seed, or the sea a ship, or any bowl food [p]or drink[p],

---

[a] S** has Ardat; A, Ardad; C, Ardas; M, Ardaf; Syriac 'rpd; Ar.1 'r''t or 'r''b; Ethiopic follows Syriac. Ardat may be derived from 'rṣ ḥdš, "new land" (cf. StB, IV, 2, 812, n. 1).

[b-b] Latin de herbis agri, "of the herbs of the field"; Syriac 'qr ddbr', "roots of the field."

[c] So C, M; S, A have saturitatem, "fill."

[d-d] Ethiopic and Ar.1 "I opened my mouth" (active voice).

[e-e] Syriac mry' mry, "Lord, my Lord"; so also Ethiopic.

[f-f] Based on Hebrew infinitive absolute construction as in Syriac.

[g] Syriac adds syny, "Sinai."

[h] Syriac wl' 'br bh 'nš, "through which no man has gone."

[i] Syriac adds b'r'', "a land."

[j] Omitted by Ethiopic.

[k] Latin ecce=Heb. hnh, "behold."

[l] Syriac adds dzdyqwt', "of righteousness."

[m-m] Armenian "I will be glorified in you."

[n] With C; S, A have servaverunt, "keep," in the sense of safeguard; Syriac nṭrwhy, "observe it."

[o-o] Lit. "this is the rule [or experience]"; Syriac nmws', "law," "principle."

[p-p] Omitted by Syriac and Ethiopic. Armenian of vss. 33–35 is missing.

and that what was sown or what was launched or what was placed in [them] is lost, 35 they are lost while in fact their containers remain. However, with us it has not been so; 36 we who received the law will be lost because we have sinned, together with our heart which received it; 37 for *the law*ᵃ is not lost but endures in ʳits majestyʳ.

The vision of the despondent woman

a. The woman's misfortune

38 While I was saying these things to myself, I looked up and saw a woman ˢon my rightˢ who was wailing and crying loudly; she was deeply grieved ᵗin spiritᵗ, her clothes were tornᵘ, and dust was upon her head. 39 Then I dismissed the thoughts that were ᵛoccupying meᵛ, turned ʷtoward her and said to her: 40 Why ˣare you weeping? Whyˣ are you grieved in spirit? 41 She said to me: My lord, allow me to bewail myself and continueʸ [my] lamentation because I am very bitter in spirit and deeply depressedᶻ. 42 I replied to her: What has befallen you? Tell me! She said to me: 43 I, your servant, was barren and bore no child though I was marriedᵃ for thirty years. 44 I prayed to the Most High night and day, every hour and every day, for thirty yearsᵇ. 45 Then after thirty years

> God heard me, your handmaid,
> ᶜTook note of my disgrace,
> Gave heed to my distressᶜ,
> And gave me a son.

I, my husband and all ᵈmy neighborsᵈ, rejoiced greatly over him and gave homage to the Almighty. 46 Iᵉ nurtured him with great

---

ᵃ⁻ᵃ Syriac "your law," *nmwsk;* so also Ar.² and Armenian; this and preceding verse omitted by Ethiopic.

ʳ⁻ʳ C, M have *honore,* "praise," "glory," "esteem"; S, A have *labore,* "work," "validity"(?); Syriac *btšbḥth* "glory," "honor."

ˢ⁻ˢ Omitted by Ar.² and Armenian.

ᵗ⁻ᵗ Syriac *bnpšh,* "in her soul," as Latin, Ethiopic, Ar.¹; omitted by Ar.² and Armenian.

ᵘ Ar.² adds "her hair was disheveled and her curls plucked out."

ᵛ⁻ᵛ Latin *cogitans* but omitted by M.   ʷ Ar.¹ adds "my face."

ˣ⁻ˣ Omitted by C.   ʸ C has *abiciam,* "resign [or deport] myelf to."

ᶻ Ar.¹ adds "for the lamentation of my heart is full of bitterness for me, and I have fallen into much humility and disrepute."

ᵃ Syriac *hwyt 'm gbry,* "I was with my husband"; so essentially Ar.¹,², Ethiopic; Armenian follows Latin.

ᵇ Ar.¹ adds "to give fruit to my womb."   ᶜ⁻ᶜ Omitted by Ar.².

ᵈ⁻ᵈ Syriac *bny mdynty,* "children of my city."

ᵉ Ar.² *rbtn',* "we brought up" and adds "and he attained maturity." So also Armenian.

pains. [47] After he was grown up, I spared no efforts to take a wife for him, and made a marriage feast [for him][f].

10 [1] Then when my son went into his bridal chamber, he fell over dead. [2] So [g]we all extinguished[g] our lights and [h]all my neighbors[h] began to console me; I remained calm until the evening of the second day. [3] When they had all [i]ceased consoling me[i] [j][because they thought][j] I was composed, I arose in the night, fled, and came, [k]as you can see[k], to this field. [4] I am not going to return to the city again but remain here, and I shall neither eat nor drink but lament and fast incessantly until I die.

> b. *She is told to bear her sorrow bravely, and if so — accepting the judgment of God — she will receive back her son*

[5] Then I[l] interrupted the ponderings with which I was occupied until now and replied indignantly[m] to her as follows: [6] [n]O most unwise[n] of all women, don't you see our plight and the things that have happened to us? [7] How Zion, the mother of us all,

> [o]is overcome with grief[o],
>
> plunged into humility,
>
> [p]wailing bitterly[p]!

[8] [q]So there is reason for all of us to lament, to be sad and to be grieved, but you grieve over [the loss] of just one son[q]. [9] For instance, consult the earth and she will tell you that she is the one

---

[f] Syriac adds *wbsm' rb'*, "and a great banquet."

[g-g] Syriac *w'n' dyn shpt 'nwn lšrg'*, "but I overturned the lights."

[h-h] Syriac *klhwn bny mdynty*, "all the sons of my city"; other MSS have "all the people of my [the] city."

[i-i] Syriac *wmn btr ddmkw*, "after they had fallen asleep."

[j-j] Syriac *wsbryn hww*, "and they thought"; some variation on the theme in other versions.

[k-k] Omitted by Ethiopic.

[l] Ar.[2] adds *el Usair*.   [m] Omitted by Ethiopic and Ar.[2].

[n-n] Syriac *ṭb pkyhty 'ntt'*, "very unwise are you, O woman."

[o-o] Armenian "Jerusalem is groaning greatly."

[p-p] Reading with C, *luget*; Bensly text reads with S, *lugete*, "imperative," and apparently takes it with next verse; so also Syriac *hš' dyn lmt'blw mtb''*, "now it is necessary to weep"; Hilgenfeld thinks the Latin is based on a misreading of the Greek *pentheite* for *penthei te*. Ar.[1] follows Syriac.

[q-q] As it stands, the Latin is difficult; perhaps the quotation by Ambrose (*de excessu Satyri* 1:2) gets at the meaning: *et nunc, quoniam omnes lugemus et tristes sumus, quoniam omnes contristati sumus, tu vero contristaris in filio*, "and now, while all of us lament and are sad, while all of us are gloomy, you are in fact gloomy over a son." Syriac *'nt gyr m'q' 'nty 'l br' ḥd hnn dyn klh 'lm' 'l 'mn*, "you are grieved over one son but we over the whole world, over our mother." Our rendering is only an approximation, not definitive. Cf. especially Ar.[1].

who ought to be grieved over*r* so many that germinate*s* upon her. 10 From her all have sprung *t*in the beginning*t*, and others will come, and nearly all go straight to perdition and a great number of them will come to doom. 11 Who, therefore, ought to lament the more? She who has lost such a great number or you who mourn over one*u*? 12 *v*Should you say to me*v*, My misery is unlike [that] of the earth because I have lost the fruit of my womb

To which I gave birth in travail,

And [which] I bore in pain,

13 Whereas the earth [generates] in *w*its own way*w* — *x*the multitude living in it goes out as it came in*x* — I would reply to you, 14 Just as you gave birth in travail, so the earth from the beginning has given her fruit, man, to him who created her.

15 Therefore keep your grief to yourself,

And bear gallantly your calamities.

16 For if you accept as right the verdict of God*y*, you will get back your son in [his] time and be highly extolled among women. 17 So go [back] to the city to your husband. She said to me:

c. *The response of the woman*

18 That*z* I will not do, nor will I enter the city*a*, but I will die here*b*.

d. *Further remonstrance of Ezra*

19 Then I undertook to speak to her further as follows: 20 *c*Do not carry out*c* that resolution*d* but *e*permit yourself to be persuaded*e* because of the calamity of Zion, and to be consoled because of the distress of Jerusalem. 21 For you see how

r Syriac is quite literal here.

s Syriac *dhww*, "who are"; so also Ar.*1*; all others as Latin.

t–t M and Vulgate have *ab initio*, "from the beginning," which is better than *ex . . . initia*.

u Ar.*1* "your only son."   *v–v* Ar.*2* "then she said"; other MSS with Latin.

w–w Syriac *kynh d'r' '*, "according to the nature of the earth."

x–x Syriac *'zl swg' ' d't' lh 'yk d't'*, "the multitude who came to her passes away as it came."

y Ethiopic adds "who sees you." Ar.*2* of verse is obscure.

z With Syriac *hkn'*.   *a* Syriac adds *wl' lwt gbry*, "and not to my husband."

b Ar.*2* adds "in this field."   *c–c* Syriac *l' 'ntt', l' 'ntt'*, "no woman! no woman!"

d Latin *sermonem*, "word"; Syriac *ptgm'*, "word," "matter" — both refer to the word or declaration of the woman in vss. 4, 18.

e–e Ar.*1* "console your heart," *'zy qlbk*.

Our sanctuary[f] has been demolished,
Our altar[g] has been thrown down,
Our temple has been destroyed,
22 Our [h]stringed instruments[h] have been laid low,
Our hymns have been stilled,
Our exultation has ceased,
The light of our candlestick[i] has been extinguished,
The ark of our covenant[j] has been plundered,
Our [k]holy vessels[k] have been contaminated,
The name [l]we bear[l] has been profaned,
[m]Our nobles have suffered abuse,
Our priests have been burned,
Our Levites have gone into captivity[m],
Our virgins have been debauched[n],
Our wives have suffered violence,
Our [o]just men[o] have been dragged away,
Our [p]little ones[p] have been abandoned,
Our youths have been enslaved,
Our brave men have been rendered impotent.
23 And worst of all,
[q]The seal of Zion has been deprived of its glory[q],
And given over into the hands of those who hate us.
24 So cast off your great sorrow,
[r]and put aside your many griefs[r],
that the Almighty may spare you,
the Most High grant you rest
and repose from your sufferings.

---

[f] Syriac *mqdšyn*, "sanctuaries."
[g] Syriac *mdbḥyn*, "altars"; other versions have singular.
[h-h] *psalterium*. Syriac *tšmštn*, "service," "liturgy"; others have "psalmody."
[i] Syriac *mnrtn*, "menorah."   [j] Syriac *dytq'* (Greek *diathēkē*, "testament").
[k-k] Syriac *qdyšyn*, "masculine holy men"; but, as Violet and Gunkel indicate, Latin *sancta* is to be preferred as rendered in our translation.
[l-l] Ethiopic "our name."
[m-m] Ar.² diverges considerably; it begins with "our nobles" but omits "priests" and "Levites."
[n] Ethiopic "killed."   [o-o] Syriac *ḥzynn*, "seers."
[p-p] Syriac 7a 1 has *wdyqyn*, which has been emended to *wzdyqyn*, "and the just ones."
[q-q] Substantially as Syriac; Ethiopic "Zion is sealed and her glory departed"; Ar.¹ "the seal that was in Zion was smashed"; Ar.² omits reference to seal.
[r-r] Omitted by Syriac.

Identification of the woman

a. *The city replaces the woman*

25 As[s] I was speaking to her,
          quite suddenly her face lit up
          and her appearance was 'like a flash of lightning',
so that I was too greatly terrified to approach her[u]; while I pondered what this might be, 26 she suddenly let go a fearfully loud cry so that the earth quaked at the sound [of it]. 27 When I looked up, the woman was no longer visible to me but a city was being built at the place on conspicuously massive foundations. I was afraid and cried with a loud voice as follows:

b. *Uriel's interpretation*

28 Where is Uriel, the angel, who came to me before? For he is the one who brought on me this great bewilderment;
          My prayer[v] has come to naught,
          And my plea [but] a taunt.
29 As I said this, [w]the angel who came to me before appeared to me and when he saw me 30 lying there like a corpse[x], deprived of my senses, he took hold of my right hand, consoled me, set me on my feet, and said to me:
          31 What is the matter with you,
          Why are you so disturbed,
          What has so[y] confused your mind,
          And your thoughts[y]?
I replied[z]: 32 Because you deserted me so utterly. I followed your direc-

---

[s] Lit. "it came to pass."
[t–t] Syriac *dmwt' dbrq'*, "likeness of lightning."
[u] Syriac adds *wlby ṭb tmyh hw'*, "and my heart was utterly stupefied." So also Ethiopic and Ar.[1].
[v] Latin S, C, M have *finis*, "end"; so also Syriac (*ḥdty*), Ethiopic, Ar.[1]. A has *fletus*, "weeping." Violet suggests corruption of text going back to Hebrew where *tklty* was read for *tplty*, "prayer." See note in NEB in loco. But *finis* can also be rendered with Gunkel *Absicht*, "purpose," "aim," "goal." Ar.[2] is unintelligible.
[w] Syriac inserts here the adjectival clause at the beginning of vs. 30: *'l 'r'' 'yk myt'*, "upon the earth as dead."
[x] Syriac takes *'l' r''*, "upon the earth," of preceding verse with vs. 30; so also apparently Ar.[1,2].
[y–y] *sensus cordis tui*, "thought of your heart"; Syriac *'štny r'ynk wmd'h dlbk*, "your mind so moved and the thought of your heart."
[z] Syriac adds *lh*, "to him."

tions, *went out* into the field and* I saw what is impossible for me to explain. He said to me: 33 *Stand up like a man* and I will teach you. So I said, 34 Speak, my lord, just do not desert me, *lest I die in ignorance*,

35 Because I have seen what I cannot understand,
    And *I have heard* what I cannot grasp —
36 Or is my mind tricked*,
    And my spirit in *a trance*?

37 Now, therefore, I *beg you to explain to your servant *this confusion*. 38 He responded to me as follows:

    Listen to me and I will teach you,
    And I will inform you about the things you fear,
because the Most High has revealed to you great secrets*. 39 For he has seen your *upright way*,

    How you grieved incessantly for your people,
    And lamented greatly over Zion.

40 Here, then, is *the meaning* of the vision: about the woman who appeared to you a little while past, 41 whom *you saw* weeping and began to console* her 42 and then saw no longer in the form of a woman, but who appeared to you as a city being built, 43 and who told you about the loss of her son, this is *the meaning*: 44 This woman whom you saw is Zion which you now see as a finished city. 45 When she informed you *that she was sterile for thirty years

---

a–a Omitted by Syriac.

b S, A have "and I see"; omitted by C, M; Syriac has on the margin *ḥzy*, "behold."

c–c Syriac *qwm 'l rglyk*, "stand upon your feet"; Ethiopic, Ar.¹ and Armenian follow Latin.

d–d Latin *frustra*, "disappointment," "frustration"; Syriac *dl' 'mwt dl'bzbny*, "that I die not out of my time"; so also Ar.¹,²; Ethiopic "die on the spot"; Armenian follows Latin.

e–e Reading *audivi* with C, M; S, A have *audio*, "I hear"; so also Syriac. Ethiopic and Ar.¹,² follow C, M.

f Syriac *md'y mkdb ly*, "my mind deceiving me."

g–g Syriac *ḥlm' hw ḥzy'* "a dream that is a vision."

h Ar.¹ adds *'bdk*, "your servant."

i–i Syriac *ḥzw' hn' dhyl'*, "this powerful, terrible vision."

j *mysteria*, "mysteries"; Syriac *r'z'*, "mysteries," a word (*rz*) occurring frequently in Qumran materials.

k–k Syriac *ltryṣwtk*, "your uprightness"; so also Ethiopic and Ar.¹. Following this Syriac adds *dsgy m'q 'nt 'l 'mk*, "how much you have been disturbed concerning your people," simply a doubling with the next clause.

l–l Syriac *mlt'*=Heb. *dbr*, "interpretation" or "meaning."

m–m Omitted by Syriac.

n Active voice as in 10:49; 12:8.

o–o Syriac *pwšq'*, "interpretation"; cf. Qumran *pešer*.

p Syriac adds *'l npšh*, "concerning herself, her soul."

it was because for ᵃthree thousandᵃ years no offerings were offered in her. 46 Then, after ʳthree thousand yearsʳ Solomon built the city and offered offerings — then it was that the sterile [woman] bore a son. 47 When she told you that she exercised [extreme] care in his upbringing, that was [the period of] Jerusalem's inhabitationˢ. 48 When she told you ᵗthat my son died as he entered his bridal chamberᵗ, and ᵘthat misfortune befell herᵘ, that represents the destruction of Jerusalem which has come about. 49 Now, you saw ᵛher figureᵛ, how she sorrowed over a son, and you undertook to console her because of the things that had happened to her — ʷthese were the things to be disclosed to youʷ. 50 So when the Most High saw

> That you were sad in spirit
> And that you wholeheartedly lamented for her,
> He displayed to you herˣ splendorous glory
> And the radiance of her beauty.

51 For that reason I urged you ʸto stayʸ in the field where no house had been built, 52 because I knew that the Most High was about to show youᶻ these things. 53 For that reason I told you to go into ᵃa fieldᵃ where there is no building foundation, 54 because no edifice constructed by man could stand in the place where the city of the Most High was about to be revealed. 55 Hence you must not be afraid, and do not let your heart be terrified. But enter and behold ᵇthe splendorᵇ andᶜ ᵈmagnitude of the buildingᵈ as far as the range of your eyes can encompass. 56 Afterwards you will hear as much as your ears are capable of hearing.

ᵃ⁻ᵃ Armenian "many"; Latin C, M have *tres,* "three"; A** has *tria milia,* three thousand; so also Syriac, Ethiopic, Ar.¹,².

ʳ⁻ʳ So Syriac, Ethiopic and Ar.¹; omitted by Ar.² and Armenian; Latin *annos tres,* "three years."

ˢ Syriac *'wmrh,* "habitation"; so substantially all versions.

ᵗ⁻ᵗ Versions nearly all have direct discourse here.

ᵘ⁻ᵘ Omitted by Syriac.

ᵛ⁻ᵛ Latin *similitudinem eius.* Syriac *dmwth,* "likeness"; omitted by Ethiopic and Armenian.

ʷ⁻ʷ So Latin.

ˣ Omitted by C, M.

ʸ⁻ʸ Syriac *dtqw' ly,* "await me." Ar.² omits vss. 51, 52, 54.

ᶻ Syriac adds *klhyn,* "all," as do all the others except Latin.

ᵃ⁻ᵃ *Agrum,* "territory," "place"; Syriac *'tr',* "place"; the idea seems to be "virgin soil."

ᵇ⁻ᵇ Syriac *nwhr' dtšbwḥth,* "the light of its glory."

ᶜ S, A, C *vel,* "or"; M and others have *et,* "and."

ᵈ⁻ᵈ Ethiopic="the strength of its walls," and omits remainder of verse.

57 You are indeed more fortunate than many,

And you have a name with the Most High as few [do].

58 But you must remain here tomorrow night 59 when the Most High will show you in those dream visions what the Most High will do for those who live on earth in the last days.

NOTES

9:26 *proceeded into the field*. Cf. Hermas *Similitudes* 9:1:4 where Hermas was carried to Arcadia to a conical shaped mountain for a better perspective; and Balaam in Num 23:13.

Ardat. Obscure. The Armenian Ardab is said to be a grain measure. It could be a place name of a small locality near Babylon. Cf. the river (wadi) Chebar in Ezekiel (1:1) where the prophet had his visions, or the river Ahava in Ezra (8:15, 21, 31). It does occur in the Tutmose III list of cities destroyed during his fifth campaign to Palestine; it is described as a place of grain and pleasant trees (Pritchard, ANET, p. 239). It is mentioned a number of times in the Amarna Letters where it is located in the vicinity of Tripoli or Byblos (see note by O. Weber and E. Ebeling in J. A. Knudtzon, *Die El-Amarna Taflen,* II [Aalen: Zeller, 1964, reprint of 1915 ed.], 1156 f.). It is also mentioned in Letter No. 20, reverse line 5, in *Ugaritica V,* Mission de Ras Shamra, XVI (Paris: Geuthner, 1968), 72; see comments ibid., pp. 663 f., 684. Perhaps there is some eschatological significance in the term which escapes us at present. Syriac was doubtless influenced by OT passages such as II Kings 18:34; 19:13 || Isa 10:9; 36:19; 37:13; Jer 49:23. For various theories about location and significance see Box, in loco (cf. also II Bar 47:1), and Erwin Preuschen, ZNW 1 (1900), 265 f.

27. *I experienced*. Lit. "my heart was troubled just as before."

28. *my mouth was opened*. Note passive voice indicating an almost involuntary, automatic reflection on the problem the seer could not put aside — perhaps because his questions were not satisfactorily answered and could not be resolved, at least not yet.

29. *revealed yourself . . . in the desert*. Doubtless reminiscent of such passages as Exod 19:9; 24:10; etc.

to us. Not in the versions outside the Latin where all manuscripts have it.

left Egypt. Cf. Judg 11:16.

entered the trackless . . . desert. For expression see Ps 107:40; Jer 2:6.

30. Reminiscent of Pss 50:7; 105:6; I Chron 16:13; Deut 5:1; 6:4; Isa 1:2; 1QM 10:3.

seed of Jacob. See II Esdras on 3:19; 8:16; "seed of Israel" in CD 12:22; 1QH 6:15 "an everlasting planting."

31. *sowing in you my law*. Cf. 4:28 ff. for the evil sowing; Sir 4:12 f. where the planting is wisdom. For the idea at Qumran see Maier, *Die Texte vom Toten Meer,* II, 90.

eternally glorified. Cf. Sir 24:16 f.; I Macc 2:64; II Bar 54:21b. The underlying Greek was probably *doxa*, "glory" which signified the light, splendor and glory of the heavenly world. Cf. *kbwd 'wlm* or *'d* in 1QH 3:4; 11:27; 13:6; 1QSb 3:4; for what possession of God's gift meant to Qumran community see 1QS 4:6–8. Jeremiah (31:33) speaks of the Torah to be written on the hearts of men.

32. *our fathers . . . did not observe it*. Cf. Num 32:13; Neh 9:29.

directives=legitima. Cf. 1:24; 7:24. Heb. *toroth*, or *ḥuqqim*.

fruit of the law. Cf. 1QH 8:20 ff.

it could not [be destroyed]. Cf. I Bar 4:1.

33. See NOTES on 7:68; 8:35; I Enoch 81:5. What was sown in them was the seed of the law (vs. 31).

35. *they are lost*. I.e. the contents of the soil, sea, bowl.

36. *we who received the law*. Here it is the vessel that is destroyed, its contents saved. Cf. II Bar 14:19.

our heart which received it. The idea seems to be that sinners and their hearts, which were the recipients of the law (*eam*, referring back to *legem*), will be lost. Gunkel's translation brings out the meaning: "We who have received the law must perish because of our sins together with our heart in which it [sin] was committed; but the law does not perish. . . ." Cf. 1QH 4:10; CD 20:9; and the recurrent phrase "stubbornness of heart" in Qumran writings; II Bar 32:1.

37. *in its majesty*. Cf. Rom 7:14: I Bar 4:1–2; Pseudo-Philo 11:3. Perhaps the term majesty or dignity has too many modern implications to render adequately the character of the law in the mind of our author: it is the lasting, effective, directive, proven, moral quality of the law.

38. *saying . . . to myself*. Lit. "I said in my heart" (cf. Ps 10:6).

on my right. Cf. 4:47. The right side was of significance in the ancient world. In Ezek 4:6, the prophet was commanded to lie on his right side to bear the sins of Judah for forty days (4:4 f., for those of Israel, three hundred and ninety days while lying on the left side). See also Mark 10:37, 40; 16:5; Luke 1:11; the side of blessing and good fortune (Matt 25:34; John 21:6).

dust was upon her head. Sign of misfortune (cf. II Sam 13:19; Isa 61:3). On the mourning woman cf. Anat's lamentation for the death of Baal, in a very different context (UT, 62:1 ff.).

39. *thoughts . . . occupying me*. Lit. "the thoughts on which I was thinking."

41. *bitter in spirit*. Lit. "bitter in soul." Cf. *mrt npš* in I Sam 1:10; 22:2. The first part of the story reflects contact with the language of I Sam 1.

42. *What has befallen you?* Heb. *mh hyh lk* (cf. I Kings 14:3), "what was to you," "what is the matter with you?"

43. *thirty years*. Cf. Marcel Simon, "Retour du Christ et reconstruction du Temple dans la pensée chrétienne primitive," in *Aux sources de la Tradition Chrétienne* (Neuchatel and Paris: Delachaux et Niestlé, 1950), p. 254, n. 3.

44. *prayed*. Cf. I Sam 1:10, 15.

night and day. Cf. Judith 11:17 where the same order is found. This is typically Hebrew (cf. Gen 1 "evening and morning"); in Qumran literature it is usually "day and night."

45. *my disgrace . . . my distress*. To be barren was so regarded in Israel (I Sam 1:6, 10, 11, 15, 16; Luke 1:25).

my neighbors. Lit. "all my fellow citizens."

the Almighty. Latin *fortem*, "the strong one"=*ton ischuron* in LXX=*ḥyl* in Hebrew. May be a veiled indication that the later misfortune was not regarded as a judgment of God. As in the case of Hannah, it merely points to the fulfillment of a religious, ritual obligation after the reception of the blessing of God.

46. Cf. Hannah's dedication of Samuel and the entrusting of his upbringing to Eli (I Sam 1:26–28).

47. *I spared no efforts*. Lit. "I came to take." Note the mother's marriage arrangements for her son, contrary to Hebrew practice. Gen 21:21 is not quite parallel.

made a marriage feast. Lit. "I made a feast day." For description see Roland de Vaux, *Ancient Israel* (New York: McGraw-Hill, 1961), p. 33; Tobit 8:19; Matt 22:2. Cf. *mšth* of Judg 14:10.

10:1. *fell over dead*. Cf. Tobit 6:13; and ch. 8.

2. *extinguished our lights*. For lights connected with the marriage feast cf. Matt 25:1 ff. The removal of lights was an indication of misfortune (cf. Rev 2:5).

my neighbors began to console me. Lit. "rose to console me" (cf. John 11:19). See NOTE on 8:45.

I remained calm. Not the calm of composure but a sign of the depth of the mother's grief; she was shocked beyond words or lamentation, dumbfounded.

3. *When they had all ceased*. Lit. "It came to pass when all had ceased to console me that I might be calm," but meaning is best expressed by the Syriac as may be seen from the translation here given.

4. Here the story of the woman ends. But vs. 10 may reflect a further development of the idea involved.

5. *ponderings*. Latin *sermones;* Syriac *mḥšbty*, "plans," "thoughts"; this expression appears out of place since it occurs in 9:39.

7. *Zion, the mother of us all*. Note definition of Zion as Jerusalem in Armenian. Zion is identified as mother in Isa 50:1; cf. Hosea 2:2; Gal 4:26.

overcome with grief. Lit. "grieved in grief."

plunged into humility. Lit. "humiliated by humility."

wailing bitterly. Lit. "she laments" or "wails most powerfully."

8. As textual note *q–q* indicates, the translation is very uncertain. See NEB rendering which is quite free. The idea is fairly clear — Ezra and his associates rightly mourn because of their great loss; the woman mourns a much lesser loss. Violet connects the last clause with the following verse: "since you are sad over one son, ask the earth. . . ."

9. *consult*. Lit. "ask" (cf. 5:46). Zion and the earth have every reason to mourn as they have suffered great loss.

10. *in the beginning*. From Adam on, i.e. from the first of creation, with more still to come.

13. *in its own way*. Lit. "the earth [generates] according to the way of the earth."

living in it. Lit. "present in it."

14. *from the beginning*. See NOTE on 10 above. Cf. Gen 2:7 f.; Rom 8:18–22 which reflects the belief that the creation (the earth) was also brought forth in travail.

16. *accept as right the verdict of God*. Cf. Pss Sol 3:3; 4:9; 8:7; Luke 7:35 (of wisdom).

get back your son. She will get another son who will satisfy her deepest longings as the mother of a son, though a resurrection could be referred to obliquely.

be highly extolled. Cf. Gen 30:13; Judg 5:24; Ruth 4:14 f.; Luke 1:42; Judith 13:18.

18. *That . . . do*. Lit. "That I will not make," *faciam*, *"bd*.

20. *resolution*. Lit. "word," i.e. what she threatened in vs. 18; cf. Heb *hdbr hzh*, "this thing."

calamity of Zion . . . distress of Jerusalem. May be a reference to situation in time of writer, or a general recollection of the disasters that had overtaken both on numerous occasions (cf. Sir 48:19, 24; II Bar 5:1), to depict current conditions.

21. *Our sanctuary . . . Our altar . . . Our temple*. Cf. II Chron 36:19; Lam 1:10; 2:7; I Macc 4:38; the descriptives of an earlier day are used by the writer to portray the situation in his day.

22. For whole verse see Lam 4:1 f.; I Macc 1:39; 2:7–12; II Bar 5:1; 10; 11:2.

stringed instruments. Cf. Isa 24:8.

The light of our candlestick. Cf. I Macc 1:21; 4:50; indicated the cessation of religious services (for description see Exod 25:32; 27:20; Lev 24:2–4).

The ark of our covenant. Not referred to after the destruction of Solomon's temple or in the temple furniture inventory in the Maccabean period (cf. Jos. *Wars* 1:152). This is a hint that our author was thinking of the Babylonian conquest.

Our holy vessels. The utensils used in connection with temple rites and services. The author may have had in mind Dan 5:2 f. They are given in I Macc 4:47–51. Cf. further Ps Sol 2:3 where the sons of Jerusalem are said to have defiled the holy things, *ta agia kuriou*.

The name we bear. Lit. "the name which is called over us." God had given them his name (II Macc 8:15; Ps Sol 9:18; II Esd 4:25) which meant that they belonged to him; they were his heritage. Cf. 4Q, Words of the Lights, col. 2:12 (RB, 68 [1961], 200).

Our nobles. Jos. *Wars* 6:271 says no class was spared in the Roman conquest of Jerusalem in A.D. 70. Cf. the same treatment by the Babylonians, II Chron 36:17. The thought expressed here may reflect the situation depicted in II Kings 24:14 and 25:12.

priests . . . burned. Perhaps a play on the burning of the temple, although some priests may actually have been cremated when it was destroyed (see Jos. *Wars* 6:271; 6:316 for an instance of this during the Roman conquest).

Our virgins . . . Our wives. See Judith 4:12; Lam 1:4; 5:11.

Our little ones. Cf. Lam 1:5, 18; 2:11.

23. *seal of Zion.* May refer to the seal of the city. Cf. Jer 22:24; Hag 2:24; Esther 3:10; 8:2; I Macc 6:15; Ps Sol 2:6. The War Scroll from Qumran (1QM) speaks of insignia on various instruments (col. 3) and the inscriptions on the standards of the various divisions of the hosts of the Sons of Light (cols. 3, 4). The seal of Zion has been interpreted as the symbol of its independence of which the city was now deprived. Cf. further Box, p. 229.

given over. Cf. Pss 44:12; 106:41; Neh 9:27.

24. *cast off.* Lit. "shake off." Cf. Isa 52:2; I Bar 4:25 f.

the Almighty may spare you. Cf. Lam 3:31–33; II Bar 84:10.

25. *her face lit up. . . .* Cf. Rev 12:1; 21:9 which the figure of the trans-figured woman here recalls. Visions of such phenomena are known elsewhere in apocalyptic literature (e.g. Dan 10:6).

27. *a city . . . built.* The new or heavenly Jerusalem. Cf. vs. 42; Rev 21:10. A frequently recurring figure in apocalyptic literature (I Enoch 90:28–29; II Esd 13:36) and present in the Talmud (Tannith 5a; Baba Bathra 75b). For further references see Moore, II, p. 342, and cf. Hermas *Visions* 3:4–5. See now the following passage from Nag Hammadi Codex VI, page 1, line 24, to page 2, line 7:

"After we had set sail, we continued to have a good journey for a full day and night. Then a storm arose against the ship and drove us to a small city that lay in the midst of the sea. I, Peter, then inquired of several people of the place who stood at the wharf about the name of the city. One of them replied and said to me? 'The city is called

> the truth strengthens you (you city) for patience,
> and the counsel of your ruler, who is in you,
> brings the palm branch for the heart of your people.' "

From the German translation by Hans-Martin Schenke in *Theologische Literaturzeitung* 98, no. 1 (January 1973), col. 16.

massive foundations. Cf. Rev 21:9–21; Heb 11:10.

I was afraid. Cf. I Enoch 21:9.

28. *My prayer has come to naught.* In 9:29–37 the seer prayed for the revelation of Israel's coming glory. Now because he failed to comprehend the vision due to human limitations, he thought his prayer had been rejected. As the interpreting angel explains later the vision was actually the divine answer to his prayer.

29. *the angel . . . appeared to me.* Cf. Dan 8:15.

30. *lying there like a corpse.* Cf. Ezek 2:1 f.; Dan 8:17 f.; Rev 1:17.

set me on my feet. See 5:15; 6:13, 17.

31. *What is the matter with you.* Cf. 9:42.

Why . . . disturbed . . . confused your mind. Cf. 9:40.

your thoughts. Lit. "the thoughts of your heart."

32. *your directions.* Lit. "I did according to your words."

I saw what is impossible . . . to explain. Cf. II Cor 12:4.

34. *in ignorance.* The meaning seems to be either lest he die in frustration or without realizing the import of what he had seen.

36. *my mind tricked.* Cf. Deut 11:16; Jer 20:7; Acts 10:10 (Vulgate); warning against in Sir 34:1 ff. What is in question here is not the reality of the vision but its meaning which the seer cannot fathom without assistance.

37. *this confusion.* Lit. "this [mental] aberration." Cf. *in excessu meo,* Ps 115:2 (Vulgate) [116:11H].

38. *Listen . . . teach you.* Cf. Job 33:33; Ps 34:11.

things you fear. The transfiguration of the woman.

39. *your upright way.* Cf. Aquila on Isa 57:2 *orthotēta,* "straightness," "uprightness"; or *rectam viam,* "right way" of II Peter 2:15 (Vulgate). The idea is present in numerous forms and variations in Qumran literature.

40. *the meaning.* The interpretation or explanation.

41. *weeping.* See vss. 9:38, 40.

console her. See vss. 9 ff., 20 ff.

42. *woman . . . appeared to you as a city.* See vs. 27.

43. *loss of her son.* See vs. 1.

44. *Zion.* I.e. the heavenly Jerusalem. Cf. Rev 21:2, and see NOTE on vs. 7. On the theological and stylistic significance of the transformation of the lamenting woman into a city see Westermann, ZAW 66 (1954), 78 f.

finished city. Lit. "a built city." On Zion as the beloved city see Sir 24:10 f.

45. *thirty years.* See NOTES on 9:43 f. There is no variation here in the versions; all have "thirty" which represents a hundredth of three thousand as indicated in the next clause.

three thousand is said to mark the years between creation and the building of the temple; again all versions have that number except the Armenian and Latin C, M. The number refers to the time between the Creation and the building of the temple (cf. Ass Mos 1:1 f.). Gunkel (in loco) adopts the C, M reading (so also Wellhausen) in line with the Latin reading in next verse and interprets the three years as the time that elapsed between the beginning of Solomon's reign and the building of the temple (I Kings 6:1).

offerings were offered. There were offerings before Solomon's temple was built but the reference here is to those offered in the temple complex.

46. *after three thousand years.* See textual note ʳ⁻ʳ. If the three thousand figure is followed the interpretation would be the same as that noted in vs. 45; so also if the Latin reading of three is followed. Manuscript L has after three thousand an explanation: *qui sunt tres etates trigintaque generationes,* "which are three years and thirty generations," counting thirty generations from Adam to Solomon and three years into Solomon's reign. (For the reckonings of time in apocalyptic literature see Volz, pp. 167–71). Thus we get three thousand years as the time from creation to Solomon; thirty years as thirty generations; three years as the time after the beginning of Solomon's reign.

Solomon. Box reads David to make this reference conform to 3:24, although there is absolutely no manuscript evidence for it (APOT, II, 607). Solomon did not build the city, nor did David for that matter — he added to it. But the name of David became associated with Mount Zion because he took it from the Jebusites (II Sam 5:7 — Jerusalem was thereafter referred to as the city of David. However, the reference does not appear to be primarily to the "city" of Zion but to the religious institution of "Zion," which was not on Mount Zion, as the mention of oblations shows. Before that for thirty years (generations) the woman (Zion) had been sterile.

47. [*extreme*] *care*. Represents the constant watch of prophets and others to preserve the cult from pagan incursions.

Jerusalem's inhabitation. I.e. so long as the temple and cultus remained.

48. *my son*. Not daughter as might be expected and often in OT — daughter of Zion (cf. also 4QT 29).

49. *her figure*. Box translates "the [heavenly] pattern of her." Cf. Heb 11:10, 16; 12:22; 13:14 for reference to the heavenly city. According to Exod 25:9, 40, Moses was shown the pattern or model of the tabernacle which he was to follow in building; it is this model or copy to which the author of Heb 8:5 referred. For only uses of word, *tbnyt*, in Qumran see 1QM 10:14 where the reference is to the pattern or shape of Adam and 4Q (Strugnell), no. 40, 24:3 where it is used in the phrase *tbnyt ks' mrkbh*, "the model [or structure] of the throne chariot." It is employed some fifteen times or more in OT, especially in late documents. Vulgate uses the same term as here in Exod 25:9; in Exod 9:40 *exemplar*. It was this heavenly pattern (the original) that was shown to Ezra.

50. *her splendorous glory*. Cf. Ezek 10:4; Heb 1:3; Wisd Sol 7:25 f. (of wisdom); I Bar 5:1 ff.

her beauty. Ps 50:2. Because of his deep concern the seer was given a glimpse of the heavenly city with all its glory and beauty. This is the reward for his devotion and marks the focal point of the vision. Cf. II Bar 4:3, 4; 32:2–4; I Enoch 90:28, 29; Rev 21:10 f.

53. *no building foundation*. Human foundations were inadequate for the building of God's Zion. Cf. I Cor 3:11.

54. *no edifice constructed by man*. For exposition cf. Volz, p. 337.

55. *enter and behold*. As Paul had entered and seen indescribable things, so the seer was commanded to enter the city and see its splendor and magnitude (cf. I Cor 2:9; II Cor 12:4). The seer is relating an experience which could not be described. He was after all limited by his humanity and could claim only so much as his eyes could encompass. The next verse again stresses the limitations of ear and eye. See Gunkel's quotation of Uhland's hymn on "Die verlorene Kirche (The lost church)," Kautzsch, APAT, II, 390.

57. *more fortunate than many*. For expression see Ruth 2:20; I Sam 15:13.

you have a name. Lit. "you are called [named] by the Most High." Cf. I Bar 5:4; Isa 45:3, 4.

58. *tomorrow night*. Lit. "the night that shall be after tomorrow." The great apocalyptic visions were night visions (cf. Dan 2:19; 7:2; Zech 1:8).

59. *dream visions*. Lit. "visions of/in dreams." One of the methods of revela-

tion (cf. I Sam 3). See Oesterley, pp. 128 f., for discussion of apocalyptic visions.

last days. Common expression in Qumran literature (cf. 1QpHab 2:5; 1QSa 1:1; 4QFl 1:2, 15, 19).

COMMENT

[Preparation for the vision, 9:26–28] This is part of the framework of the book and as such provides the setting for the conversations and experiences of the fourth vision. Carrying out the suggestion of the interpreting angel, the seer withdraws to the field — Ardat — where he spends seven days, presumably in meditation. But in the end his mind returned to the theme that troubled him before.

[Audible meditation on the permanence of the law, 9:29–37] In vs. 7 above, works and faith were stressed as essentials for salvation. That which gives direction to both is the law,[1] i.e. the Torah of the Hebrew way. In ch. 4:28 ff. the evil seed sown in Adam's heart has been dealt with. Here the other side is taken up as the writer tends increasingly to lean toward the interpreting angel's side. There is a sense in which Ezra becomes the *advocatus diaboli* while the interpreter assumes the view of the writer. This passage is in the form of a meditation which takes place in the quiet and undisturbed retirement of the seer himself.

His mind goes back to the Mosaic experience in the course of which God revealed himself to Israel in the desert where he called upon his people to give close attention to his word (law, way). At that time he sowed in them the law (Torah) which would everlastingly glorify them if they permitted it to bear fruit. Later developments, however, demonstrated that the very ones who received the law failed to keep it, even disregarded it. What did that do to the law? Did it perish? The conclusion to which his meditation led was that the law could never be destroyed since it was God's but rather that those who received it and failed to keep it would be destroyed. While the principle involved did not follow the general rule of the preservation of the container, though the contents were spoiled, it was nevertheless true. In the case of those who received the law, the container or recipient is lost while the law sown in them remains imperishable. The law continues in its validity and character. E. Brandenburger[2] has summarized Esdras' contention quite well. He points out that for II Esdras the human heart is the place or soil into which the two types of seed — that of the law and the evil sprout — are sown, each in the hope of bearing fruit. Which of the two is successful depends on the free choice of the one into whose heart they have been introduced. The triumph of the evil seed or sprout issues in the fruit of destruction and death. That of the law results in eternal life. Implicit in the argument of II Esdras is doubtless the view that man in every historical situation has to make his choice, though man here may be confined to Israel. That idea would appear to dispute

[1] On the place of the law in apocalyptic works see Bousset, ch. IV.
[2] *Adam und Christus* (Neukirchen, 1962), p. 33, n. 1.

the inevitability of evil. Yet, as Harnisch remarks, "The idea of the inevitability of evil is carried ad absurdum with the help of the concept of the law."[3]

[The vision of the despondent woman, 9:38 – 10:24. The woman's misfortune, 9:38 – 10:4] The interruption of the seer's meditation by the vision of the woman marks the inception of a new element in the ongoing story of our book as we learn later on. His attention was attracted by a distraught woman lamenting bitterly and deeply grieved in spirit. Her hair was disheveled, her clothes torn, and she had dust on her head — symbolic of her condition. Ezra put aside his thoughts and engaged her in conversation. She told him of her great misfortune at being unable to bear a child for thirty years after the beginning of her marriage. But she never gave up praying. Finally the Lord answered her prayer and gave her a son. She and all her neighbors were overjoyed at this turn of events and performed all the thanksgiving rites demanded by the occasion. She exercised great pains in his upbringing as was befitting for a mother whose offspring was the fruit of prayer. When he was grown up she saw to it that he had a wife and, in connection with the marriage ceremonies, once more carried out the religious and social customs required.

But then the hopes and dreams of the years evaporated. Misfortune struck like lightning out of the clear blue sky: in the very midst of the marriage festivities the son was taken by death. The mother was dumbfounded and despite the consolations offered by the neighbors, she refused to be comforted. Like Rachel of old (Jer 31:15; Matt 2:18), she wept for her son and rejected comfort. That is why she wandered to the field where the seer was meditating. There she had determined to remain and fast to death. She would not return to the city (place).

[She is told to bear her sorrow bravely, and if so — accepting the judgment of God — she will receive back her son, 10:5–17] While the seer's ponderings continued to be interrupted, he entered into a dialogue with the woman. He took her to task sharply because she was overwhelmed by the loss of only one son. Ezra (and those with him) had every right, even duty, to lament the incomparable loss of a vast multitude. The terrible plight in which Zion found herself was justification for grief and lamentation. The woman's misfortune, on the other hand, was comparatively insignificant, yet she appeared inconsolable. The parallel drawn between the earth and the woman is not quite relevant. It compares the *fruit* of the earth with the child of a woman, and places undue emphasis on numbers. The author seems to be aware of this when he raises the hypothetical objection of the woman (vss. 12–13). Nothing is said of the travail of the earth, though it may be taken for granted by virtue of the common conception that it did bring forth in pain. It gave its fruit to him who created it just as a mother presents a child to her husband. Then he exhorts her to bear her grief bravely and to accept the divine verdict. In so doing she will regain her son in one way or another and receive the acclaim of her neighbors (as before). Just who the figure of the woman represents has been

3 Harnisch, p. 172.

disputed but Kabisch has argued strongly that it is not *aiōn outos* (this age) but *aiōn ekeinos* (that age),[4] that is, the new, heavenly Jerusalem.

[The response of the woman, 10:18] The response is a virtual repetition of the statement in vs. 4, but a bit more curt.

[Further remonstrance of Ezra, 10:19–24] In this toned down discourse Ezra appeals to the woman not to carry out what appears to be a firm resolution, but to permit herself to be persuaded because of the calamity of Zion and the distress of Jerusalem which the seer details in the following three verses. The rather lengthy and detailed passage is composed of biblical and apocalyptic reminiscences put together in much the same way as were the hymns of the Chronicler and some of the Qumran psalms. The form reflects the author's favorite concept of seven — vss. 21–23 contain twenty-one (three times seven) statements.

Attention here is focused entirely upon Israel. The broad, universal concern revealed in earlier chapters has given way to a seemingly narrower one, as the seer laments the fate of his people. Yet he is not so pessimistic as a superficial reading might indicate.[5] In his final appeal to the woman he bids her to cast off her great sorrow and put aside her many griefs in the belief that the Most High will spare her and grant her repose from her sufferings. So while there is pessimism and despair the situation is not a hopeless one. It represents the writer's reflection on the events of both 587 B.C. and A.D. 70.[6] On the one hand he is profoundly disturbed by the recent history of his people but, on the other hand, he has not lost hope. As Israel survived the terrible ordeal of 587 B.C., so she will eventually be spared from this one if she can but give the Almighty the opportunity and ear to speak to her heart.

[Identification of the woman, 10:25–59. The city replaces the woman, 10:25–27] The transfiguration of the woman represents a conception other than that held in some circles which held to the view of a rebuilt or renewed Zion located at the old locale. Ezra here aligns himself with the authors of I Enoch 90 and II Bar 4; all three look for the descent of the new Jerusalem from heaven in a completed state to where it already existed. Ezra met the woman in a field where no buildings existed before. That is where he then saw the city being built "at the place" on massive foundations.[7]

[Uriel's interpretation, 10:28–59] Utterly bewildered, the seer calls for the angel whom he blames for getting him into this predicament. Just as he was expressing disappointment because his prayer was being ignored Uriel appeared and administered what amounts to a rebuke to him. Ezra replied that the confused state of his mind was due to the angel's desertion of him just

---

[4] Kabisch, pp. 83–85.
[5] Cf. Keulers, pp. 32–35. He thinks there are twenty-one laments in vs. 22, but to get that number there requires considerable adjustment and textual emendation. He may be right but the present text hardly permits the addition of the two additional laments necessary.
[6] See K. G. Kuhn in TWNT, I, 514, and H. J. Schoeps, "Die Tempelzerstörung des Jahres 70 in der jüdischen Religionsgeschichte," in *Coniectanea Neotestamentica* 6 (1942), 1–45.
[7] For the ramifications of this conception see Volz, pp. 336–39.

when he needed him most. He had followed precisely the instructions of the heavenly interpreter but saw things which he could not explain. Urged to becalm himself, Ezra pleaded not to be left in the lurch again lest he die without an explanation of what must have been an important revelation. After all, his mind might have tricked him by vain imaginings; he could make no sense out of what he had seen in the vision. Uriel agreed to interpret for him the fearful things he had witnessed, for the Most High had disclosed to him great secrets which had not been revealed to anyone except the chosen few. He was one of the latter because of his way of life and the profound concern he had always expressed for the people.

The woman he had seen weeping and tried to console and then was transfigured into a city was none other than the heavenly Zion. Her period of sterility represented the time from creation to the construction of the temple. That was when she bore her son whom she brought up with great care and pains — the period of Jerusalem's habitation. The death of the son represents the destruction of Jerusalem which has taken place (cf. vs. 20).[8] What Ezra had seen was a likeness (similtudo) and was thus given a glimpse not only of her glory and beauty but of the heavenly disappointment over the misfortunes that had befallen the earthly Jerusalem. Ezra was not alone in lamenting her fate. The whole thrust of the vision was the confirmation of the seer's concern but also the fact that what God had in mind was beyond human comprehension. He could not grasp the full meaning of what he had seen; only so much as his eyes and ears were capable of comprehending. He was one of the fortunate few to whom these things had been shown.

In the preceding passage (9:26–10:59) the seer was advised to prepare himself for further revelatory visions disclosing to him what the Most High has in store for those who live on earth in the last days. He was told to wait two nights. This he did as the first verse of the vision (10:60–12:3a) indicates.

[8] See Box, pp. 233 f. for a discussion of the various views dealing with the identification of the woman and the son. Box's position that the woman stands for the heavenly Jerusalem and the son for the earthly one appears the most cogent at present. It is doubtful if Wellhausen's view of the son as messiah can be maintained (Skizzen und Vorarbeiten, VI, 219, note).

THE FIFTH (EAGLE) VISION (10:60–12:51)

The vision of an eagle with twelve wings and three heads

10 ⁶⁰ So I slept that night and the next one, as he had directed me.

11 ¹ Then, in the second night, ᵃI had a dreamᵃ [in which] I saw an eagleᵇ coming up out of the sea; it had twelveᶜ featheredᵈ wings

ᵃ⁻ᵃ Latin *vidi somnium*, "I saw a dream."
ᵇ Syriac *nšr' drb brbwth sgy*, "a great eagle in its exceeding greatness." Cf. Dan 7:3.
ᶜ Ar.² *'šrh*, "ten" but apparently *'thr* dropped out. This MS has twelve in vs. 22.
ᵈ Omitted by all but Latin versions.

and three heads. 2 As I kept looking, it spread out its wings over[e] the whole earth, so that all the winds of heaven blew upon it and [f]the clouds[f] gathered around it. 3 Moreover, I observed rival wings spring up out of its wings that became [g]puny and petty[g] wings. 4 But its heads were dormant; the middle head was larger than the other heads though it too[h] was dormant as they were. 5 Then I saw that the eagle flew[i] with its wings to gain dominion over the earth and its inhabitants. 6 I saw, too, how everything under heaven was subjected to it so that no one resisted it — not a single creature on earth. 7 As I kept looking, the eagle rose upon its talons and spoke[j] to its wings as follows[k]: 8 Do not all stand guard at the same time, sleep each one in its place and stand guard in turn[l]; 9 but the heads are to be kept till last. 10 When I looked again, I noticed that the voice did not come from its heads but from the middle of its body. 11 I counted its rival[m] wings[n] and found there were eight [of them]. 12 When I looked on the right side I saw one wing rise and it [o]held sway[o] over the whole earth. 13 Then after its rule ended it disappeared so that even [p]its place[p] was no longer visible. Then the next one rose up and held sway for a long[q] time. 14 As its rule came to its end and it disappeared, just like [its] predecessor, 15 a voice spoke to it [r]as follows[r]: 16 [s]Listen you[s]! you who have held sway over the earth for such [a long] time, [t]to this proclamation[t] before you are about to depart: 17 No one after you will hold sway for so long as you [did], not even half as long. 18 Then the third [wing] elevated itself, held sway like [its] predecessors[u] but it too disappeared[v]. 19 And so it was with all the wings, each one in turn assuming leadership and then likewise disappearing. 20 As I kept looking I

[e] With Ar.[g] 'ly; and Armenian. Others have "in."
[f–f] Latin omits nubes ad eam, "clouds to it"; Bensly supplies it from Syriac 'nn' lwth, "clouds to it."
[g–g] Syriac dqdq' wqtyn' wz'wr', "minute and small and little."   [h] Latin ipsa.
[i] Syriac pqd "commanded," reading Greek ephē, "said" for eptē, "flew," according to Hilgenfeld.
[j] Lit. "sent a voice"; Heb. ytn qwl, "give a voice."
[k] Syriac adds zlw 'štltw 'l klh 'r'', "go, take dominion over all the earth" and before next verse hš' dyn šlw, "but now remain quiet."
[l] Syriac adds wbzbn zbn tt'yrwn, "awake [or watch] from time to time."
[m] Syriac z'wr', "little."   [n] Ethiopic "heads."
[o–o] Ar.[1] "circled over the face of," perhaps mistaking h'm for hkm, "rule," as Violet suggests.
[p–p] Ar.[1] "its track, trace."   [q] Omitted by A, but present in all the versions.
[r–r] Latin dicens, "saying."   [s–s] Omitted by Ar.[2].
[t–t] Syriac hd' sbrt' 'stbr, "this is the announcement I will announce."
[u] Syriac adds 'l klh 'r'', "over the whole earth."
[v] Syriac adds 'yk qdmy', "like the earlier ones."

saw in the course of time, the *other wings* on the *right side*
set themselves up to take the leadership*; some of them held sway
but disappeared at once, 21 while others of them set themselves up
but did not achieve leadership. 22 Later* I looked and saw that the
twelve wings and *the two winglets* had disappeared, 23 so that
nothing was left of the eagle's body except the three dormant heads
and *the six little wings*. 24 As I kept looking I saw that two of
the six winglets* disengaged themselves [from the rest], and remained under the head that was on the right side while the four
remained in their place. 25 Then I observed that these sub-wings*
plotted to set themselves up to achieve leadership. 26 As I kept on
looking, one set itself up but disappeared at once; 27 then a second,
and it disappeared more rapidly than the preceding one. 28 While I
continued to look the two remaining ones themselves plotted to assume rule. 29 At the time they were plotting*, one of the dormant
heads — the one in the middle and larger than the other two —
awoke. 30 Then I observed how *the two [other] heads were conjoined with it 31 and [how] the head with its conjoiners* turned
and devoured the two sub-wings that plotted to rule. 32 This head
subdued the whole earth, *held ruthless sway* over all its inhabitants and exercised more power over the world than all the wings
that preceded it. 33 After this I looked again and saw the head in
the middle disappear suddenly, just as the wings had done. 34 However, the two heads that held sway over the earth and those who
inhabited it remained. 35 While I was looking I saw the head on the
right side devour the one on the left. 36 Then I heard a voice saying
to me: Look in front of you* and contemplate what you see*. 37 When
I looked I saw what appeared like a raging lion [coming] roaring

---

w-w Latin *sequentes pennae*, "the following wings" i.e. the others that were left.
Syriac *gp' z'wr'*, "little wings."
x-x Five Ethiopic MSS have "left side"; Ar.*1,2* omit.
y Syriac *l'r' '*, "of the earth."   *z post hoc*, "after this."
a-a Ethiopic "two heads"; Ar.*2* omits.   *b-b* Ethiopic "its six heads."
c Ar.*1* adds "which came out and arose above the twelve wings and were exalted."
d Ethiopic="six heads"; Syriac omits the number six; Ar.*1* "these elegant [ones]";
Ar.*2* "seven"; so there is considerable difficulty with the numerical notation.
e Ethiopic "heads." Syriac *gp' z'wr'*, "little wings" and adds *'rb' '*, "four"; so also Ethiopic and Armenian. The Latin term *subalares* occurs four times: 11:25, 31; 12:19, 29.
f Syriac adds *dnštltwn 'l 'r' '*, "to rule over the earth."
g-g Syriac unintelligible. Other versions, in substance, like Latin.
h-h Syriac *mkk*, "humiliated." Ar.*1* "tormented," *'dhb*.
i Syriac adds *'zr'*, "Ezra."   *j* Syriac adds *šwlm'*, "the end."

out of the forest and I heard it talk *k*in human language to the eagle*k*. It spoke as follows: 38 Now you listen and I will speak to you*l*! The Most High declares to you: 39 Are you not the only one of the four beasts left that I appointed to hold sway over my world so that through them the end of my*m* times might come? 40 You are the fourth that has come and *n*you have subdued*n* all the preceding beasts,

> Holding sway over the world with *o*great terror*o*,
> And over the entire earth with the utmost oppression;
> You lived for so long in the world with duplicity;
> 41 You have not judged the earth with truth.
> 42 You have oppressed the meek,
> You have injured the peaceful,
> You have hated those who speak the truth,
> You have loved liars,
> You have destroyed the homes of the thrifty,
> You have razed the walls of those who did you no harm.
> 43 Your arrogance has reached the Most High,
> And *p*your haughtiness*p* the Almighty.
> 44 The Most High has considered his times;
> Now they have come to an end;
> His ages have attained completion.
> 45 Therefore, you eagle, you will vanish,
> With your horrible*q* wings,
> With your evil winglets,
> With your malicious heads,
> With your ghastly talons,
> With your whole sinister body.

46 Thus the whole earth will be relieved and delivered from your power; then it can hope for justice and the compassion of him who made it.

12 1 While the lion was speaking these words to the eagle, I looked 2 and saw that the remaining head had vanished*r*. Then the two wings

---

k–k Omitted by Ar.².   *l* Syriac adds *nšr'*, "O eagle."   *m* Only in Latin; Ar.² "all.'
n–n Latin *devicit*, "he has subdued," probably a mistake for *devicisti*, "you have subdued"; other versions have second person.
o–o Syriac *b'ml' sgy' '*, "with great pains."
p–p Missing in Syriac text, but present in all other versions.
q Syriac *mrym'*, "highest."
r Syriac adds *mn šly'*, "suddenly."

which had gone over to it arose and set themselves up to rule but their reign was weak[s] and tumultuous. 3 When I looked again they had vanished, the entire body of the eagle went up in flames and the earth was aghast.

Request for and interpretation of the vision

a. Weakened by his dream-vision ordeal, Ezra pleads for strength

Then I awoke because of [t]intense excitement[t] [u]and great fear, and said [v]to myself[v]: 4 See here, you are responsible for this experience of mine because you are prying into the ways of the Most High.

5 Besides, I am [w]mentally exhausted,
And I am greatly impoverished in spirit[w];

there is not left in me the slightest strength by virtue of the great fear[x] I encountered this night. 6 Now, therefore, I will pray to the Most High to uphold me to the end.

b. Ezra's prayer

7 So I said, O Lord, Lord, [y]if you please[y], [z]if I am accounted by you more just than the many[z], and if my prayer has assuredly come up [a]before you[a], 8 uphold me and disclose to me, your servant, the interpretation and meaning of this awful[b] vision so as to put [c]my mind[c] completely at ease. 9 [d]You have already regarded me worthy to be shown the end of days and the conclusion of times.

c. Interpretation of the vision

10 [e]Then he answered me: This is the interpretation of this vision [f]that you saw[f][e]. 11 The eagle you observed coming up out of the sea is the fourth[g] kingdom that appeared in a vision to Daniel, your

[s] Syriac *šwlm'*, "end."   [t-t] Lit. "great mental aberration."
[u] Ar.[1] adds *w'lrjfh*, "and trembling."
[v-v] *spiritui meo;* Heb. *npšy*, "my soul."
[w-w] Latin *animo . . . spiritu;* Syriac *npšy . . . rwḥy;* one is omitted by Ar.[2] but it is difficult to tell which.
[x] With S, A; C, M have *terrore*, "terror"; Syriac follows the former with *dḥlt'*.
[y-y] Latin *si inveni gratiam ante oculos tuos*, "if I have found favor before your eyes" — a Hebraism.
[z-z] Ethiopic "if I am greatly blessed with you." Ar.[1] adds *wrf'tny z'yd' 'n qdry*, "and you exalted me beyond my worth." Ar.[2] has greatly simplified the verse.
[a-a] *ante faciem tuam*, "before your face"; Heb. *lpnyk*.
[b] Syriac *dḥz't* "which I have seen," perhaps a mistake for *dḥyl'*, "fearful."
[c-c] So Latin; Syriac *npšy*, Ethiopic, Ar.[1] "my spirit"; Ar.[2] adds *qlby*, "my heart."
[d] Syriac is a rhetorical question.
[e-e] Omitted by Ar.[2].   [f-f] With C, M and Syriac *dḥzyt;* S, A omit.
[g] Omitted by S.

brother. 12 But it was not interpreted to him in the same way that I now interpret [it] to you or *h*as I have interpreted [it]*h*. 13 Indeed, days are coming when a kingdom will rise on earth that will be more dreadful than all the *i*kingdoms that existed before it*i*. 14 Twelve kings will hold sway over it, *j*one after another*j*. 15 The second to assume power will hold [it] longer than [any other one of] the twelve. 16 This is the interpretation of the twelve wings*k* you saw. 17 About the voice *l*you heard*l* speaking*m*, which did not come from its heads but*m* from the middle of its body, 18 this is the interpretation: *n*Following the period of that king's reign*n* no inconsiderable struggles*o* will arise so that it will be threatened with falling, yet it will not fall then but again recover its earlier [power]. 19 About the eight*p* sub-wings you saw springing*q* from its wings, 20 this is the interpretation: eight kings will arise in it *r*whose times will be short and whose years will pass quickly*r*, two of them falling 21 close to the middle of its time, while four will be reserved for the time when its end-time draws near; two, however, will be preserved for the end. 22 About the three dormant heads you saw, 23 this is the interpretation: in its final days the Most High will raise up three kings*s* who will restore*t* many things in it and exercise dominion over the earth 24 and its inhabitants with greater harshness*u* than all who were before them. For this reason they have been called eagle's heads, 25 because they are the ones who will bring his [the eagle's] ungodliness to a head and bring about his end. 26 About the larger head you saw disappearing — one of them will die on his bed *v*but nevertheless in anguish*v*. 27 As for the two remaining ones, *w*the sword will consume them*w*. 28 For the sword of the one will consume his

---

h–h Omitted by Ethiopic and Ar.*1*.

i–i Ar.*2* *mlwk 'l'rd*, "kings of the earth."   *j–j* Omitted by Ethiopic.

k Ar.*1* adds *'lnśr*, "of the eagle."

l–l Syriac *dḥzyt*, "which you saw"; so also Ethiopic and Ar.*1*.   *m–m* Omitted by Ar.*2*.

n–n Syriac *dbynt zbnh dmlkwt'*, "in the middle of the time of the kingdom"; supported by Ethiopic and Armenian.

o Syriac *plgwt'*, "divisions."

p Omitted by Ethiopic; Armenian "many."

q Latin *coherentes*, "adhering"; reading here with Ethiopic, Syriac, Ar.*1,2*.

r–r Ethiopic "whose years [will be] evil and their days short."

s Latin *regna* "kingships"; reading follows Syriac *mlkyn* and other oriental versions. The Latin reads Greek *basileias*, "kingdoms," for *basileis*, "kings."

t Reading plural with Syriac *wnḥdtwn*, Ethiopic, Ar.*2*, and Armenian. Ar.*1* "and in their days will be much turmoil and many changes."

u Latin *labore*, "distress," "trouble"; Ar.*2* *šdydh* "violence."

v–v Omitted by Ar.*2*.

w–w Ar.*2* "shall go down [fall] in war."

companion but in the end he too will fall by the sword. 29 About the two sub-wings you saw *going over* to the head on the right side, 30 this is the interpretation: these are the ones the Most High has reserved for its end; this rule *will be* short and full of turbulence, 31 as you saw. The raging lion which you saw [coming] *roaring out of the forest, speaking to the eagle, taking it to task for its injustice, and all its words which you heard*, 32 he is the anointed one whom the Most High has reserved till the end *of days, who will arise from the seed of David, come and speak* with them,

> Upbraid them for their wickedness,
> Condemn* them for their injustices,
> And confront them directly with *their insults*.

33 First he will present them alive for judgment, and then, after upbraiding them, he will destroy them. 34 But the *remnant of my people* who are left* in *my land* he will set free with compassion and grant them joy until the end, the day of judgment about which I spoke to you at the beginning. 35 This is the dream you saw and this is its interpretation.

Command to write down the vision, and the seven-day interval

36 However, you alone have been deemed worthy to know this secret of the Most High. 37 Therefore record everything you saw in a book, put them in a safe hiding place, 38 and teach them to the prudent ones *of your people* whose minds* you know are capable of grasping and preserving these secrets. 39 But as for you, stay here

---

– So with S, A**; C, M have *crescentes*, "springing up"; Syriac, Ethiopic, Ar.[1,2] with S, A**.

– So with M, A**, Syriac and Ethiopic. Other MSS have *erat*, "was."

– Omitted by Ar.[2].

– Omitted in Latin and supplied here from Syriac *dywmt' hw ddnḥ mn zr'h ddwyd wn't' wnmll 'mhwn;* this is also substantially present in all other oriental versions.

b So with Syriac and other oriental versions; omitted by Latin.

c–c Ar.[1] *jhlhm*, "their folly."

d–d Latin *residuum populum meum*, "my remaining people."

e Latin *salvati sunt*, "have been saved"; Syriac *l'my dyn d'šthr*, "but my people who is left" — our rendering follows this as do Ethiopic and Ar.[1].

f–f Syriac *bthwmy*, "border," "territory"; Ar.[1] *twr gdšy*, "my holy mountain" — reading Greek *'oros* for *'oros*, "boundary." Latin has *fines meos*, lit. "my land," "borders."

g Ar.[1] adds *wf'lfhm'*, "and intelligent ones."

h Armenian adds "of God."

i Latin *corda*, "hearts" which stands for Heb. *lbwt* as seen from Syriac *lbwthwn*, "their hearts."

seven days more so that whatever vision the Most High sees fit to reveal to you may be revealed to you.

Popular reaction to Ezra's seven-day absence

40 Then he*ʲ* left me. When all the people heard*ᵏ* that the seven days had elapsed and that I still had not returned to the city, they all assembled, from the least of them to the greatest of them, came to me, and addressed me as follows:

41 In what manner have we wronged you,
ᴵIn what manner have we mistreated you*ᴵ*,

that you have forsaken us so utterly to linger in this place? 42 You alone of all the prophets are left to us,

Like a grape from the vintage,
Like a lamp in a dark place,
*ᵐ*Like a safe harbor for a ship in a tempest*ᵐ*.

43 Are not the misfortunes that have befallen us sufficient*ⁿ*? 44 Therefore if you abandon us, how much better it would have been for us too to have been consumed in the conflagration of Zion! 45 For we are not better than those who perished there. And they wept profusely*ᵒ*.

Ezra's response

46 I responded to them as follows:
*ᵖ*Be confident*ᵖ*, O Israel,
Don't lose heart, O house of Jacob.
47 *q*For you are kept in mind*q* before the Most High,
And the Almighty has not forgotten you forever*ʳ*.

48 I have not abandoned you and I will not withdraw*ˢ* from you, but I retreated to this place

ʲ Armenian "angel."
ᵏ Syriac *ḥzw,* "saw." Ar.² omits everything between "heard" and "from."
ᴵ⁻ᴵ Omitted by Ar.².
ᵐ⁻ᵐ Latin *portus navi salvatae a tempestate,* "harbor of a ship saved from a storm"; translation is a free rendering of Syriac *lm'n' dḥy' l'lp' m' dqym' bmḥšwl',* "a harbor of life for a ship that stands in a storm." The whole clause is omitted by Ar.².
ⁿ Syriac adds *'l' d'p 'nt tšbqn,* "but that you too should have left us"; Ar.² follows Syriac. Probably omitted by haplography from Latin.
ᵒ Reading with Ar.² *šdyd';* others follow Latin *voce magna,* "with a loud voice," "loudly."
ᵖ⁻ᵖ Ar.² "rejoice," *'frḥ;* all of first colon omitted by Armenian.
q⁻q Latin *memoria vestri,* "memory of you"; Ethiopic and Armenian "our memory."
ʳ With Syriac *l'lm;* Latin *in contentione,* "in strife" — reading Greek *eis agōna* for *eis aiōna,* "forever."
ˢ Syriac *wl' šbq 'n' lkwn,* "and I am not abandoning you."

To pray about the desolation of Zion,
And to seek compassion for the disgrace[t] of our sanctuary.
49 So go away now, everyone of you, to his home[u] and I will come
to you after these[v] days.

Interlude

50 Then the people set out for [w]the city[w] as I advised them [to
do]. 51 But I remained in the field for seven days as he instructed me
and ate only flowers[x] of the field; my diet consisted of greens in those
days.

[t] Ar.² *ṭḍ'ḍ'*, "overthrow," "plundering."
[u] Ar.² inserts *w'mkth šb't 'y'm*, "and I will stay seven days."
[v] M has *octo*, "eight."
[w-w] Ethiopic "houses," though many MSS add "of the city." Ar.² *f'nṭlq 'lš'b*, "and
the people went away" but omits "for the city."
[x] Ethiopic "fruit."

NOTES

10:60. *that night and the next one.* The period of sleep indicates the importance of the ensuing vision, which required extraordinary preparation.

11:1 *I had a dream.* Cf. Dan 4:5, 9; 7:1; 8:1 "a vision appeared to me"; II
Bar 36:1; I Enoch 86:1.

an eagle. Cf. 12:11; Ezek 17:3, 7 (see Walter Zimmerli, *Ezechiel:* Biblischer
Kommentar Altes Testament, XIII, 5th ed. [Neukirchen: Erzrehungsvereins
Neukirchen Kreis Moers, 1958], 378 ff., and L. P. Smith, "The Eagles of Ez.
17," JBL 58 [1939], 43 ff.); Jer 48:40; 49:22; Dan 7:4 the beast like a lion
with eagle's wings, a symbol of Babylon (see E. Unger, in RLA, I, 37); the
woman given the wings of an eagle in Rev 12:14; Ass Mos 10:8; Sib Or 3:611.

coming up out of the sea. The construction "coming up from" is found in
Gen 41:2; Dan 7:3; Rev 13:1; the sea is often associated with evil so that the
eagle, representing the wicked power of the time, is said to come out of it
(cf. Philippe Reymond, *L'eau, sa vie, et sa signification dans l'Ancien Testament* [Leiden: Brill, 1958], pp. 182 ff.).

twelve feathered wings and three heads. In Dan 7:6 the beast has four
wings and four heads and in Dan 10–12 twelve kings of Greece have been
counted. The eagle (symbol of Rome) was referred to as coming out of the sea
by the author (i.e. out of the Mediterranean); the wings and heads represent
the kings involved in his conception.

2. *spread out its wings.* Here the wings of conquest (vss. 4, 5); elsewhere
in OT the symbol of ownership or protection (cf. Ruth 2:12).

winds . . . blew upon it. Cf. 13:2; Dan 7:2; Zech 2:6; 6:5; I Enoch 18:2.

clouds gathered around it. Reference is not clear. Sometimes clouds sym-
bolized the divine presence, sometimes the approach of a destructive storm
(cf. II Bar 53).

3. *rival wings*. Latin *contrariae pennae*, i.e. opposite, contrary, conflicting wings. Cf. Dan 7:8. The meaning seems to be provincial governors or high ranking officials who rebelled against the emperor. The fact that they sprang from the wings themselves would indicate that they were connected with imperial rule.

puny and petty wings. I.e. they were quickly squelched.

4. *heads were dormant*. Not troubled about the wings or because their time had not yet come.

the middle head. See NOTE on vs. 29 below.

5. *flew with its wings*. Violet renders "spread out his wings." Ar.² supports that rendering but the Latin here is *volavit*, "fly," though it can mean "spread"; in vs. 2 Ar.² has *expandebat*, "spread out"; Armenian "raised its wings." See textual note *ⁱ*.

to gain dominion over. Lit. "in order that it might reign over." The world-wide dominion of Rome is stressed here; while there were usurpations and uprisings here and there, the Roman eagle remained (cf. vs. 6).

7. *talons*. Cf. Dan 7:19 *ṭpr'*; and vs. 45 below. May stand for the imperial armies. This feature is ignored in the interpretation of the vision in ch. 12. A feature of *Hrgb*, the father of eagles in UT, 1 Aqht 105 ff. For an illustration of an eagle with talons see O. M. Dalton, *The Treasure of Oxus*, 3d ed. (London: The British Museum, 1964), fig. 25 — from fifth–fourth centuries B.C.

8. *Do not all stand guard. . . .* They are to exercise rule in succession, not simultaneously, as *in turn* indicates (*per tempus*).

sleep. I.e. remain inactive until the time comes (cf. the thirty-five shepherds in I Enoch 90:1).

9. *heads . . . last*. They represent the climax of the eagle's rule in the vision of the seer.

10. *the voice did not come from its heads*. They were not yet in position of power.

from . . . its body. From the empire itself relating the course of its history, its Caesars.

11. *eight*. Note that vs. 1 has twelve wings and three heads. Vs. 22 has twelve wings and two winglets. The numbers are the same in all versions with the possible exception of Ar.² in vs. 1 (see textual note *ᶜ* at 11:1).

12. *the right side*. But cf. vs. 20 and see Box's note, in loco — he thinks this is an interpolation since nothing is said of the significance of right and left sides. Were the wings originally reckoned in pairs? See criticism of the pairs idea by Kabisch, pp. 159–61, but Wellhausen (*Skizzen und Vorarbeiten*, VI, 241 ff.) insists it is the only tenable hypothesis. The Ethiopic of vs. 20 may be a correction.

one wing. Heb. *hknp h'ḥd*. Cf. vs. 26 and Rev 13:3 (head) for expression.

13. *its place was no longer visible*. Cf. Pss 37:10; 103:16; Job 7:10; Rev 2:5, for the disappearance of the church at Ephesus unless people repent. May refer to change of dynasty.

held sway for a long time. A long reign.

17. *No one after you . . . half as long.* Reference is to the long reign of Augustus.

18. *held sway.* For expression see II Kings 14:5; Dan 11:5.

19. *all the wings.* I.e. those mentioned above on the right side.

20. *right side.* See textual note *ᵃ⁻ᵃ*. The left side is required by context.

21. *not achieve leadership.* Their efforts were abortive.

22. *twelve wings and the two winglets.* With the exception of the two winglets, the number is the same as in vs. 1. The wings certainly represent Roman emperors but just exactly which ones is uncertain. Box thinks that "according to the original significance of the vision," the six Julian emperors are meant plus the two conspirators, possibly Vindex and Nymphidius, in the latter part of the reign of Nero. For another view, see Oesterley, pp. 144–47. But Suetonius also refers to twelve Caesars.

23. *three dormant heads.* Generally regarded as referring to the Flavians: Vespasian, Titus, and Domitian. At this point in the vision they had not yet become active.

six little wings. See interpretation in 12:20, 29 ff.

24. *two of the six winglets.* Considerable disagreement as to who they were — Gunkel thinks of Mucianus and Tiberius Alexander; Oesterley thinks of Agrippa II and Berenice; Violet suggests Nerva and Trajan.

26–27. Who is meant is again uncertain. Box suggests either Galba and Piso, or Galba and Otho.

28. *the two remaining ones.* Box mentions Civilis and Vitellius.

29. *one of the dormant heads — the one in the middle.* Violet thinks it is Vespasian.

larger than. I.e. Heb. *gdwl mn,* "great from," and thus here "older than." So translated, Violet's interpretation is correct, since Titus and Domitian were the sons of Vespasian.

30. *the two [other] heads were conjoined with it.* See preceding NOTE.

31. *devoured the two sub-wings.* Otho and Vitellius?

32. *subdued the whole earth.* Probably refers to the pacification of the empire by Vespasian.

ruthless sway. If Vespasian is referred to, the seer's vision was colored by events that took place in Judea following the suppression of the Jewish revolt (A.D. 66–70) rather by the general policy of the emperor.

33. *the head . . . disappear.* Vespasian died rather suddenly on June 24, A.D. 79, after only a short period of declining health.

35. *the head on the right side devour the one on the left.* Cf. 1QpHab 3:11 — "an eagle avid to devour" — for expression. The head on the right must be Domitian and the one on the left Titus. Whether Domitian assisted Titus out of this world, as a widespread tradition had it, cannot be proved.

36. *I heard a voice saying to me.* A favorite expression of apocalyptic writers.

in front of you. A way of underscoring the importance of what follows. The Syriac addition of "the end" is interpretation and points to the messianic intervention in world affairs, i.e. to the future to which the writer now turns after his long excursus on history.

37. *like a raging lion.* Cf. Ps 22:13b; Dan 7:4; I Peter 5:8; Rev 5:5; 10:3; Apoc Elijah 25:5; for interpretation see 12:31 f.

39. *one of the four beasts.* Cf. Dan 7:3 ff.; Apoc Ezra 5:2; for interpretation see NOTE on 12:11. See COMMENT at 12:10–35.

40–44. Represent a bill of particulars detailing the indictment of the Most High against the fourth beast.

40. *the fourth that has come.* Rome.

with duplicity. Latin *dolo,* "guile," "deceit," "trickery," etc. Cf. 1QpHab 3:5. Indictments by the Lord precede execution of judgment (see Schrader, p. 511).

41. *not . . . truth.* Lit. "you have judged the earth not with truth."

42. Note the opposite of the qualities the Lord demanded of his rulers. Cf. Prov 31:8–9.

loved liars. Cf. Asc Isa 4:10.

44. *His ages have attained completion.* The course of the times is predetermined so that history itself has little, if any, meaning except as the stage upon which the prepared drama of the Most High is played out. Cf. Lorenz Dürr, *Ursprung und Aufblau der israelitisch-jüdischen Heilandserwartung* (Berlin: Schwetschke, 1925), pp. 31 f.

45. *ghastly talons.* Cf. "Hymn to Ninurta as a God of Wrath," lines 2, 3 (Pritchard, ANET, *Supplementary Texts and Pictures,* p. 141), and Gilgamesh epic 7:4:19 (*ṣu-pur a-ri-e ṣu-pur-a-šu,* "his talons were like those of an eagle").

46. *justice . . . compassion.* After the judgment the rule of the Most High will ensue; its characteristics are "justice" and "compassion," the opposite of the duplicity and cruelty of the rule of the various kings represented by the eagle.

12 : 2. *the remaining head.* Probably Domitian.

the two wings. Uncertain. See NOTE below on vs. 29.

3. *the entire body of the eagle . . . flames.* Cf. Baal's destruction of the eagle (UT, 1 Aqht 114 ff.).

said to myself. Note conception of the writer and the way he interpreted his inquiry into the problems of life that disturbed him.

4. *prying into the ways of the Most High.* Cf. Hab 2:1 ff.; 1QpHab 7:1 ff. with different views on the legitimacy of the inquiry. On the ways of the Most High see Job 26:14; 38; *et alia.* The OT is full of prayers imploring the Lord to show his way to his servants and the prophets exhorted Israel to seek (obey) his way. But there was also the awareness of the fact that his ways were "past finding out" (Rom 11:33), cf. Isa 45:15; 55:8.

5. *mentally exhausted.* Lit. "fatigued in mind."

impoverished in spirit. Lit. "feeble or weak in spirit." Cf. Dan 7:15. Note reference to mind and spirit (Syriac *npš* and *rwḥ*) and see I Thess 5:23. Not too much ought to be made of the dichotomy here because of the poetic parallelism involved.

6. *uphold me to the end.* I.e until the seer has received the interpreter's explanation. Cf. 1QH 1:32; 4:36.

7. *if you please.* Cf. Luke 1:28; 18:14. See textual note ᵛ⁻ᵛ. Oesterley (in loco) points out three steps in the seer's approach to the Lord: one, appeal to his favor, two, justification in his sight, and three, prayer for desired objective.

prayer . . . before you. Cf. 6:32 (Gunkel, but Oesterley disputes it because this is a separate vision). See above Introduction, V. The Unity of the Book, on latter point.

8. Ezra prayed for: (a) strength, (b) interpretation and purport of the vision, (c) the full satisfaction of his curiosity about the end-time, since his request had been answered only in part by the vision of Zion.

interpretation. Cf. Gen 40:12, 18; Eccles 8:1; frequent reference in Qumran literature, the *pešers*, especially that on Habakkuk.

meaning. Latin *distinctionem*, lit. "distinction," then "meaning," Syriac *pwršnh*, "its significance."

completely. Ezra was partially satisfied with the vision of Zion but he desires full knowledge of the divine plan.

9. *the end of days . . . times.* This vision is not concerned with that problem. The seer has *already* been apprised of that, as he indicates. The attribution of the verse to a redactor by Box, Oesterley, and Kabisch seems unwarranted because the author does not connect the end of days to this vision which deals specifically with the fall of Rome.

10. *Then he. . . .* Who is "he"? M, S, L, at the beginning of the verse, have *et venit ad me angelus*, "and the angel came to me," which is undoubtedly an interpretation since there is no other textual warrant for it.

11. *eagle.* Cf. 11:1 and NOTE there.

the fourth kingdom . . . Daniel. See Dan 7:7, 19. There the fourth kingdom represented the empire of Alexander (see commentaries, especially Montgomery and Porteous, and H. L. Ginsberg, *Studies in Daniel* [New York: The Jewish Theological Seminary of America, 1948], ch. II). Here the author reinterprets it so as to make it apply to Rome, an interesting illustration of later interpretation of scripture — see also the *pešarim* of Qumran.

12. *not interpreted to him in the same way that I now interpret* [*it*]. I.e. he interprets it now to refer to Rome, not to Greece as in Daniel. Descriptions in NT (Luke 21:20; Rev 13:1 ff.) indicate as much, though the term "fourth kingdom" does not appear there. There is some evidence for it in other literature, e.g. Ps Sol 2:29; II Bar 39:5. The Babylonian Talmud, Aboda Zara 1ᵇ, interprets the fourth kingdom of Dan 7:23 as referring to Rome. Violet thinks the whole verse is a gloss by a Greek reader.

13. *days are coming.* Note use of prophetic phrase — a common expression in Amos, Jeremiah, et al. Recall the setting assumed for the book: Ezra in Babylon.

more dreadful. The situation involving the Jews and Rome was regarded by the apocalyptists as representing the acme of cruelty and oppression; the authors of the period lived through much of it and the last such experiences are always worse than those that preceded them.

14. *Twelve kings.* Cf. 11:1. The interpretation may be based on a tradition reflected in Suetonius *Lives of the Twelve Caesars.*

15. *The second.* Cf. 11:13b–17. The first one is virtually ignored here (cf. 11:12–13a). The second has been identified with Augustus who reigned longer than any other of the twelve Caesars of Suetonius.

Suetonius' twelve Caesars are: Julius Caesar, Octavius Augustus, Tiberius, Gaius Caligula, Claudius, Nero, Galba, Otho, Vitellius, Vespasian, Titus, and Domitian. *The Lives of the Twelve Caesars by Suetonius.* Edited with notes and an introduction by Joseph Gavorse. New York: Random House, The Modern Library, 1931.

16. *the twelve wings.* Cf. 11:12–31.

17. *the voice . . . from the middle of its body.* Cf. 11:10.

18. *Following the period . . . reign.* This (Latin) text obscures the connection intended; the Syriac (see textual note *n–n*) preserves a somewhat forced one if *mṣʿth,* "its middle," of vs. 17 is interpreted by *bynt,* "in between," (Latin *inter*) in vs. 18. Historically the situation referred to may be that at the conclusion of the Julian-Claudian line of emperors, i.e. after the death of Nero — an interpretation the latter part of the verse would appear to support.

19. *eight sub-wings.* Cf. 11:3, 11. See textual note *p* which reflects some uncertainty, despite the fact that there is no MS variation in the number "eight" in vs. 20.

20. *in it.* In the Roman empire. Cf. 11:11, 25. There has been a good deal of speculation on the identity of the eight kings but with a great deal of reservation. See COMMENT below.

20–21. *two . . . falling close to the middle.* Again uncertain. On *middle* see NOTE above on vs. 18.

22. *three dormant heads.* Cf. 11:1, 23, 29.

23. *three kings.* Has been interpreted as Vespasian, Titus and Domitian (the Flavians) and as Trajan, Hadrian and Lusius Quietus (see BOX, APOT, II, 612).

restore many things. Both Vespasian and Trajan did just that.

in it. See NOTE vs. 20.

exercise dominion. Cf. 11:32.

24. *greater harshness.* Violet suggests a reflection here of the apocalypists' hatred of the Flavians (cf. the references to Babylon in Revelation).

eagle's heads. The play on *heads* here and in next verse is difficult to recapture (cf. Violet's note, II, pp. 161 f., with examples of other word-plays).

25. *bring his [the eagle's] ungodliness to a head . . . his end.* I.e. bring "his ungodliness" to consummation and thus speed "his end." Once again a reflection of the hatred felt for the Flavians who were responsible for the conquest of Jerusalem in A.D. 70.

26. *larger head . . . disappearing.* Cf. 11:33.

one of them will die . . . bed. Could be either Vespasian or Trajan. The former was confronted by a serious plague and a conspiracy in the last year of his reign, yet he, despite his deteriorating condition, managed to rise to his feet and die like a soldier (CAH, XI, 12). The latter was faced with unrest in Britian, the Danube area, and the east, as well as his own declining health. He suffered a stroke at Antioch and was compelled to turn back; on the way, at Selinus in Cilicia, he died (CAH, XI, 251). For the death of Vespasian see Suetonius *Lives of the Caesars: Vespasian* 24.

27. *the two remaining ones*. Titus and Domitian or Hadrian and Lusius Quietus.

28. *the sword of the one will consume . . . sword*. Cf. 11:35. Some traditions have it that Domitian assisted in the demise of his brother Titus, who, however, actually died of a fever — perhaps induced (CAH, XI, 21). Thus he did not die by the sword. Domitian was slain by a freedman, Stephanus, in A.D. 96 (CAH, XI, 32). Hadrian, on the other hand, died of a hemorrhage in January A.D. 138 (CAH, XI, 322). On tradition that Domitian removed Titus see Aurelius Victor *Liber de Caesaribus* 10:4.

29. *two sub-wings*. Cf. 11:28, 31, 33.

30. *its end*. I.e. the eagle's.

31. *The raging lion*. Cf. 11:37 ff.

speaking to the eagle, taking it to task. See I Enoch 14:1 for divine reprimand before destruction.

32. *the anointed one*. For a discussion of this passage see Torrey, JBL 66 (1947), 233–77, esp. 259–63. This messiah is the pre-existent one as the clause "reserved till the end of days" indicates. Cf. Dan 7:13, 14; I Enoch 48:6; 62:7.

the end of days. Cf. II Bar 10:3; 25:1 — Heb. *b'ḥryt ymym*. See Volz, p. 189.

seed of David. Cf. 3:23; Sir 47:22; Rev 5:5; 22:16; Pss Sol 17:23; 18:6.

Upbraid them. . . . Cf. 13:37 f.; John 16:8–11; II Bar 40:1.

33. Parallel with the preceding verse. Cf. II Bar 40.

alive. Note the writer's conception of bringing the hostile power to judgment "alive" so as to rebuke it before destroying it. This is somewhat akin to the prophetic lawsuit where the case is argued before judgment is pronounced. Here the accused is brought in for sentence which stresses indictment before execution is carried out. Cf. Ps Sol 17:26, 27; I Enoch 48:8–10; Gunkel, *Schöpfung und Chaos*, p. 97.

34. *my people who are left*. Cf. 6:18–24; 7:27.

in my land. Observe again that the first task of the messiah is to free the land of foreign rule; that is probably what is meant by the end of days in this chapter. Cf. Ps 37:9; 4 QpPs 37, 3:9–11; II Bar 29:2; 71:1; Volz, pp. 372 f.; Klausner, pp. 340, 358 ff.

compassion . . . joy. Cf. 7:28; Sir 35:19; II Bar 29:6.

35. *the dream you saw*. Cf. 11:1.

36. *you alone*. The apocalyptists regarded themselves as unique recipients of divine revelation.

37. *record . . . in a book*. Cf. Dan 7:1; 12:4, 9; I Enoch 82:1; 104:11–13; Ass Mos 1:16; 10:11; 11:1; Rev 21:5.

put them in a safe hiding place. Cf. Efros, MKJV, p. 217, and n. 18. A characteristic of apocalyptic as the very name indicates (to reveal what was hidden). For expression see Ps 31:21.

38. *them.* I.e. the secrets preserved in the books.

prudent ones. Fellow apocalyptists?

capable of grasping. Cf. John 8:43; 16:12; 21:25.

39. *seven days more.* Cf. 5:19; 9:23; 12:40; 13:1.

sees fit. Cf. I Sam 3:18; et al.

40. *from the least . . . to the greatest.* For expression see Gen 19:11; Jer 6:13; et al. A common expression indicating the whole population, including children.

41. Cf. Micah 6:3; Mal 2:17; 3:8; Ps 106:6. Note the Latin *quid,* "in what manner," "how."

you have forsaken us. A frequent complaint which is just as often denied.

42. *alone of all the prophets.* Ezra is here and in 1:1 called a prophet. Cf. complaint of Elijah (I Kings 19:10, 14).

grape from the vintage. For figure see Micah 7:1; Hosea 9:10.

lamp in a dark place. II Peter 1:19; II Bar 77:13 f.; Matt 5:15; Luke 11:33; John 5:25.

harbor for a ship. Cf. Gen 49:13; Ps 107:29, 30. Poetic portion sounds like Wisdom.

43. *misfortunes . . . befallen us.* Cf. II Bar 77:8.

44. *how much better.* Cf. II Bar 33:3.

45. *we are not better.* Reminiscent of I Kings 19:4.

wept. Cf. II Bar 32:8.

46. *Israel . . . Jacob.* In parallelism also in 3:19, 32; 5:35; 8:16; 9:30.

47. *kept in mind.* Cf. Num 10:9; Ps 115:12.

forgotten you forever. Cf. Pss 9:19; 13:2; 74:19.

48. Cf. II Bar 33:3, Notes on 8:27 above, and references in Note on 12:5.

51. *flowers of the field.* See Note on 9:26; for phrase see Ps 103:15; Song of Songs 2:1.

greens. Latin *herba,* "herb." In apocryphal *Lives of the Prophets* 16, Daniel is said to have subsisted on a vegetarian diet.

COMMENT

[The vision of an eagle with twelve wings and three heads, 10:60 – 12:3a] Inasmuch as this was to be an extraordinary vision, it did not come immediately — it came on the second night. The seer saw an eagle[1] rising out of the sea — since the eagle was the Roman standard and it arose out of the

---

[1] The eagle was a widely used symbol in eastern Mediterranean region from the Persian period on. A beautifully executed representation adorns a golden dish, probably from Hamadan, dating from the fifth–fourth centuries B.C. (Roman Ghirshman, *Persia: From the Origins to Alexander the Great* [London: Thames & Hudson, 1964], p. 370). It occurs on coins from Cyprus from the time of Stasandros (440–420 B.C.) to Ptolemy I, Soter (310–305 B.C.). To judge from other coins, it was extremely

western sea, it doubtless represented Rome, the world power of the time. Striking in appearance, the eagle had twelve feathered wings, three rival wings (*contariae pennae*) described as puny and petty, and three sleeping heads, of which the middle was the largest. It spread its wings over the whole earth, dominating all so that none dare oppose it, and the winds of heaven blew upon it (the four winds representing the directions; but cf. I Enoch 18:1 f.; 76 where there are twelve winds, three issuing from each direction). The movement of the eagle with its heads and wings represents the course of Roman history. Since Rome was an imperial power, there could be only one emperor at any given time, so each of the heads and wings (representing emperors) remained in its place until its turn to dominate or rule. The heads were dormant at first, an important point, since they were to awaken and take power later in the vision (history) — i.e. those heads (emperors) were reserved until the period of the seer. As the vision progressed, the wings on the right ("right" is specified in vs. 20, but "left" is probably meant, varying with the version), rival wings and heads came into conflict with each other, and over-

popular in the Roman period in Phoenicia. See further J. Börker-Klähn, "Ein altorientalisches Motiv in Griechenland und seine Rückwirkung auf den Iran," *Zeitschrift für Assyriologie* 61 (1971), 124–56. Then there are the limestone relief of an eagle and two banners, erected at Hatra in A.D. 178 (*Archaeology* 25 [1972], 108) and the fact that coins struck under Marcus Aurelius (A.D. 161–180) and Decius (A.D. 249–251) at Tarsus Metropolis depict a pyramidal structure with an eagle at the apex (W. M. Ramsay, *The Cities of St. Paul* [Grand Rapids, Mich.: Baker Book House, 1960], p. 148). Cf. E. Babelon, *Catalogue des Monnaies Grecques de la Bibliothèque Nationale: Les Perses Achéménides. Les Satrapes et les Dynastes tributaires de leur Empire Cypre & Phénicie* (Paris: C. Rollin & Feuardent, 1893), plates 9, 20, 21, 31, 32, 34, 35, 36, 38, and G. M. A. Richter, *The Sculpture and Sculptors of the Greeks* (Yale University Press, 1930), pp. 115 and 460. Marius (ca. 100 B.C.) decreed that the figure of an eagle be displayed on the standard of each legion (for reproduction see *The Horizon Book of Ancient Rome* [New York: American Heritage, n.d.], p. 171. Cf. further sculptured eagle head from second century A.D. found by the Polish excavations at Palmyra (K. Michalowski and A. Dziewanowski, *Palmyra* (London: Pall Mall Press, 1970), plate 79; and Nelson Glueck, *Deities and Dolphins: The Story of the Nabataeans* (New York: Farrar, Strauss, and Giroux, 1965), plates 140–43. For appearance of the eagle in central Asia Minor (at Akkisse) in Roman times, see larnax fragment reproduced in *Anatolian Studies* XXI (1971), 144, plate XVb, and description on pp. 153 f. The eagle symbol was adopted later by Shapur as described by L. Trümpelmann, "Šāpūr mit dem Adlerkopfkappe," *Archaeologische Mitteilungen aus Iran*, Bd.4 (Berlin: Dietrich Reimer Verlag, 1971), pp. 173–85, with plate 27. For religious implications and connections of the eagle in the Syrian and Arabian world see Franz Altheim and Ruth Stiehl, *Der Araber in der alten Welt*, V, Part 2 (Berlin: Walter de Gruyter & Co., 1969), 116–19 and plate 17; René Dussaud, *La pénétration des Arabes en Syrie avant l'Islam* (Paris: Geuthner, 1955), fig. 20, p. 100, and *Syria* 26 (1949), 230 ff., and plate 11. Cf. the simile of the hawk and the nightingale in Hesiod *Works and Days* 200–10. Some features of the eagle vision recall that of Enkidu in the Gilgamesh epic 7:4:19. See the discussion by A. Leo Oppenheim, *Orientalia*, N.S. 17 (1948), 43–45. For artistic representations with interpretations cf. T. Fish, "The Zu Bird," *Bulletin of the John Rylands Library* 31 (1948), 162–71. The eagle was also a symbol of the Persian kings, as may be seen from Xenophon *Cyropaedia* 7:1.

came each other until the middle head, now awakened, overpowered all. Then even the middle head was subdued, and finally, a lion-like figure sprang from the woods roaring and addressing the eagle at the same time. The lion decreed to the eagle that its rule was at an end. The Most High had chosen four beasts to rule the world, each in turn, each after having subdued its predecessor. But all four were only agents through which God's times would come — part of his plan being carried to completion. All that had transpired under them had been a prelude to the coming kingdom of God. Now the whole world would be delivered from their power, from their acts of injustice, ruthlessness, deception, and oppression, and the hopes of the righteous would blossom into reality — the age of justice and compassion.

While the lion was still speaking to the eagle the remaining head disappeared. The two wings then usurped power, but with little success; their rule was short and tumultuous and they too vanished. With their demise the entire eagle was incinerated to the consternation of the world.

[Request for and interpretation of the vision, 12:3b–35. Weakened by his dream-vision ordeal, Ezra pleads for strength, 12:3b–6] Startled by the vision, the seer engaged in a dialogue with himself — really a typical Hebrew meditation. Getting hold of himself, he realized that what he had seen had something to do with his intense concern about the divine ways and their execution in the world and how he and his people fared all the while. His utter mental and spiritual exhaustion, together with the residual fears brought on by the vision, left him no choice but to resort to prayer to the Most High for strength to see him through, so that he might really get an answer to the stubborn problem he had raised.

[Ezra's prayer, 12:7–9] The prayer is characterized by appeal to the position of Ezra vis-à-vis God, that is, he voices his humility and asserts the sovereignty of God as the Psalmists do. But with the request for strength comes also one for further revelation by way of interpretation of the vision. Only then can his mind be at ease, his problem put in perspective, and divine justification disclosed. The same spirit that pervades the Book of Job is evident here, a subtle demand that the Most High justify his ways — he has begun to respond to Ezra's questions, now let him make that response unmistakably clear, especially in view of the fact that he has already apprised Ezra of the end of days.

[Interpretation of the vision, 12:10–35] The interpretation connects the eagle vision with the fourth kingdom of Daniel and thus illustrates the Jewish concept of the vitality of scripture which contains certain hidden meanings always susceptible to contemporary significance. One is reminded of the pešarim of Qumran. Certainly, even if this vision could be made to coincide in detail with that in Daniel — which it cannot — the time situation is different and hence required reapplication to meet the needs of the writer's time. That is why the intermediary noted that his interpretation differs from the earlier one. The dreadfulness of the vision is due to the fact that the kingdom it portrays is worse than any that preceded it. The twelve feathered wings (11:1) represent twelve kings who will reign over the kingdom. The second of the kings that arose ruled a long time (11:13–17) — indeed twice as long as any of the others. The voice that came from the eagle's body rather than from its heads (11:10) meant that the empire will continue despite the fall of its kings or even changes of dynasty. The eight sub-wings (11:11) stand for eight kings whose reigns will be short, or whose total years of power will be few. Two will fall near the middle of its time, four are reserved for its end-time, and two kept for the very end. The three heads represent the three kings the Most High will set up (note his control over history) in the last days (11:1, 4, 29–35); they will restore dominion after the period of turbulence and in so doing exercise harsher measures than their predecessors. The play on "heads" and "head" (vss. 24, 25) is reminiscent of the old riddle-type sayings found in various biblical passages influenced by Wisdom. Not much is said here about the largest of the heads (11:29–33), nor about the two smaller ones (12:34–36) except that they would be consumed by the sword (vss. 27–28). The last of the sub-wings (two of them, 11:28–31) marked the end of the eagle's rule; their reigns will be short and full of turbulence, just as the vision portrayed. Their appearance will be the sign of the end, for then the lion out of the forest will come to take over (11:37 – 12:2). The lion is the anointed one of the seed of David whom the Most High has reserved for the end of days. As in the vision itself, he presents his indictment and then destroys the eagle (the empire) itself. Then "my people" who are left in the land will experience freedom from foreign domination and great joy until the time of the final judgment. The attitude toward Rome reflected in II Esdras is in marked contrast to the pro-Roman views of Josephus who thought that "God was on the Roman side." (*War* 5:368 f.) and who predicted the coming emperorship of Vespasian (*War* 3:399 ff.). So also did Johanan ben Zakkai.

[Command to write down the vision, and the seven-day interval, 12:36–39] As with other apocalyptists, Ezra, granted knowledge of the secrets of the Most High because of his worthiness, was commanded to record what he had seen and place the record in a secure hiding place. He was further instructed to communicate the vision to "the prudent ones" among his people so that they too might know the plans of the Most High. The seer, however, was directed to remain in the field for whatever other revelations the Most High might see fit to grant him.

[Popular reaction to Ezra's seven-day absence, 12:40–45] After the departure of the angel, the people, apparently cognizant of where he was, came to meet Ezra. They inquired the reason for his prolonged stay and demanded to know whether it was due to anything they had done. They regarded him as a prophet, their last hope in that confused age. Should he abandon them, all hope would be gone and their fate sealed. There is some hint here of Ezra's own earlier argument about the futility of life without hope.

[Ezra's response, 12:46–49] The seer's reply is one of encouragement for the people — he exhorts them to be confident and not to lose heart. They have not been abandoned by him. He came to this place for the purpose of interceding for them and contemplating the misfortunes that have overtaken Zion.

They are urged to return home while he continues his retreat, after which he will come to them.

[Interlude, 12:50–51] The people follow Ezra's advice while he remains "in the field" in accordance with the angel's instruction. In the interim he maintains his dietary regimen so as to be prepared for whatever may follow.

Excursus on the Eagle Vision (chs. 11 – 12). Naturally the eagle vision has occasioned all kinds of speculations on the identity of its heads, wings and sub-wings. For purposes of accounting for the present writer's views, as far as that is possible, it may be helpful to give a brief summary of some of the more significant identifications.

It is unnecessary to give here the more extreme and wholly discredited views of the past century,[2] or to do more than mention that of A. Hilgenfeld[3] who connected the vision with Greek history from Alexander the Great through the Ptolemies. He maintained throughout that the three heads were Caesar, Anthony, and Octavian. A. Gutschmid[4] and A. M. Le Hir[5] and the other scholars after or contemporary with them agree on Rome as the empire involved, but vary widely on the identity of the kings. Emperors involved extend from Caesar to Macrinus and his son Diadumenianus (A.D. 217). The twelve wings were Caesar, Augustus, Tiberius, Caligula, Claudius, Nero, Vespasian, Domitian, Trajan, Hadrian, Antoninus, Marcus Aurelius with Commodus. The eight winglets were Titus, Nerva, Pertinax, Didius Julianus, Pescenius Niger, Clodius Albinus, Macrinus, and Diadumenianus. The three heads were Septimius Severus, Caracalla, and Geta. Those who held the view that the wings were to be regarded as pairs (twelve wings=six pairs; eight winglets=four pairs) identified the twelve (six pairs) with the six Julian emperors and the eight (four pairs) with Galba, Otho, Vitellius, and Nerva. The heads represented the three Flavians — Vespasian, Titus, and Domitian.

M. J. Lagrange[6] thought the original vision had six wings on the right side and six corresponding wings on the left. The two last winglets stand for the unrest expected by the author after the demise of Domitian. Later the number of wings was doubled and two winglets added (11:22). E. Schürer[7] identified the three heads with the Flavians and accounted for twenty wings by counting the emperors from Caesar to Domitian together with all the Roman commanders during the disorders from A.D. 68–70. The two winglets referred to last did not stand for persons.

[2] For a review see Schürer, III, pp. 238 f.; Keulers, p. 116; and Hilgenfeld, pp. liv ff.

[3] "Die jüdische Apokalyptik in ihrer geschichtlichen Entwicklung," *Zeitschrift für wissenschaftliche Theologie* 3 (1860), 335–38; 10 (1867), 285; 31 (1888), 382–84 (in the two latter treatments he shifted his position from the Ptolemies to the Seleucids).

[4] "Die Apokalypse des Esra in ihre spateren Bearbeitungene," *Zeitschrift für wissenschaftliche Theologie* 3 (1860), 1–81.

[5] "Du IVe livre d'Esdras," *Études Bibliques* 1 (Paris, 1869), 139–250. For a later view along the same general lines see Barry, JBL, 32 (1913), 261–72.

[6] "Notes sur le Messianisme au temps de Jésus," RB 14 (1905), 481–515.

[7] Vol. III, 241–43.

Box's view is as follows[8]: The original vision dates from A.D. 95. The twelve wings represent the Julians, the eight winglets usurpers, and the three heads the Flavians. The wings were conceived in pairs to indicate the status and powers of these emperors. The redactor (R) who assembled II Esdras in A.D. 120 identified the three heads with Trajan, Hadrian, and Lusius Quietus and the twelve wings with the six Julians plus Galba, Otho, Vitellius, Vespasian, Titus, and Domitian. For a discussion and rejection of this pair-theory cf. Keulers, p. 118.

Gunkel[9] held that the twelve wings, six on the right and six on the left, represented twelve emperors. Those on the right he identified as Caesar, Augustus (who reigned longer than any of his successors), Tiberius, Caligula, Claudius, and Nero; those on the left (who ruled only a short time) represented Galba, Otho, Vitellius, Vindex, Nymphidius, and Piso. The three heads he identified with the Flavians, the middle one being Vespasian, the one on the right Domitian, and the one on the left Titus. He went on to say, however, that identification of the eight winglets or sub-wings is quite another matter. Four had gone under before Vespasian, two were killed by him and two allied with him. But who were they? The two allied with Vespasian *may* have been the prefects of Syria and Egypt — Mucianus and Tiberius Alexander — but as for the others, the author was better acquainted with the period than we are!

Keulers[10] believed that II Esdras was written in the year 30 after the fall of Jerusalem. The three heads stood for the Flavians, the two winglets for the weak Nerva and Trajan whom Ezra (II Esdras) did not know. The second wing which ruled longer than the rest was Augustus. There is not room enough for sixteen (ten wings and six winglets) between Augustus and Vespasian, so the number has somehow been corrupted. To explain the corruption he resorted to Lagrange's interpretation of the number — each side of the eagle had three wings and three rival wings. Then a Christian interpolator of the third century A.D. added 11:11 and 11:20–23 whose meaning Keulers expresses this way: "Two of them perished when the middle (head) approached (12:20 f.). He altered the numbers in 11:1; 12:14–16 from six to twelve, and in 12:20 from six to eight. That explains why the number of rival wings in 11:3 is not given; since the rival wings sprang out of the larger wings, it follows that their number was the same as that of their parent wings. The two rival wings in 11:22 who are not once mentioned as reigning, were in-

---

8 APOT, II, 612b.
9 APAT, II, 345.
10 Cited in n. 1, pp. 119–22. Cf. the somewhat similar date and view of Rosenthal, pp. 55 f. The first and second rulers are Julius and Augustus Caesar. The three rulers are the Flavians. The head that devoured the two preceding ones is Vespasian who did away with Otho and Vitellius. The head with more power than the rest of the wings was Vespasian. The two remaining heads were Titus and Domitian. The right-hand head that devoured the one on the left was Domitian who, according to popular belief, murdered his brother Titus. The downfall of the third head reflects the murder of Domitian. The pair of sub-wings stand for the successors of the murdered Domitian, i.e. Nerva, etc. The roaring lion points to the salvation of Israel. For application of this interpretation to the matter of date see Rosenthal, p. 68.

serted by the Christian author since he did not yet quite come to terms with the doubling of the wings. Historically, then, there is no further difficulty: the six wings are the six Julians, the three heads the three Flavians, the six rival wings Galba, Otho, Vitellius, Civilis, Nerva, and Trajan."[11]

Oesterley,[12] with nearly all the above interpreters, agrees that the eagle stands for the Roman empire. The six wings on the right are Caesar, Augustus, Tiberius, Caligula, Claudius, Nero. The six on the left are Galba, Otho, Vitellius, Vindex, Nymphidius, Piso. The eight rival wings are: two, Herod the Great and Agrippa I; four, Eleazar, John of Gischala, Simon Bar-Giora, and John the Idumean; two, Agrippa II and Berenice.

Torrey[13] held that the basic number of wings was originally eight (11:11) which was increased to twelve, doubtless for the sake of later history. The three heads were the Flavians. Three plus eight (original wings) equal eleven, which a later editor increased to twelve, a sacred number. Writing in the time of Domitian, he resolutely believed that the next emperor would spell the doom of Rome, so he increased the number from twenty to twenty-three (11:11; 12:19), allowing for the continuation of the history of the empire if necessary — probably in line with the indefiniteness of apocalyptic witness.

H. H. Rowley[14] is not specific. He simply says that the eagle vision represents Daniel's fourth kingdom and stands for the Roman empire. The wings and heads indicate Roman emperors. The three heads represent the three Flavians.

It appears to the present writer that the authors mentioned above are too specific, simply pleading for a particular literary hypothesis. While there may have been some additions and alterations in the text, it is hardly legitimate to speculate too much on such bases. It seems clear that the eagle vision is concerned with the Roman empire, whose insignia was the eagle.[15] It also appears fairly certain that the three heads stand for the three Flavian emperors — Vespasian, the middle head, Domitian, the right, and Titus, the left. The twelve wings also stand for Roman emperors, but just which ones is not certain. The one who is said to have ruled longer than any of the others is probably Augustus. The one before it then must have been Caesar. It is *possible* that the twelve wings include the generally accepted rulers from Caesar to Domitian, i.e. Caesar, Augustus, Tiberius, Caligula, Claudius, Nero, Galba, Otho, Vitellius, Vespasian, Titus, and Domitian.[16] The identity of the eight rival wings, or winglets or sub-wings, cannot be determined with any degree of certainty. The three heads, also reckoned with the wings, may stand for the rulers who lived in the author's time. It is always wise not to attempt a too specific identification of apocalyptic figures in the absence of other compelling evidence that warrants it.

Apart from the eagle, the main feature of the vision is the figure of the

---

[11] Keulers, pp. 121 f.
[12] Pages 144–47.
[13] Pages 120–21.
[14] *Revelance of Apocalyptic*, pp. 96 f. [BIBLIO II].
[15] The Talmud too refers to Rome as an eagle (Sanhedrin 12a.).
[16] Cf. Brun, ZNW 26 (1927), 133 ff. [BIBLIO II].

lion (11:37 ff.) who, in the explanation, is identified as *unctus*, "the anointed one," "the messiah" (12:32).[17] He is held in reserve until "the end of days," i.e. until the eagle was about to be destroyed. He is connected with the seed of David which is elsewhere associated with the tribe of Judah. The lion symbolism appears to be based on Gen 49:9. The Yalḳuṭ Shimoni on that passage is interesting: "Judah is a young lion (Gen 49:9), that is the Messiah ben David who will come forth out of two tribes; his father is from Judah and his mother from Dan, and both together were called lion, as it is said: A young lion is Judah and, further, Dan is a young lion (Deut. 33:22)." The metaphor occurs also in Gen 37:33; I Macc 3:4; II Macc 11:11; 1QSb 5:29.[18] The connection between the messiah and the lion may be due to the common association with the tribe of Judah. It is also possible (with the same connection) that the house of David had a lion on its banner or insignia. In view of the lion's supposed royal traits, the link may go back to the house of David, and have been carried on after it lost its throne. The question of the lacuna in the Latin text of 12:32 or the addition transmitted by the other versions cannot be answered conclusively. The fact that "the Most High has reserved (him) till the end of days" points to the pre-existent messiah, while the addition "of the seed of David" combines that figure with the Davidic messiah.[19] As Moore has remarked,[20] the function of the messiah after the fall of Jerusalem (A.D. 70) was to denounce the Roman empire and destroy it.

[17] For a discussion of the messiah in the context of the Jewish national hope see Bousset, pp. 222–32.
[18] For references to the characteristics of the lion reflected in the Bible and elsewhere in the ancient world see W. Michaelis in TWNT, IV, 256–59.
[19] See C. C. Torrey, JBL 66 (1947), 262–63. He points out the messiah is not referred to elsewhere in II Esdras, in II Baruch, or in I Enoch as the scion of David. See further D. B. Macdonald, *The Hebrew Philosophical Genius* (Princeton University Press, 1936), p. 39.
[20] Vol. II, 333.

THE SIXTH VISION (THE MAN FROM THE SEA) (13:1–58)

A dream vision

13 1 Then after seven days, *I had a dream* in the night. 2 *I saw* a wind* rising from the sea that stirred up all its waves. 3 As I kept looking *that wind brought up out of the depths of the sea something resembling a man and* that man *was flying* with the clouds of heaven. Wherever he turned his face to look, everything he looked upon shook, 4 and wherever the voice from his mouth sounded all

a–a Syriac *wḥzyt ḥzw'*, "I saw a vision."   b–b So with C, M; omitted by S, A.
c Syriac adds *rbt'*, "great," "strong"; so also Ethiopic, Ar.[1], and Armenian.
d–d Wanting in Latin MSS by homoioteleuton; Syriac *rwḥ' 'sqt mn lbh dym' 'yk dmwt' dbrnš'*, which is followed in the translation. So also substantially other oriental versions.
e–e S, A, C, M have *convalescebat*, "was growing strong"; translation follows Syriac *prḥ*, and other oriental versions.

who heard it melted*f* as wax melts when it comes in contact with
fire. 5 Afterwards I saw an innumerable host of men gathered together
*g*from the four winds of heaven*g* to wage war against the man*h* who
had arisen out of the sea*h*. 6 As I continued to look, *i*he carved out*i*,
for himself a huge mountain and flew*j* upon it. 7 But when I tried to
see the region or place from which the mountain was carved, I was
unable [to do so]. 8 Afterwards I saw that all who had assembled to
him to fight him were terrified; nevertheless they ventured to fight.
9 When he saw the onrush of the approaching multitude, he did not
so much as raise his hand, or take a spear, or any other weapon of
war. I saw only 10 how he discharged from his mouth, as it were, a
torrent of fire and from his lips a *k*flaming blast*k*; and from his tongue
he poured forth a *l*gust of sparks*l*. All of these were joined together —
*m*the torrent of fire, the flaming blast, and the powerful gust*m*.
11 *n*Then it descended upon the onrushing host that had determined
to fight and cremated all [of them]*n*. Suddenly nothing of the innumerable host was apparent except powdery ashes and the smell of
smoke, so that *o*I was astonished when I saw it*o*. 12 Afterwards I saw
the man himself come down from *p*the mountain*p* and summon to
himself another, peaceful host*q*. 13 Many persons of [different] appearances joined themselves to him — some were joyful, some sad,
some in shackles, *r*some leading [others] of them as offerings*r*.

Request for interpretation of the dream vision

Then I was awakened *s*by excessive fear*s* and prayed to the Most
High as follows: 14 From the beginning you have shown your servant
*t*these wonders*t* and *u*considered me worthy*u* so that you accepted

---

f So with Syriac *šyḥ'*; Latin *ardescebant*, "to take fire," "be inflamed."
g–g Ar.² *'ṭr'f 'l'rṣ*, "ends of the earth"; so also Armenian.
h–h Omitted by Ar.².   *i–i* Ar.¹ *ṣn'*, "made."
j Syriac adds *wqm*, "set or place oneself."
k–k Ar.² *mthl ryḥ thrq*, "like a burning wind."
l–l Ar.² *mthl ryḥ thb*, "like a powerful wind."   *m–m* Omitted by Ar.².
n–n Ar.² omits.   *o–o* Ar.² *w'ntbht fy rwy'y*, "and I awoke in seeing."
p–p Ar.¹ *mn 'lsm''*, "from heaven."
q Ar.¹ according to Hilgenfeld, "he concluded peace and covenant with those who
were at peace, those who came to him."
r–r Omitted by Ethiopic. The text of Ar.¹ is uncertain here (see Ewald, *Das vierte
Ezrabuch*, p. 44).
s–s Omitted by Ar.².
t–t Ethiopic "your glory." Ar.¹ adds "understanding." Ar.² *'nt 'ḥbbtny w'tyt 'ly*,
"you loved me and came to me" for the first part of the verse.
u–u Syriac *wkd l'šw' 'n' ḥšbtmy*, "and although I was unworthy you regarded me so,"
(i.e. worthy).

my prayer. 15 Now disclose to me the interpretation of this dream also, 16 *for I was just thinking* how dreadfully those who survive will fare in those days but how much more dreadful [it will be] for those who do not survive! 17 *For those who do not survive are sad* 18 because they *know what is on deposit for the last days but cannot enjoy it. As for those who survive — 19 woe to them — inasmuch as *they will undergo* *great perils* and many exigencies, as these dreams attest. 20 *Nevertheless it is *better to* attain these [things] despite the danger than to vanish from the world like a cloud without seeing what will take place at the end*.

Interpretation of the dream vision

21 He* answered me as follows: I will give you the interpretation of the vision and also unravel for you *the things you spoke about*. 22 *Since you mentioned those who survive *and those who do not survive* this is the interpretation: 23 *the one responsible for* the peril in that time will himself protect those who may encounter that peril — that is, those who have works [to their credit] and faith in *the Almighty*. 24 Be assured, therefore, that those who survive are far more fortunate than those who have died. 25 The interpretations* of the vision are these: the man you saw rising from the depths of the sea 26 represents the one whom the Most High *has kept* for many ages through whom to deliver *his creation* and he himself *will create [the new] order* for those who survive. 27 About the wind

v–v Ar.² *wqlt,* "and I said."

w–w Ar.² omits. Verses 17–18 omitted by Armenian.

ª Ethiopic and Ar.¹ insert "not."

y–y So with C, M; S, A have *viderunt,* "they have seen," "undergone."

z–z Ethiopic "pain"; Ar.¹ *ṣ'wb't kthyrh,* "many [or great] difficulties." Ar.² omits all except first phrase of verse.

a–a Ar.¹ has the words but misunderstood the whole verse. Ar.² has been corrupted beyond recognition.

b–b *facilius.* Hilgenfeld thinks this is a mistake for *felicius.* The underlying Hebrew is *ṭwb,* "good."

c Armenian "the angel."

d–d Ar.² *m'ḫṭr bb'lk,* "what has occurred in your mind."

e Verse omitted by Ar.².   f–f So with Syriac and Ar.¹; Latin omits.

g–g Syriac *dmsybr,* "who endures," "tolerates," "suffers"; Ar.¹,² unclear. Armenian "happiness shall be to those who come in those days" (see note by Violet, II, 179, on Armenian).

h–h Syriac *mrym' whyltn',* "the Highest and the Almighty"; so also Ethiopic and Ar.¹; Ar.² *'l'ly* "the Highest."

i Singular in all versions except Latin.

j–j *Conservavit* with A; others have *conservat,* "keeps."

k–k Ethiopic "the world"; Ar.² *lyḫlṣ mn k'n lh,* "to deliver the one who belongs to him."

l–l Syriac *n'br,* "lead over."

and the fire ^mand the tempest^m you saw discharged from his mouth
28 and his destruction, without spear or implements of warⁿ, of the
onrushing multitude that came to fight him, this is the interpretation: 29 now, days are coming when the Most High will ^obegin to
deliver^o those on earth, 30 trepidation^p will seize the inhabitants of
the earth 31 and ^qthey will plan to attack one another^q, city^r against
city, ^slocality against locality^s, people against people, and kingdom
against kingdom. 32 Moreover, when this takes place, the signs to
which I directed your attention earlier will come about and then ^tmy
son^t, whom you saw as a man rising up^u, will be revealed. 33 Then,
when all^v peoples hear his voice, everyone without exception will
leave his land^w and their internecine war, 34 and unite into an innumerable host, as you saw, ^xdetermined to come and fight him^x.
35 But he himself will take his stand on the summit of ^yMount
Zion^z. 36 Moreover, Zion, ready built, will appear and be manifest to
all^a, as you saw [concerning] the mountain carved out without
hands. 37 My son himself^b will berate for their impiety the peoples
who have come [against him] — these are the ones who approach
like a storm — confront them face to face with their evil designs^c and
with the tortures they are to undergo — 38 these are like the flames
— and crush them effortlessly with^d the law — these are like the fire.
39 And about your seeing him^e collect another, peaceful host^f —

^{m–m} Omitted by Armenian and Ar.².
ⁿ Ar.² adds *wbqwl fmh śhq,* "and with the word of his mouth crushed."
^{o–o} Ar.² *mftqd',* "visit."
^p Syriac *twht',* "confusion"; Ar.¹ adds *whyrh,* "and bewilderment." Ethiopic omits
entire verse.
^{q–q} Ar.² "and they fight one the other."
^r Reading *civitas* with M, Ethiopic, Ar.¹, Armenian.
^{s–s} Ar.¹ *mskn 'ly mskn,* "habitation against habitation."
^{t–t} Ethiopic "that man"; Ar.¹ *ft'y,* "my boy," "youth"; Ar.² *'bdy,* "my servant."
^u Ethiopic, Ar.^{1,2}, Armenian add "out of the sea"; Ar.¹ *qlb 'lbḥr,* "heart of the sea."
^v Omitted by Ar.² and Armenian.
^w Ar.¹ *qwlh,* "his speaking"; Ar.² *d'rt ṭrqh',* "their ways will change" but text is not
clear.
^{x–x} Ar.² *ltn'wnwh,* "to resist him." Verses 34–40 are only partially preserved in
Armenian.
^y Ar.¹ adds *'lmqds,* "holy."   ^z Ar.² *'ljljlt 'lty lṣhywn,* "Golgatha to Zion."
^a Ar.² adds *mn yrth',* "who inherit it."
^b Ar.² adds *'ldhy mnkm',* "who is from you."
^c Syriac *'bdyhwn,* "deeds"; so also Ethiopic.
^d Latin *et,* "and"; here with Syriac *bnmwsh,* "through, with the law." Ar.² adds "be-
cause they have fallen away and sacrificed to devils, and he will crush and pulverize
the transgressors; and he will cast them into the fire of Gehenna, but he will respect
those who have kept his commandments."
^e Syriac adds *qr',* "call," "summon."
^f Ar.² *'l'mh 'lġrybh,* "the foreign people."

40 these are the ten*g* tribes who were taken captive from their land in the days of King Hoshea*h*, whom Shalmaneser, the king of *t*the Assyrians*i*, led away into captivity and transported them across the river*j*; thus it was that they were transferred into another land. 41 But they decided to leave the multitude of peoples and proceed to a more remote region where no human species ever lived, 42 and there perhaps observe their ordinances which they did not observe in their*k* land. 43 So, when they passed through the narrow entrances of the Euphrates River, 44 the Most High performed miracles*l* for them and held back the courses of the river until they had crossed over. 45 The way through that country, which is called Arzareth, required a long trek of a year and a half*m*. 46 Since then they have lived there until the last time. *n*Now that they are about to come again*n*, 47 the Most High will again *o*hold back the courses of the river that they may be able to cross over*o*. That is why you saw a multitude assembled in peace. 48 But those of your people who have survived, who will reach the limits of my sanctuary, *p*will be saved*p*. 49 Therefore when he*q* is about to destroy the host of assembled peoples, he*q* will protect the people who survive 50 *r*and show them many great portents*r*.

Further question and explanation

51 Then I said, O Lord, Lord, tell me this: why did I see the man rising up out of *s*the depths*s* of the sea? 52 He replied to me: Just as no one can search out *t*or perceive what may be in the depths of the sea, so no one on earth will be able to see my son or those who are

---

g Syriac *tš' ' šbtyn wplgh*, "nine tribes and a half"; cf. II Bar 62:5; so also Ar.*1* and Armenian. Ethiopic "nine"; Ar.*2 bqyh 'lqb'nl 'ltš'*, "the rest of the nine tribes."
h So with C and some representatives of A; others, including Syriac and Ar.*2* "Josiah"; wanting in Armenian.
i–i Ethiopic "Persians"; Ar.*1* has been augmented considerably by obvious glosses.
j Syriac adds *prt*, "Euphrates." Ar.*2* omits everything between "Assyrians" and "river."
k Ar.*2 'lqdš*, "the holy."
l So with Syriac *tdmrt'*, "miracles," Ethiopic, Ar.*1,2*. Latin *signa*, "signs," "portents."
m Syriac adds *swph d'lm'*, "at the end of the world."
n–n Omitted by Ar.*2* and Armenian. Syriac *whydyn twb d'tydyn dn'twn*, "now again when it will be that they come."
o–o Ar.*1* "cut off [the sources of the river] that they may not be able to cross over."
p–p With Syriac *n'hwn*, "live," "be saved"; omitted by Latin and all other versions.
q Ar.*1* as first person ("I").   *r–r* Omitted by Armenian.
s–s Omitted by Ar.*2* and Armenian.
t Syriac adds *škh*, "discover"; so also Armenian.

with him except in the time of his[u] day. 53 This is the interpretation
of the dream you saw. For this reason you alone have been informed:
54 Because you have relinquished your [own interests],
And devoted yourself to mine;
You have explored my law,
You have dedicated your life to wisdom,
And you have called understanding your mother.
56 That is why I disclosed this to you, for there is reward[v] with the
Most High. But[w] after three more days I will speak to you about other
things and relate to you [x]weighty and amazing things[x].

Waiting in the field

57 Then I continued to walk across the field, glorifying and praising
the Most High exceedingly[y] for the wondrous things he keeps doing
in [his] time, 58 [z]and because he controls the times and what
happens in them[z]. So I remained there three days.

[u] So with Syriac bywmh; Ethiopic "in his time and in his day"; other oriental
versions follow Syriac closely.
[v] Omitted by Ar.[2] and Armenian.   [w] With Syriac dyn; Latin enim, "for."
[x–x] Syriac tdmrt' 'ḥryt', "the last wonders [or miracles]"; Ethiopic "a wonderful
thing"; Ar.[1] follows Syriac; Ar.[2] 'šy'' 'ḥr, "other things." Perhaps Latin is hendiadys
and ought to be rendered "tremendously amazing things."
[y] Latin multum; omitted by C, M and oriental versions.   [z–z] Omitted by Ar.[2].

NOTES

13:1. Then. Lit. "it came to pass."
I had a dream. Lit. "I dreamed a dream." Often in Hebrew Bible as
ḥlm ḥlwn (cf. Gen 37:5, 9, et alia).
in the night. Cf. Gen 40:5; Job 33:15; vision of the night, Dan 2:19; 7:2, 7,
13; Zech 1:8.
2. wind rising from the sea. See Dan 7:2; II Esd 11:1 f. The wind was the
messenger of the Lord (cf. Pseudo-Philo 21:2).
3. depths of the sea. Lit. "heart of the sea."
resembling a man. Cf. the kdmwt bny 'dm, "according to the likeness of
the sons of man," of Dan 10:16; of kmr'h 'dm, "resembling or like the appearance of a man," in Dan 10:18. For figure see Dan 7:13; Ezek 1:5;
I Enoch 46:1; COMMENT on THE FIFTH VISION, fn. 18, above; cf. Bousset,
p. 266, n. 1; André Caquot, "Les quatre bêtes et le 'Fils d'homme' (Daniel 7),"
Semitica 17 (1967), 37–71, esp. pp. 50 ff.; W. F. Albright, From the Stone
Age to Christianity (Garden City, N.Y.: Doubleday Anchor Books, 1957),
pp. 379 f.
was flying with the clouds of heaven. Cf. Isa 19:1; Dan 7:13; Rev 1:7. The

idea, though not the wording, is old, as may be seen from Ugar. *rkb 'rpt*, "rider of the clouds," which is an epithet for Baal.

turned his face to look. Cf. I Enoch 89:30; Ps 104:32; cf. Hab 3:10.

he looked upon. Reflects Greek *up' autou*=Latin *sub eo*.

4. *voice from his mouth . . . all . . . melted as wax.* Cf. Pss 46:6; 68:3; 97:5; Isa 64:1; Micah 1:4; Judith 16:15; I Enoch 1:6.

voice . . . sounded. Lit. "voice went out."

comes in contact with fire. Lit. "senses or feels fire."

innumerable host . . . to wage war against the man. See Volz, pp. 223 f.; cf. I Enoch 56:5–8; Rev 20:7–9; Ezek 38, 39.

5. *the four winds.* The four directions or quarters of the earth (cf. Ezek 37:9; Dan 7:2; 8:8; Zech 2:6; 6:5; Rev 7:1).

6. *carved out . . . a huge mountain.* Cf. Dan 2:45; Rev 8:8. The mountain represents a new Zion (Rev 14:1). In II Bar 36 the mountains are destroyed. Elsewhere, as in Rev 21:2, it is a new city, a new Jerusalem. Perhaps the idea is reminiscent of the mountain of the gods in oriental mythology. For the use of Dan 2:45 in Christian literature see J. R. Harris and Alphonse Mingana, *The Odes and Psalms of Solomon* (Manchester University Press, 1920), II, 307 ff. For mountain idea in the ancient world in general see W. Foerster in TWNT, V, 475–82.

7. *I tried to see the region . . . I was unable.* Because it was not of this visible world; it belonged to the heavenly world just as does the new Zion, the new Jerusalem, that it represents. For possible connections with Irano-Babylonian mythology see Oesterley's note, p. 150.

8. *assembled . . . to fight him.* Cf. Ezek 38:14 ff.; 39.

terrified. For figure see I Sam 14:15; Ezek 26:16 f.; Isa 64:2. On fear before the divine theophany in apocalyptic and Qumran literature see TWNT, IX (1970), 201 f.

9. *weapon of war.* Heb. *kly mlḥmh*, as in Hebrew Bible and a number of times in Qumran literature. Note the emphasis on the rejection of human implements of war. Cf. Philo *On Rewards and Punishments* 16.

10. *discharged from his mouth.* For potency of the divine word see Dürr, *Die Wertung des göttlichen Wortes*, pp. 110 f. Cf. Isa 11:4; 55:11; Ps 18:8, 13; Rev 11:5; 19:15; II Thess 2:8; Heb 1:3; Ps Sol 17:27; I Enoch 62:2; Jer 5:14. The threefold description of the oral method of destruction is drawn from storm terminology current from Ugarit and the oldest literature of the OT (cf. I Sam 22 ‖ Ps 18; Hab 3).

flaming blast. Widengren (VTS, IV, 237) sees Iranian influence here. Cf. II Thess 1:7 ff.; Ps 104:4; Heb 1:7; on destruction of adversaries by furious fire, Heb 10:27.

11. *cremated all.* Cf. Dan 7:10 f.; Ps Sol 17:39; Joel 2:3; Sib Or 3:72 f.; Hosea 6:5; II Peter 3:10; and cf. Jerome *Against Rufinius* 3:31 where these characteristics are attributed to Bar-Cochba; and the Gog-Magog prophecy in Ezek 38, 39, esp. 39:6, 9–10a.

powdery ashes. For figure see II Bar 36:10.

smell of smoke. Dan 3:27 "smell of fire." Perhaps total destruction is stressed with only the faintest evidence remaining and even the smoke gone, except for the odor. Smoke from the mountain on the north was a sign for the end of Babylon (*Lives of the Prophets,* Dan 21).

12. *summon . . . another . . . host.* After destruction of enemies, the messiah summons his own host. Cf. Hosea 11:10 f.; Isa 11:12; II Bar 72; Ps Sol 17:28.

peaceful. See Philo *On Rewards and Punishments* 16.

13. *[different] appearances.* Lit. "faces of many men." The explanation follows — they reflect the mood of those who joined themselves to him.

some were joyful. Gunkel remarks: "Jews and pagans, pious and godless."

some in shackles. I.e. those that were taken captive (cf. Isa 42:7; Sib Or 3:352 ff.).

some leading . . . offerings. Perhaps a play on Isa 66:20; Ps Sol 17:34.

excessive fear. Lit. "a multitude of fear."

prayed to the Most High. Note prayer is directed to God, not to the interpreting angel, though the usual introduction of "O Lord, Lord" is missing.

14. *From the beginning.* I.e. from the time of the first visions. Cf. 8:63.

these wonders. Perhaps *terata,* with Hilgenfeld. Ar.² "secrets."

considered me worthy. Cf. 9:24 f.

15. *this dream.* Syriac has *ḥzw',* "vision."

16. *I was just thinking.* Lit. "I was just considering in my mind"; probably Heb. *blby,* "in my heart."

how dreadfully. Lit. "woe [to those who]"; cf. Ezek 7:26; 16:23; Rev 8:13; 18:10.

those who survive . . . those who do not survive. Cf. Matt 24:40 f.; I Thess 4:15. The reference is to those who are alive at the time of the coming of the messiah and experience the woes and to those who have passed on before, who know the joys to be experienced but are unable to partake of them (vs. 18).

18. *what is on deposit.* Recall the treasuries of various kinds mentioned elsewhere in II Esdras (cf. Ps 31:19).

enjoy it. Lit. "fall in with."

19. *undergo.* Lit. "see."

these dreams attest. The visions already related and interpreted.

20. *like a cloud.* Cf. Job 7:9; 30:15. The thought is that it is better to suffer the perils of the messianic age and so enter the kingdom of God than to pass away before and not enjoy it. As Oesterley remarks: it is "better to suffer and then enjoy, than not to suffer nor enjoy."

21. *the things you spoke about.* What the seer contemplated in vss. 16–20.

23. *the one responsible.* Lit. "the one who brought on." The messiah is referred to (cf. Test Levi 16:5).

will himself protect. Cf I Enoch 48:4.

works . . . and faith. See NOTE on 9:7; I Enoch 102:4; II Bar 14:12 do not mention faith; cf. James 2:24 f.

24. *those who survive . . . more fortunate.* See third NOTE on vs. 16 above. The interpreter supports Ezra's conclusion.

26. *kept for many ages.* Reference is to the heavenly messiah of I Enoch 37–70, not to the Davidic messiah (cf. vs. 52). See note by Box in APOT, II, 618, and Macdonald, *Hebrew Philosophical Genius,* p. 39; but see Schrader, p. 378.

to deliver his creation. On the Latin misreading, *per semetipsum,* of Heb. *'šr bw,* "through whom," see Wellhausen, in *Skizzen und Vorarbeiten,* VI, 236, n. 1. Cf. Pseudo-Philo 51:5; Ps Sol 18:6, and Ryle and James, *Psalms of the Pharisees,* p. 149, note on vs. 6. On the origin of the idea of the messiah as deliverer or savior, see G. H. Dalman, *Die Worte Jesu* (Leipzig: Hinrichs, 1898), pp. 242 ff.

he himself will create. Lit. "he will arrange [or put in order] those who survive." As the text now stands it appears to mean that the messiah will arrange or create the new order for those who survive (cf. II Cor 5:17).

27. Cf. vs. 10.

28. Cf. vs. 9.

without spear or. Lit. "he held neither spear nor."

29. *days are coming.* Cf. 5:1; 6:18. Fragments are extant of a Sahidic source for vss. 29–46. See Violet, II, 385–95. Violet (II, 181) thinks vss. 29–31 form an oracle like the Sibylline Oracles.

30. *trepidation.* Lit. "failure of mind." Cf. *furore mentis* (=*btmhwn lbb,* "confusion of heart-mind") in Vulgate of Deut 28:28.

31. *attack one another.* Cf. Isa 19:2; Matt 24:6 f.; Böhlig and Labib, *Die koptisch-gnostische Schrift,* paragraph 174:5 ff.

city against city. Note variants for "against" in Latin text.

32. *signs.* Those mentioned in other chapters (cf. II Bar 25).

directed your attention earlier. Lit. "showed you before."

my son. Cf. 7:28, 29; 13:37, 52; 14:9; I Enoch 105:2; and Schrader, *Die Keilinschriften und das Alte Testament,* p. 378.

will be revealed. Cf. Dan 7:13; Matt 24:30; Mark 13:26.

33. *his land.* Lit. "his region."

internecine war. Lit. "the war which they have with one another." Here they are represented as fighting one another; in vss. 8, 9, and 34 they form a coalition against the messiah. The latter is not referred to in the apocalyptic chapters of the Gospels (Matt 24; Mark 13; Luke 21).

34. *unite into an innumerable host.* Lit. "an innumerable multitude will be gathered (*colligetur*) in one (*in unum*)." It is difficult to capture the meaning of the clause in translation since both the uniting of the nations into an innumerable multitude and the assemblage of the multitude in one place are involved. The former is characteristically apocalyptic (cf. Ezek 38, 39; Joel 4:11 f.; Zech 14:2), the latter almost equally so (Rev 16:16; Joel 4:12).

35. *summit of Mount Zion.* Cf. Ps 2:6; and the Ugaritic 'Anat 3:25–28.

36. *Zion . . . will appear.* The appearance of the new Zion or new Jerusalem is common in apocalyptic literature (cf. 7:26; II Bar 4:2–7; 32:2; I Enoch 90:28–29; Rev 21:2, 10).

ready built. Cf. 10:27.

mountain . . . hands. Cf. vs. 6.

37. *My son.* See third NOTE on vs. 32.

berate . . . the peoples. Cf. 12:32; Isa 11:4; 66:15.

who approach like a storm. Cf. vs. 10. Note that 37–38 do not really interpret vs. 10. In vss. 10 and 27 the fiery forces come from the mouth of the messiah. Here it is the opponents of the messiah whose approach is like a storm.

the tortures they . . . undergo are compared to the flames.

38. *with the law . . . like the fire.* Possibly judgment by fire is meant. The law is the standard of life or death, depending on one's choice. The thrust of the interpretation is that the messiah will annihilate totally the opposing host.

39. *another, peaceful host.* See vs. 12. Test Reuben 6:8 speaks of "all Israel." See next NOTE and cf. Sanhedrin 110b with Mishna, and Gemara with note by Rosenthal, p. 62, n. 7.

40. *ten tribes.* Certain circles in post-exilic times were intent on maintaining the figment of the twelve tribes though enumeration was not consistent. Probably the number twelve was more significant than the names assigned to the tribes. The ten (or nine, or nine and a half) tribes will be gathered by the messiah to participate in his salvation (cf. Rosenthal, pp. 62 f. and esp. n. 7 for a summary of the Akiba-Eliezer debate as related in Sanhedrin 110b; Moore, II, pp. 368 f.; and Box's summary of Bousset and Volz in *Ezra Apocalypse,* in loco); Test Joseph 19:2–7 (Armenian text); Ass Mos 2:4 f.; the disposition of the nine and one half tribes is dwelt upon in the Epistle of Baruch (II Bar 78–84). The Qumran community referred to the number twelve (cf. 1QS 8:1; 1QM 2:2, 3; 4QpIs^d 3 f.). See Nikiprowetzky, *Revue des Études Juives* 128 (1969), 20 f., for discussions of point raised by Marc Philonenko, J.-C. Picard, J.-M. Rosenstiehl, and F. Schmidt, *Pseudépigraphes de l'Ancien Testament et Manuscrits de la Mer Morte,* I, Paris, 1967.

Hoshea. The last king of the Northern Kingdom (732–724 B.C.). Gunkel thinks the reading, "Josiah," of most MSS goes back to the Hebrew.

Shalmaneser. Shalmaneser V (726–722 B.C.); for biblical account see II Kings 17:1–6; II Bar 62:5 agrees with II Esdras. II Esdras and II Baruch may well reflect the actual historical situation in view of the strong evidence of Shalmaneser V's conquest of Samaria presented by Hayim Tadmor, "The Campaigns of Sargon II of Assur," *Journal of Cuneiform Studies* 12 (1958), 22–40, 77–100, esp. 37–40.

across the river. Cf. the biblical expression *'br hnhr,* "across the river," in Josh 24:2, 14, 15, et al. A. M. Dubarle, *Judith* (Rome: Biblical Institute Press, 1966), I, 115 f., and n. 22, on Jean Malalas' (fifth century A.D.) discussion of the ten and two tribes. Cf. Jos. *Antiq.* 9:277 ff.

41. *they decided.* Lit. "they devised for themselves this plan"; Heb. *y'ṣw 'ṣh,* "they planned a plan."

a more remote region. As Gunkel remarks, this conception stems from the fact that they were not found in any of the familiarly known lands (cf. Jer 23:3 f.).

human species. For expression see Gen 3:15; II Macc 7:28; Acts 17:26. Cf. Jos. *Antiq.* 11:133; on the concern for the ten "lost" tribes see also II Bar

77:19–22. The tenth petition of the Shemoneh 'Esreh (Eighteen Prayers) reflects the same conception: "Sound the trumpet loudly for our deliverance! Raise a banner for the assembling of our exiles! Praised be you, Lord, who gathers your scattered people Israel." For further references see Bousset, p. 237 f.

42. *ordinances*. Latin *legitima*, "laws," "statutes." Verse envisions a new beginning in observance of the laws which they neglected in their land. Possibly a justification for the continued concern for those exiles and their hoped for deliverance in the messianic age.

43. *narrow entrances of the Euphrates River*. Not clear but see Gry, II, 385, for conjectures on origin of expression. It may refer to crossings of branches of the Euphrates whose crossings were interpreted in an Exodus context as the following verse seems to indicate.

44. *courses*. Cf. Josh 3:14 ff. Perhaps that is why the place of exile of the ten tribes is inaccessible. For expression cf. Job 28:11; UT, 49:I:5; 51:IV:21; 2 Aqht 6:47.

45. *Arzareth*. Contains and conceals the Heb. *'rṣ 'ḥrt*, "another land," as in Deut. 29:27. First proposed by Schiller-Szinessy in the *Journal of Philology* 3 (1870), 114, and since accepted by most scholars. For other views see Violet, II, 185 f.

a long trek. Lit. "a long way," "of a distance [journey] of one year and a half." The Mishnah uses this passage in connection with the ten tribes (Sanhedrin 10:3). The tenor of these verses dealing with the ten tribes accentuates the belief in the remoteness of their place of exile and the fact that there was no contact with them.

46. *until the last time*. The Ethiopic text has "until the last [or end of] days." I.e. they lived and continue to live there (perfect of duration). Cf. Dan 2:28 *b'ḥryt ywmy'*, "in the last days."

to come again. See first NOTE on vs. 40.

47. *the Most High will again*. A second exodus from exile (cf. Isa 11:15 f.).

That is why. Because of the intervention of the Most High; the man summoned to himself the peaceful host (vs. 12).

48. Most commentators think this is an interpolation but it could equally well be a summary affirmation applying to those who remain (survive) of the ten tribes and reach the limits of his sanctuary.

49. *the people who survive*. Here the descriptive includes all Israel, i.e. those of the diaspora and those who remained in the land.

50. *many great portents*. Heb. *npl'wt rbwt gdlwt*.

51. *tell me this*. Questions about details of a vision are common elsewhere (Rev 7:13; I Enoch 23:3; 24:5; 27:1; II Enoch 7:3; 10:3 f.; 18:2; Hermas *Visions* 3:4:2).

depths of the sea. See first NOTE on vs. 3.

52. *perceive what may be in the depths of the sea*. An expression found in Pseudo-Philo 21:2.

my son or those who are with him. No attendants are mentioned in the vision or in its interpretation. Presumably they are the angelic hosts (cf. Matt 25:31) as Gunkel and Oesterley think, though the righteous who have been saved cannot be ruled out (cf. I Enoch 105:2). See Gunkel's comment on the verse — he thinks it runs counter to eschatological teaching which held that the messiah came from heaven. Some kind of astral mythology may underlie the passage.

in the time of his day. The day of the messiah is a common conception in Jewish literature.

53. *informed=inluminatus es.* Occurs some dozen times in Pseudo-Philo in the same sense.

54. *relinquished your [own interests].* Cf. Mark 10:29 f.; Luke 18:29 f.

explored my law. Lit "inquired into." Cf. Ps 119:94; and often in the sense of meditation on law (Josh 1:8; Ps 1:2; etc.).

55. *dedicated your life to wisdom.* Lit. "disposed [or adjusted] your life in [or by] wisdom." Syriac *dbr,* "led your life." Cf. Prov 2:2; 4:5; Eccles 1:17; 8:16.

understanding your mother. Cf. Prov 7:4; both wisdom and understanding are feminine and often personified. Cf. 11QPs^a 18:5 ff. (see *The Psalms Scroll of Qumran Cave 11* by James A. Sanders, DJD, IV, 1965). The mother expression applied to other aspects is found in Jer 2:27; Hermas *Visions* 3:8:5. The Targum for Prov 2:3 is *ky 'm lbynh tqr',* "for you shall call understanding mother."

56. *reward.* Cf. Heb 11:6.

57. *across the field.* Cf. 12:51. Box thinks these verses are misplaced (see in loco).

58. *he controls the times.* Apocalyptic determinism.

happens. Lit. "what things have been produced."

in them. In the times.

COMMENT

[A dream vision, 13:1–13a] The eagle vision was politically oriented; this one is religiously oriented. After a seven-day interval the seer had a dream vision in the night. He saw a storm wind that appeared to rise from the sea, convulsing the waves as it did so. As he continued to look, the wind brought up out of the depths of the sea a figure resembling a man whose vehicle of flight was the clouds of heaven. Wherever the figure looked, the object of his vision reacted with trepidation and turmoil. The sound of his voice produced utter discomfiture for all who heard it. Mobilized to attack him was an innumerable host representing all the nations of the earth. But the man from the sea prepared for his bulwark a huge mountain to which he flew on his cloud chariot. (Ezra was thwarted in his efforts to see the place whence the mountain was hewn because he was not of this [i.e. the dream] world. It was the new Zion of God). Despite his awesome and terrifying appearance, his opponents dared to engage him, only to be met not with the normal weapons of defense, but with torrents of fire and storm that issued from his mouth. They were burned completely by the flaming gust. After their destruction, the man descended from the mountain and gathered to himself a peaceful host. They wore all sorts of countenances reflective of the conditions imposed upon them by their oppressors (who had just been destroyed).

[Request for interpretation of the dream vision, 13:13b–20] Startled into wakefulness, Ezra resorted to prayer to the Most High. On the basis of previous experience with divine communication, he pleads to be shown the interpretation of this strange vision. He was troubled not only by its strangeness but by the problem that haunted him before. He wrestled with the thought of how dreadful those who remain in the last days will fare but he thought it even more pathetic for those who do not remain. The latter are sad because they are cognizant of what is in store for them but cannot enjoy it. Those who remain will indeed suffer great dangers, as this and previous dreams indicate, yet it is preferable for them despite the perils involved. To disappear from the world without experiencing what will take place at the end is beyond comprehension. For a similar conception see Heb 11:35b, 39–40.

[Interpretation of the dream vision, 13:21–50] While it is not so stated explicitly, the context suggests that the response to the seer's prayer comes by way of the interpreting angel although the request or prayer was directed to the Most High himself. The respondent offers not only to explain the vision but also to unravel the thoughts of Ezra. The interpreter begins with the latter and points out that the one who is responsible for the dangers of the age will see to it that his own are protected against them. So those who survive are better off than those who do not (see NOTE on vs. 20); despite the sufferings to be endured, against which they are in reality hedged, they will be able to enjoy salvation. Those who do not survive are cognizant of the blessings of salvation but cannot experience them.

The explanation of the vision follows. The man rising from the depths of the sea represents the messiah whom the Most High has kept hidden through many ages but who will be revealed at the right time. He is the instrument through whom the Most High will deliver his creation and provide a new order for those who survive. The wind, fire, and tempest let go from his mouth are reminiscences of the storm-god imagery current at many places in the Old Testament. The weapons of the messiah are not those of men; they are the forces of nature commanded by his mouth. Certain signs or, perhaps better, certain worldly phenomena will mark the *beginning* (note the indefiniteness) of the delivery of those on earth.[1] Panic will seize men and nations — which in itself will be a harbinger of things about to take place. Moreover the other signs (see NOTE on vs. 32) too will point up the trend of the times. But the capstone of it all will be the manifestation of "my son,"[2] the signal for

[1] This indefiniteness may be seen also in Mark 13:7–8; Matt 24:6–8; Luke 21:9 where the significant qualifications are "but the end is not yet" and "this is but the beginning of the sufferings."
[2] See Volz, pp. 213 f., and esp. p. 220 f.

Armageddon. At the same time Zion (the New Jerusalem) will appear for all to see — a sign of encouragement for the faithful, of the end for opponents and oppressors. "My son" will first berate those who have set themselves against him and will present the indictment. Here is where the interpretation takes a different twist. Earlier the storm characteristics (vss. 10, 27) were instruments of destruction issuing from the mouth of the man rising from the depths of the sea. Now the situation is reversed. The approach of the allied host opposing him is likened to the storm; the tortures they are to undergo are like flames; those crushed by the law are crushed as if by the fire. The peaceful host is composed of the ten tribes who are a new exodus coming out of exile to a new promised land. In their exile they underwent a desert experience in which they relearned the ordinances of the Most High that they had earlier neglected. Through miraculous intervention by him they will come back again. Just as in the exodus experience, the same one who had led them into the desert school will lead them back. Finally all who reach the limits of his sanctuary (i.e. the ten tribes[3] and the two tribes — all Israel) will be saved. The hand that reaches out to destroy the enemy is also the protective hand that preserves those who survive. In fact the one who destroys is the one who saves, so that the act of destruction becomes the saving act.

[Further question and explanation, 13:51–56] There was certainly a reason for the question posed here, although the interpretation of the dream vision had already dealt with the significance of the man rising out of the sea, as well as his identification. Now, however, the seer asks just *why* he saw "the man rising up out of the depths of the sea." While it is true that apocalyptic writers often interject questions on details (see NOTE on vs. 51), this one appears to have a particular thrust. Elsewhere the son of man, messiah, is depicted as coming from heaven (cf. Acts 1:11; Matt 24:30; Mark 13:26; Luke 21:27; Dan 7:13). Verse 52 is not altogether responsive to the question but it does stress the concealment of the messiah until the Most High chooses to reveal him "in the time of his day." Furthermore the pre-existence of the messiah is clearly in the mind of the interpreter.[4] No one can probe the depths of the sea to explore its secrets or rise to heaven to discover the mysteries hidden by the Lord. But the messianic secret will be revealed at the time chosen by the Most High. A few have been informed about it, though in enigmatic terms and ways, because of their faithfulness to the Most High as shown by the direction of their thoughts and lives (vss. 54–55). That is part of their reward. More is yet to come after due meditation on what has just been made known to the seer. More tremendously amazing things will be disclosed to him.

[Waiting in the field, 13:57–58] For what he had heard and seen in this and other visions, Ezra praised the Lord. Yet it was not only for these disclosures but rather for the continued activity and plans of the Most High that he glorified him. He is now convinced that, despite appearances, the Lord con-

---

[3] For other references in pseudepigraphic literature to the nine and a half (ten) tribes, see M. R. James, *Apocrypha Anecdota* [BIBLIO II], reprint, pp. 86–108.

[4] On the conceptions of the pre-existence of the messiah in apocalyptic see Bousset, pp. 264 ff. and Volz, p. 219.

trols the times and what happens in them — for all are carefully designed to execute his purposes and plans.

Observations on the visions of destruction. Visions five and six deal with social units or groups rather than with individuals, as was the case with the preceding ones. The over-all conception prevalent for both has been set forth most clearly by Gunkel,[5] of which the following is a summary.

Gunkel thinks apocalyptic images such as are involved here are generally based on tradition, rather than on imaginative creations of the author. This tradition may have been transmitted in either written or oral form. Here we have two separate traditions essentially parallel as may be seen from the fact that both sketch the destruction of the last enemies of Israel through the intervention of the anointed one and have certain aspects in common, as, for example, the rebukes in 11:38–46; 12:32–33; 13:37–38. At the same time there are significant differences. Vision five has the anointed one destroying the Roman empire, Vision six has him annihilate the assembled people of the earth who are hostile to Israel. Then there is his grace bestowed only on the remnant of those in the holy land in Vision five, on the lost ten tribes in Vision six. The former is a contemporary apocalypse, the latter has to do with traditional eschatology. The earlier visions center about the individual, these about political hopes. It is rather striking that the portraits of things to come did not take into consideration the great catastrophe of Israel which had just taken place and so perturbed the author. Even in the reference to the Roman devastation of the homes and walls (11:42), there is no mention of the temple or the promise of the return of the exiles to the holy land.

The two visions appear to reflect contact with Dan 7 where the first beast was "like a lion, with the wings of an eagle" (vs. 4) though the wing identifications in II Esdras resemble those of the horns of the fourth beast (vss. 7–8, 19–27). The "something resembling a man" (13:3) is reminiscent of the "one like unto a son of man" who approaches the ancient of days and is given everlasting dominion. However, nothing is said in Daniel about his coming up out of the sea[6] when the winds stir it up or of his "flying with the clouds of heaven."

Where the writer of II Esdras got the various facets of his visions is obscure. But he may have been indebted to many sources whose origin he himself may not have known or whose meaning he did not understand. Nevertheless he fitted them into a portrait that conveyed his thoughts at the time. That he had some difficulty in the interpretation (vss. 21–50) suggests at least some expansion along rabbinic lines. Perhaps some of the material involved has been drawn from floating tradition of the most varied sources.[7] But specifics must not be pushed too far in such identifications.

---

[5] In APAT, II, 346.
[6] Cf. the mythological "primeval hill" in Egyptian thought — Adolf Erman, *Die Religion der Ägypter* (Berlin: W. de Gruyter & Co., 1934), pp. 61 f.; and the caveat of Abdel-Aziz Saleh in *Mitteilungen des deutschen archäologischen Instituts, Abteilung Kairo* 25 (Wiesbaden: Harrassowitz, 1969), 110–20.
[7] See additional notes in Oesterley, pp. 144–48, 158–64.

THE SEVENTH VISION (THE LEGEND OF EZRA) (14:1–51)

Conversation with the voice from the bush

14 1 Then *a*on the third day*a* as I was sitting under an oak tree, 2 a voice came out *b*from a bush opposite me*b* and said: Ezra, Ezra! *c*Here I am Lord, I replied. When I rose to my feet*c*, he said to me: 3 I revealed myself *d*from a bush*d* and spoke to Moses when my people were enslaved in Egypt. 4 *e*Then I sent him *f*to lead*f* my people out of Egypt*e* and*g* brought them to Mount Sinai. I kept him with me *h*for a long time*h*,

5 I told him many*i* wonderful things,

Showed him the secrets of the times,

*j*And disclosed to him*j* the end of the times.

I instructed him as follows: 6 These things you are to make known, but those [you must] keep secret. 7 I command you now*k*:

8 *l*The signs I showed [you],

The dreams you saw*l*,

The interpretations you heard —

keep them in your mind*m*! 9 For you will be removed from [among] men and henceforth be with *n*my son*n* and those like you until the times are terminated,

10 *o*because the world has lost its youth,

and the times are approaching old age*o*.

11 *p*For the world-age is divided into twelve*q* parts; ten parts of it have already passed, with half of the tenth part gone, 12 but two [parts] of it remain after the [second] half of the tenth part.*p*

---

a–a Ar.*1* *'lywm 'lr'b'*, "the fourth day"; Ar.*2* *wb'd 'lywm 'lth'lth*, "and after the third day"; so also Armenian; others "on the third day."

b–b Ethiopic "from opposite this tree"; Ar.*2* *mn thth'*, "from under it."

c–c Omitted by M.

d–d Ar.*2* *fy twr śyn'*, "on Mount Sinai"; perhaps, as Gunkel observes, a misreading of *syny*, "Sinai," for *snh*, "bush."

e–e Omitted by M.

f–f With C, Syriac, Ar.*1,2*; S, A, Ethiopic, Armenian have *eduxi*, "I led."

g Syriac adds *w'ytyh lmdbr'*, "and I brought to the desert"; so also Ar.*1* "out of the desert."

h–h Lit. "many days"; Ar.*2* *'rb'yn ywm' w'rb'yn lylt*, "forty days and forty nights."

i Ar.*1* *'zymh*, "great," "extraordinary."

j–j With Syriac *whwyth*, Ethiopic and Ar.*1*.　　*k* Syriac adds *'zr'*, "Ezra."

l–l Omitted by Ar.*2*.　　*m* Syriac adds *wtś' 'nwn*, "and conceal them."

n–n Ar.*1* *ft'y*, "my youth"; Ar.*2* *'bdy*, "my servant."　　*o–o* Omitted by Armenian.

p–p Vss. 11, 12 omitted by Syriac. Vs. 12 omitted by M.

q So also Ar.*2*; Ethiopic has "ten"; Ar.*1* "the greater [part] of its years."

13 Now, therefore, set your house in order,
^{r}Caution your people^r,
Console their humble ones,
^{s}Teach their wise ones,^{s}
Renounce forthwith mortal life,
14 Put ^{t}earthly cares^t away from you,
Cast away from you ^{u}human burdens^u,
Divest yourself at once of ^{v}feeble nature^v,
Put aside your distressing cares,
And hasten to get out of these times.

15 For worse evils than any you have yet experienced will take place; 16 the weaker the world becomes by reason of age, the more numerous become the evils befalling its inhabitants.

17 Truth will become more distant,
And falsehood draw nearer.

The eagle you saw in your vision is already preparing to come.

*Ezra's prayer for the spirit's help in reproducing the Scriptures
and the Lord's response*

18 I responded as follows: ^{w}Let me speak^w before you, Lord. 19 If I proceed, as you ordered me [to do], to instruct the people now living^x, who will admonish those yet to be born?

20 For the world lies in darkness,
And those who live in it [are] without light.

21 ^{y}Because your law has been burned^y, no one knows what has been done by you or what is yet to be done. 22 If you please, now, grant me your holy spirit that I may write down everything that has been done in the world from the beginning, the things that were written in your law, so that men may be able to find [their] way^z and that, in the last times, those who want to live ^{a}may do so^a. 23 He replied to

---

$^{r-r}$ Omitted by Ethiopic.
$^{s-s}$ With Syriac *wskl lḥkymyhwn;* Ar.^{2} *'krm,* "honor" for "teach."
$^{t-t}$ Ethiopic and Ar.^{1} have "mortal thoughts"; Ar.^{2} *'lkfr fy 'lmwt,* "the thought of death"; Armenian "confusion or perplexity of mind."
$^{u-u}$ Syriac *mḥšbt' dmwt',* "thoughts of death."
$^{v-v}$ Syriac *kyn' dkryhwt',* "nature of sickness"; Ethiopic "put on that which does not die"; Ar.^{1} "the weaknesses of this nature subject to sufferings, sicknesses and darkness"; Ar.^{2} *śmt 'l'tw,* "airs or signs of pride."
$^{w-w}$ Reading with Syriac *'mll;* so also Ethiopic, Ar.^{1,2}, Armenian.
^{x} Ar.^{2} adds *r'ytk,* "your flock," "herd."
$^{y-y}$ Omitted by Ar.^{2}, which substitutes the following for the remainder of the verse: "and there is not present a wise man, or one with insight, or one with skill to distinguish between good and evil." Ar.^{2} lacks all the remaining verses of this section.
^{z} Armenian "ways of redemption [or salvation]"; Ar.^{1} *śblk,* "your way"; Ethiopic "path of life."
$^{a-a}$ Ar.^{1} *yślkwn fy wṣ'y'k,* "walk in your commands."

me as follows: Go[b], call the people together, and tell them not to look for you for[c] forty days. 24 In the meantime equip yourself with a good supply of writing tablets and engage Saraiah, Dabriah, Shelemiah, Elkanah[d] and Ariel — those five because they can write rapidly[e]. 25 Then you shall come here and I will light the lamp of understanding in your heart; it will not be extinguished until what you are to write is finished. 26 When you are through, you must publish some [of your works] but deliver others in secret to the wise men. Tomorrow at this time you must begin to write.

Ezra's address to the people

27 So, setting out to do as he[f] commanded me, I assembled all the people and said: 28 Listen[g], O Israel, to these words! 29 Formerly our fathers were foreigners in Egypt but were liberated from that place 30 and received the law of life which they did not keep [and] [h]which you too transgressed[h] after them. 31 Then [i]the land in the territory of Zion[i] was given to you as a dowry; but you and your fathers [j]committed iniquity[j] and repudiated the ways which [k]the Most High[k] commanded you [to observe]. 32 [l]Since he[l] is a just judge, he withdrew, [m]in time[m], what he had given to you. 33 Now you are here[n] while your brothers are [o]still further away[o] than you.

34 If, therefore, [p]you will control your inclination[p]
and [q]discipline your mind[q],
You will be kept safe while alive
and [r]be accorded mercy after death[r].
35 For [s]judgment comes after death,
when we will be restored to life again;

---

[b] Reading *vade* with C, M and oriental versions.
[c] Ar.[1] *km'l*, "end of."   [d] So with Syriac *hlqn'*; Latin *Ethanum*.
[e] Ethiopic "skillful in writing."
[f] Armenian "the Lord."   [g] Ar.[2] adds *mny*, "from me."
[h–h] Ar.[2] *kfrtm b'llh*, "you defected from God."
[i–i] Ar.[1] omits "territory of Zion"; Ar.[2] *ṭwr śyn'*, "Mount Sinai."
[j–j] Armenian "were rebels."
[k–k] Syriac *mwš' 'bdh dmry'*, "Moses, the servant of the Lord."
[l–l] Syriac *mrym' dyn*, "but the Most High"; so also Ar.[1,2].
[m–m] Ar.[1] *'zmnh 'lkr'mh w'ln'mh*, "time of favor and grace."
[n] Syriac adds *b'wlṣn'*, "in tribulation."
[o–o] Ar.[2] *'qṣy 'lmsrq*, "farthest east"; Syriac *b'r'' 'ḥrt'*, "in another land."
[p–p] Ar.[1] *'ḥbśtm 'tqkm*, "restrain your freedom."
[q–q] Ar.[2] *w'w'ytm 'lḥkmt fy qlwbkm*, "and keep wisdom in your hearts."
[r–r] Ethiopic "and not die"; Ar.[2] *tkhlṣwn mn 'ldyn*, "you will be delivered from the judgment."
[s] Ar.[2] *'l'ly*, "[the Most High] will consign all men to judgment after death."

Then the name of the just will appear,
and the deeds of the wicked be exposed.

36 *Let no one approach me now* or seek me for forty days.

Ezra's experience in the field

37 So I took the five men, as he[u] had ordered me [to do], and we set out for the field where we remained[v]. 38 Then, on the next day, a voice called to me as follows:

Ezra[w], *open your mouth,
And drink what I am giving you to drink.

39 When I opened my mouth, a cup full of what looked like water but whose *color was firelike* was handed to me. 40 *I took and drank it*; as I was drinking of it

My intellect exuded understanding,
Wisdom increased within me,
Because my mind retained [its] memory.

41 So my mouth was opened; it remained closed no longer. 42 The Most High, also gave understanding to the[b] five men so that they wrote down what was spoken, *in a series of characters* which they did not understand. *They kept at work* forty days.

43 They wrote during the day,
And ate food at night;
But I spoke by day,
And did not remain silent at night.

44 *Ninety-four books* were written in the forty days[g].

---

t–t Omitted by Ar.[2].   *u* Ar.[2] *'l'ly*, "the Most High."
v Syriac adds *d'mr ly*, "as he said to me"; Ar.[2] *km' 'mrny 'l'ly*, "as the Most High told me."
w Syriac, Ar.[1,2], and Armenian repeat the name — "Ezra, Ezra." See NOTE on vs. 2.
x Ar.[2] "and I answered, Here I am! And he said to me . . ."
y–y Armenian "its color was [like] water."
z–z Ar.[2] *fkr'th*, "and I sipped it"; the Berlin fragment (quoted with Latin translated by Gildemeister in *Esdrae liber quartus Arabice*, pp. 40 f. [BIBLIO II]) follows Syriac from which it may have been taken.
a–a Ar.[2] *wntq f'y b'lḥkmt*, "and my mouth uttered wisdom."
b Syriac *hnwn*, "those."
c–c Latin *ex successione notis*, "in succession," "in character." Syriac *bywbl' bktybt' d'twt'*, "in a series of letter signs"; Ethiopic "as [or with] signs"; Ar.[1] "after the arrangement of signs of the successive matters"; Ar.[2] "their script was foreign [or strange]," *kt'bthm ghrybt*; Armenian "they wrote in turn," *alternis*.
d–d Lit. "they sat"; Syriac *ytbt*, "I sat": so also Ar.[1], *jlśn'*, "we sat [remained]."
e–e Omitted by Ar.[2]; Armenian "and at night I ceased" (note omission of negative!).
f–f So with Syriac, Ethiopic, Ar.[1]; Berlin fragment, Armenian, Latin, S, M have 904; A, 974; C, 970. The confusion in the Latin may be due to the similarity between *nongenti*, 900, and *nonaginta*, 90.
g Ar.[2] ends with vs. 44.

Command of the Most High

45 Then when the forty days were ended, the Most High said to me: Publish *the twenty-four books* which you wrote first for the worthy and unworthy* to read; 46 however you must withhold the seventy last* books and hand them over to the wise men among your people,

47 For in them is *the spring of understanding*,

The fountain of wisdom,

And *the river of knowledge*.

The response of Ezra and his translation

48 And I did so* [in *the seventh year*, *the sixth week, after five thousand years three months and twelve days of creation*. 49 After he had written down all these (things), Ezra was removed and taken *to the place* of those like him. 50 But he was called *the scribe of the knowledge* of the Most High for eternity of eternities*. 51 The first discourse of Ezra is finished.]

h–h With Syriac *hlyn 'sryn w'rb'' ktbyn*, "these twenty-four books"; Latin omits; Ar.¹ follows Syriac.
i Syriac adds *min 'm'*, "of the people."
j Omitted by Syriac. Ethiopic omits "seventy."
k–k Ethiopic "light of lights"; Ar.¹ *khmyrh 'lhkmh*, "the leaven of wisdom"; Berlin fragment has *'rwq 'lbr*, "vein of piety."
l–l Ar.¹ *w'lbhr 'lw's' 'ldhy 'lm'rfh*, "and a wide sea of knowledge."
m Here the Latin version ends. What follows is preserved in the Syriac, Ethiopic, Ar. ¹, Berlin fragment, Armenian.
n–n Ethiopic and Armenian "fourth year."
o–o Ethiopic "in the fourth year of the weeks of the year after the year of the creation in the five thousandth year, in the tenth of the darkness, in the third month and twenty-second day thereof." Ar. ¹ "and I lived seventy-six years after the five thousand twenty-five years of the work of creation, in the third month and twenty-second day thereof." Berlin fragment "In the seventh year of the sixth week and after five thousand years, three months and twenty-two days El-Useir was removed. . . ." Armenian "in the fourth year of a week of years after five thousand years of the creation of the world, and two months of days."
p–p Ar.¹ *'rd 'l'hy'*, "land of the living (or life)"; Armenian "company (or band)."
q–q Ar.¹ *w'd' 'ln'mwś w'lfhm w'lm'rfh*, "the author of the law and the understanding and the knowledge."
r Ar.¹ Armenian, and some MSS of Ethiopic add "Amen."

NOTES

14:1. *oak tree.* Cf. II Bar 6:1; 77:18 where *the* oak tree is designated. Likely a well-known oak tree somewhere in the vicinity of Jerusalem. It is not the Oak of Mamre at Hebron.

2. *voice . . . from a bush.* Cf. Exod 3:2 f.

Ezra, Ezra. Note the repetition of the name, meant to attract the attention of the person called. Cf. Exod 3:4 (of Moses), I Sam 3:10 (of Samuel).

Here I am. As response of Moses (Exod 3:4) and Samuel (I Sam 3).

3. *I revealed myself.* Present participle plus finite verb stands for Hebrew absolute infinitive construct; lit. "revealing I was revealed." Gunkel renders "I have already revealed myself once before at the bush." Vss. 3–4, as noted above, summarize Exod 3.

4. *a long time.* Lit. "for many days" (cf. Exod 34:28). On verse see Pseudo-Philo 53:8.

5. *many wonderful things . . . secrets of the times . . . the end of the times.* Such knowledge was traditionally associated with Moses. Cf. Ass Mos 1:16 f.; 10:12; 11:1. The material on the subject has been assembled by James, *Lost Apocrypha of the Old Testament,* pp. 42 ff.

6. *These things . . . those.* The former refer to the Torah (cf. Deut 5), both written and oral; the latter to apocalyptic writings. (See Jub 1:26; Rev 10:4). Cf. revelations to Valmiki (H. M. Buck, in *Search the Scriptures* [Leiden: Brill, 1969], p. 84).

7. *command.* Lit. "say."

8. *signs . . . dreams.* Or signs and visions. Violet (II, 191) thinks the former refers to Visions one through three, the latter to Visions four through six; Vision seven he calls instructions (*Aufträge*). He calls attention to a similar situation in Hermas *Visions* 5:5:5 f. Certainly the signs, dreams and interpretations include what has been set forth elsewhere in our book.

keep them in your mind. Lit. "put in heart"; cf. Isa 41:22; Hag 1:5, 7 for expression. The idea is that Ezra is to take them seriously.

9. *removed from [among] men.* According to the Apocalypse of Esdras, Ezra dies (ch. 6). As Oesterley notes, Ezra is regarded above as a kind of second Moses, which may account for the idea expressed here. The title Assumption of Moses, an apocryphal work, suggests the same idea though there is no hint of such a phenomenon in that work.

removed from. Greek *analambanō,* "to take up." Cf. Syriac *'nt gyr mštql 'nt min bnynš',* "for you are being taken away from men." He is to remain in the heavenly world until the last times. Cf. 7:28; 14:49; II Bar 13:3; 48:30; 76:2.

my son. Cf. I Enoch 48:2, 3; 70:1; 105:2; Pseudo-Philo 48:1. See above Notes on 7:28, 29; 13:32, 37, 52; and Macdonald, *Hebrew Philosophical Genius,* p. 39; Volz, p. 213.

those like you. Cf. I Enoch 39:6, 7. Reference is apparently to choice persons like Enoch and Elijah.

the times are terminated. The messiah is thus relegated to the end-times rather than as regent upon earth before that time (cf. I Enoch 45:3 f.). Above (7:28 f.) he is said to reign on earth four hundred years and then die.

10. *the world has lost its youth. . . .* The senescence of the world is a common idea in apocalyptic literature (cf. 4:27; 5:50 ff.; 14:17; II Bar 85:10).

11–12. See textual note *ᵖ–ᵖ*.

world-age. The world history.

twelve parts. I.e. periods (cf. Pseudo-Philo 19:15 and James's note, pp. 131 f.; II Bar 53:6 and ch. 54 where more detail is given). For discussion of the problems see A. Jeremias, *Das Alte Testament im Lichte des Alten Orients*

(Leipzig: Hinrichs, 1906), pp. 223–26; Volz, pp. 165–72, and Volz, *Die biblischen Altertümer*, pp. 443 f.

13. *your house*. Your people's house (cf. II Kings 20:1; Isa 38:1 for expression). The underlying idea is to follow the commandments of the Lord, to follow his directions. Note the parallelisms in the following cola.

Caution. Hebrew probably *ykḥ*, "advise," "reprove" as found in OT and Qumran (cf. Prov 9:8, 9; 19:25).

mortal life. I.e. corruptible, perishable life (cf. Rom 1:23; I Cor 15:53 f.; I Peter 1:23).

14. *earthly cares . . . human burdens*. Cf. II Cor 5:4.

hasten to get out. Ar.[1] has passive voice, suggesting harmonization with vs. 9. Vss. 13–14 place the burden squarely on Ezra.

15. *experienced*. Lit. "have seen happen" (cf. 5:2).

16. *weaker the world*. The belief expressed here is found elsewhere — cf. Gen 6:4; II Esd 7:47 f.; Philo (*Of the Creation of the World* 49) and Lucretius (*Of the Nature of Things* 2:1150 ff.) discuss the same point.

the more numerous. Lit. "so much will be multiplied over its inhabitants' evil" (cf. Ps Sol 5:6 for expression).

17. *Truth . . . more distant*. Cf. 6:27 f.; 7:33b where truth is said to remain or to be revealed. Jeremiah (7:28) complains about the truth as having perished and been cut off. Cf. further Isa 59:14 f.; I Enoch 91:5–7.

eagle. Perhaps a scribal reference to ch. 11.

preparing to come. Lit. "hastening to come."

19. *admonish*. Cf. 7:49, the second time the interpreter has instructed Ezra.

yet to be born. Cf. Rom 9:11.

20. *world lies in darkness*. Cf. II Bar 46:2; 77:14.

without light. I.e. without the Torah. For the Torah or word as light see Pss 19:8; 119:105; Prov 6:23; frequently in apocalyptic writings (cf. II Bar 18:1, 2; 19:3; 59:2) and Jewish literature. Cf. further Isa 60:1; II Cor 4:4; II Peter 1:19.

21. *your law . . . burned*. Cf. 4:32. The sacred scrolls doubtless perished with the destruction of Jerusalem in 587 B.C. (cf. II Kings 25:9). I Macc 1:56 and Sulpicius Severus (*Chronica* II 19:8 *sacra etiam legis et prophetarum volumina igni cremata*) record the burning of the sacred books at the time of the desecration of Jerusalem by Antiochus Epiphanes in 167 B.C. Josephus (*War* 2:229) says a book of the law was burned at Bethhoron during the troubles when Cumanus was procurator of Judea (A.D. 48–52). He also mentions the burning of *to te archeion*, "the archives," in A.D. 70. The Greek term indicates a building where books, records, etc. were kept. It was standard procedure to burn sacred books in the ancient world during conquests. Cf. A. S. Pease, "Notes on Book-Burning," in *Studia Munerosa*, eds. M. H. Shepherd, Jr., and S. E. Johnson (Cambridge, Mass.: The Episcopal Theological School, 1946), pp. 145–60.

what has been done . . . what is yet to be done. The author is here thinking of history and eschatology. See below NOTE on vs. 26.

22. *grant . . . holy spirit*. Cf. Ps Sol 17:42; Wisd Sol 9:17; Asc Isa 5:14; Ps

51:11; Jub 1:21; Test Benjamin 4:5; Test Judah 24; 1QS 8:16; 1QH 7:6; 9:32; 12:12; 14:13; 17:26; 1QSb 2:24; 4QDibHam 5:15 (see NOTE on vs. 30); CD 2:12 and references in J.-D. Barthélemy and J. T. Milik, *Qumran Cave I*, DJD, I (1955), 123, and J. H. Charlesworth, "Les Odes de Salomon," RB 77 (1970), 541 ff. It is doubtful that more than the OT conception of spirit is meant here.

written in your law. Law here in the broadest sense (OT) as in John 15:25; I Cor 14:21; cf. Nötscher, *Zur theologischen Terminologie der Qumran-Texte,* p. 116.

that, in the last times. . . . Cf. II Bar 76:4.

23. *forty days.* This is part of the Mosaic pattern followed elsewhere in the chapter (cf. Exod 24:18; 34:28; Deut 9:9, 18). See below NOTES on vss. 42–45 and II Bar 76:4.

24. *writing tablets.* Cf. Jub 32:21. The Latin *buxos*=Greek *puxia*=Heb. *lwḥwt,* "tablets [of stone]."

Saraiah . . . Ariel. As has been pointed out by others the five scribes may reflect influence from the five disciples of Johanan ben Zakkai in Pirqe Aboth 2:10 (cf. Rosenthal, pp. 40 f., 57 ff.; J. Neusner, *A Life of Rabban Yohanan ben Zakkai* [Leiden: Brill, 1962], p. 71). The names themselves are well known in the OT. Note that Baruch also selected five persons to whom he narrated the divine assurance (II Bar 5:5).

25. *understanding in your heart.* Note the heart as the seat of understanding; NEB renders *corde,* "mind."

26. Cf. second NOTE on vs. 21. Again the apocalyptist's understanding of the revealed and hidden books, the former referring to the OT, the latter to the Apocrypha.

28. *Listen, O Israel.* Expression only in Deut (5:1; 6:4; 9:1; 20:3) and Mark (12:29), in Vulgate.

29. *Formerly.* Lit. "in the beginning" or "at first."

our fathers . . . in Egypt . . . liberated. The great experience of slavery in and deliverance from Egypt, celebrated in the Torah, prophets and hymnal literature.

30. *law of life.* I.e. the Torah for life, intended to direct those who have received it and know it as the way of life and salvation. Cf. Sir 17:11; Rom 8:2; II Bar 38:2; Ps Sol 14:1; for other references see M. Gertner, "Midrashim in the New Testament," *Journal of Semitic Studies* 7 (1962), 277, n. 2; cf. "The Book of Life" in 4Q 6:14 (see next NOTE).

they did not keep [and] which you too. Cf. 4QDibHam, col. VI, 5 ff. (Maurice Baillet, "Un recueil liturgique de Qumrân, Grotte 4, 'Les paroles des luminaires'" RB 68 [1961], 211).

31. *the land . . . of Zion.* The land is named after the earthly dwelling place of the Lord.

committed iniquity and repudiated Cf. Judith 5:18; CD 3:4 ff. Common complaint of the prophets.

32. *just judge.* Cf. Ps 7:11. One of the functions of the Lord was to judge

his people and he was always regarded by his devotees, though not by some of those sentenced by him, as judging justly.

he withdrew. Cf. Judith 5:17 f.

33. *you are here.* I.e. in Babylon.

your brothers. The ten tribes exiled in 721 B.C.

still further away. See textual note *d–d;* Latin "your brothers are further within [than] you." See 13:40 ff.; II Bar 77:4, 5.

34. *control your inclination.* Keep passions in subjection.

discipline your mind. Lit. "instruct your heart" (cf. Ps 16:7).

kept safe while alive. Cf. II Bar 78:7.

35. *judgment comes after death.* Cf. Heb 9:27; Pirqe Aboth 4:29.

restored to life again. Apparently refers to resurrection after which judgment will take place.

the name of the just. The name represented the quality and characteristics of the person bearing it; hence the expression really means the manifestation or demonstration, the survival quality, of just persons. Cf. Prov 10:7; Sir 41:11, 13 for the same general observation on the just and the wicked.

38. *Then.* Lit. "it came to pass."

Ezra . . . drink. As Sigmund Mowinckel remarks (*The Old Testament as Word of God* [New York: Abingdon, 1959], p. 10), this is a pictorial description of revelation; Cf Ezek 2:8 and *passim.*

39. *color was firelike.* The cup was full of inspiration. Cf. the firelike tongues of Pentecost (Acts 2:3), and Gunkel's observation: "the cup is filled with the holy Spirit." Cf. Sir 15:16; Matt 3:11; eating the scroll in Rev 10:9 f.; Philo *On Who Is the Heir of Divine Things* 51–52; Ode Sol, 19. The language sounds somewhat sacramental. Cf. Lidzbarski, *Das Johannesbuch der Mandäer,* p. 82: "Elizar opened his mouth and said to Aba Saba, O Aba Saba! When Johana receives the Jordan, I will be his servant, be baptized with his baptism and be marked with his sign. We will take his Pihta [cultic term for piece of bread], drink his mambuha [the Mandean sacramental drink, generally water] and ascend with him to the place of light." See also *Ginza,* p. 19.

40. *intellect . . . Wisdom.* As Gunkel remarks, this is an excellent description of the condition of the spirit of wisdom.

within me. Lit. "in my breast." Cf. John 7:38, 39.

mind retained [its] memory. Possibly a reminder of the difference between Ezra and the ecstatics; the former retained consciousness and memory while the latter were generally deprived of both.

41. *mouth was opened.* Cf. Ode Sol 36:7. Common figure in Bible (cf. Isa 51:16; 59:21; Jer 1:9; Ezek 33:22; Exod 4:11–15; Deut 18:18) and Qumran (e.g. 1QH 10:7; 12:33; 18:10).

42. *understanding.* Same word as in vs. 40. The five scribes were endowed with the same quality as Ezra. Their function, however, was to write down what Ezra spoke — he was the mouth of the Lord, as was Moses before him.

in a series of characters. See textual note *c–c.* Translation is conjectural because text is far from clear as to meaning. For different renderings see commentaries and translations most of which appear to follow the thought of the Armenian.

which they did not understand. Generally interpreted as referring to the Aramaic script whose invention was attributed traditionally to Ezra — a new script to which they were not yet accustomed. For a different interpretation see Volkmar, *Esdra Propheta,* pp. 208 f. Cf. St. Jerome *Prologus Galeatus* (Foreword to I and II Kings) — "It is certain that Ezra, the scribe and teacher of the law, after Jerusalem's capture and the rebuilding of the temple under Zerubbabel, invented other letters which we now use. . . ." See further Sanhedrin 21b.

They kept at work. Lit. "they sat." See Test Job 51:4 on the whole verse.

43. *day . . . night.* For occupation with the law cf. Josh 1:8; Ps 1:2; 1QS 6:6 f. Here, however, is a different conception — the endeavor to complete the assigned work within the limits of forty days (cf. II Enoch 23:6).

44. *Ninety-four books.* I.e. the twenty-four books of the Hebrew canon and seventy apocryphal books. See below NOTES on vss. 45–46. There is a synagogue at Tadif, some forty kilometers east of Aleppo — on an inscription dating from the late Middle Ages, the Synagogue of Ezra the Scribe. The ruler or president of the synagogue is referred to as being responsible for the holy books, the Haftara scrolls and as having built the storage rooms and the Torah receptacles. F. von Oppenheim, *Inschriften aus Syrien, Mesopotamien und Kleinasien* (Leipzig: Hinrichs, 1913), p. 176.

45. *twenty-four books.* The canonical books of the OT, as may be seen from Talmudic and Midrashic references. They were the books open to all. Cf. Rev 22:10.

46. *withhold the seventy last books . . . the wise men among your people.* Cf. Dan 8:26; 12:4. These were the secret or hidden books of the apocalyptists, open only to the initiate or "the wise men." They were obviously valued more highly by the apocalyptists than the canonical books.

47. *fountain of wisdom.* Cf. I Enoch 48:1; 49:1; Odes Sol 6:8 ff.; Sir 24:30; Prov 18:4.

river of knowledge. Cf. Ode Sol 26:13.

48. As textual note *o–o* indicates, there is a rather wide variation in the figures. Furthermore, the Ar.[1] reading shows that both the age of Ezra and the time, in the history of the world, when he was taken away are involved. For a comparision of the biblical, apocryphal, and Qumran systems of dating, see J. Meysing, "L'énigme de la chronologie biblique et qumrânienne dans une nouvelle lumière," *Revue de Qumrân* 6, no. 22 (1967), 229–51.

49. *the place of those like him.* I.e. the place where the messiah and his associates were (cf. 6:26; 7:28; 13:52; 14:9). Observe the use of the third person in the conclusion.

50. *the scribe.* Cf. I Enoch 12:3b; 15:1; II Enoch 22:11. For a study of Ezra as scribe see Schaeder, EdS, and for the meaning of scribe, ibid., pp. 39–59; Volz, pp. 93 ff.

COMMENT

[Conversation with the voice from the bush, 14:1–17] The writer's introduction to the last so-called vision imitates the Moses story (Exod 3). While Ezra was sitting under an oak tree, he was addressed by a voice coming out of a bush opposite that place. Just as the voice from the bush summoned Moses to attention by repeating his name, Ezra is accosted. In response to the latter's proper deference, Moses' mission was recalled, especially the fact of his extended sojourn with the Lord during which many wonderful things were revealed to him (cf. II Bar 59:3 f.) including the secrets of the times and their end. The main purpose of this rehearsal of history was to impress on Ezra that Moses had been commanded to make known certain revelations at once (the Torah) and at the same time keep others secret. The disclosures entrusted to Ezra in the preceding visions were of the latter type and he was told to keep them to himself; they were primarily for him and not for general information. Because he was one of God's elect, he, like the prophets, was admitted to the intimate council of the Lord. In any case the divine message pertained mostly to him.

The seer is told that he, like Moses (cf. II Bar 59:3 ff.), will be removed from the company of earthlings, not just to hear God's secrets but to remain in the company of his son[1] until the termination of times.[2] The author thinks of Ezra as belonging to the associates of the messiah, as the phrase "those like you" indicates,[3] who were giants of faith (cf. II Esd 6:26; 7:28; 13:52; 14:9). The impression created by vs. 10 is that the end is near. It is not too clear from vss. 11–12 that that impression is confirmed. The world-age is divided into twelve parts[4] of which nine and a half have already elapsed; only two parts remain. Note the relative nature of the calculation; five-sixths of time is over, one-sixth is still to come. But there is no indication as to just how long each part was in the past or will be in the future, though the implication is that the parts are of equal duration.

Following the observation that the times are approaching old age and the statement about the divisions of time, Ezra is instructed to prepare for his own position in the plan of the Lord. He is charged to set his house in order, to caution, console and teach, to renounce this corruptible life, extricate himself from earthly cares and burdens, and do everything possible to divest himself of human appurtenances so as to get out of these times posthaste. For, as apocalyptic writers in general thought, the world was getting worse by the minute; greater evils were on the way. By reason of age, and with its natural weakness, the world was susceptible to more numerous and more heinous evils.

[1] On the conception of the pre-existence of the messiah in II Esdras and II Bar see Volz, pp. 202 f.
[2] See Volz, p. 189, for a discussion of the theme.
[3] Cf. Bousset, pp. 232 f.
[4] Evidently the reckoning of time is based on the twelve-month scheme. The twelve scheme is followed elsewhere, e.g. II Bar 27; 53; I Enoch 90:17; Apoc Abraham 29 ("twelve hours").

That is why truth appeared to recede while falsehood and lies appeared more rampant. Reference to the eagle vision may be redactional but it nevertheless reinforces the writer's view that the fourth and last beast of Daniel (ch. 7) was about to make his appearance.

[Ezra's prayer for the spirit's help in reproducing the Scriptures and the Lord's response, 14:18–26] This passage marks the beginning of a narrative whose influence was felt for many centuries in both Jewish and Christian circles. Although it is enshrouded in legendary accretions it rests on the basic fact that the Ezra of the fifth–fourth centuries B.C. was responsible for editing and introducing the Pentateuch in its present form.[5]

The voice from the bush seemed to the seer to be concerned only with the present, and in view of the general impression of the visions the end of times was at hand so that there would be no extended future. But since two of the twelve parts of time still remained, Ezra inquired of the Lord who would instruct those yet to be born. The world is in darkness and its inhabitants are without light (the Torah). He could instruct those now living but future generations would remain without hope since the Torah had been burned and hence what the Lord had done or what he would yet do would remain unknown when the seer was taken away. For that reason he prayed for the Lord's holy spirit to chronicle the law (i.e. the history of Israel) as a guide for those whose desire it was to live in the last times (in the two parts still remaining). In response to his prayer, the Lord directed him to assemble the people and inform them not to look for him for forty days during which he was to equip himself with the necessary writing tablets, summon the five best scribes available and proceed to the place of revelation. He was told that he would be given inspiration to carry out his task and that it would not cease till the objective was accomplished. Afterward he must publish some of the works (the history of Israel) and deliver others (the secret books) to the wise men who could interpret and presumably release them at the proper time.

[Ezra's address to the people, 14:27–36] No time is lost by the seer in preparation for the duty laid upon him. The whole passage is based on the Moses prototype, especially as suggested by Deut 27 – 31.[6] The main points in the tradition are given: Israel's sojourn in Egypt, deliverance therefrom, the revelation of the divine way through the Torah which was observed neither by the fathers nor the generation to whom Ezra is represented as speaking. Despite deliverance, underscored by the gift of "the land . . . of Zion," the fathers and they persisted in iniquity and thus showed their contempt for the ways of the Most High.

A just judge, like the Lord, could not ignore those affronts. That is why he

---

[5] Cf. Neh 8–9 and *Ezra · Nehemiah,* AB, vol. 14, p. LXXIV. See also R. T. Herford, *Pirke Aboth,* 3d ed. (New York: Jewish Institute of Religion, 1945), pp. 19–22, and Moore, I, 8 ff. For the influence of the Ezra tradition on Jewish and Christian writers see H. E. Ryle, *The Canon of the Old Testament* (London: Macmillan, 1892), pp. 239–72. The Koran (9:30) accuses the Jews of saying "Ezra is the son of God." The basis for such an accusation is unclear. See note by George Sale, *The Koran* (Philadelphia: J. W. Moore, 1853), p. 152, and Simon Szyszman, "Esdras — Maître des Sadoqites," in *Proceedings of the Twenty-Seventh International Congress of Orientalists at Ann Arbor, Michigan* (Wiesbaden: Harrassowitz, 1971), pp. 152–54.
[6] Cf. Judith 5:6–19; Acts 7:2–53 where the same general ideas are voiced.

withdrew what he had given them. Their land, their dowry was in the hands of others now, while they are "in Babylon" and their brothers still farther away. Nevertheless, despite these tragedies of dislocation, the situation was not so hopeless as it appeared — especially for those who will take seriously the advice of Ezra. Although it may be too late for recovery in this world, there is hope in the world to come for those who control their passions and discipline their minds; they will be preserved while alive — amid the temptations of the world or, according to another interpretation, after death — and be granted mercy in the post mortem judgment. They may rest assured that judgment will come; it will bring the righteous to life again. Moreover the respective values of the just and the impious will be made apparent to all.

[Ezra's experience in the field, 14:37–44] Taking with him the five scribes, Ezra retired to the field where they remained until the task to which he had been summoned was complete. The portraiture of divine inspiration is unique.[7] A voice bade him open his mouth and drink — a cup full of liquid with firelike color. That was the writer's way of indicating the effect of the movement of the spirit upon the seer, conferring upon him the powers requisite for carrying out his commission. The gift of the spirit invested him with understanding, wisdom, and memory.[8] But the power of communication was shared also by the five scribes who were endowed with understanding so that they transcribed what was spoken by Ezra in characters they themselves did not understand. The forty-day period conforms to the Mosaic precedent (Exod 24:18; 34:28; Deut 9:9, 11, etc.), forty being a favorite figure in the Old Testament.[9] The ninety-four books produced included the canonical and apocryphal treatises.

[Command of the Most High, 14:45–47] When the forty days' work of transcribing the ninety-four books was finished, Ezra was commanded by the Most High to publish or make available the twenty-four books written first. Despite the seemingly greater importance attached to the remaining seventy by the apocalyptists, the characterization of the former as first — however that may be interpreted in the different versions — appears to give the canonical writings some kind of priority.[10] The theory was that these books were capable of being understood by all; in them the law given for the guidance of all Israel was revealed (cf. 14:30). The seventy other books were to be withheld from the general public and delivered only to the wise, for they alone could profit from them. The author's description of the significance of these books expresses the views of the school of apocalyptists.

[The response of Ezra and his translation, 14:48–51] The conclusion of our book, following Ezra's declaration of obedience to the divine command, was omitted from the Latin when chs. 15 and 16 were appended. Most of it is from another hand as the use of the third person indicates.[11]

---

[7] Cf. Bousset, p. 396, with references to other literature on inspiration.

[8] In contrast to this, "the wine of their intoxication" of the Deceiver and the Error in Odes of Solomon (38:13) makes the partakers "vomit up their wisdom and intelligence" and "deprives them of understanding."

[9] Baruch was directed to instruct the people for forty days (II Bar 76:4).

[10] Perhaps only priority in time is implied in view of the strong affirmation of vs. 47 (cf. Bousset, p. 154, n. 1.).

[11] See Apocalypse of Esdras, ch. 6.

III. SIXTH EZRA
(15:1 – 16:78)

The author is directed to speak and write down the words the Lord is putting
into his mouth

15 1 *a*Proclaim, now, *b*to my folk*b* the prophetic words which I am

about to put into your mouth, says the Lord, 2 and have [them]
preserved in writing because they are reliable and dependable. 3 Have
no fear of cogitations against you; do not let the incredulities of
opponents disturb you, 4 because every unbeliever will die in his unbelief*c*.

Evils to be brought on the whole world, God's people to be delivered again
from Egypt, and Egypt stricken

5 I am going to bring calamities upon the whole earth, says the
Lord — sword, famine, death and ruin — 6 inasmuch as wickedness
has engulfed the whole earth and their noxious works have reached
[their] consummation. 7 Therefore, says the Lord, 8 I will not remain
silent about their impieties which they carry on so wickedly, nor
tolerate them *d*in their evil deeds*d*. Verily, innocent *e*and just*e* blood
cries out to me and the souls of the just clamor incessantly. 9 Surely
I will vindicate them, says the Lord, and take to myself all the innocent blood from among them. 10 Look at my people being led to
the slaughter just like a flock; I will no longer permit them to live in
the land of Egypt*f*, 11 but I will lead them out with a powerful hand
and uplifted arm, and I will hit Egypt with plagues as [I did] earlier

Note: Because the textual differences in chs. 15 and 16 are not too important, only
the most significant variations are given. Where the meaning is substantially the same
the structural and morphological differences have been ignored. So also Latin syno-
nyms.
a Title of S is *Incipit liber quintus Ezrae.*
b–b C, M have *populi mei,* "my people"; S, A *plebi meae,* "my folk."
c C, M add *et omnis qui credit fide sua saluus erit,* "and everyone who believes will be
saved by his faith." Cf. Heb 2:4 which may be the basis for the addition.
d–d Omitted by A.   *e–e* Omitted by A.
f C adds *advenam,* "foreigners," "strangers."

and lay waste its whole land. 12 Let Egypt, together with its foundations, wail because of the plague[s] of chastisement and castigation which *the Lord* will bring upon [it]. 13 Let *the farmers who till the soil* wail because their seeds will fail [to germinate] *and their trees will be ravaged* by blight, hail, and a fearful constellation. 14 Woe to the world and those who inhabit it! 15 For the sword has come, and their doom; nation will rise to fight against* nation, with sword[s] in their hands. 16 Unrest will plague men; one group will overpower another, disregarding their king and the chief of their magnates *in their power*. 17 A man desiring to enter a city will be unable [to do so], 18 for, because of their arrogance, cities will be in disarray, homes destroyed, and men apprehensive. 19 A man will have no compassion for his neighbor when making *an assault* against their homes with the sword or despoiling their possessions *because of dearth of food and great tribulation*.

Oppressors of God's chosen ones and sinners among the latter will be subject to disaster by virtue of their sins

20 So, says God, I am summoning all the kings of the earth *to respect me* — * from *the sunrise and from the south*, *from the east and from Lebanon* — and to restore again what they have given to them. 21 Just as they have done continually to this very day to my elect, so I will do and I will return *payment to their purse*. The Lord God* says further: 22 My right hand will not spare sinners and *the sword* will not cease [pursuing] those who shed innocent

g–g C has *deus,* "God."
h–h C has *cultores terrae,* "farmers of the earth."
i–i Omitted by M.
j With A; others have *super,* "over," "against," which may reflect Heb. *'l.*
k–k C, M have *inpotentia sua,* "his [their] weakness."
l–l S, A, C have *ad irritum,* "to empty or dislodge," which Bensly thinks correct, through the conjecture *ad impetum,* "to assault," is printed.
m–m M omits.
n–n S has *ad me vendum,* "to come to me"; A, C, M have *ad movendum,* "to turn," "move," "stir."
o A, C, M add *qui sunt,* "who are."
p–p A has *ab orea et a notho,* "from the north and from the south." Both are Greek words.
q–q C has *ab euro et libie,* "from the east and west." Cf. Bensly, p. lxvii, who inclines toward C.
r–r Cf. Luke 6:38 (Vulgate) in *sinum vestrum,* "in your lap," "bosom," "purse"; see recent translations.
s So C, M; S, A have "God"; Gildas has "my Lord." [Gildas was a British church father whose *Epistola* is said to date from the middle of the sixth century. His texts of Sixth Ezra are quoted by Bensly, MF, pp. 36 ff.]
t–t C has *rumfea mea,* "my sword."

blood upon the earth. 23 Fire *has spurted forth* from his wrath and consumed the foundations of the earth and the sinners *have been burned* like straw. 24 Woe to those who sin and *do not observe* my commandments, says the Lord; 25 I will not spare them. Away with you, apostate* sons, do not defile my sanctuary. 26 Because* the Lord* knows all who sin* against him, therefore he has consigned them to death and slaughter. 27 For now *evils have come upon the whole earth and you will remain in them; God will not liberate you because* you have sinned against him.

A vision dreadful

28 Then — a vision dreadful, and its direction was from* the east! 29 Nations of Arab dragons* will come out in many chariots and from the day of departure *their buzzing* will be manifest throughout the earth so that all who hear them will be afraid and alarmed*. 30 The Carmonians, raving in anger, will come out *like wild boars* from the bush; they will approach in great strength to wage war against them and devastate a portion of the territory of Assyria with their teeth. 31 Afterward the dragons, remembering their origin, *will triumph*; should they turn around, conspiring by virtue of their great strength, to hunt them down, 32 they too will be confounded and silenced* by their strength, and turn their feet in flight*. 33 *In the territory of Assyria* *a highwayman* will lie in wait for them and

u–u With S, A and Gildas; C, M have *exiet,* "future."
v–v C has *incendentur* and M *accendentur;* S, A have *quasi stramen incensum,* "as burnt straw."
w–w S, A have *observant;* C, M have *custodiunt* (both have essentially the same meaning).
x With A and Gildas; S has *a potestate,* "without authority," obviously a mistake.
y Omitted by A and Gildas.
z So S, C, M; A and Gildas have *deus,* "God."
a Reading with M, *derelinquunt;* and S, *de[..]linquunt;* A and Gildas have *peccant,* with same meaning.
b C, M and Gildas add *multa,* "many."
c Reading with S, C, M; A has *propterea,* "therefore."
d C has *ad,* "toward."
e Omitted by C, M. M has *et arabunt in currus multos,* "and plow with many teams."
f–f S has *sic flatus eorum,* "so their snorting"; C has *et ibi planctus eorum,* "and there their lamentation."
g A adds *repetentur,* "be attacked anew"; C, M have *formident,* "be terrified."
h–h C, A omit.
i–i C, M have *convalescet,* "recover."
j C, M have *timebunt,* "will be apprehensive."
k C adds *et faciem suam ad aquilonem,* "and their face to the north."
l–l A has *et averterit orio assiriorum,* "and he will remove or turn away [from] the territory of Assyria."
m–m C, M have *obsessor,* "besieger."

kill one of them. Then fear and terror will seize their host and vacillation their kings.

The appearance of ominous storm clouds

34 Then — storm clouds from the east[n] and from the north to the south! Their appearance is exceedingly frightful, full of wrath and tempest. 35 They will slam one against another and hurl down a host of stars, including their own star, so that blood from the sword [o]will reach[o] to the belly of a horse, 36 the thigh of a man, and [p]the hock[p] of a camel. Great fear and trembling will take place over the earth 37 and those[q] who see that wrath will quake and trembling will seize them. Following this copious rainstorms will develop 38 from the south and north, with another [moving in] from the west. 39 Winds from the east will become strong and expose[r] it and the cloud he stirred up in [his] wrath, and the star [s]will be driven furiously[s] by the east wind to bring about destruction in [t]the south[t] and west. 40 Huge and powerful clouds, full of wrath, will be raised up, together with [u]the star[u], to [v]lay waste[v] the whole earth and those who live in it; they will pour out over [w]every valley and hill[w] a terrible star 41 [with] fire, hailstones, [x]flying swords[x], and torrents of water so that all the fields and brooks will be filled with the copiousness of those waters. 42 They will demolish cities and walls and mountains and hills and trees of the forests and [y]hay of the meadows[y], and [z]their grain[z]. 43 They will keep right on going as far as Babylon and lay her waste. 44 They will converge [a]upon her[a], surround her, and pour out upon her the star with all its fury so that the dust and smoke will rise to heaven, and all around her will bewail her[b]. 45 [c]Those who escape will serve those who have laid her waste.

[n] C adds *ab occidenti*, "from the west," supported by M *oriente et occidente*.
[o–o] A omits *erit*, "will be" and has *sanguinem*, "blood," in the accusative following *effundent*, "pour out," here rendered "hurl down."
[p–p] C, M have *poples*; A, S have *suffrago*, both with same meaning.
[q] C, M add *omnes*, "all."
[r] C, M have *repellent*, "hold back"; Bensly thinks *retrudent*, "thrust back," ought to be read in S, A for *recludent*, "reveal," "expose."
[s–s] *violabitur* (meaning is conjectural — see Bensly, p. lxxi).
[t–t] A, C, M have *natum*, "rising" — from the east.
[u–u] C, M have *calagnis* or *calignis*, "mist," "cloud," "darkness."
[v–v] C, M have *exterminent*, "exterminate, perhaps banish, drive off limits."
[w–w] C has *omne altum et excelsum*, "every depth and eminence"; M *omne monte altum et excelsu*, "every high and exalted mountain."
[x–x] M omits.   [y–y] C, M have *erbas camporum*, "grass of the fields."
[z–z] C, M have *tritticum ipsorum*, "their wheat."
[a–a] C, M have *in unum*, "together," "in one."
[b] C, M add *donec funditus eradicent illam*, "until they annihilate it utterly."
[c] C, M add *ceteri*, "others."

Asia has become like Babylon

46 You, O Asia, companion in the splendor of Babylon and her personal glory! 47 Woe to you, you scoundrel, because *d*you have emulated her*d*; *e*you have adorned your daughters with incest to delight and glory*e* *f*in your lovers who have always lusted after you*f*. 48 You have copied the odious whore in all her works and designs*g*. Therefore, God says: 49 I will send calamities upon you, widowhood, poverty, famine, sword and pestilence to destroy your houses, [to bring them] *h*to ruin and death*h*. 50 The glory of your manhood will wither like a blossom when the flame that is emitted will rise over you. 51 You will become weak and wretched through *i*blows, smitten with wounds*i*, unable to submit to your masters and lovers. 52 Would*j* I proceed against you so zealously, says the Lord, 53 if you had not always*k* murdered my chosen ones, exulting with applause and cheering*l* over their dead *m*when you were intoxicated*m*? 54 Beautify your face! 55 The hire of a harlot will be in your purse, hence you will receive your reward*n*. 56 Just as you will do to my chosen ones, says the Lord, so God will do to you and give you over to calamity. 57 Your children*o* will perish with hunger, you will fall by the sword, your cities will be leveled, and all your [people] will fall in the field with the sword; 58 those who are in the mountains will die of starvation, devour their own flesh and drink [their own] blood because of hunger for food and thirst for water. 59 Most unfortunate one! You will come and suffer still more adversities. 60 In passing by they will de-

---

d–d C has *qui similis facta es illius,* lit. "who you have been made like her."

e–e C, M have *ornando filias tuas ad questum ut placēas et sis gloriosa,* lit. "by adorning your daughters to coo as you please and be proud."

f–f C, M have *penes amatores tuos,* "in the house of your lovers," etc. S adds *fornicari,* "to commit harlotry" after *semper,* "always."

g A line appears to have dropped out of S, A by homoioteleuton but has been preserved by C, M as follows: *secuta es illa placitura potentibus et principibus eius et ut gloriosa fias et placeas in fornicationibus eius,* lit. "[in her designs] you have followed after that one about to gratify her magnates and chiefs that you may be made proud and be pleased in her harlotries."

h–h Omitted by C, M.

i–i C adds *flagellis,* "flagellations" and omits *et mastigata a vulneribus,* "and smitten with wounds."

j C adds *ergo,* "therefore," M has *ego,* "I," with S, A.

k S, A have *in omni tempore;* C, M *semper,* both with same meaning.

l S, A have *dicens;* C, M *deridens,* "scoffing."

m–m C, M have *ebria facta,* "made drunk."

n C, M add *in sinus tuos,* "in your purses."

o S, A have *nati;* C, M *filii,* with essentially the same meaning.

stroy the tranquil*p* city, devastate a portion of your land, *q*and remove part of your glory*q* when they return again from*r* overthrown Babylon. 61 You will be charred by them like *s*dry straw*s* and they will be to you as fire. 62 *t*They will consume*t* you and your cities, your land and your mountains, all your forests and fruit trees they will burn with fire. 63 *u*They will lead away your sons as captives, acquire your possessions as booty*u*, and damage your beautiful face.

Malediction against Babylon, Asia, Egypt, and Syria

16 1 Woe to you*v*, Babylon and Asia; woe to you*v*, Egypt and Syria! 2 Gird yourselves with sackcloth *w*and cloth of goats' hair*w*, bewail your sons and grieve over them, because your destruction is near. 3 The sword *x*has been unleashed*x* against you; who is there to turn it away? 4 Fire has been unleashed against you; who is there to extinguish it? 5 Calamities have been unleashed against you; who is there to hold them back? 6 *y*Can anyone ward off a hungry lion in the forest or extinguish a stubble-fire once it has started to burn? 7 *z*Can anyone deflect an arrow shot by a powerful bowman? 8 The Lord God sends calamities; who can hold them back? 9 Fire will go forth from his wrath; who is there to quench it? 10 He will flash forth lightning; who will not fear*a*? He will thunder; who will not tremble? 11 *b*The Lord*b* will threaten; who will not be utterly overcome by his presence? 12 The earth quakes to its very foundations, the sea rages to its depths, its waves are perplexed; so also are the fish by his presence and by the glory of his power. 13 *c*Because his right arm that draws the bow is powerful, his arrows which he discharges are sharp, and

p So S, M; A has *oditam;* C has *odiosam,* "hateful."

q–q S, M add *et partem glori[a]e tuae,* "and part of your glory [pride]," but omitted by C.

r S has *ad,* "to."   *s–s* With A; S, C, M have *stipula,* "stubble."

t–t With S, C, M; A has *omnes hii comed[e]unt,* "all these [will] consume."

u–u With S, C, M; A has *et natos tuos captivabunt et honestatem tuam spoliabunt,* "they will take captive your sons and despoil your virtue."

v C has *vobis,* "you" (plural); S, A, M have *tibi,* "you" (singular).

w–w Omitted by A, C.

x–x S, A have *inmissus est;* C, M have *missus est;* the former is a bit stronger but essentially both mean the same.

y M omits verse.

z Omitted by Gildas. In vss. 3–12 Gildas follows A as pointed out by Bensly, p. lxxiii.

a C adds *eum,* "it."   *b–b* Gildas has *deus,* "God."

c–c A has *quoniam fortis gloriae; qui tendit sagittam et acumen eius acutum quae dimisa est ab eo non deficiet missa super fines terrae,* "because of the power of glory; who shoots an arrow with sharpened point that discharged by him will not miss [when] sent over the ends of the earth." If it goes back to a Greek original, *dextra* (=*dexia,* "right hand") is not very different from *gloria* (=*doxa,* "glory").

they will not miss [the mark] when they are once shot to the ends of the earth*c*. 14 Now, calamities are sent out and will not turn back until they come upon the earth. 15 Fire will be kindled, and it will not be extinguished until it devastates *d*the foundations*d* of the earth. 16 In the same manner that an arrow discharged by *e*a strong*e* bowman does not return, so the calamities that will be sent upon the earth will not return. 17 Woe to me! Woe to me! Who will rescue me in those days?

The beginning of sorrows

18 The beginning of afflictions with *f*much lamentation*f*!
The beginning of famine when *g*many will die*g*!
The beginning of wars when powers will be apprehensive!
The beginning of misfortunes when all will tremble*h*!

19 *i*In these*i* [conditions] what will they do when misfortunes come? 20 Now *j*famine and calamity*j* and tribulation*k* *l*and distress are sent*l* as *m*lashes for correction*m*. 21 Despite*n* all these things they will not turn away from their iniquities; *o*and they do not always remember the lashes*o*. 22 Indeed produce will be *p*so cheap*p* on earth that they will consider themselves to be certain of peace; but then misfortunes *q*will germinate*q* on earth — sword, famine *r*and great confusion*r*. 23 *s*For many who live on earth will perish of starvation*s*, and the sword will destroy *t*the others*t* who survive starvation. 24 The dead will be cast off like dung with none to mourn them because the earth will be left desolate and its cities will be razed. 25 *u*No one*u* will be left to till the soil or sow it. 26 Trees *v*will bear fruit*v* but who

---

d–d A has *frumenta*, "grain."   *e–e* A omits.

f–f A has *copiosi suspirantium*, "an abundance of those sighing."

g–g A has *multi x disperient*, "many will perish."

h A adds *ab eis*, "because of them."   *i–i* A omits.

j–j A has *famis plaga*, "calamities of famine."

k A has *tribulato eius*, "its, or his, tribulation."

l–l A has *tanquam mastix*, "just as a whip or scourge."

m–m S, C, M have *flagella in emendatione*; A has *castigatio in disciplina*, "castigation for discipline."

n A has *super*, "above."

o–o A has *nec super plagas. memorantur sempiterna*, "nor above all plagues; they are always remembered."

p–p A has *brevi*, "short [in supply]"; and omits *sic*, "so."

q–q A has *superflorescent*, "blossom all over."   *r–r* A omits.

s–s A has *et aporient vitam super terram*, "and they will render life on earth uncertain."

t–t A has *quae*, "who" (feminine).

u–u A, C add *agricola*, "farmer."

v–v With S, *ligna dabunt fructus*. A has *fructiferabunt*, "will bear fruit"; C adds *suos*, "their."

will gather it? 27 Grapes *will ripen* but who will tread* them? In
[various] places there will be a great emptiness; 28 one person will
ardently long to see another person or to hear his voice. 29 But only
ten from a city will be left, and two from a field [and they are the
ones] who have hidden themselves in *dense thickets* and the
clefts of the rocks. 30 In the same manner as three or four olives are
left *on several trees* in an olive grove, 31 or as *[a few] bunches
[of grapes] are left* in a harvested vineyard by those who carefully
search out the vineyard, 32 so, in those days, three or four will be left
by those who search out their houses with the sword. 33 The earth
will be left empty, its fields *become brier patches*, and all its highways and byways will become overgrown with thorns so that even
sheep will no longer traverse them. 34 Young women will wail because they have no bridegrooms, women will wail because they have
no husbands, their daughters will wail because they have no support.
35 Their bridegrooms will be decimated by war and their husbands
will perish with famine.

Appeal to the servants of the Lord

36 But* hear these things and mark them well, O servants of the
Lord! 37 Here is the word of the Lord; welcome* it [and] do not
discredit* what the Lord says: 38 Indeed calamities *are approaching*
and *are not deferred*. 39 Just as *a woman* pregnant with her
child* in the ninth month*, when the hour of her delivery* approaches, two or three hours before that suffers* excruciating* pains
around her womb and the child comes forth out of the womb, it will

---

w–w A has *tradet se ad vindemiam,* "the grape will yield itself to vintage."
x A has *adligabit,* "bind" or "gather."
y–y A has *silva,* "woods."   *z–z* A omits.
a–a A has *et subremanet racemus patens,* "a bunch of grapes remains exposed."
b–b So with C, M; S** A** have *invertabunt,* "will be plowed up" or *invertaverunt,*
"have been plowed up."
c S, A have *vero;* C, M *igitur,* "then," "therefore."
d C, M *sumite,* "lay hold of" — a bit stronger than S, A *excipite,* "welcome."
e C, M emends thus: *a domino et molite increduli esse,* "from the Lord and do not
will to be unbelieving."
f–f C, M have *protinus venient,* "will come forthwith."
g–g C, M have active verb.
h–h So with C, M; omitted by S, A.
i With C, M; S, A have *filium,* "son."
j C, M add *in utero . . . habens,* "carrying in the womb."
k C, M add *ubi ceperit,* "when [it] shall have begun."
l With C, M, *patitur.*
m Omitted by C, M.

not be deferred for a minute, 40 so the calamities *n*will not delay [their]*n* coming upon the earth, so the world will writhe*o*, and pains *p*will accompany*p* it.

The word: prepare for the worst

41 Listen to the word, O my people; prepare yourselves for the combat *q*and in the [coming] calamities*q* you must be just like strangers*r* in the earth — 42 he who sells as one who escapes, and he who buys as one who will lose; 43 he who is engaged in trade as one who makes no profit, and he who builds as one who will not occupy [the building erected]; 44 he who sows as one who will not har-vest*s*, and so also he who prunes [the vine] as one who will not gather the grapes; 45 *t*those who marry as though they will be without sons, and those who do not marry as though they were widowed*t*. 46 For those who work, work without results, 47 since aliens will gather*u* their fruits, carry off their wealth, destroy [their] homes, and *v*take captive their sons*v*, *w*because they bring forth their children for captivity and famine*w*. 48 Those who carry on trade do so for gain; the more they decorate their cities, their homes, their possessions and their persons*x*, 49 so much the more *y*angry I will be with them*y* on account of [their] sins, says the Lord. 50 In like manner as *z*a reputable and very chaste woman despises a woman [who is] a harlot*z*, 51 justice will despise iniquity, when she decorates herself, and will accuse her to [her] face when he comes to vindicate him who scrutinizes every sin upon earth.

n–n C has *tardabitur,* "evil delayed"; M follows S, A.
o C, M have *parturit,* "will be in travail."
p–p C, M have *circumcingunt,* "surround."
q–q C, M have *ab[p]tate vos ad mala,* "get yourselves ready for calamities."
r C, M have *incole,* "sojourner."
s C has *secet,* "reap"; M follows S, A.
t–t C, M has *qui nubtias faciunt, quasi filios non habituri, et qui nubtias non faciunt, quasi viduitatem servaturi,* "those who are married as those not about to have children, and those who do not marry as those who are about to remain in widowhood."
u C, M have *manducabunt,* "eat."
v–v C has *filios ipsorum captivos ducent,* "they will lead away their sons as captives."
w–w C has *ideo sciant qui nubunt quoniam in captivate et fame filios generabunt,* "therefore those who are married may know since they will produce children in [for] captivity and famine."
x C has *faciem,* "face," "beauty"; M has plural.
y–y C, M has *zelabo illos zelo,* "I will be jealous of them with jealousy"; perhaps reflects a Hebrew construction "I will be very jealous of them."
z–z C, M have *zelot fornicaria mulierem idoneam et bonam valde,* "a prostitute is jealous of a reputable and very chaste woman."

Wickedness will be removed from the earth

52 Therefore do not desire to imitate her or her works[a], 53 for iniquity will presently be removed from the earth and justice will rule among us. 54 Let the sinner not say that he has not sinned[b] because he will burn coals of fire on the head of him who says: I have not sinned before God and his glory. 55 Surely the Lord[c] is aware of all the works of man — their machinations[d], their thought, and their minds. 56 [He] who said: [e]Let the earth be created, and it was created; let the heavens be created, and it was created[e]. 57 By his word the stars were fixed, and he knows the number [f]of the stars[f]. 58 [He] who explores the abyss and its treasuries and has taken the measure of the sea and [g]its contents[g]. 59 [He] who has confined [h]the sea[h] in [i]the midst of the waters[i] and by his word suspended the earth over the water. 60 [He] who stretched out the heaven like a vault and set it upon the waters. 61 [He] who has placed fountains of water in the desert and lakes on the mountain tops releasing rivers from the heights for the earth to drink. 62 [He] who has formed man, placed a heart in the center of his body, and invested him with breath, and life, and intelligence, 63 and the breath of God[j] Almighty who created all things and explores secrets in hidden places[k]. 64 Surely[l] he is aware of your machinations and what you think in your minds. Woe to sinners and those who want to conceal[m] their sins. 65 For that reason the Lord will thoroughly scrutinize their works and expose you all[n]. 66 You will be dumbfounded when your sins are unmasked before the public and [your] iniquities will stand as your accusers in that day. 67 What are you going to do? How will you conceal your sins before God and [o]his angels[o]? 68 Indeed God[p]

---

[a] C, M adds *neque malis cogitationibus eius,* "nor her evil designs."

[b] C adds *neque iniustus iniustitiam fecisse,* "nor the unjust done injustice."

[c] C, M add *deus,* "God."

[d] C, M add *malas,* "evil," and have a different order but same idea.

[e-e] C, M reverse the two clauses.

[f-f] C, M have *ipsarum,* "of them."

[g-g] C, M have *fundamenta,* "foundations."

[h-h] C, M have *seculum,* "world."

[i-i] C, M have *inter aquas et aquas,* "between the waters and the waters."

[j] C, M have *dominus,* "the Lord."

[k] C, M take *certe* from the following verse and read *certa,* "nameless," "fixed."

[l] C, M omit; see preceding note.

[m] S, A have *occultare,* "hide"; C, M *celare,* "hide."

[n] C, M add *in illa,* "in them."

[o-o] C, M have *gloria eius,* "his glory."   [p] C, M have *dominus,* "the Lord."

is judge; fear him. Have done with your sins, forget your iniquities, and never again engage in them; then God*q* will support you and free you from all tribulation*r*.

Subjection to indignities a test for the chosen

69 For indeed the flaming wrath of *s*a vast throng*s* is kindled over you*t* and they will drag some of you away and feed [you] *u*food sacrificed to idols*u*. 70 Those who give in to them they will hold in ridicule, in reproach, and in contempt. 71 *v*[From] place to place and in neighboring cities*v* there will be a great tumult against*w* those who revere the Lord*x*. 72 *y*They will be like maniacs, sparing no one, in despoiling and looting*z* those who still revere *a*the Lord*a*, 73 because they will loot *b*and despoil their*b* possessions and throw them out of their homes. 74 Then the testing of my chosen ones will be at hand*c* — like gold that is tested by fire.

The promise of the Lord

75 Listen, my chosen ones, says the Lord, the days of tribulation have arrived but I will deliver you from them. 76 Do not be afraid nor waver*d* since God*e* is your leader. 77 As for you, keep my commandments and precepts, says the Lord God*f*, let not your sins overwhelm you or your iniquities overcome [you]. 78 Woe [to those] who are shackled by their sins*g* and *h*covered up*h* by their iniquities*g* as a field *i*is so overrun*i* with bushes and its seed-bed*j* so overgrown with thorns that one cannot *k*get through*k* it. It is set aside and given over to be consumed by fire.

q C, M have *dominus*, "the Lord."   *r* C, M have *pressura*, "distress."
s–s C, M omit here and place in following clause: *et turbalunt vos multi populi*, "many people will throw you in disorder."
t C, M add *et disripient res vestras*, "and they will plunder your things."
u–u C, M have *et cibabunt vos de sacrificio*, "and they will feed you sacrificial [food]."
v–v C, M have [*in*] *locis per vicinas civatates*, "in places throughout nearby cities."
w S, A have *super*, "over"; C, M *supra*, "around."
x C, M have *deum*, "God."
y C, M add here *aporiati enim homines, a malis suis*, "for men [will be] unstable [and] because of their misfortunes."
z C, M have *exportandum*, "carry away."   *a–a* C, M have *deum*, "God."
b–b Omitted by C, M.
c C, M add *et tolerantia ipsorum*, "and their endurance."
d C, M have *formidetis*, "be terrified."   *e* C, M have *dominus*, "Lord."
f C, M omit.   *g–g* Omitted by M.
h–h C, M have *cooperiuntur*, "overwhelmed."   *i–i* C, M have *conclusus*, "confined."
j C, M have *semita*, "path."   *k–k* C, M have *transibit*, "has not traversed."

Notes

15:1. *Proclaim.* The person addressed is not named but is doubtless to be understood as Ezra.

my folk. I.e. the common, ordinary people.

the prophetic words. Chs. 15–16 imitate OT prophecies (cf. Rev 1:3; 22:18).

put into your mouth. Cf. Isa 51:16; Jer 1:9.

2. *preserved in writing.* Lit. "cause that they be written on paper (papyrus)"; frequently in OT. Cf. II John 12 *chartes,* "paper," as here (=*carta*); Jer 43:23 (LXX 36:23). For history of papyrus as writing material see David Diringer, *The Hand Produced Book* (London: Hutchinson, 1953), ch. IV.

reliable and dependable. Cf. Isa 30:8; Rev 21:5; 22:6; 1QH 11:7. Reliability and dependability of the prophetic words were accentuated by putting them in writing; they are valid and true despite the possible delay in fulfillment (cf. James Muilenburg, "Baruch the Scribe," in *Proclamation and Presence,* eds. J. I. Durham and J. R. Porter [London: SCM Press, 1970], pp. 226 f.). Cf. conception of Jer 31:33 where the Torah is to be written on the heart whence are the issues of life (Prov 4:23).

3. *cogitations.* Cf. Deut 31:21; Lam 3:60, 61 (Vulgate); Odes Sol 24:10; 25:3; 32:3; 1QH 2:35 f.; and on triumph over opposition, Ode Sol 28.

4. *every unbeliever . . . unbelief.* Cf. IV Macc 12:4; Num 20:12; Odes Sol 42:5a. For addition see textual note *e* and cf. Luke 7:50; 18:42; Eph 2:8; II Tim 3:15; I Peter 1:5.

5. *bring calamities upon the whole earth.* Lit. "bring evils upon the circle of the earth [or world]." First part of expression quite common in Jeremiah (e.g. 6:19; 11:11, 23; 29:15 ff., etc.) but rare elsewhere. The sweeping inclusion of "the whole earth" is typically apocalyptic; see Isa 13:11; 18:3; 24.

sword, famine . . . ruin. A cliché found, with some variation, in the prophets (cf. Isa 51:19; Jer 14:12; 21:9; 42:17; Ezek 16:21; Rev 6:8; Ps Sol 15:8; 4QpPs 37, 1:9; 4QpIs^b 2:1).

6. *wickedness has engulfed the whole earth.* Cf. Gen 6; I John 5:19.

reached [their] consummation. Lit. "have been filled up," i.e. they are ripe for judgment (cf. Gen 15:16; 1QM 14:7; 1QS 10:24).

8. *remain silent.* Cf. Ps 83:1; Isa 65:6 f.

tolerate them. Lit. "endure." Cf. 3:8, 30; II Bar 11:3; Pss Sol 2:1; 17:27, 29.

blood cries out. Cf. Gen 4:10; Job 16:18; Isa 26:21; Ezek 24:7b. See W. R. Smith, *The Religion of the Semites* (New York: Meridian Books, 1956), p. 417, n. 5, for further observations on unavenged blood. Innocent blood is often referred to in OT.

souls of the just. Wisd Sol 3:1; CD 1:20.

9. *vindicate.* Lit. "avenge." Cf. Hosea 1:4; I Macc 9:42 (where the Maccabees Jonathan and Simon avenge the blood of their brother John); Deut 32:43.

take to myself all the innocent blood. Since blood meant life, the passage means the divine acceptance of the lives of those who were guiltless.

10. *slaughter just like a flock.* Cf. Isa 53:7; Jer 51:40; Ps 44:22, Acts 8:32.

11. *a powerful hand and uplifted arm.* Cf. Deut 26:8. Figure used in Jer 21:5.

Egypt with plagues. Doubtless a reference to the plagues described in Exod 7 ff., threatened in a new situation. Riessler ([BIBLIO II], p. 1286) thinks of the Jewish persecution by Ptolemy XIII (Auletes) after his restoration with the help of Gabinus in 55 B.C. Others think of the terrible hardships experienced by the Jews in Alexandria, as related by Eusebius *Church History* 7:21, 22, in the period of Gallienus (A.D. 260–268). Some event of oppression is in the mind of the writer but it may very well be simply subsumed under the well-known historical Egyptian sojourn and may actually have taken place elsewhere in the world (but see vs. 11). Hilgenfeld, p. 208, points to the Christian persecution in Egypt referred to by Eusebius.

12. *Let Egypt . . . wail.* As it did when the firstborn were slain (Exod 12:30); Wisd Sol 18:10; 19:3; Sib Or 5:507 ff.; I Enoch 89:20.

plague[s] of chastisement and castigation. Cf. Wisd Sol 19:13 ff.; Sib Or 3:314–18, 348; for plagues in Revelation see H. P. Müller, "Die Plagen des Apokalypse" in ZNW 51 (1960), 268–78.

13. *seeds will fail.* Cf. Joel 1:17; there was widespread famine in Asia Minor in A.D. 93. Cf. Rev 6:6; M. I. Rostovtzeff, *The Social and Economic History of the Roman Empire,* 2d ed. (Oxford: Clarendon Press, 1957); II, 599 f.

trees . . . blight, hail. Cf. Ps 105:33; Joel 1:7, 19; Hag 2:17; reminiscent of the hail and locust plague visited against the Pharaoh (Exod 9:22 – 10:11).

fearful constellation. Perhaps a comet. Cf. Sib Or 3:334–36; Rev 8:10 f.

14. *Woe to the world.* Cf. Rev 8:13; 12:12. Riessler (p. 1286) suggests the disturbances following the death of Julius Caesar in 44 B.C. Cf. I Enoch 99:4.

15. *the sword.* Often referred to in OT as the weapon of destruction. Cf. Ps Sol 3:13.

nation . . . against nation. A common expression in apocalyptic literature (cf. Matt 24:7; Mark 13:8; Luke 21:10; Isa 19:2; Zech 14:13).

16. *Unrest.* I.e. instability, wavering.

one group will overpower. A time of utmost confusion, party strife.

disregarding their king. Cf. 1QpHab 4:2–3, 5–6.

17. Cf. Eccles 10:15 (but here the situation is different); and Ps 107:4. These prognostications are free and general observations imitating such materials as those found in Isa 22; 24:10, 12; Jer 4:29; 14:18.

18. *men apprehensive.* Cf. Luke 21:26; Ps Sol 13:5.

20. *all the kings of the earth to respect me.* Cf. 1QM 12:14; 19:6.

from the sunrise. Difficult; see textual note *p-p* and reference there, and vs. 34 below.

restore. Lit. "to turn and to restore." Cf Zech 14:14. Appeal to the rulers of the earth to give up what they have wrongfully acquired.

21. *as they have done . . . so I will do.* Cf. Judg 15:10, 11; Deut 19:19 — a kind of *lex talionis.*

payment to their purse. When *sinus* is used of a person it refers to bosom, so lit. "I will give back to their bosom" (cf. Ps 79:12; Isa 65:6; Jer 32:18; Luke 6:38; I Enoch 100:7).

22. *spare.* Cf. Jer 13:14; II Peter 2:4 ff.

shed innocent blood. Cf. law against shedding innocent blood in Deut 19:10; the phrase occurs often in OT; cf. Jub 6:7–13; 7:28–33; I Enoch 9:1; 99:6.

23. *Fire . . . from his wrath.* Cf. 16:9; Deut 32:22; 1QM 14:1; Matt 3:7.

consumed the foundations. Cf. 1QH 3:27 ff.; Sir 10:16; 1QpHab 10:13 ff. for whole passage; Test Zebulon 10:3; Sib Or 5:418.

burned like straw. Cf. Exod 15:7; Isa 5:24; Joel 2:5; Nahum 1:10; Matt 3:12.

24. *Woe to those who sin.* Cf. Isa 3:11; Micah 2:1.

25. *apostate sons.* Lit. "sons of apostasy [or wickedness]." Cf. Isa 1:2; Ezek 20:21.

defile my sanctuary. Cf. Lev 20:3; Ps 79:1; Lam 1:10; Ezek 5:11; 23:38; I Macc 1:21, 37; 1QpH 12:9; CD 4:18; 5:6; 20:23.

26. *the Lord knows . . . sin.* Cf. Amos 5:12.

death and slaughter. Cf. Pss Sol 3:13; 13:10; 15:11, 13, 14; 17:27 f.

27. *evils . . . upon the whole earth.* For expression cf. Judith 2:2.

remain in them. In the evils upon the earth.

28. *vision dreadful.* Cf. Hosea 6:10; Jer 23:14; I Enoch 21:2, 7.

direction . . . the east. Reference is probably to the Syrian wars of the late third century A.D.

29. *Arab dragons.* The figure may reflect Num 21:6; Isa 30:6. The nations of Arab dragons stand for a loose confederation of peoples operating in the North Arabian desert with its center around Palmyra, but as serpentine symbolism in the Arab world was widespread more may be involved. See Glueck, *Deities and Dolphins,* pp. 353–56, 479–85 and plates 140–42, 152 a, b. At Petra has been found the figure of a serpent sliding up over a horse and striking its rider (R. Brünnow and A. von Domaszewski, *Die Provinca Arabia,* I (Strasbourg, 1904), 180 and fig. 207.

buzzing. Cf. LXX of Jer 46:22 where Egypt is said to make a noise like a hissing serpent (cf. Herodotus 2:75); and Sanhedrin 97b (Baylonian Talmud).

30. *Carmonians.* The Carmonians were the Sassanians under Shapur I, named after the southern province, Kirman of the Parthian empire, next to the Iranian plateau. Cf. Herodotus 1:125.

wild boars. Cf. Ps 80:13; cf. James, *Apocrypha Anecdota,* 2d ser. [BIBLIO II], p. 55. Refers elsewhere to Edomites (I Enoch 89:12, 42–49, 66) and Samaritans (I Enoch 89:72). For illustrations of wild boars see *Encyclopedia of World Art,* VII (1963), plate 212; Richter, *The Sculpture and Sculptors of the Greeks,* pp. 113, 457. See now the Miletus relief in M. A. Beek, *Atlas of Mesopotamia* (London: Nelson, 1962), p. 88, fig. 170; the gold figurine of a wild boar from a tomb near Ordzhonikidze in the Dnepropetvosk region of southern Russia dating from fourth–third centuries B.C., in *The Illustrated London News,* July 1972, p. 51; and the hunting scene in the Dumbarton Oaks Collection tapestry in K. Wessel, *Koptische Kunst* (Recklinghausen: Bongers, 1963), fig. 133, p. 240, which dates from the age of Herakleios (A.D. 610–641).

Assyria. Syria.

31. *their origin.* Lit. "their nature."

32. The addition in C (see textual note *k*) may come from Dan 11:17–19.

34. The addition in C (see textual note *n*) may well be right in view of the upheaval in the middle of the third century A.D.

storm clouds. The hordes of invaders, perhaps Goths (Riessler).

35. *hurl down.* Lit. "pour out."

stars . . . star. Perhaps *sidus,* "star," ought to be rendered "storm," so that the translation would read "pour out a host of storms, including their own storm." So both Riessler and H. Weinel in *Neutestamentliche Apocryphen,* ed. Hennecke. But see Oesterley's interpretation (in loco) which takes *their own star* to mean "one of the military leaders" (cf. Sib Or 3:334).

blood . . . to the belly of a horse. Cf. I Enoch 100:3; Rev 14:20.

38. *another.* Lit. "another part."

39. Rendition is somewhat conjectural.

40. *lay waste the whole earth.* Apocalyptic announcement of the end of the world which was thought to be preceded by great turmoil and confusion.

every valley and hill. Both Riessler and Weinel render "high and exalted ones"; Oesterley has a similar interpretation. Our version reflects the storm and flood image.

41. *flying swords.* Sib Or 3:673; Lactantius (*Divine Institutes* 7:19) mentions a sword falling from heaven as the beginning of bloody vengeance. Here there is a combination of storm and the unleashing of armies. For a rain of flaming fire see Sib Or 5:274, 377 f. and vss. 61, 62 below.

43. *Babylon.* I.e. Rome. Riessler thinks the original prophecy was occasioned by the Arab attack on Herod the Great with its subsequent bloodbath (cf. Jos. *Antiq.* 15:5:1–4).

44. *the star.* If Riessler is right, the star could originally have referred to Herod, but this is by no means certain. May reflect knowledge of and veiled reference to the ill-fated Bar-Cochba movement, A.D. 132–135.

dust and smoke. Cf. Rev 18:9; 4QpPs 37, 3a:8.

45. *Those who escape.* Lit. "those who remain over, after the conflict." Observe that the Arabs did precisely that, according to Josephus (*Antiq.* 15:5:5).

46. *Asia.* May refer to Odenathus and his court.

companion in. I.e. partaker of the splendor and glory of Rome with the idea of replacing her in the east.

splendor . . . glory. Cf. Isa 13:19; Rev 17:4 f.; Dan 4:30.

47. For characterization of Rome here cf. Rev 14:8; 17:4, 5; 18:2, 3.

emulated her. Cf. Rev 17:2.

48. *odious whore.* Cf. Rev 17:16.

49. *widowhood.* Cf. Isa 47:9 for loss of children and widowhood announced for Babylon.

famine, sword and pestilence. Often in predictions of the prophets (cf. Isa 51:19; Jer 11:22; Ezek 6:11; 7:15).

50. *wither like a blossom.* For figure see Isa 28:1, 4; 40:6–8.

53. *my chosen ones.* Probably refers to Jews, not Christians (cf. I Enoch 45:3–5; 49:2, 4; etc.).

with applause. Lit. "exulting by clapping of hands."

intoxicated. Cf. Rev 17:2; III Bar 4:17.

54. *Beautify.* Lit. "decorate or adorn the beauty of your face."

55. *hire of a harlot.* For expression see Deut. 23:18; Micah 1:7.

57. Vss. 57–59 found in a Greek papyrus of fourth century from Egypt (see Hunt, *Oxyrhynchus Papryi*, Part VII, no. 1010, pp. 11–15).

hunger . . . sword. Cf. CD 3:9 f.

58. *devour their own flesh.* Cf. Jer 19:9.

drink . . . blood. Cf. Rev 16:6.

hunger for food . . . water. Cf. Amos 8:11; a mark of divine favor, concomitant of salvation was an abundance of food and water (cf. Isa 49:10; Rev 7:16).

59. *Most unfortunate one!* Lit. "unhappy in the highest (degree)," cf. Rev 3:17.

63. *your beautiful face.* Lit. "the beauty of your face."

16:1. *Babylon and Asia . . . Egypt and Syria.* The whole extent of the Roman empire.

2. *sackcloth and cloth of goats' hair.* A sign of mourning (cf. II Sam 3:31; Amos 8:10; Isa 50:3; Jer 4:8; Rev 6:12).

your destruction. Cf. Ezek 7:5 ff.

3. *sword . . . unleashed.* Cf. Ezek 21:8 ff.; 1QM 15:3; 16:1; 19:4, 11. On form see I Enoch 97:3.

4. *Fire.* A figure occurring frequently in the prophetic literature (cf. Jer 11:16; 15:14; Ezek 20:47; Hosea 8:14; etc.).

5. *Calamities.* Lit. "evils"; also a common prophetic expression (cf. Isa 47:11; Jer 2:3; 25:32; 45:5; Micah 1:12; etc.).

6. *lion in the forest.* Cf. Jer 4:7; 5:6; 50:44; Amos 3:4; Micah 5:8.

stubble-fire. Cf. Isa 5:24; 47:14; Joel 2:5; Nahum 1:10.

7. *arrow . . . bowman?* Cf. Ps 127:4; 1QH 6:30; 2:26; Jer 50:9.

8. *The Lord God sends calamities.* Cf. Amos 3:6; Isa 45:7; Jer 4:6; 6:19; 19:2 f., 51; etc.

9. *Fire . . . from his wrath.* Cf. Ps 89:46; Jer 4:4; 15:4; 17:4; Ezek 38:19; 1QM 14:1.

10. *lightning.* II Sam 22:15; Pss 18:14; 77:18; 144:6; UT, 51:v:70.

thunder. A fairly common figure in the OT as the voice, *qwl,* of God; also frequent in Ugaritic literature, associated with the storm-god Baal. Cf. also 1QH 1:12; 3:35; I Enoch 59; 69:23.

12. *The earth quakes . . . foundations.* Cf. II Sam 22:8; Ps 18:7; Isa 24:18.
sea rages. Cf. Ps 89:9; Jude 13.
also are the fish. Cf. Ezek 38:20.
the glory of his power. Cf. Isa 2:10, 19, 21; 1QH 15:20, 21; Hab 2:14.
13. *right arm . . . is powerful.* Exod 15:6.
draws the bow. See NOTE on vs. 7 above.
arrows . . . sharp. Ps 120:4; Isa 5:28.
are once shot. Lit. "begin to be shot."
14. *calamities . . . will not turn back until . . . earth.* Cf. Jer 30:24; and inscription on pursuit trumpets in 1QM 3:9; 11:10–11, "his wrath will not turn back until they [sons of darkness] are destroyed."
15. *Fire . . . devastates the foundations of the earth.* Cf. 1QH 3:29–31.
17. *Woe to me!* Cf. Job 10:15; Micah 7:1.
Who will rescue me. Cf. Rom 7:24.
18. *The beginning of afflictions.* Cf. Matt 24:8; Mark 13:8.
19. *what will they do . . . come?* On form see I Enoch 97:3; cf. vs. 3.
20. *lashes for correction.* Cf. Hab 1:12; Heb 12:6; Prov 3:11, 12. A common prophetic conception.
21. *they will not turn.* Cf. Isa 9:13; Jer 2:30a; Amos 4:9; Hag 2:17.
22. *so cheap.* Cf. II Kings 7:1, 16, 18.
certain of peace. Cf. I Enoch 94:6; 96:4–6; just when they think they are secure by virtue of abundance, ruin will come (see Luke 12:16–21).
24. *cast off like dung.* Cf. Jer 8:2; 9:22; 16:4; 25:33.
25. Cf. II Bar 10:9 ff.; Gen 2:5.
26. *Trees will bear fruit.* Cf. Lev 26:4, 20. See II Bar 21:14 for form.
gather. vindemiabit, used of gathering grapes.
27. Cf. II Bar 10:10.
great emptiness. Cf. Isa 6:12.
29. *ten from a city.* Cf. Amos 5:3; Isa 6:11 ff.
two from a field. Cf. Matt 24:40 f.; Jer 3:14, "two from a family."
clefts of the rocks. Cf. Isa 2:21.
30. *three or four olives.* Cf. Isa 24:13. Note the form of "three or four" here and in vs. 32; also Amos 1 and Ugarit.
31. *bunches [of grapes].* Cf. Isa 17:6; Obad 5; I Enoch 32:4; Micah 7:1, no cluster left; Rev 14:18; Jer 49:9.
33. *earth . . . left empty.* The idea, in more limited scope, is common in the prophets (cf. Isa 6:11; Jer 25:38; Ezek 14:15 f.).
brier . . . thorns. A favorite combination of Isaiah (5:6; 7:23 f.; 9:18; etc.).
highways. Cf. Isa 33:8.
34. *Young women will wail . . . bridegrooms.* Cf. Ps 78:63; Jer 7:34; Rev 18:23.
36. *mark them well.* Lit. "know or understand them."
37. *do not discredit.* No exact parallel expression but cf. John 20:27.
39. *a woman pregnant . . . child.* For figure see Jer 4:31; 13:21; etc.; Isa 13:8; 21:3; 26:17; I Enoch 62:4; I Thess 5:3; Rev 12:2; 1QH 3:7, 8, "like a woman bearing her firstborn child, when her birth pangs come suddenly

[upon her] and with excruciating pain upon her birthstool [she] agonizingly expels the foetus from the furnace [pudenda]"; cf. also 3:10 f.; 9:7.

40. *accompany it.* Lit. "hold it in all around"; perhaps C, M are more meaningful here.

41. *prepare yourselves for the combat.* Latin is *pugnam* which appears to have a more general meaning here; cf. C, M which have *bellum,* "war" or "battle."

strangers in the earth. Cf. Ps 119:19; Heb 11:13; I Peter 2:11.

42. *he who sells.* Cf. Sir 37:11; Isa 24:2.

who will lose. Cf. Philip 3:7.

43. *engaged in trade.* Cf. Ezek 27:9; I Cor 7:30 f.

makes no profit. On merchandise figure see James 4:13; for opposite, i.e. to trade with profit, see Ezekiel's oracle against Tyre (ch. 28).

builds . . . not occupy. Cf. Zeph 1:13.

44. *sows . . . not harvest.* Cf. Micah 6:15; Deut 28:38; Hag 1:6.

prunes . . . not gather the grapes. Cf. Deut 28:39; Micah 6:15.

45. *those who marry.* Cf. I Cor 7:25–29, 32–34 for reminiscences of expressions here.

without sons. Cf. Ps 109:9; Jer 18:21.

widowed. Cf. Ezek 22:25.

46. *without results.* Lit. "without good reason." Cf. Jer 51:58.

47. *carry off their wealth.* Cf. Obad 11; Lam 5:2.

destroy [their] homes. Cf. Ezek 26:12; Zeph 1:13.

48. *do so.* Lit. "carry on trade."

gain. Lit. "plunder" or "booty."

52. *her or her works.* Refers to iniquity personified. For expression cf. Rev 18:4 ff.

53. *iniquity . . . removed.* Cf. Zech 3:9; Test Levi 18:9.

justice will rule. No exact parallel but cf. Isa 42:4; II Peter 3:13.

54. *sinner not say.* Cf. 3:35; 7:46, 48; I John 1:8; Jer 2:35; Prov 30:20.

coals of fire on the head. Cf. Prov 25:22; Rom 12:20.

55. *aware of all the works of man.* Cf. Isa 66:18; Rev 2:2 and often elsewhere; Sir 15:19; 39:19.

their thought. Ps 93:11; 139:1–3.

their minds. Lit. "their hearts." Cf. Ps 44:21; Luke 16:15; I Sam 16:7.

56. *earth be created.* Play on creation by the word. Cf. Isa 45:12; Ps 148:5.

57. *stars were fixed.* Cf. Jer 31:35; 1QH 1:12; I Bar 3:34.

number of the stars. Cf. Ps 147:4.

58. *explores the abyss.* Cf. Sir 16:18; 42:18.

its treasuries. Cf. 6:40; 7:77; 8:54; Ps 33:7.

59. *confined the sea.* Cf. Job 38:8; Prayer of Manasseh 4.

suspended the earth. Cf. Job 26:7; I Enoch 69:17; Ps 136:6.

60. *stretched out the heaven like a vault.* Isa 40:22 (LXX); Hebrew "curtain"; Job 9:8; quoted in *Apostolic Constitutions* 8:12; the expression "stretch out the heavens" occurs a number of times in Isaiah, Jeremiah, and Zechariah.

set it upon the waters. Cf. Ps 24:2.

61. *fountains of water in the desert.* Cf. Ps 107:35; Isa 35:6 f.; 43:19 f.; 48:21; 1QH 8:4.

lakes on the mountain tops. Cf. Isa 41:18; Ps Sol 17:21.

62. *breath, and life.* Cf. Wisd Sol 15:11.

63. *explores secrets.* Cf. Jer 23:24; Amos 9:2; Dan 2:47; Ps 139; Prov 15:11; 1QH 1:25.

64. *aware of your machinations.* Cf. Job 21:27; Ps 94:11; Isa 66:18; I Cor 3:20; Sir 42:20; Wisd Sol 1:6 ff.

think in your minds. Lit. "in your hearts." Cf. Esther 6:6; Prov 23:7.

66. *sins are unmasked.* Cf. Hosea 7:1; Lam 2:14; Isa 59:12; Job 20:27; Ps Sol 8:8; II Bar 83:3; Luke 12:2; I Cor 4:5; Heb 4:12 f.; 4QpNahum 3:3.

before the public. Lit. "before men."

iniquities . . . your accusers. Cf. Num 32:23; Jer 2:19.

67. *conceal your sins.* Cf. Ps 69:5; Jer 16:17; Ezek 8:16 ff.

68. *God is judge.* Cf. Pss 50:6; 75:7; Heb 12:23; II Macc 12:6; II Bar 5:3; 48:39.

Have done with your sins. Cf. Isa 1:16. Sounds like the Hindu injunction "Be done with self . . . cast off worldly desire in mind and body."

free you from all tribulation. Cf. 1QS 11:13; 4QDibHam 2:14.

69. *wrath . . . kindled.* Cf. Ps 124:3; Sir 16:6; Ps Sol 2:25–28.

drag . . . away. Cf. Dan 11:18; I Bar 4:26.

food sacrificed to idols. Cf. Acts 15:20; 21:25; I Cor 8:1 ff.; 10:19; Rev 2:14, 20; II Macc 6:7; IV Macc 5:2.

70. *ridicule . . . contempt.* Cf. I Bar 3:8; Neh 5:9; Ps 79:10 ff. Those who are weak-spirited give in but are then laughed at, reproached, and held in contempt by those who beguiled them.

contempt. Lit. "trampled upon." Cf. Dan 8:13; 1QH 6:32; Isa 63:18; Rev 11:2.

71. *place to place.* Lit. "place to places." Because of variant in C, M and rather awkward expression in S, A it is difficult to arrive at the exact meaning of the expression. There may be more than meets the eye because of the rabbinical interpretation of *mqwm*, "place," as the place of the Deity.

COMMENT

[The author is directed to speak and write down the words the Lord is putting into his mouth, 15:1–4] The discourse recorded in this chapter is couched in the form of a prophetic summons, presumably to Ezra, to proclaim the prophecies (predictions) about to be put into his mouth. They are to be delivered at once but are meant for times other than the present for the prophet is commanded to write them down.[1] Because writing was regarded so highly and as so significant in certain areas of the ancient world, and the prophetic words were of such singular importance, it was of special value to commit them to permanent material to ensure their preservation

[1] Cf. Jer 30:2; 36:2 ff.; Hab 2:2; Rev 1:11, 19. Cf. David Diringer, *The Alphabet* (New York: Philosophical Library, 1948), p. 17.

for future generations or for the times for which they were intended. No adverse plans of enemies or unbeliefs of opponents must be allowed to deter the prophet-writer. Unbelievers will perish in their unbelief but the words of the prophet will remain because they are reliable and dependable.

[Evils to be brought on the whole world, God's people to be delivered again from Egypt, and Egypt stricken, 15:5–19] The universal perspective of the seer is noteworthy. The Lord informs him that he is about to bring judgment upon the whole earth because of its wickedness.[2] The world's perpetration of evil has reached its fullness, its cup is running over. Hence he has resolved to act because of the involvement of his people. There is no castigation of Israel, only of her oppressors whose shameful deeds brought pitiful cries of anguish from the innocent and unjust sufferers. If the piece is late and of Christian origin one can think of the persecutions which Christians endured at the hands of their enemies; if it is Jewish the author could have had in mind any one of a number of periods. The reference to Egypt as a surrogate for the oppressor suggests the latter origin. Here, it is interesting to observe, Egypt has replaced Babylon, though the latter reappears in vs. 43. The prophet's statement — the whole earth, the world — seems to indicate that Rome was the real villain. The upheaval visualized reflects a period of confusion and near anarchy such as sometimes ensues in the wake of a weak rule or a change of dynasty.

[Oppressors of God's chosen ones and sinners among the latter will be subject to disaster by virtue of their sins, 15:20–27] The viewpoint reflected in the preceding passage is regnant here too. Both the enemies of God's people — their oppressors and the sinful people themselves — come under judgment. The Lord appeals to the kings of the earth to acknowledge him and restore to the rightful owners what they have taken from them. Since there is no response and they keep right on doing what they have always done, they are promised their reward. As they have done, so it shall be done to them. Here is a distinctly sub-Christian outlook, at least from the standpoint of reprisal for evil (but cf. Matt 7:2b); the eye for eye, tooth for tooth principle is clearly evident as may be seen from vss. 22, 23. Yet the criterion for divine judgment is the same for all sinners — the commandments of the Lord. Apostate sons[3] are placed in the same category as recalcitrant kings, for the Lord knows all who sin against him. Because of their apostasy, the chosen people are participants in the evils that have become world-wide and they cannot expect special treatment. They will not be liberated because they too have sinned against the Lord.

[A vision dreadful, 15:28–33] After the cryptic manner of apocalyptic, the writer gives us a glimpse of the history of his time. He may well have reworked an older story, as Riessler suggests,[4] to make it applicable to his time

---

[2] The whole passage echoes the thought of Ascelepius III, 24b ff., of the Hermetic corpus (cf. Walter Scott, *Hermetica*, I [Oxford: Clarendon Press, 1924], 341 ff.).

[3] Riessler (pp. 1286 f.) thinks of Hyrcanus and his cohort Antipater whom the Jews opposed strenuously (see Jos. *Antiq.* 14:8:4; 14:9:3).

[4] Riessler, p. 1287. The high priest, Karder, boasts of the victorious sweep of Shapur I over Aneran (not Iran) in an inscription found at Naqš-i-Rustam (*Archaeologische Mitteilungen aus Iran*, N.S. 3 [Berlin: Reimer, 1970], 261).

and purpose. In that case, the redacted story can be explained on the basis of political events transpiring in the reign of Shapur I (A.D. 240–273). About A.D. 259, after fifteen years of relative peace, war between the Sassanian king and Rome broke out once more. A number of Syrian cities were taken by Shapur, among them Antioch. A year later he defeated the Romans near Edessa, and captured the emperor Valerian and seventy thousand of his troops.⁵ Shapur took advantage of his triumph and, in a campaign to the west, devastated Syria and Cappadocia. But during the return, he was assaulted and battered by the Palmyrene prince⁶ Odenathus, the husband of the famous Zenobia. Odenathus was, in all probability, of Arab descent (cf. the name Udhaynah, "little eared"), and his army was composed of Syrian and Arab tribesmen. As Odenathus' move was a bold attempt to liberate Valerian, he was regarded as a friend of Rome whose empire was now in a precarious state in both east and west. Because of his virtuous, if abortive, action, the emperor, Valerian's son and successor, Gallienus (260–268), recognizing realities, gave Odenathus the status of *dux Orientis* in A.D. 262, i.e. emperor of the eastern provinces of the empire.⁷ He disappeared under mysterious circumstances in A.D. 267.⁸

Looking at the passage in the light of historical events, it would run somewhat like this. The Carmonians (Sassanians, or the Persians under Shapur I) came from the east. They rushed like wild boars from the bush and attacked the imperial forces (Romans under Valerian) in force. They then waged war against the cities of Syria, devastating a considerable portion of them. On their way back, they were intercepted by the Arab dragons (Odenathus with his Syrian and Arab tribesmen), buzzing out of the desert, and pursued to the very gates of their capital. The dragons will thus overcome the boars, i.e. triumph or prevail. Should they (the Persians) turn, relying on their great strength, to hunt them (Odenathus and his hordes) down, they (the Persians) will be confounded and silenced by their (Odenathus and his tribesmen) strength and turn (the Persians) in flight. Verse 33 probably refers, in part, to the mysterious murder of Odenathus. The last part of the verse might reflect the situation brought about by Aurelian's conquest of Zenobia's empire,⁹ the vacillation referring to the failure of her allies and other enemies

⁵ For representation on monuments see J. Gagé, "Comment Sapur a-t-il 'triomphé' de Valerian?" *Syria* 42 (1965), 343–88; and H. von Gall, "Die Mosaiken von Bishapur," *Archaeologische Mitteilungen aus Iran*, N.F. 4 (1971), 193–205 and plates.
⁶ Roman Ghirshman, *Iran* (Baltimore: Penguin Books, 1954), pp. 292–94; CAH, XII, *infra*, pp. 169–80.
⁷ See the Palmyrene Inscription published by G. A. Cooke, *North Semitic Inscriptions* (Oxford: Clarendon Press, 1903), no. 130, pp. 290 f., where he is referred to as *mlk mlk'*, "king of kings." But observe Cooke's discussion. For position and wealth of Palmyra see Michalowski and Dziewanowski, *Palmyra*.
⁸ Cf. Edward Gibbon, *The Decline and Fall of the Roman Empire*, Everyman Library reprint (New York: Dutton, 1925), I, 294 f.; CAH, XII, 176.
⁹ Gibbon, *Decline and Fall*, I, 296 ff. It could equally well reflect the uncertainties created by the general imperial instability; as M. I. Rostovtzeff (*A History of the Ancient World*, II, *Rome* [Oxford: Clarendon Press, 1928], 309) has noted "between A.D. 235 and 285 there were twenty-six Roman emperors; and only one of them died a natural death." Or perhaps the Gothic invasions.

of Rome to come to her rescue out of fear born of Aurelian's earlier suc-
cesses in the west and elsewhere.

[The appearance of ominous storm clouds, 15:34–45] If the foregoing
situation is the one that gave rise to the prophecy-apocalypse, this passage
would represent a continuation. The political situation is described in terms
of a series of storms breaking over the world that are harbingers of the end
of the world (vs. 40). This becomes even clearer if Manuscript C is correct
in adding "from the west." Anarchy is the only word that can be used to
characterize conditions in the empire after the death of Severus Alexander
(A.D. 222–235) until the reign of Aurelian (A.D. 270–275). The Germans struck
from the north, the Goths and Sarmatians in the lower Danube valley,
the Sassanians in the east, followed by the Palmyrenes in the desert.[10] The
Christians were relatively free from disturbance until the third century when
they came under severe pressure. Maximian, Decius and Valerian actively opposed the Church as well as individual members[11] of the Christian cult. Such
persecution had a double-edged effect — it spelled death to many but at the
same time solidified the endangered communities.

The specifics of our passage are hardly recoverable but the general course
of events is clear. The writer interprets them as divine judgments — the
sword and wrath of God — brought upon the earth because of sin. He ends
by reiterating that those who escape destruction by the political involvements
of the time will be subject to those who prevail in the end — another way of
reaffirming what was said in vs. 27.

[Asia has become like Babylon, 15:46–63] This is apparently a denuncia-
tion of Asia (Syria) under Odenathus for associating with Rome. His splendid
victories over Shapur and the Sassanians in all probability saved the eastern
provinces of the empire. Had Shapur been more discreet and joined hands
with the Palmyrene these provinces might have been forever lost to Rome.
But such was not the case. Odenathus was thus compelled to deal with
Shapur on terms set by the Sassanian: warfare. The former demonstrated
his sagacity and power, no doubt inspired by his noble wife, Zenobia, by
twice pursuing the enemy as far as the gates of Ctesiphon. He was regarded
as a colleague by Valerian and given, as we have seen, extraordinary recognition by the weak Gallienus. Odenathus' acceptance of these high honors
led the writer to the severe condemnation here expressed. Tagged as a companion or partner in the crimes of Rome, Odenathus was castigated for
relying on wealth, power, luxury and debauchery characteristic of "Babylon."
The severe judgment pronounced upon Asia here was all too soon in being
realized. After having brought most of the other uprisings in the empire under
control, Aurelian turned his attention to the eastern provinces now in the hands
of Palmyra. (Under two weak rulers, Claudius Gothicus and Quintillus,
the empire had fallen into disarray between 268 and 270, and Odenathus
had taken advantage of the situation to seize control of the east.) Upon the
death of Odenathus, Zenobia herself assumed power, but with her husband's
demise the Roman status granted him also came to an end. When, however,
the imperial authorities sent one of their generals to deal with her she forced

---

[10] See Rostovtzeff, *History of the Ancient World*, II, ch. XXI.   [11] Ibid., p. 349.

him to retreat to Europe with the loss of most of his troops and his reputation. At the height of her power, she had firm alliances with the surrounding states of the Arabs, Armenia, and Persia, and exercised dominion over Egypt. Her combination of "the popular manners of Roman princes" with "the stately pomp of the courts of Asia"[12] evoked both fear and respect on the part of her subjects and the neighboring principalities. No wonder the Romans decided to subdue her at the earliest opportunity.

On his way to the east Aurelian rewon Bithynia, Ancyra and Tyana, and by apparently feigned leniency created second thoughts in the minds of Zenobia's Syrian subjects. Aurelian met Zenobia's forces in battle at Antioch and, later, at Emesa. The queen's army gave an excellent account of itself; the Roman army was no match for her arms in direct engagement. Had they not resorted to the ruse of affected disarray and thus divided and weakened her soldiers by pursuit and harassment, the Romans would have lost the campaign. Zenobia was twice defeated; and she failed in an attempt to raise a third army, but did not give up the fight. Aurelian was compelled to lay siege to her capital at Palmyra, no easy task, considering its location and the necessity for fending off guerrilla attacks on both army and supplies by Arabs who were as familiar with the desert as he was not. Even when he reached the capital, he thought it wise to offer terms of surrender which were contemptuously rejected by the proud and determined queen. She hoped for aid from Persia and famine in the Roman army. However, the death of Shapur and the arrival of reinforcements from the west and south for Aurelian evaporated that hope and Zenobia fled. She was soon captured and her city with its tremendous wealth taken over by the enemy. She was later to be paraded through the streets of Rome in golden chains, dragging herself on foot before the very chariot in which she planned to ride in triumph through that western city. But the end had not yet come. After Aurelian's departure from Palmyra, the Roman governor was slain and the garrison decimated, a bold attempt at revolt. The emperor returned at once and in a rage of resentment executed old men, women, children and even innocent, helpless peasants.[13] This final immolation was doubtless what the writer had in mind here. But it now appears that Aurelian's devastating acts did not involve the temple of Bel, for the priests seem to have supported him.[14]

[Malediction against Babylon, Asia, Egypt, and Syria, 16:1–17] One cannot say very much about this piece except that the judgment called down upon the enemy is of the most general character. The enemy is the Roman empire, especially those parts about which the author knew most or where those concerned had suffered adversity and persecution. If the preceding chapter has been correctly located in time, this one would appear to follow right after. The situation reflected is one of instability and uncertainty, with little or no hope for better times. All of this is divine retribution (vs. 8).

As may be seen from the explanatory NOTES, traditional materials were

---

[12] Gibbon, *Decline and Fall*, I, 296.
[13] For fuller description see CAH, XII, 301–7.
[14] See Michel Gawlikowski, "Inscriptions de Palmyre," *Syria* 48 (1971), 407–26, esp. 412–21.

tapped by the writer so that which he presents is a compilation from varied sources. The whole discourse is couched in the form of Wisdom — note especially vss. 6, 7:

> Can anyone ward off a hungry lion in the forest
> or extinguish a stubble-fire once it has started to burn?
> Can anyone deflect an arrow shot by a powerful bowman?

— and reminds the reader of such passages as Amos 3:3–6; Jer 15:12; Isa 49:24. The upshot is that the Lord has unleashed disintegrating, destructive forces against Babylon (Rome) and her provinces, forces that cannot be recalled until they have accomplished their end. The only thing for the writer, and those like him, to do is to lament their lot and hope and pray for rescue.

[The beginning of sorrows, 16:18–35] This too is a patchwork of quotations and allusions reflecting extensive acquaintance with the prophets. The underlying ideas are along the same lines as those expressed in the preceding verses. Again, perhaps the outstanding characteristic is the Wisdom form. The rhetorical questions in vss. 3, 4, 5, 8, 9, 10, 11 of the previous passage and vss. 19, 26, 27 here sound very much like Amos 3:3–8.[15] The mašal-like figures in vss. 16, 30, 31 also point in the direction of Wisdom.

[Appeal to the servants of the Lord, 16:36–40] The servants of the Lord are exhorted to pay strict attention to his word. Indeed they are to welcome it and in no way doubt or discredit it because the calamities he has already announced are at hand; in no case will they be impeded. They are going to be as painful as childbirth. But, as indicated later on, the situation is not hopeless. Painful and agonizing as childbirth is, the result is a new life.[16]

[The word: prepare for the worst, 16:41–51] After previous discourse on the proximity of judgment, the Lord's people are themselves warned to be ready for its imminent inception. The word is not something to be taken lightly or with skepticism. The message urges them to get ready as for battle, though it is not clear whether as active participants in the struggle or simply as innocent victims — perhaps the latter since they are compared to strangers in the earth. The whole passage recalls the discourse of Jesus with his disciples recorded in Luke 17:22–37. In both cases those concerned are urged to put aside earthly ways — buying and selling, trading and building, sowing and reaping, and marrying — because these will have little relevance in the time of judgment. Of course it is mostly for illustrative purposes that these activities are mentioned but the deduction just noted runs through it all. It is a reapplication of the apocalyptic theme in the writer's time. The typical Wisdom form is apparent; vide, for example, vss. 42–45, 48, 50.

[Wickedness will be removed from the earth, 16:52–68] The passage begins with the assertion that sin will soon be removed from the earth and the

---

[15] See Samuel Terrien, "Amos and Wisdom," in Israel's Prophetic Heritage, eds. B. W. Anderson and Walter Harrelson (New York: Harper, 1952), pp. 111 f. On the influence of Wisdom in apocalyptic see Johannes Meinhold, Die Weisheit Israels (Leipzig: Quelle & Meyer, 1908), pp. 307 f.

[16] For possible messianic implications see Oesterley (in loco) and Maier, Texte vom Toten Meer II, pp. 72–74, with references. But though this passage may stem from such apocalyptic traditions, not too much ought be made of it except in a very general sense.

writer admonishes his hearers not to be lured into its clutches. Justice will predominate. The guilty sinner must avoid any endeavor toward self-justification or denial of his sins because coals of fire will be burned on his head.[17] No one can hide his sins or iniquities from the Lord, who probes the depth of men's thoughts and minds. Verses 56–63 are reminiscent of Job 38 f. Attempting to conceal sin is the worst possible thing to do because the Lord scrutinizes the works of man and will expose them all. The guilty ones will be chagrined when their deeds are unmasked in public and their iniquities openly accuse them. It is impossible to get away with sin, so the best thing to do is to admit guilt and then have done with sin and never succumb again. Then God will uphold you and deliver you from all tribulation.

[Subjection to indignities a test for the chosen, 16:69–74] This sounds very much like a reminiscence of actual subjection to persecution, carried out with some bitterness. Some of the victims were dragged away from their homes, others compelled to eat meat sacrificed to idols — an abomination to both Jews and Christians. As the history of Jews and Christians reveals, there were always some among them who surrendered their lightly held convictions only to be subjected to further indignities. According to vs. 72, a rather widespread area was involved. The extent of the devastation of religious communities together with the methods employed could only have been the work of sheer maniacs. The figure of testing (vs. 74) indicates that the writer looked upon the whole ghastly business as a refining process — a fairly common idea in later Jewish and Christian literature.

[The promise of the Lord, 16:75–78] The chapter concludes with an appeal, a promise, and an observation. The days of tribulation are at hand but for the Lord's elect there is promise of deliverance. They must not be afraid or waver in their position since the Lord is their guide and leader. Past sins or the sins of others, and particularly those of their persecutors, must not be allowed to overwhelm them. The antidote for such dire possibilities is observance of the Lord's commandments and precepts. The final outburst of the writer is an exclamation of woe concerning those so shackled by their sins and overgrown by their iniquities that their deliverance is impossible. They are like an uncultivated field reclaimed by nature, its former seedbed impenetrably overrun with thorns and briars, so that it cannot be utilized until purged by fire.

---

[17] There is no doubt here as to the writer's interpretation of the famous verse (25:22) from Proverbs.

INDEX OF AUTHORS

INDEX OF SUBJECTS

INDEX OF SCRIPTURAL AND OTHER REFERENCES

PSEUDEPIGRAPHIC MATERIALS

RABBINIC MATERIALS

QUMRAN

UGARITIC

KEY TO THE TEXTS

I ESDRAS

Chapter	Verse	Section
1	1–31 (1–31)*	I
1	32–55 (32–58)	II
2	1–14 (1–15)	III
2	15–25 (16–30)	IV
3	1–23 (1–24)	V
4	1–63 (1–63)	V
5	1–70 (1–73)	VI
6	1–33 (1–34)	VII
7	1–15 (1–15)	VII
8	1–92 (1–96)	VIII
9	1–55 (1–55)	VIII

II ESDRAS

1	1–40 (1–40)	I
2	1–48 (1–48)	I
3	1–36 (1–36)	II A
4	1–52 (1–52)	II A
5	1–19 (1–19)	II A
5	20–56 (20–56)	II B
6	1–34 (1–34)	II B
6	35–59 (35–59)	II C
7	1–139 (1–140)	II C
8	1–63 (1–63)	II C
9	1–25 (1–25)	II C
9	26–47 (26–47)	II D
10	1–59 (1–59)	II D
10	60 (59)	II E
11	1–46 (1–46)	II E
12	1–51 (1–51)	II E
13	1–58 (1–58)	II F
14	1–51 (1–48)	II G
15	1–63 (1–63)	III
16	1–78 (1–78)	III

* Verse numbers in parentheses are those found in English versions generally.

DATE	ISSUED TO